THE SPIRIT OF INDUSTRY AND IMPROVEMENT

The Spirit of Industry and Improvement

Liberal Government and Rural-Industrial Society, Nova Scotia, 1790–1862

DANIEL SAMSON

McGill-Queen's University Press

Montreal & Kingston · London · Ithaca

© McGill-Queen's University Press 2008
ISBN 978-0-7735-3353-0 (cloth)
ISBN 978-0-7735-3354-7 (paper)

Legal deposit second quarter 2008
Bibliothèque nationale du Québec

Printed in Canada on acid-free paper that is 100% ancient forest free
(100% post-consumer recycled), processed chlorine free

This book has been published with the help of a grant from
the Canadian Federation for the Humanities and Social Sciences,
through the Aid to Scholarly Publications Programme, using funds
provided by the Social Sciences and Humanities Research Council
of Canada. Funding has also been provided by the Advancement
Fund and the Humanities Research Institute, Brock University.

McGill-Queen's University Press acknowledges the support of the
Canada Council for the Arts for our publishing program. We also
acknowledge the financial support of the Government of Canada
through the Book Publishing Industry Development Program
(BPIDP) for our publishing activities.

Library and Archives Canada Cataloguing in Publication

Samson, Daniel, 1960–
    The spirit of industry and improvement: liberal government and
    rural-industrial society, Nova Scotia, 1790–1867 / Daniel Samson.

    Includes bibliographical references and index.
    ISBN 978-0-7735-3353-0 (bnd)
    ISBN 978-0-7735-3354-7 (pbk)

    1. Nova Scotia – Economic conditions – To 1867. 2. Nova Scotia – Social
    conditions – To 1867. 3. Coal mines and mining – Nova Scotia – History –
    19th century. 4. Nova Scotia – Rural conditions. 5. Agriculture – Nova Scotia
    – History – 19th century. 6. Liberalism – Nova Scotia – History – 19th century.
    7. Industrialization – Nova Scotia – History – 19th century. I. Title.

    HC117.N8S24 2008   306.309716'09034   C2007-907052-3

This book was typeset by Interscript in 10/13 Baskerville.

Contents

Acknowledgments

This book was a long time in the making, and thus the debts are many. Aside from my father, of whom more later, the major sources of funding for this work were the Social Sciences and Humanities Research Council and Queen's University. Additional funding was provided by McGill University, the McGill Institute for the Study of Canada, the Brock University Advancement Fund, the Humanities Research Institute at Brock University, and monies made available by the Canada Council's Academic and Scholarly Publishing Program. I would also like to thank Joan McGilvray, Jonathan Crago, and Robert Lewis at McGill-Queen's University Press for their efforts on my behalf. Loris Gasparotto made a fine map. Archivists at the National Archives in Ottawa, the Bank of Nova Scotia Archives in Toronto, the Beaton Institute at Cape Breton University, the Public Archives of Prince Edward Island in Charlottetown, the Dalhousie University Archives and the Killam Library Special Collections Room in Halifax, and the Public Record Office in London, UK, were helpful and patient, and I thank them for their efforts. One archive, however, stands out: Nova Scotia Archives and Records Management. The staff there – and I must thank in particular Barry Cahill, Allan Dunlop, and John MacLeod – offered first–rate support and a warm sense of common purpose.

There are so many friends and colleagues who provided some form of support that it's impossible to try to cover them all. Special mention must be made of Jim Kenny, Bill Parenteau, and Rusty Bittermann, three close friends and Maritime historians. I can't imagine doing what I do without their counsel. Evelyn Morin, Peter McInnis, Nancy Forestell, Winnie MacInnis, and Rich Ludlow were equally important, even if studying the wrong places in the wrong centuries. Katia Kissov gave me a desk to work at and many other wonderful distractions. Gail Chmura, Ernie Forbes, David Frank, Des Morton, Sue Morton, Del Muise, Rosemary Ommer, Bryan Palmer, Bob Shenton, Tom Summerhill, and Graeme Wynn each offered important support along the way. Jack Little, Alison Forrest, Michelle Stairs, and two anonymous reviewers commissioned by MQUP offered very helpful comments on the manuscript. Ian McKay supervised the thesis upon which this book is based. He's the best.

My mother didn't live to see this work, but her vision of Cape Breton and its history shaped mine and pushed me to understand our past. My father continues to remind me repeatedly that I don't know everything about L'Ardoise, Judique, and assorted other locales in northern Nova Scotia. All my life, his cheerfully cantankerous politics compelled me to try to better understand my world and to ask questions of the past and the present. If we disagree on many answers, we agree on the importance of asking the questions and the value of the debate. This work seeks to understand the place of ordinary people in the history of their world. It was inspired by the lives of my Acadian and Highland Scot ancestors and their compatriots who built a new world in Cape Breton/Île Royale in the eighteenth and nineteenth centuries. It comes from stories about my grandparents: a cooper named Joseph Samson Sr and his wife, Katie, and a blacksmith named Dan Tom MacInnis and his wife, Jessie. These were people with very big hearts, of whom many still tell tales. I could not do this work only as an intellectual exercise; it was inspired by good hearts and great stories.

I dedicate this book to the memory of my mother, Ann (MacInnis) Samson, to the present of my father, Joseph Samson, and to the future of my son, Francis Samson. I hope this book helps Francis understand something of where we came from.

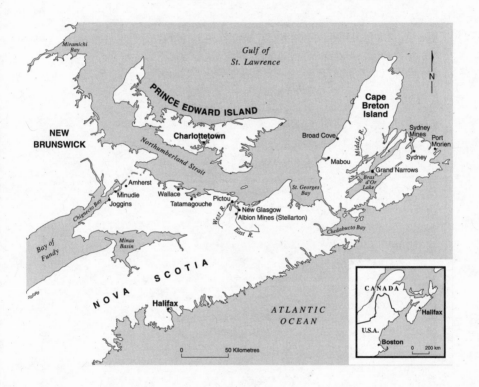

THE SPIRIT OF INDUSTRY AND IMPROVEMENT

Industry and Improvement

The idea is to write into the history of modernity the ambivalences, contradictions, the uses of force, and the tragedies and ironies that attended it.[1]

Anne of Green Gables, certainly the most famous piece of literature to come out of Maritime Canada, begins with a farm household's need for supplementary labour. Anne, as almost everyone from Summerside to Osaka knows, is an orphan from rural Nova Scotia, and her adoptive "parents" are farmers whose frustrations with the local labour market (wages are high and the only available workers are "those stupid halfgrown French boys" who run away as soon as they have enough money to get to Boston) drive them to adopt a little "boy" to assist them in their toil on the farm.[2] That she is not a boy causes no small amount of anxiety. While the narrative focuses on school-time activities, romance, walks in the "Haunted Woods," and our heroine's eventual accommodation to adult sensibilities, the household labour of a farm girl structures Anne's daily and seasonal activities. *Anne of Green Gables* is escapist fiction, and we would surely be mistaken to emphasize the suffocating, adult features of her world. But much of what Anne escapes from is the banality and drudgery of farm work. Indeed, it is useful to remember here that hard work and proper attention to industrious endeavour are central aspects of Anne's less imaginative adult nemeses.

Lucy Maud Montgomery was concerned much more with describing what was in Anne's head than with what she was doing with her hands. The imaginative terrain of farm girls may be beyond our grasp as historians, but how many didn't dream young girls' dreams? The question may be a reminder that we have read rural history in much the same way that we have read *Anne of Green Gables*: we have followed the main lines of the narrative but left its margins unexplored. In the case of *Anne* – and indeed for rural history – the margins of the story-as-told may be crucial to determining its larger form. Few would argue that this novel would be a good source for an agricultural historian. Yet if we remain attentive to those brief glimpses of the day-to-day activities of our bonded-labour heroine – that is, to the margins of the text – and to the even briefer glimpses of the wider rural world, something of the material context of the Maritime Provinces is present. Her position as a girl who was supposed to be a boy and the consequences of this for the working of the farm form the tension that drives the novel's narrative from the beginning (her selection and the reasons for adopting a child), through the main body of the story (Marilla's ongoing frustrations with Anne's inability to concentrate on her work), to the tragic conclusion (Matthew's death while working and the explicit suggestion that he might have lived longer if Anne had been a boy). To focus on this aspect of the novel is perhaps to rob the story of much of what made – and continues to make – it one of the most popular novels ever written; to ignore it, however, is to miss a vital underpinning of the construction of the story.

Today, Anne and Avonlea stand for a time when life was simpler and the world was greener. Most everyone recognizes that the novel glides over the harsher aspects of life on a farm. Everyday life on a farm is present but muted; work and workers appear only, as Raymond Williams observes of the rural English novel, as part of the landscape. Despite Anne's travails, the novel's bucolic vision mitigates, or at least adds charm to, a decidedly bittersweet tale.[3] It is ironic that this novel, which has become part of a popular genre that represents "the Maritimes" as somehow set apart from the modern world, was written at the height of the region's participation in the modern industrial world. Only a few miles away from Avonlea were steel mills, railcar plants, glass works, coalmines, and numerous other large-scale industrial facilities. In 1909, the year after Montgomery published the novel, a massive and bitter representation strike ripped apart Nova Scotia's coal towns for almost two years. Indeed, the region's historiography would suggest that industrialization, urbanization, progressive reform movements, and modern states were the dominant features of life in the region. As Ian McKay observes, by the early twentieth century "public lives [were constructed] around the problems and challenges of capitalist modernity."[4] Avonlea may have been even less idyllic than we thought.

I do not wish to contest this point. Indeed, one of my main purposes in this work is to explore the ideas and activities that secured the creation of a modern industrial society in the region. What I wish to illustrate is twofold. First, staying with Anne for a few more moments, it is important to allow that part of the context that Montgomery set for her heroine was very real. However idealized Avonlea may have been, there was another quite different world lying in the shadows of the pitheads, steel mills, and factories, one that we must better recognize if we are to have a fuller understanding of these particular locations of modernity. Second, we also need to recognize that the events that brought Anne to Avonlea were not the pernicious effects of modernity's penetration of a traditional countryside but were instead rural aspects of the modern world. Supplementary labour, both waged and unwaged, had been a critical component of the north-western Atlantic rural economy since its immersion in the world of European empires.[5] The nineteenth-century countryside was different from that of our "modern" world but not so different that we should simplify its development by applying notions of an uncomplicated, linear process of "modernization," with its attendant binary of "traditional" versus "modern." To be sure, the region's countryside changed over the course of the nineteenth century, but its origins in a "traditional" past are not clear.

In this book I argue that the making of modernity in rural Nova Scotia was a fragmented and contested process and that distinct class interests led and defined a series of debates on the future direction of social development in the province. Many people resisted these changes. Practices not in keeping with the ideals of liberal modernizers existed throughout the countryside. Often these practices – as innocuous as how well one's fields were fenced or how straight one's rows were ploughed – were the products of tradition (i.e., they bore the certainty of past practice) and sometimes of poverty (e.g., an old hoe was cheaper than a new plough). Such resistance to change often disturbed the economic and political aspirations of local elites. Herein lies our story. Following Dipesh Chakrabarty (however modestly, for his agenda clearly extends well beyond the reach of this work), I seek to understand the "ambivalences, contradictions, the use of force, and the tragedies and ironies" that attended the advent of modernity in this relatively small corner of the colonial world. Modernity came to Nova Scotia with the beginnings of European settlement. The bounding, enclosure, and commodification of the land, which occurred with colonization, the marginalization of Aboriginal peoples, and the land's resettlement by Europeans marked a radical transformation of its use and place in human society.[6] Yet these "Europeans" were far from a coherent group, and their ideas and practices varied dramatically over time and place. If we might, at some level of abstraction, understand European expansion as carrying property and capitalism to the New World, we must also acknowledge that on the ground few Old World migrants understood their world through the lens of John Locke.[7] If there was a "transition to capitalism" in colonial Nova Scotia, we would best understand it as the gradual diminishment of the capacity of poor and middling settlers to achieve competency through means other than a complete reliance on the market. The process was uneven and protracted, and we had best understand the varieties of experience and their different meanings rather than subsume such a messy story under a convenient, if misleading, label.[8]

British North America was never "traditional," at least not as a type that we could set against "modern." I will describe a series of locations where evidently traditional and modern practices met, clashing, merging, or existing side-by-side. There were, to be sure, transitions under way in rural Nova Scotia in this period, some of which might be usefully placed along a modernizing trajectory. But there are two major problems with understanding Nova Scotia's history in this manner. First, such an approach typically emphasizes an abstract, and externally animated, modernity that shapes the story – thus missing the dynamism of the countryside itself. Positing capitalism as a many-tentacled monster, many writers have described it as "penetrating" the countryside from without, as "invading and conquering" an older traditional world.[9] When we examine the ideas and activities of rural people, we can see that capitalist modernity grew from within the countryside at least as much as it "penetrated" the countryside from without – that modernity's seeds were firmly planted in many rural practices.[10] Second, a normative modernization approach misses the contested and contingent nature of many of these changes. Thus while capitalist modernity emerged within the countryside, it did not do so naturally, inevitably, or unopposed. Today, in the twenty-first century, we have difficulty imagining a world where capitalism does not influence almost every aspect of our lives. Yet an examination of the countryside on the eve of capitalism's greatest triumphs makes clear that in this corner of the Western world, as in many others, there were innumerable obstacles to change and consolidation. These obstacles were political and ideological, overt and passive; most often resistance came from the poor, but as we shall see, it could also come from elements of the middle and ruling classes and sometimes even from the state. There was a liberal-capitalist project under way *in* the countryside. But as Ruth Sandwell has argued for rural British Columbia, any such project was contested, its direction was unclear, and its success was in no way certain.[11] A history that assumes modernity's eventual and complete victory cannot explain how it happened.

In Nova Scotia there are two standard versions of the tale. One is liberal and the other is Marxist. Both are laments. Charles Dunn's nostalgic account of "the rural life" in postwar Cape Breton exemplifies the liberal account. He adheres to all the major tenets of the traditional-urban typologies of a modernization theorist[12] and describes a traditional, peasant-like life "common to the Gaelic country people." They were a "happy people" who had resisted the lure of the city. For Dunn, the historical question becomes how to explain why others left. After all, who would abandon the idyllic existence of the poet-farmers who comprise his account? Dunn's view of the transformation of the countryside venerates those who remained and faults those who left, but the major source of explanation (and blame) is posited as lying with modernity's seductive charms. Some, such as the rural artisans, are portrayed as victims who were pushed out by the pressures of "mass machine production," the "showy product," and the "hypnotism of advertising." Others abandoned the idyll, seduced by the "lure of the city." These were "unreflective" types who were ignorant of what they gave up for "easy work, ready cash, the latest conveniences, and the latest fashions" in Halifax, Boston, and Montreal. The acceptance of modern ways hurt even those who remained.[13] "Many farms today," laments the Harvard academic, "might not be lying idle if the owners had not so readily accepted the many machine-made products offered them and then found that all their land and cattle could not yield returns enough to pay the price … luxury is a greedy and extravagant mistress."[14] For all its melancholic nostalgia, Dunn's account is history with a verdict: the absolution of those whom he so admires requires the condemnation of others. Innocence is the mark of the folk. Indeed, Dunn configures these country people as having been so innocent that they did not act; they only responded, and they did so within the narrowest of possible realms. They are types: Highlanders, farmers, the folk. They are "simple," "primitive," "peasants." Dunn's subjects are, on the one hand, victims of a world that is changing around them and, on the other, prisoners of their own culture, apparently unable to think their way out of either traditional or modern problems.[15]

The economic transformation of the nineteenth century also underpins one of the earliest Marxist accounts of the history of the Maritime countryside. Colin McKay, much like Dunn, describes a "rural revolution" marked, most centrally, by a change from traditional to modern capitalistic conditions. Like Dunn, McKay also emphasizes the transition from independent subsistence – where "a certain harmony pervaded their economic life" – to dependence on the market. Artisans and home production were squeezed out by factories and mass production, while farmers themselves became specialized producers who no longer produced for their own family's use or processed their own produce but sold their raw materials. Improved transportation and storage facilities not only better facilitated access to long-distance markets but also connected farmers to other producers, effectively requiring them to produce on the terms of the market or not at all.[16]

McKay's much richer account differs from Dunn's primarily in its emphasis on the needs and power of capitalism, the reach of markets, and the active role of state policies. At the same time, the basic conceptual models employed by both writers are effectively the same. Like Dunn, McKay describes a traditional society altered by the forces of capitalist modernity, and he represents this modernization as a pernicious and largely external process. Both condemn modernity's assault on the countryside, and both celebrate the older, uncompetitive, and communal ways. These core notions continue to exert a powerful influence.[17]

Regional historiography has changed dramatically since the time of Charles Dunn and Colin McKay. Historians have since focused most of their attention on Atlantic Canadian society as seen from its towns and cities in the years between 1880 and 1930. By reinserting the region into the main streams of Anglo-American historiography, these historians have shown that Atlantic Canada, far from being on the periphery, experienced "the great transformations" of the modern world: a preindustrial period was followed by the emergence of industry and by the eventual consolidation of industrial capitalism.[18] Although the work of T.W. Acheson, D.A. Muise, Ian McKay, and others has taken the discussion back earlier than the National Policy tariffs and post-1879 industrialization, it has not broken with the focus on urban and industrial change. The countryside, while in some ways central to their arguments, forms only a background to their urban and industrial stories. Given the emphasis on the supposed rural blockages to development, it is surprising how little historians have explored the connections from a rural perspective. The major exceptions here are the local studies by Rusty Bittermann and others, which suggest that these impediments in no way fully thwarted rural producers from exploiting markets, wealthy farmers and merchants from diversifying into wage-labour-based manufactories, or the emergence of social classes in the countryside.[19] In the region's outports and countryside, most notably in mining and shipbuilding, nascent industrial facilities were in place by the 1830s.[20] If "industry" was not itself creating a working class, the process of class formation was nevertheless well underway. Most centrally, these writers have highlighted a dynamic countryside, one where change and vitality were the stuff of everyday life. An exclusive focus on urban industry thus seems partial and incomplete. These more recent rural studies, however, describe small communities and focus almost exclusively on economic matters. By contrast, I seek here to move out from this local economic focus in order to explore some of the cultural and political effects of a socially differentiated society. The countryside was one of the grand theatres for the modern drama that was nineteenth-century Nova Scotia.

In Nova Scotia the examples of miners (especially coalminers) and of farmers (as nebulous an identity as this might be for many in Nova Scotia) can help us to explore this division. These people lived in a locale that we can refer to as the "country of coal," a term borrowed from David Frank that will be employed as shorthand throughout this book.[21] The coalfields determined the limits of this geographical area, which runs along the northern shore of the province from the western-most coalfield located at the Joggins in Cumberland County, along the Northumberland Strait past Pictou and Inverness Counties, to those at Sydney Mines and Cow Bay in eastern Cape Breton. Agriculture here was uneven. Parts of the country of coal had poor quality land, but the area also contained some of the best soil and market access in the colony.[22] The mining and farming householders who peopled the country of coal comprised two of the most important social groups in the colony. Although agriculture was never as successful in Nova Scotia as it was in Canada or New England (northern Nova Scotia farms were only about two-thirds as productive as their Upper Canadian counterparts), at mid-century farming was nevertheless the principal occupation of fully two-thirds of the province's people and the second largest industry in terms of importance to the formal economy.[23] Merchants and farmers marketed significant quantities of livestock, dairy products, and hay as well as smaller amounts of grain and vegetables both in the industrial towns and garrisons and in Newfoundland. Coalmining, by comparison, was not as prominent in this period. Not until after the 1880s and the development of the integrated coal-steel complexes in Pictou and Sydney did the industry come to assume its role as the leading industrial sector of the economy and as the principal revenue generator for a *rentier* state. Nevertheless, many understood coalmining to be a vital resource for the future. As early as the 1790s some far-sighted state agents and investors saw the importance that coal could have for the development of markets for the province's farms and fishery. By 1839 almost £300,000 had been invested and well over one thousand men employed. Service industries such as brick works, iron foundries, and sawmills were in place, and increasing numbers of farmers found markets for their forest and agricultural products.

Mining and farming also nicely represent two sides of the divide between urban and rural, industrial and pre-industrial, waged and unwaged, and modern and traditional. Farmers come as close as any group to defining rurality, while historians have regarded miners as the "archetypal proletarians."[24] Coalminers, and the coal industry, have also played a central role in the region's post-Confederation historiographical renaissance. Historians have emphasized coalminers' roles in forming an industrial society and now understand much more about their day-to-day lives as workers, within families, and as community members.[25] Yet we know very little about their lives and roles before about 1870.[26] Enclosure of the province's coalmines in 1827 by the General Mining Association's restrictive state-sanctioned monopoly is alleged to have effected a separation between the mines and the countryside in which they were situated; as run by the General Mining Association, the mines operated as a limited "enclave" of industrial production, socially and economically insulated from their neighbouring communities.[27] In this book I argue that these mining centres were more fully integrated into the countryside than these writers have described. The nineteenth-century mines, as run by the General Mining Association, may well have checked the wider development of a coalmining industry in the colony, and they may have insulated some aspects of life in the mining towns from the social regulation of the state. But these were relatively unimportant beside the mines' effects on politics and society in these communities.

Nova Scotia was a colony of conquest. It was a French colony, Acadie, held by the British – effectively, after the Treaty of Utrecht in 1713 and, unreservedly, after the final defeat of France in North America in the Seven Years' War. The conquest of Acadia solved a military problem for the British, but ruling this new colony created a problem of government. At a time when many colonial officials were already concerned that the existing colonies of British North America were far too

democratic and far too adrift from the concerns of Parliament and the
Board of Trade, the prospect of governing French Catholics added a
cultural dimension to their thinking and compelled a basic redesign of
the structure of colonial administration. The creation of a highly centralized form of government in the 1720s met both concerns. Under
the revised structure, power lay principally in the capital – never too
far from the eye, or the hand, of the imperial centre.[28] Unlike in New
England, local government was highly restricted, with almost all areas
of local administration conducted in the capital. Over the next few decades Britain eased its tight control, although only partially. For those
who were not adherents of the Church of England, for example, constitutional convention relaxed requirements on taxation for the state
church, in effect allowing some accommodation of dissenters' expectations. This accommodation of cultural difference emerged as a cornerstone of government across British North America, but it came at the
expense of local democratic institutions. Government remained highly
centralized. The province's Assembly administered almost all local
matters, effectively concentrating all political power in the capital and
creating minor fiefdoms in the electoral districts of the colony. The appointed executive – the Legislative Council and lieutenants governor –
could, and did, dominate the Assembly, adding yet another element of
strong, centralized government. The lessons of centralization and accommodation – and their failures, most notably the collapse of accommodation that led to the expulsion of the Acadians between 1755 and
1758 – were not lost on imperial officials over the next half-century as
the conquest of Canada and the loss of the Thirteen Colonies framed
the narrative of state formation into the nineteenth century. Centralized paternalist government was a program premised on balancing the
expectations of colonial inhabitants with the requirements of imperial
policy – of reigning in democracy and local autonomy without completely alienating settlers. Although not often explicitly posed as such,
the problem of government in Nova Scotia – whether in the 1750s
(the final period of the Acadians and the beginnings of protestant colonization), the 1780s (the period of the Loyalists), or the 1830s (the
period of reform) – was always how to define the boundaries between
authority and freedom or, in other words, the limits of liberalism.

These years saw the beginnings of the consolidation of liberal, capitalist modernity in Nova Scotia.[29] At the heart of this history were innumerable smaller stories in which some people attempted to alter
others' "traditional" (i.e., existing) social, cultural, and economic

practices. Invoking the legitimacy found in the science of political economy, standing on a belief in the inherent good of enlarging the wealth of individuals and the nation, and quite willing to employ the full powers of the state in the process, those who would change existing ways were intent on making the New World in their own image. They were undoubtedly genuine in their desire to improve the world, but they would do so, as Raymond Williams observes, through the destruction or alteration of "habits or beliefs inconvenient to innovation."[30] Eighteenth- and nineteenth-century disciples of progress termed this process "improvement." Agricultural improvement, in particular, was the product of the European movement to advance the interests of the nation – and the nation's elites – through the expansion of agricultural productivity. Such improvement was understood to include a diverse range of changes – technological, cultural, institutional – but a key concern was to remove the obstacles formed by smallholding peasants and common fields by transforming these older forms into modern capitalist agriculture.[31] Employing the terminology of C.A. Bayly, we can describe improvers as "agrarian patriots" – those members of Britain's agricultural elite who equated advancement of their own lands with the advancement of the nation and the empire.[32] Nova Scotia had no "feudal" past, but it clearly had settlers whose ideas and practices were at odds with the radical individualism promoted by its improving elites. Provincial improvement writers, ranging from the Glasgow-educated John Young to local intellectuals such as the Mabou merchant William McKeen, found in the countryside not only an object for study but also a location for elite intervention. Ranging from the banal (building a road was a mark of improvement) to augmenting the wealth of the nation-state, such intervention also included individual improvement through self-help and voluntary societies (e.g., missionary, literary and scientific, and agricultural). Although typically directed at relatively modest endeavours, these measures effectively linked individuals to local, national, and even imperial considerations. Nova Scotia's improvers understood they were part of a broader and grander movement.

Improvers were not liberals – at least not in any clear and consistent fashion. Although inspired by some liberal ideals, their worldviews were more complex, embracing both a forward-looking sense of innovation and progress and a backward-looking emphasis on order and regulation; they understood that the New World offered new conditions and challenges, but they wished to reproduce an Old World society.[33] Balancing these contradictory forces was crucial. Early modern political debate focused on extensions of individual liberties and their regulation. The broader sense of "government" outlined by Michel Foucault suggests the bases on which the people understood, legitimated, and distinguished between freedom and regulation.[34] Foucault has opened up the term "government," removing it from its narrowly institutional references and reasserting an older, more generic sense of "government" as directing, guiding, regulating, and generally exercising both liberty and restraint in the ordering of activities. In the early modern period, government increasingly came to form an intellectual problem; the questions posed about government shifted away from those based in the practices of rule and the maintenance of authority through politics and coercion (as in Machiavelli) and toward ones based on managing large populations (as in Malthus), where the guidelines for rule broadened and became more complex: "how to govern oneself, how to be governed, how to govern others." Foucault sees a "double movement" underway, characterized, on the one hand, by increased state centralization and, on the other, by the dispersion and fragmentation caused by the break-up of feudalism and the religious upheaval of the Reformation and the Counter-Reformation. It is, he argues, "at the intersection of these two tendencies that the problem comes to pose itself with this peculiar intensity, of how to be ruled, how strictly, by whom, to what end, by what methods, etc."[35] Governmentality outlines the process of sifting through liberalism's key tension between freedom and regulation – between the assertion of autonomy and the acceptance of authority. Liberal government, then, meant that the state governed individuals; yet liberal government also charged individuals with responsibility for their own wellbeing, which they were to demonstrate by acting through socially acceptable norms and patterns. In the colonies, such basic questions were usually at the forefront of most political discussion.

Colonial Anglo-American liberals grappled with the fundamental issues of freedom versus restraint and the rights of the individual versus the commonwealth.[36] Following the tumult of the American and French Revolutions, the intellectual climate would appear to have swung toward freedom and the individual, and an increasingly vocal North American middle class appears to have accepted most of liberalism's core precepts, including the primacy of the (free) individual.[37] In Nova Scotia, as elsewhere, issues such as religious dissent and restrictive mercantile regulations persistently pushed the issue of freedom and independence (as well as a reactionary response) onto the political table.[38] For the most part, colonial intellectuals looked almost instinctively to Britain for the conceptual language by which they would construct the liberal edifice. In the 1820s and 1830s liberal newspapers such as the *Colonial Patriot* (in Pictou) kept readers abreast of the great reform measures of the time that were being adopted elsewhere in the empire and urged that similar measures be adopted by the colonists of Nova Scotia.[39] Yet despite a rhetoric that often emphasized freedom, the "rights of Englishmen," and a "freer scope to the popular influence," many provincial reformers were more apt to emphasize economic reform, the freedom of property, and of course improvement. Although often invoking notions of rights and the Constitution, some colonial newspapers represented liberalism and politics more as bases for the ordering of economic affairs and as an expression of British patriotism than as offering a sphere for negotiating power. In 1847 the *Cape Breton Spectator* said nothing about freedom or democratic principles (much less about equality) when its editorialists defined liberalism as being about "good government," proper "administration of the laws," a "rational system of public education," and the "good order of society."[40] In colonial Nova Scotia liberalism's triumphant consolidation was still some time away.

By the early nineteenth century Nova Scotia's self-described liberals saw self-government as central to both political and individual wellbeing. Many understood the connection between an adult male's self-control and propriety, on the one hand, and his capacity for political sovereignty, on the other. Conversely, a lack of self-restraint was a sign of irrationality, of what was commonly referred to as the "tyranny of impulse." This concern for self-government emerged in the works of advice givers on family and domestic issues, on poor relief, on "Indian" policy, on agricultural improvement, and notably on temperance: they warned that the inability of individuals to govern their own actions was not only a social evil but also marked an unpreparedness for political self-government. This was especially important in the colonies, where elites typically fretted less about settlers not having enough freedom and more about their having too much. Nova Scotia's greatest agricultural improver, John Young, observed that putting "man" back into nature posed threats to a civilized order. Because Nova Scotia farmers were unable to demonstrate improved ways, they were unworthy of the freedom of self-government. Those who understood freedom's necessary logic were obligated to govern those who resisted improvement's innovations and rationality. Freedom, it would seem, was available to all, but one had to demonstrate one's responsible, self-governing ways to claim it.

Having successfully hived off equality and a universal freedom, Nova Scotia liberals were themselves free to pursue their own improvement through the limited democracy of responsible government – that is, by shifting responsibility from the executive to the Assembly while retaining the centralized organization of the state. The most important influence, here, was the ability of elite-led, middle-class men to assert their claim to represent the best interests of the emerging nation-state. Notably, they were able to maintain a hold on the legitimate use of power while simultaneously proclaiming their stewardship of civic virtues such as independence, respectability, propriety, and later sobriety. This agenda was a product of a transatlantic debate about and conceptualization of government and the public sphere, while the material conditions and possibilities of Nova Scotia gave it a particular form and shape. It emerged at least as much from rural-agricultural society as it did from a nascent, urban-industrial bourgeoisie, or ruling class. Political life was led by urban and rural elites, fuelled by capital earned in both rural and urban production and exchange, conceptualized through masculine and ethnically restrictive ideas about civil society, and conditioned by class struggle in the towns and countryside of the region. Social difference and inequality, at least as much as political ideology and urban modernization, gave shape to the key political-cultural divides; in rural colonial Nova Scotia, where inequality appears to have been more sharply marked than elsewhere,[41] the outcome would be a weakly democratic society.

This book is an effort to understand the material and discursive bases for government in a rural, nineteenth-century, colonial context. In particular, I will explore some of the larger conditions of politics and class identity as well as some of their everyday bases. In Canada there are few models for such a project. To date, studies of nineteenth-century state formation have suffered from two major problems. First, they have assumed that the emergent urban-industrial world was the sole source of progress and the growth of the state. Many writers, for example, have posed the debate over Nova Scotia's reluctance to enter Confederation as an economic contest centred on urban-industrial issues.[42] Kenneth G. Pryke, for example, rightly argues that pro-Confederates "combined an appeal to nationalism with a belief in progress," but he links "progress" exclusively to manufacturing industries and the urban middle classes. Similarly, Rosemarie Langhout describes the colony's early railway expansion as a kind of state-capitalist project driven by the ideas of a few key figures in the capital.[43] Neither of these works are wrong. Both highlight critically important features of state formation, but each is a good example of a limited sense of where, and therefore of how, to locate the operation and significance of ideas and political power in colonial societies. As we shall see, rural elites were modern men; they understood, believed in, and worked for progress just as much as did their urban colleagues, though often with different indices. Their struggles to advance this agenda against the opposition of many others shaped the Nova Scotia countryside; their struggles shaped modern Nova Scotia.

Second, Canadian nineteenth-century studies have centred on the elite's aspirations more so than on concrete descriptions of the efforts to implement their plans (and much more so than on voices from the countryside).[44] The broadest work to date, *Colonial Leviathan* (1992), an anthology edited by Allan Greer and Ian Radforth, is much better at appraising high-level systems of administration and control than at discussing either resistance or negotiation. While the editors refuse to choose between state formation as a cultural phenomenon and state formation as an institutional development, most of the essays are very much in the latter camp, occupied with describing the development of railways, police, a governor, and administrative finance.[45] These are clearly important factors in the creation of modern states, yet there is much more. Graeme Wynn's "sceptical" essay, which concludes the collection, is more effective. He places the story on the ground and emphasizes the cognitive, spatial, and effective territory that the state had yet to conquer and the discrete locations and possibilities that had yet to be united or reached by the state's still poorly developed penetration of civil society.[46] Yet at the same time, although Wynn raises the right issues, he appears to underestimate both the presence and the capacity of the state, even in the earlier nineteenth century, while also underestimating the level of popular resistance prevalent across the towns and countryside of the region. To be sure, the state was not as extensive, or as powerful, as it would become later. Compared with the twentieth-century state, this seems clear enough. But where do historians go from there? How do we measure the state's "penetration of the civil realm"? If the state was a hybrid, Janus-faced creation in the mid-nineteenth century, when did it change? When was society not liberal?

This study too pays more attention to elite aspirations than to the alternative visions of a rural class whose voices were either ignored or written over in the surviving textual evidence. Yet following the cultural shift apparent in recent western Canadian works by Tina Loo, R.W. Sandwell, and Adele Perry, we can shift our focus on the colonial state to include the role of everyday local political questions as well as larger questions of ideology in forging the institutions and practices of colonial society.[47] By extending the range of our grasp, by reaching slightly deeper into the countryside, and by reading across a more diverse base of evidence – that is, by listening for more voices and not restricting ourselves to obviously "political" or "rural" evidence – we can better gauge both the breadth of liberalism's hold on the popular imagination and the obstacles and negotiations that it necessarily encountered. The focus, then, while including the still forming institutions of the state, will be more on public discourse, local practices, and the growth of civil society. Nova Scotia's state-supported agricultural societies, for example, attracted most members of the local rural elites as well as others who aspired to the respectability of such public-sphere activity. Although these improvers lacked the authority of the state to intervene in the same manner, for example, as the education inspectorate in Canada West described by Bruce Curtis, these two groups of men occupied much the same level of society, served similar purposes, and sought related ends. Operating under the sanction of the state, both groups were tutelary agents for the diffusion of order and moral improvement and for the integration and coordination of centre-local state activities.[48] The focus will be on a broader and consequently inferior realm of local elites in communities across the country of coal, a group who were nonetheless very much on the front lines of political management during the period. Based on brief glimpses, as encountered in occasional petitions and court proceedings, of the alternative positions of the poor, the political opponents, and the apostates, we can establish some sense of the variety and difference, as well as occasional resistance, that characterized the too-often uncluttered historiographical road to improvement and liberal progress. However, unlike in the case of Bittermann's exploration of the Escheat Movement in Prince Edward Island and Greer's study of the Lower Canadian rebellion, we do not have available to us a concentrated package of documents produced through this alternative vision that could relate for us the immense political importance that moments of resistance held for the document-producing elite.[49] Thus we have no basis for describing a single, articulated alternative to the liberal course of "progress" and "order," only a number of moments when this path was rejected and occasionally demonstrated to be fraught with peril. This book highlights the quite different positions of the poor, the variety of elite positions available, and the fragile nature of the emerging middle-class government of Nova Scotia.

In an effort to cover both the material and the discursive bases of government in rural and industrial society, we must cover a lot of northern Nova Scotia's famously stone-filled ground. The first three chapters survey the history of British-led farm settlement, various early forms of mining, and colonial improvement writers. Conceptually, these chapters form a kind of point of departure for what is to come. To speak of "agriculture," "industry," and even the state in this period is to speak of still forming social structures that were being shaped both by the practice of settlers and by the interventions of elites, intellectuals, and the imperial state. In this radically open context, chapters 4 and 5 then pursue two examples of rural-industrial change in the form of private state-supported enclosures of coalmines and grindstone quarries in the 1830s and 1840s. The next two chapters describe something of the practices of, and ideas about, the everyday lives of farm and mine families. Here, the emphasis is on the linked features of families' material capacity and their ideas about self-government. Chapter 8 examines the activities of rural merchants and the critical importance of credit and capital in fostering economic progress in rural communities while sharpening the lines of class that structured local politics. The early bases of civil society and the state-supported vision of improvement expressed by its many disciples across the provincial countryside form the focus of chapter 9. Finally, chapter 10 examines the politics of the antimonopoly initiative, particularly the campaign to end the General Mining Association's control of all the colony's mines, as an expression of a maturing, yet still complex and contradictory liberalism in the elite politics of pre-Confederation Nova Scotia. In all these cases, we see the negotiation of the divide between freedom and authority, how material capacity and cultural power provided legitimacy for positions in this contest, and how the state shaped and benefited from these processes. Nova Scotia politics, long held to be the preserve of old guys chewin' apples while sittin' on the front steps of country stores, emerges here as more complex, more modern, and much more connected to the major currents of the North Atlantic world. Those old guys might have been sittin' on the steps, but we can begin to see that their conversations were more interesting and more significant than historians once imagined.

1

Land and Settlement

"Rambling" through eastern Nova Scotia in the summer of 1829, the Halifax newspaperman Joseph Howe was struck by the "rapid increase of population, and commercial and agricultural improvement."[1] Crossing Mount Thom, on the road from Truro to Pictou, he was well pleased to observe that "towns and villages have risen where [once] roamed the moose and the bear, and a numerous population have scattered the blessings of cultivation over a wide extent of country that was then little better than a howling wilderness." Much of this "howling wilderness," however, remained: "The view from Mount Tom [sic] is very extensive, but the widespreading and still unfelled forest ... occupies the largest portion of it." From his vantage above Pictou, he saw not only "some of the finest and most populous settlements ... scattered along the banks of the rivers" but also the "deep solitudes, [and] the unbroken wilds of nature." The road from Antigonish to St Mary's was "dull and wearisome," a "solitary and rather uninteresting ride of forty miles." After St Mary's he endured "a long ride over an indifferent road," marked here and there by a "few farms and a mill or two, but no object of special attention." And beyond this lay "a wilderness – the road over which you pass being almost the only evidence of man's industry."[2]

Still, Howe was truly impressed with the progress of settlement, and in their combination he marvelled at both the "unspoiled" natural beauty of the shore and the "neatness, order, and taste" found in the "painted cottage, the bending orchard, or the tasty garden."[3] Howe's narrative gives us some sense of just how thinly developed Nova Scotia was, even after sixty years of active British settlement. It is also a useful reminder of the limits of what we can and cannot know about this early part of the province's history. Howe's journey was partial; his account relates only what caught the eye and the interests of a single man as he travelled a single road across the province. The view was circumscribed not only by the limitations of his route but also by what he selected from his limited view and presented for his largely urban audience in Halifax.

That same year, Captain William Moorsom, a British naval officer recently stationed in Nova Scotia, travelled through much the same territory. Standing on the same hillside that overlooked Pictou, he took in a rather different view. Moorsom found less to comment on here, noting only the "fine view of the forest country" and the "white buildings of Pictou."[4] Unlike Howe, who frequently paused to describe and reflect on what he saw, Moorsom's "sketches of a young country" are more like a tourist's postcard impressions, based in part on what he believed before arriving in the province. As he admitted, he had grown up with Old World visions of New World savages, monstrous beasts, and crude, near-savage colonists. These expectations, of course, were a foil for what was actually to come, as he quickly shifted to a discourse on the "progressive habits" of the settlers. Reflecting on the "character of the peasantry," he described their "honest independence, respect for the laws, and contented minds" – a combination that "breathes happiness in every well-shingled tenement."[5] These were his general impressions. Taken from afar, they comprised social landscapes – formed in quick, broad strokes – of a barbarian world punctuated by an optimism about the capacity for Britishness to be reproduced overseas. Whenever he paused to capture more detail, however, elements closer to his childhood expectations re-emerged. Stopping for the night at an inn near Manchester in Sydney (now Antigonish) County, he delighted in describing the "unshaven visage and rough figure" of the proprietor, an "old beldame humming a nursery requiem" to a "half-naked infant," while a younger woman "with a face and head half-European, half-Indian, and clothed apparently in nothing but a loose gown, without any under garments, strode round the hearth." Up close, savagery re-emerged and the progressive habits of the peasantry gave way to the combination of pleasure and danger that is often evoked by the "other." That from a distance he had seen the peasantry as possessing "a higher standard of simplicity, virtue and intelligence" than the "most accomplished scoundrel from the purlieus of the British metropolis" neither dampened his titilation at primitive sexuality nor prevented him from fearing for his life during his night at the inn.[6]

This chapter examines the margins of settlement in Nova Scotia in the late eighteenth and early nineteenth centuries. Most of the focus is on describing how the rural poor established themselves on the land, how and where they acquired it, their various forms of tenure, and some of the prevalent strategies for seeking independence. The point here is simple, but it has important repercussions for the remainder of this study: contrary to the imagined descriptions of the levelling effects of settlement, the settlement process did not in fact level. Rather, it resulted in a most heterogenous and stratified province, settled by many peoples of different ethnic backgrounds, means, and desires who had arrived at different times and had settled in areas with differing capacities. Neither isolated from broader social forces nor transformed members of "frontier" societies, settler communities were marked by a tension between an older (often pre-migration) communitarianism and the emergent conditions of a burgeoning world market, economic and political liberalism, and the regulatory impulse of a state in formation. While some practices nurtured a kind of defensive traditionalism, others encouraged or facilitated a directed modernization. Sometimes, these were embodied in the same forces.

A SOCIAL GEOGRAPHY OF SETTLEMENT

Because Nova Scotia represented the northern limit of agricultural settlement in eastern North America, its capabilities were uncertain and uneven. As Graeme Wynn has demonstrated, the colony was a land of "bounded possibilities."[7] Settlement primarily followed the coast, inland waterways, and valleys. By 1800 the basic settlement pattern of the province had been established, and it would not vary substantially over the next hundred years. Wynn describes three basic zones. First, around the coast were hundreds of small fishing settlements where agricultural was normally limited to small gardens for domestic use. Farther inland, typically cutting into the peninsula along river valleys, were the principal agricultural settlements. This second zone, the largest in terms of both area and population, was characterized by mixed farming. Some of this farming was market-oriented, but at this early stage much of it was oriented toward self-sufficiency. Finally, the third zone was also agricultural, but here, on longer-settled farms on some of the best land in the region, such as the Fundy marshlands, cattle, butter, and grain provided important surpluses for sale in the markets of Halifax and Saint John.[8] Less an area than a number of discrete locations, these farms on marshes and fertile intervales represented the near-immediate initiation of commercial farming in the colony and a no-less-swift integration into the North Atlantic market.[9] In a province of "bounded possibilities," such locations were not widespread. Any understanding of rural life in Nova Scotia must recognize the environmental limits that its lands imposed. While containing numerous pockets of rich farmland, much of the province's interior is rocky and hilly. Most of the pockets of prime land are at the bottoms of river valleys; the land quickly turns coarse and stone-filled as one moves out of the valleys.[10] Nova Scotia was an agricultural-settlement colony where extensive settlement was possible. But it was on the northern edge of viability and also possessed large swaths of poor soil. It was not, as many remarked, a "wheat country," so farmers faced greater challenges than were found in Upper Canada and in the north-eastern United States.

Yet these environmental factors did not completely determine the social structure that emerged in Nova Scotia. The second basic geography of settlement was shaped by variations within these larger zones, where specific social and historical factors, such as the quality of the land, the timing of settlement, access to markets, and the settlers' cultural and economic capacities, all mediated the relationship between the land and the incoming human population. As Rusty Bittermann's description makes clear, the Cape Breton community of Middle River was outside Wynn's commercial farming zone, but portions of the valley held substantial farms that allowed their owners a prosperous life. Others lived on backland sites above the richer valley bottoms and eked out a spare existence, often more of it coming from wage labour than from their land. Clearly, some part of the explanation for this socially stratified community is to be found in the simple fact that the more prosperous households were on better lands. Yet in asking why these settlers acquired these superior sites and why they were able to turn them to such advantage, Bittermann convincingly argues that the outcome was not due so much to the site itself or to the settlers' initial capital as it was to the combined effects of the timing of settlement (especially in an area where good land was limited) and to the capital available to these settlers. In short, these were not wealthy men who simply purchased good farms but were moderately capitalized householders who arrived when good land was still available; good land and moderate capital could be made to work.[11] Bittermann provides a rich counter-scenario in which farm specialization, capital accumulation, and markets for farm products and labour are superimposed on what was once imagined to be a poor and essentially homogenous rural society. Mindful of some of the environmental boundaries, I thus further pursue the issue of social heterogeneity here by exploring some of the multiple bases on which rural Nova Scotia was settled.

By 1800 most of the prime marsh, intervales, and upland sites on mainland Nova Scotia were occupied. Cape Breton still had some good locations, but even these were disappearing quickly. The Middle River settlers of Bittermann's account (who settled the valley around 1807) were probably among the last to be afforded an opportunity to settle on good riverfront land. As Lord Selkirk observed in 1803, newcomers and second-generation settlers around Pictou were already moving to other parts of the province in search of good land. Partly cleared farms in the area were available at between 10s and 20s per acre, but few could afford the £50 to £200 required to purchase farms of 100 to 200 acres.[12] Thus most immigrants after 1800 were moving farther up the rivers. Settlements such as St Mary's (about twenty miles up the East River), Merigomish, the Miré (ten miles east of Sydney), the inland valleys around Mabou, Margaree, River Philip, and the areas north and east of Truro were growing, but given their distance from the coastal towns, market-oriented farmers faced numerous obstacles. Poor settlers, unable to purchase good land, were equally unlikely to possess the means to develop their "free" grants. Whether the desired end of moving inland was to obtain a bare subsistence or to reach markets, it would be many years before success could be achieved.

Land, of course, was never really free, although for a time it could be had at a very small cost. Before 1817 grants were available only to loyalists and retired soldiers. Between 1817 and 1827 a 100-acre grant could be had for the quite minimal price of £5, although little good land remained at this point. In 1827 orders were issued requiring that new grants be auctioned, and this certainly introduced a differentiating process. Yet even in the ten-year period when the almost-free grants were available, the land that was granted seldom held good farming prospects. Any land that became available after 1827 was either poor or expensive.[13] Thus even in the period of "free" grants, the differences between the capitalized settler who purchased land and the poor settler who obtained a grant continued to form the same crucial differentiating process. Additional peril came from the maddeningly slow process of confirming title, in some cases taking anywhere from eight to fifteen years.[14] Reforms improved the process after 1817, but for some the difficulty was much more than insecurity and inconvenience. Crown-land records document numerous cases where a licence was not recorded and another settler was given full title to the

land. In other cases, the grantee arrived to find others already established on the land – either believing that title had been granted or simply squatting – who adamantly refused to give up what they had already
improved. In this administrative mess, squatting became an important
strategy for obtaining land, especially in Cape Breton. In 1814 the lieutenant governor reported that over 60,000 acres were illegally occupied; by 1837, after the arrival of a torrent of immigrants in the late
1820s and early 1830s, the surveyor of Crown lands estimated the
number of squatters on Cape Breton to be about 20,000, more than
half the population of the island.[15] Encroaching on Mi'kmaq lands was
another common strategy. Surveying was inconsistently employed in
the best of circumstances, and Mi'kmaq lands were at the bottom of a
long list. Numerous coercive strategies were employed by settlers, including downstream damning of fishing rivers and the simple but effective use of gunpoint. Courts were often sympathetic to small-scale
improving settlers but rarely so if they were Aboriginal.[16] However obtained, such marginal lands seldom brought prosperity or even permanence, but for the increasingly poor settlers arriving after the
Napoleonic Wars, it offered possibilities.

Almost every chronicler of settlement in Nova Scotia has observed
that the first agricultural settlements were beside the marshlands and
along the banks of major rivers that flowed inland from the sea.[17] In
Pictou County initial European settlement was heavily centred on the
West, Middle, and East Rivers. While the largest waves of immigration
into the area did not begin until about 1800, the principal nodes of settlement were already established at the towns of Pictou and New Glasgow and for a few kilometres up the three major rivers. Writing in 1827,
"Philo Antiquarius" recalled how early settlers "sought suitable locations
on which to settle ... They explored the different rivers ... and finding
the soil near their banks to be the most fertile ... they seated themselves
upon it."[18] In some areas, settlement was blocked by large speculative
grants taken up by wealthy colonists in Pennsylvania and New England
in the mid-eighteenth century. Some of this land was escheated with the
arrival of the Loyalists after 1783, but many of the refugees who were
granted lands near Pictou had to travel 20 kilometres up the East River,
where they finally found suitable intervales near what became Springville. Between the settlers and the speculators, by 1800 there was very little good land available near the towns of Pictou or New Glasgow, and
as late as 1829, Joseph Howe could still remark on those "immense
grants which retard the settlement of the country."[19] Seeking good land,

timber, transportation, and sometimes a good mill site, the early settlers had obtained much of the best land available in the county well before immigration swelled in the years after 1800.

Travelling through Pictou County in 1803, Lord Selkirk moved from the mercantile and ship-building centre of Pictou up the West River and then overland on his way to Halifax. Observing the advance of settlement up the river and the extent to which the best lands were already granted, he described how these earlier settlers not only had first chance at land but also possessed the means to develop it. Now, twenty or so years later, many of the established settlers had made substantial improvements, and their homesteads showed "every mark of comfort." Some, such as a settler named McKay, had built "good comfortable farmhouses," purchased additional lands for their sons, and were concerned more with markets and prices for their surplus goods than with carving out a greater place on the land. McKay had "built a new Stone house ... keeps 12 Cows – from which he sells annually 8 or 10 Cattle (as supposed 5 to 7000 wt at 3d to 4½d per lb. on 4 quarters – rest for butchers – to Halifax). Dairy produce is reckoned worth 2£ per Cow – but of this the consumption of a large family takes a great share – 30 sheep. McKay has about 100 acres clear – besides farms for several of his sons." For the more recent arrivals, choice locations were increasingly scarce, and settlers "who have capital prefer paying rather than go to back lands, as all the front lands are granted & none but back [land] can be had from Govt."[20]

Selkirk's comparison with more recently settled farms gives us some sense of the stark differences that had emerged within these first few years of settlement and that would continue to mark these areas for years. Still on the river, he observed the house of a settler named McIntosh, whose land was "upon the top of a steep bank." McIntosh had "2 or 3 acres cleared, mostly planted with Potatoes – sowed 15 bushels – besides a small pickle of Oats, too late and will not ripen. – The potatoes are not a good crop in general, the land not being very good – hemlock etc." The McIntosh household was clearly unlike the "comfortable farm" that he had described earlier. Farther up the river, he found another "Highlander settled about 14 years ago who has done but little" living in a "miserable" house on land "which would be good meadow but is full of stumps"; having no oxen of his own, he had to hire a neighbour's, "paying a day by a day of his own labour."[21]

Selkirk understood that many of these less developed farms were simply new and that their occupants had not yet had time to improve their lands. But like so many later writers, when he sought to explain the variations, he turned to culture, emphasizing the idle "habits of the Highlanders." "The old settled Highlanders," he continued, "even those of 10 or 12 years date have in general cleared as much as they want & do little more – being not ambitious of making money so much as living comfortably."[22] While noting that others had "purchased 100 acres for 100 guineas," he was unsympathetic about the difficulties faced by householders from Perthshire who "had been turned out of their farm 3 years before they emigrated" and had spent their only money, £60, "in the dear years ... [and] landed without a penny." Granted land but lacking the money to establish themselves, both the wife and her husband were "obliged to work for hire" before finally clearing enough land to plant five bushels of potatoes in the spring of 1802. Although now on the farm, the husband still occupied "full half his time employed at wages off the farm to make up the articles he had got on credit."[23] Much of this farm household's progress now rested on the husband's wages and the wife's unpaid labour in the fields. Selkirk's account gives us some sense of how the combined effects of timing and capital made tremendous differences in the fortunes of individual settler households. Time would magnify this effect. As early as 1803 those comprising "the redendent [sic] population arising from natural increase" were searching for good land elsewhere, "as all the front [land] was occupied." Some purchased sites, but with improved land in the area selling for between 10s and 20s per acre, many others were forced to either move elsewhere or seek grants on the poorer land of the rear settlements.

Farm formation was slow and costly, and most settlers faced tremendous obstacles in achieving the much-vaunted state of independence. In a few instances, a settler could clear as much as six acres in a single year, although this very much depended both on the site (its terrain and forest type) and on the ability of the settler to purchase equipment or hire labour. A much more likely figure would be one to two acres per year.[24] But whether one was settling on a prime intervale near a market town or on upland soils well upriver, farm formation costs could mean that it would be some time before a household could provide for itself, much less produce a surplus. Independent of the cost of land, an 1839 report estimated that farm start-up costs would be at least £50.[25] This would be for basic provisions, and additional requirements could add anywhere between £20 and £50 within the first year or two. But few, even in this period before the truly impoverished immigrants arrived in the 1830s and 1840s, could find this capital investment without turning to the labour market. In many areas of northern Nova Scotia, the difficulties of farm formation would be overcome very slowly. Compared with the older settlements, such as those around Amherst, recent settlements were perhaps less stratified, but the differences between the poor and the comparatively rich were still evident.

Settlement proceeded more slowly in Cape Breton than on the mainland. In 1801 it was estimated that there were only about 2,500 people on the island. The census of 1827 showed the total population to be less than 19,000 (compared with more than 100,000 on the mainland). With most of the good farmland already granted, those arriving in the 1820s – especially those pushed out by the collapse of the Scottish kelping trade after 1825 – were compelled to seek land on the semi-mountainous, rocky, and wretched soils of the back settlements.[26] While these factors would form important ingredients of Cape Breton's later history, even in the 1820s the generalized poverty of the poor farm-based economy was striking. Along the Bras d'Or Lakes, where some of the best farm opportunities lay, there were few farms with more than 20 acres in cultivation when the census takers came round in 1827. At Benacadie and Grand Narrows (south of Sydney at the northern head of St Andrew's Channel and the only Cape Breton returns to have survived from the 1827 census), the average cleared acreages were 15.8 and 12.3 acres respectively. Between the two settlements, only 9 of 152 farms had more than 30 acres in cultivation, while 128 households did not own even a single horse. At Grand Narrows, 3 of 4 households owned three or fewer head of cattle, and only 11 of 76 had more than five head (the largest herd numbered twenty). Barely 1 in 10 households had more than two pigs. Many residents in the town of Sydney would have owned this much livestock.

Yet, as small as the figures were, the distribution of these farm products was not uniform (table 1.1). Disaggregating the census data by farm size offers a portrait of some dismally poor farms. Only three farms in Benacadie had more than 30 acres in cultivation, and it is to these farms that we must turn to find more than a fractional horse (1.7 per household). But the jump here is quite large. These three farms averaged 21.7 head of cattle, 31.7 sheep, and 5.7 pigs. Such numbers, although by no means spectacular, would have been quite respectable in the 1851 census, twenty-four years later.

It should not be surprising that there was such a clear correlation between acres cleared and farm stock. Although a more recently settled

Table 1.1
Farm sizes and average numbers of livestock, Benacadie, 1827

	Acres (cleared)			
	1–10	11–20	21–30	30+
Farms	31	26	16	3
Horses	0.1	0.4	0.5	1.7
Cattle	1.6	5.7	9.6	21.7
Sheep	2.7	10.6	15.9	31.7
Pigs	1.7	3.2	5.7	5.7

Source: Nova Scotia, Census of 1827, Nova Scotia Archives and Records Management, microfilm.

area, Benacadie shared the same pattern with older settlements. At the bottom end of this spectrum, most settlers were probably only recently on the land and cannot be expected to have possessed much. But in the two middle ranges we find farm households whose acreage tells us that the occupants must have been settled for at least ten years. Of these, only one household in two owned a horse, and with livestock holdings of three pigs and ten or fifteen sheep, the potential for either food or exchange was not great. Moreover, of those comparatively established farms, three of the forty-five households owned half the horses in the settlement, almost one-third of the cattle, one-seventh of the sheep, and one-eighth of the pigs. These declining fractions are significant. They illustrate clearly that while poor farm households owned some stock, this was relatively less likely to be capital-enhancing stock (i.e., horses and cows) and more likely to be stock for household use (i.e., pigs and sheep). In other words, the stock kept by poor households was for subsistence, not accumulation. Most of these farms also produced 100 to 300 bushels of potatoes and 20 to 50 bushels of oats. A moderate-sized household of five to seven could live on the upper end of this range but not on the lower. Any other basic goods could have been provided only through merchant credit, timber sales, or off-farm labour. While by no means wealthy, the few comparatively prosperous farms were in a much better position not only to subsist but also to obtain credit – usually on better terms – and to invest in their own farms. The future of these moderately prosperous farm householders looked much more secure than for those on the smaller farms. Some of the latter undoubtedly persisted, but the struggle must have been enormous. Others were compelled to move on.

Settlers who lived their lives according to the ideals of the independent yeoman appear to have been more the exception than the rule.[27] Poor settlers clearly required off-farm wages, and prosperous farmers depended on this labour to harvest their crops and ship their products to market. "Farming" in northern Nova Scotia seldom conformed to the prevailing images of this livelihood. Participation in the farm-based rural economy meant taking part in a wide variety of productive activities. Besides actual farming – here meaning only tillage and husbandry – men, women, and children might also hire themselves out for day labour on others' farms or for fishing, shipping, lumbering, tanning, household service, or milling, or they might engage in many other types of occasional waged employment. Already by the 1820s market forces determined the demand and price for agricultural labour. In 1822 George Ross, secretary of the West River Agricultural Society, observed that an unusually successful crop had resulted in a "low price of farm produce," which in turn "caused our members to employ as few labourers as possible." For prosperous, market-oriented farmers, the issue was not whether to hire labour but how many they could afford not to hire.[28] For the poor, such labour was a lifeline. Credit, debt, and their relationships with local merchants could determine their capacity to survive.

MERCHANTS AND SETTLERS

Credit was essential to the rural economy of colonial Nova Scotia. It was also controversial. Many contemporary observers thought that credit was a vice and too easily obtained. Whether the issue was the potential for political "ledger influence" or the "moral degradation" of debt, most critics pointed to credit and debt when they discussed the slow progress of the province's farming communities. Competency, as "Mephiboseth Stepsure" and a host of other commentators observed, derived from industry, dutiful attention to one's own farm, and good moral behaviour, not from merchant credit or from working the timber camps.[29] Many historians view the merchant as a kind of pariah, feeding on the meagre but numerous scraps of profit to be found in these poor communities, or (worse) as the germ of an ever-advancing sphere of capitalist social relations.[30] But the simple truth was that credit was essential to both settlers and merchant-capitalists. Merchants, lacking adequate supplies of labour, could turn to credit as a means to obtain the products that they needed for export; while settlers, lacking adequate access to capital, could turn to credit as a means to obtain the goods necessary for their own self-provisioning. Merchants and settlers negotiated what Daniel Vickers aptly describes as a "productive if unequal compromise" that facilitated degrees of subsistence and capital accumulation.[31]

In the northern half of the province, the timber trade was an important source of cash and credit for farm households.[32] Settlers arriving with little or no capital might be able to obtain a land grant soon after arrival, but few were in a position to actually begin working the farm. Many settlers and tenants purchased essential supplies and sometimes even their land with timber.[33] For many others, participation in the timber trade meant hiring themselves out. Work typically could be found close by, but many travelled as far as the Miramichi Valley in northern New Brunswick to work in timber camps. There was a regular traffic in labour around the Gulf of St Lawrence. Along these shores coastal vessels carried trade goods, the mail, and migrant workers to and from the western shore of Cape Breton, Antigonish County, Pictou, Tatamagouche, and Prince Edward Island as well as up to the Miramichi.[34] Many, of course, were able to combine timbering with clearing their own land, although this depended greatly on the period, the location of the land, and of course the settler's capacity not to work others' lands. Much of the timber came from indiscriminate cutting, and some settlers found that their saleable timber had already been removed. As early as 1803 Lord Selkirk observed that the "depredations" on the forest were already so great that "the trade must soon decline unless a new channel is found." The forest frontier always preceded settlement, and lands near navigable waters were culled of their valuable timber long before settlers arrived.[35]

The shore along the Gulf was dotted with dozens of small timber yards and wharfs where merchants assembled their cargoes for the British market. But some men quickly came to dominate large portions of the trade. In the first two decades of the nineteenth century, the major timber baron on the Gulf shore of Nova Scotia was Edward Mortimer, the "King of Pictou," who shipped as many as eighty loads of timber to Britain each year from various ports along the shore from Baie Verte to Charlottetown and Pictou. Many merchants vied for positions within this often-lucrative trade, but Mortimer resisted them: any

man who intruded on his "legitimate domain" would find "he did not
hesitate to use measures to crush him."[36] In the 1870s James Patterson
recalled that Mortimer's "influence" in the county was great. As his
role as a "public benefactor" grew, people "look[ed] to him almost as
if the money came from his own pocket."[37] Although he is reputed to
have died broke, at the height of his career Mortimer was said to have
been worth £100,000.[38]

Mortimer cast his credit net well into the countryside and as a result
drew much of the county's trade into his hands: "By the system of credit
which prevailed, [Mortimer] had almost every inhabitant of the county
in his books, and thus, in a measure, under his control ... Not only were
goods pressed upon them, but also they were kept in ignorance of the
state of their accounts, as a means of securing a continuance of their
custom ... For example, after men had agreed to give their timber or
produce to other parties, he would have no hesitation in persuading
them, or concussing them, into giving it to him." But Mortimer's power
was not exercised freely. It was negotiated through the complex and
stubborn entanglements of paternalist rule. Mortimer's "influence ...
with the country people," Patterson learned when he conversed with
those "who recollected that period," was that of a man who was both
ruthless and kindly: "He celebrated many of their marriages ... and on
such occasions he and Mrs. M. danced with the common people, and
mingled freely with all ranks in a manner that gained their good
will ... Though he wished to have people in his books, and loved the
power that gave him, yet he was never disposed to deal harshly with
them. On the contrary, his inclination was rather to act the Lord Boun-
tiful."[39] This pattern of embedded dualities – of kindness and wrath,
forgiveness and punishment – was a common characteristic of early
nineteenth-century social relations. In this period before the modern
state, authority was articulated largely locally – by wealthy merchants
and politicians who possessed the ability to give credit, employment,
and access to land – but also through the wider realms of political and
market possibilities.

The duality of the paternalist's role as caregiver and disciplinarian
must also be emphasized, as well as the central place that such relations played in governing early colonial society. But it is equally important not to restrict the influence of such men to these implicitly local
("personal") domains. On one level, the "King of Pictou" clearly understood the power afforded him by reciprocal "face-to-face" obligations in combination with debt dependency. On another level,

however, he must also have understood the wider scope for applications of power beyond this narrowly "personal" social context. This
merchant's power extended well beyond "ledger influence" and the
coercive potential of economic interests. Mortimer's wood might
come from Pictou County farms, but it was sold in the North Atlantic
market; his "concussing" was not only harsh but also had the support
of the state. Indeed, formally, it was very often the state that was doing
the concussing. As one of the three presiding magistrates in the local
quarter-session courts, Mortimer meted out imprisonment, stocks, and
even lashes for debtors and petty thieves while at the same time determining the allocation of road monies available each spring from the
Legislature.[40] This rural justice of the peace, judge of the Inferior
Court, and distributor of state largesse might be lampooned in Halifax
as "our oat meal Emperor from the East," but even those who mocked
him could see the breadth of his power.[41] Others felt the raw brutality,
and the gentle hand, of his power in the most material fashion. The
power of the "oat meal Emperor" was local but drew from the power of
the colonial state and from the community's embeddedness in the
North Atlantic colonial economy.

Mortimer was probably somewhat exceptional. Few merchants had
Mortimer's reach or his power; few too were quite so ruthless. But by
keeping farm households in their debt, many merchants gained the
necessary leverage to obtain as much timber as they could contract for.
Most merchants combined the timber trade with their stores. William
Matheson of Roger's Hill, Pictou County, divided his time between
contracting with settlers to obtain timber and contracting with British
merchants for ships to get the timber to market. James Marshall of West
River was one of several dozen men who paid their debts to Matheson
with timber. In 1825 Marshall obtained credit from Matheson for almost £100 worth of provisions. The following summer he repaid about
half this value through his labour (two days rafting, helping to build
Matheson's boom), in cash (£20), and by delivering twenty-eight tons
of timber (£22.2.19½).[42] Cumberland County merchant William
Harper combined the timber trade with the export of grindstones. In
1831 thirty-eight men delivered between 10 and 142 "sticks" of timber
to Harper's boom on the Petitcodiac River, which he had purchased
for between 12s and 15s. Most often, Harper "paid" by cancelling
debts.[43] Yet account books, with their harmonious presentation of balance, give us little sense of the potentially coercive side of the process.
In 1831, for example, Harper offered James King a way to clear his

debts: "Sir, you owed me the first of June last £19-9-6 and if you will get me by 1 June next ... and deliver at my boom on or before that date Either red pine that will girth 11 inches or upwards and squared well agreeable to Law or white pine that will girth 15 inches and upwards ... If you Chuse to Comply with this you can save cost & trouble both to you & me & buy your debt."[44] This was not necessarily comparable to Mortimer "concussing" his debtors, but it certainly carried a hint of threat. It was clear to some merchants that the portent of gaol, especially for someone whose property could be at stake, would prove a forceful incentive. These small inputs could add up quickly: in 1829 Harper exported 1,500 tons of timber. With cash in short supply, hundreds of settlers wintering in the woods used tools, oxen, and provisions advanced on credit. Men such as William Harper supplied them with credit and waited for their return in the spring.

Merchants' success depended on their ability to obtain an obligation from a producer; this, in turn, was largely determined by the producer's economic position. Once in debt, a farm household had to pay back the merchant, but merchants were also constrained by the amount of credit that they could offer. This could give settlers a small edge by allowing them to spread their debts among several merchants (a practice that Mortimer resisted as strongly as he could). Most merchants understood that they had to expect small losses in order to realize larger gains. But there was always a balancing act between overextending credit, and thereby succumbing to their own creditors' fortunes, and extending too little debt to obtain full shiploads of timber for export to Britain. If merchants were unable to develop an adequate base of the debt-dependent settlers or to finance enough debt, they might not be able to obtain their product. As some timber merchants learned, this could mean half-filled ships in Nova Scotia and angry creditors in Britain.[45]

Timber was but one of a number of products available for even poor settlers. Other merchants were embedded much more fully into the local economies, without necessarily giving up any ties to the wider markets of the North Atlantic. Thomas Roach, for example, owned and operated one of the largest farms in the province. In 1827 his farm at Fort Lawrence, near Amherst, Cumberland County, had 330 cleared acres, which produced almost 500 bushels of grain, 84 tons of hay, and over 1,000 bushels of vegetables; much of this would have been feed for his eleven horses, thirty cattle, and eighty-seven sheep. He was also a merchant and drew on a much richer range of products for exchange and export.

Roach's store formed a central point in the economy of the Cumberland Basin.[46] While the rich farmland in the area was especially noted for its marshlands – and thus for cattle and dairy production – Roach's accounts included the full range of the basin's products: butter, cheese, vegetables, cattle, timber, grindstones, coal, fish, cloth, and cordwood.[47] With his business interests ranging so widely, with such a large farm to manage, and with his public duties as justice of the peace and later as a member in the House of Assembly, Roach employed one or two agents to carry on his business affairs away from the immediate locality. Most of his producing customers exchanged directly with Roach. William Man, for example, gave Roach fifteen cattle, three oxen, and a few pounds of beef to put against his account for "Sundry goods" and interest charges totalling £63 in the fall of 1804. John Fawcett Senior sold Roach between 8 and 11 firkins of butter, and between 300 and 500 pounds of cheese each autumn between 1803 and 1806; his son, John Junior, also sold between 5 and 9 firkins per year, as well as between 100 and 200 pounds of cheese. Such amounts brought in between £35 and £60 each year.[48]

More often, there was a remarkable variety to the bases for exchange. Thomas Chapman was listed in Roach's account book as a blacksmith, and part of his exchange came from his livelihood. Roach sold him some dry goods and loaned him £30 in the spring of 1806, against which he charged interest in the fall and then again in the spring of 1807. Chapman repaid part of his debt through his trade, repairing one plough and plating another, shoeing some horses, and "mending a pair of tongs." But that fall he also sent Roach two barrels of mackeral and a firkin of butter.[49] Martin Bent was listed as a farmer, and most of his credits were farm products such as potatoes and butter (1804, 4 firkins; 1809, 9 firkins; and 1810, 9 firkins). But such farm products were not enough, and so one year Bent also cut and hauled 60 tons of lumber, helped Roach inspect his butter supplies, and worked day labour – some of it listed simply as "Day Work," some of it specifically described as being in Roach's mill. Bent was also credited for a few yards of cloth each year. If, as was usually the case, it was his wife making the butter and weaving the cloth, she was responsible for producing at least half the household's exchange value.

Just as this value production was hidden within the household, waged labour was often obscured within these exchanges. Roach had at least two or three full-time male employees and one female household servant at any one time. But he employed many more than this on an occasional basis, and in this generalized exchange economy, it is often difficult to differentiate between exchanges of goods, services, and labour. Indeed, many of his "customers" were, effectively, semi-regular employees. Most of those credited for grindstones had only this product for exchange, a point that makes clearer that what they were really selling was their labour.[50] Roach, like many other merchants, also derived direct and immediate benefit from his public commissions. As overseer of roads and purveyor of the government bounties for clearing land and grain production, he had the best opportunity to pocket these monies himself. The overseer chose who worked on these publically funded projects, and not surprisingly those in his debt very often found employment. In 1809, for example, Roach garnered at least £30 from these sources, a not unsubstantial sum in a cash-poor province.[51]

The area around Amherst Township – including here the estates around the Cumberland Basin and Westmoreland County, New Brunswick – had a much stronger agricultural economy than did most of northern Nova Scotia, and it is interesting to observe that even here timber was an important supplement to the farm economy.[52] Yet the distribution of both timber and the other major products highlights the very different conditions faced by people of varying material circumstances. For many in this relatively rich and well-developed area, Roach provided access to goods that offered some measure of choice in their lives: clothing, flour, cotton, tea, books, paper, iron. Their regular return of a variety of farm products and even cash suggests that the relationship was reasonably balanced; credit was more a convenience than a necessity. For many others, however, that they returned with only (or nearly only) grindstones or timber suggests that they had little else. Typically, these customers used their credit to obtain not only provisions but also chains, rope, hammers, axes, and codlines – in most cases, the tools that they needed to make their labour productive. Not surprisingly, the combination of large prosperous farms and freely accessible resources drew a large pool of the landless and land-poor to a location where they could eke out an existence in semi-legal trade, in agricultural day labour, and on credit. This area not only had better farmland but was also longer settled and more proximate to markets in southern New Brunswick and New England. Here, where British-led settlement dated from shortly after the expulsion of the Acadians, the same general pattern of a stratified social structure appears evident. This was not, then, at least not yet, a society headed toward a shared competence or prosperity. It was a society involved fully, if not completely, in the market economy of the North Atlantic world; it was one where a rural class structure was forming and solidifying.

ALTERNATIVE SETTLEMENT STRATEGIES

Before 1800 many immigrants became tenants on some of the large landed estates established in the province in the second half of the eighteenth century. Between 1749 and 1773 over 5 million acres were granted to land companies, groups of settlers, and lumber and fishing interests. Many were "planters," placed on the land by well-organized, and sometimes well-capitalized, New England immigration associations.[53] Once in the colony, however, the lure of private ownership meant that keeping these new tenants was often difficult. Collecting rents was even more so. In this northernmost agricultural colony, visions of establishing a system of neofeudal fiefdoms were rarely realized, and few estates were commercially successful.[54]

Yet in some parts of the province, estate settlements played a significant role in colonization, and a number of agricultural communities were nevertheless brought into being, most notably on the fertile marshlands at the head of the Bay of Fundy. Resettling the decades-old farms of expelled Acadians was an attractive option for many. British agents attracted a diverse group of tenants, ranging from the dirt poor to the well-capitalized. Bernard Bailyn argues that in the 1770s the movement to Nova Scotia was "dominated by established householders, farmers for the most part, not destitute at the point of their migration, not forced out by abject poverty."[55] Desiring "men of substance" who would improve their lands and not wishing to pay the transportation expenses for prospective tenants, estate agents tried to be selective. Agents working for J.F.W. DesBarres found a number of relatively well-capitalized households in Yorkshire willing to relocate to Nova Scotia; neither wealthy nor impoverished, they were middling farmers and tenants who desired a more solid footing than that promised by the modernizing British countryside. On arriving, however, many of these settlers saw that they could buy their own land. One of DesBarres's Yorkshire settlers was a man named George Dixon who immigrated to Cumberland County in 1772, where he bought a 2,500-acre farm near Amherst for £260 and spent another £210 on livestock and provisions. Emigration agents travelling through the area in 1773 found Dixon and a number of other "Old England farmers" improving their positions and becoming "men of substance."[56]

Some of these moneyed migrants prospered as tenants. Another Yorkshire migrant, John Harrison, arrived with his family in 1774 and rented land at River Hébert from either Edward Barron or Michael Franklin for £20 per year.[57] Most tenants paid £5 to £8 per year, an indication that Harrison obtained a much better lot. Moreover, his household possessed the means to make even this high-rent farm a profitable undertaking. Ten years later, the Harrisons, together with seventeen households, received a grant of almost 10,000 acres on the Maccan River. By the first decade of the nineteenth century, the family had established itself with over 1,000 acres of farmlands, a gristmill, and a sawmill. While perhaps not typical, the Harrisons were representative of at least some of their fellow Yorkshire settlers. Some, to be sure, remained tenants and could hardly be said to have prospered in Nova Scotia, but many were clearly unlike the impoverished settlers who arrived in increasingly large numbers in the early nineteenth century. By 1803 the Harrisons' extended household produced almost all its own requirements and marketed surplus livestock, grain, and maple sugar. John's son Luke operated gristmills and sawmills and hoped to add a fulling mill. Later, in 1818, Luke's younger brother, William, purchased 700 acres of upland and 44 acres of marshland at Maccan from J.F.W. DesBarres for £525; he was also a justice of the peace and sat on the executive of the Cumberland Agricultural Society, two sure marks of achieved status.[58] At the turn of the nineteenth century the Harrisons were apparently contented with their present circumstances, and their future must have seemed quite unbounded.

Few tenant lives contained such possibilities. In part, this situation reflected the general condition of estate agriculture in Nova Scotia. J.F.W. DesBarres was one of the few successful estate owners. A partner in a group that was granted over 100,000 acres in four locations across Nova Scotia, DesBarres too had visions of tying his and his family's futures to landed wealth in the colonies. Unlike his fellows, however, DesBarres managed to attract a good number of tenants to his lands and also seems to have had agents who were much better at working his estates – that is, better at placating an often restless tenantry and even, on occasion, at collecting rents. Like many of the land developers in Nova Scotia, DesBarres had a number of Yorkshire families on his estate. Michael Keiver, for example, leased 1,000 acres at Nappan, agreeing to pay 1,200 pounds of "prime Cumberland butter" (worth approximately £30) per year. Keiver also assumed responsibility for maintenance of the farm, increasing the height of the dykes by one and a half feet and building any "new dykes and aboiteaus [*sic*] that may be wanted."[59] The stipulation of a quantity of butter rather than a cash price reflects the limits of the market. One-third of the produce was a common demand of these estate owners. These products, in turn, were marketed in the towns, timber camps, and fishing centres along the shore. In a number of ways, then, estate owners, improving freeholders, and even a number of prosperous tenants were operating under the same constraints and possibilities. In this sense, they all moved to position themselves as best they could and often adopted the same general procedures, particularly the adaptive mixtures of commercial and barter arrangements necessary for primary accumulation under these primitive market conditions.

Tenant life held variable advantages and disadvantages for people of greatly varying circumstances. For some rural poor – particularly the dispossessed Acadians – tenantry was one of the few options for getting onto the land. For others, such as the Harrisons, it was a stepping stone: a near fully operational farm for a comparatively low cost that provided quick access to an already existing rural economy, smoothing their way to full ownership and greater prosperity. For many others, perhaps most, tenantry was somewhere in the middle. In 1816 Angus McEacharn and his brother-in-law, Laughlan McMillan, left estates on Prince Edward Island and "took up land" – that is, squatted – at St Andrew's Channel in Cape Breton. Four years later, they were joined by two other "native[s] of Prince Edward Island," both requesting land at the same location.[60] We know little of these people, but for those whose ages we know – Dougald McDonald was 28, and Lachland Curry was 21 – this record suggests that they were either the sons of tenants who wished to own their own land or possibly younger sons who could not assume their fathers' leases. We have no definitive evidence that this represented some form of organized group settlement, although the circumstances – four households from PEI all requesting land in the same place at the same time – certainly suggest that it was. Nor is there any record of their continued life there. If they were anything like Lord Selkirk's Scottish tenants, they too had come from a background where at least some fields were shared and where the "clannish disposition of the Highlanders" induced them to "congregate" more than their landlord thought advisable. And it is quite likely that this predisposition informed their choice of location as well as how they settled. At least two of the three initial householders that Bittermann describes at Middle River were once tenants on Prince

Edward Island. Apparently dissatisfied with the prospect of resuming their new lives in the old manner, they crossed the Gulf of St Lawrence to Broad Cove, Inverness County, and then petitioned for and were granted lands above the Mi'kmaq reserve on the Wagamatcook River. Within ten years – through a combination of grants, purchases, and encroachment on Mi'kmaq lands – these settlers controlled much of the best land in the valley.[61] In Pictou County another group of sons of German Swiss tenants – from DesBarres's estate at Tatamagouche – settled on lands at Smiths Point near River John. Drawing perhaps on their experiences as tenants, they set out a plan "of living in a town and having their farm lots outside ... [and] laid out for themselves small lots." Outside their "town," they "took up land for farming purposes, but ... continued to live together at Smiths Point, thus strengthening each other's hands."[62]

Most grants by the Crown were to an individual, almost always male, so it is difficult to discern collective patterns within such settlements. Quite often, however, we find as many as twenty names – presumably, heads of households – applying for large tracts of land. Other applications, however, suggest several householders applying for land in the same area. In 1809 and 1810, for example, land-grant reports show a number of large family-centred petitions and grants. In one case, 3,900 acres were granted to eleven individuals near Havre Boucher in Antigonish County. All were Acadian and several bore the same surname: five Le Vendres (Levandiere), three Fougeres, one Maret, one DeCoste, and one Benwaugh (Benoit). But they were not alone. In this two-year period almost half the grants – and all the grants over 200 acres – were made out to more than one person, most often to a group of people sharing the same surname.[63] Such a strategy allowed extended kinship units to begin on the land with a substantial acreage, far more than individual householders could develop in their own lifetimes but sufficient to provide for an already expanding family as well as for future generations.[64] In all these cases, the families appear to have chosen lands suited to their backgrounds and future possibilities. Some sought access to the shore fishery, others chose marshlands that they believed to have grazing potential, while others looked for still unexploited timber. Once on the land, many groups of settlers often continued to act more as communities than as individuals. Indeed, as we shall see, while their everyday social relations were often fractious, such settlers, when viewed through the eyes of their social superiors, often presented a troublesome unanimity.

In Cumberland County, at Minudie, J.F.W. DesBarres induced a few dozen impoverished Acadian families to settle on his estate at the head of the Bay of Fundy. DesBarres, who is best known as the author of *The Atlantic Neptune*, a remarkable set of charts for most of north-eastern North America, was also the governor of Cape Breton and later Prince Edward Island.[65] His tenants' knowledge of the construction and maintenance of dykes (*aboiteaux*) and their skill in the other methods of marshlands agriculture proved invaluable. This area around the head of the Bay of Fundy had been an important Acadian settlement before their expulsion.[66] DesBarres's French Swiss ancestry aided his recruitment of Swiss French Protestants for the estate at Tatama-gouche, and his command of the language helped him to people Minudie with Acadians.[67] But in the longer term DesBarres's facility served less purpose because he seldom visited the estates. At Tatama-gouche his agent, Wellwood Waugh, ran the estate as though it were his own, and conflict soon emerged with the French tenants. In September 1795 the tenants petitioned DesBarres, complaining that the "prevelages that you left us to Enjoy [are] being either taken from us or Embaizled by Your agent ... [and that] he has Engrossed the princaple part of the Meadow."[68] Over the next ten years Waugh's position on the estate remained controversial: some tenants resisted him, while others supported him. DesBarres himself took both Waugh and the tenants to court, but Captain John Macdonald – a landlord from Prince Edward Island whom DesBarres had hired to report on the management of his estates – praised Waugh's improving ways.[69]

In his 1795 report, Macdonald drew his friend's attention to Waugh's organization of successful cattle sales in Halifax, his recruitment of new tenants, and the sawmill and timber sales that he had organized on the French River, noting that Waugh and his sons were "very active, industri-ous, and as fit for any business by sea or Land. They do their own Iron work – have erected a grist mill ... also a saw mill ... which if I remember well may make about 200,000 feet of boards a year." The tenants, on the other hand, saw a man "engrossing" their cattle and their marshlands, "hindering us from fishing in your River and making Shugar for the use of our Familys," and "turning our Childring [children] out of your lands and put[ting] in Strangers." Macdonald noted these complaints but took the side of the local improver. Although unsure of the exact nature of the charges, he nevertheless observed that if the estate was to prosper, it would be necessary to take a firm hand in organizing the tenants' ac-tivities. "Whatever tends to regulation is proper," he maintained, "and

when an Individual has to transact with & regulate a Number of ignorant people, it is impossible he can please them throughout ... low people are averse to regulation; they readily suspect agents, who are too
frequently interested, and they do not relish those things at the hand of
agents, which might be taken at the hands of the Master." Macdonald,
who was facing his own unruly tenants in the 1790s, believed in improvement and had no time for the tenants' pretended rights. These "low
people," and moreover the estate, would ultimately benefit from
Waugh's industry and improvement.[70]

Like most landlords in the colonies, DesBarres faced the dilemma
posed by tenants who were either too poor to improve their lands or
too wealthy to resist the temptation to move onto freehold lands.[71]
Once they were settled, their combined efforts could prove serious obstacles to their management. In this instance, and on numerous other
occasions, DesBarres viewed the tenants' actions not only as inappropriate to good agriculture but also as "Collusive" and as an indication
that they were in an illegal "Combination."[72] The tenants' actions were
probably more defensive than intended to wrest control from their
landlord. Yet this should not obscure how central such collective strategies were in the settlement process. Indeed, such collective strategies
were in some ways outcomes of how the state, and social convention,
managed settlement. Whether their strategies created economic or political problems, the tenants were now obstacles to good order. They
would become objects for improvement.

Beyond the estates, settlement was given form and shape by a range of
selection processes. Most settlers were in some form or another selected,
commented upon, and categorized as to their suitability as immigrants.
Estate agents had fairly clear criteria for their choices – although they
did not always follow them – but the state's criteria were less clear. For
many colonial officials, it was critical that the colony choose some types
of settlers over others. Although not completely arbitrary, the process
was highly theatrical, a demonstration of the power – and the benefi-
cence – of government. Governor Ainslie revealed his understanding of
this symbolism when he insisted that individual land petitioners appear
before him personally "for the purpose of judging whether they are
likely to carry [out] with effect His Majesty's gracious intentions." Settlers, one report argued, should be drawn from those who were best "fitted by nature" to life in Nova Scotia.[73] In Cape Breton, Governor
Macormick attempted to recruit and obtain assistance for Cornish settlers around Sydney Mines because they were "accustomed to Fishing

and Husbandry as well as digging in Mines."[74] In the summer of 1802
Lieutenant Governor Wentworth ordered that 370 Catholic Scots from
Barra be removed to Pictou Island because he believed they were "bred
to the fisherys [*sic*]."[75] Thus it is not entirely clear what he had meant
when, a year earlier, he had informed the Duke of Portland that settlers
were "recommended to such situations as may be useful to themselves
and to the public."[76]

Ethnicity was an important consideration. It was, of course, common
for nineteenth-century Europeans to identify nationalities as "races"
with clearly defined characteristics that determined behaviour. This
tendency heavily influenced which groups were targeted for emigration and how immigrants were dealt with upon arrival. Writing to
Nathaniel Atcheson, the London-based memorialist for the British
North American Merchants Association, W.H.O. Haliburton outlined
the capabilities – and thus the desirability for settlement in Nova Scotia
– of various nationalities. His descriptions corresponded well to common nineteenth-century representations, the views of a middle-class
British male:

> The Irish are strong and ... are often the best Laborers, but, in gen-
> eral, are not inventive or quick of apprehension, and are much ad-
> dicted to strong Liquors. The English are the Best, and natural
> Farmers and Mechanics, but are the least likely to come abroad. The
> Germans are the most industrious and persevering in every thing
> they undertake ... [T]he men *will* drink, and are mulish if you inter-
> fere with them in their manner of doing their work [and] are not
> willing taught; the German women are the best Settlers America
> ever knew, laborious, persevering and prolific as Rabbits. The New
> Englander would be the best Settlers were they steady'r. There are
> no such Ax man [*sic*] in the world besides, nor a people, in any de-
> gree so inventive which quality, to a new settler is invaluable ... but,
> in general, they are liable to shift about from one place or occupa-
> tion to another, and ... [are], in general, inveterate Republicans.
> Black people are good House servants, and make very good com-
> mon hands on board vessels; they make but indifferent Country
> Labourers – and never become the Masters of others – they are
> quick and inventive in the small way, never with great – tractable,
> cheerful, and good tempered, of much value in towns, very little
> in the Country; sober, honest, industrious, but not often laborious;
> love their own Society and are very talkative.[77]

Such assumptions guided the thinking of many elite figures in the colonies.[78] Although state officials wished both to encourage more immigrants and to stem the flow of emigrants from the colony, they could be selective. In 1815 the Assembly worried that more "refugee negroes" would arrive in the province. The African Americans were, they explained, people "whose habits &c are uncertain," and they petitioned the governor "to prohibit the bringing [sic] any more of these people into the colony." Irish Catholics, and to a lesser extent Scottish Highlanders, were a concern too. When Governor Wentworth was asked to explain reports of people leaving Nova Scotia, he replied that he was quite sure such reports were exaggerated; if any were leaving, they were only "useless Irishmen" and thus not a major concern.[79] Those Irishmen who remained, however, were a concern. With their well-known "indolence and attachment to ancient customs," the Irish were commonly regarded as potential hindrances to the improvement of the country. Desirability could turn on class as well. In Britain, of course, class was the centre of the debate on reform, poor relief, and colonization; the selection process there hinged on economic calculations of a person's worth. In Nova Scotia colonial improvers were certainly attuned to the importance of locating capitalized settlers, but character, especially national character, could be equally important.[80]

Crown officials often directed where immigrants could settle on the basis of such characterizations. Not only the general area would be determined on this basis but also the quantity and quality of the land that they would be granted. At Tracadie, in Antigonish County, the better tracts of land for farming were close to the shore, thus affording access to the fishery. Acadians applying for land before 1790 received about 30 per cent less land in their grants than did Anglo-Celts. Most of the land around the harbour – 4,000 acres – was granted to four absentee New Englanders; thus the Acadians were not only granted inferior lands but also denied access to the shore.[81] The Acadians, however, did better than twenty-five African American Loyalist families who between them received 3,000 acres of hilly, stone-filled upland. The result for Tracadie's geography was a series of concentric semicircles around the harbour demarcating class, ethnicity, and future economic possibilities.

When African American Loyalists and Jamaican Maroons arrived in 1784 and 1802, the Crown presumed that the former slaves would make better labourers than settlers. In the case of the Maroons, Wentworth thought them unsuited for farming. He also believed that there was a great demand for a wage-labouring population, so the Maroons were granted small plots of land where, it was assumed, they could raise garden vegetables and work day labour.[82] The former slaves were granted land (however small and poor) and improved legal status (however ineffective), but many remained tied to various forms of un-free status – in "share-cropping" or "limited service by indenture." Twenty years earlier many employers had protested the removal of many of the African American Loyalists to Sierra Leone. Given a severe shortage of labour and its accordingly high price, the African Americans were considered by some to be a blessing – a group of workers who could be paid significantly less than standard wages – while white workers often violently opposed the black workers' place in the market. By 1815, although the price of labour was still considered high, a much broader cross-section of European Nova Scotians believed that the introduction of more "refugee negroes" would only "lend to the discouragement of white labourers."[83] As Haliburton's comments suggest, African Americans were rarely considered potential "settlers"; they were labourers. This categorization shaped their futures as much as any other.

Those African Americans at Tracadie were particularly poorly placed. Settled on miserable land, they suffered all the more due to their separation from their own community, their limited access to other resources, such as the city or even waged work, and the apparent hostility of their largely Catholic Acadian neighbours. A few of these African Americans actually died of starvation in the first few years of the settlement.[84] The census of 1827 illustrates the disparity. Farms owned by settlers of European descent averaged 33.9 acres, whereas for the African Americans the figure was 18.7 acres. The latter also had far less produce and livestock.[85] It is clear that many were hanging on to their farms by casting widely into the rural economy. Most farmed the miserable soil; some found work as servants and day labourers in the village. By 1817 their numbers had increased to over two hundred, and a small church and school were in operation. Four years later a Baptist evangelist offered them a religion that they could make their own.[86] When another Baptist missionary came through the settlement in 1832, he was dismayed by the "irregular" practices that had evolved and refused communion to some church members. This was but one of numerous instances when African American Baptists exhibited a distinctive, collective response to their social and economic segregation. They had not been given good ground, but they were making it their own.

Over the next decades African American settlers would be an ongoing "problem" for the colonial administrators, and most in the community resisted every effort at reform. Consistently, they found strength and comfort in a collective response to the individualist assumptions of European administrators and colonial practice.[87] Where a racist society was unwilling to accommodate itself to African American settlers – except as a potential source of cheap labour – they carved out their own place, and they did so as much on their own terms as the state and their competitors in the labour market would allow. It was this shared and purposeful sense of common identity, what James Walker describes as their "communal consciousness," that supported them in their new northern home.[88]

Although the experiences of African Americans were extreme, a similar pattern of community-based collective practices could be seen around the province. Bound by ties of religion, family, kinship, ethnicity, or place of origin, groups of two to twenty households petitioned the Crown for larger blocks of land so that they might found some form of shared settlement. Acadian communities – whether based on the fishery, farming, or both – organized themselves, as they had for generations, around the principle of mutual aid. Before the expulsion, "Acadian settlements demanded a community, rather than a familial labour force," a communal orientation epitomized by the building and maintenance of an extensive system of dykes and by marshland agriculture. Their expulsion in 1755, argues Naomi Griffiths, was a policy not for the extermination of those who were Acadian but for the "eradication of the idea of an Acadian community."[89] It did not work. As we shall see, long after the expulsion, this idea of community-based identity exerted a powerful influence on the ways that they organized their lives.

It is not difficult to imagine how perplexing all this was to the liberal-individualist imagination. If, for some, collective strategies provided an alternative route to successful settlement, for others such practices were considered obstacles to industry and improvement. Indeed, these community-centred systems of mutual aid exemplified what Thomas McCulloch's protagonist, Step, rails against in the *Mephiboseth Stepsure Letters*.[90] Why, Step often asks, are they not tending to their own affairs? There was little to be gained from such defensive, insular postures, when an energetic, self-improving, young colonial man (the liberal subject was invariably male) might find such unparalleled potential in the New World. To fall back on older corporate ways was to be primitive, weak, and unmanly. The liberal improver saw value, including human value, in productivity, and productivity could be made better only by what Joyce Appleby refers to as the "radical reductionism" of liberal moral philosophy: the likelihood of individual economic gain.[91] Such collective strategies became obstacles to the emergent liberal program, an ancient vice that needed to be dealt with before it took greater hold.

When Captain John Macdonald inspected J.F.W. DesBarres's estate at Minudie in 1795, he was dismayed by what he saw. With the exception of the magnificent dyked marsh – which the tenants called Champs-élysées – his general impression was one of complete failure: "There were spots ... here and there, carrying crops of poor pease – and of the worst oats I ever saw – and as good hay as I ever could wish to have ... Going on I found the Marsh hay and the upland equally good and luxuriant – the pease crop as poor as that mentioned above – and the oats wretched, thin, and not above a foot high ... indeed, in all my expedition I did not see a stalk of tolerable oats."[92] However, the primary problem identified by Macdonald was not the quality of the land or even the skill of the tenantry but the social geography of the settlement. Macdonald pointed to the spatial organization of the estate. He was particularly troubled that the tenants' households were "huddled in the form of a village," with the common fields radiating out from the centre. Rather than each household occupying its own land, the tenants ploughed the same fields and treated the dyked marshlands as commons. "I hold it to be adverse to the progress of Improvement," Macdonald continued. "Every one should have his own plantation apart and live upon it."[93] Here was the Lockean program for improvement.

Such common-fields agriculture reflected not only the poorer circumstances of this particular settlement but also the Acadians' general experiences in Nova Scotia over the past forty years. Some of these tenants had probably experienced their people's expulsion from the province in 1755, and it certainly remained part of their collective memory. Because they lacked the material resources to act outside this community, the estate's rich lands – which some may have once owned! – offered them the possibility of a shared independence, while the absenteeism of the estate's owner gave them the opportunity to shape this independence in their own manner. As one improving commentator noted, the estate was characterized by a "most irregular" organization. Twenty years later it would be differently organized, but in the eyes of another improver the practices of the Acadians remained much the same. Stephen Oxley, president of the Cumberland Agricultural Society, observed that Minudie was populated by "Acadian French who follow a mode of culture peculiar to themselves; and their prejudices are so deeply rooted ... that very little hope can be entertained of their conversion to a new system."[94]

Were these self-directed and well-planned efforts simply anomalies rooted in estate agriculture, particularly when the estate had an absentee owner? Certainly, the very nature of their tenure provided these people with a basis for collective activity. But evidence from other communities suggests that such practices were commonly employed. Village-centred plans were prevalent in other Acadian settlements. T.C. Haliburton's description of Marguerite (Margaree) in the northwest of Cape Breton in the mid-1820s sounds remarkably similar to what Griffiths describes for the period before the expulsion and what Macdonald described at Minudie: "[T]he land on both sides [of the river valley] is possessed by descendants of the French colonists. In no part of Cape Breton are these people altogether dependent on agriculture; even at Marguerite, occupying large tracts of the best land, they congregate in villages, and their attention is divided between the pursuits of agriculture, or rather grazing and potato planting, and the fisheries of the coast and river."[95] Ethnicity, historical identity, and the material effects of being a dispossessed people were the crucial factors here. Much like the African American Loyalists, Acadians were a people whose ethnicity delimited their possibilities and whose experiences – both the dispossession of the past and the success of their new arrangement – encouraged them to act together.

These collective responses were not limited to groups such as Acadians and African Americans who faced overt and systematic discrimination. In 1847 James Boyle Uniacke, attorney general and member for Cape Breton, recalled his observations of the pattern displayed by the thousands of poor Highlanders who had immigrated to the province over the past twenty years. Immigrants "without any sort of connection to the province [were] almost without precedent." The more typical pattern, he recollected "consisted of friends following out those who preceded them ... They go out to Relatives and Friends from the Islands, Highlands and other parts of Scotland, some of whom have been settled fifteen or twenty years ... so that there is a Disposition to receive them kindly, and to aid them as far as they have it in the power."[96] Once in the colony, family, kin, or often simply people from the same area made substantial efforts to assist newcomers, a pattern that in turn fostered the community-based mutualities of support and obligation. Often this was informal, such as friends writing to friends, but it could also be much more systematic. Works by Rosemary Ommer and Maureen Molloy emphasize the way that older kinship patterns and kin relations established through marriage provided critical sources of emotional and material support.[97] In some cases, aspects of Highland *clann* systems survived the crossing of the Atlantic and lived on in rural Cape Breton late into the nineteenth century. Although the *clann* system lacked the formal institutional structures of the Old World, a number of its communal features survived because they provided practical solutions to the myriad and often immense difficulties of settlement and exile. Without these formal structures, given the difficulties posed by the new social and economic context, the fate of the *clanns* in the New World may well have been an inevitable, although gradual, disintegration. Elsewhere, the demise of collective practices was actively encouraged.

Across the province in the 1820s rural improvers "congregated" in their own collectivities – the state-funded agricultural societies – so that they might combat the habits of "ignorant and lazy" settlers such as the Highlanders in Antigonish commented upon by the Reverend Thomas Trotter and the Acadians at Minudie described by Stephen Oxley.[98] In some places, the decline of such collectivities was much more aggressively pursued. Macdonald's report on Minudie recommended means by which DesBarres might attack the Acadian tenants' village-centred practices. In 1796 Desbarres ordered his agents to rewrite leases and to recruit, in Macdonald's terms, "a better class of tenants." Between 1796 and 1811 several new agents were hired and fired, a number of new and apparently wealthier tenants were recruited, and DesBarres and his lawyers served notices to quit on dozens of tenants.[99] By 1815 the now elderly DesBarres was trying to rewrite the original terms and conditions, written in 1775, by pleading that his intentions had not been exactly the same as the seemingly precise words of the lease suggested. "The Acadians," he recalled, "were *employed* in erecting the Dykes and aboiteaux ... [and] at that time I permitted [them] to settle on my lands ... [as] tenants at will."[100] But neither Macdonald's modernizing advice nor DesBarres's shifting memory could completely change forty years of practice – or some clearly written leases.

The ongoing reports, the frequent replacement of agents, the numerous court cases, and the renegotiation of leases all illustrate both

DesBarres's inability to manage his estate and many tenants' abilities to maintain their relatively strong position. Evictions and suits could be threatened and even effected, but this did not always mean that the tenants left or that back rents were paid. Yet in many ways the modernizing strategy seems to have worked, although only with the support of the state. By 1827 Minudie had changed. Over the intervening twenty years, dozens of legal actions, innumerable eviction notices, and the regular – if not always enthusiastic – support of the local sheriff had meant that many of the older Acadian tenant families were eventually forced off the estate, that new tenants were brought in, and that parcels of Minudie – and the adjoining Nappan and Maccan estates – were sold.[101]

The Minudie reflected in the census manuscripts for 1827 appears to have been quite different from the one that John Macdonald described in 1795. It was no longer a community of similarly impoverished tenants; there remained people whom the earlier descriptions might still fit, but we also find people whose property and holdings suggest wealth. In fact, we see a fairly dramatic range encompassing poor tenant farms, middling freehold and tenant farms, and large commercial farm enterprises.[102] The property descriptions also indicate that the village-centred organization observed by Macdonald had been dismantled and that most households now held freehold title. The households can be divided into three fairly clear groups. The first group comprised "middling" farms (but these would still have been quite large farms in the Cape Breton communities examined earlier). They had between 20 and 60 acres of cleared land, grew some grain and a range of vegetables, and owned at least two or three horses as well as some cattle, sheep, or swine. In total, they represented just over 30 per cent of the households in the district. They were not poor. Most would have existed above or slightly below the range of basic household self-sufficiency. Several had household servants, and certainly at the upper end of the range, many produced some substantial surpluses for sale. Yet at the lower end of this group, self-sufficiency would have been a difficult achievement; some in these households must have supplemented their livelihoods to make up the difference.

There was some demand for agricultural labour in and around Minudie, much of which would have been driven by our second group. In 1827 thirty-seven farms in the district (25 per cent) had more than 60 acres under cultivation; eleven were working over 100 acres. These larger farms each produced between 2,000 and 3,000 bushels of grain and vegetables as well as several hundred tons of hay and owned between 5 and 12 horses, as many as 85 head of cattle, and over 100 sheep. Such farms could not have been worked relying on family labour alone. Some had quite substantial payrolls. In the 1790s Edward Barron's labour expenses at harvest time were over £50.[103] Thirty years later, with the increased number of large farms in the district, there must have been a strong demand for harvest work.

Finally, then, the third group would have been supplying much of this labour. This group was composed of those households that had either no land or only a few acres in cultivation. Sixty-three of Minudie's households (43 per cent) had fewer than 20 acres; of these, thirty-eight (26 per cent) had no land at all. The householders' names indicate that many were or had been tenants or the children of tenants, so they would have had access to the estate's common resources. The standing of others, those listed as "manufacturer of grindstones," is less clear. If they were tenants, they were ones who lacked any property other than their homes. Signing a lease for a grindstone quarry did not provide farmland, so these households' only participation in running the agricultural side of the estate would have been as agricultural labourers. Some of the agricultural tenants, however, also cut grindstones. And some held leases that allowed access to both quarries and land or even held two separate leases.[104] The family histories of these landless quarriers too were varied. As suggested by the surnames, some were Acadians, even descendants of the original tenants, some of whom had probably been evicted in the past few years. Others were itinerants who were regarded as "settled" only because the census taker had found them on the land on a given day. Whatever their individual histories, most were somehow products of the potential for revenue that DesBarres and his children later attempted to realize and of the already tight market for good farmland.

Over the ten or fifteen years after the Franco-American Wars, larger markets, increased immigration, and a spirit of industry and improvement created the conditions under which the DesBarres family attempted to put its estates on a sounder productive footing. At this still early phase in the estate's improvement, it was only a modest success. But tremendous obstacles had been overcome, not the least of which, as Macdonald had warned his friend, was the intractability of a people whose different ways were well established. But the results spoke for themselves. Whereas earlier the estate had been populated by a group of similarly impoverished people who governed their own lives and practices and consciously refused to disabuse themselves of their allegedly mistaken ideas, now there was an identifiably ordered social structure comprised of middling settlers, wealthy farmers, and land-less labourers. Improvement, Macdonald might have observed, had brought order to the estate. But improvement was little more than a set of ideas and practices that were supported by some people in their efforts to make the world look as they felt it ought to look. In the strictly instrumental sense of the state's role in having sheriffs forcibly remove tenants (or threatening to do so), the enclosure of Minudie could not have taken place without the support of the state, at least not legally. Here, on this relatively insulated pocket of plantation-style industry and agriculture, the market, the state, and the ideas of pos-sessive individualism and improvement combined to rationalize the productive regime. This estate-based example is not an anomaly, for it is by no means the only example. These forces combined to order much wider swaths of the New World. At the same time, we would do well to note that the marsh, the startlingly beautiful Champs-élysées that left John Macdonald fairly babbling over its magnificence, re-mains to this day a community pasture. Not all illiberal obstacles had been removed. And as we shall see in chapter 4, after the death of J.F.W. DesBarres another improver would discover how deeply seated the settlers' older habits were.

CONCLUSION

The foregoing details something of the range of circumstances that were in place in the first major period of British-led settlement. Settle-ment was not a levelling process. If as some writers have argued,[105] ru-ral Nova Scotia was *less* stratified than the Old World, it was not uniform. For every Cape Breton bard who sung in praise of his new-found freedoms and the potentialities of his north-western Atlantic home, there was another lament for the old country and another con-demnation of the bitter cold or of a ruthless merchant.[106] To be sure, the social structures of rural class would intensify over the course of the nineteenth-century, but the modernizing forces acted on existing structures. The patterns evident in these initial moments emerged from the structures of colonization in both the New and Old Worlds and from the broader existence of markets and capital, which shaped the settlement process on a land of markedly variable terrain. These patterns were, in short, the consequences of enclosures, of improving ideologies, and of the entry of a land of bounded possibilities into a market for goods and labour that spanned the North Atlantic world.

Once settlers were on the land, the differential conditions in large part determined the options open to them and thus the strategies that they pursued. Most settlers appear to have been seeking some form of propertied independence. In seeking much the same goal, the poor settler and the comparatively wealthy one embarked on different activities. With some money and some capital, the latter might buy an existing farm or a choice lot and move directly toward full-time farming. This householder too would cut timber in the winter for sale to the merchants, but there was less immediate economic need for him to do so. Where the poor settler might be compelled to direct such income toward immediate requirements and basic provisions, the more prosperous settler could look to the future. Clearly, posing this as a bifurcated system risks oversimplification; it was not. But so long as we remain mindful of the range of positions in between, this sense of two starkly contrasting paths may be useful. These paths formed the differential pressures that facilitated capital accumulation not only on farms but also in the mercantile sector, a point that becomes clearer in the case of "merchants" who moved beyond their stores and into productive realms. Yet even here we can see their employment of labour and capital in ways that might anticipate diversification. Whether they were able to diversify was heavily dependent not only on their desire for acquisition and on the possibilities of growing markets for goods but also on the existence of a ready supply of labour throughout the countryside and on the crucial need of some settlers for wages.

We have seen some of the obstacles that the settlement process posed to the formation of a liberal society. Most centrally, these came from settlers, especially the poor. While improvers such as McCulloch, Captain John MacDonald, and the local agricultural societies advocated the precepts of modern political economy and science, innumerable settlers were not in a position to even begin this process and may not have been interested in doing so in any event. Regardless of how the improvers said things ought to be done, many were living their lives without the improvers' assistance. DesBarres's settlers were certainly not typically situated, but their responses to material and social problems were not unlike those of their fellow Acadians near Margaree, the African Americans at Tracadie, and perhaps thousands of Highland Scots throughout Cape Breton and the mainland. Strengthening each other's hand was, at least for a time, as important to many of these people as the development of markets, scientific agriculture, and liberal dreams. Others were already living a middling existence, improving their farms, and moving toward commercial agriculture, but they were doing so on their own terms. And the state itself was an illiberal obstacle here too. Even so basic a liberal fundamental as the security of property could not be assured. Governors, politicians, and state officials alike allowed the colony's land policy to fall into disarray, and squatters and legal applicants alike were often completely without secure tenure. Unable to protect property, those who governed attempted by some other means to project a semblance of proper government. But it was partial and theatrical. Whether the prospective settlers had to demonstrate that they were not thieves or to demonstrate their suitability to the governor, the state selectively intervened in the lives of the poor, offering the firm, guiding hand of the paternalist master.

Finally, some of the evidence casts additional light on the characterization of early nineteenth-century settlers as actors whose decisions were driven largely by economic calculations of "predicted gains and losses."[107] Most made such calculations. But an effort to describe this tendency as the norm would be highly misleading. The frequency of plainly communitarian practices suggests the need to refine our ideas about settlers' economic motivations. While communitarian undertakings should not be romanticized and the profit motive should not be castigated so as to suggest opposing worldviews, some clearly believed that it was necessary to make such a strong distinction, that "low people" did not know what was in their best interests. Improving farmers, such as Captain Macdonald and Stephen Oxley, were part of a transatlantic movement to improve agriculture through science and altered social organization. Their assessments of the obstacles to improvement and their prescriptions for change would be highly influential. These men led on the ground. As in Britain and America, they in turn were led by a group of writers and activists who sought to modernize agriculture. Liberal historiography would have it that these pragmatic intellectuals saw the future, but as we shall see, they too were a varied group, foretelling different routes to different futures.

2

Discourses of Improvement

In July 1818 John Young, a Glasgow-educated merchant living in Halifax, began writing a series of letters to a Halifax-based newspaper, the Acadian Recorder, on the subject of agricultural improvement. Over the course of the next two years, "Agricola," as he identified himself, outlined a plan designed to move the province from its "low and degraded state" and into the modern age. Agricultural societies were the key. Based on society members' "noble and enlightened" examples, Nova Scotians would "construct [their] future prosperity on the solid and permanent basis of Agricultural improvement."[1] There was no shortage of advice givers in Nova Scotia newspapers in this period, but Young's letters stand out because they were clearly and directly the push that initiated the province's first sustained attempts at agricultural societies and improvement. In Nova Scotia agricultural societies were a state-supported movement that made "improvement" a central underpinning of ideas and practices within both the countryside and government circles in Halifax. Through local agricultural societies and a central board, Young's plan institutionalized certain liberal ideas and practices in the countryside and in the state.

Agricola held no monopoly on didactic purpose. Young was but one of a number of writers, including Thomas McCulloch, Joseph Howe, Titus Smith, and T.C. Haliburton, identified as contributors to the province's "intellectual awakening" in the second quarter of the nineteenth century.[2] Whereas Haliburton was an arch-conservative who nonetheless spent much of his career promoting "progress" through economic and technological innovation, McCulloch's work for moral and educational reform has been described as having "the most profound intellectual ... influence" on the province's "nascent liberalism."[3] While all of these men promoted reform, Young and McCulloch shared a particular interest in improving the behaviour of country folk. Indeed, they are part of an oft-noted group of men who "urged better farming techniques" on their fellow Nova Scotians. This is true. But they had very different ideas about how and why the changes should be made. Both espoused liberal ideals, elements of which might more unambiguously be identified as liberalism later in the century. Young read Adam Smith and advocated the ideals of Smithian political economy, but working within a narrow economic liberalism, he said little about individual liberty or equality. McCulloch, by comparison, was concerned less with policy than with individual self-improvement, not simply in terms of material life but also in terms of conduct, propriety, and respectability. These differences were important. And they represented but a few of the many directions available to those who wished to chart a course for the future.

This chapter outlines two elite visions of the countryside, one presented in John Young's *The Letters of Agricola* and the other in Thomas McCulloch's *The Mephibosheth Stepsure Letters.*[4] Although the two works are very different – Young's being a manual for improved agriculture and McCulloch's a satirical examination of a fictionalized Pictou Township – their authors held similar didactic purposes. Both men were members of the provincial elite, both were educated at universities in Scotland, both looked around and saw a provincial economy in shambles and a people badly in need of instruction and improvement, and both pinned much of the province's lamentable condition on the weakness of its agriculture and, more particularly, on the deficiencies of its farmers. However, each man's version of liberalism imagined a different future economy and society in the colonial context. These were not the only versions of such didactic ambitions, and as we shall see in later chapters, varioius interests within both elite and non-elite circles envisioned the province rather differently again. The intention here is merely to outline two major interpretations that shared some bases, held wide currency, and in some of their particulars, might be said to have triumphed in the ideological contests for social hegemony that arose later in the century. Although many professed to be adherents, "liberalism" meant a number of often quite contradictory things in this period. How these liberalisms competed with each other and how they competed with decidedly illiberal views form central components of our view of the countryside. These men held clear ideas of where Nova Scotia should have been headed, but they did not approach improvement in the same way or conceive of it in the same terms. However, both articulated a reform program for the betterment of the province, situated their schemes in the countryside, struggled with the contradictions and paradoxes of the liberal political subject, and described what they believed to be the cultural preconditions of good government. Moreover, among those in colonial society who wielded political power, their views were widely applauded and upheld, so they deserve our attention.

IMPROVEMENT AS ENTERPRISE

Young was not the first person to call for improvement nor even the first to attempt to establish agricultural societies.[5] His writings, however, spurred the first major reforms in agriculture in colonial Nova Scotia and gave rural liberalism an institutional and intellectual base. With the serialized publication of *The Letters of Agricola*, elements among local elites and within the state found common terrain on which to reform colonial society. Educated in the liberal, or "Common Sense," tradition of the Scottish enlightenment, Young viewed himself as part of a "Scots specialty" that promoted agricultural improvement as the key to progress.[6] A Halifax merchant by day, his evenings were apparently spent reading Adam Smith and *The Edinburgh Review*, works on soil chemistry, works by James Anderson and Arthur Young, and any other agricultural treatises that he could obtain. Before coming to Nova Scotia he had worked for Sir John Sinclair, president of the British Board of Agriculture and one of the principal architects of the Scottish enclosures, and these years would exert a great influence on his later activities.[7] His only public comment, a short work criticizing high wages during a period of industrial unrest in Glasgow in 1813, fixes his economic thought firmly in a market-based approach.[8] Attempting to take advantage of the prosperous wartime conditions of the colonies, he brought his family to Halifax in 1814. Four years later, the hot wartime economy having cooled dramatically, he began writing a series of public letters urging the "enlightened and scientific" men of Nova Scotia to change farmers' "ignorance and inactivity" and bring the province's agriculture out of its "low and degraded state."[9] Collected together in book form in 1822, the letters' influence would continue into the second half of the nineteenth century.

Most of Young's work, in fact, was concerned with the "principles of vegetation and tillage," including such technical matters as crop rotation, soil, manure, and convertible husbandry. But *The Letters of Agricola* was equally designed to articulate and promote a particular social, political, and economic view of society. As Vernon Fowke noted fifty years ago, Young's concerns centred on mercantile and national issues. Indeed, as we shall see, for Young these issues were very much two sides of the same coin. But to dismiss Young as a Halifax merchant who exemplified the "mercantile mentality" or as a man whose individual "actions and aptitudes ... undermined his position as an impartial spokesman for farmers" is to miss the complexities, contradictions, and even the erudition of his argument.[10]

Young divided his subject into "three great parts": the principles of vegetation and tillage, the management of livestock, and "all the miscellaneous matter connected with agriculture ... which either further or keep back its improvement."[11] The first two parts occupy most of the work. But the part on "miscellaneous matter" reveals his purpose, his vision of the improved countryside and its historic necessity, and his rationale for improvement. While the concerns of most practical farmers related to crops, land, debts, and markets, Young began by noting that he had long "beheld with no small indignation the constant and unceasing drain on our specie for the purchase of American produce." This was the central economic issue. The adoption of his "system," he argued, would bring about "an immediate improvement in our implements of husbandry, by a flow of wealth into the landed interest, by an additional demand for labour, by a progressive population, and, finally, by that most enviable of all situations – independence of American supplies for our own consumption."[12] This context is crucial. While much of the work discusses technical matters directly related to better farming techniques, he wanted to elevate the issues beyond their status as everyday practice. It was not only the indignity of buying essential foodstuffs that concerned him. Young also argued that the province would not be economically viable if a better balance of payments was not achieved. This is the "mercantile" background on which most writers have commented, and it clearly was a central part of his argument. Nova Scotians understood well the "fluctuations" and "accidents" that attended a colonial economy. The period of the American and French wars was one of "unexampled prosperity," but after 1815 the province fared poorly during the international recession that ensued. In his first letter, Young argued against the view "that this province cannot thrive, but during war." Nova Scotia's "increasing poverty," he insisted, "may be traced to ignorance and inactivity, not to the niggardliness of nature, nor the want of physical capabilities."[13]

Young turned frequently to the theme of reversals in the "natural order" – an order that was at once "natural" yet required careful human
guidance. In the final letter, he concluded "that when things proceed
in this natural tenor, the accumulation of national wealth is more
certain ... than under any possible inversion of it."[14] Agricultural improvement offered more than the chimerical "speculations of commerce"; it was "solid and permanent," the "foundation" on which
Nova Scotians could "construct our future prosperity."[15] Broader economic stability would also reduce and maintain the cost of labour. If
the province could supply its own flour, the "price of labour [would]
be uniformly regulated by that subsistence, and the workman [could]
only accept of such wages as will enable him to live and rear a family."[16] Clearly, there were a number of benefits to be gained from improvement. But here we should examine not only Young's diagnosis
and prescriptions but also his prognosis for the future health of the
province. In particular, we need to explore exactly what he thought a
healthy body politic looked like. As he argued in the first letter: "That
colony must always be poor which buys its own bread and must be lia-
ble to many accidents ... That portion of the globe which cannot produce bread for its people is no place for the multiplication of the
species, or for the expansion of dignified and independent sentiment."[17] The first part of the passage is unambiguously economic;
Nova Scotia would be poor so long as it imported flour. But as the second part suggests, it was not simply poverty that concerned him. What
was his vision of the improved society?

Many, Young acknowledged, argued that "this Province cannot
thrive" because "its own soil is so unblest by nature as to be incapable
of feeding the present population." However, the "great defect" was
not the soil but the "want of general and scientific principles." The
problem could be traced to the provincial farmer, where a "stupid and
contented indolence lies at the bottom of our poverty." In his estimation, most Nova Scotia farmers were unskilled in even the rudiments of
good farming practices. The settler worked the land in a "sluggish tor-
por" and "aspires to nothing more than the *independence of poverty*. He
rears his miserable hovel ... [and] plants a few potatoes to eke out a
miserable existence ... His ambition rises not above the possession of a
little herd ... and of a patch of ground where the energies of vegetation waste themselves in rank and poisonous weeds."[18] Travelling
around the province, he questioned farmers on their knowledge of scientific farming, on which agricultural works they had read, and on

their familiarity with the Scottish *Farmers Magazine,* but the "only answer [he] received was the broad and vacant stare of inanity." His solution – "the first grand step towards internal improvement" – was the encouragement of agricultural societies that would "excite a principle of emulation ... and would gradually introduce a more effective and enlightened mode of practice."[19] Young's program, then, was not merely technical. It was not simply a matter of better farming; it was a matter of "improvement," a key term of the Scottish enlightenment.

The discourse of improvement was a central feature of liberalism in the late eighteenth and early nineteenth centuries. "Improvement" was an inherently positive term that denoted not only progress and betterment for individuals and the nation but also the legitimation of capitalist consolidation and practice.[20] It encompassed a complex bundle of ideas, but its core elements included notions of paternalism, science, and proper government all wrapped in a profit-driven, "Common Sense" political economy. Young's discussion of improvement borrowed from a host of agricultural writers. The most important influence, however, was not James Anderson or Humphrey Davy but Adam Smith. Like Smith, Young looked to Britain as a historical referent for economic progress and national development. As Nova Scotia was a "young country," however, its history posed something of a problem. Before the British, there were only the "wandering and barbarous tribes," and during "the first settlement" – that is, the French colony of Acadia – "the most valuable lands were taxed far beyond their natural strength."[21] For the improver, then, Nova Scotia farmers had no local historical legacies on which to draw, except the improper practices of Natives and French "peasants." But with proper instruction Nova Scotia farmers could draw on the civilized experiences of Britain.

Agriculture's place in advancing human society was a standard enlightenment theme. More particularly, however, Young followed Adam Smith's four-stages model of the development of "civilization." He described the historical movement from hunting and gathering to "shepherding," to husbandry, and finally to commerce: "Grazing draws forth no energies of the mind ... the Arab in the desert can tend his flocks and herds and leave their multiplication to the instinctive appetites of nature; it is only the first step from the savage life ... 'Tis the plough which awakes his dormant faculties."[22] Dealing with a largely British population, Young easily set up "the Arab" and "barbarian tribes" – and implicitly too the French – as the inferiors in his comparisons. But Nova

Scotia was not a society of "husbandmen." The colony's "emigrant" population was composed "mostly of mechanics" and others drawn "from
the dregs of society." If they were to be husbandmen, the dregs would
have to be taught. But from neither the press nor the Legislature had
there "emanated ... lights to direct the husbandman in his efforts."
Looking to the success of agricultural societies in England, Scotland,
and America, he argued that their "inspired example" was the answer.
Agricultural societies – composed of "men of liberal views" who "magnanimously offer on the altar of public utility ... the inspiring influence
of the example" – would "rapidly dispel that total ignorance, which, like
the gloom of midnight, has cast over us a darkening mantle."[23]

Young brought together science and political economy, arguing that
the interests of the nation would be best dealt with by educated and public-spirited men who could impart the proper methods of science to an
ignorant population. His principal task was to correct the "total ignorance of the very first rudiments of the science," and the letters are laced
with scientific terminology. This language was an important feature of
the program. Improvement required the knowledge and expertise of a
trained expert: "Agriculture is not an *Art*," he opined in his first letter,
"which may be acquired like other mechanical trades by patient drudgery and plodding dullness." Provincial farmers' "ill-directed and unenlightened efforts may ... obtain a stunted and ungenerous crop," but
lacking the "knowledge of soils, the application of composts and manures, the structure of implements, the habits of plants, and ... [the]
philosophical improvements to which husbandry has been indebted
during the last century," they were doomed to "waste the profuse liberality of nature, and wait the menacing and sure approach of penury."[24]
Young also understood that Nova Scotia farms, like any other farms, had
particular needs, so a central component of his plan was a program of
experiments designed to understand what worked best in the province.
This was good science, although all such experiments were also to include a "reckoning" of the costs involved; at base, the end was economic, not scientific.

Young's deployment of the discourse of science highlights the importance of class, and much of the argument hinges on culture and social
position. Young was arguing for the place of his class (a class of educated
and moderately wealthy men) and for their role as social leaders by demonstrating how much science (and of course men of science) could
bring to the "ignorant and unlettered boor[s]" who made up most of
the province's farmers. The extensive use of scientific terminology

meant that most of the letters were expressed in a manner that few colonial farmers would have understood. Indeed, it might be argued that its opacity was a mark of its wisdom: less-educated but aspiring members of the middle class might not know what it all meant, but they knew it sounded impressive. Young was very good at suggesting what characteristics marked this better class of men. Scientific farming required the manner of a gallant middle-class man. Nature, after all, was a woman, and the "ignorant and unlettered" farmer "wants the talents and address to court vegetative nature in her coyer moods, to draw forth her latent beauties, and induce her to display the full luxuriance of her charms. These she reveals only to those ardent and scientific admirers, who penetrate her sequestered recesses, who study her in all the windings and mazes of vegetation, and labour to acquire the knowledge of soils, [and] the application of composts and manures."[25] Agricultural improvement – clearly, at least in this illustration, the domain of men – was much like seduction. Not to improve, he argued, "betrays a want of manly firmness." Yet, equally clearly, it was not simply a masculine sphere but also one of cultured and educated middle-class men.[26]

This cultural particularity can also be seen in Young's patrician vision of the "improved" rural landscape. There were two senses to his use of the term "cultivation": first and more obviously, as the cultivation of the soil; second, as a signifier of advanced culture. When Young discussed the cultivation of the soil, he saw more than fields of wheat: "The seasons themselves frown on a people who live in the midst of woods and morasses, and nature hides her charms from their sight; for they are only displayed in the verdant meadow and the winding valley, in the cultured hill and the planted and ornamental woodland. The rude and unchastened luxuriance of the forest can never be allied to the pleasing ... attractions of rural scenery."[27] Primitive peoples – presumably not only Natives but also settlers in their first "rude" efforts – did not advance civilization. The imagined landscape of the improver featured the "verdant meadow ... the cultured hill and the planted and ornamental woodland." It was a vision very much out of step with what he saw in Nova Scotia.

The second use of cultivation – as an advanced cultural condition – situated people within this larger landscape. "Agricultural pursuits," he wrote, and the "pleasures of the country life" were the stuff of poets, the "relaxation of the nobleman and the retreat of the philosopher. The merchant or manufacturer whose mind has been broken down by the strain of business, regards them as the solace and enjoyment of his summer years ... [there] he can escape the smoke of the city [and] inhale the fresh country air." Young allowed that as a still immature colony, this form of country life might be premature. But therein lay a potential future danger. The settler was not "the improver." The settler was "devoid of all the previous training to constitute a farmer ... With the forest he has to struggle for subsistence ... [and] he is not in a condition to acquire a relish for convenience, far less for refinement." The provincial farmer, mired in the "morasses" of the forest, needed to be taught this "taste for convenience and refinement." Young's vision of this better life was clear. For him, the farm of the "improver" was not just a house and fields but the "ornamental pleasure-ground – the shrubbery, the lawn, the tasteful villa, the substantial family seat"; it was not just cultivated fields but a cultivated lifestyle. In Nova Scotia these "sublime" images were "as yet ... without import."[28] Indeed, as shown in the last chapter, this was a very long way from the reality of rural Nova Scotia at this time. Young's vision goes beyond improving the quality of the existing rural landscape; it is much more firmly rooted in recreating what he saw as virtuous in the British landholding class. His patrician vision of the rural landscape was that of an enclosed Nova Scotian agriculture. The issue was how to communicate this cultivated vision to those who could effect it.

Agricultural societies would be the main vehicles of improvement. They would be formed by men of high principles – men "raised above the petty calculations of sordid interest" – who would "cheerfully lend their services, and extend their patronage to a project which promises to construct our future prosperity." Young repeatedly reminded his audience that improvement would "increase ... capital in the hands of the agricultural classes," put more money in circulation, and increase the national "opulence" – factors that "[led] to glory, independence, [and] wealth."[29] The examples provided by such noble men, together with the rewards and premiums provided by the local societies, would "prove powerful stimulants in all the agricultural districts."[30] Emulation – "the inspiring influence of their example" – was the key point here. The status of those who took up this noble challenge would, in his estimation, rise, further securing their place in local society. Like all heathens, Nova Scotia farmers needed to be proselytized, not so that they could enter a community of equals but so that all would assume their proper position under the guiding hand of the cultured middle-class male.[31] Thus he called on "men of liberal and enlightened views" to assume the "patriotic undertaking" of forming societies, "setting a noble example," "rousing the enterprize, and facilitating the progress" of the province's farmers.[32]

In the two final letters, Young explained how agricultural improvement would affect the "national prosperity" and the "employment of capital." Again following Smith's stadial thesis, Young asserted that the "natural progress of opulence in every free state ... seems to be; first, the introduction of agriculture ... next the erection and increase of towns ... and last of all foreign trade." Nova Scotia, he argued, had reversed this "natural" path: "Our great error hitherto has been in exalting mines and fisheries above land, or rather in encouraging and promoting the former to the exclusion of the latter. Let us reverse this general system of conduct, let us return to the natural principles of national opulence ... and our prosperity will move forward with accelerated motion."[33] Here, Young went beyond criticism of the abilities of Nova Scotia's farmers, directing his words at those who shaped policy. Clearly, his audience was comprised not of "peasants" but of merchants, politicians, and other men of influence, who would organize the agricultural societies and direct the province's economic course. Farmers, he insisted at one point, were the "progenitors of all modern nations,"[34] although it is clear that when he used the term "farmer" he meant something more like "gentleman farmer." Most Nova Scotia farmers, apparently, were "peasants." The improving farmers would build the nation.

The argument around nation, political economy, and the culture of good government underpinned all of Young's work, as it did that of the Scottish improvement writers. Scottish rural improvers in the late eighteenth century, argues T.C. Smout, "believed that the highest good was the 'national opulence' ... and nowhere was the hunt for opulence more closely allied to the language of patriotism than in the literature of rural improvement, where the interest of the improver and his country were constantly assumed to be identical."[35] Young never described Nova Scotia as a nation, but his frequent comparisons of this "infant country" to other "nations" make clear that he imagined some form of autonomous existence.[36] Food and the satisfaction of hunger – the "most clamorous, unceasing and urgent demand of nature" – were absolutely basic. These were "the most pressing wants of the state," and Nova Scotia's national future lay in its ability to feed itself. "That country which does not feed itself," he maintained, "is doomed to poverty and degradation."[37] Nova Scotia must look to the examples of the great nations of the past and the present: "It is the agriculture of Great Britain ... which has swelled her resources, magnified her power, and supplied the expenditure of her foreign operations ... The preponderance of France and the weighty grandeur of Germany rest on the weighty basis of the plough; the American States have risen to importance by the same means; and Nova Scotia is poor because from a false and pernicious estimate of her soil and climate, she has hitherto neglected her true, her best, her only interest."[38] Nation, government, and economy – "the extent and condition of its territory" – were intertwined. Nova Scotia's national future lay in "building the political fabric on the foundation of the plough."[39]

Young wrote much about this foundation but occupied little of his time describing the finer features of the "political fabric." Yet even when the discussion appears technical, his assumptions are clear. One of the most telling of Young's letters is the twenty-seventh, one of several titled "On Manures," for it is here that we can see the historical vision that informed his thinking. Although, like most of his writing, this letter does discuss its title, it speaks more to the correct use of government than to the correct use of manures. It provides a story of how improvers "broke the crust of custom."[40] Young recalled how, while travelling through the Highlands in 1806, he encountered "an emaciated but venerable figure ... in the last decrepitude of old age" who described for Young the "wonderful" changes he had witnessed in his lifetime. His earliest memory was the "great riot" of 1724 "in consequence of the landed proprietors beginning to enclose their estates ... The small tenants were turned out [and] great distress was felt in the country." The tenants, the old man recalled, "rose in a mob ... and proceeded to level all these enclosures." The old man's father was one of those arrested in the disturbances and "banished to the American plantations for his crime." He went on to describe how his life "from my birth up to 1745 was miserable in the extreme: the lower classes were ill fed, ill cloathed, and ill lodged." Much changed in Scotland after the suppression of the Jacobite rebellions of 1745, but for the old man the major changes came with "the introduction of potatoes and lime." Young understood the benefits of potatoes, but the old man had to explain the larger significance of lime as both mortar and fertilizer: "Houses acquired permanence and the labours of one generation were enjoyed by the next ... If to this fossil we are indebted for the stability of our town, we are under greater obligations for the unprecedented effects on the power of the earth ... after its introduction the farmers became rich, land advanced in value, the produce was multiplied tenfold, population increased, and the counties quickly rose to their present unexampled prosperity."[41]

In a colony with an "immense abundance of lime, although hitherto much neglected," there was much to be learned in this letter "On Manures." Lime allowed the village both to improve production and to better regulate reproduction; not only did its people become wealthier, but this wealth endured. The greater lesson, however, was the possible parallel between Old and New Scotland: just as the old country's underdeveloped agriculture had been improved after 1745, so too might the wonderful effects of improvement and enclosure – and indeed conquest – be seen in the new country in one man's lifetime. Improvement had "raised Scotland to opulence and independence," and the same could be true in New Scotland. As for most of the Scottish rural improvers, 1745 represented new opportunities more than conquest. As Smout remarks on the nationalism of the Scottish improvers: "getting rich was almost the same thing as being patriotic." But this was different. Here, in this poor old man – clearly one of the "lower classes" – who had suffered the loss of his father through the enclosures, was the exemplification of how even the poor could be seen to have benefited from the paternal hand of advanced British culture. While it had been painful, it had been in their best interests.[42] Captain John Macdonald might well have said much the same to the tenants at Minudie.

Should we evaluate Young's aims based on his admiration for the enclosures? While he did not advocate enclosures as a remedy for Nova Scotia's troubles, he admired their successes and noted them as exemplifying improvement. Part of this success, he maintained, could be duplicated in Nova Scotia by adopting some of their more important, and perhaps less objectionable, techniques: the improved agricultural technologies, most obviously, but also renovated political technologies such as the properly ordered configuration of civil society. Of particular note, here, was his urging that there be a properly conducted "statistical account" of the province.[43] Modelled on Sir John Sinclair's reports on the Scottish enclosures,[44] Young's statistical account would embrace soil surveys, assessments of inland navigation, the "nature and legality of ... tenures," the "moral habits of the people which impart a pernicious influence to industry ... and to sum up all, every circumstance which has a tendency to accelerate or retard [the province's] rising prosperity." The information required here was detailed, although not to the extent of the individual- and household-level data of a modern census. The proposed account, rather, appears to have been visualized as a kind of geographic and social topology that would outline both the actual and potential locations of economic practice, the existing and required strategic facilities, and the types of people who did or would occupy these locations (whether farmers or fishers, pastoralists or horticulturalists), while commenting on their industriousness, their morality, and whether they were Britons or others. Young, like his mentor, was using "statistical" in its older – although still current – usage to refer to "knowledge of state."[45] Here, much as in the work of the French physiocrats and German cameralists whom Sinclair admired, "statistical" meant the acquisition, possession, and use of knowledge for policy and government.[46] If "such a body of evidence ... [was] collected," it would be "so rich, varied, and important that the [Central] Board [of Agriculture] could with certainty adopt and prosecute such measures as would overthrow every barrier to improvement; and its appeal to the Legislature on momentous occasions would come sanctioned with such authority as to be quite irresistible."[47]

In Nova Scotia enclosures might not occur, at least not exactly as in Scotland, but an encloser's account could provide the kind of knowledge and legislative support that rural improvement required.

Young's championing of independence through enclosure reminded his audience that improvement could have important rewards for them beyond the status that they would gain from their selfless acts. Sinclair's account "paved the way for those rapid and unexpected strides which Great Britain took in the cultivation of her territorial soil [i.e. Scotland], and the same causes here would be productive of the same effects." The "vital" issue here was the "acquisition" of knowledge; ultimately, it was also the willingness of people – whether part of the group of potential improvers or peasants – to accede to the guiding hand of the paternal improver. While the Nova Scotia improvers might face short-term costs, their services would improve the national economy, safeguard its future prosperity, and assure them of their proper place in the colony's future. Young knew that there was much more at stake here than the proper use of manures. Directed through a state-supported board, improvement societies could influence the realignment of state policy and also bring government to bear within the farming communities of the province. Improvement was statecraft.

Admiring the enclosure movement, advocating its techniques, and accommodating its nationalism, Young belonged to that very class-specific group of colonial nationalists for whom nation meant economic independence and strong government. It did not mean throwing off the chains of colonial dependency; it meant an economic independence for the province's emerging rural middle class, alignment and integration with a metropolitan elite, and a tiny slice of the glory and status associated with empire. This specificity is clear from the attributes that he assigned to the improver. He appealed not to the "privileged orders" of society nor to the peasants but to the "enlightened and provident" men who composed the province's "better classes."[48] Young was clearly speaking for the necessary guiding hand of the province's educated middle class. And as seen earlier, there were clear economic motives for his argument, although there were clear limits too. Profit and accumulation, for example, although frequently discussed, were not to be the primary determinants of improvement. He was most concerned to convince provincial elites of their duties and responsibilities, and his invocation of the language of civic humanism distanced the cause from any selfish motivation: "What duties," he reminded them, "are obligatory on us ... if we really love the soil on which we tread, and endear it with the name country?" "Our first great duty," he continued, "is to encourage Agriculture" because it is "in every age and in every place ... the prime source of national prosperity and grandeur."[49] Here, the "patriotic undertaking" of improvement was the adoption of the high ground of moral leadership in pursuit of a national wealth that the middle classes would define and from which they could undoubtedly profit. But the undertaking was by no means unambiguously "economic." Although improvers would achieve financial gains – he was unapologetic on this point – duty, not mere self-interest, propelled the improver.

Numerous comments throughout the letters suggest a certain ethical repugnance at aspects of what we would call capitalism, although, it needs to be added, always as compared with husbandry and the "country life": "Abstracted from all ideas of profit, there is an inward complacency in these peaceful pursuits which ... tends to hush the ruder passions. The strifes of ambition, the torments of rivalry, and the contentions of gain follow not the track of the plough." Among the "peaceful occupations," one does not find the "rivalships of business, the collision of commercial arrangements, the jealousies of capital, [or] the grasping selfishness of cupidity ... which disturb the harmony of society ... Among farmers there have never been ... the secrets of trade, concealments, distrusts and all that loathesome brood of passions which have raged in commerce since the first dawn of civilization." These remarks seem more antimodern than anticapitalist, more a romantic evocation of the therapeutic effects of country living than a condemnation of capitalist practice. It was the potential excesses of commercial affairs that he found unsavoury and the moderating effects of rural life that he found most appealing.[50] Young might be seen as occupying an older discursive ground where agriculture possessed a social virtue that commercial life still could not claim. The virtue that could be achieved through self-restraint maintained a crucial role in his political economy.[51]

For the most part, however, Young was not even a consistent antimodernist, much less an anticapitalist. Improvement, for example, included creating employment for labourers so that they became "consumers" of "either the rude produce of the land or of the manufactured commodities"; changes that encouraged such activities were part of "progress." He was not against factories or industries; it was simply that, according to the stadial thesis, "in the natural order" of the development of capital "the industry of the country will pre-exist ... that of the town."[52] Young's concerns about markets, and the frequency with which he invoked the critical importance of increasing the supply and thus reducing the price of labour, suggest that at minimum he understood the importance of wage labour and a society structured by a social division of labour. Yet his view was complex, composed of an elaborate mix of older and newer ideas. Duty could be invoked as an abstract ideal, wealth might be decadent and offensive, but there was no questioning the vital importance of a substantial and propertied middle class. What mattered for Young was this historic vision, which hinged equally on civic duty and middle-class prosperity.

Clearly, Young's imagined countryside was manufactured in Britain. Yet in delineating his aspirations within a European-Smithian model, Young had to make some allowances for the province's position as a colony and for its population of "emigrants." Because Nova Scotia "labour[ed] under a want of Capital," he continued, its people must turn to the plough: "no nation can carry [trade] on without holding some production of its soil or its industry as the materials of commerce. Neither of these we possess in any quantity ... It is on the internal resources of the country alone that we must place our reliance."[53] Husbandry, in the "natural order" of social development, always preceded commerce; as this colony lacked other "products of commerce," agriculture must form the basis of all future development. In theory, it would be "impossible to reverse this order, without abolishing the political laws of society." In practice, however, Smith's stages and his invisible hand would be less than helpful. While directed toward internal improvement – that is, within Nova Scotia – Young's version of improvement was an externally oriented program that looked to Europe for the proper course of progress. Indeed, his modernization program can be understood only as a particular variant of the larger program of colonialism.

In Nova Scotia, as in both Scotland and Ireland, agricultural improvement was also a tool of empire. Agricultural societies were the seedbeds of what Christopher Bayly terms "agrarian patriotism," by which he means the national ideals of an integrative, "moral community" of great landowners, yeoman farmers, and professionals in Britain before about 1840.[56] In the colonies, of course, this had a different meaning than it did in Britain. Yet for both colonizers and colonial elites, improvement's concerns became the justification for conquest and settlement – for the replacement of barbarity by civilization – and once in place, for governance in terms of both national and class subordination. Civilization entailed order. It was the ability of some to control nature and to plan a civilized society that supported their claim to power: "Like the Sovereign of the Creation, [the husbandman] commands, and ... is obeyed; he speaks, and it is done. The weeds, which are the natural inmates of the soil, disappear at his bidding; the grasses spring up and form a carpet for his feet; the corns are subject to his power ... the features of a rugged and forbidding territory are transmuted into the beautiful and sublime, and soften under the influence of his transforming smile."[57] So great was the transforming power of the improvers' dominion that even Nova Scotia's notoriously extreme weather could be civilized. Settlement had already "meliorated" the climate, and he predicted that it would continue to "gradually become milder, till it attain[s] that temperature which it is destined to enjoy." Settlement, improvement, and the resulting climatic amelioration were part of the civilizing process; just as in ancient Greece and Rome, "the vine and the olive [would] shoot here in exuberance."[58]

The stadial thesis did not mean that progress was inevitable. "The naked and trembling savage surveys the rugged and unpolished features of nature with a stupid amazement," Young argued, "*and foresees not*, that in the progress of improvement his more intelligent offspring are destined to subdue the unprofitable luxuriance of the forest, to drain the noisome and unhealthy fen, to level the inequalities of the surface, and to collect and pile the stones that infest and cumber the ground into durable and sheltering fences."[59] The improver could "foresee"; he "possess[ed] the gift of forethought, of well-directed labour, or of applying apt means to the completion of important ends." To improve was to think about the future; it was a key mark of the improver.[60] That the Briton could foresee the fences to be built justified the conquest of North American "savages" – just as it allowed the improver to direct the activities of the peasant.

Young also critiqued the colony's chaotic settlement system. Improperly ordered settlement discouraged improvement. Like the "savages" and the "irrational tribes" whom "nature has rendered ... obedient to the appetites," the settler sought "refuge from despair by plunging into the forest, and cultivating the soil to answer the cravings of indignant nature." "He" became a "self-taught farmer," but "[w]ithout skill, without capital, [and] without the benefit of instruction ... [he was] ready to run into every blunder which ignorance has invented, and which the vicious culture of the country has lent the sanction of authority."[61] Peopling the colony was critical, but it meant little if settlers ran into the woods and lived according to their appetites. The future prosperity of the province depended on recruiting a "better class of settlers," who would then create an additional demand for labour. This "demand," he argued, "would naturally absorb the emigration which to this province has been hitherto nearly useless and unavailing."[62] Anticipating the Wakefieldian argument, Young pointed out that the current practice of "shovelling out paupers" was of dubious value in the Old World; in the New World it was clear that it created only poor smallholders.[63] Yet where Wakefield would later see the market eventually capitalizing poor emigrants, Young left them under the caring arm of the improver. Young envisioned the Central Board of Agriculture also functioning as a centralized employment agency for immigrant agricultural labourers. Understanding that the "price of labour must be uniformly regulated," Young maintained that "labour [could] never fall to its proper level" until improvement created this demand.[64]

Unwilling to separate fully the political from the economic, and desirous of fostering a British-modelled agricultural market for goods and labour, Young outlined a political economy of colonization and governance that anticipated something of the method and rationale of systematic colonization.[65] "When things proceed in this natural tenor," he argued, "the accumulation of national wealth is more certain and rapid than under any possible inversion of it; and those legislative provisions which have been enacted with a view to accelerating the public prosperity by changing this order have universally proved injurious and ineffectual."[66] Given the proper encouragement, the national wealth would progress. However, again following Smith,[67] Young also had reservations. His cautious views on human nature and his ambivalent remarks on some forms of economic activity highlight this uncertainty. And this is where the real juggling act took place for the improver: the trick was to encourage "enterprize" without promoting avarice, to promote immigration without wasting it in the "*independence of poverty,*" to plan the future while looking to another world's past, and to argue for laissez-faire while recommending regulation.[68]

Young's liberalism might be seen to anticipate a more fully developed late nineteenth-century variety, but only in some ways. He advocated a form of liberal modernization, but it was of a curiously colonial sort, a kind of patrician economic liberalism in which, unlike what we see in Wakefield, the fostering and quite visible human hand was not assumed to be temporary. It was probably this hybrid character that explains the popularity and success of Agricola among the local elites. In bringing the weight of European practice to bear on a New World issue, in premising colonial-national prosperity on the ideas of Adam Smith and the Central Board of Agriculture, in articulating his plan as a program by which the rural middle classes might gain some control over the direction of their futures, and in situating all of this future success on the surety of science and political economy, Young offered something for an entire range of aspiring members of the elite and for the elite-led middle classes. To see how such a program could be implemented, we must turn to the role of the state and civil society.

Improvement was a duty and thus also a constituent part of civic virtue – of subordinating one's private interests to the public good. Ultimately, Young's concerns were directed at correcting what he saw as improper regulation. Improvement's modernizing effects would be felt not only in better farming but also in the good government promised by a well-regulated civil society. Thus in calling for the leading men to form societies that would offer direction to their communities, Young was soliciting the enlightened men of Nova Scotia to step forward and assume their role in inculcating civic virtue. Someone had "to direct the husbandman in his efforts," and someone had to guide the legislative hand. It was not the market that would make these determinations but the men of a particular class. On the issue of the government of the economy, Young pronounced himself laissez-faire, but on broader issues of governance, no invisible hand was invoked in *The Letters of Agricola*. On the contrary, the future of Nova Scotia would be secured by the guiding and quite visible hands of the public-spirited middle classes and the state. Laissez-faire and strong government were not antithetical. Nova Scotia was "approaching an eventful epoch" that promised a "new age – full of promise and pregnant with improvement."[69] But it was not the ordinary settler, whose "poverty ... modifies alike his feelings and his conduct," who would create the future in Nova Scotia. Husbandry could be where "our active powers find full scope for exertion," but it could also, he added, be brought to bear where "must needs call in the aid of the understanding to guide and direct."[70] Recognizing that the national wealth was "merely the aggregate of those capitals held by individuals," he understood the importance of increasing capital in the hands of even smallholders. The problem, of course, was that this was not being done. Colonial farmers had to be brought up to the task by science, good government, and the noble and patriotic example of their social superiors.

For Young, as for many other writers of the early nineteenth century, improvement was much more than an economic issue. It was also a matter of police and social regulation. It is important that we situate this language accurately if we are truly to understand Young's message. First, as Young's cultural allusions suggest, improvement was about the production and reproduction of social meaning. Meaning, here, was framed through metropolitan emulation and acculturation, so an improved society was like an idealized Britain: settled, cultivated, and orderly. Second, given the significance that Young attached to emulation, tutelage, and superior social positions, it seems unwise to remove his use of the term from the context of moral and social regulation. Improvement was about better farming and about economic policy, but it was more about the necessary knowledge and conditions for social and political dominance. It was, after all, the only way that Young could conceive of achieving a properly organized country; when one came from the centre of the world, emulation made sense in so many ways. Transferred to the peculiar conditions of the New World, improvement became at once a justification for conquest and a program for the creation of a new state, the maintenance of order, and the reaffirmation of class rule.

IMPROVEMENT AS A MISSION

Thomas McCulloch's satirical sketches of a fictionalized Pictou County offered a form of improvement distinct from that offered in Young's *Letters*. In some ways, their programs were complementary and directed toward the same ends. Both focused on the farmer, arguing that improvement was necessary and that an improved agriculture held the key to the province's future. Both too raised the issue of agriculture's importance to the future viability of the nation and to good government.[71] Crucially, however, they differed both in their methods and in their rationales. It was on one of the most basic liberal principles – individualism

– that they differed most fundamentally, and here we see Young, the Smithian, emphasizing features very different from those espoused by McCulloch, the evangelical Presbyterian. Young favoured laissez-faire and other liberal economic premises, but politically he looked back to an ordered society with his paternalistic, top-down notion of emulation. This notion had little connection to evangelical Christianity. Where Young envisioned an ordered, paternalistic society directing its peasants to rational (i.e., nationalist, scientific, and economic) industry, McCulloch saw a society in which individuals, driven by a moral imperative, were their own guiding forces for improvement.

Much of *The Mephibosheth Stepsure Letters* was occupied with arguing two central points. First, "industry" – that is, hard work – was vital to proper behaviour. Second, any one person's duty was to God and family, and the best way to attend to this duty was to look out for one's own best material interests through industry. "Parson Drone," the sage minister of "our Town," outlined the argument: "The deity has endowed man with active principles; he has placed him in circumstances, in which activity expended upon industrious pursuits, acquires property; and property enables him to enjoy the comforts of life, and to be the friend of every good and benevolent design ... It is the industrious and benevolent Christian, whom his lord esteems; the man who combines religious principle and worship with active industry and diffusive benevolence." God – not nature, or science, or "man's rational faculties" – had placed "man" in a society where property not only could, but also must, be accumulated. Only through the accumulation of property was humankind then able to move beyond "domestic enjoyments" to the larger world of politics, government, and the other arenas of the public. While for Young these were the starting points – their viability demanded industry and improvement – for McCulloch they were the ends attained by the moral imperative to finish "*the work thou gavest me to do.*" It was the "industrious and benevolent christian" who would receive Christ's "salutation," "[w]hether he be found prostrate at the altar of God, or rolling logs in his field."[72]

Morality, then, was the fundamental consideration. But in terms of an individual's activities, looking after one's own wellbeing was fundamental to one's ability to act morally. McCulloch repeatedly emphasized the importance of individual work and industry, but these were not enough. He continually reasserted, more than any other point, that one had to mind one's own affairs. Having decided to clear some new ground, "a number of young people" approached Stepsure and "proposed to make a frolic of the business." Stepsure, however, graciously declined his neighbours' offer, recognizing after "a little consideration ... that the profit of a frolic would be dearly purchased." He knew that the offer was kind and would be a "great help," but he would then owe each of them a day, and perhaps they might have "expect[ed] something more than ordinary eating and drinking." Stepsure then recounted his own successes, all marked by modesty, thrift, industry, and of course, "looking after my own affairs," all in marked contrast to the hardships of his neighbours:

> Many of my neighbours, it is true, have not been so successful. Still, though we differ in our modes of farming; I must say of them, that they are in general a good sort of people, and very helpful to one another. Indeed, if they did not assist each other, their life would be very miserable. I am always at home looking after my affairs, and never fail to have good crops: but my neighbours so often meet with bad land, hard labour, and poor returns, that they are obliged to spend much of their time in mutual visits, for the purpose of unburthening their minds and keeping each other in heart.

Stepsure took great delight in satirizing those "public duties and private necessities which call[ed] a farmer from home." When the Supreme Court met, he was amazed at the "public spirited" attention of the people in dutifully attending the trials and "taking care that the lawyers should not ruin the country." Although professing to admire their vigilance, Stepsure, of course, "stayed at home and wrought many a good day's work upon my farm; and this had a wonderful effect upon its improvement."[73]

Minding one's own spiritual affairs was equally important, for the material and the spiritual were inseparable. Saunders Scantocreesh – another of the didactic characters – jeered those "exceedingly religious" women who "spent most of their time" "running about the country, pretending to convert sober, industrious folk," "[i]nstead of minding their own affairs, and living comfortably like other decent folk." Mrs Sham, Scrantocreesh declared, should have shown a "little christianity at home, by lessening the misery in which her idleness, ill management, and ill nature had involved her family."[74] Time spent occupied with others' affairs was time wasted; moreover, "Every man who works for his neighbour, knows time to be money. I, therefore, determined to make it money by working for myself." The home – and minding one's own home – figure centrally. These women could be criticized not only as wives but also as Christians because they failed in their domestic duties. After condemning Mrs Sham's domestic failings, Scrantocreesh turned to Clippit, Mrs Sham's spinster sister. If she really wanted to be a Christian woman, she should "find a husband for herself, and get children as the bible bid her."[75]

The home underpinned McCulloch's political economy of improvement. Again we hear from Parson Drone:

It is ... to *home* that human beings must look for the commencement and perfection of social duties and social enjoyments. Nature has established a relation between female and male, which constitutes a basis for duty; and a feeling of duty produces exertions of energy, which exalt the mind and give it exalted pleasures ... But let me earnestly beseech you to beware of every thing which interrupts domestic society; for I tell you from this sacred book ... that the person who is often from home, whether upon business or from any other cause, is in danger of returning a worse man and to fewer enjoyments.[76]

Here, paralleling nature's active agency in creating separate male and female spheres, the home created a space for the reinstatement of women as important participants in the economy. When Stepsure married Dorothy, Drone explained to the groom the "duties of the married life." The man's primary task was to "keep want on the outside," and Drone's advice reminded Stepsure "that I had no time to lose, and must work harder than ever ... By these means, fields and crops rose very fast about my little hut."[77]

Parson Drone "did not forget Dorothy" and had some advice for her too. "Young women," he explained to the bride, "are not sufficiently aware of the connexion between female happiness and home":

Dorothy, if you wish to enjoy true comfort yourself, make your husband happy, by making his house his home ... You must ... bring your catechism to bear upon the matrimonial state: And, as I told Mephibosheth to chace [sic] want from his house, I now tell you, that domestic happiness, though helped by plenty, depends very much upon who lives in the house, and upon what use is made of plenty when it gets to the inside. In short, Dorothy, if you wish to live a comfortable life, be a domestic woman; and when your husband shows industry without, let him see that ... he has got contentment, cleanliness, and economy within.[78]

Although the boundaries were clear and the chain of command unquestioned,[79] Drone's precepts inserted the wife's labours into the
range of necessary activities for "improvement." After detailing
Drone's advice, given many years earlier, Stepsure readily acknowledged "that the prosperity of our family is not more indebted to my
labours without, than to her thrifty management and economy
within."[80] The two were complementary, if still hierarchical: it was necessary for the man's industry to allow the woman's economy; and the
woman's economy was necessary to allow the man to be contentedly industrious. Note too how this complementarity parallels the role of
"comfort" – clearly meaning both material comfort and the contentment to be found in the spiritual home – in facilitating both religiosity
and domesticity.

What completely different representations of the countryside! Compare, for example, McCulloch's description of the proper farmer's house
as a "little hut" with Young's "the tasteful villa"; McCulloch's emphasis on
private responsibilities with Young's public duties; or McCulloch's admon-
ishing farmers to labour with Young's desire that the elite "extend their
patronage to a project which promises to construct our future prosperity
on the solid and permanent basis of Agricultural improvement." McCulloch too envisioned a future prosperity, but it would be built on individual, Christian initiative, not on the enlightened and patriotic activities of
the rural elite. Both also portrayed rural society as peopled by clearly defined groups: those who improved their lots and those who sunk into misery and poverty. And toward the end of the first "book" (letter 17),
Stepsure informed his readers that he, like so many Nova Scotians, had
been impressed with *The Letters of Agricola*, which had "suggested to me a
great many improvements which my present system of farming needs."[81]
But it seems worth noting that from the tremendous cultural distance of
Young's vantage point, a real-life Mephibosheth Stepsure might well
have been one of those in whom Young saw nothing but the "broad and
vacant stare of inanity." Indeed, Stepsure readily acknowledged that he
had never heard of Smith, Ricardo, "Du Say," and the French econo-
mists (although undoubtedly McCulloch knew them at least as well as
Young), a point that highlights the differences between Young's broader
program and what McCulloch saw as the knowledge required for improvement. Fundamentally, of course, spirituality separated the two
worldviews: Young may have been moralistic, but rationality and duty to
one's country impelled his improver; for McCulloch, God and hard
work went hand in hand. Both programs stood on respectability, but

Young's was an aggressive, public respectability – where "men of liberal and enlightened views" "magnanimously offer[ed] on the altar of public utility ... the inspiring influence of the example" – not the modest, private respectability that McCulloch valued. In fact, the showy display of one's status that Young envisioned was just the kind of conduct that Parson Drone might have condemned. "Many of our people," he counselled Stepsure, "are eager for honour; but they seek not that honour which cometh from God ... [A] fool exalted to dignity, is merely a fool more conspicuous." This may be the crucial difference between the two writers. McCulloch argued that one could find respectability and improvement by securing the "means of domestic enjoyment": "every religious man," with but a "little hut" on a "small" plot producing a "little crop," "never fail[ed] to secure respectability."[82] Young wanted rather more.

Here, we can pursue these two writers' emphases on the role of the individual and, more particularly, on the idea of duty to oneself. Both writers attempted to situate their individual audience members within a community. In the case of Young, it was the nation-state; in the case of McCulloch, it was a community of Christians (although he might have allowed for a Christian nation). But the didactic messages called not on communities to act but on individuals; it was individuals in the aggregate whom both were addressing. Here is where both writers emphasized the effects of an individual's actions, those who would be affected by their activities, and to whom one was obliged. In arguing that these aggregations of individual actions were what mattered – locally, nationally, materially, spiritually – they were asserting individual responsibility to the community, to the family, and to the self. It was McCulloch – not Young, the liberal political economist – who most clearly and most emphatically placed the onus on individuals to look after their own self-interest before looking after others. The recognition that self-interest could be in the public interest was a critical underpinning of Adam Smith's political economy. But here, if we want to locate the liberal individualist, we need to look to the writer who cites the Bible, not *The Wealth of Nations*. Young's individuals were already men of substance whom he urged to lead their lower brethren. Ultimately, it was the masses who made up the national aggregate, but part of the blame for their "ignorance and inactivity" could be laid at the feet of their social superiors.

Here, then, we see the very different understandings of the place of the individual in government. While there was paternalism in McCulloch's admonishments and a certain recognition of the role of the individual in Young's prescriptions, paternalism mattered much more to Young in the same way that individual self-reliance mattered more to McCulloch. McCulloch, perhaps following Smith, understood the benefit to the community that arose from self-improvement; yet no one made it clearer than Young that duty to one's community also benefited oneself. Duty, obligation, and the subordination of oneself to a greater good emerge as strongly held and shared concepts in both authors' world-views. Whether one's obligation was to God or the state, one had a duty to perform, an obligation to contribute to the society in which one found oneself, in whatever position this might be. One also had to learn to subordinate oneself to greater powers for the greater good; whether God or the "invisible hand," there were conditions acting on one's will that imposed important constraints. It was in this crucial location, between subordination and self-government, and between discipline and action, that the modern political subject could be seen to emerge. To discipline oneself in such a way as to be self-governing yet governable was to become a liberal subject. Both men seem to have understood this, even though they approached the issue quite differently.

As there were different visions of improvement, so too were there different routes to self-government. Young's program was about one social group being the rightful leaders of others; there is no sense that the poor could govern themselves. Indeed, the major message of the book is that they must be well governed, that they must be shown the true course, and that they must follow this course. McCulloch too saw a true course that must be followed, but a crucial distinction lay in any one individual's apprehension of this course. For McCulloch, individual independence – the sort that came from hard work, minding one's own business, and knowing one's relationship with God – could put someone on this course. McCulloch's expression of the Christian dissenters' emphasis on individual choice aligned him much more clearly with the ideals of republican civic virtue. It also highlighted an important distinction between the forms of government envisioned for rural societies: whereas one was patriarchical and led by elites, the other was individualistic and led by virtuous, independent Christians. While both would play an important role in rural societies, it was the former that would most characterize elite approaches to government in rural Nova Scotia in the first half of the nineteenth century.

We will pursue these agrarian-patriotic plans into the countryside and explore their impact across a broad cross-section of the province's emerging rural middle classes. Over the next forty years, the disciples of agricultural improvement and industrial colonization would become faithful servants to these undertakings and activists in their proliferation, seeking not only to discipline the activities of farmers, workers, rural producers, and merchants but also to integrate these activities into an economy and society that was governed through the understood needs and criteria of a capitalist liberalism. Aspects of this agenda were foundational in the construction of the colonial liberal project. There were additional ingredients as well, most of which were much more grounded than the imagined communities of either Young or McCulloch. Variants of their two broad perspectives – one based in government by paternal elites, the other rooted more clearly in individual self-government – would attempt to shape the debate on government in rural Nova Scotia. Yet the complexity of this world was much greater than either of these men allowed. Rural Nova Scotia was not a gentrified agrarian England nor a quietly domestic countryside. It was much messier, and they alone would not set the terms of the debate. Alongside and within the improvers' imagined landscapes, there were other worlds – those of rural work, the timber trade, domestic manufactures, and an emergent mining industry. It is to some of these worlds, conceptually distinguishable but integrally connected, that we must turn to understand something of this messiness. Improvers were not the only colonists who understood the importance of self-government.

3

The Open Field that Was Early Mining

On the eve of the last day of the 1799 election, the Reverend Dr James McGregor stoked the already heated flames of provincial town/country politics by entertaining the "country party" candidates in his home with a fire. This was no ordinary fire. It burned coals hewn from McGregor's lands on the East River of Pictou County. We know nothing of what was said or what impressions were made that evening, except, as the nineteenth-century historian George Patterson tells us, that the coals were "quite a novelty" and portended to be "an important event for the Province."[1]

Coal's future importance was still many years away. Yet the symbolism of that evening is striking. McGregor had not simply invited three politicians to share his table or even his good fortune for having coal in the ground below it. He had brought together the three most noted members of the "country faction" – Edward Mortimer of Pictou, James Fulton of Londonderry, and William Tonge of Hants – men who were about to lead rural Nova Scotia's political battle against Halifax's Loyalist "merchantocracy" and its dominance of provincial politics.[2] All three were merchants whose trade came from the country: Mortimer was the major timber dealer on the Gulf shore; Tonge too bought and sold timber, as well as exporting gypsum (i.e., plaster of paris) to New England; and Fulton invested in timber, gypsum, and shipbuilding.[3] It is hard not to imagine McGregor and the candidates discussing the possibilities that coal held for the future and, moreover, their possible role in shaping this future. They had no idea just how big coal would be, but they knew a marketable product when they saw one.

Elsewhere, in dozens of locations around the province, hundreds of others were already engaged in mining and quarrying. For many country people, coal, gypsum, and grindstones were part of a package of products – fish, timber, potatoes, hay, coal – that together provided some part of their households' subsistence. At the eastern end of the Bay of Fundy, itinerant quarriers and tenants on the bordering estates cut grindstones and building stones; further south, near Windsor, many others quarried gypsum from the river banks of Hants and Colchester Counties, as well as in Cape Breton. While trade in these articles often ran afoul of the colonial state, it was considered an important component of the province's economy. The government-run coalmines at Spanish River (Sydney, in the still separate colony of Cape Breton) and a single iron mine near Annapolis represented the only state-sanctioned mining in the first decade of the nineteenth century. The others were small-scale, labour-intensive, and illegal. Indeed, as J.S. Martell argues, early coalmining "was not an industry in any real sense until sometime after 1784 and was not established as one of the foundations of the Nova Scotia economy until the 1840s."[4] From the perspective of the industrial organization of the future, Martell is right. Yet, as we shall see, these mines were better organized and more significant than Martell's account might allow.

The various forms of mining that were being practised also represented the possible paths that still lay open for resource-based production in the years to come. Private capital, with the support of the state, would eventually dominate the field, but policy discussions, customary use, and common-law considerations continued to hold out the possibility that any one or all of the alternatives – the state, private merchant's capital, and independent petty producers – might operate legitimately. Indeed, the distinctions between these alternatives were not always clear. Over the course of the next half-century, private interests, the state, and advocates of industry and improvement would compel a radical simplification and clarification of this open field. In doing so, they would more clearly define private rights and public interests, while further disciplining the colony's peoples to such government.

Coal was among the minerals reserved in all Crown lands in Nova Scotia, with the state taking great interest in developing and controlling a potentially revenue-producing product.[5] Yet how this development would occur was not clearly articulated. Throughout this period, particularly in Cape Breton, control of the legal production of coal would be traded back and forth between merchants and the state itself. The two groups demonstrated a clear unity of purpose, a sharing of resources, and ultimately a fundamentally mercantilist recognition that their combined efforts best suited the exigencies of industrial practice in a colonial context. At the same time, the Crown also held ownership for the people. Thus many people believed that coal was a public resource that might be freely employed for their own use. This tension between Crown ownership (which leant itself fully to state-merchant cooperation, but with at least the potential for common use) and capitalist development (which treated coal as a restricted resource to be controlled by a limited property regime) established divergent views on resource use and exploitation. In many areas of Nova Scotia some resources were not only still available on an open-access basis but also successfully governed as commons. Many poor settlers made such resources important components of their subsistence. But very quickly, coal – together with other publicly owned resources such as tidal flats, grindstones, sea marshes, and gypsum – came under increasing pressure from merchant-capitalists who wished to control larger portions of trade in these products. In Nova Scotia, home to many who had fled the enclosures of land and resources in the Old World, new enclosures were already under way as some attempted to increase their holdings at the expense of the poor. These pressures increased rapidly over the course of this period, establishing the context for a struggle between the moral economy of the poor and the new political economy of improvement.

Production and marketing were organized by what we can call "state-merchant enterprise," another curious colonial hybrid that united older and newer models for governing the economy. Against a tendency in Atlantic Canadian historiography to conflate "merchant capital" and "mercantile," the second part of this chapter explores the rearticulation of mercantilism as central to understanding some forms of economic activity in this period and as a conceptual key to better understanding colonial Nova Scotians' conception of society. The close connection between merchants and the state has long been acknowledged as a distinct feature of colonial economic development.[6] Although this connection is typically represented as a form of colonial venality or as a necessary collaboration under the primitive conditions of the time, we shall describe it more as deriving from a colonial-military *raison d'etat*. In his classic account Eli Heckscher describes mercantilism as government principally guided by the state's first interest – power – and thus as a locus where "all economic activity [must be] subservient to the state's interest."[7] Economic activity in this formulation was rarely separable from political or governmental activity. Like diplomacy and other more patent forms of state, it was at the service of, and indeed an activity of, statecraft. This chapter examines the very early period of this history in Nova Scotia and reveals the simultaneous existence of an open field of independent producers and an already patterned tendency toward state-capitalist directed monopoly and regulation. Poor people's eventual dispossession, and their reconstitution as waged labourers, forms a crucial episode in the history of mining and quarrying in rural Nova Scotia. Justified by the logic of enclosure and the rhetoric of improvement, these events signalled victories on the road to the consolidation of liberal-capitalist practice.

SMUGGLERS AND PRODUCERS

The history of coalmining in the eighteenth and early nineteenth centuries appears to be one of fits and starts. Until the final conquest of Acadia, this intermittence is understandable. Amid innumerable wars, and with colonial powers passing either the peninsula or Cape Breton Island back and forth, it is unlikely that any large-scale efforts were even possible. Throughout all these changes, most coal was mined and marketed illegally. The most important minerals, including coal, gold, silver, and lapis lazuli, were specifically reserved from all grants of land made in Nova Scotia after 1783. This meant that, legally, mining could occur only under a lease from the Crown. Yet in the 1770s and early 1780s, "smugglers and unauthorized persons ... carried off large quantities of coal" from Cape Breton to Nova Scotia and New England.[8] Most of Nova Scotia's known coalfields outcropped along the shore. And while we should not underestimate the difficulty of transportation and marketing, it required little capital or skill to locate the coal, dig it out of the cliffs, load it onto scows, and transfer it onboard a coastal vessel. These independent producers demonstrated that there were markets for the province's mineral resources throughout the region and beyond.

There were hundreds of small-producer operations around the province. Coal, grindstones, and most significantly gypsum outcropped along the shore in the mainland counties of Hants, Cumberland, Colchester, Pictou, and Antigonish, as well as on most of Cape Breton Island. In the existing histories of resource development in Nova Scotia, these producers from the eighteenth and early nineteenth centuries are invisible, as they fall outside a developmentalist logic that insists players must have a legitimate lineage to nineteenth-century capitalist firms or entrepreneurs in order to claim a place in the story. Yet for a time these producers stood centre stage. These small-scale operations hindered the capitalist consolidation of trade and production, while their numbers made them a significant political force, both locally and in Halifax.

Hundreds of small coastal traders ranged up and down the Atlantic Coast from Newfoundland to New York. These small vessels were the main source of supplies in the small villages and outports dispersed along the region's coast. Most engaged quite strictly in legal trade, but many carried illegal cargoes of fish, gypsum, coal, and numerous other local products. In the 1770s a group of smugglers were operating abandoned French coal works at Cow Bay near Sydney until they were driven off by troops from the garrison at Spanish River. By 1785 these troops were working the mine and supplying the garrison at Halifax. But other markets for coal remained, and the smugglers simply moved on to any of the many harbours in the vicinity where they could continue to load coal relatively free from any risk of interference. In 1788, despite the presence of troops and armed naval vessels, Governor Macormick of Cape Breton reported that during the summer fifty-four ships had loaded coal illegally east of Sydney at Lingan. This, he admitted, was only at one place, and he had no idea what was occurring "at the many other places open to such depredations."9

Smuggling was a vexatious issue in most colonies.10 This was particularly so in the still separate colony of Cape Breton. In the 1790s and 1800s there were hundreds of miles of unsettled coastline, and most of the governors' reports made some reference to "depredations" upon the government's revenue. Coal was the most important source of revenue for the colony, so many of its officials had a direct stake in suppressing its illegal trade. The young colony's very limited resources meant that enforcement proved difficult. As the colony had only two small schooners and no men to spare for "excursions" along the coast, few smugglers were actually caught, fewer captured and tried, and fewer still convicted. Although active in the dozens of small harbours and along the hundred miles of irregularly patrolled coast, smugglers were gone by the time a report reached Sydney and the (aptly named) *Hope* had been sent out to catch them. Officials' reports, always emphasizing their good government, were compelled to send out mixed messages. In 1796 a surprisingly sanguine David Mathews, president of the Cape Breton Council, informed the colonial secretary that he had successfully suppressed the trade. James Miller, the superintendent of mines, offered much less confidence, observing that most of the smugglers had simply moved over to the island's sparsely settled west coast, where they could "steal Coals without risque." More men and resources were required if there was to be any hope of regulating the trade.[11]

The basis for Matthews's optimism was a new certification system for coal exports initiated by his government. With cooperation from Nova Scotia officials, a few boats were seized at Halifax, but the new policy made only the slightest dent in the trade. In fact, in many instances state practices actually encouraged smuggling. The refusal of the Colonial Office to invest in better equipment for mining and loading the coal, combined with the burden of the new licensing system, meant that legal traders spent as much as a week in Sydney loading their vessels, while the Crown's duty of 2s per chaldron allowed smugglers a comfortable margin to undersell legal coal. Thus the permit system only deterred illegal sales to the legal mines' principal market, the garrison in Halifax. It could not police those "Harbours of little notice" around the region that were the smugglers' main market, "much less those of the States of America." It was the international market and the interstices of the regional market that the smugglers filled, supplying small towns and villages "accustomed heretofore to get Coals from hence, and it may be presumed will in future have still more occasion for Them." Governor Wentworth of Nova Scotia – no enemy of regulation – observed that the new rules created a "heavy discouragement to the industry of the Country, and tend[ed] almost necessarily to create habits subversive of the control and regulating of trade."[12] Smuggling was a mark of bad government.

Even if a smuggler was caught, the law may not have been applied fully. In the ports receiving the coal, few were keen to prosecute those who supplied their communities with such valuable products. In the summer of 1800 a report on the "regulation of trade" in New Brunswick and Nova Scotia detailed the principal trade of each of more than twenty ports as well as the extent of the "practice of illicit trade." The report's author, George Leonard, recognized that little could be done to curb the practice because it was both widespread and important to the local economies. The deputies in each port that he visited were "zealous to promote the views of government … but being deficient in the means of enforcing the Laws of Trade they can only hold up threats."[13]

And idle threats at that. Because stealing coal was a crime against His Majesty's property, the law required the attorney general himself to lay charges. Private suits were possible, but the only compensation was the smuggler's cargo, and few were willing to risk privateering for a load of coal. Moreover, even if such measures worked, there was little chance of a prosecution in a place where, as one official explained, "a Jury [was] very tender where poor people are concerned in a Trade which cannot be conceived to be injurious to any." Smugglers, in this context, were not criminals. Like many jurors, they were poor people who were engaged in a popular and often vital trade. In the case of coal, the illegal traders sold their products for less in a domestic market that the official trade ignored. The "fair British Traders" who complained most loudly were distressed because of the unwanted competition in markets that they believed were their own. Smugglers were easier targets than the large British vessels that often arrived in Halifax or Saint John with several tons of coal as ballast.[14]

Smuggling represented a major component of the coal market well into the 1820s. We have no firm data on the smugglers' numbers or their share of the market; indeed, given how much of the demand was itself clandestine, any such data would be largely speculative. But there is sufficient evidence to make reasonable estimates. Most smuggling ships were shallops, small vessels capable of carrying between 10 and 30 chaldrons (15 to 45 tons). Macormick's report of fifty-four vessels at Lingan in the summer of 1788 would warrant an estimate of about 1,000 chaldrons. Lingan was a favoured location for the smugglers, but it was only one of at least a dozen locations where coal could be mined easily. Coal was also shipped down the Bay of Fundy along with loads of gypsum, grindstones, fish, and timber, most often to Passamaquoddy Bay, where such extra-legal trade between the United States and the British colonies was centred.[15] Simply working with the figure of 1,000 chaldrons – and taking into consideration that Lingan was only one of several locations – we might double it, yielding an estimate of about 2,000 chaldrons per year.[16] If this estimate is at all accurate, then in the years between 1790 and 1820 smuggling would have represented between 30 and 50 per cent of the region's coal trade.

This estimate is certainly conservative. There were numerous techniques for working the margins of the legal trade. Many smugglers, for example, obtained permits, but through forgery and bribes each smuggler could use his one permit for several loads. Alternatively, as Superintendent Miller observed, the inspector was often not at his post, sometimes at moments apparently convenient for the smugglers. These lines between the legal and illegal coal trades become still less clear when we consider the extent of the informal local trade in coal around the province. In 1803 coal dug near Londonderry was being sold to blacksmiths along the Parrsboro shore, and King's College at Windsor was attempting to obtain a supply from the same seam. Along Pictou's East River, coal was "carted from 1200 to 2000 yards to the River, laden in Boats and transported three miles on safe water to the vessels which export them" – a description that suggests much more organization than was attributed to the smugglers. In 1811 Governor Prevost of Cape Breton observed that coal outcropped in many parts of the colony and that these "veins of coal are partially wrought by the proprietors of the Soil whereon they are found for their supply of fuel and their neighbours, notwithstanding the restraining clause inserted in all Grants to prevent such practice." In Cumberland County, Thomas Roach, the merchant-farmer at Fort Lawrence (just across the Cumberland Basin from the Joggins) whom we met in chapter 1, accepted locally wrought coal as payment for goods, either using it himself as fuel or exchanging it again with local blacksmiths.[17] All of this was before the Colonial Office sanctioned mine openings in mainland Nova Scotia.

Indeed, when the first recorded licence was granted in Pictou County, competition was immediate. In 1817 John McKay obtained a lease to the mines on the East River, although he claimed to have been working the mines since at least 1807.[18] In the same period Adam Carr worked a seam on the other side of the river and "sold the Coal to the Inhabitants of the Place." Carr, like the coastal smugglers, had no licence but filled a market that the authorized producer was unable to meet or for which the producer's price was too high. But state-sanctioned markets could be capricious. In 1820 we find the same Adam Carr on the other side of the issue. Now, having obtained his own lease, he was seeking the state's protection, complaining that "persons" were "raising coals on their own lands and other lands in the vicinity … for their own use and in many instances sparing them to their neighbours."[19]

Other evidence suggests something of the depth of people's unwillingness to allow anyone to monopolize a freely accessible resource, although the point was inconsistently upheld and carried mixed meanings. Take, for example, the petition from Edward Mortimer, S.G.W. Archibald, S.B. Robie, and William Lawson, who also protested McKay's "exclusive Licence." They argued that the state should "allow that most necessary article to be raised in more than one place as [otherwise] an Individual will have it in his power, to charge any price he might think fit and supply only whom he pleased." Given that the petition came from prominent merchants and politicians, this is hardly evidence of popular resistance to monopoly; indeed, they were probably more concerned with not possessing the monopoly themselves than with its existence. This too may explain the 1820 petition of the elite-dominated East River Agricultural Society for permission to dig coal. This petition emphasized these elites' experiments with burning lime with local coal but also added a request for "permission for those who have no firewood on their lots but coals to dig them for family use."[20] Such petitions represent one side of the coal question at this time: here, antimonopoly sentiments were rhetorical devices intended to open new possibilities. The proto-liberal commitment to free and open markets was often selective.

Illegal mining continued after the state opened the mines for legal production and sales, but the new regime would change conditions. In granting its first licence, and by making the licence exclusive, the state had not so much created a monopoly as asserted control over its domain by more clearly defining as legal and regulated what previously had been only reluctantly tolerated. Regulation ended a free market, but it made business possible. As George Smith argued when refusing the petition of the East River Agricultural Society, "If the petitioners are granted the Prayers of their Petition, the same indulgences will be expected by all the inhabitants of the District for like purposes."[21] Such indulgences would not be allowed by the Legislature and certainly not by someone, such as George Smith, who was already investing in local mines himself. Smith knew that the profitability of coal depended on a restricted supply, so he sought exclusivity. If people could mine where they liked, there would be a limited market for coal. Such liberal indulgences did not make for good government.

At the eastern end of the Bay of Fundy, coal was simply one of many products – most notably gypsum, timber, and grindstones – exchanged in both the formal and informal economies. And it is here that the extant record gives a fuller sense of how mining and quarrying fitted into the economy and society of Nova Scotia in the early nineteenth century. Grindstones had been cut along the Cumberland shore since the early eighteenth century. The shore around the Cumberland Basin abounded with a hard-grit sandstone, ideally suited for grindstones. The best location was just below the DesBarres estate at Minudie at a place known as the Joggins.[22] Coal also outcropped along the shore there, but it was exposed to the tides and thus of poor quality. The grindstones produced there, however, were known to be the finest on the eastern seaboard of North America. As we saw in chapter 1, when DesBarres settled his estate in the 1770s, he was principally interested in its marshes and agricultural potential, but he was clearly aware of the stones' potential value. In 1784 DesBarres laid out a detailed plan for the production and marketing of grindstones. He estimated that 1,500 stones could be manufactured each year; each stone would cost about 4s but could be sold in Saint John and New England for about 7s6d. The quarriers were to be tenants living on the estate, as well as farmers and itinerant workers from around the region of the Bay of Fundy. The itinerants would be "paid in goods consisting of provisions," while tenants could put grindstones against their rents and any surplus could go against provisions.[23] Thus the 4s cost would be partly carried by the producers.

The 1784 plan was never effectively carried out. When it came to collecting rents, DesBarres had no more success with quarriers than he had had with his landed tenants. In 1799, for example, one of the few years that saw a substantial portion (75 per cent) of the estate's rents collected, most residents paid with cows, butter, barley, wheat, and peas but seldom with grindstones. Throughout the 1790s DesBarres's agents demanded payments for their absentee employer but with very limited success. Few quarriers paid for the privilege of cutting on the tidal flats; most paid only for "camping" on the adjacent shore.[24] Transient "manufacturers of grindstones," as they were labelled in the census of 1827, were in a better position to avoid rents than were the tenants. Yet as we shall see, many tenants resisted paying rents that they felt were improper or unjust. Of £140 due in 1810, less than £50 was received. In 1807 DesBarres's son negotiated new leases for inland quarries, an attempt to consolidate the estate's hold on the better sites. But even this limited strategy failed. These seven leases represented only a tiny fraction of the many hundreds of men who quarried not inland but on the exposed tidal flats along the shore.[25]

Conditions, and therefore rules, were radically different on the foreshore. The tides along the eastern end of the Bay of Fundy are among the highest in the world, ranging from 12 to 16 metres. At low tide, the immense tidal flats offered local people access to valuable products such as seaweeds, kelp, and shellfish, as well as the option of establishing large-scale weir fisheries and, along one stretch of the shore, producing grindstones. The shore and its resources were used freely by anyone along the coast, and few people saw any distinction between gathering seaweed and cutting grindstones. Over the next forty years, however, struggles over access to the seashore would involve both the provincial and colonial state, independent producers, and nascent capitalists in a protracted and often violent conflict.

DesBarres, as well as later proprietors, found themselves on messy legal terrain. Common-law tradition reserved tidal flats – the foreshore – for the Crown. Property lines on the seashore extended only to the high water mark, and the only bases for any claim of ownership were a grant from the Crown that specifically included the foreshore or some other proof of "ancient ownership" or use. Otherwise, the shore was assumed to belong to the Crown. DesBarres's grant contained no such clause.[26] Nor could he demonstrate ancient use. As "A Farmer" observed, during DesBarres's lifetime "every person had access" to the shore. "In some cases," he continued, "the persons so employed was charged Campage that is a rent for erecting Camps or huts on the Upland but not as a rent for Quarrying the stone ... DesBarres wished to possess this reef, but never exercised any right of ownership." Many others shared this understanding of how the shore had been regulated. Local people had long been in the practice of cutting stones and were exercising a claim based in their notion of customary use. But this understanding of custom and use went well beyond the quarriers. The customary exercise of shore rights was an ancient privilege, well recognized under British law, and both petty producers and the state guarded their rights jealously. Hundreds of farmers routinely gathered seaweed from the shore for fertilizer. Fishers used the shore to salt their catch, and many, including some of DesBarres's tenants, set weirs on the flats.[27] For these farmers, fishers, and quarriers, the shore was Crown land and therefore public; they had administered its use and could continue to do so. The location of most of the quarries between high and low water marks created opportunities for poor workers and tenants as well as legal difficulties for anyone attempting to control the trade. Thomas Black, who in 1836 had been working the grindstone reefs for over forty years, understood that "all had equal rights" to quarry stones on the shore.[28] Such customary practices would soon come under attack.

When Captain John Macdonald made his report for DesBarres in 1795, he mentioned only briefly the valuable grindstone ledges along the shore. If he had more fully focused his attention on these ledges, he might have noted that like the fields and marshes the ledges too were treated as commons. An elaborate and carefully administered workplace had evolved there in the past one hundred years. Each spring quarriers descended upon the shore of the Minas Basin. The stones were cut at low tide. They were then tied to log rafts, floated to the surface on the rising tide, and either hauled up on shore for finishing or loaded onto small shallops or schooners just offshore, which would transport them to Saint John, to New England, or depending on the international trading climate, to the illegal British/American trading zone at Passamaquoddy, between Maine and New Brunswick.[29] This shore-based regulation was in fact formalized and governed by an association referred to as "the Fraternity." In the 1830s Simon Newcomb, recalling a lifetime working on the shore, explained how hundreds of tenants and itinerant workers cut grindstones from April until November. Work sites, marketing, and disputes were all administered jointly. Quarriers were under "no Control while there," Newcomb recalled, "except, Such Laws and Regulations as were made by the Fraternity, on the Spot." William Chapman also explained how the quarrymen regulated access to the shore so "that no one should interfere with the occupation of another in a seam or quarry previously opened."[30] As an open-access commons, the grindstone ledges between the low and high water marks were open to use by anyone. Most of the extant petitions note the frequency of "strangers" working the shore, and there were occasional conflicts and petty encroachments, especially over work sites. As was the case for English "commoners" into the nineteenth century, the rational solution to such disputes was to provide some form of policing through collective self-government.[31] We know little more about the Fraternity, except that with no state or mercantile regulation and support, it oversaw production in an industry that shipped between 10,000 and 20,000 grindstones per year to New England. In doing so, the quarriers' Fraternity successfully managed the commons.

Prior to DesBarres's death in 1824, any sort of consolidation in the grindstone trade took place after production, and even this appears to have been quite limited. Although several merchants were emerging as important players in the trade as early as 1810, there were probably dozens similarly engaged. The example of Thomas Roach illustrates both the limited concentration of the market before the 1820s and the great potential that nevertheless existed. Like most rural merchants, Roach was at the centre of a network of producers and buyers; his customers and his agents supplied him with large quantities of butter, cheese, cattle, timber, grindstones, coal, and plaster as well as with smaller amounts of cloth, cordwood, fish, berries, vegetables, and other farm produce. Along with dozens of other merchants in the area, he formed a central link between the various products of the countryside and the local, regional, and international markets accessible from the Bay of Fundy.

Each year Roach provided his customers with a wide variety of agricultural products (butter, homespun, cattle, timber, and fish) as well as several hundred tons of "plaster," a few chaldrons of coal, and several hundred grindstones. Many of these transactions appear to have been conducted under the standard conditions of the truck system: goods were advanced on credit with the promise of return in some other goods. Hugh Boyd, for example, was advanced £12 in December 1805; then, in October 1806, he returned with 160 grindstones at 3s each (£24). Boyd, like many of the grindstone traders, also made some purchases from Roach, most of which were either food or supplies for the job (usually tools and rope). In some cases, the trade appears to have been less formal than truck, encompassing a wide variety of exchanges. Stephen Ward, for example, sold butter, furs, and occasional day labour but was also credited for a "1/3 share" of 67 grindstones.[32] Most years Roach credited customers with two or three hundred stones, although each year between 1804 and 1808 he gave credit for between eight hundred and a thousand. Again, there was great variety among the items exchanged, but most of the grindstones that he received came from persons who had nothing else to exchange.[33]

While much of this trade was illegal, it was not unknown. Several government reports described the grindstone and gypsum trade and even noted its importance to the rural economy. Gypsum was also quarried by farmers on their own lands, especially in the area between Windsor, Nova Scotia, and Shepody Bay in New Brunswick. Commenting on a downturn in trade and a shortfall in agricultural produce in the spring of 1802, Governor Wentworth observed that the trade in grindstones and gypsum was an exception and that this trade was actually booming. Alhough the trade generated no revenue for the Crown, Wentworth estimated that it would "yield part of the means of payment for bread, flour, and corn necessary to this Country."[34] Asked to comment on New Brunswick legislation intended to curb smuggling, Wentworth rejected the need for such a measure, as smuggling did not, in his opinion, "exist in the degree and in the manner they [the New Brunswick Legislature] imagine." Moreover, he continued, it would cause producers great harm: "It is supposed by restricting the exports to larger vessels and more distant ports, that more freight will be obtained [and] more tonnage and Men employed. If this is the case, it could not compensate disfranchising the smaller vessels hitherto employed, and depriving the People who own Plaister Rocks, in small creeks and inlets where small vessels only can take it, from the sale of their property, which is too cheap to bear lading in boats and transferring again into vessels."[35] Wentworth was no advocate of laissez-faire, and this is one of the few times when he sided against the regulation of anything, much less defended the position of smallholders. But as with the Pictou coalfields, there was statecraft at work here too. To be sure, Wentworth recognized the importance that this trade held for local petty producers. But the former governor of New Hampshire was no Thomas Jefferson. As we shall see, Wentworth was also working to maintain Halifax's political and mercantile dominance. One way to protect the power of the capital was to prevent consolidations of power in the hinterland.

Wentworth's brief flirtation with support for the poor reflected his experiences with William Tonge, one of the more important rural traders. Tonge was a substantial farmer, a gypsum trader, a member of the Legislative Assembly, and a leading player in the so-called "country party." He was also one of the men entertained with the coal fire in Dr McGregor's home that evening in 1799.[36] In 1803 Tonge attempted to introduce restrictive shipping rules for the gypsum trade similar to those under consideration in New Brunswick.[37] Tonge's bill would have restricted participation to vessels over 40 tons, thus effectively eliminating the small coastal traders. The bill passed the House, but Wentworth refused to sign it. Tonge then attempted to have the town of Windsor made a customs port, and to do so he played on his rural constituents' resentment and mistrust of Halifax merchants and politicians. In the winter of 1806–07 he organized a series of meetings and petitions complaining of the onerous and sometimes – it was alleged – illegal burden imposed on rural producers by the Halifax customs officials. In effect, he wished to represent himself as a "tribune of the people" while also, as the leading merchant in the area, attempting to consolidate a larger share of trade. Wentworth's defence of the small producers would undergo a radical change. At present, a "demagogue," a man whom Wentworth described as "the miniature of the Abbé Sieyes," led the country people, and they wanted a "popular superintendence" of a customs house at Windsor so that they might smuggle more easily. After the stormy spring session of the Legislature and several letters from London, we find Wentworth – now sounding much more like the antidemocrat he is known as – invoking much less sympathy for the rural small producers, who seemed entirely under the sway of their representative: "Popular meetings are convened in the Country, composed of uneducated tradesmen, laborers, and farmers, who *from the nature of their industry* cannot possibly have real information, who are persuaded to sign or make their mark to anything, often without knowing the Contents, and almost always deceived in its object and consequences."[38] These agitations, like the "corresponding societies, Clubs and Committees professing reform" that Tonge was alleged to have established, struck at the core of Halifax's political control over trade and at Wentworth's belief in the established order. Tonge's capacity to achieve a "popular superintendence" threatened to enhance power outside the capital. Halifax's weak capacity to police an important trade threatened its capacity to govern. The city's merchants undoubtedly lobbied Wentworth on this matter. But it was the anarchic, potentially democratic impulse that the governor most feared. Within the week, Wentworth ordered the sheriff of Hants County "to suppress and disperse all such meetings" and sent word to other areas that he would "dismiss any magistrates who allowed such meetings."[39]

On one level, this was a personal battle between the capital's elite and a local paternalist – in other words, between court and country. On another level, however, it was an additional component of an ongoing struggle over governance and the ability to exercise power. Like most eighteenth-century Tories, Wentworth saw democracy as mob rule; it had wreaked havoc in France, and the former governor of New Hampshire had first-hand knowledge of its destructive power.[40] Rural dwellers, "from the nature of their industry," could not be knowledgeable in affairs of the state. Most of them were "interested" in the trade, which, in combination with their general ignorance, made them poor judges: "the shoemaker, the Tanner, the Farmer, the Tailor, the labourer and the Peasant are all directly or indirectly interested in the trade of Fish, Plaister of Paris and Stone." And they were all, apparently, illiterate and easily led astray by a dangerous rural demagogue who would usurp the king's authority. In the period of three years under Tonge's menacing influence, Wentworth magically transformed propertied "People" (whose smuggling amounted to a "trifle") into a group of farmers, fishermen, and peasants ("all engaged more or less in smuggling") who threatened the authority of the Crown. Whereas earlier Wentworth had dismissed the need for greater control, now he believed that more ships were needed to suppress "Practices which always tend to disobedience and opposition to the Laws."[41] This control would come from Halifax, not from someone believed to direct a "popular superintendence." The governor might tolerate small-scale smuggling to the extent that it facilitated peace in the countryside. But he would not allow it to be consolidated and made an instrument of power. He would not allow threats to his capacity to govern the capital's hinterland.

State-directed mining began in the French period. Coal, required by the garrisons at Louisbourg and by the smaller centres on the Bay of Fundy, was mined at Spanish River (Sydney) and the Joggins (in what became Cumberland County).[42] These were small mines, pits really, worked by the local garrisons. Little changed after the British conquest. During the American Revolutionary War "the mines at Spanish River" – an open pit "worked by His Majesty's Troops at the lowest Rate of Wages" – were worked to supply the garrisons at Halifax. Not until 1784 did the newly created colony of Cape Breton begin to operate the mines at Sydney on any scale beyond digging coal directly from the bank.[43] Four hundred acres were reserved at North Sydney for the purpose of coalmining, and workers drove a level into the seam and constructed a wharf.[44] For the first two years of operation the government itself worked the mines. Production was limited and the few dozen "miners" – a mixture of professional miners, Irish fishermen from Newfoundland, itinerant workers, recent arrivals not yet or only recently on the land, soldiers, and convicts – produced only a few hundred chaldrons of coal per year. These were sent to Halifax in exchange for produce.[45]

At a time when the fledgling colony was struggling to find revenue, the Cape Breton Legislature looked to the coalmines as a potential source, and indeed as a possible base, of the future prosperity of the island. If Spanish River was made a free port and the mines developed, Governor Macormick believed, it "would cause such an Influx of Inhabitants with their Stock and other property as would establish a fund of Wealth and Commerce … As the Mines are almost inexhaustible, shipping would soon be employed by the Merchants … and the Settlement become consequented to Great Britain." In 1793 the Colonial Office sent James Miller, an Irish mine manager, to Cape Breton to report on the state of the mines and to prepare a "plan for working and Exporting [coal] in the future." Envisioning Sydney as "a proper English mine," Miller set out an elaborate series of plans for shafts, levels, pumps, shipping facilities (as opposed to the single, unprotected wharf now in place), and a large stone breakwater capable of sheltering the mines from flooding. It seems a sound plan, but the secretary

of state for the colonies balked at the required expenditure of over
£5,000 (sterling). Instead, Miller was appointed to superintend the existing works, and the council was to budget £100 each month to effect
"what improvements are deemed necessary." The proper development
of the works would have to wait "until the quantity of Coals exported
will ... provide for the Expence."[46] In Sydney it was no development
without money; in London it was no money without development.

Miller's plan for the mines went against the needs and expectations
of almost everyone involved. The Colonial Office's task was not to invest in dubious, and expensive, schemes that might create returns
down the road. Duties on exported coal and fish were the only significant sources of revenue – the so-called "Casual Revenue" – for building roads and bridges and for funding other measures needed to open
the countryside, costs that would otherwise come from the meagre
funds that Parliament allocated the tiny colony. Revenue, however, was
also needed to provide the salaries of government officials, so most salaries came directly from the coal duties. By 1820, the last year that
Cape Breton was a separate colony, the total revenue from the mines
after paying the wages of the miners was £1,040. Of this, over £500
went toward salaries for inspectors and other administrators and almost £400 toward expenditures for equipment and other expenses,
leaving a surplus of only £108.12.9. In effect, as far as local state officials were concerned, the mines existed to pay their salaries.[47]

The mines were leased to two merchants, Richard Tremain and
Jonathan Stout, in 1792 for a term of seven years – apparently because
they were the "only respectable merchants in the place."[48] Despite the
faint praise, the lessees of His Majesty's coal mines dominated coal
production over the next decade. The leasing arrangement made
them responsible only for the operating costs; they leased the mines,
not the rights to the seam. All the development work – shafts, levels,
wharfs – was financed by the state and worked by men hired by the superintendent of raising coals, James Miller. The lessees rented the facilities, hired labour to dig the coal, and shipped it to Halifax and
St John's. Tremain and Stout appear to have been singularly concerned with protecting and maintaining their hold on this contract,
demonstrating no desire to expand the works or their market. Their
investment involved very few fixed costs: the government owned (and
had paid for) the actual works, their workers were charged for everything from rum and picks to their room and board, and the mines relied exclusively on independent coastal traders to get their coal to

market.[49] Not only did this reduce overhead costs – by shifting the charge for the vessels onto the owners – but it also reduced their risk of overproduction. Coastal traders purchased the coal from the lessees and then resold it in Halifax. If no coal was needed immediately, the vessels had either to dump the load or wait until someone would buy it. The lease required the lessees to guarantee to meet the demand of the garrison, and this was the only function that either colonial offi-cials or Tremain and Stout appear to have considered. Small wonder, then, that the smugglers were so successful.

Production fluctuated wildly during the 1790s and 1800s but sel-dom rose much above the bare minimum required to meet the annual supply for the garrisons of Halifax and Newfoundland. In 1796, for ex-ample, there was a shortfall at Halifax; the next year, however, there was an oversupply. David Mathews, president of the Legislative Council and a close ally of the lessees, fairly glowed in reporting how well Tremain and Stout were fulfilling the contract (as well as how well he had supervised them). The particular character of state-merchant en-terprise emerges nicely from some of Mathews's report to the Duke of Portland (the colonial secretary) on this occasion: "I have the satisfac-tion to inform Your Grace that the Contract for Coal for the supply of the Garrison at Halifax was very early in the season completed, and such an overplus laid in for the Inhabitants as that several small vessels have been six weeks there without being able to dispose of their Car-goes, which gives me great pleasure to find that the exertions of the Contractors for working the Mines to supply all demands for Coal has had so pleasant an effect."[50] One supposes that the owners of these vessels took less pleasure. Miller too found all this puzzling. It seemed to him that it would be in the best interests of both the mines and the lessees if they made some effort to expand their market. In his last re-port, he found it "remarkable" that the lessees still had not established their own yard in Halifax or in "large Towns in the States." But so long as vessels continued to carry away a guaranteed minimum quantity of His Majesty's coal, their owners appear to have been quite contented. The two merchants sent four petitions to the Colonial Office in this pe-riod, none of which even broached the possibility of expanding pro-duction or of countering the smugglers' dominance of the smaller, lower-priced markets. Rather, they requested that their margins be im-proved either by an increase in price or by a reduction in the duty. [51] There is no indication that Tremain and Stout were at all unhappy with the general terms of the arrangement, and when their first lease expired in 1799 they lined up quickly to renew it. Clearly, such a situation also stemmed in part from restrictive British colonial policies, but there is scant evidence in Cape Breton of nascent industrialists striving to break free of these mercantilist limits.

Tremain and Stout were merchants, and the classic notions that we often associate with merchant capital – of "buying cheap and selling dear" and striving for control of trade through monopoly – held true despite their apparent venture into proto-industrial mining activities. As the owner of one of the two major mercantile houses in Cape Breton, Richard Stout dominated the island's supplies trade outside of the fishery. His partnership in the coalmines with Halifax-based Tremain was simply one component of his dominance of trade within the colony. Coal also gave them a stranglehold on the carrying trade between Nova Scotia and Cape Breton. The ships carrying coal to Halifax returned with provisions that in such a young colony were in limited supply and great demand. Tremain became an important force in Halifax mercantile and political circles; he was a close associate of Governor Wentworth and "enjoyed a secure place within the local oligarchy."[52] Tremain's influence with Wentworth appears to have been matched by Stout's relationship with David Mathews. Stout exerted a strong influence on local politics well before his appointment to the Cape Breton Council in 1797. Miller often complained that part of the reason his work had been slowed was interference from Mathews and Stout. On one occasion, the the Duke of Portland mildly rebuked Miller, reminding him that Stout had no obvious connection to the government of the island. Miller agreed but embellished his reply by including a description of the "*Dramatis Personæ*" who made the "deep Tragedy" that was, in his view, Cape Breton in the 1790s. Everyone had a part in this tragedy, although some parts were more demanding than others: as president of the council, Mathews stood "behind the scenes or mixed with the audience," several officials "stand as mutes" or appeared to have been "engaged on another stage," and a number of others "may be painted on the Back Scene." Only one person stood out: "Mr. Stout, Resident Contractor for the Colliery and Merchant, directs how the players have to perform their parts, but does not appear on Stage."[53] In Miller's eyes, the merchants and the state were very close indeed.

During this early period in the colony's history, there were few cash-paying customers, and correspondingly there was little profit to be made. But with sufficient will and resources, an aspiring merchant such as Stout could monopolize most of whatever limited possibilities existed by consolidating them in one neat package. Public concerns never seem to have entered his calculations. Despite his place on the council, we do not find Stout writing to the Duke of Portland to extol the virtues of the colony, nor did he – as Miller and other minor officials did – comment on problems posed by the system of land tenure or by the inadequate roads, which prevented "industrious farmers" from bringing their produce to market.[54] Quite the opposite. Stout supplied his mine employees with produce imported from Halifax, he was one of the councillors who voted down a proposal for import duties to protect local produce, and he was said to be earning higher profits from provisioning his men than from the mines themselves. Miller was the only government official in Cape Breton who commented on such things; he was also the only one who found it odd that the principal merchant of the colony – and the principal supplier of the colonial government's needs – was appointed to council, where "he will of course be a party to Auditing his own accounts."[55]

Labour shortages were an additional problem. Reliance on hired labour – "a few neighbouring farmers and [men from] the crews of vessels" – meant that workers were not always available. Both Miller and the lessees employed Newfoundland fishermen who wintered at Sydney but who normally returned in the spring "to their favorite employment."[56] In July 1795, attempting to explain why so little progress had been made that summer, Miller explained that both he and the lessees could hire farmers at the end of spring but would lose them when they were "busy making Hay." Writing in November, he noted the return of the "colliers": "The Harvest being now got in, and fishing but over they are beginning to pick up men pretty fast."[57] Such irregular availability of workers, Richard Brown later observed, resulted in a poor quality product. Shipping occurred principally in the autumn, before the harbour froze. While the most important production period should have been summer and autumn, the mine's reliance on seasonal workers meant that the peak period was instead the height of winter. Thus coal raised in December might not be shipped until the following autumn and then not burned for months after that.[58] This long exposure to the weather, combined with at least two rough transports between the face and the furnace, meant that much of the coal was in poor condition by the time it was actually consumed. But this mattered little to the merchants who sold it or to the officials who regulated the trade. All that mattered was that a directive had been received to obtain three or four thousand chaldrons, to be delivered at Halifax, and a few hundred more, to be deposited at St John's. Whatever the quality, both the price and the market were guaranteed.

Yet some of the evidence on both the source and ability of the men who worked in the mines is contradictory. Some of the "colliers," for example, were local labourers and a few were carpenters, masons, or blacksmiths. However they described themselves, on any one day they could be employed in their craft, working underground, or cutting timber. A complete "Monthly Pay List" from 1800 provides a window on the workforce at the mines in this period.[59] The mines employed a total of forty-nine men between 11 February and 15 March 1800. Together they produced 725 1/3 chaldrons of coal and were paid a total of £160.7. 1/2. The account lists twenty-four of the men as "miners" receiving piece rates. The remainder included three blacksmiths, a carpenter, a cooper, two sawyers, four labourers, a cook, a clerk, seven cart drivers, a gin operator, a "Topman," a "Bottom man," a groom, and a "gin driver," all of whom were paid either a monthly salary, a daily wage, or in some cases both. The monthly salaries were very low and could not have been for full-time work. Presumably, they were available full time but worked less frequently, as the highest paid among them earned less than the average of all the miners. Even a labourer on daily wages earned 3s or 4s per day, and skilled workers earned 5s – and in one case 6s – per day.

This is a simpler division of labour than can be found even by the middle of the nineteenth century.[60] Most notable is the crude division between miners – that is, anyone working underground – and everyone else. Yet it also seems surprisingly sophisticated in light of the many descriptions that portray these men as *only* farmers and fishermen. Indeed, it is clear that a more sophisticated workforce was emerging. When we examine how the men were paid, it becomes clear that within the category "miner" there were a number of divisions. Miners generally earned significantly more than their fellows on the surface. In one month most aboveground men made about £2.18, while most miners received £4 or £5 and as much as £7.7.0. They were all paid piece rates but not at the same rate. Eight of the "miners" did not actually cut coal; they were paid 1s per chaldron to "haul" the coal to the gin. Distinctions were also made among those who cut the coal. Coal "Cut to the Rise" was valued at 1s6d per chaldron, while coal "Cut to the Deep" obtained 1s9d per chaldron.[61] There was some overlap here (e.g., men who were paid for cutting in both locations, men who both cut and hauled coal), but the descriptions certainly suggest that clear workplace distinctions were being drawn. The piece rate differential seems particularly striking, as it suggests, at minimum, recognition of varying conditions and probably also negotiated rates on the part of the miners. Such distinctions suggest a more highly organized work-force than we might have imagined.

In some ways, then, this was a workplace governed by experienced miners who could, at minimum, regulate some skill designations as well as some control over the production process. Miller often la-mented the shortage of "regular bred" colliers, but occasionally, usu-ally when he was describing progress on the new works, he would note that he had "experienced miners" conducting the task of advancing the level, while the task of clearing the floor behind them was termed the "work of common Labourers." These men were paid by the day, but again distinctions were made, often clearly on the basis of ability. The "Head Miner" was paid 4s6d per day, while the others received 4s; the "two best labourers" earned 3s6d per day, while the remainder re-ceived 3s. Tremain and Stout paid all their men by the day, but the men cutting coal were expected to produce 2 chaldrons per day, and "a Premium was given for whatever was cut over and above that quan-tity." As early as 1796 there seems to have been something of an ap-prenticeship system developing. One year later, in what may be Nova Scotia's earliest coal strike on record, Miller's men refused to work, as they were concerned that the roof of the new level might collapse be-cause it was not adequately secured. Miller dismissed their actions based on their lack of experience – "the men never having been accus-tomed to such works." But just one month earlier Miller had admitted cutting back on timbering the roof to lower his costs; thus the men's actions suggest much more knowledge about mine conditions than his comments allow.[62] Many, if not most, of these men may well have been principally farmers and fishers, but they were certainly learning aspects of the craft on the job.

Miller died in 1799 without having completed his planned improve-ments. Yet for all his failings, he implemented a much stronger organi-zation at the mines than had existed when he arrived in 1793. Much of this was based on the essentially sound plan that he had attempted to enact between 1794 and 1799, although some of his success was per-haps achieved unwittingly. Much of it too was due to the gradual emer-gence of a higher-skilled workforce. Despite the seasonality of their employment and the apparent indifference of the employers, a coterie of skilled workers was emerging; they were learning what they could from James Miller as well as from Alex McCowan – the "regular bred" miner – and, moreover, gaining experience and skill through their own ingenuity. Over the next few years a few more "regular bred" miners would make their way to Sydney to work in the mines.[63] They too would add their professional skills to this workforce and perhaps encourage the development of the colliers' pride in the craft. And while they might take immediate notice of the comparatively primitive state of the mines, they would also find a workforce not completely unlike that to which they were accustomed.

THE STATE AND THE YEOMAN

In the colony of Nova Scotia a different path was taken. Nova Scotia was an older, better-established, and significantly wealthier colony than Cape Breton. Nevertheless, in the 1790s and 1800s few Halifax merchants seemed interested in operating the mainland seams. The major deterrent was the short (seven-year) leases offered. Given the high capital costs of starting and operating coalmines and the relatively low value of the product, it is doubtful that anyone would risk such a major investment with so narrow a timeframe. Shifting imperial trade policies added further uncertainty.[64] Leases also fixed prices, and price inflation during the wars with the French and the Americans between 1794 and 1815 added to the vagaries of large investments.[65] In the colonies, war could foster economic booms, but peace could wipe out fortunes overnight.

In 1802 Wentworth attempted to improve the available terms. Without prior consultation with London, he granted the Halifax merchants Forsyth, Hartshorne, and Boggs a lease to all the mines in the colony. In his report seeking approval he felt obliged to justify two key points. First, he argued that private individuals should operate the coalmines because "such speculation ... require[d] the zeal, industry and acuteness of private interest to render them successful." Unlike in Cape Breton, at no time did officials advocate government-run mines. Second, if private interests were to develop the mines, the leases would have to be extended to twenty-one years. Because of the "nature of the business," Wentworth explained, "it must be attended with heavy expence and large advances of capital." He proposed a graduated scale with rent increased over seven-year increments, recommending that the "first seven years at least" be viewed as a period when the investment should be allowed to take hold, the emphasis being on the promise of greater revenue later in time.[66] Wentworth might also have defended a third, potentially controversial, point: the exclusivity provision granted to the proposed lessees. Wentworth's proposals were rejected, but the fact that the monopoly clause elicited no comment reinforces the view that both the mercantile elite and the state saw exclusivity as consistent with colonial policy.

Acceptance of the 1802 lease would have represented something of a patronage coup. The reasons for the Colonial Office's refusal were not made clear, although the secretary of state's request for more information on the "nature, extent, and location of the Coals" suggests that the office wanted to know just what was being given away.[67] Wentworth's reply envisioned possibilities beyond merely supplying the garrison at Halifax. After noting a number of potential problems, Wentworth concluded: "Should, however, enterprise and ingenuity hereafter prevail over these difficulties consumption and export to the United States will follow."[68] Wentworth's offer of an exclusive lease to (now) Forsyth, Hartshorne, and Smith – all members of the Executive Council – was bald politics, having very little to do with competition, ingenuity, or enterprise. At the same time, in terms of capitalist practice, it was also rational, progressive, and in theory directed toward greater future expansion. Yet it is not clear that there was any liberal-capitalist design here. Wentworth, more so than most colonial officials, was determined to promote state policy. If this meant freeing merchants to pursue larger ends, so be it. His method, particularly its monopolistic aspects and its centredness in Halifax and in merchant elites, suggests a broader statecraft at work. In light of Wentworth's design for the gypsum trade, the real meaning of this lease may only have been confirmation of the Halifax merchant elite's hold on the resources of the colony. Economic expansion was a desirable end only if it met state needs.

While the outcome was different than in Cape Breton, the basic features of state-merchant enterprise were still in place. Wentworth dropped the issue of leases altogether until 1806, when he broached the subject once more, tentatively and very generally. The Colonial Office replied, equally briefly, that "nothing further could be done ... without very deliberate consideration."[69] Beginning in 1810 the Halifax Committee of Trade sent a series of petitions "praying that the collieries be opened." Led by William Sabatier, chair of the committee, and L.M. Wilkins, the speaker of the House, and aided by Nathaniel

Atcheson, the committee's agent in London, they urged the king's ministers and the lieutenant governor, Lord Dalhousie, to take up such varied issues of importance to the colony as encouragement of emigration, aid to the fisheries, timber preferences, the regulation of navigation, and year after year, the opening of the coalmines. But like Wentworth's petitions a decade earlier, the answer was always a desire for more information.[70]

The merchants' patience is noteworthy but not really remarkable. After all, the merchant elite, the Halifax Committee on Trade, and the Legislative Council were by and large comprised of the same people. They were the men who would operate the trade and who would also regulate it once it was in place. In 1808 Attorney General Richard John Uniacke outlined for the Legislative Council the guidelines under which coal reserves should be managed. On the crucial issue of ownership of the resource, he was most careful to observe that surface ownership was not an impediment to proper development of the subsurface wealth. While some earlier grants had not specifically reserved coal for the Crown, he cited numerous (English) legal precedents for the Crown's retention of ownership even in grants where the Crown had not specifically reserved it.[71] On the matter of whether grants had specifically to exclude coal, Uniacke would ultimately prove to be wrong, but he was certainly correct to emphasize the Crown's normal reservation of all rights to subsurface mineral. In most cases, the Crown could certainly enter lands, search for coal, and even expropriate lands if it wished. For prospective investors and those who sought protection from unscrupulous landowners and traders, the issue was that ownership of the soil conferred no rights to subsurface minerals; the state would determine how coal would be produced and who would produce it. This politicization of what might have been a more neutral process meant that merchants' connections with, and presence in, the Legislature would ensure that when London granted permission to open mines, they would determine who would gain legal possession. When the Colonial Office finally assented to the province's requests in June 1815 and opened the legal path to mining in Nova Scotia, a legal regime favourable to the development of local merchant capital was already in place.

Interestingly, however, the petitions from Halifax were not the final factor in prompting the Colonial Office to allow leasing of the mainland mines. Nor did the decision result from the extraordinary market conditions created by the War of 1812. Despite complaints of fuel shortages and the innumerable petitions, the authorization came after the war had ended. It was the fortuitous arrival of more African American refugees who had served His Majesty's empire against their former masters that changed the official position in the Colonial Office. Believing the African Americans to be unsuited to a life on the land, the Colonial Office sought new possibilities by which these new immigrants might not become charges on His Majesty's revenue. The government of Nova Scotia too was concerned about the newcomers. Ironically, it was the colonists' fretful and alarmed petitions regarding these troublesome newcomers that finally secured them permission to lease the province's coalmines, where the labour of the African American refugees might, the officials surmised, be put to good use.

In the spring of 1815, at the behest of both the House of Assembly and the Legislative Council, the lieutenant governor wrote to the colonial secretary, Lord Bathurst, complaining that there were "already many negroes in Nova Scotia ... which must lend to the discouragement of white labourers." They were, he continued, a people "unfitted by Nature to this climate or to an association with the rest of His Majesty's Colonists," and he asked that His Majesty "prohibit bringing any more of these people into this colony."[72] The petition also wondered what to do with the African Americans who were already there. A week later, and entirely by coincidence, another dispatch was sent praying that the coalmines be opened. In his reply, Bathurst explained that as for "any further Introduction of colored Population into the colony," "the termination of the war with the United States ... has in itself effected the object which the Provincial Legislature has in view." He then artfully joined the problem of the African Americans already present to the question of opening the mines so that both issues could be addressed in one stroke:

> As far as regards the Free Negroes already landed in the Province
> I cannot suppose that the Difficulty of providing them with occupation in a Colony where the Demand for Labour is necessarily great can be of long duration. But if difficulties have hitherto existed a remedy will surely be found in those new sources of occupation which the opening of the Coal Mines is calculated to afford. On the latter subject, I have much satisfaction in communicating to you the acquiescence of his Royal Highness in the wishes of the Province as recommended by you.[73]

This was both more and less than the province had bargained for. Nevertheless, unfounded assumptions regarding the nature of the provincial labour market – combined with the racist concerns of the Legislature and the equally racist assumptions of the Colonial Office – had opened the province's coalmines for development. As for the "refugee negroes" themselves, it is unlikely that any so much as entered a legally operated coalmine in their lifetimes. Of course, there was more than bald racism here. Equally important to this story was the assumption that a command economy and society could, as it did with settlers, simply direct the refugees to these mines and begin production. In opening the coalmines, as in resettling these refugees, London reminded Halifax who determined the imperial state's interest. The decision had less to do with liberalization than with statecraft and the paternal regulation of subject peoples.

The province advertised for bids on the Pictou coalfields in December 1816. There is no record of the bids, but Dalhousie apparently granted the lease to John McKay, who mysteriously had "heretofore been permitted to work the mines in that quarter."[74] A self-described collier who had learned the "art of mining" from his father, McKay did not actually make the bid himself: it came from Lawrence Hartshorne (one of the original merchant applicants from 1802) and Thomas Boggs, Halifax merchants and members of the Committee of Trade who referred to themselves as the "agents" of John McKay. The nature of McKay's production in the previous ten years was not made clear. McKay claimed that in "about 1807" he had "received a licence from Wentworth to dig Coals for the use of the Inhabitants of Pictou" and that he had "obtained another licence" during the Prevost administration (April 1808 to September 1811), which allowed him "to dig and raise Coals ... and to export them to any Port."[75] He and his father, William, raised the coal on William's land near what would become Albion Mines. Initially, he remembered, the mines were worked "upon a Small Scale, at an inconsiderable expence." But following the expansion of markets with the War of 1812, "coals were then in very great Demand and bore a high price ... Your Memorialist was induced to extend his Business, and he employed a great number of Labourers ... when wages were at the highest rate, and expended large sums of money in sinking Drains to carry off water ... and in making permanent Roads and Bridges."[76] But the wartime conditions did not last. Coal prices fell by 50 per cent after the war, while labour costs decreased less, and he found himself owing "large sums of money" to his employees and his creditors, including Hartshorne and Boggs.

McKay's lease drew a quick response from Edward Mortimer – the "King of Pictou" – and others interested in developing the mines.

Mortimer, S.G.W. Archibald, S.B. Robie, and William Lawson, all solid members of the merchant elite, petitioned Dalhousie in February 1817, protesting McKay's "Monopoly of the Pictou Coal Mines." They wished "to allow that most necessary article to be raised in more than one place"; otherwise, "an Individual will have it in his power to charge any price he might think fit, and supply only whom he pleased."[77] The antimonopoly argument sounds shallow, especially coming from Mortimer, the man who "had nearly the whole trade of the place in his hands." Their indignation was short-lived, as they were soon offered another opportunity. Within the year, McKay's debts had landed him in prison, forcing Dalhousie to reopen bids on the mines.[78]

This time the Crown accepted separate bids for the Cumberland coalfields near the Joggins. Dalhousie also divided Pictou County in two, issuing one lease for the west side of the East River (the area worked by McKay, which went to Mortimer) and another for the inferior seam on the east side (which went to Hartshorne, Boggs and Co.). Samuel McCully, a wealthy farmer and merchant in Amherst Township, obtained the Cumberland County lease.[79] Among the bids on the more valuable Pictou County leases, Mortimer's was the highest, but it gained him only part of the lease. Governor Dalhousie had decided that it would be best to spread the rewards around and offered Hartshorne and Boggs the less desirable west side of the East River. Hartshorne was by this point no longer on council, but he remained a respected member of the Halifax merchant elite and served on a number of public and private organizations, including, of course, the Halifax Committee of Trade.[80] Mortimer too was an important political and commercial figure, whose particular prominence had derived from his role as a leading figure among the "country party" over the past eighteen years. By dividing the lease, Dalhousie found a way both to reward the lobbying efforts of the Halifax merchants and to appease an important "country" member.[81] Mortimer, whose enemies still mocked him as the "Oatmeal King of the East," had achieved what Tonge had not.

McKay did not give up easily. Having invested, he claimed, over £1,700, he spent several years asserting his right to the seam under his land and later demanded compensation. As had Miller at Sydney, McKay appears to have established the infrastructure for a proper coalmine. His men had cut a shaft and a level that a later assessment by men "well qualified for the purpose" determined could produce "for many years to come."[82] Coal carts were constructed and a road was cut through to a wharf on the East River, where lighters were loaded and the coal carried to a loading ground outside the town of Pictou. He also built an office, housing for his miners, and a blacksmith shop. While it is not clear how many men he hired or who they were, they included a number of men who each claimed between ten and twenty years experience in mining in Sydney, East River, and England.[83] McKay's miners too tried to block Mortimer's claim. When Mortimer attempted to assume control of the pit, McKay's "colliers ... threatened to take possession of the Pits." Unsuccessful, they then filled the mine entrance with coal carts, boards, and debris, delaying Mortimer's possession for several months.[84] In the end, this mobilization of paternal local power mattered little because Mortimer died within the year, and William Smith (of Halifax) and George Smith (of Pictou) assumed the lease (this was the same George Smith from the 1802 lease in Sydney; he had removed to Pictou, where he would remain into the 1830s). By 1820, after a brief scramble for control, Halifax merchants had a secure hold on the Pictou coalfields. Their hold was controversial, and legally tenuous, but it was made possible and later enforced by the state.

McCully's lease of the seam at the Joggins (in Cumberland County near Minudie) was less contentious, at least in Halifax. Given the struggle that later ensued over access to the adjacent grindstone quarries, it is surprising that no one resisted his exclusive right to the coal. In part, this is probably attributable to his limited activities undertaken there. A report from 1821 describes the mine as not much more than an extension of McCully's farm. The investigator, Richard Stewart, an Annapolis County farmer, reported, for example, that McCully raised only a few hundred chaldrons per year. While McCully "occasionally hired men to assist at the rate of from Four to Five Pounds per month," Stewart was "unable to ascertain the price of working the Mines as it was generally performed by McCully and Family." Unable to compete with English coal brought to Saint John as ballast, McCully limited and eventually quit production.[85] Equally striking here, however, is not the small scale of the mine or McCully's apparent ease of movement onto the seam but the person who had undertaken the venture. McCully was a farmer, not a merchant. And while his £400 investment pales beside even McKay's, it seems incongruent with "farming" in this period. Of course, McCully was no poor dirt farmer. He was one of those more substantial Yorkshire settlers drawn to the area in the

1790s. He owned a large farm and also engaged in shipbuilding. Six years later, in 1827, his property (slightly upriver at Maccan) was described as having 150 acres in cultivation. He owned 40 head of cattle and 7 horses, and his annual production of 250 tons of hay suggests that he owned a good piece of marshland.[86] As he was a farmer with six sons, £400 might have gone toward purchasing some additional property rather than toward a risky, and ultimately disappointing, mining venture. Yet as we have already seen, and as we shall see again, many farmers were both willing to invest outside their farming interests and capable of doing so.

The mines that opened were not, properly speaking, coalmines. McCully's mine at the Joggins was an "adit," a horizontal shaft cut into the bank where coal outcropped along the shore. In terms of technology, capital investment, and workers' skill, these mines resemble quarries more than the government-run mines at Sydney. Yet for all its crudity, McCully's mine was quite remarkable. A farmer, with his sons and a few hired men, built a loading ground with a wharf, wagons, a blacksmith's shop, and sleighs to haul the coal (which probably had some kind of wooden rails), and he cut two levels into the seam. Ships arrived and coal was carried off to market. Although lacking equipment and experience, they nonetheless made a substantial attempt to bring a mine into being. However primitive, these pits represent the early colonization of the coalfields. Perhaps it should be viewed as a foolish venture into the unknown. But how unknown? These outcrops had been productive for at least one hundred years; McCully had not, as McGregor claimed to have, "discovered" the seam; he was mobilizing local knowledge and attempting to bring capital to bear on it. There was a market (a city of some 15,000 and then an entire nation) a few hours away by trade routes that were almost as old as European colonization itself. The only difference – although hardly an insignificant one – between McCully and hundreds of smugglers was a licence from the state.

The state's involvement was the signal event here. Because the state attempted to condition fundamentally all activities in the province's coalfields, its involvement must be understood as an effort to impose a radical restructuring on the existing modes of mining. It is in this context that we can view the "expert" testimony of the four men called to give statements on the events surrounding the dispute between McKay and Mortimer in 1818. Obviously, the immediate purpose of their testimony was to bring information to bear on a matter that the state had not directly created. With respect to the potentially criminal actions of McKay's men, their testimony was no different than that of any witness in any trial. With respect to the value of McKay's works and his claims for compensation, by comparison, their authority was the reflection of an acquired expertise, or competency. One of these men, Adam Carr, was the son of an English miner who had come to Nova Scotia about 1810. Speaking on another occasion, he began by citing his authority. Stating that he was "brought up to the Business of a miner from his Infancy," he then detailed the different mines in which he had worked.[87] Similarly, although with less authority, the others also stated their experience. Clearly, that they were asked to testify and the manner in which they responded demonstrate that both these men and the state recognized the importance of specialized mining knowledge. Temporary, presumably unskilled workers must have performed some part of the labour, but again we detect the presence of a core of artisans settling the mining frontier. We also see the state's efforts to administer this process not only through the licensing procedure but also through its ability to employ the authority of others – that is, through its adjudication based on what it acknowledged to be expert testimony. As these men were drawn into the political struggle for control of the coalfields, they were also literally written into the state's assertion of its governance. But these testimonies also highlight local understandings of the men's achievements, which emphasized their competency and propertied independence. The men were, in effect, understood in much the same terms as the independent agricultural yeomanry around them; they were regarded as something akin to the "independent yeoman," the mythical figure of the US countryside characterized by his sturdy and honest independence.[88] They were not rich, but their industry and improvements had brought them respect among their fellows. The state's rule fixed an outcome here, as its authority prevailed, but it had been compelled at least to be seen to rule through popular conceptions of right.

A few "miners," a couple of licences, some "expert" testimonies, and the occasional visit from an inspector: these factors may well seem relatively unimportant. But they were important. Here, we can see the tension between the state's desire to regulate and broad-based notions of yeomanly rights and property. It was also important that the state be seen to be at least asserting its control not only over its resources but also – through its centralized control of resources and people – over its larger domain of government. Typically, critics posed these assertions as protecting resources that "may eventually produce a source of

Wealth to the Colony."[89] Although posed in general terms for the greater good, such assertions were equally well understood by some to sanction their efforts to administer others' activities, while others understood these assertions to restrict their access to resources. Such pronouncements of regulative power were often unenforceable and at best weakly enforced. Yet their logic, their constant reassertion, and their justification pushed in the same direction: consolidation, regulation, control, and ongoing efforts by the state to extend its hegemony. In the context of colonialism and the British state, this was nothing new. But in this young colony, wherein state control faced such challenges as undeveloped communications, dispersed resources, and popular resistance, such initiatives represented a newly intensified effort at surveillance and regulation.

CONCLUSION

In 1825 there was little evidence of the promise portended in the meeting at the Reverend McGregor's home twenty-six years earlier. Mining and quarrying continued to be carried on in a century-old fashion. Clearly, there were a number of reasons for this. First, and probably foremost, investors put very little capital in any form of mining. This not only reduced the size of any one operation but also limited the application of technology (it did not, however, exclude capital or even limit the application of labour). Rather than large-capital, intensive works, mining operations in this period were extensive, employing innumerable hands in dozens of small and illegal pits along the coast of northern Nova Scotia. Capital was available. Witness the range of investments from farmers such as McCully and McKay and from merchants such as Mortimer, as well as the industrial investments of Cunard, Boggs, and others on the Halifax Committee of Trade who sought to extend their reach by investing in mines, canals, and iron works. What was not available was the effective security that capital investment demanded: the guarantee of property, the regulation of markets, and protection by the state.

A focus on state-merchant enterprise illuminates for us the limits of power in colonial society. In an age when the British state's capacity for control was by no means complete, we should not be surprised that the governors of this young, weak colony would be so limited in their coercive or regulatory capacity. Nor should we be surprised that in a colony where the memory of war, revolution, and republicanism was still fresh, many officials held restrictive mercantile concepts of what was in the best interests of their society. Such a focus also illuminates the locations of power in a colonial context. While power was often negotiated through paternalism, clientelage, and the family, these affairs were not wholly localized; the larger arena of colonial politics, as much as local contests, could be brought to bear on social relations. The lines distinguishing the regulation of trade from the regulation of society were very faint. Whether in the form of petty exchange conducted in "harbours of little notice" or larger-scale smuggling on the Bay of Fundy, the production and exchange of illicit commodities could and did continue despite the opposition of the state. (Indeed, it is clear that coal smuggling was fostered by the state's restrictions on markets.) And it was this opposition, this independence of action and even thought, that most disturbed colonial officialdom. To contain the trade, it would be necessary to contain the traders. The mercantile benefits were evident, but no one missed their social dimension.

Enclosures were underway in this period, but the effective enclosure of resources, much less the consolidation of capitalist social relations, was far from complete. What we do see are settlers, merchants, and the state each identifying resources and attempting to employ them in their own particular manner. As McGregor and friends dined, they could foresee their future place, but much work needed to be done. The only future truly portended in this period was that the state would seek to administer and control the direction of development. The particular direction that this ordering enterprise might take was as yet uncertain. Only two things were clear: first, in 1825 mining remained an unenclosed field where small producers, merchants, and the state all continued to vie for control; second, state-based improvers were attempting to impose their own order on this field. Private capital's colonization of the coal seams was undoubtedly premature but not because of any inherent limitations on their abilities to develop an industry. It was premature because they did not yet have the full support of the state. The state could protect its hold on the mines at Sydney but only because of its proximity to these mines. If we turn our attention to the shores beyond the state's vision, we find hundreds of freeholders and itinerant miners, quarriers, farmers, and traders who held effective possession of the colony's minerals.

These political struggles highlighted the place of rural politics in a centralized colonial state. Not only did they occur away from the colony's cities, but in most cases they took place on or around farms well outside the capital and therefore away from the surveillance of the state. In coping with their inability to govern their hinterland, state officials had to find ways to bring the countryside within their domain. Nova Scotia's heavily centralized state institutions were designed to exercise control over its hinterland, but in practice this was exceedingly difficult. State officials might have tried to co-opt key figures among the rural elite. Tonge, for example, might have been an ally in extending centralized control, but officials saw only a threat to the established order. The coalmine leases issued after 1817 were indications that the state was attempting to consolidate its control through private hands – but these were Halifax-based hands. At the same time, another rural rebel would attempt his own enclosure, again without the support of the state. As we will see in the next chapter, he would spend the subsequent twenty years battling the independent producers whom he wished to remove and a state that as yet saw no value in protecting his industry and improvement.

4

Enclosing the Commons at Minudie

In 1837, while other events were unfolding in the government of the Canadas, a revolution in government was also underway along the grindstone quarries of Cumberland County. As we saw, the tenants on the estate at Minudie had formed a small, self-governing community. They had been able to build and maintain an extensive system of dykes, farm thousands of acres of land, and successfully regulate access to an otherwise open and competitive resource on the grindstone reefs of the Cumberland Basin. Members of the largely Acadian population at Minudie and elsewhere along the shore were regularly criticized by their fellow settlers for their "ignorance," peculiar habits, and indifference to the broader world of markets, as well as for their apparent inability to follow the ways of economic, political, and moral improvement. The general description applied equally well to the grindstone quarriers, some of whom were from Minudie, while others came either from the surrounding countryside of Cumberland County or from New Brunswick's Westmoreland County. Richard Stewart, the Annapolis County farmer sent by the colony to report on the McCully's coalmines at the Joggins, was probably representative when he dismissed the entire community as "a few miserable beings ... who exist by making grindstones."[1]

The residents of Minudie nevertheless survived, and a fourth generation of Acadian settlement started new households in the village beside the magnificent dyked marsh referred to as the Champs-élysées. But the death of J.F.W. DesBarres in 1824 opened new possibilities as his heirs tried to re-establish control. They would sell the estate in 1831, and for the next seventeen years the new owner too would attempt to consolidate control along the shore. The enclosure of

Minudie was marked by a combined intervention of the state and capital in what had been a self-governing community. Together, these forces represented a heightened effort to order, direct, and regulate social and economic relations that, for generations, had been self-governed and self-regulated.

RESOURCES AND DISSENT

We have spent much time discussing the state's view of petty production and smuggling and not nearly as much time considering the actual producers. Part of the reason for this is simply a problem with sources, particularly a problem of whose voices they allow us to hear. It is something of a constant battle to examine the tactical considerations of colonial officials at any one time. The ability to do so might give us greater insight into the views of producers by helping us to distinguish between the truths and fictions, whether positive or negative (although they were almost always condescending), that structured colonial officials' representations of the people and their activities. Yet the state's view remains both essential and useful. Most centrally, its descriptions highlight the tremendous anxiety that illicit trade caused colonial officials and the equally great amount of energy expended attempting to quash it. While London was never as generous as local officials wished in supplying the resources that they felt necessary, the desire to suppress smuggling remained the single biggest concern of Cape Breton officials and preoccupied their Nova Scotia counterparts only slightly less. Even if many of these officials were inclined to exaggerated fears of the masses and their alleged "democratical" influences, they correctly perceived in the countryside an independence from formal government. Smugglers knew that they were operating outside the law, and the many settlers who comprised their market must have known this as well. Such economic lawbreaking continued because people knew that they could get away with it, given the state's very limited reach, and because they had come to regard smuggling as a critical part of how they provisioned their lives.

These ongoing debates on how best to better regulate trade illustrate the prevailing concern with the establishment and maintenance of order and with the proper exercising of power – in short, with governance. Not only did smuggling demonstrate a disregard for the rule of law – a disregard that, as we saw earlier, juries were occasionally willing to condone – but it also brought the perpetrators directly into contact with the "evils" associated with democratic republicans. There is little evidence of any mass movement toward republican democracy, but people's innumerable assertions of independence certainly contributed to official anxiety. The independence of the governed caused fear among the governors.

Much of this fear can be attributed to Halifax's isolation from its domain. There was simply too much going on in the countryside for the state to be able to exercise its will. The state's ability to exercise power in this period was frustrated by a poor knowledge of its own territory. Orders, reports from agents in the countryside, and statistical tables and reports such as the census, as well as the reports by George Leonard, Titus Smith, and Richard Stewart, were efforts to identify, classify, and categorize what Halifax ostensibly governed. That the colonial state lacked the means to establish a general system of such identification and fix normative procedures is certain. While the state strove to enforce such a system, its operation and implementation (for example, the circulation of lists of smugglers, the requirement that settlers appear before the governor, and the numerous agents sent out to report on various subjects) were more ad hoc than systematic. Each report reflected an attempt to learn how to read the province's social and even physical landscapes through a prior understanding of governance. Thus each report (and each ordinance in its wake) also sought to define "what was" in terms of "what should be." Together, the reports formed a program for governing Halifax's domain. By mapping these landscapes and by identifying subjects and practices of governance, they enacted specific and limited mechanisms to effect their objectives. Colonization, no less than settlement, was episodic in Nova Scotia. Thus it required the elaboration of practices institutionalizing a more general practice of governance and the routinization of such practices among both the governed and the governors.

This is a quintessentially colonial story. In their day-to-day concerns about their subjects, colonial officials in Nova Scotia drew very much from the same well of official ideology and practice as did colonial officials throughout the empire. Obviously, those in Nova Scotia were dealing primarily with peoples whose "otherness" was not as generally apparent as it was, for example, in the case of the colonization of South Asia or in the colonizers' construction of North American "Indians."[2] But knowledge of the ruled is a necessary condition for any governance. The "white" settlers of North America, like their rulers, were also primarily European; thus the settler and the administrator could assume certain cultural affinities. Even here, however, as British historians have noted, there were often significant gulfs in terms of perception.[3] This was the case particularly where Britishness was perceived to have been compromised in primitive colonial settings. Thus when we examine the actual relations between the governed and the governors – as we might if we were examining relations between the British working class or rural labourers and the British state – we see that there was a tremendous social (even cultural) distance between them. In state documents such relations were typically expressed in hierarchical dichotomies (e.g., high vs low, refined vs degraded) and also in subtler gradations (recall, for example, Haliburton's particular, multiple, and ethnically based criteria for determining the desirability of prospective immigrants). These taxonomic gradations were important, for in this remarkably (and for some frighteningly) plural society understanding people's positions and capacities was critical to rule. Smuggling was but one of many areas where the state recognized its incapacities and thus also perceived threats to its authority. Religious dissent, not surprisingly, was also a particularly troublesome area. Radical evangelicals, the more moderate Presbyterian anti-Burghers, and Roman Catholics were perceived not simply as undesirable but also as "calculated to create ... a want of respect for the established forms of worship, and of the British Government & Constitution." This comment was prompted by a request for £100 for an Acadian school. In debating this petition, one member of the House of Assembly equated the request with a dangerous slide into republicanism (an outcome that, the members could observe rather smugly in the spring of 1815, had produced "baleful effects ... so severely felt").[4] The foundations of the political and moral order appear to have been at stake here.

In Nova Scotia the state steered a kind of middle course between two forms of governance. One reflected an assumption of difference, as in the state's attempt at – and belief in the possibility of – a totalizing knowledge of the ruled based on culture, such as we see in the administration of indigenous peoples. The other reflected an assumption of similarity, as in the state's focus on more common European measures. Because there were some similarities in the backgrounds of the rulers and the ruled, the types of knowledge required were not so much about cultural features (which officials presumed to understand) as about identifying the social locations of those who peopled Halifax's domain. There was also a need for knowledge that would enable the state to identify the various gradations in the people's activities (e.g., fair traders vs smugglers, the propertied vs tenants, freeholders vs squatters, husbandmen vs peasants). Other categories refined, and sometimes confused, the view. Thus within the category of settler, there were several subtypes with their own peculiarities based sometimes on "race" (e.g., the Highlander, the Irish, the Acadian, the African), sometimes on class (e.g., the peasant, the farmer, the yeoman, the gentleman farmer), and sometimes on ideology (e.g., the rural demagogue, the democrat, the radical, the anti-Burgher, the evangelical). As demonstrated by the cases of the Acadian school, the "refugee negroes," the smugglers, the squatters, and the numerous other marginal colonization figures, these people could exist and even persist. In Halifax, such categories functioned as boundaries of rule, constraints on which a stable nexus of power and knowledge could be constructed. These constraints, however, were themselves frustrated by the combination of the limited knowledge of the state's actors, the resistance of the people, and the instability of the very categories that state officials sought to impose. The centralizing impulse of the state could reach the hinterland, but seldom did anyone know how to marshal this impulse when it got there. Patronage, paternalism, and the occasional recourse to force remained the state's most important tools; thus the Acadian school, for example, got its money one year but not the next. If it was petty politics, it was petty politics within a grander symbolic order. Yet as the cases of Mortimer, Tonge, and the mere existence of Acadians illustrated, this ad hoc approach to governance also meant that control was often out of the central authorities' hands.

It is at this broad level of state formation that we can best see both how the state was effectively quite weak and how its agents attempted to impose themselves where they could. Yet equally striking in all of these cases is how these discourses of rule converged in the complementary ends of merchants and the state. While unable to exercise a broad and integrated hegemony, the state could effect particular ends in coordination with those who best met its larger ends; colonization was, after all, a product of colonialism, and the empire was built on the twin pillars of trade and conquest. Where merchants desired to consolidate their hold on a particular branch of a trade, they could find common ground with state officials who desired to consolidate their rule – and, of course, vice versa. Obviously, this was no certainty, as faction and politics still mattered. But it was among these peoples that common interests *could* be formed. The smuggler, for example, not only denied the fair trader his market but also negated the state's authority and undercut its revenue. Thus smuggling was an issue not simply of trade or revenue but also of how to govern a populace that was "daily becoming more and more habituated to the violation of the laws."[5]

This goes some way toward explaining the logic of the state's actions, but it is less helpful in explaining the emergent spirit of capitalism that suffused some merchants' efforts. Here, it seems important to return to the idea of state-merchant enterprise. While many of Halifax's merchant elite were singularly concerned with protecting their trade-centred positions within the provincial economy, there were also many who at least desired to enter different productive domains, and there were some who wanted to start manufacturing. Of course, the commodities produced in mining and quarrying were not especially different from those of the timber trade or the fishery; the key difference was that in even a relatively small coalmine there was a significantly higher capital investment. Like good capitalists, the merchants were willing to invest if the conditions were right. In the still young colony, merchants looked to the state to guarantee their position either through some form of official monopoly or through effective monopolies in the form of various regulations to protect the "fair trader," but often these same traders (such as the Halifax merchants with whom William Harper dealt) were also involved in illegal trade. In seeking ways to shore up their positions, merchants travelled many routes. But we must resist seeing these routes in strictly economic terms. The merchant elites' base was broader than economic transactions; these merchants were men who could seek "mercantile" regulation one day and invest in iron works the next. Moreover, they were also rulers – not merely of trade policy but also of people. And so long as these multiple roles existed in the colony (and thus were also subject to imperial-mercantile management), these men would continue to see their own best (private) interests and the state's interests as fundamentally the same.

Tonge's case is a good example. Because he represented a threat to Halifax's control, he was unable to secure regulation of the gypsum trade. He then attempted to mobilize local support by trying to bring the superintendence of customs under local jurisdiction. Dependent equally on local merchants and access to only one significant staple, rural petty producers could understand and rally behind an argument that would wrest some power from the distant hands in the capital. But to view Tonge as a laissez-faire free trader is to overlook his original goal and that of many other merchants. If trade had truly been free, small-producers and smugglers would have continued to dominate the market. Here, Tonge and the Halifax merchants agreed. The issue was how to assert stronger control over shipping, and it was for this reason that eventually some agreement was found between these two normally antagonistic parties.[6] Merchants too employed the rhetoric associated with the fear of republicanism-by-association, but it is much less clear that their motives were either conservative or reforming.

It is important to note that all of this regulation took place in the realm of trade, not production. Tonge's gypsum bill (and the similar legislation passed in New Brunswick)[7] understood that production was the domain of small producers; the issue was the carriers. The goal was to funnel the product (as both commodity and source of revenue) into centralized hands, not to assume control of production. Not only was there no real need to control production, but it would have been virtually impossible given the extent of the gypsum fields. So long as independent producers of gypsum and grindstones could not finance their own marketing, they were left with only two choices: dealing with local merchants or dealing with smugglers. As we saw in the cases of William Harper and Thomas Roach, neither of whom actually owned grindstone reefs, their positions as merchants allowed them to arrange for ships (and also to gain some leverage over producers through supplies and credit). Gypsum appears to have worked much the same way, although there is another important distinction in this context. Unlike grindstones, gypsum could be found along creeks and rivers all through Hants County as well as in parts of Colchester, Pictou, Antigonish, and Inverness Counties; it was effectively an open-access resource. So long as the landowner – or whoever was digging the gypsum – had access to a small vessel (or even a cart to get to a navigable river), he could exchange his product, and merchants could take over the trade from there. The great merchants of Halifax came to understand this. Whether because of armed interventions on the sea or because of the country people's apparent compliance with the will of a demagogue, it was clear that government was potentially at stake here.

Coal was different. While coal outcropped in many locations around the province, the small open pits employed by the smugglers and landowners could not sustain production beyond limited local markets. Smugglers and other independent producers could form a major part of the market only so long as legal production and markets were restricted. Once merchants and the state recognized that there were commercially viable seams and markets for the product and that it was a potential revenue generator, the infrastructure would be developed. Once enclosed, coal required a substantial investment but also offered a potentially huge market. In his 1825 application for all the province's mines, Cunard offered £6,000 per year, almost twice what the province had obtained from the mines to this point in even the best of years.[8] As the cases of Cunard, Boggs, and Mortimer illustrate, in seeking more products to trade, merchants were not detered from seeking new ways to obtain products or from spending large sums of money to do so.

The grindstone trade contained the same potential for regulated production because, as with coal, good locations were limited. The best were within an area fifteen kilometres long and a few hundred metres inland at the Joggins. Ownership, or even effective possession, of such a relatively small piece of land held forth the possibility of controlling much of the market. If this land could be possessed, production could be increased and independent producers marginalized. And this is exactly what happened; illegal production continued well beyond this period, but its place became increasingly peripheral. The key point here, however, is that in the first quarter of the nineteenth century this was simply not taking place. No efforts were made to regulate or control the production *and* marketing of gypsum or grindstones. There was no need for such regulation. So long as the markets for these products were primarily in the United States, so long as producers had no independent access to transportation, and moreover, so long as there existed a dependent class of producers, merchants could control the trade simply through their domination of credit and exchange.

Yet small producers' continuous assertions of independence were critical checks on merchants' leverage, while the state's ineffective regulation of the resource economy also provided many opportunities. The tactics of those who engaged in illicit production and trade need not be seen as either defensive or proactive. The former view would lead us to describe producers as victims, while the latter would surely romanticize their activities; both would reproduce the social distance between rural householders and their elites. The point, of course, is that producers' illicit practices were neither exclusively defensive nor proactive but both. Debt dependency was a crucial limit on rural people's lives, but resistance was possible; conversely, producers' resistance placed limits on state-merchant enterprise, but we should not blithely inflate this observation into an assertion of their independence. Producers' efforts were attempts to maintain some independence within the larger structures of dependency, while merchants and the state attempted to enlarge their own spheres. For aspiring "great merchants" and the state, the ability of smugglers, smaller merchants, and farm-based and landless producers to maintain their place in the trade was a grave concern, for it threatened both the regulation of markets and a crucial basis for governance. The two were seldom separable. This relationship changed over the course of the next few decades, but the interwoven existence of market regulation and government ensured that the shared concerns of merchants and the state would form the logic of consolidation and enclosure.

The resistance of producers was facilitated by shared customs, similar positions within the agricultural/settlement economy, and decades of regulating the trade on their own terms. Like agricultural commoners in England and fishers in Newfoundland, these producers successfully established systems for regulating access, resolving disputes, and maintaining the general government of common resources.[9] Much of this history is inaccessible, but sources on the grindstone quarries at Minudie, in Cumberland County, suggest that resistance was rooted in a collective strategy for maintaining broad-based access for as many producers as possible. Disputing some people's claims to larger shares of quarry grindstone and associated resources, many of the residents of Minudie and the surrounding countryside countered the market-economy plans of local improvers seeking enclosure with a defence based on what some writers have termed a "moral economy," understood as an ethic rooted in custom and practice that set clear limits on exploitation and expropriation.[10] The plans of those who would emulate the enclosures of England and Scotland by bounding the seashore of Nova Scotia were pitted against the petitions, protestations, and occasional physical challenges of the poor tenant proprietors and grindstone makers who worked along the Cumberland shore. Although their resistance ultimately failed to prevent the enclosure of their worksites, their actions and the responses of the would-be enclosers reveal the still flimsy hold of liberal ideals and the occasional violence that necessarily undergirded improvement's benign and rational face. What would happen if an encloser attempted to control both distribution and production?

THE ENCLOSURE OF MINUDIE

J.F.W. DesBarres, who rarely so much as visited his estates at Minudie, Nappan, Memramcook, and Tatamagouche, died in 1824, opening up a number of new possibilities for those who recognized the market potential of his lands. Some individuals immediately attempted to consolidate control of the estate's resources by means of enclosures. This process would see wealthy, politically powerful men obtain, by law or by violence, ownership of the shore and remove the tenants and transient quarriers. Much of the plan, which was effected through evictions and actions of trespass on the people who had worked these lands for several generations, was carried out in courtrooms and legal chambers. DesBarres's death placed the estate in the hands of three lawyers: James Stewart, J.W. Johnston, and Henry Bliss. These were powerful men, and the tenants, we might think, had little chance of holding out against the full weight of the law.[11] But combined with some rather blurry aspects of the common law, sympathetic juries, and the state's lack of certainty about its own best interests, the tenants' resolve kept the enclosers at bay for some fourteen years.

Chief among these enclosers was Amos Seaman, the "Grindstone King" of Cumberland County.[12] A substantial mythology has arisen around Seaman and his industrial-paternalist utopia. One "golden age" account describes him as a kindly and benevolent ruler, a man who unceasingly gave to and cared for his tenant-employees like he did his own children: "Under the ownership of Amos Seaman, Poet, dreamer and shrewd man of affairs, Minudie became a utopia. It pleased him to make it so. This green spot at the head of the Bay of Fundy, he loved with all the intensity of his passionate nature. King Seaman, as locals came to know him, had the monopoly of the stone trade in America ... Here was the interest of his heart."[13] Seaman's planned empire was to be located on the "foreshore," the legally ambiguous tidal flats between the low and high water marks, so his "utopia" would be founded on a protracted and often violent conflict not only with the poor tenants who had possessed the estate since the 1760s but also with the state. The tenants understood law (or notions of rights) and productive relations in ways greatly at odds with the views of their new landlord and increasingly so with those of the colonial state.

DesBarres's modernizing strategy had paid some dividends, although for the most part not until after his death. As Captain John Macdonald had prophesied, changing generations-old habits occured slowly and at great cost. The larger, better capitalized farms of the area were turning toward the area's best possibilities, cattle and butter, and their expansion through the 1820s and 1830s increased the already high-priced market value of the dyked marshes and their adjoining uplands.[14] The estate continued to run as before, but the following decade would see a contest between the tenants, transient "manufacturers of grindstones" (as they were described in the census of 1827), the heirs of the estate, the estate's lawyers, and a number of prospective enclosers who saw an industrial future on the Minudie shore. Because DesBarres's legal estate was so entangled[15] – and with his children grabbing for as much cash as they could get as quickly as they could get it – the estate's lawyers were open to most any offer if it would bring in some cash. Thus in 1825 they leased all the quarries to Seaman and a recent tenant named William Fowler for ten years at £30 per year. Seaman and Fowler then sublet portions of the reefs to whoever would take one, including Joseph Read.[16] This partnership did not last long, and Seaman and Joseph Read would eventually become the dominant players in the trade.[17]

Seaman's strategy for enclosing the grindstone reefs is unclear. As a local resident, he must have been aware of the difficulties attending any such operation. Notwithstanding this history, he took a lease from DesBarres's lawyers and attempted to manage the shore in this manner for the next five years. Compared with the remainder of the estate – and with past results – Seaman and Fowler did fairly well. In 1827 they collected £60. But they were owed another £50, and this was their best year.[18] Indeed, in general, Seaman's experiences were little better than DesBarres's had been. However, farms in the area (including his own) produced substantial surpluses, and on this basis we find Seaman trying to obtain free-port status for Minudie in 1837. Although his bid was unsuccessful, Seaman's argument is worth examining. Additional imports, he observed, would allow for an increase in revenue, suppression of smuggling, and expansion of the grindstone trade. It would also, he maintained, encourage growth in the existing exports of "hay, pork, beef, and other agricultural produce," which local farmers were already selling in the southern United States. Opening new markets for trade had had a "stimulating effect" on producers, and it seems to have benefited some local farms.[19] For Seaman, free-port status would have allowed him additional exports with which to supplement his still insecure hold on the grindstone trade. Capturing trade was Seaman's strategy, although primarily (if not only) because his possession was not certain.

We do not know much about Seaman's activities in this period. We do know, however, something of what was transpiring elsewhere on the estate. All through the late 1820s and early 1830s, the estate's lawyers were unable to collect more than a small portion of the rents on the remainder of the estate. They were admirably single-minded in their determination to collect rents, distrain debtors, or simply "remove all the paupers and squatters from the estates," but they were often unsuccessful in court or unable to physically remove the tenants. Between 1824

and 1836 the lawyers managed to evict and remove roughly one-third of
the original tenant families. The process, however, was slow, and many tenaciously held onto their homes and property.[20] The lawyers sold a number of parcels of the estate for whatever they could get, but obtaining
possession of these lots was seldom easy. In 1829 Stewart sold eleven lots
at Tatamagouche. Four of these, however, were still claimed "by possession" by four tenants (one of whom – an old man named George
Milliard – was an original tenant settled by DesBarres about 1770). One
of the lots was sold to "persons named J & D Nelsons," but "another
pauper ... got on it and said he would hold it by possession." For Stewart,
it was just another instance in a long series of tangled legal affairs that,
however remunerative, sorely tried his patience.[21]

In some of these cases, the purchasers were already landowners and
were expanding their holdings. Some of these holdings were substantial; William Campbell, for example, purchased over twenty lots at
Tatamagouche, paying almost £2,000 for over 3,000 acres.[22] Often,
the purchasers were expanding at the expense of evicted tenants. Unable to pay his rent, James Welch's lot at Maccan was sold by Stewart to
a man named Ripley. Welch implored Johnston to examine his unjust
treatment: "I petition you for my rights ... Mr St[ew]art [is] undermin-
ing a poor old man ... and if this land is taken away from me I know
not what to do ... I want nothing more than what is right and just[;] I
wrong no man, [and] Ripley has more land than he can work ... but
his covetous disposion want to [take] my lot of land."[23] Welch, according to the census of 1827, was a poor man, and he had little else but
his rights. The lawyers continued in their attempts to collect rents, occasionally demonstrating some patience but more often than not ap-
pearing at each session of the circuit court with a new list of tenant
ejections. It is difficult to determine how many tenants were removed;
almost every one of the lawyers' letters makes mention of at least one
attempted eviction, but the references are not always clear – as to the
persons, which estate, whether they are tenants or mortgagees – and
we seldom have any sense of the outcome, only the intention.

The nature of the tenants' resistance is also not clear. When Sheriffs
Robert Dickey and Joshua Chandler went to collect rents or to serve
notices of eviction, they went armed. Violent resistance was not common, although on two occasions Johnston and Stewart urged the magistrates "not [to] permit blood to be shed on any account."[24] In 1826
an agent named Thomas Blenkhorn died from a gunshot wound in his
leg while attempting to evict a quarrier, but both men's relationship to

the larger story is unclear. If nothing else the event would have served to remind officials of the potential for a strong defence.[25] Perhaps our best indication of what might have transpired on these occasions can be imagined from Thomas Roach's comment on his remuneration for surveying the estate in 1827. The estate's lawyers had questioned some of Roach's charges, but the Fort Lawrence merchant and onetime member for the county quickly shot back, noting that the "humiliation and suffering I endured [making the survey] were such that I consider myself very poorly paid."[26] Although violence was always possible, less overt forms of resistance were often just as effective, being sufficient enough that the lawyers' more usual efforts were directed not at removing the tenants but at disciplining them.[27] In 1829 Stewart obtained an order against David Mattatal (a former tenant still in possession of his house and barn) not for the money but as an example. Mattatal was "a pauper and but little if anything can be obtained from him, yet as his example was a bad one so ... I thought the interest of the estate required that [the other tenants] would be deterred by the punishment of Mattatal."[28] The lawyers agreed that it was best to force one suit through rather than fight all the tenants at one time. In part, this was obviously a financial consideration; their best interests would be served by making the tenants pay, not by forcing them off the estate. But as the lawyers now knew well, there was also the prospect of the tenants resisting collectively, a prospect that did not bode well for their plans. "If the tenants combine," they explained to James Luttrell DesBarres, "we shall be compelled to ... involve the Estate in as many lawsuits as there are tenants."[29] There was little sense in evicting those who might be persuaded to pay or in prolonging an already lengthy legal battle. Stewart, Johnston, and Bliss were also doing their best to put the estate's finances in order – in effect, attempting to achieve by force of law and the state what Macdonald had proposed thirty years earlier.

The lawyers sold what they could of DesBarres's property while still maintaining as many rent-paying tenants as possible, and, they were clear, they would remove those who stood in their way. A number of tenants, however, simply refused to move. By 1833 there was exasperation in the lawyers' letters. "[T]he squatters are incorrigible," Stewart fumed, "I really do not know what to do with the Minudie tenants ... little or nothing was paid by them last fall, and now ... not a man has come forward with a dollar." The situation at the quarries was identical: "all the people at the Joggins refuse to pay any rent or acknowledge our title to the quarries."[30] The whole situation was "irksome," complained Johnston. He too was at a loss over how to deal with the "uncontrollable determination of ill-disposed persons, paupers chiefly, to assert a title to the property," much less how "to *dispossess* intruders."[31] The cases were complicated by the innumerable leases that seemed to exist for many – if not most – of the tenants, some dating from the 1780s and 1790s, others from the period between 1806 and 1815, and still others written by James Morse, another heir's lawyer, after the patriarch's death. Depending on the case, the estate's solicitors used one lease or another in an attempt to prove their claims. In the case of Jean Gould's family, Stewart recommended putting forth its nonadherence to an eighteenth-century lease as a basis for ejection, while in another case he wished to ignore this same lease. This tactic, of course, posed further problems, and Johnston cautioned his partners that it was "difficult to uphold the principle of resorting to it for one purpose and invalidating it for another."[32] Yet in pursuing evictions or actions for trespass, the lawyers generally proceeded in whatever direction was necessary. In 1831, despite realizing that their power of attorney may not have been valid, the strategy was simply to avoid the issue. "[S]ay nothing of the anomalous nature of Seaman's possession," Johnston reminded Stewart, adding that it "will hardly be made out to be exclusive and general ... as may be requisite."[33] They were good lawyers, aggressively putting the interests of their clients first and saying only what needed to be said.

On the estate proper, Seaman faced many of the same difficulties that DesBarres had encountered over his lifetime at Minudie, especially a tenantry used to much more independence than their masters wished. But the tenacity of the tenants' hold on the farmlands would be nothing compared with the political, legal, and social struggle that the new landlord would face on the shore. Although the grindstone quarries were his principal object, Seaman initially leased the entire estate and attempted to establish authority on the shore by virtue of his possession of the adjacent lands. Through the estate's solicitors, Seaman launched a trespass suit in 1831 against James Rutherford, a tenant quarrying at the Joggins. The outcome of the trial appears to have been representative of local opinion: although urged by the judge to return a verdict in favour of Seaman, the jury was unable to reach a decision, and the suit was discharged.[34] The solicitors then moved to evict Rutherford from the estate. Unable to persuade him to remove of his own accord, they balked at forcing him off, fearing the response that doing so might draw from the other tenants. Stewart urged his colleagues that if they lost the Rutherford trial, as he now supposed they would, they should move their actions to the Supreme Court in Halifax, where he expected that they would receive a more sympathetic hearing.[35] Stewart was right: the case was lost and Rutherford remained on the estate, working the ledges, while Seaman and his solicitors continued to try to have the case retried through 1833. Stewart viewed the Rutherford case as crucial both for Seaman's ability to work the shore and for the estate's future saleability. Unless they were able to assert ownership of the grindstone reefs, all they would have was a large farm with a few hundred acres of good marsh – valuable but not the fortune that they believed possible. Thus Johnston urged Stewart to continue applying to have the case retried; unless they were successful in making this claim, "all the persons who last year held quarries under Seaman will enter without license ... [and] our possession will be lost."[36] Seaman launched several such cases, and all were lost. Convinced that he could own the shore, he took stronger steps. In 1833, together with a Boston merchant, known only as "Mr. Lombard," Seaman purchased the entire estate for £8,000.[37] Yet ownership did not in itself change the productive relations on the estate. The quarriers mobilized against the new owner, and most continued to work the shore without his consent.

In a series of petitions in the 1830s, the quarriers requested that the provincial government intervene to protect their rights to use of the shore. In each case, the petitioners were clear that what was at stake was a generations-old custom of use and their ability as "poor people" to provide for their households. Francis O'Regan, for example, had "settled" just down the coast from Minudie at Lower Cove and in classic yeoman fashion had attempted to forge a living from the land:

When I first came [1826], there was not any person wintered in Lower Cove, but one family, so you may easily judge what my situation was then; having 8 small children ... and not even a blazed Road to travel ... I commenced work as a Farmer, but to my mortification my Land was cold, barren and would not produce enough to sustain nature, notwithstanding my industry and frugality. I was then obliged to set my wits to work, and by some other method than Farming, to get a living for my family.[38]

Francis O'Regan was not to be an independent yeoman; despite his industry and frugality, he was still poor, so he began cutting grindstones. At first it was a fair success. "[T]hinking that I might work out the rest of the days in peace," he purchased land beside the shore, built a small house, made a garden, and commenced working a quarry. But now others sought to monopolize the shore, and he petitioned for his rights to the quarry that he had "discovered." The same story could be told in any number of places along the Cumberland shore. An 1833 petition from twelve quarriers concluded by asserting that Seaman "wish[ed] to engross the whole of the Grindstone Trade to the utter ruin of a number of poor families."[39]

Seaman's actions flew in the face of a century of practice on the shore. Recall that some of these stonecutters described a system of regulating production and a perception of work and property relations best understood in the context of the self-government of commons. Crews of stonecutters operated independently on the ledges. Each staked out its own territory, but usually in a regulated (if not necessarily cooperative) manner. The quarriers' Fraternity, as we saw, mediated conflicts, and "quarrymen made regulations for their own Government in respect to the Shore in Order that no one should interfere with the occupation of another."[40] The Fraternity governed entry and protected possessions. "[A]bout forty years ago," one quarrier recalled, "it was usual for Individuals to open quarries on any part of the Shore which suited their convenience so long as they did not interfere with the possession of some other person."[41] These were rules, constructed as required, that governed rational use and provided protection and management of both the resource and those who wished to exploit it. These corporations, like the village-centred, cooperative arrangement of the farmlands of Minudie, were remarkable illustrations of self-government and the regulation of commons; they enabled a community that was poor to provision itself through common resources.[42]

Many of the quarriers understood the important role that custom played in determinations of common law. Thomas Black, for example, recalled both the nature and the context of customary use on the shore: "no claim or demand for rent for use of the quarries was ever made by any person … The Shore and the ledge of stone thereon were considered by all those who resorted there for the purpose of quarrying as belonging to the Crown or the Publick in which all had equal rights."[43] Similarly, Thomas Chapman was quite clear on the legal basis for his quarrying on the shore. He had been quarrying for over forty years in 1835 when he described how the inhabitants of Minudie and others along the Joggins shore "conceive[d] it to be their right to take stone from the Soil and Freehold of His Most Gracious Majesty."[44] They were not alone. It was this basic position that was upheld by a number of local magistrates and in the Cumberland County sessions of the Supreme Court.[45] Despite repeated attempts, Seaman's lawyers were thwarted in their efforts to have the low water mark recognized as the boundary of the estate. Part of this determination was certainly grounded in local knowledge and tradition. Juries in the area, perhaps like those sitting in judgment of the coal smugglers in Cape Breton, were probably reluctant to convict poor men trying to earn a living, and they treated these cases no differently than they had treated the evictions and actions for trespass in the 1820s. Stewart saw it differently. "*The country is strongly prejudiced against us*," he complained, attempting to explain why the lawyers could not win over local juries.[46] But there was much more than a stubborn unwillingness behind the tenants' successes.

The state also resisted Seaman's claims for a number of reasons. First, there was the issue of precedent. As the surveyor-general, John Spry Morris, argued early in the case, allowing one person access to Crown land "would encourage individuals to take an unauthorized possession of the Crown Property, and would go far to establish a principle that the Government have determined not to admit."[47] Here, potential revenue was the central issue. Lieutenant Governor Sir Colin Campbell, no less, maintained that he "fe[lt] it [his] duty ... to make [the trade] available in aid of the Casual Revenue,"[48] so Morris was under pressure to obtain as much revenue as possible for such lands. Although the land itself was "rocky and sterile," its location adjacent to the grindstone quarries made it more valuable than even the magnificent marshes just up the coast.[49] The second reason, however, was simply that the petitioners were right: the foreshore was a commons. The basis for both their petitions and the decisions that supported them were clearly established in common-law tradition, and legal officials in Halifax followed this interpretation exactly. In 1832 two law officers summarized this position, forcefully arguing that "grants of the Crown are always construed strictly in this particular. We are of the opinion that the Line of the Highwater mark on the shore ... must be considered the Boundary ... This space, which is defined in the books as the Sea Shore, is by Common Law vested in the Crown for the Public Benefit."[50] As far as local officials were concerned, this was a straightforward case. Seaman protested the decision, noting the money that he had already invested and the great potential for loss. Colonial officials, however, were not moved, and the case continued for several more years.

The key legal issues were outlined in two series of statements generated in 1836 and 1837. The first comprised petitions and recorded statements intended to demonstrate that DesBarres had never exercised any
control over the shore between high and low water marks. Some petitioners remembered working on the shore in the eighteenth century and described it as unencumbered by demands from the estate's agents, while
entry, possession, and production were all regulated by the quarriers
themselves.[51] The second series of statements was generated in response
to the first. The respondents denigrated the petitioners' credibility and
commented on their "incident imbecility of intellect" (both Seaman and
the lawyers regularly commented on the "ignorance" of the Acadian tenants and how they were "much misled").[52] Seaman generated statements
"adduce[d] from the oldest men of this County ... who have worked on
the Shore." These individuals, not surprisingly, said the opposite: that
rent had always been paid and that quarriers, both resident and transient, understood and accepted that the shore was the property of
DesBarres (although they were much clearer on the first point than on
the second).[53] Both sides attempted to show ancient usage.

> Nehemiah Ayer ... saith that he ... is Eighty two years of age and
> recollects working when a boy with his father quarrying and making
> grindstones at Lower Cove, South Joggins in the County of
> Cumberland before the American Revolutionary War ... that
> upwards of Fifty Years ago, he commenced working there on his
> own account, that he quarried stone on the Ledges or reefs between
> high and low water mark and boated the said Stones to the adjacent
> Upland to Manufacture into Grindstones and that he always paid
> rents to the late Governor DesBarres or his agents, when demanded
> for the privilege of quarrying on said reefs and camping on the
> Upland and always understood at the time he worked there that
> the reefs belonged to Governor DesBarres.[54]

Ironically, Seaman was willing to employ the record of the tenants' use
for his own case while at the same time attempting to prove that the tenants had acknowledged DesBarres's ownership.

Clearly, there were two quite dissimilar memories of past practice on
the shore. To understand why this was so, we first need to recognize
the social relations from which these memories emerged. One of the
petitions came from the Cumberland County sheriff, Joshua Chandler.
The sheriff's appointment was owed to Johnston, and given that he was

a man of considerable property who was himself once interested in buying shore properties, it is not surprising that he would corroborate Seaman's version of the shore's history. Edward Baker, another of Seaman's witnesses, owned the adjoining estate, and he was certainly not going to allow his own tenants any potential manoeuvring room.[55] Such a motive for assisting Seaman might, on the surface, appear not to have influenced the tenants, farmers, and even the odd quarrier who spoke in support of Seaman's claim. But assuming that they were telling the truth, they could have been interested in obtaining freehold access to the shore too. We need to remember the range of small-scale petty encroachments underway both on the shore and on the farms of the surrounding countryside. In part, it was against such transgressions of the commons that the quarriers' Fraternity had been directed, and in many ways the Fraternity appears to have broken down, a point that should not surprise us in this tumultuous period following DesBarres's death. The case of Joseph Read is an obvious example here. Read and Seaman ended up in competition because the latter was attempting to drive all the independent producers off the shore. But to poor tenants such as James Soy, John Tipping, Francis O'Regan, and a number of others, Read was no different than Seaman. He was an encloser who sought to "monopolize" a part of the shore, and they attempted to sue him for "defrauding" them of their possessions.[56] Read eventually won his case, but within ten years he had shifted his operations to the New Brunswick side of the Cumberland Basin. By the 1850s Read and Seaman would control almost the entirety of trade in industrial and agricultural grindstones from Florida north.[57] If Read had not been trying to break into Seaman's monopoly, he might well have been writing supportive affidavits too.

In our attempt to understand the discrepancies between accounts of past practice on the shore, the second thing we need to remember is that we are looking at a debate, a contest of words. If one side was exaggerating and prejudicing its evidence as best it could (as was almost certainly the case), so too was the other. There were no disinterested parties here. Indeed, there seems little need to decide who was being truthful. The shore was certainly big enough that some were better able to avoid payment, while others may well have been willing to pay in the hope of obtaining access to better sites. The Fraternity appears to have been intended primarily to prevent abuses, so there is little reason why it could not have accommodated both practices. In fact, we might remark on how little the petitions actually differed in detailing

practice on the shore. Both described a fairly autonomous work setting. Seaman's supporters consistently affirmed that they paid rent and
that they understood the shore to be part of the estate, but no one ever
claimed that DesBarres controlled the shore or directed production in
any way. If these affidavits give us a picture of petty capitalists collecting
rents and hiring waged labourers, we also need to remember the ways
of the Fraternity. Charging a fee to those who employed workers and
charging rents to "strangers" may have been revenue generating, but
there may also have been ways to restrict entrance and to protect both
the commons and small producers against the potential abuses of a
capitalist regulation.

The tenants' petitions regarding their rights of use went beyond legal issues. The core of their complaints was a critique of the new government that Seaman wished to impose on the shore. Indeed, as we
can see in an 1837 petition signed by 129 residents of Minudie, the
tenants in effect constructed a critique of the new political economy:

> Your petitioners ... submit that numbers of the poor inhabitants of
> the County resort annually to these quarries in the Summer Season
> to raise grindstones, building stones, and the like and that many
> procure their livelihood in this way – and if the Government should
> allow Mr Seaman thus to make a monopoly of the quarries which ex-
> tend for some miles in front of his lands it would not only seriously
> prejudice those who are immediately depending on them for a Sub-
> sistence but would materially injure the County at large by throwing
> So great a part of its Exports into the hands of one individual.[58]

This is the way that the area's economy was, and continued to be, governed, as described by those who knew the area and who lived by its
practices and customs. The shoreline, which in their conception of the
"public benefit" was for the benefit of the public, seemed increasingly to
have been monopolized by one man. Consequently, an antimonopoly
argument was central to their point.[59] But this argument was presented
through a clear understanding of the state's responsibility to protect the
interests of the poor. And Seaman was not poor. Seaman was represented in the petitions as a "wealthy man," the owner of a "rich Company," while his partner, Lombard, was an "opulent alien merchant";
together they "hop[ed] to monopolize to themselves the exclusive privilege of manufacturing and exporting Freestones from this Country."
The petitioners, in contrast, were the "poor inhabitants of this County,"

"dependent chiefly on the manufacturing of Grindstones for the Support of ourselves and our families, which grindstones we exchange for flour and produce."[60] The law was vital here. But so too was a reliance on paternal compassion, a popular sense of justice, and perhaps the broader sense of antimonopoly sentiment occasioned by the General Mining Association (GMA) in this same period. The tenants and quarriers had a good case, even if their enemy was powerful.

Seaman's strategy in response to these petitions was sound, timely, and knowledgeable. In addition to his remarkable achievement in raising the money to capitalize his venture, he also, by building bridges between the old and new political economies of government, artfully linked his methods to the needs of the provincial government. Recalling arguments that could have been made by Wentworth during the gypsum debates of thirty years earlier, Seaman emphasized the two key issues of regulation and revenue. In a petition dating from 1839 he stressed how "numerous persons" had quarried "large quantities of grindstones ... without authority and paying no rent therefore to the Government." Knowing too how little was understood of the trade, he also briefly described the methods of production and distribution while noting the problems faced by individual producers as well as the other potentially baleful effects of an unregulated trade:

> Grindstones so obtained are shipped to the United States and the owner thereof not having sufficient capital to enable them to hold the property for fair prices but requiring immediate returns, are obliged to sell at any price, and the American dealers taking advantage of their necessities, generally purchase their grindstones at prices insufficient to afford a fair remuneration for the labour expended ... and the sellers are frequently compelled to take American goods as payment, which are in consequence introduced into this province without payment of duties to the injury of the fair trader and in fraud of the Revenue Laws.[61]

Selflessly defending the interests of labouring men and the country, Seaman walked a very high road indeed. Enclosure, he argued, would be good because economies of scale would improve the quality of the product and the leverage of the vendor, smuggling would cease, and the revenue would be enhanced. The United States, he reminded the Legislature, "depend altogether" on Cumberland Basin stones and could pay a substantially higher price "if the trade was properly regulated." Seaman also insisted that the "public benefit" meant the largest possible revenue to the public's representatives. "How unavailing," he remarked of the present situation, "how utterly unproductive to the Crown."[62]

Repeatedly, Seaman attested to the public benefit that would accrue if private gain was established as the guiding principle. Claiming "an interest in the stone trade as well as the benefit of the Country as for myself," he argued a few months later that the state of the grindstone trade could "never be brought up until those ledges are just under the control of some person."[63] In 1839, through Stewart, Seaman lobbied the Legislature to initiate a direct superintendence of the grindstone ledges by appointing a customs agent or inspector who would allocate quarrying spaces and collect a tax. Seaman, ever interested in the public welfare, volunteered to provide this superintendence "for a small commission." He was not given the position, but if he had been, it would have been a classic, if extreme, example of state-merchant enterprise.[64] In addition, Seaman was also able to link the issue of revenue to another high road, that of national interest. While government officials could equate the price that a piece of land might obtain with the interests of the Crown, Seaman was willing to go one step further and claim that the change would be for the "benefit ... of the whole Province."[65] He was dangling the prospect of revenue *and* emphasizing the improvement of the country that would accompany any such consolidation of trade. These were the areas where the state and merchant capitalists could find common understandings.

In one sense, the eventual decision to support Seaman's claim to the shore might well have signalled nothing more than a bourgeois government's support for private property. In part, this was clearly true, but in another way it is misleading for us. The arrival of the new lieutenant governor, Sir Colin Campbell, reaffirmed patrician ways. The unabashedly anti-reform governor had little room for democracy and government by freeholders, and even men of "enterprize and energy," as he described Seaman on one occasion, were seldom suitable.[66] He was not, to be sure, one of the new-style utilitarian governors. As Phillip A. Buckner observes, Campbell "bridle[d] at appointing the 'preachers', and [other] men 'without one hundred pounds at stake in the province'" and was in fact recalled by the Colonial Office in 1840 for his failure to implement even the more moderate reforms of the Durham Report.[67] Thus he was not impressed by the fact that his new solicitor-general was also Seaman's attorney (Johnston). As he remarked to Lord Glenelg: "The services of several learned Gentlemen of this Province appear to be introduced to give weight to Mr Seaman's claim, but I believe ... that a good fee would secure the service of most legal men."[68] Campbell felt that it was his "duty ... to make [revenue from Crown land] available in aid of the Casual Revenue," but in the face of the claims and counter-claims, he determined that he would "personally examine the reef" in the summer of 1836. The visit, although a remarkable gesture of power that showed him to be governing, was brief. He did not even venture onto the shore but nonetheless emerged more confident in his earlier opinion. One month later, the Crown was prosecuting Amos Seaman for trespass.[69]

Seaman's peril was brief. In 1838 the secretary for the colonies, Lord Glenelg, reversed the orders to prosecute and affirmed the property claim. We do not know Glenelg's rationale. His orders simply stated that it should be thus, and it was. Campbell, perhaps aware that he had taken the politically incorrect stand, defended his position by arguing that he had no animosity against Seaman and offered to make the new grantee a magistrate as well.[70] In the end, politics and property may have been the only factors that really mattered. But we must remember that before Glenelg's intervention, in the fourteen-year period between Seaman's first lease in 1824 and the reversals announced in the memorandum of 1838, the critical issues revolving around customary and common law had been maintained as much by the persistence of the quarriers as by the Crown.

Lord Glenelg's intervention marked the final defeat of the tenants. Although smuggling and illegal quarrying would continue, Seaman now had the law on his side and could much more readily bring the power of the state to bear on any who would enter his close. In some respects, he had won several years earlier. Certainly, many quarriers must no longer have worked the Joggins shore simply to avoid Sheriff Chandler. Even if the courts had sided with the quarriers, few were willing to go to gaol to prove the point; they were trying to earn a living, not build a new Jerusalem. And perhaps just like Seaman, they were seeking security of tenure; the security once provided by the Fraternity was now in the hands of the state. Some of the quarriers had already shifted their strategy in this direction by 1835, when they urged the province to divide the shore into "convenient lots ... in order that your Petitioners may not be entirely deprived of an opportunity of exercising their trades."[71] By this time, Seaman had already gained effective – if not legal – control of most of the shore immediately in front of his property, had established his "factory," and by one report had "150 men employed" cutting grindstones.[72] That so many accepted waged employment rather than continue (or perhaps join) the struggle is a reminder of the dire need of many of these people. It could also help to explain some of the inconsistencies found in the contemporary descriptions that remain to us.

The major difference, of course, was the meaning that could be drawn from these descriptions. The tenants put forth their arguments rooted in terms of justice and fairness. Desiring the protection of what they had (and being comprised in part of a people who had already lost a great deal),[73] they sought what was both lawful and equitable. But they were unable to counter the ideologues' belief that the benefit of the many could be tied successfully to the interests of so very few. It is noteworthy, then, to observe the extent to which this was also a discursive contest over the meaning of such fundamental concepts as justice and interest. For the tenants, it was clear and unaltered greed that would allow one man to monopolize the wealth of the shore; for Seaman, it was commonsense that he could improve the quality of the grindstones by placing the shore "just under the control of some [one] person."[74]

The grindstone quarries were only the beginning for Seaman. By the mid-1840s he had successfully turned his mercantile trading company into an industrial operation that employed close to two hundred waged workers; a scattered series of independent worksites were now under one supervisor, and the shore work was no longer conducted on the shore but in a "factory." He also purchased an additional 1,500 acres of land, built a steam-powered gristmill valued at over £4,000, made an unsuccessful bid to open coalmines at the Joggins (immediately adjoining the quarries), and by 1850 had consolidated the shore-based weir fishery of the Cumberland Basin just as he had gained control of the production of grindstones. When his gristmill burned in 1846, he rebuilt, this time adding a steam-powered sawmill.[75] And even if he did stand aloof from the agricultural societies, the local executive was still pleased to observe that, "prompted by a spirit of rivalry" with those estate farmers around him, he was importing cattle and producing a fine breed.[76]

Seaman always saw bigger as better. In describing the shad fishery to Moses Perley in 1850, Seaman noted the important changes that had been introduced in the past "fifteen years," modestly neglecting to mention his purchase of the estate fifteen years earlier.[77] He remembered when no fish had been prepared for export – the "people who followed this fishery being content with securing sufficient for their own wants, and perhaps a barrel or two for their neighbours." Now, the shad were marketed in Boston (undoubtedly exported by Seaman on his own ships)[78] and cut and cured in the "method preferred by the American merchant." The export market also meant that the "energies and enterprize of our fishermen" were more clearly directed at the fishery, and this new attention had had a "wonderful effect in stimulating our fishermen to greater exertions." Looking to the future, Seaman saw that the proposed railway to Canada meant that "a new field would be opened to our fisheries": "We consider our shad fishery to be only in its infancy; and not a doubt can be entertained, that when a larger field is opened, and improvements introduced in the modes of capture and cure, that the trade will become extensive, of great importance, and highly lucrative." Seaman certainly knew highly lucrative ways, and he died a very wealthy man. But we need to take even greater note of his improving spirit, most centrally his firm belief that his own improvement carried improvements for others. If unlike so many of his neighbours, he did not see fraternal organizations as the means by which such disseminations should occur, he certainly believed in righting the wrong course.

CONCLUSION

For a time, Amos Seaman was an agent of disorder. In this, he stood with a great many more. Smuggling, the mobility of the unimproved settler, religious dissension, and other forms of anarchic, individualistic, and nonconformist behaviour could be easily equated with greater evils such as radicalism, republicanism, and Jacobinism. Here, the unwillingness of a man like Amos Seaman to play by the mercantile rules – or even that of a man like Tonge who wanted to establish his own terms within these rules – could be set apart and identified as not merely impolitic but dangerous; such actions represented a loosening of bonds, which might have "baleful effects" on government.[79] Government and enclosure could involve very different, even antagonistic, conceptions of economy and society and of the state's place in their regulation. State-merchant enterprise sought to maintain these distinctions by finding unities of purpose between public and private interests. One task of the liberal improver was to reconcile these differences by making private investment more useful to the state. Seaman, in this context, represents someone who stepped more fully outside the bounds of the mercantile structure. He wanted, and moreover needed, the protection of the state, but he did not want its interference. The place of the state in such a liberal conception should be at arm's length – detached but still within reach. Seaman was merely one of many enterprising nineteenth-century men anxious to escape the state's embrace but quick to rely on its authority.

For all his ingenuity, ambition, and capital, and despite the early obstructions posed by the state, Seaman's consolidation and enclosure simply could not have occurred without the state's support. The real change came in the state's acceptance of his different conception of the "public benefit." The contested shoreline became an issue in the changing legal conception of property and public welfare. Local officials had some interpretative leeway but were expected to exercise this latitude in a manner that would best serve the public's (i.e., the state's) interest. The law of the seashore had always been open to some exceptions, and as Moore's history makes clear, new exceptions were increasingly frequent, especially after about 1790.[80] Officials' decisions, then, while grounded in common law and often sympathetic to local conditions, ultimately determined how their society would distribute resources and how claims to these resources would be administered. Eventually, the Colonial Office accepted an interpretation of the law that favoured a liberal notion of what was in the interest of the common weal. The new interpretation would be one that was in line with classical political economy's acceptance of private interest as being commensurable with public benefit. But as we've seen, for many years the state maintained the more strictly defined interpretation of this branch of the common law. It may well have been an anachronistic conservatism – an unwillingness not to tamper with what appeared firm – that continued to protect the quarriers' hold on the shore. In combination with the resolve of the quarriers themselves, this reverence for tradition also meant that for a time the Crown maintained and protected a broader conception of how property rights could be distributed. This may have been done only to retain the state's hold on valuable, revenue-generating properties, but for the quarriers, for a time at least, it was enough.

Seaman's actions were clearly those of an encloser. It is of course ironic that the government should at this time have taken such a stand in support of one man's monopolizing of one mineral trade at the very same time as its battle with the monopoly of the General Mining Association was at its height. But liberalism's history is one of ironies and tragedies. As we shall see, the local government's struggle with the GMA was not so much against monopoly as it was for national self-determination and control over its own territories and revenues; it was less an issue of political economy than one of government. The enemy there was not monopoly per se but its effects in a particular context. The tenant and transient quarriers, however, were defending more than economic rights and utility; they sought to address the distinction between public and private rights. Theirs was an attack on the disruption of practices that had successfully regulated common property. They defended neither a simple legal position nor a naive, backward-looking nostalgia for a "golden age." Theirs was a pointed defence of their customs and an equally pointed attack on the arbitrary mechanism of their dispossession. They cited generations of past practice to articulate their own "ancient use" and the legitimacy of their claim. In the face of Seaman's capital, his access to powerful support, and his certain determination, they called on the state for support. For tenant-quarriers, "strangers," and even for a time the state, Seaman was the "intruder."[81]

It was most unlikely that Minudie's tenants and the transient quarriers had any real chance of victory in this struggle. The state's support was far too self-interested for the tenants to have found sustained patronage. Remarkably, however, especially as a prosperous farmer and merchant and having built his case on the solid foundation of national self-determination, revenue, and apparently strong politics, Seaman too was unable to move provincial officials. Even allowing for a narrowly revenue-centred notion of "the interest of the Country," Crown land officials, in particular, had a remarkably short-term sense of what would be in the best interest of the country. What was clear in all of this, however, was that poor, independent producers were not to be admired for their industry. They were protected by the state's need to be seen to uphold the law, not by customary notions of right or by the virtue of their industry and improvements. They would not acquire, as had Adam Carr and John McKay, a yeoman-like status for their labour. And unlike later provincial political figures, they would not receive praise for their resistance to monopoly. They were a "few miserable beings," and their positions as people who could govern some components of their own lives were severely and suddenly undercut.

5

Industrial Colonization and
the General Mining Association

Enclosing the province's coalmines was a much simpler process than enclosing the quarries at Minudie – although a more complicated tale. The story of the General Mining Association (GMA) and its place in the history of the provincial coal industry has been told before.[1] Formed on the basis of a "Royal Donation" from King George III to his son the Duke of York "to relieve him from his Embarrassments,"[2] the lease gave the duke the mineral rights to the entire province. The GMA was a group of London investors who subleased the mineral rights from the duke. In exchange, the duke would pay off some of his debts and get a cut of the future profits. The association invested more than £200,000 over the next ten years and quickly elevated the province's mines out of the "worse than useless" state in which the firm's engineers had found them.[3]

Studies of the GMA generally emphasize its foundational, but limited, impact on Nova Scotia, especially in relation to the coal industry's "take-off" in the late nineteenth century. The most nuanced of these studies stresses the ambiguous role played by the company, which effectively created a modern "industrial" coalfield through increased employment of skilled labour, capital, and technology while also hindering local or indigenous development through the exercise of monopoly rights on all mineral production in the colony, thus retarding market formation for both labour and commodities.[4] This view of the GMA as a conservative force reflects the company's later strategy much more than its early plans and activities. The GMA's operations were not so much "enclaves" – a metaphorical term suggesting fragmentation, insulation, or separation – as what we might call industrial colonies. "Planted" in classic colonial form, with their own class structure, social organization, and systems of production, marketing, and infrastructure, they stood out from the surrounding society. But in many ways these coal towns were in fact only a variation on imperial settlement programs. To be sure, they were in some ways aberrant, but in other ways they were harmonious with and indeed may have epitomized the patterns of colonial development. The early history of the GMA offers a fine example of how agents of industrial colonization forged essential links between British and colonial labour, capital, and states. Together, the GMA's operations made up an industrial plantation, one very much integrated into the fabric of the provincial countryside and into the patterns of colonial political culture.

In Pictou, Jotham Blanchard, editor of the *Colonial Patriot*, a leading reform paper, was ecstatic about the arrival of the British firm in 1827. He was particularly impressed with the manager, Richard Smith. Blanchard, a regular promoter of improvement through emulation, saw in Smith "a useful illustration of the way wealth and respectability are acquired in Britain." The GMA would provide many valuable lessons (although Smith, who was in Nova Scotia only because he had lost the family fortune and who would later embarrass the firm by organizing an electoral riot, was perhaps not the best model).[5] The most important lesson was less about how to acquire wealth and respectability than about a large capitalist firm's capacity to establish order and bring the local state onside. But it was also controversial. As was the story of Minudie, this is another tale of enclosure, although with some notable differences; now the displaced were not "some miserable beings" on a hinterland shore but included some of the Halifax elite. That this was an age of liberal reforms when monopoly and the royal prerogative found few defenders also made the GMA a target of reformers. Yet also instructive was the firm's ability to bring some order to the countryside through industrial settlements and a willingness to police its own frontiers. Because the GMA was "planting" industry and population while serving the interests of the state, it also had many powerful friends in Halifax and London.

THE ATLANTIC WORLD

In the spring of 1825 the commercial centre of the British Empire was in an uproar. A serious depression in trade was underway, William Huskisson had just introduced changes in the Navigation Acts, Parliament was debating Wilmot-Horton's proposals for state-assisted emigration, and

British investors were in the dying days of a maniacal rush to invest in Latin American mines following the various wars of independence, which had suddenly opened this field for investment. British capitalists, many with money "burning holes in their ... pockets," were putting their money in a host of foreign ventures, much of it, Eric Hobsbawm observes, "rashly, stupidly, some of it insanely invested."[6] By summer, rumours were spreading that the British government was on the verge of bankruptcy, the Latin American venture bubble had burst, enthusiasm for foreign investment had crashed, and London finance capitalists had stepped back to reassess their monstrous calamity.[7] From the vantage point of British investors in the summer of 1825, the wisdom of any foreign investment was highly questionable.[8] In the colonies, while some called out for British investment, others expressed ambivalence. T.C. Haliburton described the recently formed New Brunswick and Nova Scotia Land Company as just another of the "mad bubbles" made possible by the "unbounded wealth of our parent country, of that monstrous capital which seek[s] rent in the most remote parts of the world."[9]

That summer two apparently unrelated developments moved precariously nearer each other, and they did so on a course heading for Nova Scotia. The first of these was one of the British investments in Latin America. A group of London investors, headed by the wealthy jewellers to the royal family, Phillip Rundell and John Bridge, had formed the General South American Mining Association, obtained mineral leases in Brazil, were negotiating for another in Colombia, and had sent out men and equipment to assess the possibilities for exploitation and development. The second was that Prince Frederick, the Duke of York, who was the second son of George III and a brother of George IV, realized that his creditors were, as he aged, becoming increasingly anxious about his debts. The duke quickly needed to raise about £70,000. These two developments, although apparently unrelated, were to merge because of a pin, a rather elaborate pin. Twenty years earlier, in an age of industrial expansion, Frederick had observed an older, more genteel form of prodigious expenditure in purchasing an ornate pin – the Shield of Achilles – from none other than Philip Rundell and John Bridge. In keeping with his usual practice, he purchased the pin on credit. The duke was well known to be "improvident in pecuniary matters" – not to mention his "love of pleasure ... [which] did not always respect the moralities of private life" – and this was but one of many debts that he carried for most of his days.[10] By 1825 the jewellers were part of a queue dunning the duke, and he was selling any assets that he had in order to raise some much-needed cash. One of these assets was a lease to all the mineral rights in Nova Scotia, an apparently forgotten gift from his father.[11] Frederick was indeed a very busy man and had never shown much interest in colonial mining. The jewellers, who had by then greatly expanded the sphere of their investments, were interested.

In 1824 the GMA – now Rundell, Bridge, Bigg, and Rundell – had formed the General South American Mining Association on stock nominally valued at £2,000,000.[12] Little is known of the firm's Latin American venture except that it was eventually abandoned; as to why it was abandoned, the extant evidence points in opposite directions.[13] The re-emergence of the duke's lease was a happy coincidence for both parties: the improvident duke negotiated a 25 per cent cut on the GMA's Nova Scotia returns,[14] while the jewellers solidified their venture in foreign mining. Their investments now spanned a massive triangle from London to Brazil to Nova Scotia. It was a classically colonial investment, characterized by *ancien regime* wealth (or at least credit), money from the luxury trades, and an empire desirous of financial returns from military conquest. Yet it was also something new. As J.R. McCulloch, one of the most important improvement writers, observed: "discovery," conquest, and settlement were the stuff of history; now, with the application of capital, "the true discovery" of the New World could begin.[15]

As in all colonial enterprises, the GMA's investments would place it in an industry where the state was a key player, but this was especially so in the extraction of minerals. Within the eighteenth-century colonies, the state played the role of caretaker of His Majesty's natural resources, not only owning them but also administering their use and sale. The state claimed continued ownership of subsurface minerals and directly administered several areas of production. In the eyes of the state, ownership of land meant nothing to the prospective subsurface developer. Formally, the arrival of the GMA did not end this arrangement, but it did alter it. The state would continue to administer the mines but in a much less direct manner. Whereas before the re-emergence of the duke's lease, the colonial state had administered every aspect of the king's resources, in 1827 it effectively relinquished to the developers all of the direct responsibilities of mine administration. As we shall see, this distinction was not always clear, but it was clear enough to remove the state from any of the direct production functions that it had previously exercised. Thus what also emerged in 1827

was a series of guidelines for regulating the proper spheres of the state
and capital in resource development in the British North American
colonies. Relying as it did on particular types of markets, being produced under radically different conditions, and requiring the creation
of a modern industrial complex on site, coal was very much unlike the
other established colonial staples such as cotton, sugar, wheat, timber,
fish, and furs. The GMA, then, brought about the transfer of many
modern industrial practices to the colonies. Throughout the period of
the firm's innovations, the state – both local and metropolitan – was a
crucial ally. At the same time, segments of the provincial elite struggled
to break the firm's monopoly. The GMA offered capitalist innovation,
but it did so while relying on state support and resisting efforts to push
its operations onto more firmly liberal ground.

The original lease to the Duke of York guaranteed exclusivity but specifically excluded all currently leased mines as well as lands where mineral – specifically coal – rights had not been reserved to the Crown in
the original grant.[16] The GMA, therefore, bought out the existing lessees and assumed those operations in Sydney and Pictou.[17] The mere
presence of this large new firm with its tons of equipment, steam engines, and hundreds of skilled miners – not to mention the prospect
of quick and easy money – was apparently enough to make the local
firms submit. The GMA had obtained the best sites (at least for immediate production) and could now be assured that it had obtained
a complete monopoly. But its success actually meant much more.
Over the next year, the GMA managed to get all the leases (its own
sublease, plus one each from Sydney and the East River) completely
rewritten as one lease with two sets of conditions: one specified by
the terms of the duke's original lease and the other assumed after
the GMA's arrival in Nova Scotia. Of course, the existing mine sites
were among the best. They now fell outside the terms of the duke's
lease and thus also outside the firm's arrangement with his estate.[18]
This was a very clever move and offered the company the best of
both worlds: it had maintained the exclusivity arrangement (including Cape Breton), it now had the best mine sites at a better rent to
the Crown than under the duke's lease, and it had excluded the better locations from the duke's 25 per cent cut. The GMA's activities
outraged the administrators of the duke's estate – costing the company almost thirty years in Chancery Court[19] – but this appears to
have been a sound business calculation. In June 1827 when Richard
Smith and the miners arrived from Britain, the GMA had a lease on a

site *beside* a coalmine in Pictou County; by the autumn of 1828 they controlled all the coalfields of Nova Scotia.

At Pictou the firm began sinking a new shaft within days of Smith's arrival, while a second engineer, Richard Brown, was assessing the requirements for Sydney Mines. Would-be competitors in Cape Breton were impressed not only by their new rival's skills and capital but also by the terms of the GMA's lease. Smith and Liddell, the lessees at Pictou, bowed out almost immediately (notwithstanding the Treasury Office's reluctance to allow them out of their remaining twelve years). Their "small mines," wrote George Smith in a petition praying for release, were no match for the "superior skills and Capital of His Royal Highness' Sub-lessees." These factors, together with the "very favorable terms on which [the company will] work the Mines[,] will make it impossible to compete with such powerful rivals."[20] And very favourable terms they were. Samuel Cunard, who had attempted to obtain a lease for Sydney Mines in 1826, had offered £3,000 per year for the first three years and £6,000 per year for the remaining twenty-seven years of a thirty-year lease.[21] Smith and Liddell had been required to pay their rent plus 3s6d per chaldron. The GMA's lease (here on reserved mines) entitled them to mine coal on the adjoining property at no rent and to pay only 1s per chaldron for the first five years of the lease. As Sir James Kempt argued on their behalf, "under these circumstances ... [it was] quite impossible for Messrs Smith and Liddell to continue to work the mines without ruin to themselves."[22] Moreover, they were giving up the mines "in accordance with the wishes of His Majesty's Government," a reference not only to the proclamation of a year earlier but also to Kempt's ongoing support for the firm's activities; "otherwise," they continued, "they would have resisted any interference until relieved of the liabilities which they were under and a remuneration made for the outlay of capital."[23] Undoubtedly, George Smith was being rather disingenuous here. It seems unlikely that they would have, or could have, resisted for long. But he certainly highlighted the new conditions under which the mines of the province would be conducted: large capital, advanced technology, a skilled workforce, and state support.

This scale was important. In an era when dozens of British-financed, South American mining companies were drowning in their own watered stock, the GMA was undoubtedly a much more solid venture. Rundell, Bridge, Bigg, and Rundell needed very little convincing that there was profit in Nova Scotia, nor did their other investors. At the end of 1827 the firm had over £100,000 in hand, a lease, engineers, about two hundred miners, and equipment on site in Nova Scotia. Three years later, the iron foundry was in operation, a brick plant was producing for construction throughout the region, the wharves had been completely rebuilt (on a much larger scale), and two steam engines were in operation. By 1839 almost £300,000 had been invested, a railway was under construction, and well over one thousand workers were employed.[24] Who were these men who invested so heavily in what must clearly have been a risky venture at a time when the best tip available for investment in overseas mines was "don't"?

The shareholders in the GMA were not drawn from the monied elite of Great Britain, the "moneyocracy" as Marx referred to them, although Rundell was certainly rich and owed his own wealth to this group. With the exception of the senior Rundell, none of the men were particularly wealthy or well known. Several of the shareholders, however, were moderately wealthy, middle-class men who aspired to be men of leisure, and they perhaps fitted something of the mold of what P.J. Cain and A.G. Hopkins refer to as "gentlemanly capitalism."[25] Three made their way into the *Dictionary of National Biography*, and occasionally one or another of the investors, having attended a charity ball or a concert, would show up in *Blackwood's* or *London Magazine*.[26] John Wright was a partner in a small bank in London. The younger Rundell too entered banking and brought in his partner John Bigge; they also had investments in coalmines in Durham.[27] Two of the directors, Edward Blount and the president, Edward John Littleton, were members of Parliament. Littleton – later Baron Hatherton – was a "country gentleman," the owner of a substantial estate, and the MP for Staffordshire, a point that probably explains a good deal of the GMA's mine-manager hirings.[28] Another of the pre-Nova Scotia directors, Andrew Belcher – son of the province's first chief justice and now resident in London – was a Nova Scotian. Older and not nearly so wealthy as he once had been, he apparently still had enough money to speculate in South American mines.[29]

With the exception of the senior Rundell's wealth and Littleton's more moderate wealth and very moderate political clout,[30] the resources of the men who comprised the directors of the GMA were quite unextraordinary. They were the kinds of men, not fabulously wealthy but with money and some political influence, who might have a few hundred, and some a few thousand, pounds to invest in a foreign mining venture. Some had obtained their money "by dint of hard labour"; others had inherited it, obtained it in marriage, or in the case of Littleton, both.[31] And with the obvious exception of the two seniors – Rundell and Bridge – as well as Belcher, they were also quite young. By 1842 the principals had not changed:[32] at least two were sons of the other principals; J.B. Foord would still be secretary in the 1870s, discussing affairs with Richard Brown Sr in London and corresponding with Richard Brown Jr at Sydney Mines; and the solicitor Thomas Farrer would negotiate the lease of 1827 and renegotiate it in 1858.[33] In politics, most appear to have been conservative, or at least certainly not reformers. With the exception of Littleton's later conversion, most appear to have been Tories. Blount, Littleton, and both Rundells were certainly Tories, and Robert Stewart spoke proudly of his "conservative principles."[34]

These men were a hub for a wider circle of friends and business associates. Neither Robert nor David Stewart, for example, show up in any GMA material as directors or board members, but we know that they were influential shareholders who at meetings could occasionally force the agenda to effect changes in the firm's policy.[35] The Stewarts were Scottish investors with substantial holdings not only in lands in Prince Edward Island, New Brunswick, and Nova Scotia but also in Ireland and the United States. They were also active promoters of British North American commercial ventures such as the Bank of British North America, land companies, and PEI estates, as well as advocates for joint-stock companies and associations such as the North American Colonial Association of Ireland, the London-based Prince Edward Island Association, and the New Brunswick and Nova Scotia Land Company.[36] It was through such associations that the Stewarts came into contact with John Bainbridge of the London-based timber merchants Bainbridge and Brown, who was an associate and friend of Samuel Cunard's and later the provincial agent for Nova Scotia in London;[37] G.V. Duval and Thomas Farrer, directors of the GMA; R.W. Hay, the undersecretary for the colonies; Lord Selkirk, a fellow estate holder in PEI; and a number of MPs, bankers, and investors whom they felt that they could call on for support when necessary, including Edward Gibbon Wakefield, Lord Durham, and Edward Ellice.[38] The Stewart letter books are a remarkable testament to two brothers' locations at the centre of a small but world-striding empire, where bankers, politicians, speculators, and the odd wealthy heiress converged, if only briefly, to play their small parts in the colonization of British North America.

Given the GMA directors' affiliations with so many colonial associations, it is not surprising that they also developed strong ties within the colonies. John Bainbridge, while not necessarily the driving force, was central. Bainbridge was a London-based merchant and agent. He did business with both Joseph and Samuel Cunard from the early 1820s, having secured for the latter the position of commercial agent for the East India Company in the Lower Colonies. By 1828 he was, along with Halifax MLA Charles Fairbanks, representing the promoters of the Shubenacadie Canal Company in their efforts to secure loans from Parliament and investors in London.[39] As the provincial agent for Nova Scotia, he must certainly have known of the GMA, and the opportunity to sell canal stock brought him to its doors in 1828. And willing hosts its directors were. That fall Bainbridge and Fairbanks sold 1,200 "Preference Shares" in the Shubenacadie Canal at £22.10 per share. Of the £27,000 worth of shares sold, £9,877.10 worth were purchased by eight GMA board members, who thereby joined such distinguished Nova Scotians as Samuel Cunard, Andrew Belcher, and Mather Blowers Almon.[40] And the financial interest might have been reciprocal, for by 1831 Bainbridge appears to have become a shareholder in the GMA as well. That winter he and David Stewart were discussing plans for revising Bainbridge's estimate for the GMA's finances over the next few years, a conversation that they mixed with their plans for the New Brunswick and Nova Scotia Land Company (Stewart was a director and Bainbridge the managing director) and for land deals in Prince Edward Island.[41]

David Stewart does not seem to have purchased shares or become in any way involved with the Shubenacadie Canal Company, but it was one of the few colonial investments on which he passed. Earlier in 1831 Stewart had visited the mines at Pictou and Sydney after settling his affairs in Prince Edward Island. While in Nova Scotia, he not only studied the works themselves but also aided Smith in some form of secret land transaction, met all the prominent local politicians, investigated the proposed St Peter's Canal, and assessed the countryside surrounding the coalfields for possible settlement lands. The Stewarts were men with fingers in many pies, all of which, including the GMA, involved land. When David Stewart surveyed the proposed route for the canal at St Peter's, he was also looking to assess the "waste lands" surrounding it, just as the correspondence between Bainbridge and Fairbanks on the Shubenacadie Canal raised the as yet unresolved issue of the "uncultivated lands near the line of this communication."[42] Stewart often spoke of how his "connections in Nova Scotia" gave him access to over 80,000 acres in the province as well as over 100,000 acres in PEI, while the New Brunswick and Nova Scotia Land Company purchased almost a half-million acres of land in New Brunswick in 1835.[43] Such large amounts of land, and the capital to support it, made the brothers powerful players in the colonies and in the various colonial associations to which they belonged.

Stewart's connections in the province were many. While better situated politically in Prince Edward Island, where he held his estates, he evidently knew Bainbridge, Cunard, and probably Andrew Belcher before he visited Pictou in 1831. While in Pictou, however, he wasted little time before meeting almost anybody who mattered in local politics.[44] Such political connections were a vital aspect of doing business. His meeting with George Young was particularly fruitful, not commercially but in terms of other contacts in the government and the Halifax business community. They met when both were returning from PEI, where Young had been prosecuting another landlord's tenants for nonpayment of their rents and where Stewart had been trying to "settle" with his. It was a coincidence that they got on the same boat back to Pictou, but as the circumstances make clear their meeting was hardly unexpected. The two would continue to correspond for years on matters of personal interest (colonial affairs and education) and business (the Bank of British North America and the GMA). In 1835 Young, Cunard, and Robert Stewart would all become involved with the new Bank of British North America. The following year they would form a joint-stock company, the Prince Edward Island Land Company, and purchase Lord Selkirk's estate in Prince Edward Island for £10,000 plus another double lot (60,000 acres) for £12,000.[45] It was a mark of colonial politics and business that the agent for the GMA – and a strong Tory – could do business with one of the leading reformers in the province and the brother of a man whom the GMA had humiliated so thoroughly in the election of 1832. It was another mark of colonial politics and business that the partnership lasted less than a year and "left ill feelings with the Youngs."[46]

Another major connection in the colonies was through the Bank of Nova Scotia, which would be the GMA's bank from 1832 through most of its existence. The bank brought together most of the colonial merchants and businessmen who had strong contacts with the mining venture. Not only did it concretize business dealings in the colony, but it also afforded the GMA a solid base with the province's Tory elite. Included here was Andrew Belcher; his business had recovered somewhat in the past two years, probably bolstered by his lucrative position as the Halifax agent for the GMA. He was one of the original directors of the bank, which brought together some of the wealthiest merchants in the capital, including other prominent Tories like J.W. Johnston (future premier), William Lawson, James Boyle Uniacke, brothers William and Henry Bliss, and Mather Blowers Almon.[47] Cunard remained aloof from all of this until 1834. However, determined to somehow get in on the coal trade, he found his opportunity in early 1834 when Belcher's debts caught up with him again. He owed over £12,000, much of it to Cunard, who foreclosed that winter.[48] Coincidentally, this occurred at the same time as Richard Smith was recalled to Britain, so Cunard obtained not only the position of Halifax agent for the GMA but also that of general manager of the firm's British North American operations.

What is most interesting about this collection of men is not their wealth, although this certainly mattered, but the way that they forged and maintained the links between British and colonial labour, capital, and states, links that would be necessary both for the creation of wealth and for the realization of their envisioned projects. Together, their plans also belie any clear division between landward and seaward investment strategies. Samuel Cunard made his early money in the timber and East India trades, but this did not prevent him from investing in the Annapolis Iron Company, the Shubenacadie Canal Company, the GMA, and each of the province's first three banks; nor did it prevent him from moving quickly into steamships and attempting to acquire the coalmines at Sydney. Although he never supported a bill to protect local industry or agriculture while he was a member of the Legislative Council, this may say as much about his particular interests as it does about his being an example of conservative merchant capital. While Cunard was rejecting trade protection for agriculture, the Stewarts were promoting the sale of PEI wheat and barley in the London market; while Cunard and George Young were buying agricultural estates in PEI, George's brother William Young was plotting the demise of the GMA.[49] Ten years later Almon, Uniacke, W.A. Black, Cunard, and William Young formed the first managing committee of the Atlantic and St Lawrence Railway (later the Halifax and Quebec Railway).[50] That they had particular (or personal) differences did not mean that they could not share particular interests. Most important, they all shared the desire to gain greater access to the wealth of the colony and were prepared to invest in the infrastructure necessary to achieve it.

These programs were bound by more than common parties at their helms. The Stewarts, the GMA, George Young, and even the head of the Cunard Steamship Lines all understood well that colonization was a land-centred practice: one had to own, and control, land in order to people it; and one had to people it in order to make it pay. The GMA sold the program, politically, as in keeping with the twin objects of post-Malthusian colonial policy: depopulate the overpopulated areas of the United Kingdom, and populate the settler colonies.[51] But how exactly this was to be done was another matter. Enormous political and intellectual battles continued to be waged over this issue throughout the period treated here. Few of these colonization ventures had good reputations, and the ongoing reports of poor Britons being treated like cargo in both the laissez-faire and "assisted" programs, which had gone on for the past thirty or more years, meant that these new companies had to legitimate their actions by demonstrating that they were at least humane, if not humane *and* cost-effective.[52] Land policy in Nova Scotia had been a miserable failure, and the province, especially Cape Breton, was plagued by poor immigrants and thousands of illegal squatters. Systematized emigration practices promised to bring order to a chaotic muddle.

If the GMA is understood, then, as a colonization program rather than as a simple mining investment, we can see its more complex role in the colony, a role that was understood by colonial administrators and investors alike. The issue that we should be attentive to here is more complex than a focus on "economic development" allows; we should also recognize the role of the company in establishing governable societies and in aiding in the reconciliation of progress and order.[53] For adminstrators, the case was clear. For example, Wilmot-Horton's plans for "assisted emigration," the dominant model of the 1820s, turned more on the concerns of Malthus than of Smith, emphasizing the vital link between the welfare of a population – particularly the wellbeing of the "lower orders" – and the proper management of a society, not simply an economy. In contrast, Wakefield's "systematic colonization" was explicitly designed to encourage the creation of an economically viable society, specifically one with classes and the capacity for capital accumulation.[54] Yet it is important to observe that he envisioned not only creating an economy but also recreating civilization – or more precisely British society – abroad. These were not merely colonies but also, as he famously observed, "extensions of an old society."[55] Wakefield, as is well known, saw peril in the unrestricted access to land that he believed characterized North American settlement. This peril is typically portrayed as economic, the fear being that unrestricted access to cheap or free land prevented the creation of a class of waged labourers (a class of people who could not afford land), which in turn weakened the capacity of a rural landowning class to accumulate capital. But it is equally important to recall that the concern here was not simply markets but markets as they related to the conditions necessary for good government and social cohesion. Wakefield, like so many colonially minded men of the nineteenth century, had a vision of the colonies as providing what Britain could not guarantee. His program was addressed to young men, such as himself, who were ambitious and educated but only moderately capitalized. To be clear, this program was about becoming wealthy. But to be equally clear, it was as much about glory as about gain; it was about playing a part in and contributing to the grandeur of empire. Wakefield, and the men who invested in the GMA, were very much like-minded men.

PLANTATION INDUSTRY

Colonization programs brought with them a vision of government, an imagined ordering of the chaos that was Crown-lands policy in Nova Scotia at the time. And this was exactly how they were sold. The issue went beyond what we would term economic development, emphasizing as well the peopling of the province's wastelands in an orderly, programmatic fashion. Thus, for example, when the directors of the Shubenacadie Canal Company described their firm's intended impact, they highlighted how they would provide access to "the value and fertility of the districts around the Bay of Funday [sic], and bordering on the Shubenacadie, and the abundance of their agricultural produce, timber, coals, building materials, lime, gypsum, slate, and other minerals."[56] The canal would then bring this frontier within the ambit of capital by bringing these "great internal resources" into operation, thus "contribut[ing] to the consumption and exports of Halifax." In addition, the company would not only provide access to this frontier but also, if it obtained possession of "a grant of the uncultivated lands near [the canal]," put people in contact with those resources by settling hitherto unsettled lands. The canal company, like the land companies and the GMA, had several tacks for different audiences (the directors also noted, for example, that the canal would greatly improve the movement of troops should the United States invade by way of the Bay of Fundy). But the ability of the venture to open up new areas for settlement was always a vital component of the company's plans. Interestingly, the GMA took almost exactly the same approach, emphasizing not only its fairly obvious advantages as an operator of mines but also its not-so-obvious role as colonizer. For land companies, colonization was a given, although the path toward it was not always clear. As systematic colonization increasingly came to hold sway over the course of the 1830s and 1840s, it was ever more important to demonstrate how well the settlement was planned and provisioned. The GMA had its lines well rehearsed long beforehand. But before we pursue the issue of colonization, we need to turn briefly to the firm's lease, as it was the foundation for its entire colonial approach.

The lease was a powerful tool for the GMA, but there was still room for both interpretation and negotiation. Alone, it cannot explain why the British government acquiesced so readily to the company's terms on the lease and in other matters over the years. In part, the answer is obvious: although it was never merely a lapdog, the British state often bowed before capital. Certainly, whether it was seeking concessions or protesting state action, the GMA was always quick to point out the extent of its investment. As well, in part, the answer lies in the royal prerogative, although it was much more easily dealt with (both legally and politically) than the term might suggest. Indeed, no one in either the Treasury or Colonial Office seemed overly enthusiastic about the royal connection, except in law. The answer, rather, seems to lie within the broader contours of colonialism, more specifically within the British state's willingness to alter the rules precisely because the location was a colonial possession. In many ways this is an obvious point. Certainly, the GMA was a foreign venture, and as we have already seen, it was part of one of the British Empire's greatest overseas-investment rushes. Indeed, in its framing and in its final structure, it held many of the hallmarks of any overseas trading monopoly, such as the Hudson's Bay Company or the East India Company, both of which, while under assault, had had their charters renewed in the five years before the GMA was founded.[57] Yet with its exclusivity based in production, not trade, it also held many of the hallmarks of a proprietary land company.

When the Treasury approved the duke's blueprint in 1825, the venture was given exceptional latitude not merely because of the royal prerogative but equally because the GMA was a colonial venture. Treasury officials reasoned that the grant was in a "Foreign Colony ... hitherto wholly unexplored," that the cost would be very high "in a Country where roads and other means of ready communication are in a considerable degree unformed," and that "the greater proportion of the Miners and other individuals to be employed must be sent from this Country and provided with habitations and the means of subsistence."[58] These conditions were unusual, and the company was therefore entitled to unusual terms. In a decision that the acting official observed "may be considered as generally applicable to grants of Mines and Minerals ... in any of His Majesty's Foreign Colonies," the Treasury ruled "that the reservations *usually* made in grants of Mines in Great Britain do not afford any just criterion whereby a satisfactory decision might be formed," so peculiarly colonial terms were required.[59] Specifically, the venture should pay only a nominal rent for the first five years (£1 per year), with no royalty, and for the remaining thirty-one years the rent would be £1 plus one twentieth part of the minerals or (on coal) 1d per ton. Ten years earlier the same board had limited George Smith and William Liddell's term to fifteen years, fixed their rent at £370 per year, added a royalty of 3s6d per chaldron, and expected payments to begin in the next quarter. As the ruling's preamble detailed – and as its conclusion certainly guaranteed – the conditions applied to the GMA were different. Ultimately, however, the issue had little to do with creating coalmines, joint-stock ventures, or the requirements of large-scale capital investment. The case for exceptional treatment rested on the *additional* problems that a *British* firm would encounter in a primitive colonial context and on the benefit that could then be obtained from its remedying such problems through colonization. To be sure, property considerations mattered, but population as much as pure economics was figured among the basic criteria for the board's decision. As Rundell himself observed, by encouraging "whatever may increase and employ the population," the GMA also promoted the internal development of the colony.[60]

The argument was repeated again and again over the next thirty years. Almost every letter, statement, or petition to come out of the GMA, whether from Richard Smith in Pictou, Samuel Cunard in Halifax, or Edmund Waller Rundell in London, emphasized that the firm was not only a foreign mining venture but also an agent of colonization, of "extend[ing] society to distant places."[61] An 1828 GMA petition that picked up the issue of surplus population and the importance of planned colonial settlements could have been written by Wilmot-Horton himself. When petitioning for the inclusion of Cape Breton in the lease, the directors emphasized what they had already accomplished: they had brought with them "many unemployed families ... erected houses and otherwise provided for the sufficient comfort of settlers and ... given them and many other new settlers otherwise without employment profitable occupation." And more could be done. The GMA, they concluded, was providing both for the "increase in the internal strength of the Colony" and for the "public benefit of the Empire." Such actions complemented the good government of Britain, and indeed of the empire, because they encouraged not only the colonial virtue of improved population management at home by transferring the distressed classes overseas but also the good government of Nova Scotia by promoting the twin liberal virtues of sound economic policy and an increased population.[62]

Three years later, fearing a reduction in the duty on British coal exports, the GMA's directors again petitioned for their rights "as British subjects working upon British capital in a British colony." This time they detailed much more precisely their role in assisting emigration and benefiting the empire. The firm had, "to the great advantage and improvement of the Colony, planted new collieries and consequently formed new settlements of population in places where none before existed … [it had] erected furnaces, established wharves, laid down railroads, sent from this Country numerous workmen from the distressed and overinhabitated districts, in most cases with their wives and families, all of whom are employed and paid by the Association, lodged in houses built by the Association, [and] supplied with Stores found by the Association."[63] It was a carefully crafted argument, referencing a number of important colonization issues. The final comment was significant: these settlers were not charges upon either His Majesty or the colonies. The parenthetical comment about wives and families was clearly important too (they did not have to read Malthus to know that removing only men was only so helpful), as was the commonplace reference to the "overinhabited districts," although in 1831 this also had particular currency in the ongoing debates over the Reform Bill and the New Poor Law. The foregoing was but one of several arguments forming the directors' petition, each intended to make a particular point about their claim for protection. But each of the GMA's petitions during this period consistently emphasized four themes: the revenue that the Crown derived from its lease, the size of the its investment, its contribution to relieving distress at home, and its peopling of the overseas colonies. The directors justifiably boasted that, whereas so many overseas-settlement programs had proved to be either failures or scandals, the GMA had indeed planted, populated, and moreover paid for new settlements. They had indeed founded, as one writer observed ten years later, "a colony of miners."[64] Here, just as had been expressed by Wakefield, Captain John Macdonald, and John Young, was the transatlantic movement of ideas and practices so often lionized in public discourse, resulting in the re-creation of British order and government overseas.

In some ways, the language used here was strategic, a rhetoric chosen simply because it resonated in some politically useful fashion. Thus it may have reflected more what the GMA's proponents felt that they should say they were doing than what they were actually doing. This distinction may be misleading, and they may well have been convinced of their own rhetoric. In a number of ways, moreover, such language did reflect the firm's actual plans and practices in the colonies – how the GMA's members envisioned their estate's future, as well as its place in the future of the colony. Simply in terms of marketing, for example, we can see that their early ambitions were great. Whereas historians have emphasized the firm's excessive reliance on exports to the US market,[65] it is important to observe that its original plan included a local market.

The GMA's directors seem to have understood that their imagined industrial complex meshed well with the emerging tenets of colonial policy, and for a time at least, they believed that their enterprise could create its own market. While the US market was pursued from the first day of the company's existence, there was an additional plan for the encouragement of a market within the province. Exports to the eastern US did form a central part of the GMA's market plans. This was obvious from its early efforts to have Sydney and Pictou made free ports in the summer of 1828, just as Samuel Cunard had attempted to do two years earlier when he made this a condition of his obtaining the Sydney lease.[66] The GMA's directors made the point more explicitly in a petition three years later when Parliament was considering removing export duties on British coal, a move that they feared could ruin the GMA in the US market. From the "outset of their establishment," they argued, "the Association had not alone in view the remuneration to be found in the Colony itself ... but was chiefly encouraged by the hope of establishing Nova Scotia Coal in the markets of the United States."[67] And this, certainly, was no empty rhetoric; the firm had agents appointed in most major US ports from Baltimore to Portland by 1829, as well as depots in New York and Boston. At the same time, the petition was careful to note that injury to the GMA's market in the US might "even in Nova Scotia, incapacitate them ... from bringing to maturity their present system and plans."[68] The directors acknowledged that the GMA was more reliant on the US market than the Colonial

Office might like, but they also reminded their overseers that it was on such trade that the firm's larger program rested. If by the mid-1840s the firm looked to be focused exclusively on the export of coal, this was because the broader components of its plan had failed, not because it was locked in a narrow mercantile mindset.

In a colony where a new gristmill was worthy of note, the works envisioned by the GMA were on a scale never before witnessed. In Pictou in the summer of 1827 Richard Smith, following up on an earlier survey, investigated the mining and manufacturing possibilities of the province and described the GMA's "intended weighty establishment."[69] This earlier report laid the groundwork for the first decade's plan, noting the combined presence of coal, iron, limestone, and clay. The uses for coal were clear enough, but given that lime and ironstones were also available, a foundry or iron works appeared possible, while the clay seemed well suited for brick making. (Indeed, it was on the basis of the long-term, fixed-capital costs involved in building an iron works that Jonathan Parkinson, the solicitor for the Duke of York, had the lease extended from thirty-six to sixty years.)[70] Smith, drawing on his background in Black Country coal and iron works, described an immense industrial complex embracing a coal yard, iron foundry, and brick plant. These, in turn, would require roads, housing for workers, and wharves for shipping the coal. Smith was an engineer, so we might forgive his excessive enthusiasm for building more and bigger. But the GMA's financial calculations must have been predicated on just such a plan. Exports to the US would be key, but the firm foresaw much more than a mine and a wharf.

Much of this planning was actually fulfilled. Within three years, the iron foundry, a brick plant, and the colony's first steam engines were in operation, and new and larger wharves had been built. Ten years later the first railway would be in operation. The GMA's impact in the first few years was substantial but, at the same time, restrained by the nature of the enterprise and by the uncontrollable vagaries of investment in a colonial society. Until the 1840s the company brought almost all its men and much of its equipment from Britain. A few local men were hired, and the company occasionally felt the need to advertise for seasonal workers. But coalmining required skilled colliers, and few were to be found in Nova Scotia at this time.[71] Most manufactured equipment – even rope – was still coming from Britain as late as the 1860s.[72] The one product that Nova Scotia could supply well in the 1820s was timber, especially rough timber, which was the only requirement for pit props (supports for the mine roof).[73] Combined, the mines also provided a nicely concentrated market of between seven and twelve hundred men and their families. In 1838 figures supplied by the managers of Albion Mines showed that the GMA expended almost £9,600 per year on provincial agricultural produce.[74] However, while company officials were quick to point to the "ready market" that farmers found for their produce in and about the mines, either the supply was inadequate or the company preferred the terms elsewhere; the company had its own farm at Bras d'Or and continued to import substantial amounts of produce from New England.[75]

The GMA's wages were also an important contribution to the local economy. As the company was again quick to point out, its employees were paid in cash, which meant that miners became very desirable customers among local merchants.[76] At both Sydney Mines and Albion Mines, there were company-run stores, but the men do not appear to have been obliged to purchase their goods there. The purchases of local produce and timber, combined with the over £44,000 in wages paid out in 1838 at Albion Mines, made a substantial addition to the economy of Pictou County. If we allow for the extra items that the GMA purchased for the railway construction underway when the report was made and also factor in the wages paid out at Sydney Mines, then during the late 1830s the GMA was putting about £66,000 per annum directly into circulation in Nova Scotia. There were also ancillary benefits, such as obtaining free-port status for both Pictou and Sydney. It is not clear how this long-pursued goal was accomplished, but locally there was no doubt that the GMA's success illustrated the leverage exercised by metropolitan commercial capital in the halls of Downing Street. Local merchants quickly joined the trade. For some, it provided a substantial addition to their business, and between the spring of 1831 and the end of 1833, at least fourteen different Pictou merchants shipped coal mined on the East River. Private correspondence among Bank of Nova Scotia officials noted the possibilities for more ship construction for the coal trade.[77]

The GMA's program for the internal development of the province complemented colonial policy, a point that again and again the firm employed as best it could. "One great object of colonial Policy," Rundell reminded R.W. Hay, the undersecretary for the colonies, "is the encouragement, by all possible means, of whatever may increase and employ the population, [and] one of the most effectual that can be devised towards its speedy attainment in Nova Scotia is the extensive *consumption* of coals."[78] In this particular petition, Rundell's immediate objective was neither "improvement" nor economic development. The GMA was looking to have the royalty removed from coal sold to its own foundry; it merely wanted to reduce its production costs. At the same time, the firm offered to extend a similar benefit to all "smelting houses, Cupolas, Foundries & Forges that may be established on the East River of Pictou, not belonging to the Association," whereby these facilities would pay a reduced royalty of only 6d per chaldron (rather than 2s).[79] Obviously, this proposed subsidy for local use was good business practice for the GMA, a way to increase local sales. But the petition is singularly remarkable as one of the few assessments of the coal industry to stress not only its immediate and direct effects but also the longer-term role that it *might* come to play.

The GMA's activities may appear unexceptional, even banal. But we should compare them with the thoroughly mercantile logic of the alternative position adopted in Halifax. In reply to the GMA's petition, a committee of the Legislative Council argued that the "least objectionable mode by which the exportation of coals could be promoted" was not free-port status for Sydney and Pictou but a higher duty and transhipment through Halifax.[80] This conclusion, of course, makes sense only according to a narrowly conceived mercantile logic of maintaining stable revenue. Employing the logic of eighteenth-century mercantilism, the merchant-councillors believed that the trade existed to provide certain revenue. It was not even suggested that more production could occur or that it might be good if it did. Council felt that the trade could be improved through better regulatioin, which meant channelling all traffic through Halifax and then adding customs fees to pay for the additional costs. If at this point there was a vision of what we might call development, it came not from the state but from the GMA, whose directors saw the desirability of creating not only an industrial enclave but also an extended local market for the firm's product.

The wider proposal for a release from the royalty on local sales was rejected, although not on its demerits. The Treasury assented to removing the royalty on coal mined for the GMA's own use but not to removing the royalty on coal sold locally. R.W. Hay agreed that such a plan might be beneficial but discouraged Rundell from pursuing the issue so soon after the lease had been finalized.[81] In addition to their concerns over the conditions of trade, Treasury officials were sensitive to how the measure might be received in Halifax, where there would be alarm over any potential infringement on the Crown's Casual Revenue, four-fifths of which was derived from coalmines. The GMA's scheme might have been seen as little short of picking the pockets of the lieutenant governor, the attorney general, the solicitor general, and the provincial secretary (whose salaries ate up four-fifths of the Casual Revenue). The coal revenues were not monies to be toyed with. Throughout the province's negotiations with the GMA, the Colonial Office, and the lawyers for the Duke of York, the issues of how the rent was to be obtained and how much was to be obtained were central. But again the matter was political and only barely economic. The Board of Trade, perhaps as a sop to the province, recommended that a duty be placed on coal exports. Kempt and the Legislative Council, which up to this point had been amenable to most suggestions, firmly balked at this one. Aiming high, Kempt explained that "Any Export Duty imposed by Parliament would necessarily check demand for the exportation of Coals, increase their price to the consumer, and diminish the hereditary revenue which the King received from his Mines." From the point of view of the producer and the consumer, it mattered little whether a duty rather than a royalty was added to the price of the GMA's product. But it was Kempt's final point that was the more important issue; to the governor and his council, how the revenue was collected mattered a great deal. A royalty would go to the Casual Revenue, controlled by the governor and council, whereas a duty would go into general revenue and thus, as Kempt noted ominously, "be at the hands of the Assembly."[82] As the negotiations over whether the GMA would pay £3,000 or £3,300 (and over whether it would be in Halifax currency or sterling) dragged on for months, no one even mentioned that Samuel Cunard had offered £6,000 per year for Sydney Mines alone. The council possessed a curious form of *rentier* mentality; so long as councillors were paid their salaries, they appear to have been content. Not until the achievement of responsible government in 1848, which established a connection between revenue and popular politics through patronage, would a rent-maximizing *rentier*ism (and thus a concern for development) emerge.

CONCLUSION

The GMA was a curious hybrid enterprise: a British mining company, rooted in *ancienne regime* wealth and born in an investment rush on foreign mines, that shifted its location to a settler colony and created an industrial colony. Whereas investing in Brazil might have produced a certain Latin romance and a more publishable adventure story, Nova

Scotia promised security of tenure, British law, and a more stable political climate. Both ventures would have presented the GMA with the difficulties of any overseas operation, but Nova Scotia offered a more attractive investment climate, as well as a special challenge. This was no adventure in Latin American plunder; it was a coalmine. The payoff would not be instant riches. It would take longer and require a heavy capital investment. Starting from scratch, the GMA sought to build an entire industrial-social infrastructure: mines, railways, wharves, homes, roads, a foundry, and a brick-making plant. But we need to be clear that it was also not a proto-typical, indigenous industrial enterprise. The structures of the operation, the backgrounds of the principal figures, and in many ways their understanding of the principles and practices by which they would be guided were all clearly rooted not only in colonialism but also in colonization programs as then understood. The GMA was not merely an investment strategy, or a foreign mining venture, or a colonial enterprise: it was a hybrid industrial scheme adapted to the social and economic peculiarities of a settler colony and to the political expectations of the colonial and imperial states. The firm's directors were not inclined to look backward. They aggressively pursued what they deemed the profits and potentialities of the colonial future, although they did so in the curiously Janus-faced manner of industrial colonization. They could not have foreseen that just as systematic colonization was ill-suited to the emergent liberalism of the settler colonies, so too was industrial colonization, as the future would demonstrate.

The first major blow to the GMA's plans came in 1841 and 1842. The "field" that the company had entered eighteen years earlier was radically changing. To the south, the Reading Railroad had been completed (connecting the Pennsylvania coalfields with the industrial northeast and reducing by US$1.50 per ton the cost of shipping coal to the seaboard), while the US Congress had placed an additional duty of US$1.75 per ton on imported coal.[83] The effect on the GMA was immediate. The ships that normally carried its coal to the US simply did not arrive. The company had shipped 21,000 chaldrons in the first six months of 1842, the part of the year that was normally the slow season, but the figure for the second half of 1842 was a mere 8,400 chaldrons – most of which went to other British North American colonies. That autumn Samuel Cunard was again petitioning London for a further reduction in the GMA's rent.[84] While the trade reversal showed some recovery the next year, the effects were still substantial. In part, the

recovery was due to increased recognition that Nova Scotia's bitumi-
nous coal was only partly in competition with Pennsylvania's anthracite
coal, but it was also due to the fact that the GMA had dramatically low-
ered its price. In combination with a series of strikes (themselves very
much related to this turnabout in the market and to the reduction in
the company's price for coal), the inferior quality of the local iron ore,
and the weak colonial market, the reduced price put an almost immediate halt to further expansion and development of the local works.
However, the new political economy of the market changed neither
the GMA nor its desired ends. "The mercantile context," writes Ian
McKay, "imprisoned industrial development in the perpetual realm of
the short-term."[85] This was undoubtedly true in the 1860s and 1870s.
But such a conclusion seriously underestimates the anticipated long-
term plans and possibilities of the company until at least 1842. The
GMA offers much for the historian of nineteenth-century Nova Scotia.
If in some respects the company's history explains the dependence of
the late nineteenth-century coal industry on state assistance, in another respect it offers important insights into the colonial imaginary
that was "improvement." In Nova Scotia's future, John Young saw
"shrubbery," a country home, and the agrarian landscape of the Scottish lowlands; Richard Smith saw foundries, row houses, and Britain's
industrial midlands. Both saw that, guided by science, capital, and the
leading men of the country, a great and certain future lay ahead.

6

A Colony of Miners

Albion Mines stood out from the surrounding countryside. Writers of travel accounts routinely paused to describe the village, and several contrasted the red brick houses, smoke, and blackened landscape with the neighbouring farms. George Wightman, a Windsor-born engineer sent from Halifax by the House of Assembly to investigate the operations of the General Mining Association (GMA), described the village as "a colony of miners." His comment was meant to highlight the village's difference. Pointing to the workplace in particular, he attempted to show how the miners' work habits were inappropriate to the colony: their wages were too high ("more than is accordant with the current prices of labour in this country"), and the company's business strategy was "not on a par" with local practice. The company's owners, managers, and workers were "applying the maxims and practices of England to a country under different circumstances."[1]

Wightman was an improver. Trained as an engineer, the friend and ally of Joseph Howe applied his utilitarian ideals to plans to bureaucratize road construction, cost overruns on the Shubenacadie Canal, and reforms to the land system in Prince Edward Island.[2] Like John Young, Captain John Macdonald, and the many others who focused their attention on agricultural practices, Wightman trained his eye on inappropriate activities and sought to apply better systems. His report on Albion Mines attempted to portray an anomaly, one that could be changed given the appropriate technique and patience. Certainly, there were differences in the ways that things were done at Albion Mines, and at Sydney Mines too, compared with elsewhere in Nova Scotia, and we should not be surprised that Wightman picked up on them. After all, looking for difference was the stock approach of the travel writer, and of the missionary, as it accounted for the peculiar – and usually aberrant – ways of the natives. Whether one was selling one's book or raising money to spread the Gospel, illustrating difference best conveyed the perceived problems. As we have seen, the coal towns at Sydney Mines and Albion Mines were planted with specific intentions that required specialized tasks and that produced fairly obvious differences compared with the surrounding countryside. Their inhabitants were digging coal, not potatoes. But how different? Can we view the mining societies as separate enclaves within the colonial countryside? Or can we detect more uniformity with their agricultural neighbours than the term "enclave" might suggest?

ORDERED TOWNS

It is difficult to "see" the miners in either of the mining towns; it is even difficult to locate miners in the census manuscripts. The major problem relates to how individuals were identified and categorized. In the period under discussion, only the 1851 census is of much assistance, but there was no category for coalminers, and the manuscripts for Cape Breton are missing.[3] Outside of a few professions (clergyman, lawyer, and school teacher), the census used only generic categories: one was either a merchant, a farmer, or a mechanic. The following discussion risks conflating colliers with any independent artisan in the area, as well as with most labouring employees of the GMA. Nevertheless, at least one-third of these men were skilled colliers, and at least half would have been underground employees of some sort.[4] We can learn a fair bit by briefly turning to their census returns.

The first and most obvious point that we should observe is that the Albion Mines census district itself stands out, even compared with the towns of Pictou or New Glasgow. The proportion of "mechanics" in Albion Mines was much greater than in any other district, and there were far fewer farms. A one-in-three sample from four districts on the East River (Albion Mines, New Glasgow, Hopewell, and East Branch) located a total of 293 farms, only 24 of which (about 8 per cent) were in the Albion Mines district. Almost two-thirds of Albion Mines' heads of households were described as mechanics. On the West River (excluding the town of Pictou) only 16 per cent of the householders listed themselves as mechanics. In the agricultural districts on East River, the figure was even lower at 10.5 per cent. Not all these Albion Mines mechanics were in fact miners, but it is obvious that miners gave this population a very different character.

So what did it mean that mining households so heavily populated this district? Here, the census is less helpful, but it does provide us with a few fairly clear points. The most obvious difference from farmers was the miners' weaker ability to provide their own food. Some, perhaps even most, of the mining households probably kept small gardens either outside their homes or in a common field behind the row houses. These would have been a vital component of these people's lives, an effort to reduce their spending on food and defer something of their reliance on wages. None of these gardens, however, were deemed worthy of note by the census enumerators. There were no formal instructions to enumerators on this point, but it was common to mark a single acre as the lower limit in the nineteenth-century census; none of these gardens would have been close to one acre. Nevertheless, despite the small gardens, a number of other "rural" practices were maintained. Almost 40 per cent of Albion Mines' miner-headed households owned one or more cows, while one household in eight reported producing anywhere from 40 to 96 pounds of butter. About 40 per cent also reported cloth production, averaging about 26 yards of fulled and unfulled cloths and flannel. By way of comparison, East River farm households produced an average of 49.8 yards each year, and the proportion of households producing was much higher at 88.5 per cent.

Some of these figures may be surprising. That Albion Mines was composed mostly of miners should not surprise us. Nor should it surprise us that "urban" workers employed "rural" tactics such as gardening and raising animals to supplement their waged income.[5] Alan Campbell describes Lanarkshire miners as "incompletely proletarianized" and notes that mid-nineteenth-century mine officials worked hard to "erode the rural trappings" (particularly animals and firearms for hunting) of life in the district's Scottish mining towns.[6] But the extent of the "rurality" in the industrial village of Albion Mines might nonetheless seem startling. Certainly, the cloth production seems higher than we might expect, if only because the raw material would not have been easily accessible. There were also more cows roaming the backfields and laneways of Albion Mines than we might have expected. The common pattern was for households to have one milch cow and one "neat" cow (for meat). With limited storage possibilities, we must presume that they purchased a beef cow in the spring for slaughter in the fall and sold, shared, or somehow exchanged what they did not consume themselves. It also gives us a slightly better sense of the contribution of women and younger children in these households. If we can presume that women tended the cattle and the garden and made the cloth and butter, in addition to tending to the children, the cooking, the washing, the stove, and the house itself, it is evident that while this work was not as dangerous as mining, it was at least as demanding. It was also important from a simple (household) finance perspective. Much as was the case for the victims of enclosure across Great Britain, opportunities for the employment of dispossessed women usually declined as families moved to the industrial towns. This was particularly true in coal towns, where there were not only fewer "female" jobs but also more men willing to take on any form of waged work. There would certainly have been some incentive to turn to home production or to outwork if it was available.[7] If sold, the cloth produced by these miners' partners would have represented as much as £10 per year, more than two month's wages for a male labourer doing surface work or working the loading docks downriver from the mines. If it was not sold, as the moderate participation figure suggests was more often the case, such cloth would have meant at least a substantial savings in purchased clothing.[8] There was nothing inherently "rural" about weaving cloth or having a cow or two. But we might also note that one commonly assumed difference between rural and urban households is the latter's greater use of and access to consumer products. It is certainly worth noting that these women, whether migrants from the surrounding countryside or Staffordshire, did not fully immerse themselves in the possibilities of the "Big Store" (the company store at Albion Mines, where it was said anything could be had).[9] Whether this was by choice or necessity is not clear, but as with poor farmers and smallholders, domestic production lessened reliance on wages, cash payments, and merchant credit.

One major difference between farm households and mining households stood out on the census forms. Enumerators were asked to note both the assessed and "probable" values of each household's holdings. It is entirely possible that, in Albion Mines, the enumerators simply never bothered asking about property values while going through a village dominated by company-owned red brick houses, but if the figure offered us is accurate, home ownership was very low. In Albion Mines only two "mechanics" in our sample were listed as having holdings with any "probable value" – an average of less than £1 per household. (Some miners in Sydney, however, appear to have purchased lots for houses from the GMA in the 1850s.)[10] Even a small farm, say less than 25 acres, on the East River was worth just under £130 (over

£200 on the West River), while a backland farm with little improvement could still fetch £30 to £50.[11] In a colony where capital was increasingly important to anyone's betterment, this difference mattered.
A few years later, a Cape Breton County farmer observed that the
material life of miners compared favourably with that of poor farmer-
fishers; the miners, he commented, "work well ... are never in want,
and always well clad."[12] Cash wages might allow one to be "well clad,"
but apparently remuneration was not substantial enough for one to
purchase property. Thus miners could look forward to little security
or independence.

It will be instructive at this point to turn briefly to the village of New
Glasgow. In 1828 New Glasgow was a few merchants and a customs
house. By 1851 it was not yet the thriving industrial town that it became in the last third of the century,[13] but it was growing rapidly and
on its way to surpassing Pictou as the commercial centre of the county.
At the heart of this growth was a substantial shipbuilding industry that
attracted hundreds of skilled and unskilled workers to the area after
the 1830s.[14] In 1851 we find that roughly 40 per cent of New Glasgow's heads of households described themselves as mechanics, while
44 per cent described themselves as farmers. This is not as proletarian
as Albion Mines (where 74 per cent were mechanics), but for the time
and the area it certainly made New Glasgow stand out against the surrounding countryside. Again, as in Albion Mines, we have no information by which to determine with any more specificity exactly what these
individuals' skills might have been except for the hints that they left in
the manuscripts. Sadly, even these are not particularly helpful in the
case of New Glasgow because the enumerator there did not record
what the numerous small mills and factories (employing between
three and forty people) actually made or did. Like those of the Albion
Mines "mechanics," these New Glasgow households probably also had
gardens, but our sample located thirteen with farm acreage (i.e., an
acre or more), several of which had between 5 and 15 acres, and nine-
teen with more than two cows. Most mechanic-households produced
30 to 40 yards of cloth, and many produced a firkin or two of butter.
New Glasgow (District 13) lists an average "probable value" of £241.10
for all the mechanics in New Glasgow. In a world – indeed, a county –
where great merchants and wealthy capitalists bought and sold land
and other commodities for thousands of pounds, £241 seems paltry.
Within these communities, however, it is rather impressive. Compare
this figure, for example, with the average value of £234 for a *large* farm

(more than 45 acres improved) on the East River, this being an average property.[15] In New Glasgow, as with the farms, there was a tremendous variety in the value of mechanics' households, ranging from a
large cluster valued at around two hundred pounds to some valued at
three, four, five, seven, and twelve hundred pounds. Almost 90 per
cent of these were assessed at more than £50. As with the farmers,
there were substantial differences within the category. But unlike the
"mechanics" farther upriver in Albion Mines, most of these mechanics
had, as one writer believed, "aspir[ed] after something more than an
ignoble existence" and accumulated some small amount of property.
Such a mechanic had "procure[d] respectability to himself."[16] Respectability was earned, but the measure was property – and property
certainly marked a clear difference between the "mechanics" (i.e., the
miners) in Albion Mines and those in New Glasgow.

Before 1858 and the expansion of the coal industry, the miners did
therefore form something of a cultural enclave within the countryside.
But were they, as some have assumed, isolated – that is, were they apart
from the broader world of culture, politics, and even their more immediate neighbourhood? To be sure, there was intercourse between the miners and everyone else, but it was limited and the miners often stood apart,
consciously, to protect their hold on their workplaces and, less consciously although not unknowingly, through their beliefs and practices.
In the early years of the mines, almost all of the skilled men – the colliers
– were imported from Great Britain. Some had probably worked in several mines before emigrating, and the steady stream of workers arriving
kept them well abreast of goings on at home.[17] And not all the Britons
working in the mines had come straight from another isolated coal town.
These were men who came from the south of Scotland and the north of
England, and they continued to correspond with people in the old country as well as with others who had moved on to the US. Take, for example, Peter Barrett's account of his own life. He was one of three brothers
who arrived in 1866, the sons of a couple who alternated between farm
labour and Methodist preaching. The three young men left their employ
as farm labourers to work in coalmines in Staffordshire in order to earn
the money for the crossing. Over the next ten years, all three would continue to live their lives centred on coalmining, moving from Nova Scotia
to Pennsylvania and then briefly to Upper Canada before returning to
Nova Scotia; they also purchased land and farmed to the best of their
abilities. Barrett, like millions before and after him, travelled the routes
of the transatlantic labour market. When he was in Philadelphia, three

shysters whose scam preyed on newcomers tried to take his money. As Barrett quickly figured out, many had been robbed before him, and plenty more would follow.[18]

An earlier account can allow us to see traces of this transatlantic movement. In December 1835 James Madison, a miner in Sydney Mines, replied to a letter from his brother-in-law, John Stevenson, in the coalmining town of Pottsville, Pennsylvania. This one letter captures a remarkable slice of the transatlantic movement of people. Stevenson had reported that he and his family were well and, moreover, that there were "great wages" available in Pottsville. Such favourable reports only made "life on this cold island" less bearable, and Madison, together with his father and several others, were now "earnest about leaving." Stevenson was not the only former GMA miner in the US:

> Since I last wrote several have left the place for the United States. Such as John White, George Kehoe, John Dubben, John Foley, Michael Osmond, and a great many others. Indeed, the Mines is thin of people to what it used to be. There is only about 12 houses that pays Rent occupied. And some of the shantees are deserted. Letters have been received from most of them, and they all send good accounts. Peppet and Wilson have both left and gone to Boston. Most of the others went to Boston. James Andrews and Richard Richards is working in a Tunnel 6 miles from New York at 1 Dollar and a half per day, and 30 more men is wanted. A letter has been received from Isaac Brown ... John Day is in Pittsburgh, also David Thomas, John Davies, and [illegible], and John James [and] Kenny Anderson is gone to the Missouri Territory.

Having received news, Madison then had to pass on information to others within Sydney Mines. He read "Brother's" letter to "Mitchell & wife," who had not heard from their son James, who had also gone to Pottsville. And there were also other greetings to be passed on to what must have been at least ten former Sydney Mines residents now in the same Pennsylvania mining town. He also had news from the old country to pass along:

> Our friends in England are all well. Jacob Vickers has got a little daughter. Her name is Margaret. John Armstrong is no better for his voyage to New York ... The letters from Staffordshire, South Wales, and Scotland say that times are very prosperous. One letter

from Staffordshire says that wages were never so great, nor work
so plenty as at this time.

Finally, Madison turned his attention back to his and his family's futures. His father certainly wished to leave Cape Breton, although the
son was less sure. He sought "Brother's" advice:

> Anthony talks of leaving in the spring ... But I think it would be pref-
> erable for you to write and send us word about the state of things in
> the Spring. You are on the spot and you will know what the look out
> is for work. Send us word what sort of winter you have had, the
> wages, and the prices of wearing apparel ... and any other informa-
> tion which may be good and proper for us to know. Our women
> people wish to know what sort of house you have and whether [illeg-
> ible] you were previously acquainted with for neighbours. Now you
> know this place, and you gained some knowledge of the state of
> things where you are and other places and send us your advice
> whether you would recommend us to leave this place or not. You
> know we are now worse of[f] knowing every particular, and if things
> continue to look dark, we can then act accordingly.

They were unhappy in Sydney Mines; they were not as well paid as they
had expected, and "Mr. Brown" was now "pinching at every end" in order to reduce operating expenses for the company.[19] Given too that
they probably had access to newspapers and perhaps the odd book (this
family had a Bible with which they were teaching the children to read),
these people were as well in tune with the world as any working person
could be. Their points of contact were quite fantastic – Pennsylvania,
New York, Boston, Staffordshire, Wales, and Scotland – and the information, while in many ways banal, was the stuff of life for a migrant worker.
They could hear about the wages that their friends were now receiving
in the US and about the state of the labour market at "home."[20] They
could also have read about the wars on the continent, the Chartists, and
Captain Swing.[21] These people were not isolated.

But having had worldly experiences does not guarantee maintaining
one's worldliness. In some ways, the mine villages themselves were physically isolated. Certainly, Nova Scotia was not New York or London, but
then again neither were Pottsville or Staffordshire. What about within
Nova Scotia? Were the "enclaves" so insular as to make these towns isolated? Coalminers have always been regarded as a "breed apart." They

were the archetypal proletarian,[22] the extreme in nineteenth-century social relations. Historians and contemporary social commentators alike drew from a rich base of mining stereotypes when they represented coalminers and the coalmining family as a separate and notoriously fertile breed. One mid-nineteenth-century English observer commented that migration was neither a necessary nor a useful component of the coalmining labour market because "Pitmen must be bred to their work from childhood," adding that there was little need for either training or recruitment in this "notoriously prolific section of the population."[23] We have only poor figures for Nova Scotia miners' vital statistics before 1865, but we do know that in some ways they were segregated. In Pictou one commentator described the village of Albion Mines as an island of skilled workers who "fix their prices and will not consent to admit any other persons into the works."[24] Clearly, this was a comment on the workplace, not the community, but the two locations were vitally linked. In the mining villages, the workplace and many broader cultural activities intermeshed.

Economic life in the coal towns centred almost exclusively on the coalmines. There was little else. The mines provided a market for merchants, farmers, and traders from around the province as well as for shipping interests. Stores, homes, and wharves were built, and businessmen were drawn by the lure of coal and coastal trading vessels. What set the coal villages apart was their planted, town-like atmosphere. Within two years the brick manufactory at Albion Mines had produced enough bricks to build several rows of houses for miners at all four mines, and several log-framed houses were built as well. The company also built lavish homes for the managers: Mt Rundell, at Pictou, and Beech Hill, at Sydney Mines.[25] Mt Rundell, built for Richard Smith, overlooked the works in appropriate paternalist fashion, while Beech Hill still commands the entrance to Sydney harbour. Both were very impressive homes for their day, rivalling most anything in Halifax, and outside the capital they were matched by very few. The presence of these orderly villages, characterized by patent hierarchies that extended from managers' mansions down to workers' red brick houses and log huts (a distinction that almost certainly represented status within the mine), was a real mark of difference. Anyone visiting the East River after about 1830 could not possibly have failed to observe the works, the village attached, and the manner in which they were organized.

The GMA treated its employees quite differently than most other employees of the time were treated. In many ways, this was good. Certainly, in terms of pay, the company's well-experienced managers treated their employees as the valuable and skilled workers that they were. It was not out of chauvinism that the GMA brought miners from Britain but because it knew the value of skilled employees.[26] Coal cutters, the men most responsible for the quality and quantity of coal removed, could earn 10s per day, while even loaders earned 4s. Boys, very often the sons of the colliers, could earn anywhere from 1s6d to 3s depending on their age. Outside the mines, few skilled workers could obtain more than 4s per day; farm labourers typically received 2s or 2s6d, and this rarely in cash. The company also provided housing at a low fixed rent, and coal was either free or available at minimal charge.[27] The housing was inexpensive, although variously described as "neat [and] well furnished" or as "low Dirty, dingy houses."[28] The drawback, however, was that Nova Scotia's export season (especially at Pictou) was limited to the period from April to January. Thus few men were paid such high wages year-round. Even in summer, the peak shipping season, if demand was down, the need to produce for the next year was minimized, and even regularly employed men might obtain only a few days per month.[29]

The managers ran their operations, including their men, tightly. Discipline was emphasized. All employees were expected to produce to their best abilities and also to conduct themselves well above ground. At Sydney Mines, Richard Brown "mustered" his men twice a year as lieutenant colonel of the militia. When faced with a poor showing, as in 1834, Brown promised the provincial secretary that in future those who did not attend would be "severely punished" and that he would "preserve order" among his men. Indeed, failure to muster would be punished in the same way that he punished insubordinate employees: offenders would be dismissed.[30] At the same time, he could be a protector and could "lecture" an underground manager "on his conduct toward the men."[31] Typically, such paternalist actions cut both ways. On a range of day-to-day concerns, the miners were very often able to fix their own terms of employment without resorting to a strike. Brown's diaries from the early 1830s to the late 1840s record a consistent pattern of men setting their own days and hours of working. In 1849 Brown recorded that the "pits [were] idle" on ten separate days. Three were because of poor shipping and one because of a mechanical problem, but the remainder, save for one on "account of the races," were due to St Patrick's Day, a meeting of the "friendly society," the procession of the Temperance Society, and a "fast day."[32] Even the lieutenant colonel had to give a little slack.

Individually, the GMA and the managers exercised a substantial power over the day-to-day lives of the men from their wages to their housing conditions, the number of helpers that they could obtain, and the safety of the workplace itself. Yet the miners, with their high skills and relative scarcity, maintained a strong bargaining position. The company was, in many ways, held captive by the skill of its employees – the only explanation for the tremendously high wages that they were offered. Few incidents relate the two-sidedness of the relationship between master and men better than Richard Smith's recollection of the early days of Albion Mines. After returning to England, Smith recalled that the gas at Albion Mines, and thus the danger of explosions, was greater than anything he had witnessed before. Smith described his first few times in the Nova Scotia mines and the experience of entering a seam where the gaseous emissions were so great that they sounded "like a hundred thousand snakes hissing."[33] Although the miners were all well experienced, none had ever worked in such strong gas before – but they knew exactly what it meant. While Smith's work was on the surface, he understood that he had to be the first down the shaft every morning: "It [the gas] was very alarming and I had to go every morning with the men ... as I would not ask them to go where I would not go myself."[34] Smith, Brown, and the underground managers set many of the conditions, but the miners could set some too. A few years later the *Colonial Patriot* waxed lyrical about the strength of the relationship between Smith and the miners and about the "parental care" that he offered them: "He seems to look upon them as his own children," the newspaper observed, "and they upon him as a kind protector."[35] Parental, paternal, perhaps even kind – the metaphors seem to fit. But few children insist that their parents put their lives on the line as a condition of consent.

Paternalism characterized most employment relations in early nineteenth-century North Atlantic societies.[36] What marked these Nova Scotia paternalisms, however, was the effects of insular work in the industrial plantation, most notably the advantage exercised by the men through their unusual positions as highly skilled men in a highly regulated labour market, and the effects of a segregated life in the industrial plantation. Two miners' parades, one in 1833 and another in 1841, give us some sense of the clear cultural differences and similarities between the inhabitants of the industrial villages and their neighbours. They also reveal something of how the miners both understood and appreciated their place in their new home.

In December 1832 a fire shut down Albion Mines for almost six months. A year later the miners of the village staged a parade in commemoration of the incident, which had killed fourteen horses.[37] The circumstances of the fire were suspicious. Believed to be the work of "incendiaries," the fire remained a mystery. A two-month local investigation and an additional inquiry by the solicitor general had been unable to find the guilty parties. On Monday, 31 December 1833,[38] a few hundred residents assembled outside the main shaft. The men had constructed, on top of a coal sled, a tableau with "a mixture of the coal charred by the conflagration, and a quantity of the bones of the horses suffocated in the pits." Standing amid the ash and bones were "two Effigies, and on a board attached ... the characters INCENDIARIES was [sic] written large." Fourteen horses were harnessed as a team to pull the sled, with a man alongside each horse and boys mounted and carrying flags. The parade then marched off in fourteen "orders," each with a flag and a horse. The first flag read "Anniversary," followed by "Fire," "Starvation of 500 persons," "Indignation," "14 Horses Murdered," and "Cruelty," and the seventh advertised the "£300 Reward." These were followed by a silent group of three carrying identical black mourning flags "bearing the skeletons of horses," followed by "Justice," "Punishment," "Pillory," and "Gridiron." The parade made the circuit of the GMA's property, "slowly ... [and] a large concourse of people then assembled in an orderly and peaceable manner on the spot immediately over where the fire had been below." After the parade the people reassembled with Richard Smith and some unnamed government officials, turning from the condemnation of past acts to a celebration of what had been good, and of the New Year to come, with a meal of "roast Beef and plum-pudding and Beer." After offering three cheers for the king, the president, the council, the House of Assembly, the GMA, the solicitor general (who had investigated the fires), and the coal trade, they offered "3 deep groans of abhorrence of the vile incendiaries and their abettors, if it be possible that such there be." Having cast the light of suspicion into the wider community, they then made clear their general goodwill by offering cheers for the success of the "surrounding neighbourhood ... the general prosperity of the land we live in ... [and] the Ships Trade and Commerce." All they desired, as they noted in their cheer for "the Constitution," was rights to the protection of "its laws and justice."[39]

It was a remarkable display. Clearly, their anger was most evident. Although they did not burn the effigies (Smith had asked them not to), the display of charred coals and bones, the black flags with skeletons, and the text ("Justice," "Punishment," "Pillory," and the delightfully medieval "Gridiron") made certain that any viewers would understand the magnitude of this crime and the colliers' complete support for the charges made by their superiors. Indeed, in some ways the parade seemed to have been as much for their superiors as for themselves. The miners also offered cheers "for the success of the Albion Mines," "the coal trade," and "Richard Smith, Esq." That they should wish their own industry well is by no means surprising – indeed, we might expect that they should be strong advocates of anything conducive to their industry's prosperity.[40] It is also in this context that we can understand the inclusion of Smith, who, like the trade and the GMA, assumed the role of provider. In a similar expression of dependence, they also exhorted their "comrades in Sydney and Bridgeport" to "treat with equal indignation, every attempt to injure and destroy the property of their employers, and to deprive themselves of honest labour and daily bread."[41] Here, the messages became more complex, and we can begin to see the multiple strategies contained in their actions. That there was condemnation and moral outrage is certain. That there was a slightly defensive edge is also evident, a sense that they were, especially in their comment on the abettors but also in the message to their "comrades" in Cape Breton, asserting their own complete innocence in the matter. Although the investigation never turned toward any of them,[42] the men seem to have felt it necessary to at least reassert their loyalty and remind their employers of the ties binding employee to employer. In this sense, then, the parade would seem to have been for the benefit of Smith and the Board of Directors, and perhaps the Sheriff too, as much as anyone. Indeed, that the parade was confined to company property seems rather more insular than such a public display might have warranted. Parades were common public displays in both town and country.[43] It seems odd that on this occasion they confined their display to themselves and their masters, literally under the gaze of Mt Rundell. In the paternalist order of the mine village, many actions were both acts of self-expression and paternal performances.

Another parade, six years later on the opening of the South Pictou Rail Road, suggests a broader public presence, a greater scope for worker self-activity, and a clearer assertion and affirmation of the miners' own importance. Although remaining within the bounds of paternalist performance, the mineworkers seem to have constructed a stronger place for themselves within the company's celebratory representation of itself.[44] The parade was but one element in a daylong celebration to mark the opening of the railway. Starting at 6:30 in the morning, the steamship *Pocahontas* travelled back and forth between New Glasgow, Pictou, and the Loading Ground, below the mines where the railway ended, carrying what appears to have been half the county to the site of the celebrations: "Ladies ... *rigged* original emphasis out in their finest attire," together with their "gallant beaus," paraded down the main street, while the Volunteer Artillery Company marched and fired regular volleys across the river. The major show, after the parade, was the first run of the trains. The *Samson*, the *Hercules* (appropriately strong names), and the *John Buddle* (in due respect for his assistance)[45] were on display for the entire morning and afternoon, before they were "cleared of the vulgar throng ... [and] filled with those to whom the gentlemen of the Association had sent tickets of admission." Two trains, each with thirty-five cars and carrying 700 "souls," delivered the celebrants to the Loading Ground and later carried them back to their departure point – a total of almost 10 miles – "at a rapidity varying from 10 to 20 miles per hour."

Over the course of the day, the GMA put on no less than three large meals, including an outdoor banquet, "opposite the office," of "1200 lbs of Beef and Mutton, 6 hhds. of Ale, with Bread and vegetables in abundance" for a total of 750 workmen. Later, the Masons – who appear to have been acting in a capacity somewhere between security and ushers – and the Artillery Company were fed beef "washed down with Brandy." In the evening, the GMA put on another, much more "sumptuous" affair for the 150 invited guests inside the converted Engine House, while "the Ladies" were entertained at Mt Rundell by "Mrs Smith." At a time when temperance was emerging as a popular force in the county, the wine, brandy, and ale, not to mention the "copious libations of Champagne" during the many toasts, flowed freely with scarce a comment from the pro-temperance press. It was a time for celebration: the railway had come to Nova Scotia.

The parade, to be sure, was part of the company-sponsored affair. But this parade suggests that the miners had a much greater role in organizing it than the previous one. Again, the procession was organized into orders, this time ten. Each of these represented a group of workmen. First came 100 horses "mounted by their respective drivers – horses and men decorated, [and] carrying flags." They carried two "devices" (i.e., banners) and a flag: the first was a large crown surrounded by a rose, a shamrock, a thistle, and a mayflower, with the motto "Long life to Queen Victoria"; the second was a depiction of "2 horses with 2 wagons coming out to the pit bottom, meeting 2 Colliers going in to their work, with picks under their arms," with the motto "Success to the coal trade; as the old cock crows the young one learns." The parade continued, with each order representing similarly the enginemen, the colliers, the freemasons, the foundrymen and blacksmiths, the bricklayers and stone masons, and the carpenters, followed by bagpipers and, finally, the Albion Mines Band.

Each device carried its own message, and in most we see the same play between an assertion of self and an ultimate dependence on the GMA. The enginemen's motto, for example, was:

Long may the Company flourish,
And their servants rejoice;
May Steam Navigation never fail
To burn our Coal and send us sail.

The carpenters' device simply read, "The Albion Mines and Joseph Smith, Esq," while the bricklayers' said, "Success to Locomotive Engines, and All the Trades belonging to the Albion Mines." We also see the sense of craft pride found wherever we examine craftworkers in the North Atlantic world. The foundrymen and blacksmiths did not look to the coal trade so much as assert their common ties with other engineers and knowledge workers; their device represented Archimedes and James Watt with the motto "Ours and for Us; Knowledge is Power." All the mottos and devices contained the common symbols of their trades (engines, trowels, and the square and compass) and expressed their connection to a broader Atlantic world of trades.

While expressions of craft and collective pride poured from these texts, they contained only weak assertions of class solidarity. Only the colliers articulated an explicit expression of solidarity with their motto, "United we stand, when divided we fall, Unanimous as Brethren." The parade itself may have recognized some intercraft solidarities, but there was little sense that anything beyond this was binding the crafts. The issue here was more corporate than particular – that is, while the paraders separated themselves within their particular crafts, their point of unity seemed to be less their affinity as workers, or even workingmen, than their affinity as workmen in the coal trade. To be sure, there was an expression of working-class independence here, but it is doubtful that these men would have recognized it as having political consequences beyond their immediate audience. The newspaper account also noted as remarkable the "good order" with which the men conducted themselves; both in the parade and in seating and unseating themselves from dinner, they moved with an apparently military-like precision. This should not be surprising. Both Joseph Smith and Richard Brown were militia leaders, and as we have already seen, Richard Brown routinely paraded his miners.[46] In some sense, then, the parade may have been very well rehearsed.

This is not to argue that these workers were wholly subservient to a coercive paternal order. The following summer (1840) there would be a major display of independent action – a strike to protest a wage cut. And two years after this strike, there would be another, during which the colliers and their families would turn the paternal order on its head, threatening violent confrontations and terrorizing the residents of Mt Rundell.[47] Nevertheless, we need to recognize the context of workers' dependency and the limits of even those strongly positioned within the lower end of a paternal social hierarchy. The same scarcity of workers that leveraged their wage-bargaining position also entailed their own limited access to new employments; although there was the possibility of moving elsewhere for work, such movement was not as easy in the monopolized coal industry as it would have been in Britain or in other industries within the colony. For miners in Nova Scotia, protesting with one's feet meant finding a berth aboard a train bound for New York or Philadelphia and the money to transport one's entire family. As we have already seen, this was common enough, but it was perhaps one upheaval too many for most families. Whatever their skills, whatever their pride, whatever forms of resistance they might engage in, they were employees, not independent artisans; they were proletarians whose workplace allowed them to act as artisans, hire their own men, and apprentice boys, but they were still employees whose craft position relied on foreign trade, international duties, and the economic prosperity and stability of the industrializing US northeast. Twenty years later the *Eastern Chronicle* observed how "election after election" the employees of the GMA were "led up to the polls like sheep to the shambles ... to record their votes to suit the political views of their employers."[48] The newspaper, a good Liberal organ, was lamenting how the miners voted as much as how they were brought to the polls. That Tories did a better job of protecting the miners' right to vote certainly mattered – so did the Liberals' sending in troops to quash a strike at Sydney Mines in 1864.[49] But the miners' jobs too were on the line. Given the nature of the industry, it would have been very surprising indeed to find miners voting for antimonopoly reformers hell-bent on destroying their employer's position in the trade. Advancing the prosperity of the trade meant advancing the prosperity of the company and the security of their employment. The hypocrisy of the Liberals here was deep. There was little doubt that the company disciplined its workforce; this ordering of the mining frontier, we have already noted, was an important part of its legitimacy in the colony. What the *Eastern Chronicle* was really trying to suggest here was that the GMA turned these men into sheep – that is, that they were not good liberal citizen-workers because of the company's excessive control. But they were not sheep. Tories protected the working-class vote; Tories protected the GMA. Sensible miners voted Tory. They were far from sheep; they were sensible liberal citizens voting for their own best interests.

On another level, the parades were assertions not only of the miners' identity but also of their place within these rural societies. It is interesting, for example, that they made the gestures they did to the broader community. The second parade – celebrating the opening of the railway – was an unambiguously public event in a way that the earlier one was not; this time they explicitly made common cause with the farmers, shipping interests, and "the land" upon which they both trod. They recognized a shared fate; upon the prosperity of one depended the prosperity of the other. On this level, then, it may be true that there was some sense of commonwealth here, although not the kind of republicanism (or even proto-republicanism) that Sean Wilentz sees in New York City parades in the same period.[50] However unequal the relationship may have been, the miners were reminding their neighbours of the GMA's benefits and constructing a common producers' cause with a success that often eluded their masters. However this reflects their politics, it seems clear that the miners were not so isolated that they lacked either awareness or an appreciation of their surrounding communities.

Part of this, undoubtedly, was because there was much more engagement between the people of the mines and those from the surrounding towns and countryside than we might think. As most of the miners were Scots, many quickly joined the major Scottish churches and became active participants. In the 1830s and 1840s Presbyterian missionaries in Sydney Mines, who were often quicker to describe irreligiosity than piety, were "touched" to observe the number of collier-laymen reading at service as well as the common sight of "coal stained fingers" holding prayer books in the pews.[51] Catholics too seem to have supported their church at Sydney Mines, despite not having their own priest until the 1840s. The Presbyterians and Catholics built their own churches in the late 1830s. In a display of tolerance remarkable for schismatic eastern Nova Scotia, Catholic and Presbyterian workmen volunteered their labour in the construction of both churches.[52] In Pictou the integration was less harmonious, yet this schism did not pit Protestants against Catholics but reformed anti-Burgher Presbyterians against the conservative, state-sanctioned Church ("Kirk") of Scotland. This division cut through almost all Pictou County politics. Richard Smith too entangled the GMA in the division, as some suggested that the differences between Mt Belville (the home of Thomas McCulloch, a reformer) and Mt Rundell (the residence of the company's manager) aptly paralleled those between the anti-Burgher and Kirk factions.[53] Certainly, the parallel worked in terms of their respective positions on free will versus state-sanctioned order. While there are few indications of the division affecting life among the employees, one mineworker was killed by another following a fight in which religious difference was the basis for the dispute.[54] Whereas some men slept late on Sunday mornings following their allegedly regular drunken Saturday-night brawls,[55] others were engaged in much more respectable behaviour. Presumably, it is among the latter group that we might expect to find those who were organizing temperance balls, marching with the amateur band, attending meetings of the mechanics' institutes, and petitioning for support for a "workingmen's library."[56] Identity, religious, and class solidarities were not always harmonious, so from the outside (where almost all accounts originated) the mining villages could simultaneously appear to be both rough and respectable. Just like in the countryside, improvement's hold in the mining towns was uneven. But the existence of activists addressing temperance, unions, self-help, and other issues of working-class self-government suggests that improvement was finding a place.

Most critically, the integration of mining towns into local society could be seen in the increasing numbers of people born in the area (but not of mining parents) who came to work in the mines. Because Albion Mines was a place that drew people, the number of migrant men and women marrying residents of the area increased, as did the Nova Scotia-born population of the village. Figures for this movement before 1865 are not good, although there are a few hints in the 1851 census. None of this is surprising, of course, because we know that there was a tremendous demand for waged-work in this period and a limited supply available, especially for anything full-time. Outside of roadwork, the best opportunities for waged employment could be found in coasting vessels, the fishery, the timber trade, and shipbuilding. Wages were always important for struggling farm households, but those in search of employment were now willing to travel great distances, often on foot, to obtain good wages. Almost all of these men came from the poorer squatters' farms, where their labour was absolutely crucial. In 1857 D.B. McNab, the provincial surveyor for Cape Breton observed: "all the tradesmen and young men of the country go to the states for employment in the summer as there is no work for them at home ... Those who represent this class occupy in general, Crown land as squatters, and by means of farming conducted by their wives and children, and going themselves during the summer season to distant parts of the province or to the United States, they eke out the means of a scanty subsistence."[57] After 1858, when the GMA's monopoly was broken and the number of coalmining companies expanded quickly, there was a virtual explosion in the number of Nova Scotia-born males entering mine work and Nova Scotia-born females marrying miners. By the 1860s over two-thirds of the young men entering mining were born in the province, and over half came from the countryside, not the mine villages. These data would certainly suggest that if two separate populations – miners and farmers, village and countryside – had existed in the 1830s and 1840s, by mid-century the ties between them were growing stronger. As these figures have as much relevance for farm households as for mine households, we will pursue them more fully in the next chapter. But for the time being it is enough to note that these populations were, in some ways and on some levels, merging. That it might only have been occurring within a limited social range – miners and poor farmers – suggests that in the industrial north-eastern part of the province at least, we can see part of the major basis for class formation in this movement.

THE STRIKES OF THE 1840S

If the GMA's miners were dependent, they were not servile. During the early 1830s there were numerous indications of what appear to have been brief (one- to three-day) work actions in which the men "refused to go down" because another worker had been discharged or sometimes because of a safety issue.[58] By the early 1840s the market for coal was changing, and the miners faced the company's first attempt to deal with its own precarious position by reducing the men's wages. The coal market thrived through the late 1830s and into 1840 but came to a quick halt that summer when the men struck for a pay increase. With production below demand, prices up, ships waiting in the harbour, and little coal in reserve, it was an ideal time to strike, and the miners won a quick and relatively easy victory.[59] But the combination of the recession of the early 1840s, an increased US tariff on coal, and increased competition from Pennsylvania anthracite put tremendous pressure on the GMA's markets, and their US sales fell off. The company attempted to enforce the "strictest economy" in its operations in order to recover some of its profitability. Part of this was an attempt to roll back the advances that the colliers had earned a year and a half earlier, a move that resulted in a three-month strike in the winter of 1841–42.[60] As we shall see, the 1842 strike was the object of much comment for the "disorder" that it occasioned and had near-devastating consequences for the mines, the community, and especially the miners and their families.

The strike succeeded in preventing part of the rollback, but it was long and difficult. This was partly due to the tactical error of striking in February, but it was also due to the ruthlessness of Samuel Cunard, who handled all the negotiations.[61] The wage reductions were calculated by Foord and Cunard and announced in October 1841 – that is, near the end of the shipping season. The timing was carefully selected. The new scale would see a collier's earnings reduced by 20 per cent.[62] There would be little immediate need for production at this time of the year, as not many ships risked the North Atlantic after 1 December, and the few that did could be handled from the stored coal on hand. Details are sketchy until early February,[63] but it appears that after the company announced its intention to bring in English strike-breakers the following spring, the men offered to return to work at the old rate of wages until the new men arrived. Cunard, of course, refused this offer, knowing fully well that the men would strike again in the spring and that the new colliers might support them; downtime in February was much easier to deal with than downtime in the peak shipping season. The managers also recognized their employees' vulnerability at this time of the year, so they cut off both coal supplies and credit at the company's sublet store.[64] The *Mechanic and Farmer*, showing neither the miners' nor Cunard's savvy, condemned both: the miners for striking in the first place and the company's agent for not allowing the men to return to work "at their former rate of wages until other men could be procured, as the loss otherwise resulting to the company (to say nothing of its effects upon the community) will be much more than if the highest rate of wages had been paid until the spring." The publication's argument made sense in the short term, but Cunard (and eventually, although too late, the miners as well) knew that whatever the effect on the community, the long-term interests of the company were best served by maintaining the strike, now effectively a lockout. For its part, the *Pictou Observer* simply noted that it was "not right" that these "unfortunate men whom [the GMA] brought here from their distant homes ... are now to be seen daily stretched on the ice spearing smelts to keep their families alive."[65] The paper's sympathy, however, was limited. Although the *Observer* called for the company to "furnish the labourers with employment at the usual rate of rates, and in accordance with their agreement," it was not the sanctity of contracts, the plight of families, or even honour between masters and servants that was emphasized here but the demand that they "not inflict an injury on the people of New Glasgow by throwing the families of the Miners on the Township of Egerton." The issue was simply about keeping miners off poor relief.

In addition to this public and more visible "disorder," the strikers made clear their willingness to risk damage to the mines and possibly even imprisonment for their cause. The "negotiations" were protracted and quite irregular. The strike appears to have been what later would be called a "100 per cent" strike, where not only the colliers struck but also the boys, the surface workers, and even the maintenance crews, forcing the managers to remove the horses from underground.[66] More dramatic still, however, was the terrorizing of manager Henry Poole and his family in Mt Rundell on the night of 25 January 1842.[67] Poole claimed that over one hundred of the "wives and children of the colliers" surrounded his house that night while the men "during all the time remain[ed] in the bushes." Most of the terrorizing came from the women, who spent the evening "shaking the shutters," "using abusive language to [Poole], heaving mud and dirt at the windows ... and remaining about the house for about an hour" before going away "threatening to return before daylight." Poole offered to meet the men the next day, but it was the women who appeared, "insist[ing] upon getting their coal free of charge as they were accustomed." As later events confirmed, and as the striking families undoubtedly knew, the strike leaders would not likely retain employment. The women, then, were able to act as the men's proxy, effectively negotiating, hiding their partners' faces, protecting their families' interests, limiting the response of the managers, and adding a touch of masculine humiliation. The manager relented somewhat, offering to sell the coal. Three days later, on 29 January, the women's actions having effectively made clear the strength of their resolve, Poole agreed to meet a "deputation" of three miners, the first face-to-face meetings since the strike had begun. Following the "first outrage," the men were "quiet, without any apparent disposition to commit any further outrage."[68]

The men went back to work less than two weeks after Cunard's arrival on the scene, "they and the employer having 'split the difference.'" The magistrates arrested some of the "ringleaders," but the threatened replacement workers did not arrive, and some sense of normality returned to the village and the workplace.[69] Clearly, however, the strike was not good for the men or the community. It was not only ill-planned but also divisive. A number of men, perhaps recognizing the folly of the timing, attempted to go back to work during the strike but were prevented from doing so, their effigies burned outside their houses at night. Some, it was said, had "set off for the United States, leaving their wives and children behind them, presuming, no doubt, that they will be provided for from the Poors' fund." Indeed, they were, but those who had been "turned adrift by the Association" consumed all the township's poor-relief money, and the township was not pleased.[70] Once again, the residents of Pictou County were being asked to pay for the privilege of having this new industry in their backyard. This time, feeling called upon by "duty and humanity," they did. But the following spring they successfully petitioned the Legislature "for setting off the Albion Mines as a separate poor district."[71] It was the biggest and roughest strike that Nova Scotia or the GMA had yet witnessed, although much worse were to come. There would be more strikes, but for the next fifteen years the GMA's major difficulties would be with the provincial government and local elites, not its own workers. During these years the provincial government increased its efforts to break the company's monopoly. Ironically, the strike would form a part of the attack on monopoly.

CONCLUSION

The evidence from this period leaves us with an incomplete, and contradictory, view of this colony of miners planted on the western side of the Atlantic. If in many ways the towns' inhabitants were starkly different from their farm-family neighbours, there were already some indications that the lines were blurring. Ironically, as industry grew around the mine villages and New Glasgow, the connections to the countryside in some ways grew stronger. The miners themselves were part of this transformation, most notably as a second generation began to marry local farm-born women and as some farm-born men found work in the mines. Clearly too, all sides appear to have been cognizant of the differences, and some at least made an effort to bridge the divide. Here, the miners appear at the forefront. Although isolated and dependent, they were not sheep. Their variously expressed gestures of defiance and deference to their employers, and to the broader community, indicate something infinitely more complex. And their clear connectedness to the broader movement of labour across the North Atlantic remind us that more than capital was transforming the New World.

The defiance of these men, who some days would muster and parade, came back to haunt them and the GMA. As the parade devices proclaimed, the miners understood well that their fate was closely tied to the success of the company. The board's response to the changes in the Atlantic coal market was to attempt to shift much of this economic burden onto the miners. The mining communities' abilities to resist part of this change may have pushed the company to grow more cautious in its larger plans. Moreover, at least in the longer term, the "disorder" of the strike undercut part of the company's legitimacy. Industrial colonization had been premised in part on the GMA's ability to bring order to the mining frontier. Building mines, housing workers, and constructing railways was one thing. Strikes, riots, and draining a township's poor monies was quite another. Here was clear evidence that the GMA could not police its own affairs. As we shall see, reformers grabbed hold of the issue of disorder as a weapon against monopoly, a weapon that further weakened the company's hold.

7

Farms and Families

By the middle of the nineteenth century little of northern Nova Scotia could be characterized as a settlement society. Pictou County, like much of the area along the Northumberland shore, bore most of the marks of a settled society, no longer those of one still in the process. If we had travelled up the West River with one of the census enumerators in 1851, we would have noted some of the newer two-storey, wood-frame and stone farmhouses, and our enumerator friend – a member of the West River Agricultural Society – might have commented on the luxuriant hillside pastures and the neatly fenced fields of potatoes, turnips, and oats. The situation in Cape Breton was different. Although there too the river valleys contained numerous impressive farmhouses, the backlands were much less impressive. Thousands of new immigrants had arrived in the decades after the Napoleonic Wars, occupying whatever land they could, wherever they could find it. Most were the latest victims of the ongoing economic dislocations of Scottish society. Most arrived poor, and few observers felt that they had much chance of prospering on the worst land in a marginal agricultural colony.[1] Few defied expectations.

This period, then, was marked by an increased differentiation between the settled life of many frontland farmers and the perilously unsettled and fragile lives of the poor, the unpropertied, and those perched on the region's many stone-filled, hilly backland sites. Emphasizing the heterogeneity of experience and circumstance, this chapter explores the structures of state, society, and economy in the country of coal at mid-century. Many of the relatively comfortable farmers, as befitted their new possibilities for leisure and self-improvement, joined the reinvigorated agricultural societies as well as numerous other scientific, literary, temperance, and improvement societies that had emerged across the province. These societies and their activities form the subject of a later chapter. But the subjects of these two chapters are very much related. As one writer observed in 1847, the current interest in agriculture was not new at all. Disputing a letter from "Homo," who maintained that Cape Bretoners took no serious interest in farming, "Sounds and Tongues" drolly replied: "Why, dear Sir, there is nothing so much attended to – give only a bond, and you will soon learn that single interest, and double interest upon interest will be punctually attended to."[2] This chapter pursues an outline of the social structure of agriculture and farm families at mid-century. These structures were stabilizing in some areas and chaotic in others, an unevenness that highlighted ongoing problems of governance in the colony.

MISMANAGING POPULATION

The basic patterns of land and labour established by the time of the 1827 census did not fundamentally change over the course of the following thirty years. Indeed, the basic zonal pattern described by Graeme Wynn for the period up to 1800 remained essentially intact.[3] In the northern half of the colony, agriculture continued to be the core around which most people organized their lives. Despite large fishing and industrial populations, especially in Pictou and Cape Breton Counties, farming was the principal livelihood declared by almost two-thirds of heads of households along the Northumberland shore in the census of 1851. While the social composition of the people had not changed, their numbers had grown significantly. Together with the growing numbers of native-born Nova Scotians, the wave of immigrants who arrived over these years had almost doubled the colony's population, which grew from about 143,000 in 1827 to almost 277,000 in 1851.[4] In the northeast the population more than doubled from 45,800 to 99,800.[5] In some areas much of this increase was biological. Certainly, this was true in Pictou, where immigration was a negligible factor after the 1820s but where the population nevertheless increased by 88 per cent. This was much less true in Cape Breton, where immigration accounted for much of its 190 per cent increase in the 1830s. Cumberland County's population increased by 165 per cent in the same period. While Cape Breton was receiving thousands of immigrants from abroad, Cumberland may have been Nova Scotia's frontier, receiving the province's internal agricultural migrants.[6]

These changes are indicative of two clear crises on the land in Nova Scotia at mid-century. The first issue was related to land policy and immigration and was therefore a direct result of the actions of the state. By 1840 provincial officials realized that Crown-land policy was completely unable to cope with the thousands of poor settlers who had arrived in the mid-1830s, especially in Cape Breton. Finding no way to obtain land legally, many, if not most, of these poor immigrants squatted wherever they could. Although especially acute in Cape Breton, the problems associated with squatting were evident all over the colony. The second crisis was more clearly related to biological increase, although still indirectly related to the first. By the 1850s a whole new · generation of farmers was seeking access to land. But unless they stood to inherit the family's farm (and were prepared to wait) or had the money to buy one, there quite simply was no good land to be had. These two overarching features of land use marked the general crisis in settlement, but social position determined how any one individual encountered these general conditions. Population pressures, in combination with the effective removal of land grants, major crop failures in the 1840s, and the sharpened contours of social stratification, resulted in this generalized condition, eventually culminating in massive out-migration and a dramatic reorganization of family formation practices. Those who wished to stay on the land were increasingly obliged either to stay on their parents' farms, deferring such major life-course decisions as marriage, or to migrate to find work in mining villages, shipyards, commercial towns, or beyond. We will pursue this issue later. In the meantime, we will examine the first crisis, particularly how the provincial colonial state attempted to cope with a population of squatters that had placed itself beyond the pale.

The first crisis peaked between 1837 and 1841 when thousands of new immigrants landed in Cape Breton from the north-western islands of Scotland. Swamped with migrants, the colony lacked the state machinery to ensure their orderly transfer to surveyed lots; the result was chaos. As Halifax and London officials renegotiated suitable land policies for the colony, it was clear that a gulf existed between the Wakefieldian notions now ascendant in the Colonial Office and the practical experiences of Crown-land officials in Nova Scotia. At the most fundamental level, the provincial and colonial governments agreed that individual ownership of land lent itself to an independent and morally superior people and that security of tenure was vital to proper government. As we saw in chapter 1, the control of land was heavily centralized. Rural people were to understand that when the Crown gave them land, it was an act of beneficent paternal care. By the 1840s, however, there was an emerging recognition among some colonial officials that colonization needed to be systematized in order to foster proper markets for land (which would increase its value by placing restrictions and costs on its acquisition – effectively reducing the supply) and for labour (which would decrease its value by the same means – effectively increasing its supply). The other key difference lay in the political cost of the migrants: officials in Nova Scotia knew that Britain's efforts to reduce poor-relief expenditures through emigration could fall on the backs of the colony. Thus while many in Britain remained intent on "shovelling out paupers" by allowing emigration to occur in a relatively untrammelled (yet systematic) manner,[7] the Government of Nova Scotia wanted either to end immigration altogether or to limit it to well-capitalized settlers.

As early as 1831 Nova Scotia officials suggested that the colony accept no new immigrants. Spurred by a combination of fiscal caution and local political savvy, provincial politicians saw little value in more immigrants. When the Colonial Office asked what "encouragement can be given ... the working-classes" who might emigrate to Nova Scotia, the Legislative Council replied, "very little." On the one hand, the council argued, raising the upset (base) price of land meant that "should an old settler ... conceive the lands to be valuable he would most probably outbid the Emigrant." On the other hand, waged work was not only unavailable but also unsuitable. The committee, as part of the government's ongoing efforts to pass blame onto settlers, maintained that the "poor Emigrant does not possess the ... versatility of character" necessary to compete in the local labour market and that such a settler inevitably became "a dead weight on the Community for Support."[8] Ten years later, in 1841, the issue was forced by a combination of thousands of squatters ("possessing no wealth but their labour") and speculators ("individuals who contribute in no way to the prosperity of the colony") holding thousands of acres outside the reach of improvement.[9] The Colonial Office proposed land auctions as a solution, but this created political problems in the colony. Nova Scotia officials argued that "native born Nova Scotians" were best suited to the province's colonization and population needs. As William Young explained to Lord Durham, auctions meant that the "young men of the colony [were] unable to purchase the wild lands ... [T]hose who would constitute our most valuable and hardy settlers are leaving us by hundreds, and the clearing and improvement of the country is greatly retarded." Establishing more native-born settlers – even poor ones – was better than the land hoarding that they believed was occurring.[10] Nova Scotia's problems, provincial officials argued, required a Nova Scotia solution.

The provincial government had made an active policy of discouraging the concentration of land by speculators, a policy that the commissioner of Crown lands, John Spry Morris, was still defending in 1837. It had not worked. The centralized structure and paternal aims of government meant that administrative fiat could easily overcome policy, and land continued to be engrossed.[11] Much land was in the possession of poor squatters, and other land was also in the hands of absentee landowners such as the Cunards and the Stewarts. By the mid-1830s provincial officials recognized that a crisis was imminent: residents were unable to afford land, and squatters were occupying anything that was uncultivated. And it was going to get worse. In the previous three years (1838–41) H.W. Crawley, the commissioner of Crown lands for Cape Breton, estimated that the number of "pauper immigrants" settled in Cape Breton was "not short of 3,000 … not one of whom do I think has yet purchased land." He understood that 3,000 more were expected in the summer of 1842.[12] Pictou County, by comparison, received 32 immigrants the same year: 13 adult males, 7 adult females, and 12 children. While there was little land available in the county, neither were there thousands scrambling to find a plot.[13]

The real problem, Wakefield might have noted, was that the policy was not actually being enforced: anyone could get land, auctions were not always taking place, the upset price was far too low, and squatting was pervasive.[14] As Charles Buller (together with Wakefield, assistants to Durham on his mission to Canada) pointed out, Nova Scotia did not have a problem because of squatters; Nova Scotia had a squatting problem because of errors in policy: "In Nova Scotia … emigrants on their arrival can find no employment for wages. The profusion of the government in granting its land has checked to so great an extent the prosperity of these provinces, that *the actual settlers* are too few or too poor to be enabled to employ labourers; and emigrants therefore must either proceed at once to the United States, or, in order to support himself [*sic*], must occupy the first vacant lot from the cultivation of which he can alone procure a livelihood."[15] Could the Wakefieldian program prove itself in Nova Scotia? The poor quality of the province's remaining lands ensured that a supply of labourers was available but not – as both Durham and John Young noted – as a "class of labourers" who could live by their wages alone. Lieutenant Governor Falkland was close to the mark when he noted that one of the paradoxes of life in colonial Nova Scotia was that the "labouring emigrant" was "able to procure money by his labour ... only [when] he obtains land."[16] Although overstating the case, Falkland captured something of the limitations on the development of farms and a labour market in the province. Poor farm householders spent much of their time working off the farm, thus hindering the development of their farms, but few could obtain sufficient wage labour to give up the land. At the same time, poor administration of land policy led to tremendously high levels of squatting. In 1837, *before* the immigration wave of the late 1830s and 1840s, the Crown surveyor estimated that there were 20,000 squatters in Cape Breton – half the population of the Island. The market in land was thus limited to those frontland properties where proper grants and capital expenditures combined to make these lots real (that is, commodified) properties. In general, however, the system was not, as Buller rightly noted, one that might have the desired effects of driving up the price of land or driving down the price of labour.

Colonization companies offered at least a partial solution to the chaotic land situation, but they added problems as well. By 1837 Morris had become concerned with the effects that land companies were having on the price of land as they temporarily increased demand (and therefore price) and drove poor immigrants out of the land market altogether. In the early 1830s one company's speculations (perhaps those that Stewart had been making for the New Brunswick and Nova Scotia Land Company) encouraged the cash-starved government to implement a system of land sales by auction, a system that was supposed to have been initiated in 1827.[17] The lands to be auctioned and a number of earlier-granted blocks of land, as Morris was quick to point out, were never improved. With new companies knocking on the door, it was clear that both the settlers and provincial revenue needed to be protected. Morris advocated granting land in small blocks to poor settlers for the cost of only a survey. Clearly, this was a temporary expedient, more a short-term, agrarian poor-relief measure than a vision of the future. But there was here, as we have seen elsewhere, a good deal of public sympathy for the poor. As Falkland later pointed out, while "destitution must inevitably be their portion," the "feeling was very strong throughout the community, that a settler, however poor, is a benefit to the province."[18] It may well have been such un-Wakefieldian notions that brought charges of incompetence against Morris in 1836. It mattered little because Morris, Crawley, and the province eventually achieved their ends when the Colonial Office, apparently acknowledging both the severity and immediacy of the crisis, relented (very reluctantly) by eliminating the auctions, even assenting to the lower upset price of 1s9d per acre.[19]

Some writers have pointed to this victory as a crucial turn on the road to responsible government in 1848.[20] Undoubtedly, it was a victory for provincial control, although it seems equally clear that these "reforms" were also a victory for Halifax's domination of local affairs. Only a few years earlier a committee of the Legislative Council had noted not only that these new regulations had cost revenue but also that they were threatening the governability of the province's people. As reports from the field made perfectly clear, settlement in Nova Scotia and particularly in Cape Breton was "lawless and irregular." The new regulations, the committee argued, "divested the Executive of the power and patronage of granting lands, weakened the hands of the King's Representative and continue[d] to operate injuriously to the Interests of the Province." If these settlers' "feelings are poisoned in their source and the heart soured in the outset of life by viewing Government as a hard Master or rigorous Creditor, it is long before they assume a healthful and proper state."[21] Thirty years later Samuel Fairbanks, the commissioner of Crown lands in the late 1850s, could still observe: "There is no motive to labor when the fruits of it are insecure; there is no hold upon the people when they have no certain hold upon the property which gives their family support."[22] Fairbanks was advocating for a better-regulated program, but he understood well the close connection between government and land. A healthy, happy, and therefore orderly state was basic to Halifax's centralized paternalist design of government.

The reforms made little immediate difference. The provincial officials who argued for the changes knew that they would have little beneficial effect on the existing squatter population. Speculators owned "vast portions of the best land in the province," but they did not possess them; squatters often occupied these lands, but had little chance of holding them. For these poor settlers, even the reduced upset price was quite beyond their means. Poor immigrants, Crawley explained, "squat as a matter of course, nor has the government in general the means of preventing them from doing so ... [T]hey proceed at once to the wilderness where it would be difficult to track and next to impossible to dislodge them for if traced and driven from one spot by means of an expensive and tedious legal process, they would immediately occupy a lot of land a few yards distant."[23] There was little point in the state chasing down such squatters. In part, this was because there was some public sympathy, but it was also because the effort simply had little chance of success. The theory evolved, therefore, that by eliminating the auctions and minimizing the upset price, "the children of such an individual will form a valuable addition to the population." Twenty years later, when some were still calling for the removal of squatters, the province resisted because many had in fact made substantial improvements. In 1857 John Murphy, the deputy surveyor for Inverness County, estimated that some had made improvements valued at between £30 and £60 on frontland lots and £10 and £20 on backland lots. Squatters were a problem, but as many Crown officials argued, for good or for ill, Nova Scotia's land policy was now better suited to its actual conditions.[24]

These settlers did make a valuable addition to the province's history, although not in the way that Falkland intended. Together with Morris, Crawley, and most Crown officials, he seemed to believe that the fate of such squatters and their descendants was that they should eventually become semi-independent smallholders. Over the course of a generation they might gradually earn enough to purchase their land without being thrown on the mercy of the community or, worse, the state. As most state officials acknowledged, however, such a long-term strategy did little for the squatters' immediate needs; nor did it reduce the threat of legal dispossession. These backland settlers, squatters or otherwise, were the poorest of the poor, and their economic positions were never secure, whether in terms of their "property" or their survival. Despite these existing problems, by the 1850s there were new plans afoot to bring more people into the province. Carrying within their titles the magical word "Railroad," these new proposals usually received support from the provincial government. The emergence of a number of railway and colonization schemes associated with the Halifax and Quebec Railway – including the Canada Land and Railway Association, which was then being promoted in Nova Scotia by General Mining Association (GMA) board member John Wright[25] – raised the possibility of bringing in new settlers, although under quite different circumstances. As experience elsewhere demonstrated, and as state officials' own experiences with the GMA had taught them, when settlement was contained within an industrial plantation-style program, the results could be both orderly and efficient.

Ultimately, these plans were not fully implemented (at least not as a fully organized railway colonization program such as occurred in Quebec later in the century).[26] Yet beyond the accepted wisdom of the desirability of a railway to the Canadas, in their conception these plans illustrate two basic issues that characterized many state officials' thinking on the question of continued immigration: the desire to populate the interior of the province more fully (without adding to the poor-relief rolls) and the continuation of a fundamentally paternalistic approach in doing so. In combination, the two issues came together nicely around the matter of railways. Here was a way, as Provincial Secretary James Boyle Uniacke argued, to aid the "Parent Country," benefit Britain's "suffering but Honest poor," build a railway, and instil order in the province's chaotic land system. Giving evidence before the House of Lords in June 1847, he outlined his philosophy of railways and colonization.[27] Uniacke acknowledged the general antipathy toward additional immigration to the province. He argued nonetheless that the province could still accept more immigrants if the plan was "accompanied with an organized System, and with Capital."[28] Nova Scotia offered England's poor two great opportunities: "affording them profitable employment while the line is in construction, and when completed a happy Home in a fruitful and healthy Climate." Based on his knowledge of the requirements of Nova Scotia settlers, he recommended that they be offered land (but with no title, only tickets of occupation for the first five years), that the labourers be paid at the rate of 10d per day (less than half the standard rate of 2s6d), and that one-third of each worker's wages be withheld and deposited in a provincial savings bank so that he might eventually pay for his land. "If he gets more than 10d a Day," Uniacke reasoned, "then he has more than is necessary to subsist himself and his Family. I believe if you let him have it uncontrolled he will spend it, or it will be taken away by the Temptations of those who follow such great Undertakings. If you give him an inducement to invest it in a Savings Bank, I believe he would invest it."[29] No doubt, many thought Uniacke and his supporters mad for advocating further immigration, especially in the middle of the potato famine. But this proposal for a carefully regulated "system," Uniacke and the colonization promoters would argue, was different from the existing chaos. By strictly regulating the activities and possibilities of the immigrants/workers, by tying their future positions to their present labours, and by making use of the savings banks for the "poor and working classes," Nova Scotia could (in the minds of these officials) enjoy further, and moreover better, colonization.[30] Immigration, they argued, was not the problem; it was the organization and implementation of immigration that presented difficulties. They might disagree on the precise details, but here Uniacke and the provincial official agreed with Wakefield and the Colonial Office that a correct policy ("a system") was the solution.

Such plans, however, dealt only with the future, not with those immigrants already on the land. The lives of these already impoverished settlers would plummet still deeper after 1845 when blight destroyed the potato crop, the staple food of the poor. Although nowhere near as calamitous as the Irish blight of the same period, the potato famine nevertheless caused widespread suffering and pushed many households over the edge. In 1851, when the blight finally appeared to be ending, the province still had a squatter problem, and many legal property holders had lost their land. As late as 1857 it was estimated that squatters possessed over half of Cape Breton's improved lands.[31] After the advent of responsible government, the province initiated several efforts to better regulate the administration of lands, but squatting continued to be regarded as a problem into the twentieth century.[32]

In different parts of the province different forms of agriculture prevailed. In the marshlands of Cumberland County and along the Minas Basin, butter and cattle dominated because the land was ideal for such use and because there were local and export markets available. In Cape Breton mixed farming was more prevalent, but grazing was key, not because it was ideal but because there were good markets in Sydney and St John's and because the cooler, wetter climate made many crops decidedly marginal and risky. There too we find perhaps the greatest social extremes, as the island's fiercely variable terrain articulated the range between a number of quite substantial farms (several with more than 100 head of cattle on farms with over 100 improved acres) and miserable hillside and backland locations of freeholders and squatters who raised a few bushels of potatoes and who may not have owned a horse or a cow. Such extremes existed everywhere, although in Cape Breton the numbers of both rich and poor seem particularly disproportionate. One recent study employing an estimating procedure for farm-household inputs observes that Middle River, a more recently settled and comparatively isolated census district in Victoria County, had a higher proportion of wealthy farms while also having a higher proportion of poor farms; thus the "middling" group was actually comparatively small.[33] Pictou County appears to have been less crudely differentiated, but it was marked by clear lines of social stratification nevertheless. In general, the inequalities that we could see in the 1820s and earlier had, in some

ways, been levelled, in that many more farm families had sufficient land
and stock to come close to a subsistence level of production. In other
ways, however, the disparities had actually broadened over the subsequent twenty years as social differentiation produced much sharper contours of social position.

THE SOCIAL STRUCTURE
OF THE COUNTRY OF COAL

A view of Pictou County from the 1851 census can give us some sense
of the extent of economic stratification. Pictou County offers an interesting contrast to the more sharply variegated social geography of
Cape Breton, yet it exhibits a clearly patterned differentiation. Moreover, Pictou offers us a compact view of the town-country/industrial-
agrarian divide in what are otherwise very similar physical geographies.
The most obvious feature of both East and West River farms in Pictou
County was their relatively small scale and their apparent lack of specialization. Unlike in Upper or Lower Canada, there does not appear
to have been any clearly dominant product that might be seen to have
"propelled" Nova Scotian agriculture's economic development. Nor
do we see the kind of market-led specialization that more clearly characterized farming there.[34] Indeed, a case could be made that this was,
in structure, a society marked by a relative equality of circumstance.
The differences were not dramatic. The vast majority (91 per cent) of
farms on the East and West Rivers had fewer than 60 improved acres;
only four had 100 acres or more. On the smaller side, only one-quarter
held 20 or fewer improved acres.[35] Younger households may have held
many of these smaller farms, and several (perhaps like Mephibosheth
Stepsure's)[36] were quite productive and probably provided at least a
basic competency for their householders.

Yet such figures betray little of a demonstrable variety of circumstance. Within different communities in the county, there were
marked differences in wealth, productivity, and capital resources. We
can measure, and thus describe and categorize, these differences in a
number of ways and form a picture of the social geography of material
life in these areas. There were, for example, substantial and clearly patterned differences both between the East and West River communities
and as one moved up the two rivers farther from the market towns
along the coast. The East and West Rivers were settled at about the
same time and at the same rate, and in many particulars they appear to

have been roughly similar. Soils on the West River tend to be better –
especially better than downriver on the East, where the coal areas are
covered with fairly poor podzols – but the difference is not too significant.[37] Average household sizes on the two rivers were approximately
the same (6.5 persons on the East versus 6.3 on the West), the age profiles of the households were about the same, and both rivers averaged
about 11 cattle per household (4 of which, in both cases, were dairy
cows) (table 7.1). The average East River farm was slightly larger
(36.2 acres versus 32.4); these farmers owned slightly more sheep and
swine, and they produced more peas and beans (9.4 bushels versus
3.9) and more potatoes (59.9 bushels versus 55.1). In some areas,
however, the West River farms were more productive than those on the
East. The average household on the West River produced almost twice
as much butter (228.2 lbs versus 125.1), more than twice as many
turnips (81.8 bushels versus 36), almost 50 per cent more cheese
(73.1 lbs versus 52.8), about 25 per cent more grains (211.1 bushels
versus 159.5) and cloth (40.3 yards versus 34.1), and almost 2 tons of
hay per household more than the neighbouring households 20 kilometres to the east. In short, although the East River farms were slightly
larger, the West River farms were more productive. Indeed, the average 20 acre farm on the West River produced more of several valuable
farm products than the average 30 acre farm on the East.

Most striking about these differences is the relative place that these
products held in the farm economy. Any of these products could have
been sold (and indeed any merchant's account book will provide examples of all of these). But it is notable that the West River farms produced or owned substantially more of the major farm products (butter,
grain, hay, cattle, cloth, and cheese) than their East River counterparts
in all categories except the number of cattle, where they were effectively equal. If we look at these as "average farms," the one representing the East River is undoubtedly a reasonably successful one,
supplying all of its own needs as well as having a small surplus of some
products (perhaps 50 lbs of butter, maybe 10 yards of cloth, a few cattle, and some sheep) with which perhaps to purchase other basic
goods such as tea, sugar, and implements. Using only what the census
recorded and employing standard slaughter ratios and weights as well
as prices from the Pictou market,[38] we can conclude that this average
East River farm could have sold as much as £18.16.6 worth of goods,
most of this coming from the sale of about 900 lbs of beef.[39]
Other products could have been sold as well. Timber, in particular,

Table 7.1
Average sizes and productions for farms
on the East and West Rivers, Pictou County, 1851

	East River	West River
Number of farms	146	86
Improved acres	36.2	32.4
Household size	6.5	6.3
Hay (tons)	7.6	9.4
Grain (bushels)	159.5	211.1
Turnips (bushels)	36.0	81.8
Milch cows	3.6	3.9
Cattle	10.6	10.9
Cloth (yards)	34.1	40.3
Butter (lbs)	125.1	228.2
Cheese (lbs)	58.8	73.1
Declared value (£)	186	328

Source: Pictou County, Census of 1851, Nova Scotia
Archives and Records Management, microfilm.

was not included in the census. While Pictou's participation in the timber trade had declined significantly since the 1820s, most local merchants accepted timber as payment for goods. Many farmers in the Hopewell and Springville areas were selling between £1 and £10 worth of logs every year. Our calculation also does not include the sale of hay (1 ton might have fetched another £3) or potatoes.[40] Nevertheless, we are not estimating probable total incomes; we are attempting to suggest only the range of possible differentials.

These two imaginary farms illustrate something of the social divisions that could emerge. We can see, for example, that the average West River farm would have fared a bit better than that on the East River. In terms of the potential sale of animals, the respective farms were similarly placed (the West River farm would have received about £1 more), but for animal products such as butter, cheese, and cloth, West River farms obtained almost £5 more. Although £5 was not the difference between a wealthy farm and a poor one, it could matter a great deal. This £5 might be spent on articles of consumption – tea, sugar, flour, or rum – or it might be invested in capital goods – a loom (between £1 and £4, typically around £2),[41] another plough, a dairy cow or possibly a horse (this might have taken two years), or several smaller implements, such as fanning mills or winnowing machines. If the farm family was already well supplied, it could have purchased furniture or a new carriage, joined an agricultural society, or hired a male servant for several months or a female servant for the better part of a year.[42] If a family had saved for two years, it could have purchased another ox or a threshing machine. In short, although £5 would not have represented the possibility for any major investments, it could make a significant difference – not simply in terms of meeting needs but also in terms of reproducible capital.

We can also see, however, that there appear to have been differences in how the sizes of these farms were distributed. In absolute numbers, slightly more than half of our East River sample held more improved land than the average. On the West River over 60 per cent fell below the overall average for the county. This would suggest both that the East River farms were generally larger and that there was less range in the size of farms on the West River. Indeed, if we disaggregate the data simply in terms of size in 10-acre increments, we can see that both impressions are accurate (table 7.2). Both areas appear to have a fairly large clustering of farms in the middle range but also subtantial numbers of both small and large farms. Even given the differences between the East and West River farms, these data suggest that it might be helpful to create three categories.[43]

Table 7.3 divides our sample farm populations into three categories based on acreage. On the East River, the small, medium, and large categories each comprised roughly one-third of the population. The proportions on the West River, however, were quite different: while the middle range was much the same, there were far more small farms and far fewer large ones. In terms of estimated value, stock, and production, these divisions suggest very different farms. On the West River, as we move from the lowest to the middle category, there is roughly a doubling of the average production figures, according to almost all of our measures. On the East River the increases are less dramatic, but typically production goes up by 60 to 80 per cent. Obviously, these numbers reflect differing productive capacities, which in turn affected farmers' ability to raise cash or to generally improve their exchange positions. The greater one's surplus, the more one had available for exchange. But can we be more precise? What exactly did these figures represent in terms of a farm's ability to earn?

Table 7.2
Distribution of farm sizes (improved acres), East and West Rivers,
Pictou County, 1851

Improved acres	East River	West River
0–9	10	6
10–19	13	11
20–29	25	22
30–39	22	17
40–49	32	14
50–59	29	8
60–69	8	4
70–79	2	1
80+	5	3

Source: Pictou County, Census of 1851, Nova Scotia
Archives and Records Management, microfilm.

Table 7.3
Average production based on a hypothetical three-tiered structure derived
from improved acreage, Pictou County, 1851

	East River			West River		
	Small	Medium	Large	Small	Medium	Large
Acres	<30	30–45	>45	<30	30–45	>45
Number of farms	48	54	44	39	31	16
Hay (tons)	5.1	8.1	9.7	5.6	11.4	14.7
Grain (bushels)	101.4	165.8	219.5	127.9	243.1	352.2
Potatoes (bushels)	42.4	73.1	66.4	33.9	63.6	90.8
Turnips (bushels)	27.2	39.1	41.7	54.1	92.5	115.6
Milch cows	2.5	4.0	4.5	2.9	4.2	5.9
Cattle	7.0	11.6	13.8	7.5	12.4	16.3
Cloth (yards)	25.8	38.7	42.2	30.5	47.2	51.0
Butter (lbs)	74.8	138.8	167.7	153.0	270.0	330.3
Cheese (lbs)	43.0	67.2	52.7	59.2	87.0	66.2
Household size	5.4	7.4	6.7	5.3	7.2	6.7
Value of beef and butter (£)	£11	£20.8.0	£24.16.0	£15.2.0	£26.10.0	£41.16.0

Source: Pictou County, Census of 1851, Nova Scotia Archives and Records Management;
prices from *Mechanic and Farmer,* 31 August 1842 and 30 November 1842; slaughter
ratios from Rusty Bittermann, Robert A. MacKinnon, and Graeme Wynn, "Of Inequality
and Interdependence in the Nova Scotian Countryside, 1850–70," *Canadian Historical
Review* 74, no. 1 (1993): 1–43.

Using the same estimating procedures that we employed earlier, we find that our imaginary small farm on the East River might still have earned as much as £11 simply from the sale of two beef cows. (This is not to suggest an overall surplus, only that according to the census figures the farm produced enough of some items to exchange them for something else; it may even have been, and probably was, still in a deficit position overall.) For the middle and larger farms, this figure increases to £17.8 and £18.10 respectively. On the West River these figures increase in all cases but especially on the larger farms. Again, this was not a great difference, but as our earlier example illustrates, this extra £5 to £12 might be significant for any household. Outside of beef, butter would have been the largest income generator. On the East River the average small farm might have had a few pounds of surplus butter – based on a constant assumption of 1 firkin (75 lbs per firkin) per household for use – but perhaps only enough to exchange for a few pounds of tea and some sugar. The average larger farms could have had a surplus of between 1 and 2 firkins at £3 per firkin. Some sold more. None of these "average" farms were becoming rich. However, substantial surpluses such as these every year would have meant that some farms were amassing capital.

Two other crucial issues remain unexplored here: the cost of living and the cost of creating surplus. First, especially for the smaller farms, we have to ask what they likely would have spent this money on. For the small farms, the most likely answer is essentials. If these smaller farms were not producing enough for their own subsistence, then they were expending much of any exchange value on the necessities of day-to-day reproduction. The calculations of Rusty Bittermann, Robert MacKinnon, and Graeme Wynn suggest that many of these households would need to work for wages or some other form of exchange for between 100 and 200 days each year. Farm households might have to purchase not only common store-bought articles (such as tea, sugar, flour, and rum) but also products that they might have produced for themselves (such as oatmeal, cloth, meat, and especially in the spring, even potatoes and other inexpensive vegetables). The larger farms too might have spent money or exchanged value for some of these products, but the issue is not *whether* a farm exchanged but how, why, and at what price. Again, as earlier, for the larger farms a surplus meant that after such reproductive costs had been subtracted, at least some exchange value remained that could then be applied toward improvements (more land, new seed, livestock), productive inputs (horses, machinery, labour), or even luxuries (a carriage, furniture, or new wallpaper). In other words, such surpluses could be turned not only toward day-to-day reproduction but also toward production, accumulation, and longer-term reproduction. Spending cash on oatmeal because one needed to eat was not the same as using cash to buy a threshing machine or hiring someone to help harvest one's crops.

Some farmers could, and indeed did, hire labour and even replace labour with capital by investing in machinery; they could also purchase superior breeds and seeds. They were beginning to look at farming as a business. Such men were learning that one had to invest, to expend more value, in order to earn a surplus. Take the case of John Grant, the East River miller whose account book aided our earlier price calculations. Grant's debit column centred largely on his sawmill and gristmill operations, but he also owned an 80-acre property on which he operated a substantial farm. Indeed, in the 1851 census, this miller described himself as a farmer. Situated on the northern end of Grant's Lake where it connected with the West Branch of the East River (about 5 kilometres upriver from Hopewell), Grant's farm lay beside that of his brother James. Between the two of them, they owned almost 200 acres of prime land on the best mill site for many miles. Not including the mill, the enumerator valued John Grant's farm at £300, and he paid one of the highest rate assessments in the district (10s9d). His farm produced 18 tons of hay, over 300 bushels of grain (mostly oats), 120 bushels of potatoes, 50 bushels of turnips, and 5 bushels of beans. He owned 21 cows (7 milch), 3 horses, 25 sheep, and 5 pigs, and the household produced 160 yards of cloth, 500 pounds of butter, 80 pounds of cheese, and a few gallons of maple sugar. The household also owned its own handloom,[44] as well as producing leather, shoes, soap, and candles. Grant's farm was among the most valuable farms on the river and certainly one of the most productive, generating between 50 and 100 per cent more of every recorded product than our average large farm on the East River shown in table 7.3. Our estimating procedure suggests that sales from his farm alone – that is, excluding the mill – would have generated a minimum of £55 in 1851 from sales of surplus beef, mutton, butter, cheese, and cloth.

Grant, who by 1851 was in his early fifties, and his wife, who was in her late forties, were aided in this work by their substantial family of eight children (six of whom were over the age of ten, including a daughter in her twenties). Such a large family would have provided a vitally important source of labour around the farm, especially during the harvest. Yet their labour does not appear to have been sufficient, and the account book lists numerous men, women, and children working anywhere from two or three days to several months in and around the Grant property. James Cameron, for example, came out ahead by 4s on his carding charges of £2.1.4 by paying with one small pig (8s), some "maple pickets" (5s2½d), 29 yards of cloth (12s), woven ("By your wife"), and 13s8½d in cash (not including the 1s discount that Grant gave him for this cash payment). Few, however, came out ahead when Grant tallied his accounts. William Fraser was debited £5.5.11 for carding, oiling, and sawing performed over the period June 1849 to October 1853. During this time he was credited no cash and only one item, 84 lbs of remarkably low-priced beef valued at 16s9d (about 2½d per pound for dressed meat), but he spent four days taking in Grant's hay, two days threshing, one day ploughing, and one day at Grant's lime kiln, while his three daughters spent two three-day periods working the miller's harvest (at 1s3d per daughter per day). At the end of this period, Fraser still owed slightly over £1, paying almost all of it with his and his family's labour. The long credit, the quick settlement, and the discontinuation of the account suggest that something more than neighbourly conversation might have encouraged the settling of this account.

In many of these instances, labour was the only credit that these neighbouring farmers were able to offer Grant; in 1851 Donald McKenzie was credited with 19s9d against his account of over £3 for carding, all of it coming from threshing (4 days of his own, three of son's, and one and a half of his wife's). McKenzie was not alone in offering his labour; in 1851 Grant credited about £20 for work on the farm. Limiting ourselves to a conservative estimate of Grant's farm revenue of £55 and the figure of £20 for labour, we can see that in 1851 Grant would have cleared roughly £35 on his farm alone. This is a minimum estimate.[45] These figures do not include payments in kind and other noncash forms of exchange that comprised the countryside's "web of mutual interdependence." The common (and often unrecorded) reciprocal exchanges between friends and neighbours formed a crucial component of what Rosemary Ommer has termed the "informal economy."[46] Such exchanges formed an important, in some cases crucial, feature of the mid-century "economy," and we ignore them at our peril. At the same time, we need to recognize the differential bases from which these exchanges could occur and the difficulty of interpreting the precise meaning of any one such exchange. If such an exchange was not part of the calculus of profit and loss, it equally may not have been "mutual" or "reciprocal." It may not have been coercive, but this does not mean that it was friendly or neighbourly.

There were numerous such farms throughout the north-eastern countryside. Although few families were getting rich, many were doing very well, some even passing on considerable estates upon the death of the male head.[47] On the East River, Grant's £300 estimation made his farm very valuable, but there were sixteen others estimated to be of equal or greater value. Such impressive holdings were fairly common, just not average. Surely, as the improvers would have it, all farm households could look forward to such success with appropriate attention to their lives and farms. According to our data, however, life was quite different for many households. Some of the smaller farm properties from our sample were in fact young households, just starting out and perhaps on their way to betterment. Just as many, however, were older households, so age seems poorly correlated with wealth. As table 7.4 makes clear, although entering the potentially more productive mid-life period or the less costly mature period generally meant that the farm size grew, it did not mean that one's farm was suddenly bigger and better. There was a clear flattening of the results in the older stages, but almost 30 per cent of the "mid-life" farms still had fewer than 30 improved acres. At their productive peaks, such households' ability to persist was far from certain.

Many farms produced large surpluses of some goods, often significantly more than the household's labour could meet. Thus in late summer and early autumn, larger, more productive farms required additional inputs of labour. Very often, this might come from neighbours assisting one another with the harvest or slaughter, but this seldom seems to have been the case with larger, better-capitalized farms. Large farms could not accept the irregularity of casual help and expect to harvest their crops in the narrow timeframe available. Hay left ungathered could ruin a farm that specialized in cattle; in northern Nova Scotia, where summer heat can swiftly turn to autumn frosts, a single night might ruin a fine field of oats. While most commentators agreed that there was no such thing in Nova Scotia as the class of workers whom the British referred to as "farm labourers" – that is, those who made their living as year-round employees on a farm – farm accounts such as Grant's make clear that labour was in demand and that many needed the credit available from working another's land. Of course, there was little need for a full-time labourer when even wealthy farmers' needs were so short-term and the supply so great. As one farmer from Mira

Table 7.4
Productive measures by life-stage, East River, Pictou County, 1851

	Early	Mid-life	Mature
Number of farms	33	74	44
Household size	4.4	7.9	5.7
Improved acres	27.9	36.7	41.0
Hay (tons)	5.2	8.2	8.2
Grain (bushels)	117.3	176.8	159.1
Potatoes (bushels)	56.2	65.7	53.2
Cattle	6.7	11.9	11.4
Cloth (yards)	22.9	40.9	31.5
Butter (lbs)	67.6	142.7	132.3
Cheese (lbs)	29.5	60.0	51.7
Declared value (£)	134.5	199.3	202.3

Source: Pictou County, Census of 1851, Nova Scotia Archives and Records Management, microfilm.

noted, "if I have occasion to employ two or three men, a dosen will offer."[48] Compared to the Old World, in Nova Scotia land was cheap and labour dear. But compared to New York or Upper Canada, good land was also less prevalent, and settlers appear to have been more in need of wages. Improving farmers might sometimes complain about high wages, but the suggestion here is that they should have been relatively lower.

Locally, wage labour could entail a variety of forms, although very often an entire family might be hired. Boys and girls worked the manure, harvested potatoes, raked hay, or ran errands. Sometimes the son would accompany the father on the job, for which a day's pay was not doubled but was greater than that paid for the man alone. Women, commonly noted as "the wife," also worked the harvests against their households' accounts, as well as working by the day at John Grant's looms. In Cape Breton, John Beamish Moore paid men's "wife," or "the girl," 1s6d for spinning and even paid younger girls as much as 1s6d for "work," while William McKeen took in cloth by the yard.[49] Similarly, John Grant's accounts show that young girls churned butter, threshed, and baked for him and were also hired to spin at 9d per day, while their mother's received about 1s3d for work at the loom. James Barry was able to hire women and girls for the same tasks at his mill and farm on the West River.[50] A husband and wife together in the fields could earn as much as 4s per day, or more if they had a horse, while the children were usually paid 1s or 1s3d per day. For thousands of poor farm households, the worst features of settlement a generation earlier were still present – and then some. As these householders lacked money, good land, and even security of tenure, their best prospects now lay more in wages supplemented by farming than in the opposite. Although described as farmers in the census, their material lives were not much different from those of miner householders living in company housing a few miles to the north.

Few merchants needed to or could clear their accounts exclusively, or even primarily, through wages. Thus many poor rural families supplemented their incomes from a number of often quite diverse sources. At Broad Cove, north of Mabou in Inverness County, for example, the fishery was conducted "mostly by farmers who live on the shore who after they first put there [sic] crops or seed in the ground go fishing till it is time to take them again."[51] As Rusty Bittermann has illustrated, employment opportunities were available around the region, particularly for men in shipbuilding, fishing, lumbering, and mining. Combined, these opportunities might translate into about 20,000 seasonal jobs or double this amount if we include the New Brunswick timber trade.[52] And while local employment for women might be limited largely to agricultural or domestic work, by the 1850s Cape Breton "servant Girls" were noted as an "article of export" to New England.[53] It was here that the more substantial amounts of cash and credit might be obtained that would allow someone to pay off his debts or at least to maintain the credit tether. Every spring thousands of young men, and a not insubstantial number of women, left the province to find employment in New England, where they "meet with that reward for their industry that no amount of [work] can obtain for them here."[54] Most returned in time for the harvest, but many stayed for a few more months or years, perhaps forever. Some stayed closer to home, cutting timber in the winter, often illegally on others' lands.[55] Many others, like Neil McFadgeon of West River, Pictou County, travelled north to the Miramichi timber camps in north-eastern New Brunswick for the winter before returning in the spring to put in their crops. In 1848 McFadgeon described how he, along with dozens of other peripatetic farmer-woodsmen from Pictou County, travelled by cart, ferry, and foot each autumn and spring, returning with as much as £20 in cash even after paying for food and lodging and buying new clothes.[56] But whether the jobs were away or near and whether one engaged in labour for exchange with a merchant or within the household, the onus of maintaining the household's material security fell on all shoulders. While tasks were usually shared, they were also divided by age and gender. So too were the expectations for the individual's life-course. Possibilities for the children differed greatly as adulthood approached.

"DULY YOKED": FAMILY FORMATION

Major life-course decisions, such as marriage, were often determined by the conditions described in the previous section. We can get a better sense of how these households – and this general stratified social structure – were reproduced if we examine the conditions under which households were formed. Household formation is a very poorly understood process in Nova Scotia, as it is elsewhere in the country. The literature on courtship and marriage in the nineteenth century is based primarily either on large provincial-level population samples, which cut across differences of culture and class, or on the social situations of largely middle-class diarists and letter writers.[57] The picture that emerges from this literature is one of closely bound communities, where the young man and woman (or at least their respective families) knew each other. Relationships were formed on one level through families, churches, and social institutions (such as temperance organizations) and on another level through tentative gestures and signals that were sent and received, accepted or spurned. Other work from Quebec, however, highlights the more structural features of family formation.[58] Linking changes in the economic structure of people's lives with their patterns of household formation, Peter Gossage argues that there was a strong relationship between the economic autonomy of waged labourers and family formation. When, for example, Quebec women and men left the land for work in the towns, the basis for decisions about marriage changed. No longer tied by the constraints of a propertied life, they married earlier than either bourgeois couples or those who stayed on the land. W. Peter Ward, by comparison, denies the importance of class to nineteenth-century Canadians' decisions about marriage. Relying on a mixture of aggregated census statistics and selected local marriage records, Ward argues that class formation in cities could not have had much effect on the general pattern of family formation, as the overall trend was toward increased age of marriage and declining fertility. In aggregate and over the long term, Ward is undoubtedly correct. His general outline corresponds with the pattern that we find in Pictou and Cape Breton Counties and has been

corroborated by some econometric analysis elsewhere.[59] At the same
time, it seems surprising that during a period of massive structural
shift in the movement from the countryside to the town and from
smallholder independence to wage dependence (factors that other
writers have suggested would reduce the age of marriage), the aggregate figures for age of marriage would actually be rising.[60] Indeed, if
we disaggregate the Nova Scotia figures by occupational categories
and backgrounds, an entirely different pattern emerges. The data
from Nova Scotia's country of coal corroborate the pattern described
by Gossage – an argument rooted in class formation – although, as we
shall see, the process here was more protracted. There is little doubt
that Old World patterns of delayed marriage influenced the pattern
that we see on the farms of Pictou County, but class formation was al-
tering this pattern. Just as Bettina Bradbury has traced working-class
Montrealers' survival tactics (such as gardening and keeping livestock) back to their rural roots, so too can we find a rural logic in the
patterns of household formation and courtship common to newly proletarianized Nova Scotians.[61]

One of the key social problems at mid-century was the emergence
of a large population of native-born Nova Scotians on the verge of
leaving the parental household when there was little land available
and before widespread industrialization. Starting out on life usually
entailed getting married. But there were a number of material factors
that weighed heavily on this decision. Unless one had the money to
purchase a farm or stood to inherit one, the possibilities of establishing a farm of one's own were significantly poorer in 1850 than they
had been a generation earlier. Inheritance, and its timing, was the major issue with which the aspiring patriarch had to contend. What was
left of a bequeathed estate varied widely. For the poor, there were few
bequests to be had, while for those of the middling class there might
be little for any but the eldest male offspring. Presuming that he
wanted the farm, it was usually willed to him or passed on before the
parents' (or more commonly the father's) death. Joseph Bogg, for example, a farmer in Middle River, Pictou County, left all his property
(valued at over £900), plus other monies owed him by neighbours, to
his eldest son. Similarly, Nicholas Balfour, also of Middle River, left a
small 30-acre farm valued at $580 and $92 worth of shares in a small
mill to his eldest son, with the stipulation that he care for his mother in
her remaining days; this left only $50 in cash to be divided among the
other six children. When the property was small, there was little need

to go through the trouble of stipulating the division of assets.[62] When James Donnely, a farmer near Albion Mines, died in 1864, he left an estate valued at £20, which provided very little aid for his family, especially after the assessment of £27 in debts.[63] But few owners of small farms or labourers bothered to formalize their wills because they had so little to leave. At the other end of the scale, few were as well off as Allen McLean, a farmer upriver at Hopewell, who left a farm worth over £1,600 on his death in 1857. Most of MacLean's estate went to the eldest son, but his holdings were large enough that he was able to leave the "back meadow" to his second son and over £300 to be distributed among his other children.[64]

The expectations directed at the eldest son gave him the greatest reward but also placed the greatest constraints on his forming his own household. Sons did not necessarily wait until all expectations had been fulfilled before marrying, but the pattern of late marriage suggests that for most these expectations at least delayed the trip to the altar. In Pictou and Cape Breton Counties the average age of first marriage in the late 1860s was 26.7 for men and 23.8 for women.[65] But if we limit this to men who described themselves as farmers, the average rises to almost 30 (29.9), while for women who married farmers the average age rises to 25.8. If these men were the eldest sons, as their declarations and these probate practices indicate, then it seems clear that there were fairly strong pressures on farm children to delay forming their own households; leadership of the farm household entailed a certain amount of personal sacrifice and perhaps restraint. The pattern was different for the younger sons and all the daughters. Many stayed on their parents' farms well into their twenties and often into their thirties. The lives of many young men would remain attached to the land, punctuated by spells of work around the region. Lacking both the security of the farm and full-time waged work, many young men maintained a place in the household while working to save money, learning a skill or perhaps, as became increasingly common in this period, leaving for Halifax, Montreal, or New England. Few young men, however, had the security to think of establishing their own households. There were probably many reasons for this, differing widely with individuals and the particular circumstances of the farm, but two reasons likely predominated. First, the labour of these men would still be needed on their families' farms, and there would often be some expectation on the part of parents that their children remain. Second, with limited possibilities for work in the area, leaving was in

many cases a major decision entailing a significant and often permanent relocation. It was very common for young men to leave for a winter's work in the woods, the shipyards, or wherever. Such work would
have served the dual but contradictory function of allowing a son to
begin to establish his independence and simultaneously to contribute
to his family's income. It may or may not have been enough to allow
him to think seriously of marriage, but it provided him with the opportunity to begin to resist the pull of his parent's household. It seems
likely that the tension between these two "pulls" was resolved by earlier
marriages than are seen among those who remained on the farm. Yet
even these earlier marriages were late relative to the marriages among
those who came from working-class backgrounds.

We can see something of this in a comparison of miners and farmers
who married in this period (table 7.5). Not surprisingly, following a pattern found throughout the North Atlantic world, coalminers in Pictou
and Cape Breton married at a younger age than most males and females
in their society.[66] In Cape Breton men who described themselves as miners married, on average, at the age of 25.7, while in Pictou the age was
24.8 – between one and two whole years below the overall county averages. For women in households headed by miners, the figures were 23.0
and 22.8 respectively; these figures are lower than, but closer to, the average (not surprising as we move closer to socially acceptable mini-
mums). The differences, although notable, are not really as great as one
might have expected. After all, according to the conventional wisdom,
miners were the archetypal proletarians: as workers they started and finished young, they married young, and they were notoriously prolific.
Why should it be any different in Nova Scotia?

In fact, Nova Scotia was not so different, but there are a few things
that we should note. The archetypal-proletarian thesis assumes that the
mining population under examination is a relatively stable population,
reproducing itself under roughly constant conditions. This was not the
case in Nova Scotia. Earlier, we saw that most colliers employed by the
GMA were experienced English and Scottish coalminers, imported for
their skills. These men's sons might have fit this stable, archetypal background, although as we saw in the previous chapter, the Nova Scotia
mine population also experienced significant out-migration. Moreover,
the mining population was increasingly rural and native-born. By 1861
well over half the young miners marrying had not been born in Albion
Mines or Sydney Mines but on farms in the surrounding countryside.
Thus if we disaggregate the marriage data still further by the declared

Table 7.5
Age of first marriage, miner- and farmer-headed households,
Pictou and Cape Breton Counties, 1865–70

| | Farmer-headed household | | Miner-headed household | |
	Male	Female	Male	Female
Cape Breton	29.4	25.0	25.7	23.0
(n=)	(39)	(41)	(157)	(157)
Pictou	29.9	26.1	24.8	22.8
(n=)	(92)	(99)	(134)	(135)
Combined	29.7	25.7	25.4	22.9
(n=)	(141)	(140)	(291)	(292)

Source: Nova Scotia, Vital Statistics, Pictou and Cape Breton Counties, RG 32, Nova Scotia Archives and Records Management.

occupations of the couples' fathers, we find still greater differences. As we saw earlier, miners' average age of first marriage was 25.4. But if we look only at miners whose fathers were miners, they married on average at the age of 24.3 (removing another year from the aggregate average), while those whose fathers were farmers married at 25.7 (still below the county average but a year and a half older than their fellows who were born in the town) (table 7.6). That our sample did not find any farmers who were sons of miners also gives us a clear sense of the pattern of social change in the countryside.

Farm-based women appear to have been similarly constrained, although it is not clear that they were constrained by the same factors. While most women in the countryside and in the industrial towns did eventually marry, the timing of marriage differed widely. If women, like younger sons and most proletarian males, had little opportunity to own (or marry into) property, their averages should be lower and the patterns less variable than among men. And this, in fact, was the case: for men, the range was over four years, while for women it was only two and a half. At the same time, we see an enormous variability. Many rural households in 1871 contained two or three daughters over the age of 25 (and as old as 40) who never married. Most women needed to marry,[67] and given local mores there were no obvious reasons for them not to. Evidence from earlier in the century does not suggest any particularly strong pattern of late marriage. In the 1860s farm women married for the first time as young as

Table 7.6
Age of first marriage by occupation for marrying male and by
occupation of the male's father, Cape Breton and Pictou Counties

Occupation of marrying male	Occupation of father	
	Farmers	Miners
Farmer	29.9	–
(n=)	(152)	(0)
Miner	25.7	24.3
(n=)	(130)	(81)

Source: Nova Scotia, Vital Statistics, Cape Breton and Pictou Counties,
RG 32, Nova Scotia Archives and Records Management.

18 and as old as 45. Such a wide range provided many different possible
experiences, but these figures represent the extremes of the range; most
women married in their mid to late twenties.

The evidence here suggests that some form of demographic stress was
underway in farm households in northern Nova Scotia at mid-century.
The combined effects of a limited land base and an unwillingness to divide properties among offspring greatly restricted the ability of the area
to provide spaces on the land for a growing population. The average age
of first marriage for farm women in Pictou and Cape Breton Counties
was 25.7. Presumably, like the men, these women put off marriage for
some time too. But not all women born on farms married farmers. Increasingly, many married miners as the industry grew in the 1860s. Thus
in the same period the average age of first marriage for women born on
farms who married miners was 24.0, about a year and a half younger
than the overall farm average. Marrying a miner – someone who did not
have to wait to acquire an education or a plot of land to set up his own
household – allowed some women to leave their parents' households
earlier. For women born into mining households who married miners,
the average fell to 21.4 (two and a half years below the county average
and a full four years below that of women born on farms). Clearly, having
twelve- and fourteen-year-old boys leave home to work in the mines affected the age of first marriage not only of the young men in mining
towns but also of their sisters. The possibilities of economic independence encouraged younger marriages, but it appears that the pull of
some farm actions and expectations remained evident in the practices of
those who eventually left the farm. That such a difference existed may

also have been a product of the expectations of a farm woman's parents – perhaps a desire for their daughter to marry a farmer or the household's ongoing need for her labour. But it was also related to the instability of the rural economy.

Sex ratios suggest the degree to which men in the typical marriageable age brackets were away from home. While Pictou and Cape Breton Counties were the industrializing core of northern Nova Scotia, they were not yet net importers of migrants. In the United States and western Canada during the second half of the nineteenth century, resource towns tended to have significantly more males than females, as large numbers of men moved into such areas in search of waged employment.[68] Rural-industrial Nova Scotia, however, was exporting large numbers of males. In some counties the ratios were close to typical (stable) figures. In Antigonish County, for example, the figures were stable for those between the ages of 11 and 20 and between 31 and 40, but in the critical 21 to 30 age group, the figure was much lower, at 0.84 males per every female, suggesting that many young men were away from home (whether permanently or temporarily) to seek work.[69] In Pictou County the figures deviated ever further from those of a stable population. The figure was stable in the age group 11 to 20 but then fell dramatically to 0.81 males per female in the 21 to 30 age group, and unlike in Antigonish County, the figures did not recover so well in the 31 to 40 age group. Many more young men were apparently leaving for good. Clearly, the demographic profiles of these counties suggest that some young women may well have confronted a serious problem: the limited availability of marriage partners.

There were also major differences, however, within these counties. If we compare sex ratios in Albion Mines with those in some of the surrounding farm districts, we see remarkable differences, especially in the 21 to 30 age group (table 7.7). Whereas most rural districts were losing many of their young men, Albion Mines had a significant surplus of young marriageable men, making them much more like the resource towns of the West.[70] To the extent that simple availability of potential partners was an issue, it is not surprising that the female ages of first marriage would be significantly lower in the coal towns. Such figures also suggest the limits on a discussion of female migrant labour at this point. While we know it was occurring, it had clearly not reached the same levels as it had for males. And as the only centres that seemed to be drawing young men, the mining towns offered young women few incentives, except young men. Nonetheless, if one was a young woman from Hopewell, for example, where there were only 3 men for every 5 women, the prospects of finding a suitable husband looked much better a few kilometres downriver in a mining town.

Table 7.7
Sex ratios (males per female), Pictou County, 1851

District	Age group		
	1–10	11–20	21–30
West River (District 6)	0.93	0.97	0.77
West River (District 7)	1.03	1.07	0.97
MacLennan's Brook (District 15)	0.84	0.84	0.71
Hopewell (District 17)	1.03	1.16	0.60
Albion Mines (District 12)	0.99	0.97	1.21

Source: Pictou County, Census of 1851, Nova Scotia Archives and Records Management, microfilm.

Of course, while availability mattered, the issue was not simply whether there were men to be had but also what possibilities any one man offered at any one time. If a woman wanted to marry an established farmer because this was a "type" that she desired or simply because she preferred an individual in this economic situation, there were only so many available. There were many more younger sons of farmers, as well as workers, whom she could marry. Materially, these men were not so promising: their reliance on wages, the frequency with which they left home for short-term work elsewhere, and the concomitant uncertainty about establishing their own farms surely reduced the security to be found in marrying such a man. But it might have been better than waiting for an established farmer or better than the economic uncertainty attaching itself to spinsterhood.

That many young farm women married miners and other wage-workers, and did so much earlier than those who stayed in the countryside, suggests an element of choice, the incidence of young women choosing to leave farm life. That they married significantly later than working-class women from the towns suggests that there were pressures keeping them on the farm – perhaps the desire to stay in the countryside, the availability of suitable men, the pressures of parents on their children to continue to contribute their labour to the land or to marry within the community. To speak of marriage strategies in this context is to risk downplaying the limited possibilities that local material circumstances left open to rural men and women; it is not clear that marrying late, but still at the first possible opportunity, can be considered a strategic choice. Material considerations appear to have been paramount. The only real strategy here was the short-term assessment of a potential household's long-term ability to maintain itself. Farm women in Pictou County lacked the kind of closed stable market for husbands that may have existed in longer-settled areas. With local men working all over the region, the prospect of the relative security of a working-class household in a nearby town was more acceptable, or at least available. Clearly, there was a choice between finding an acceptable local man with whom to live a farm life and the more immediate prospect of quickly establishing a household with a less acceptable man. Such an age difference suggests that many women found the latter route more promising than waiting out their time on the family's farm and running the very real risk of becoming paupers. The key factor here seems to have been economic security. Yet it is also evident that the "pull" of wage labour was itself an uncertain variable that might delay marriage for men and women.

Three major forces altered the timing of major life-course decisions for people in Pictou County in the middle of the nineteenth century. First, the limited availability of land and the few opportunities for full-time waged work in the countryside compelled many young women and men to seek opportunities elsewhere. Second, the emergence of expanded opportunities for low-skilled, waged employment in the coal and metal-manufacturing towns offered many Pictou County women and men an opportunity to establish households. The first factor restrained family formation in the countryside; the second, for most of those born in working-class households and for many from the countryside, meant that such constraints were lifted in the towns. One's position in the family – that is, one's age and gender in relation to other family members – was also important. Prior to these considerations, however, was a third factor: class position conditioned how any one individual, male or female, understood his or her location in relation to – and thus how one responded to – these factors. For the first-born son of James Donnely, the Albion Mines farmer discussed earlier who left a £20 "estate," being male and being first-born did not provide much material support for his future, while Allen MacLean was able to set up his second-born son with his own farm. Of course, being the first-born daughter did not help a woman's inheritance, but it could provide a dowry and surely conditioned her assessment of a suitable partner.

We know a good deal less about the process of actually choosing a partner. The Reverend George Patterson described an older pattern of rural couples starting life together. Having received a portion of his father's land or obtained his own grant, a young man erected a log house and "readily found some rustic maid, not afraid of labor, or of spoiling her complexion by exposure to the sun, [and] ready to share his joys and sorrows, his trials and successes." Such was the style, he wrote, in which the "majority of brides were brought home." "Duly yoked ... they enjoyed their full share of domestic bliss, and reared a race, who for vigour and worth, may shame their degenerate successors."[71] While Patterson's description seems a bit fanciful, he certainly drew attention to an essential feature of the future life for many of these rustic maids: they would spend a great deal of their time yoked, while their complexions would undoubtedly not be well served by their time outdoors working in the sun. The life of a farm woman, whether in newly settled areas or on the more established farms of the 1840s and 1850s, would be difficult, and one element in a woman's choosing of a partner was finding one who might at least minimize her drudgery. Nancy Grey Osterud's work on late nineteenth-century rural New York emphasizes the great care taken by women in choosing a husband. Given the "powerful role husbands played in women's lives, men's consideration for their wives' welfare was seen as the primary ingredient of women's happiness."[72] Certainly, this must have been viewed as an important characteristic. But not everyone was a "Miss Bennet" aspiring to find a "Mr Darcy." For many, such considerations had to be counterbalanced by, on the one hand, a desire for independence – or at least a retreat from the confines of one's parent's home – and, on the other, the material possibilities of establishing a household. A woman's choice of husband was also bound by personal considerations until the time, as Osterud writes, when she (and the general point might apply equally to men) "began to face the choice between accepting a man who was less than ideal and remaining single for the rest of her life."[73]

We can safely assume that mothers and fathers offered much advice on this theme to their children. Sadly, most of this advice is lost to us, although there was no shortage of advice proffered by the press. A Sydney writer urged his fellows to choose a "pure and virtuous female." Caution was required because "girls are beautiful blossoms that bud and bloom spontaneously ... [but] remember, too, that the fairest and sweetest flowers soonest lose their beauty and fragrance."[74] A few months later, the same writer offered "Advice to Maidens" that similarly emphasized practical issues and the guidance of their parents: "Love is an idea; beef is reality. The idea you can get along without; the beef you must have. Do not then allow any refined sentimentalism to interfere with what judicious and calculating parents call an advantageous settlement."[75] In Pictou County the Mechanic and Farmer regularly ran "Girls' Department" and "Mothers' Department" columns. Occasionally, these columns offered advice on the good marriage. Too often, this writer observed, the couple are "perfect strangers" who "rush ... into the marriage state from the mere impulse of passion without forethought or prudence."[76] Mephibosheth Stepsure too emphasized practical issues such as prospective partners' ability to provide and to "tend to their own affairs."[77] Or as another Pictou writer put it, a man should seek a wife who will not waste time and money on frills and fancy furnishings: "A man gets a wife to look after his affairs ... not to dissipate his property."[78]

Stepsure's emphasis on proper conduct and its relationship to material security was at the heart of most such advice literature, be it aimed at marriage or politically weightier matters. Marriage, like much of life, was about taming passion, exercising self-control, and engaging in proper conduct. Few people, it was argued, recognized how nearly their children's as well as their own "destiny is connected with their [own] conduct." A sound education by the parents, particularly the influence of the mother in the home, was crucial to preventing the child from "rush[ing] on the ruinous course of self-indulgence."[79] The issue, however, was not simply about individual propriety and conduct; it could be elevated quite rapidly to address broader issues of economy and government. "[O]n the proper management of children," argued a writer in the Colonial Patriot, "depends not only their health and usefullness ... but likewise the safety and prosperity of the State."[80] For these writers, the connections between choosing a suitable partner, family life, and the inculcation of proper conduct were all part of a package. These, in turn, were the foundation of good politics and government, whether of the family or the nation. As "A Spectator" wrote, "A man who has never learned the art of self-government, but is a slave to his own passions, is unworthy of confidence, and unfit to fill any prominent place in society." The properly educated child, he concluded, must be "effectually taught ... the lesson of self control."[81] It is not clear how much of this (or whether any of this) would have resonated among an audience that was not middle-class and propertied.

While we have slim evidence here of popular mores and concerns among the backland, squatter, and working-class poor, reports from missionaries suggest the prevalence of premarital sex, unsanctioned marriages, "bundling" (i.e., a couple's lying down or sleeping together while fully clothed), and other less regulated sexual activities – or what one Pictou writer referred to as the "irresistible influence" and "hell consigning sway" of "licentiousness."[82] Stepsure recalled the case of Miss Dinah: "Some time ago, along with a number of the youngsters, she went to Miss Sippit's tea party and frolic, in very good health and spirits. After a good deal of dancing, the young folks, as it was a wet night, agreed to bundle; and the poor girl has never been well since." Northern Nova Scotia has many cold wet nights, and another writer noted the particular risks of "Winter, the season of nocturnal dissipation."[83] The pattern appears widespread and of ancient origin. J.I. Little reports similar church concerns and similar premarital sexual practices among Highland Scots in the eastern townships of Quebec.[84] Work on early modern Scottish women's sexuality also suggests the prevalence of premarital sex, "irregular" marriages (a socially and legally acceptable form under Scottish law), and the active efforts on the part of the Church of Scotland to better regulate marriage into the 1830s.[85] The newspaper advice was aimed at those whose conduct was inappropriate and whose respectability might therefore be in jeopardy. Thus it might have made sense only among the propertied and reasonably well-educated middle class. Assessing the efficacy of such advice is beyond us, but its prevalence certainly suggests the public-spirited gravity attached to this weightiest of private decisions. It also suggests a perceived need.

So how did young people choose their partners? On this point, our data are even less clear. There is evidence that while selection was often limited to a local pool, it was by no means always the case that a young man or woman married a childhood friend or neighbour. Marriage notices in newspapers, usually only for community notables, often recorded weddings between one partner from Pictou or Sydney and another from Truro or Halifax.[86] The same could be true among workers or farmers who might escape the notice of the newspapers. As our earlier discussion of work patterns suggests, men travelled a great deal. And while much of this time might be spent in a work camp, a long way from any women, there were certainly opportunities to meet women by attending church or other social functions in nearby communities. Peter Barrett, an immigrant miner from England, almost married a young woman whom he met while working in Canada in 1867. On the other hand, as her farmer-father's response suggested, there might also be concern over marrying off a daughter to a complete stranger who might then take the daughter away from her parents.[87] Indeed, the marriage records indicate that few such weddings actually occurred.

Based on individuals' stated "place of residence," Nova Scotia's marriage records suggest that many young men and women found each other away from their settlements and away from their immediate neighbours, although not by a great distance. These marriage records indicate 99 marriages in Pictou County between 1865 and 1870 in which the male described himself as a farmer and for which the "residence" of both partners was provided. Of these, 45 couples were from the same community (45.5 per cent). In Cape Breton the pattern was more localized, with almost 60 per cent of "farmer" couples marrying someone from the same community. The figures among those who described themselves as miners were different, but not by much. In Pictou roughly half of the miners (69 of 139) married someone from the same community (Albion Mines accounted for two-thirds of these), and half (70 of 139) married someone from another, while in Cape Breton almost 60 per cent (98 of 167) married someone from their own community. In all these cases, however, few of the marriages among both miners and farmers were with someone from outside the county; these accounted for less than 2 per cent in both counties.[88]

Earlier, we discussed the "pushes" and "pulls" of marriage versus the parental household. These data on locations suggest that we may have underestimated some of the pull of family and the household. Certainly, few women either wanted to or could make an independent stand against the family's expectations with such limited opportunities for either property ownership or waged employment available to them. But even if it was difficult to find a suitable husband, few were about to marry a Prince Edward Island farmer or a labourer from Cape Breton just because he was there – again, whether this was of their own volition or due to parental pressure. Independence could be found in the next valley without the loss of one's family and community, vital supports in any nineteenth-century woman's life.[89]

It would seem that there were a number of opposed pressures pushing and pulling on young men and women throughout this period. We have seen that it may have been becoming increasingly difficult for a young man to establish himself on the land unless his circumstances rendered him at least moderately wealthy. If this restrained some men (and women) in the parental household, it drove more into the towns, and farther away, in search of work. Many of these, of course, stayed away, so our necessarily local window on their lives is effectively shut. As important as it was for women to find a husband if they were to have any independence (and, for many, to avoid the stigma of spinster-hood), family and the network of women's communities were power-ful centrifugal forces. Quite unlike an aggregate view or one based on the writings of middle-class diarists might suggest, there was no free market in marriage in rural/working-class Nova Scotia in this period. Much of the evidence suggests that choice for men and women alike was severely constrained by many more factors than attraction and de-sire. The field was bounded by one's position within the family, one's class, and one's gender. It was also, at this particular time, conditioned by weak local markets for goods and labour, limited availability of land, and an expanding coalmining industry. These data suggest the ulti-mately material considerations that influenced these decisions.

A few years after the period under discussion, in May 1873, a huge ex-plosion at the Drummond Colliery in Pictou County killed sixty men. As the local newspaper noted, it was not merely the loss of property that was so devastating "but the fact that so many strong men, husbands, fathers and sons, the stay and support of mothers, wives and children have been suddenly ushered into eternity." It was this loss of connections that had "thrown a sudden and awful gloom over the whole country."[90] This com-ment on the material aspects of those who were left behind points to the dependent position of the families of those who worked the mines. The women left behind – about half of the men who had been killed were married – were in an instant left without any material support. Few were employed, and most had little to fall back on for income, their bread-winners now lying dead. Many, however, had recourse to their families in the countryside, where they were born. One of these widows, Jessie Elliot, 20, had married only two months earlier, in March. She was fortu-nate enough to have the option to return to her parents' farm in Four Mile Brook. But the countryside could provide only so much for Jessie. She remarried three years later and tempted fate again by marrying another miner, twenty-four-year-old George Davis.[91] Once more, Jessie Elliot's story would unfold in the shadow of the mine.

CONCLUSION

Provincial farms had advanced significantly in the middle third of the century. Most farms on the East and West Rivers of Pictou County appear to have been successfully managing their operations. But there was no common experience. These data leave no doubt that Bittermann, MacKinnon, and Wynn are fundamentally correct in their assessment that while some farms were doing very well, the remainder either could only make ends meet or operated somewhere in the middle.[92] Those in the weakest category were least likely to persist. Of course, all these farms were able to persist for some time, but real permanence required profit. The frequency with which we see some farms clinging to lines of credit, members of farm households working off-farm for extended periods, children working for wages, young women and men marrying outside their social worlds, and farmers finding themselves in gaol and losing their land attests to an economic basis for the inability to persist. In the same way, as we examine the growth and capacity of some of these farms, the emerging markets for farm labour and products, and the growth of exports, we can see an emerging group of relatively prosperous farmers who – whatever the limits of their land or their capital – would form a permanent commercial core of northern Nova Scotia agriculture. To the extent that an ethic of permanence, rather than wealth or authority, exemplified colonial agriculture, these farms embodied many of the ideals of industry and improvement, if not always with the same enthusiasm as improvement's more devout disciples. If, as we shall see, few farm householders joined the local agricultural improvement societies, many were certainly expanding their operations through activities that required market-based production. Much like the early republican farmers described by Joyce Appleby, they developed a core of common interests that attempted to balance family, independence, and commercial activities.[93] Some undoubtedly pushed the commercial frontier harder than others; some had little room to manoeuvre.

Yet this general situation was already in crisis as population growth hit the wall of limited environmental capacity in Nova Scotia, a small territory with much marginal land. Many of these farm families were large, and the predominant practice was to pass on the entire farm, not to divide it. Those who could afford to purchase additional lands did so, but their numbers were few, and even this was a limited possibility if the household had more than two or at most three sons. Some of these householders could still provide other possibilities for their children, especially for the males but sometimes for the females too, but most could not. Again, these are the extremes, and the system was not so bifurcated as this would suggest; in between there were a range of positions, and we should not assume that every boatload of young men leaving Pictou harbour was filled with the poor and the destitute. The conditions informing why any one of these young people boarded the boat certainly could be very different.

But there was a pattern. At the level of material possibilities, any one household's position within the social and economic hierarchy of rural society greatly affected the possible avenues open to it. We do a tremendous disservice to those young people who were forced to leave if we simply attribute their removal to the apparently inherent "restlessness" of the Scot, to the overall malaise of the economy, or to the inexorable pressures exerted by a burgeoning population.[94] Sons, and the odd daughter, from middling and relatively prosperous farms undoubtedly left for their own, perhaps restless, reasons. But the pattern suggests that relative wealth provided the major context within which such decisions were made. It was not an undifferentiated mass of "farmers," "fishermen," "labourers," and "women" who left but individual farmers (or single farm households), individual fishers, individual labourers, and individual women making decisions based on their own lives, experiences, desires, and contexts. Our inability to determine why some left and some stayed obscures much of what we do know about rural society in the nineteenth century. D. Campbell and R.H. MacLean, for example, point to "farmers" giving up their farms based on census returns that showed a declining number of farmers working a greater extent of acreage.[95] Yet this trend suggests that some farmers were expanding while others were giving up their farms. There is also the assumption that those who left gave up security on the land for insecurity – and "glitter" – in the city, such as Charles Dunn's comments that urban emigrants "did not seem to miss the independence and self-sufficiency of the farmer's life."[96] Such formulations assume subsistence agriculture and uniform conditions – that most everyone in the nineteenth-century Nova Scotia countryside lived basically the same subsistence-oriented existence. This does not hold up. Some strove for a basic subsistence, some failed to achieve it, and others strove for much more. Population pressures determined that people had to leave, but population pressures did not determine which people left. Class does not explain all of this, but it certainly provides a context for a much better understanding of the partiality of the process.

It is in this context too that we can best understand the advice on marriage. This literature focused on two key considerations: the wise use of property and the regulation of the passions; marriage was not a romantic

adventure but a social and economic enterprise. This advice was not restricted to the prosperous, but property-centred values lay at the core. A
young miner or the daughter of an older one would almost certainly consider a prospective partner's potential contribution to a future household. But at such young ages and with so little property to consider, these
concerns were surely not paramount. Indeed, the differences that we see
in the data on age of marriage suggest that property, parental supervi-
sion, and class conventions meant that the sons and daughters of the
prosperous might have relatively less freedom in matters of courtship
and sexual relations. Those who valued the slow unfolding of improved
property might pause to seriously consider connections between the taming of passion and the security of property. More study would be needed
here, but the age of first marriage appears to be higher in the 1860s
and 1870s than it had been earlier in the century. If this is true, then
their additional sacrifice and restraint add another dimension to propertied farmers' embrace of the principles of self-government. Here,
class was an economic category rooted in material success. But we can
also see how people of the middling ranks might come to connect their
own lives with prescribed forms of self-governed behaviour. What was the
point of improving one's farm if a bad marriage could dissipate one's
property? These men and women came to understand that industry and
improvement also attended to the proper regulation of domestic life.

8

Merchants in the Country of Coal

If the coal industry was not yet a great engine of economic growth, the countryside around it was nonetheless an economically dynamic place. In 1854, before the effects of the reciprocity agreement with the United States improved access of the General Mining Association (GMA) to the New York and New England markets, coal accounted for only 5 per cent of the province's exports. Agriculture accounted for twice as much export value, as did shipbuilding, and these were dwarfed by the two major exports: forest and fishery products.[1] In the last chapter, we witnessed something of the degree and extent of stratification within rural society; this chapter examines a number of the countryside's more active economic actors – principally, merchants – and their economic and political activities in this period. Social stratification was an important condition for all of these activities, and as we shall see here, this structure emerged for the most part through factors within rural society. Although few "farmers" were becoming truly wealthy, the countryside was still producing wealth – if also poverty.

Because of their domination of credit and marketing, merchants stood at the centre of the rural economy. Farmers' prosperity was built on their capacity to get products to market. For most, this meant that they sold to a merchant who arranged to get the product to market. Whether it was getting the timber to Britain, the fish to Brazil, or the cattle to Newfoundland, merchants organized the exchange. Merchants connected rural producers with North Atlantic markets and brought them tools from Britain, tea from India, sugar from Barbados, wine from Sicily, and cinnamon from Madagascar.[2] Merchants, therefore, could be powerful figures. If some farmers were developing capital, most were doing so in part through local merchants' abilities to market the farmers' goods. The risks were high, but the returns could be very good. By the 1840s and 1850s some merchants were better able to reinvest in other forms of rural industry, including milling, tanning, shipbuilding, and mining. Just as improving farmers were increasingly coming to see a connection between their industry and their place in rural society, so too were country merchants reaching to extend their economic and political capacities.

THE MERCHANT OF MABOU

Even before the 1840s, when blight destroyed the island's potato crops, Cape Breton claimed the poorest of the poor, and hardship was endemic for the thousands of squatting householders and backland smallholders. Still, there were potential customers in Cape Breton, and there was money to be made. Merchants such as Peter Smyth, George Laurence, and William McKeen did their best to negotiate their way through the vagaries of exchange in such poor communities. William McKeen was the dominant mercantile and political figure in western Cape Breton for much of the middle third of the nineteenth century. His 600-acre farm, with its fruit orchards, cattle, and imported English trees and furniture, was one of the most impressive in the province.[3] McKeen's agent, Robert Hill, ran a store up the coast at Broad Cove (later the coal town of Inverness). Hill travelled the countryside from Broad Cove north into the Margaree Valley "in order to meet and converse and show our new and Cheap goods ... likewise to Circulate the Liberal Credit that I would give on all goods to good markets, the down Shore Squad in particular gathered round ... and [I] let them have some Irish Soap."[4] The competition was fairly intense, as a number of petty merchants vied for a limited amount of exchange and a very small amount of cash. The demand for potatoes in the spring testifies to the miserable conditions of many backland farms in what was becoming an important agricultural county.[5]

It was Hill's business to reconnoitre the market and to learn what the farmers and fishers were producing and what could be obtained in exchange for their goods.

I came by Mr Chisholm the Black Smith. I enquired of him if he had paid you and told him you had requested of me last fall to write him, he requested me to state to you he will pay you with thanks as soon as Mr Kinsey returns to Rebuild the bridge at his place that McKinsey

Indebted to him over Six pounds. Hugh McNeill Chimney Corner
Called here this day saying he would pay you 19-9 the amount of his
account on his return from Port Hood he is gowing shortly fishing.
James Smith has left 26 lb Butter as part payment for herrings received at Mabou what will I allow him, the farmers here of late Seem
to be more plentifull Supplied with Potatoes than they would acknowledge months ago I am Enclined to Say Potatoes would be
Scarce worth your notice, you know best, will the Pork &c be Shipt
with Daniel Kenedy, he is day Expected with a vessel, the articles we
are out of is Frequently asks for Tare will Soon be in demand likewise
Nales of all Kinds, have you any Cordag fit for Tin pints &c.[6]

Reports such as these were common and illustrate well the complexity
of rural exchange. If ledgers calculated monetary values, they only
partly captured the complex bases of production and exchange.
Matching the consumer needs of their customers with the uncertain-
ties attached to future road monies, the prospect of a good catch, potatoes, and rather meagre amounts of butter meant that Hill's work
involved much running around for often small returns.

Hill's main task was to obtain farm goods, particularly cattle for the
export trade to Newfoundland but also butter, pork, and even that rar-
est of goods, cash. His principal technique was to seek out farmers who
owed money and encourage them to sell their cattle. Sometimes he
did this with a carrot:

> Agreeable to your desire I went to several place in search of cattle,
> and poor speed I made, the Men prinsaply were from home, and the
> Cattle in the woods ... Mr Sutherland is this Instant going to Cape
> North I will send a very inviting Document to John McKinon Piper
> for him to come up with his Cattle and I will allow him Extravagant
> price all Cash and had I a horse I would gow down.

And sometimes with a stick:

> I here propose giving a few names I would propose Sueing viz
> Donald and Angus McIsaac Conaghy William Hamilton Alexander
> McLeod Cape Widow McIntire Widow McLelland S[outh] Point
> Neal McLane – if pay Cant be had from him now it never will, and all
> named here I have Notify'd frequently without any Effect ... They
> have sold me so many falsehoods that they are not to be credited.[7]

That Hill felt he had to offer cash to some and threaten others is surely descriptive of western Cape Breton's social geography at this time. Where one lived in the area around Broad Cove was often a clear mark of economic potential – and of status. In his descriptions, Hill effectively mapped his territory, dividing those who were "raskals" from those who were respectable farmers (always individuals referred to as "Mr"). There were the "interval gentry," a term that (although clearly two-sided) was intended to carry some respect at least for the relative wealth of these more prosperous farmers, while the "down shore crew" were the peripatetic farmers-cum-fishers from whom Hill often had difficulty collecting payments. As Richard Brown observed, the backlanders were those poorer settlers in the "rear of the front lots."[8] In most cases, they were the truly poor; for Hill, they were the more difficult to track down.

Hill frequently bemoaned his difficulties in collecting and noted how many of the residents of Broad Cove were quite adept at not paying their bills. But while Hill's frustrations were many, the system worked very well for McKeen. Like many merchants, McKeen effectively mixed business and politics. He was the dominant non-elected political figure in the county, and his political organizing for William Young would in later years garner him an appointment to the Legislative Council. Such a figure could command the attention of local judicial officials, all of whom were appointed, and the courts were vital tools in McKeen's business. "Squire [John] Beaton," the justice of the peace (JP), was always cooperative, if occasionally slow.

> I sued the oldest debts first … making up a Sufficiant number
> weekly as many as Squire Beaton will get through in one day, he
> wrote from Morning Earley to Sundown last Thursday and only ac-
> complished 18 single surnames. But I will have a Larger list always at
> the house and he can take his time … 18 or twenty is as much as he
> is willing to try in one day. I will insist on having 2 days of trial in
> the week from this forth as his slow way of moving we will be long
> getting through.[9]

Legally, Hill could "insist" on very little, but the JP knew on whose behalf Hill's demands were made. A few months later, frustrated by Beaton's slow hand, Hill promised his employer that he would "help [Beaton] through with his work" of serving up papers.[10] Lawsuits helped to recover costs not only directly but also indirectly, as the setting of a

court date often "weakened those Indolent wretches to a Sense of Duty."
As Hill boasted after several successful lawsuits: "these customers of
mine Sees I am now in Ernest and Butter is Coming pretty plenty."[11] In
Inverness County the more powerful merchants not only were able to
draw upon the state's support but also could direct the actions of state
officials, turning the JP into a bill collector with extraordinary powers.

There were, of course, many other merchants, but few offered the
access to goods and credit that someone like McKeen could. Thus
while there was some room for negotiation, the available manoeuvring
room was tight. Hill frequently commented on the poor quality of the
fish cure and on the low state of the butter, but he offered a range of
prices, suggesting a range of quality and therefore a range of positions
for the sellers of these products. In 1839 and 1840 Hill offered between 18s and 22s6d for a quintal of salted codfish and between £2
and £3 for a firkin of butter. John Kennedy, a miller at Broad Cove,
was insistent on receiving 8d per pound for his butter, but Hill claimed
that he "would not give 6½d." When he received good product, however, he remarked on it and offered a better price. In the summer and
fall of 1839 Hill was offering 8d per pound for butter, "but mind it
must be the very best." Sometimes, however, it was necessary to raise
the price, as was the case the next spring when the quality was good
and the demand high; Hill wanted to offer 8d per pound but was
forced to raise the price to 10d, as this was what the competition was
offering.[12] For live cattle and barrels of fish, butter, and pork, the quality was important and thus had a considerable impact on the price.

McKeen's major export market for cattle was in Newfoundland.
While his agents often complained of underweight cows, McKeen
knew from long experience that farmers had no great incentive to fatten cattle for sale when Newfoundland was the only real market.[13] The
sea journey – which could be three or four days from Port Hood – was
always hard on the cattle, and they seldom arrived fat. One load arrived in such poor condition that the agent was unable to recover the
costs of shipping them.[14] (Butter, fish, and pork, however, were less
fragile, and there were more diversified markets in which to sell them,
including Sydney, St John's, Halifax, and the fishery at Canso.)[15] But
whatever the quality, cattle were vital to McKeen's participation in the
Newfoundland trade, so local farmers had some leverage. In the summer and fall of 1840 McKeen shipped between four and five hundred
head to Newfoundland. This was good for the more prosperous farmers. When demand was high, the producers knew it: "Irish soap" was a

lure for some, but "nothing short of cash w[ould] satisfy" farmers selling cattle.[16] Others begged McKeen for mercy.

As powerful as a merchant or wealthy farmer might be, the poor could
and did often resist. There are no indications of customers ever taking
McKeen to court to recover an unfair charge, but occasionally he lost a
suit and was forced to pay costs.[17] Elsewhere, however, there were a few
cases where the poor refused to simply accede to someone else's rule.[18]
Juries often protected landholders from the encroachments of landlords and creditors. In Inverness County juries sometimes reinstated
ejected tenants, and it continued to be difficult to obtain convictions for
petty smuggling and the theft of wood, in part because such offences
were difficult to prove and in part because juries continued to be reluctant to convict the poor.[19] But actions for debts did not require juries,
and the semi-annual meeting of the Supreme Court was a virtually end-
less stream of debtors ordered to gaol. Here, local sentiment mattered
less, and men could be gaoled for owing less than £2.[20]

Avoidance was the most common method of resisting the hand of
the merchant (and often the gaoler). Very often what the bill collector
thought was avoidance was unintentional, as the men were simply
away; some were in the fields, often working someone else's land. Thus
Robert Hill was often frustrated when he went round seeking both customers and debtors, "the Men prinsapally from home" or "away at the
fish." More often, at least according to Hill, the "raskals" were "dodg-
ing" the merchants or the constables sent out into the countryside to
serve papers. Late in the summer of 1840, for example, Hill noted that
while the "Back Landers is Coming with Trifles of poor Stuff ... where
one Comes he has a number of messages from Others beseeching a
few days and they will find the way." "[B]eing scattered," the debtors
forced Hill to seek ways to find them together. Noting that "prayers
[were] to be here Sunday," he posted notices all round the interval
where the sermon was to be held.[21] Hill implied that the reliability of
the constables was not always certain, and the suggestion was that some
sought to interfere with the agent's tasks. On some occasions, such as
the case of the two "Fidlers" from Lake Ainslie, he had to find extra
constables to serve the notice or prevent them from absconding. The
previous week they had successfully "dodged the Constable," but Hill
"obtained another Constable and got them Served yesterday."[22] The
combination of a large area, a peripatetic workforce, and community
interference could make the debt collector's life a difficult one.

Debtors often simply refused to pay, leaving their fates to the whim
of judges or the patience of their creditors. It was seldom a haphazard,

ill-conceived strategy. McKeen was not merciless, and often the debtors worked his patience. Hill often criticized his master for being
"to[o] leneant," which in combination with the "habit of giving Such
Liberal Credit," meant that many were unable to pay their debts. "You
are to[o] feeling to make much money amongst those low-Scotch …
Here we find Every day a Frolick and rum will make Hay when nothing else. Such idlers I never saw."[23] "Oh what a pitty," Mill lamented,
"So much property collected annually from such a poor groop of half
starved fools." But Hill was not moved, and he spent a good part of his
letter-writing time urging his employer to be less lenient with "these
swindlers" and "miserable farmers."[24] On another occasion Hill was
insistent that three widows, McIsaac, McDougall, and McIntyre, were
playing McKeen a fool and that he should take them to court. But in
the correspondence available to us, McKeen appears to have sued
only one.[25] Hill was constantly frustrated by his master's apparently
interminable patience. McKeen, however, seems to have understood
that so long as the cattle, cloth, and butter were coming, the "raskals"
were perfect gentry.

Nevertheless, many did indeed wind up in gaol. McKeen routinely
had between four and ten men imprisoned every spring and fall. Thus
it seems surprising that there remain so few indications of overt resistance. Most of the crimes that we see in Sheriff Laurence's papers were
petty, most often crimes against property, especially trespass, not
against persons.[26] Very often these were committed against a neighbour; stealing timber was very common, and property disputes were a
part of everyday life. D.B. McNab, the Crown surveyor, certainly knew
the day-to-day battles of property disputes and what lay beneath the
friendly facade of neighbours: "Each says to his neighbour, all is well, although the storm that sooner or later will burst on many devoted head,
now enjoying fancied security, is clearly seen."[27] Some of these storms,
however, burst on the head of a prominent member of the local elite,
and undoubtedly some must have been small acts of rebellion. Few,
however, were so direct in their responses as Donald MacDonald, a
farmer from Long Point, south of Port Hood, who struck out at none
other than the county sheriff himself, George Laurence.[28] MacDonald
and his son Angus broke into the house of Hugh Johnston, Laurence's
agent at nearby Judique. In the middle of the night of 21 March 1839,
Johnston was awakened by a loud commotion coming from downstairs.
Descending, he came upon MacDonald, who made no attempt to flee
or even to cover his face but instead hollered to someone with him
that he should bring the sled up to the door. Then, pointing to several

bags of meal standing in the corner, the intruder asked Johnston who owned these oats, a curious question that suggests he knew the answer, as he surely did. Johnston replied that it was "Mr Laurence's meal," to which MacDonald announced that the merchant and sheriff of Inverness County was "a damn raskal and had robbed it from other people"; he then proceeded to march off with one of the bags. In MacDonald's estimation, the merchant had stolen the meal already, and the farmer was there to take it back.[29]

Such an overt and public act of social reprisal peeled back the thin, veneer-like surface of harmonious social relations in both town and country. Such actions also make clear how fragile the "security of peace and order, life and property" could be when the powers of police were not always at hand.[30] It was not uncommon for a state official to be met with threats or beatings or even to be threatened at gunpoint, as the deputy surveyor of Cape Breton discovered.[31] The assault on Mt Rundell was not an isolated incident.[32] Sydney newspapers commonly noted acts of vandalism on the homes of prominent merchants and farmers in and around the town. In the summer of 1852, for example, several acts of "black guardism" were reported in which the houses of "many of the most respectable and inoffensive individuals ... [were] smeared and daubed over with Coal Tar," while just outside the town geese were stolen, animals released, and vandalism committed on apparently selected houses and gardens. A week later someone threw stones through the windows of C.H. Harrington – the author of angry letters about "black guardism."[33] Such patently social crime is rarely to be found in the records, although crimes directed at socially privileged people were common in the towns and the countryside.

There were also many other acts whose meanings might have been clear at the time, but their documentary traces are obscure. In the autumn of 1841 McKeen informed Hill that his services were no longer required, and the former agent was left on his own. Lacking any money and not having planted any crops himself, he was left to beg for food, and twice that winter he claimed that no one would give him so much as some oatmeal or a pound of bread.[34] The moral economy of the poor was rooted in a sense of justice, and although it is doubtful that anyone would have allowed even the zealous agent to starve, no doubt many noted the irony with a small amount of relish. One also wonders what might have been the background to the attack on William McKeen and several members of his family in their home in 1853. On 16 February a cooper, a blacksmith, and two farmers broke "into the home of Wm McKeen at Mabou [and] assaulted and beat McKeen" and three other residents.[35] Nothing was reported stolen, and the record gives no other indication of the attackers' intentions. They might have been four drunken men on a violent binge; it could as well have been a small act of reprisal, an act of social justice against a man about whom the community had decidedly mixed feelings. Feelings about Peter Smyth, the dominant merchant in nearby Port Hood, were also mixed, but one man left few ambiguities when he cursed the merchant: "May he fall off the bridge, and may the lobsters devour his private parts."[36]

McKeen's story and the related stories of resistance illustrate a number of the tensions within rural society. Whatever the nostalgic literature might tell us, a great deal of evidence suggests that rural society was by no means uniformly serene and neighbourly. If sometimes McKeen was a beneficent paternalist, other times he fulfilled Robert Grant's recollection of merchants being "noted for craft and dishonesty [and] resorting to every petty scheme to increase their store."[37] The absence of a large market such as a coal town did not hurt these Inverness County merchants. McKeen was fully engaged in his trade, and the coal monopoly certainly does not seem to have had any impact on the Newfoundland cattle trade. That McKeen's business operated quite well independently of the GMA is not surprising. We could say the same for hundreds of merchants around the province. In McKeen's case, however, there was also the issue of the coal seams that underlay Mabou and that he, and everyone else, was prevented from mining by the GMA's monopoly. This would change.

MERCHANTS AND INDUSTRY

From the perspective of the local market, the GMA's immediate impact was not great. Whatever had been the excitement over the company and its "immense capital," up until about 1840 the GMA brought almost all of its men and equipment from Britain. A few local men were hired, and the company occasionally felt the need to advertise to obtain some seasonal workers.[38] Most manufactured goods, including such very common ones as rope, shovels, and picks, appear to have come from either Britain or the United States, a situation that did not change much until the 1860s.[39] Timber was the one product that Nova Scotia could supply, especially the rough timber used for pit props (supports for the mine roof). In some cases, such as that of the East

River miller and merchant John Grant, a merchant would gather timber from his customers and then deliver loads of it to the mines whenever he had a sufficient quantity.[40] Alternatively, the company issued contracts for the delivery of specific sizes and amounts of wood. In December 1854, for example, Sydney Mines issued twenty-one contracts valued at over £300 for various sizes of pine and hemlock lumber at the rate of 10s per 100 feet.[41] These contracts were for properly cut and milled lumber. Pit props, although a lower-value product, would have added substantially to the mines' wood requirements.

More enticing was the nicely concentrated market of between seven and twelve hundred miners and their families. The GMA bought some local farm products such as meat, butter, and wood products. But while many were quick to point to the "ready market" that farmers found for their produce in and about the mines, either the supply was inadequate or the company preferred the terms elsewhere.[42] In 1830–31 Richard Brown recorded in his diary local purchases of planks, timber, fish, lime, butter, beef, pork, oats, hay, and potatoes.[43] But the GMA also purchased and managed a farm just outside Sydney Mines at Bras d'Or for part of the company's supplies and continued to import large quantities of flour, oats, and even hay from New England. Undoubtedly, this was more true in the 1830s than it was later, but Richard Brown noted hay arriving from Boston as late as 1849.[44] We can safely surmise that part of this demand was simply for a return cargo for coal vessels, but in any case it reminds us of the limited markets created by the mines.

The GMA's wages were an important contribution to the local economy. As the company was always quick to point out, its employees were paid in cash, which meant that miners became very desirable customers among local merchants. In both Sydney Mines and Albion Mines, there were company-run stores, but the men do not appear to have been obliged to purchase their goods there.[45] Still, the GMA consumed a great deal of farm produce. Figures supplied by the Albion Mines managers for 1838 claimed that the company expended almost £9,600 on provincial agricultural produce.[46] Combined with the over £44,000 in wages paid out that year, this made a substantial addition to the economy of Pictou County. Eight or ten timber camps or small shipyards, however, might have done likewise. Whereas in these other local industries the pay was typically half cash and half credit from the merchant who owned the camp, the GMA paid its employees and its suppliers in cash – a factor that made their business very attractive.[47] The figure for expenditures listed above is undoubtedly high owing to the construction of the railway at the time. But if we suppose 75 per cent of it to represent a typical figure for the period and double it to account for Sydney, then during the late 1830s the GMA was putting over £65,000 per annum directly into circulation in Nova Scotia. No other single firm could come close to such a claim at this time.

Purchasing supplies was not the GMA's only contribution to the local economy. One of the more immediate effects of the arrival of the company was the granting of free-port status to Pictou and Sydney. Neither local nor Colonial Office records offer us precise details of how the measure was accomplished, but there was no doubt among locals that the measure came about through the influence of the London firm. Indeed, the then still enthusiastic supporters of the GMA at the *Colonial Patriot* proudly proclaimed in a headline: "Richard Smith Announces Free Port Status."[48] The free-port issue was a clear illustration of the leverage exercised by commercial capital in the halls of Downing Street. Local merchants and politicians had been petitioning for free-port status for many years, decrying trade restrictions as hindrances to economic activity.[49] In Pictou their petitions argued that the town's different orientation on the Gulf of St Lawrence, the potential prosperity of the area, and the critical importance of developing a home market were threatened by the requirement to tranship through Halifax.[50] London dithered. But within months of the GMA initiating operations in Nova Scotia, the Colonial Office had reversed a seventy-year-old policy of restricting port privileges by designating the two coalmining centres as free ports and ordering the creation of customs houses. It was not a coincidence. When Governor Kempt sent orders to "all Officers of Government, Magistrates and Proprietors of Land to afford every reasonable facility to the said Richard Smith, and those employed under him, in the prosecution of his design," he was relaying instructions from London.[51]

However the free-port decision came about, it had an immediate effect on the commerce of Pictou and Sydney. Local merchants quickly jumped at the opportunity to join the trade by chartering vessels to carry the coal to market. When the first free-port vessels arrived in Pictou harbour in May 1828, the *Colonial Patriot* hailed the arrival as the dawn of a new day for the area and noted the essential condition of trade: "in the coal trade any merchant can of course engage. Mr. Smith ... has never shown the slightest wish to monopolize all the trade from his [*sic*] establishment, but has shown the utmost liberality in affording facilities to others."[52]

While earlier coalmining ventures had focused almost exclusively on
the local market – for the most part Halifax and rarely outside New Brunswick or Nova Scotia – the GMA moved quickly to establish a trade network on the Atlantic seaboard of the United States. Within two years the
company had agents in the major markets of Boston, New York, and Philadelphia, as well as in Saint John and Halifax.[53] Their task was twofold: to
obtain vessels for the transportation of the product and to market the
product once landed. But neither the GMA nor the agents made any direct investments in these markets, and the carrying trade was available to
any reputable carrier. The GMA's role in the entire process would simply
have been producing the coal and getting it to the wharf. Shipping returns indicate that between the spring of 1831 and the end of 1833, at
least fourteen different Pictou merchants shipped coal mined on the East
River.[54] In addition, several masters also purchased loads of coal to market. But this commerce was hardly shared equally. Most of these fourteen
merchants chartered only one vessel, and if we remove George Smith –
who was responsible for four shipments – we are left with a single firm,
Ross and Primrose, which turned an already prosperous trade in timber,
provisions, and fishing supplies into one increasingly heavily concentrated on the American coal trade.[55] In this three-year period to the end
of 1833, about one-third of the coal vessels that left Pictou carried Ross
and Primrose cargoes; one-third were vessels chartered by the GMA; and
the final third were divided between the remaining thirteen merchants
and about a dozen ships' masters.[56]

These figures reflect only the number of vessels; if we examine what
type of vessels, we find that most of the larger ones – brigs, brigantines,
and barques – were chartered either by the GMA or by Ross and Primrose,
leaving only the shallops and sloops to the other merchants, with schooners divided fairly equally. Moreover, the destinations reveal that the same
two parties accounted for 60 of the 82 ships (and 30 of the 37 brigs) sent
to New York or New England. These larger vessels, of course, carried
more cargo. Thus between the GMA's direct sales (chartered vessels) and
those chartered by Ross and Primrose, two agents accounted for almost
90 per cent of the coal exports.[57] Making Pictou a free port certainly
opened new trading avenues for local merchants, and "any merchant"
might participate, but the coal trade demanded merchants with the ability to get ships, with good contacts in the prime American market, and
with the capacity to finance such operations. Many participated, but few
did so on any substantial scale, and fewer still undertook business in the
United States.

Ross and Primrose did well by the trade. But they did not expand. With the decline in the timber trade, they appear to have been content to allow coal to make up the shortfall. In Sydney, however, another mercantile house rose to be a powerful regional player by carrying GMA coal. Samuel G. Archibald ran his firm out of North Sydney, about a mile below the mines. In the mid-1820s, on the eve of the arrival of the GMA, Archibald and his then partner Peter Hall were prominent, but by no means dominant, players in the trade on the north side of the Sydney River. Before this time Archibald had shown no interest in joining the coal trade. He had never applied for a licence and rarely participated in the carrying trade, preferring to leave this to trading companies that participated directly in the transatlantic trade, such as Bown and the firm of Ritchie and Leaver.[58] Most of Archibald's business came from supplying the people of North Sydney, Sydney Mines, and the surrounding districts. The firm sold a fairly standard range of goods: tea, rum, flour, cloth, and household and farm implements. In return, the company obtained a fair portion of the area's agricultural surplus.[59] The surviving account book for 1825 lists a little over £2,000 in credits to his clients from around the area. Butter accounted for 38.5 per cent of the firm's credits. In total, almost 60 per cent of the goods that Archibald's customers exchanged were farm products (not including timber or boards): primarily butter, oats, wheat, and various meats. If we include timber products from what appear to be farms – that is, accounts that list both farm and forest products – over 70 per cent of Archibald's credits came from farm households. The labour account was surprisingly small, accounting for less than 10 per cent of his credits, while cash accounted for only 3 per cent.[60]

By the 1840s this pattern had changed dramatically. The company had expanded and now was engaged in sealing, fishing, shipbuilding, timber, and milling lumber.[61] We still see the odd bit of butter and hay being exchanged, but in the 1840s this part of the trade constituted less than 10 per cent of its credits. The firm had started building its own ships in the 1830s, and ten years later it would launch the largest vessel ever built in Cape Breton, the 1,074 ton ship *Lord Clarendon*. By the mid-1850s Archibald and his sons, Thomas Dickson, Blowers, and Charles (later president of the Bank of Nova Scotia), owned the shipyards, a marine railway, a lumber mill, a forge, and a ship chandlery, and they were financing fishing, whaling, and sealing expeditions – remarkable growth in fifteen years.[62] Whereas in the 1820s the firm had conducted roughly £2,000 in business, in 1841 this figure was over £16,000, *not* including the coal or shipbuilding accounts.

Some of this growth was certainly attributable to the new opportunities presented by the GMA and to the close ties that developed between the two companies as well as between Archibald and Richard Brown, the manager of the GMA at Sydney Mines.[63] Archibald and Co., however, was still a store and thus had a fairly typical rural clientele, including some who had nothing to offer in exchange but their labour.[64] The store also did well simply by having access to a well-paid base of customers at the coalmines. The ease with which it obtained cash from these customers would have elicited envy from merchants in town or country. The ledger includes close to £800 in cash paid directly from the "Mines Office."[65] In the case of the Archibalds at least, the GMA even guaranteed some of its employees' accounts.[66] Few profited so well by their association with the GMA. The Archibalds were clearly good businessmen.

Not surprisingly, Archibald's name was not one associated with the campaign to break up the GMA monopoly. Thus it must have been rather galling to many in the firm when Archibald and Co. (in the form of the youngest son, Charles) was one of the earliest companies to attempt to begin coalmining after the GMA's monopoly was broken in 1858.[67] Indeed, not only was this apparent apostate one of the first in the field, but his establishment was one of the few Nova Scotia-based companies that might unequivocally be termed a success. The Archibald-built Gowrie Mine at Port Morien, just east of Glace Bay, operated successfully from 1862 until its eventual sale to the Whitney syndicate in 1893.[68] Indeed, the Archibalds and their mine represent the only major example of a successful transfer from sea-based mercantile ventures to the coalmining industry in this period.

There were other, smaller attempts at such a transfer. Charles J. Campbell opened a store at Baddeck around 1845. By the late 1850s, he was said to have become the wealthiest man in Victoria County. As the MLA for most of the period from 1855 to 1867 and a member of the new federal Canadian Parliament from 1867 to 1882, he also held considerable political clout. His business activities spanned farms, his merchant store, and a shipbuilding facility that launched six brigs between 1844 and 1859. Together, his properties were valued at over £4,000, almost one-fifth of the property assessments in the entire county during the late 1850s. As the wealthiest and most powerful man in the county, Campbell no doubt thought it appropriate to have his bust, in the attire of a Highland clan chief, placed in the keystone of the new government building in Baddeck.[69] While his business grew and broadened substantially after the mid-1850s, from the time he started his own store in 1845, most of his exchange was based on the farms of the surrounding countryside.

In 1859 Campbell applied for a licence to mine coal at a place called Kelly's Cove, on the northern side of the mouth of Great Bras d'Or. Over the next four years Campbell hired 120 miners and labourers, who cut a shaft and built a small mining village named for its creator, New Campbellton. Between 1862 and 1864 Campbell claimed to have expended close to $50,000 with almost one-third ($16,400) of this spent on houses and buildings, and another third ($17,600) on a tramway, rolling stock, and a wharf.[70] For the next thirty years the New Campbellton mines would be one of the more successful, if still quite small, mines to operate in the province after the break-up of the GMA monopoly. Producing only about 40,000 to 50,000 tons per year after about 1868, Campbell's mines nevertheless survived the period of most intense competition and several severe recessions before he too sold out to the Whitney syndicate in 1893.

The costs of developing a mine, whether a large mine such as Archibald's or a smaller one such as Campbell's, were often prohibitive. Few could afford to go it alone, and an obvious solution was to form partnerships or joint-stock companies. James D.B. Fraser, a New Glasgow merchant, druggist, and activist in the crusade against the GMA monopoly, provides a good example of a smaller merchant who entered mining by the joint-stock route. Although best known as a druggist and anaesthetist, he also had a general dry goods operation and was proprietor of the Eastern Stage Coach Co., which ran between Halifax and New Glasgow, and of a small confectionary factory. In addition, he was a partner in the Pictou Gas Light Company, in the Pictou Marine Insurance Association, and together with A.P. Ross, in a grindstone and flagstone quarry and export business.[71] Although a town merchant, Fraser's business interests ranged into the countryside. His advertisements announced his willingness to accept "country produce" as payment, and one account book lists several people paying in butter, potatoes, or labour. And as the owner of a stable of stage-coach horses, Fraser could always use some oats and hay.[72] The stone quarries grew slowly and faltered several times, but by about 1845 older techniques and an unskilled workforce had been replaced by machinery, skilled quarrymen, and aggressive marketing in New York and New England.[73] Yet, as he relied almost exclusively on exports for sales and with larger, better-positioned competitors on the Bay of

Fundy, it seems unlikely that the grindstone trade alone would have generated an adequate return.[74] The fixed costs must have represented something in the order of £1,000. With grindstones selling at less than £2 per ton at the wharf, 1,000 stones would have brought in only about £300. After wages, even if partly paid in goods the business could not have been very profitable.

Part of this must be understood within the broader sphere of a colonial merchant's trade. In Fraser's case, the ships carrying most of the stones that he sent to the American northeast returned with other goods for his store – cloths, dyes, pharmaceuticals – and even if the profits on the export were low, this trade allowed him to finance other aspects of his general trade. While the usual merchant pattern was to draw as many into his exchange relations as possible so that he might obtain as many goods for export as possible, it could also work that exports merely served as a vehicle for importing.[75] The export might be only as important as the profit to be made on the returned goods. It was much the same in the coal trade. Thus for merchants such as Fraser, Archibald, George Smith, Primrose and Ross, and the host of other merchants who exported the occasional boatload of coal, participation in the coal trade was not necessarily an end in itself; it could also be a means toward accessing other markets and financing their trade. This business strategy also helps us to better understand the techniques chosen by the GMA. Although it was clearly in a better position to invest in the carrying trade, it did not have to. The requirements of local merchants allowed the company to forego such investments as well as the risks involved in the increasingly competitive coal trade of the eastern United States. These risks fell not on London financiers but on outport shipbuilders and rural merchants. They, in turn, passed part of the risk on to the farm-based rural workers who relied on such work for their households' subsistence.

Fraser's initial foray into coalmining in 1858 appears to have been financed entirely on his own. However, the outlay in costs added up, and he was quickly in need of additional financing. He turned to his partner, A.P. Ross, and for the next year and a half the two men attempted to raise enough money to place the mine on a stronger footing.[76] They obtained a lease of a site adjoining the GMA's lease at Albion Mines and commenced digging "oil coal," but they gave this up "in consequence of the discovery of oil wells in the United States." They claimed to have expended about $8,600 in the process.[77] They then turned their attention to another seam on the same property and purchased the adjacent lease of J.W. Carmichael. Throughout all of this Fraser was confident in the partnership's prospects and pleased to have learned from others' mistakes: "With the experience of the Albion Company [GMA] to caution and guide us," he explained, "I am satisfied we can work more economically than they have done."[78] But after expending another $2,400, they quickly realized that they needed still more money.

Fraser and Ross adopted two methods. After failing to raise adequate sums in New York,[79] the two looked for local money. In January 1860 Fraser showed the mines off to a number of prospective local investors and insisted that between the local contacts and the investors they had lined up in Halifax, they were well on their way. As they already owned the land, the necessary leases, and the mines themselves, Fraser estimated that it would "only require £5000" to establish the works. The Fraser Mine, as it came to be known, eventually developed into a proper mine, and it did so in part backed by local financing.[80] But once again, the operation reached a stage beyond which the operators felt that they could no longer run the mine without additional financing, and Fraser and Ross were forced to try New York and London in 1861–62. Unable to secure the funding, Fraser found himself in New England the following summer trying to sell the mine entirely, a sale that he finally effected in October 1864.[81] This sale was not unlike several others that occurred in the 1860s as the coalmines of Nova Scotia slipped out of local hands and increasingly into the hands of men from New York, Boston, and Montreal.

Whether their mines were unable to pay for themselves or these entrepreneurs were unable to raise the money necessary to allow them to do so, local owners sought to solve their problems by selling their properties and liquidating their coalmining investments for the best price that they could obtain. More often than not, this meant a sale in New York or Boston, not Pictou or Halifax. A few years afterward William McKeen, together with his sons John and David (later Senator David McKeen), took out a lease on the shore near Mabou, spent about $4,000, hired about forty men, and attempted to begin mining out under the harbour. The Submarine Mining Company was a failure, and although mining would continue periodically at Mabou for the next eighty years, the seam never fostered more than small, marginal operations.[82] The McKeens, however, probably recouped at least part of their loss. Indeed, judging by the amounts of goods charged against their employees, one supposes that the investment was not so costly as the expense column might suggest.[83] If the monopoly had removed coalmining from the hands of the province's elite as a tool of economic development, it was nevertheless returning dividends to some of "the people."

Agriculture and the rural economy were generally capable of producing wealth and investment capital, but they did not produce enough (apparently) to support coalmining operations. Or did they? The truth is that we cannot say. While the field was now open for indigenous investment, it is important to remember what these local capitalists were competing against in the GMA: a company that was still able to spend £120,000 to clear up a lingering civil suit with the estate of the Duke of York and that had (whatever its shortcomings) produced a substantial and well-engineered mining operation designed to produce at minimum operating costs for several decades.[84] Moreover, most of these costs were now behind it. For Fraser, McKeen, the Archibalds, and the other provincial merchants who moved into mining, there was a long road ahead.

MERCHANTS AND POLITICS

Agricultural improvement, observed the secretary of the River John Agricultural Society late in the winter of 1845, had brought with it "wealth, comfort, and respectability ... [W]ith industry and perseverance the farming community can command all the necessaries of life within themselves."[85] It was undoubtedly true that many could provide all the necessaries of life, but many were closer to this margin than others; some apparently required a fair bit more industry and perseverance. This was particularly true in Cape Breton, where fully one-half of the population were squatters and where the relative extremes of wealth and poverty were greater. The potato blight reached northern Nova Scotia in 1846, and by the winter of 1847 reports of starving backland settlers and Mi'kmaq were reaching the capital. On a scale somewhere between what happened in Ireland and New England (although much closer to the latter), *Phytophthora infestans* devastated Nova Scotia agriculture, straining the province's relief resources, ruining farm households' finances, and pushing hundreds of already poor families literally to the edge of starvation. For the Mi'kmaq, the crop losses of the 1840s spelled the final death of an already ineffective Indian agricultural-settlement policy.[86]

In Pictou County, late in the winters of 1848 and 1849, petitions came from various parts of the county describing the "destitute families" and "desparate cases" and warning of the "fearful consequences" that might occur if these were not attended.[87] James Henderson of Merigomish estimated that "were the whole amount of breadstuffs contained in this district equally divided amongst the inhabitants it would barely suffice to support them for six months." But it was not divided evenly, and "more than one half the people have not now what will maintain them for half that period."[88] George Smith, the Pictou merchant, had never "seen so great a call for meal and flour and those who are the most in need are the least able to purchase."[89] Few petitions or letters came from the poor themselves but from people writing on their behalf – sometimes selflessly, sometimes not. Some claimed that there was simply no flour or meal available, but the cry from most writers was for money, not food. As in most famines, the problem appears to have been as much related to distribution and price, not simply availability. As "R" from St Ann's, near Sydney, observed: "There is food to be had, it is true; but the means to purchase it is wanting."[90] Three Pictou County merchants, James Carmichael, James Crichton, and a "Mr. Yorston," claimed to have "expended the sum of £30 ... to relieve the distress at present existing among the Indians." As merchants, they always had access to a few barrels of meal or flour that they could forward to the poor. As justices of the peace with direct access to poor-relief monies, they could – and did – draw directly on the government for the sum.[91] In a cash-poor province, these merchants obtained full remuneration on products for which they might normally receive only half. One wonders too whether such relief was charged at cash prices.[92]

The potato blight hit Cape Breton particularly hard, and the stories of hardship and starvation are dramatic and often heart-rending. Potatoes were the staple of poor Cape Bretoners' lives. From the backlands of Lake Ainslie to St Ann's – where the Reverend Norman MacLeod reported starving men and women "running continually from door to door, with the ghastly features of death staring them in their very faces" – potatoes rotted in the ground.[93] Over the next three years, reports of begging and later starvation came from all parts of the island. The effects of the blight were severe, crippling many households and forcing them to sell off their cattle and go into debt simply to obtain food. Not only were crops lost, but also credit disappeared and animals starved. A number of merchants and wealthy farmers opened their stores and their pocketbooks to provide for their communities, but as many profited by the increased prices and the thousands of pounds of extra relief money voted in 1847 and 1848.[94] In Pictou there was widespread suspicion of hoarding, while in Cape Breton others observed that some merchants had "refused to dispose of [grain] at a very fair remuneration expecting of course to sell them to better advantage in the Newfoundland Market."[95] Merchants (as well as a number of farmers who shipped all their cattle rather than risk losing their investment)[96] would have reminded their critics that cattle exports to Newfoundland and Halifax brought back British grain and flour. This meant little to those who had nothing to exchange for these products.

Local elites responded to the crisis – and some were hurt by it – but few suffered. Some agricultural societies turned their attention toward distributing new seed and occasionally some food relief. But even at the worst point in the famine, other societies were importing "superior" breeding stock, new machinery, and guano.[97] The famine was an important turning point in the history of the province not simply because of its severity but because of the society upon which it was inflicted. The famine hurt all of Nova Scotia but nowhere as severely as Cape Breton; and even an apologetic history must admit that it did so unevenly. In Pictou and Antigonish Counties, crops were devastated and there was widespread hunger; in Cape Breton people died.[98]

William McKeen is still remembered in Mabou as the man who fed the poor by handing out free potatoes during the famine.[99] But a curious amnesia prevails about the fact that every act of charity in these years appears to have been recorded in a ledger and that he attempted to collect on his generosity over the next few years. Of the people who would have needed such assistance, however, few had any money afterward, so McKeen obtained a huge return in land.[100] In the ten years after the famine (1849–59), McKeen obtained twenty-three properties in court judgments and purchased another forty-eight by deeds, almost all of them in the area between Broad Cove in the north and Judique in the south. Undoubtedly, some of these were the unremarkable business dealings of a man whom the registry of deeds shows acquired almost one hundred properties between 1828 and 1865. It is equally certain that many of these judgments came about from his "benevolence" during the famine; many of these benign-looking purchases had their origins in a ledger as well. This was not uncommon after the famine, nor was McKeen the only merchant to benefit from people's misery. As late as 1862 another Inverness County correspondent observed that the combination of "unlimited credit" and the "loss of the potato crop for many years ... has thrown many of the people in debts to merchants so deep that their lands have or must go to

liquidate them."[101] It is not to impugn McKeen that we should note
that he did well through, and by, the famine; and we need not question his Christian charity. Indeed, there may well have been other motives. It is worth noting, however, that some members of the elite
responded as much out of fear as out of charity. Others operating under the same fears removed to New England or Canada, having resolved that the "little property they have may not be plundered and
devoured by the famishing populace."[102] There were also accounts of
popular anger over exports of food during the famine. The one account that we have of McKeen's magnanimity has the merchant on a
ship at the Mabou wharf, surrounded by a large, hungry, and very anxious crowd. This account suggests that he was moved by what he saw.
Perhaps this is true. Perhaps too, as he surveyed the assembled crowd,
he might just as well have feared for his life – and certainly his property.[103] For some merchants, the extra relief money may have represented some of their best years for cash sales. This would certainly
seem to have been the case with McKeen and perhaps too with the
merchants shipping the locally produced flour and potatoes to Newfoundland that "R" described at North Sydney in the spring of
1848.[104] A more remarkable illustration of the mercantile possibilities
provided by times of dearth comes from Gammel and Christie, merchants at Bras d'Or and North Sydney. In 1853 they reported sales of
600 barrels of flour; during the famine, they had been selling between
2,000 and 3,000 barrels per year, most of it paid for in relief money.[105]
Whether they profited or fled, a number of merchants and prosperous
farmers stood apart during the famine.

As leaders in the local elite, these men were also highly public figures. Few moved into electoral politics, but they were all political. We
will pursue the public lives of a broader cross-section of the emerging
rural middle class in the next chapter; here, however, it is worth briefly
sketching some of the politics of these men, lest we limit their descriptions to that of *Homo economicus*. New Glasgow's James D.B. Fraser, for
example, was active in local and colonial politics. He engaged in the
antimonopoly campaign against the GMA, and as this might suggest,
he was also a reformer and active supporter of Joseph Howe's liberal
reformers.[106] But his daily political activities touched a number of
bases, and his concerns reflected a variety of prevalent issues, as well as
a range of positions from which they might be viewed. During the famine winters of 1848 and 1849, he busied himself with three vital political matters. The first was the "fearful scarcity of food" in the back

settlements and how to secure the government's guarantee on funds that some merchants (himself included) were willing to forward for the purchase of meal and flour.[107] The second related to his investments in a cloth mill under construction just outside New Glasgow at Middle River by Robert and Alexander Fraser (who do not appear to have been his relatives). The previous summer Fraser had imported the machinery for the brothers, and "they still owe[d]" him £112. He was quite confident that the brothers' "security [was] perfectly good," but he wanted the money and was pressing the local MLA to obtain a loan for the young entrepreneurs.[108] The third matter nicely tied the first two together, as it attended to relations between the poor and the middling classes. Fed up (again) with the poor quality of the county's grand jury (by which we might safely surmise that he did not like its decisions), he quickly seized on a solution. "There ought to be," he argued in a letter to George Young, "a class of persons who would fairly represent the landed interests of the province" in matters of legal disputes over property rights, "say whose property is worth not less than £400." Even though only 24 of 600 local men "[were] ever called," he concluded that "the present qualification is entirely too low."[109] Fraser frequently wrote to Young on behalf of the poor during the years of the potato famine, and notwithstanding his own interest in gaining their relief, his sympathy seems real enough. But as with so many of the emergent middle class, both his liberalism and Christian sympathies for the poor were clearly concerned with their corporeal existence, not their political liberty. For Fraser, the poor were objects of pity, not political subjects.

McKeen, like Fraser, was never an elected official, but he exercised considerable political power within Inverness County and a fair bit beyond the county too. William Young, the MLA for Inverness and son of "Agricola," was a regular correspondent, and McKeen, together with the Reverend Alex MacDonell, the parish priest in Port Hood, organized the Scottish vote for Young in the infamous campaign against Albion Mines' manager, Richard Smith, in 1832. Over the next twenty years, McKeen continued to bring out the reformers' vote, and he played other backroom political roles throughout the 1850s.[110] McKeen's support for this leading reformer offered certain rewards; thus while they discussed a number of local political matters, the major topic was the distribution of patronage – that is, who was deserving (politically) of a road commission. As a man who made it his business to know who was up to what and who could exert pressure on some voters, he was a valuable ally, and Young usually consulted with McKeen before making any changes in the distribution of patronage. He was rewarded for his services in 1848 with an appointment to the Legislative Council.[111]

McKeen was viewed as a benefactor. Even before the famine, he cultivated the role of a paternal figure – one not caught up so much in the tumult of everyday politics and who quietly presided over all. His roles in the community were many and quite public; these included his presidency of the Mabou Agricultural Society from the early 1820s through the 1850s, his advocacy for common schools, and his leadership in the temperance cause.[112] McKeen's image was carefully cultivated. In the winter of 1843–44 a group of young men met to form the Mabou Literary and Scientific Society.[113] Together with agricultural societies, mechanics' institutes, and a range of other fraternal organizations, literary and scientific societies had become important indicators of social status for the middle classes of even small rural communities such as Mabou. There was nothing at all unusual in the formation of this society, except that McKeen himself did not join. This was not, however, because he was unsupportive. Indeed, McKeen sent along a letter congratulating the young men on their "enterprise," wishing them a secure future as an organization, and encouraging every rural village and settlement in Cape Breton to follow their fine example. The young men graciously accepted his encouragement and in suitably reciprocal form asked that he give the first lecture. Here was McKeen's favoured role. He could exercise power over magistrates, send debtors to gaol, offer mercy to a widow, feed the starving, and be supportive of all that bespoke the benefits of improvement. Even in formal politics, McKeen's role was managerial and theatrical, but quiet. On 4 November 1840, at a "Public Meeting of the Freeholders and Inhabitants of Inverness," the Reverend Alex McDonnell, Peter Smyth, J.L. Tremain, George Laurence, Samuel McKeen, and a number of other interested figures met to indicate William Young as their favourite in the upcoming election.[114] Each of the above men made a resolution, each was passed, and Young himself gave a speech. At the end of the evening, toasts were offered to the Queen, the army, Prince Albert, the governor, Lord Falkland, "Mr Young," "Mrs William Young," and "Auld Scotia with her hills and glens." William McKeen said nothing. Instead, at the commencement of the meeting, he was appointed chair, and he presided in his typically restrained manner. William McKeen did not have to speak to be heard.

CONCLUSION

Ever opportunistic, provincial government officials managed to find a silver lining in the events of the famine. They had spent the late 1830s and early 1840s attempting to stop the flood of poor immigrants coming into the province, and the famine offered an opening. In 1847 Sir John Harvey informed the Colonial Office of the severity of the situation, adding that it had become imperative to end "pauper emigration" to the province and describing the starvation and suffering in some detail.[115] The British government then ordered the information reprinted and circulated. Combined with the estimated 10,000 who left Cape Breton during the famine years, the curtailing of immigration took some pressure off the crisis in the Crown-lands office, at least for a few years.[116]

Conditions in Cape Breton were worse than on the mainland. The Island's overburdened backland settlements were unlikely to have prospered as agricultural communities in any event, and it is probable that the famine simply encouraged a number of poor settlers to move on more quickly than they might have otherwise. But many others stayed, unwilling and in some cases unable to foresake the past twenty years' efforts. Yet the exodus was not limited to Cape Breton, and all along the Northumberland shore hundreds of settlers were leaving by mid-century. Certainly, as the 1851 sex ratios suggest,[117] this movement was being led by young men searching for work in Halifax, the Miramichi, New England, Canada, and occasionally beyond. Some of these men probably returned regularly, others returned less frequently but sent back money, and others probably felt few tugs and left with little intention of ever returning.

Class was central to these people's lives. If these farm-based people were not classically defined proletarians, they were still poor people whose market positions made them dependent on and subject to the economic and political authority of others. It is difficult, therefore, to read brief accounts of resistance and not see people reacting to perceived injustices and understanding perfectly well that these injuries stemmed from others' superior social positions. Some watched their neighbours and children go hungry, while merchants and frontland farmers purchased machinery, built new houses, joined the local agricultural society, and earned cash returns by exporting flour, livestock, and vegetables. Nor is it possible to overlook the condescension and bare tolerance with which rural elites – and even, as in the case of Robert Hill, the elites' servants – regarded the poor, or unimproved, around them. These people experienced class relationships. That neither group expressed its understanding in an explicitly class-based language does not mean that there was no understanding of difference based on economic and political capacity. In the case of immigrant Highlanders, for example, there was a deeply rooted understanding of *political* authority and hierarchy, but they had left *this* form of authority behind them. Here, in New Scotland, there was still authority, but the bases for this authority were different. Formally, the men who dominated rural society in Nova Scotia held no excess political rights, except what they derived from the combined effects of their gender and their wealth. As rational men, rural elites understood that there were benefits to be had from their status, and they understood how best to claim them. As we shall see in the next chapter, they too were beginning to form associations and institutions so that they might further their own collective needs and aspirations. It was here, in the twin bases of material difference and a political project of elite-led, middle-class government, that we can best see the liberal-capitalist order emerging across the colonial countryside.

9

Improvers

Within a few months of the initial publication of John Young's "letters" on improvement, several local agricultural societies had been set up around Nova Scotia. By 1821 his letters had been brought together and published in book form as *The Letters of Agricola*, twenty-seven agricultural societies were in operation around the province, and the Central Board of Agriculture had been established in Halifax with government funding to oversee the local societies' operations. Not only did Young's writings provide the spur for these actions, but his leadership was honoured by naming him president of the board in 1819. From his position, he exercised direct influence on the local societies' affairs until stepping down in 1824. The local improvers' vision was not as grand as Young's, but even their more prosaic versions clearly accepted the self-evident necessity of improvement, as well as much of its social technology. When reading the correspondence of the agricultural societies, we find few discourses on political economy and nation building, but these writers certainly professed knowledge of political economy and of the necessity of their own leading roles. They evinced a clear vision of the future and a remarkably clear understanding of the steps necessary to achieve it. Improvers positioned themselves as the guiding lights of an as-yet-uncertain progress. While they were confident in their own expertise, they were much less sure of their fellow colonists. As one River John improver observed, "we are morally certain permanent prosperity will eventually arise," but if it did not, he added, "it shall be no fault of ours."[1]

Improvement was a key element in both directing and maintaining the claims of elite-led, middle-class men to represent the best interest of an emerging national state. Few nineteenth-century members of the provincial elite saw progress as certain. Most believed that human-directed improvement was the path to progress. Together with Young and some colonial officials, they shared a view of the world and politics as progressive, a commitment to economic change, a dedication to their own missionary function, and a belief in a kind of trickle-down theory of education and in the diffusion of knowledge. While the societies may well have failed in their immediate tasks of "improved" farming, they retain historical importance in their role as formative elements in the institutional bases of governance, the organization of middle-class masculine identity, the formation of a liberal state, the legitimation of certain forms of liberal-capitalist practice, and the consolidation of key liberal ideas that lay at the heart of governmentality. In particular, it was their ability to maintain a hold on the legitimate use of power and violence while simultaneously proclaiming their stewardship of civic virtues such as independence, respectability, propriety, and later sobriety. This agenda was a product of a transatlantic debate on and conceptualization of government and the public sphere[2] and was given a particular form and shape by the material conditions and possibilities of rural Nova Scotia.

AGRICULTURAL SOCIETIES AND IMPROVEMENT

Agricultural societies were among the key organizational bases of rural elites. Much like the many other fraternal societies springing up in the towns and villages of the region, they allowed rural men, and to a much lesser extent women, to meet, to discuss matters political and social, and to demonstrate their social rank. As state-supported bodies, such societies also brought the state more fully into civil society. They provided a forum in which the aims and aspirations of local elites and the state could be brought together and thus formed loci for rural politics and the contestation of political power and influence. In describing their societies, these local improvers give us a clear portrait of how they viewed both themselves and their functions. Most saw themselves as those who Richard John Uniacke believed understood "the true interests of this country," those who would "make every possible exertion to ... keep alive the laudable and patriotic spirit" of agricultural improvement.[3]

In December 1818, and still in the midst of Agricola's "letters," a Central Board of Agriculture was formed at Halifax to initiate a renewed effort toward agricultural improvement in Nova Scotia. The respectability of the institution reflected its august membership, which included the governor and much of the local mercantile and political elite.[4] The board's function would be "to direct and watch over the agricultural interests of the entire province" by collecting and publishing information, assisting emigrants, offering premiums, introducing new machinery, seed, and livestock, and generally "to direct the enterprize and emulation of the farmer into the channels most conducive to our prosperity." In short, the program of the Central Board was to guide and direct the local societies in their immediate tasks of improving agriculture through the larger vision of an economic prosperity. Provincial agriculture, S.G.W. Archibald argued in introducing the resolutions, was in the hands of an "ignorant" people who, since Young's letters, had been "generally awakened from that state of inaction and inattention to their best interests." Now, however, there were "a great many in our population, enlightened, opulent, and full of activity and zeal," who could forward the cause of improvement. Modelled on the British Board of Agriculture, the Central Board was designed to link the capital to the local societies. Its function was governmental, and Young insisted (following Sir John Sinclair) that it "must be regarded as the agricultural organ of the legislative branches."[5] All money would be distributed through the Central Board, and it would "exercise a wholesome vigilance and control over the others." Like Young, the board believed that Nova Scotia "was a country replete with natural resources and inhabited by a hardy peasantry." Now, added Brenton Haliburton, "the peasants require only instruction."[6] No clearer statement of the improvers' paternal design was possible.

Within the local societies, we find similar emphases. Each society was required to raise £10 through subscriptions, so there was some incentive to draw a substantial number of members. But with most societies charging 5s for membership, this meant that only forty members were needed. While often despairing of their ability to attract a broader base of participation, they uniformly boasted of their attracting the "most respectable inhabitants of the country." Twenty years later, in February 1837, the Pictou [West River] Agricultural Society formally reorganized itself when "a number of the Gentlemen of Pictou" met at the Royal Oak Tavern, established rules and regulations to govern the society, adopted a Latin motto, and set membership fees at 10s per year. They set their second meeting for June but had to cancel because the date of the sitting of the Supreme Court had been changed; almost everyone on the executive and the executive committee was either an assistant judge or a justice of the peace. Similarly, the constitution of the Inverness [PortHood] Agricultural Society called its first meeting for the day after the "adjournment of the Supreme Court" and designated the same event as the marker for all future spring meetings.[7]

But the respectability that these men found in their communities might not have been so clear in the capital, and they were sometimes forced to strike a defensive pose against any suggestions that defamed their positions. J.S. Morse, the secretary of the Cumberland Agricultural Society and a member of the Legislative Assembly, wrote specifically to counter an anonymous writer who, in a letter published in the *Halifax Free Press*, attempted to "represent our Society to be composed of the lower order of the inhabitants." He included a current membership list, which clearly demonstrated the opposite to be true: "it will be seen ... that the 'Cumberland Agricultural Society' comprises a large portion of the Magistracy and of the respectability of this county." Young, not surprisingly, echoed these assertions of the respectability of the members of the local societies. Such claims were commonly made, and as Graeme Wynn's examination of the membership of several Pictou societies illustrates, the pattern of local elite domination continued through the reorganized societies of the 1840s and 1850s.[8] Much the same was true in almost all societies.

Society members' correspondence consistently demonstrates that they knew their primary mission was to change the behaviour of those around them. And, again consistently, they stressed the same direction for change: "to induce the people to forego the unprofitable practices and modes of their ancestors" and to enter the modern world of agricultural improvement. Most societies argued that their chief object was "to shake off [non-members'] prejudices and old Customs." Provincial farmers, the improvers continued, suffered under the weight of tradition and custom, whether learned from their "ancestors" or from years of "habit." Acadians and Highlanders seem to have been particularly burdened by tradition; they were not only "bigoted in the good old ways," and "their prejudices ... deeply rooted," but also, another writer argued, "lazy."[9] These prejudices seem to have been rooted in the transference of Old World custom. In their report for 1843 the Pictou (West River) Agricultural Society outlined the problem: "Many of the worst principles of bad husbandry adopted by our forefathers are still in vogue ... the prejudices of former days remain in all their force ... [and] scarce an appearance of improvement exists. It therefore becomes your society not to relax in their exertions, and it is the duty of every member to endeavour to extend the bounds of [the society's] usefulness as far as his opportunities in his private sphere will enable him to do." Much like

Young, the local improvers narrated a possible history: the errors of the past continued, but even within their communities stood the public-spirited, who would lead them to a bright future. Changing these habits would take time, but the improvers believed that history was on their side. Few farmers were assuming the responsibility to improve their own lives. Someone else had to.[10]

Emulation was the improvers' primary method. Almost every letter in the societies' correspondence made some reference to emulation – "the inspiring influence of example." But in terms of the more immediate matters of "practical farming," the societies were very important in encouraging and in some cases introducing new techniques, breeds, information, and equipment into the province. In the 1820s most societies emphasized the better use of manures and the introduction of new breeds of livestock and new seeds, particularly wheat. Thus the societies in Pictou and Cumberland Counties spent most of their money on prizes for ploughing matches, the best crops of wheat, oats, or potatoes, and the greatest amount of acreage in summer fallow, while devoting some money in some years to the purchase of seed or livestock. By the 1840s most societies continued to offer prizes for wheat, and occasionally for summer fallow, but these prizes constituted a much smaller portion of their monies. The new emphasis was clearly on the importation of livestock and agricultural machinery.[11] Most societies quietly dropped Young's central tenet about growing breadcorns and were coming to believe that Nova Scotia was "more of a grazing country than a grain country." There were local variations. In Cape Breton both the Sydney and Middle River societies initially emphasized machinery but shifted almost completely to obtaining improved livestock breeds. For merchants and export-oriented farmers, this was clearly a sensible route because in most areas along the Gulf shore livestock and other animal products made up almost all their sales.[12] They were quite discriminating. The Mabou society sent "selected" agents of "thorough and competent knowledge" to choose particular breeds for their "high economums" [sic], "even though the cattle were somewhat enhanced in price."[13] Although there were often complaints, especially about the condition of animals brought from England, the wider movement to improved livestock was unquestioned, and the results were generally praised. The proof was in the price. In River John the society's secretary was undoubtedly pleased to report that "double the price" was offered for the offspring of imported cattle; and an East River correspondent also reported that stock in his area "now find a ready market and good prices while the product of our dairies is more abundant and of better quality."[14] This was how these men understood improvement.

Economic returns certainly provided some measure of improvement's success. If we turn to machinery and agricultural implements, a familiar pattern emerges. Again, some societies emphasized machinery more than others, but each appears to have recognized the benefits of at least improved implements and sometimes simply of greater mechanization. Several writers acknowledged the importance of the "proper implements," "by which an immense amount of grain is saved to the Members that was formerly lost." Others noted that more and better machinery was "particularly needed now when the price of labor is so high." In Cumberland County, where hay was "the staple crop," members were much more interested in mowing and raking machines, "which very much lessened the amount of labour." This was one of the favoured positions of the improvers; but here too they occasionally met with resistance. In Sydney local improvers actively encouraged members to purchase cultivators that the society had imported from Boston, but several were unhappy with this improvement. One purchaser was said to have "burnt" his, while the secretary told of another who appeared to have been lost to the cause: "I endeavoured to explain to him the imperfection of *that* Cultivator ... when he shook his head and said, 'O Sir, it is all very well to hear about these sort of new fangled things, but in all our minds now it is only a downright waste of money, for they are only got up just to give work to the *carpenters* and *Blacksmiths* – I'll stick to the old Hoe!'"[15] Although occasionally critical of particular machines, however, the improvers never wavered in their general enthusiasm for machinery.

Distributing the costs of importing machines and breeding stock obviously made a great deal of sense in communities where money and resources were scarce. It also allowed members to experiment with a variety of machines from a variety of sources, thus lessening the risk of purchasing products from unknown manufacturers. But spreading the risk also meant spreading scarce resources, and there were major difficulties sharing scarce equipment. Most societies sold their goods at auction, where usually only members were eligible to bid. In 1855 the North Sydney society spent £49.15.0 for implements, a bull, and five sheep. Having the previous year split from the Sydney society over questions of access, the new group was not about to run into the same problem; thus "all [were] sold at auction to members only" because it was felt that "these useful articles [would] be better taken care of than if vested in the Society at large."[16] The membership of any one society represented, at most, 10 per cent of the households in the area, so very few were eligible to benefit. But the societies' resources were limited, and few would have imported enough goods to repay every member's investment. The frequent reappearance of very familiar names in reports of auctions, purchases, and successful breeding "trials" suggests that such imports reached a very limited circle. Clearly, it cannot be said that the state did not provide assistance to agriculture. Indeed, much of the money made available subsidized the capital investments of *some* provincial farmers and not a few merchants. Over the course of the 1840s and 1850s the relative proportion of state funding declined as less cash was distributed among more societies. But the object of this funding remained largely the same. State assistance to Nova Scotia agriculture in this period was not a general assistance (such as might have been provided by a tariff on imported produce or by a bounty on exports); it was a form of patronage. While not the only (and perhaps not even the principal) reason for the societies' activities and successes, cash and patronage were vital aspects of fixing an agricultural presence within the state and solidifying the patterns of elite dominance of the countryside.

Status is a more nebulous measure. Membership in an agricultural society was no guarantee of any one man's elite status, although it clearly placed him in the realm of the respectable. Each society had an executive committee and a managing board. Membership on such committees was a sure sign of status. The societies' executives were composed almost entirely of members of the local elite. Many of these were men whom we might encounter if we were studying provincial or even intercolonial politics; all were dominant figures in their local communities. Domination by such a "compact" did not continue so strongly in all counties, but the general pattern of elite control did. When the Mabou society reformed in 1841, William McKeen was again president; the same was true of James Morse in Amherst. McKeen's continued leadership was a reflection of his tremendous influence. Much the same could be said of his fellows on the executive: merchants and sheriffs George Laurence and J.L. Tremain, the lawyer Hiram Blanchard (brother of Jotham, the Pictou County publisher and politician), and McKeen's brother James.[17] Within three months, however, Laurence was leading a breakaway society formed to represent the northern part of the county. Apparently anxious to provide suitable titles for as many of the respectable as possible, the new society's executive included eight vice presidents, plus a managing committee of another fifteen.[18] The societies fragmented into smaller societies throughout the province in the 1840s, enabling more localized elites to attain additional leadership roles in the communities. Increasingly too, such civil roles paralleled formal state positions. In the 1840s and 1850s being a local state official meant that one was probably also a leader in the local improvement society. Neither increased representation nor greater accessibility to funding changed the societies' narrow social base.

Not everyone, however, rallied to the cause of improvement, even among the elite. Many critics, as Young observed, focused not so much on the societies' particulars but simply scoffed at the idea that Nova Scotia could be an agricultural colony. Some attacked Young himself. In 1823 one writer in the *Acadian Recorder* observed how Young "never descends from his aerial heighth, but is always declaiming from the loftiest language of impassioned feeling."[19] Others seemed to accept the program but attacked the societies. "A Farmer" from Cumberland County, writing to the *Halifax Free Press*, complained that the society in his district "conducted their affairs ... improper[ly]," citing in particular the questionable conduct of some members of the executive. For his part, Young rejected the complaints as "trivial," arguing that the members' respectability was self-evident. Another correspondent complained that Young and the Central Board had "not turned your atension to the condition of the Hundreds of Emigrants that are now in this neighbourhood [near Merigomish]." On a few occasions, members paused to criticize aspects of the program, and local secretaries found themselves on the defensive. James MacGregor reported a number of small disputes within the Pictou society over judging at its exhibition and the relative value of some techniques versus others, charges that he dismissed. But he also observed that, as early as 1821, the society was already losing members, a condition that he blamed on a popular view of the value of societies: "Some think the whole bustle about agriculture is a contrivance to pick poor people's pockets." In Cumberland County, Alexander Stewart too noted that the early societies faced similar suspicions, although he remained confident of the future because "our motives are every day becoming better known and more justly appreciated."[20] Stewart, like most of the correspondents, understood that the first task of the improver was not simply in diffusing new techniques but also in fostering the *idea* of improvement.

Most societies were unable to attract more than a slim percentage of their constituencies. Few sustained more than sixty members, and most hovered around thirty or forty. Throughout the 1840s and 1850s a number of societies failed because they could no longer raise the minimum £10 in dues, while a number of others faltered.[21] The Pictou Agricultural Society was one of the more successful branches in the province, but as Graeme Wynn notes, even this society fluctuated between only forty to sixty members in a township that contained about two thousand households in 1851. Yet even in the face of criticism and weak support, the emulative principle was still believed to be working. As an Antigonish correspondent noted, "even those that are loud in their vociferations against Agricultural Societies shew, by their practice, that they are influenced by [the society's] example."[22] Despite such claims, it was clear that the deference so often manifested within the institutional framework of the societies would not always translate into deference from the orders of the unimproved.

These membership numbers tell us that few joined agricultural societies, but they do not tell us why. Certainly, for some, the cost of joining was prohibitive, whether it was simply an issue of not having 5s or 10s to spare or one of weighing the cost as an investment. But there were other issues. "An Experienced Farmer," writing from Cumberland County, left us one of the few extensive critiques of the workings of the agricultural improvers. He had much more practical concerns than those expressed either in the Halifax press or within the societies. His were rooted in the day-to-day difficulties of farm making in the infant colony. "Sir," he wrote after Young attended the Cumberland Agricultural Fair in the autumn of 1820,

> when you was here ... you said something about a new sistem of farming that we do not well understand. [Y]ou talk of lime mills[,] alternate croping and what not. Now as to lime, if it should enrich our land as no doubt it will we cannot afford to buy it and we are to[o] busy rearing stock and planting potatoes to go seeking limestone[.] I will tel you sir how we manage is that [we] do not join the Ag'l Society[;] we keep good stocks of cattle and often fat some oxen through the winter ... but we labour under some disadvantage for many of us owe the merchants ... [A]t that season of the year mony we must have [and] we must take what we can get for them or do worse.

Time and money, certainly two of the primary concerns of Young and the local improvers, were also foremost in the minds of many small farmers but for quite different reasons. The process of farm making was slow and expensive, and "we are not such fools as to pay 10s for

nothing[;] it is more mony than many of us can muster or if we can get
it we want to buy bread." But "An Experienced Farmer" carried his argument beyond the issue of dues. In this farmer's eyes, the societies
comprised an identifiable group. The "Agricultural class," as he labelled them, were arrogant fools, men who put their faith in improvement and the promise of markets:

> [T]hey say they are resolved to conquer all difficultys ... that the
> land will raise more wheat than they will want, [and] the surplus
> they will sell [so they can] soon get out of debt, [and] make ready
> to pay merchants who can afford to sell 50 per cent cheaper for
> prompt pay ... but we laugh at them and their Agricola plans.[23]

Such plans were the leisured design of those who dreamed of improving their farm production, reducing their costs, and market-oriented
agriculture. All of these may have been desirable ends, but many could
not afford the recommended route. Few could spare the time or the
money for "Agricola plans."

This was not passive non-participation. "An Experienced Farmer"
did not reduce the problem to poor farmers' inability to participate.
He actively rejected both the program and those who espoused it. His
position went well beyond the critiques of the merchant interests in
Halifax or the petty complaints from within the societies. While the arguments from these quarters were limited to tactical considerations regarding immediate interests, "An Experienced Farmer's" critique
struck at the heart of the problem for most settlers. He rejected the fat-
uous grandiosity of the program, not the possibility of farming; he
knew, whether Halifax merchants understood it or not, that there was
a farm economy out there that was in need of cash, off-farm wage labour, and daily toil, not cattle trysts and after-dinner toasts. We do not
know who "An Experienced Farmer" was. Despite the spelling and
grammar, something in his voice suggests that he was no "ordinary"
farmer. He may even have been a relatively wealthy and perhaps even
well-educated farmer (perhaps feigning limited literacy) who simply
opposed Young and his "Agricola plans" for any number of petty political reasons. But his awareness of the economic burden and daily concerns of the middling and lower ranks of rural society suggests that he
was indeed "experienced."

Evidence of such critiques, however, is rare. Young's ideas prevailed
among the societies and more broadly within the circles of the rural

elites. We can, for example, see some evidence of the local leaders' appreciation and understanding of much of what Young propounded on science, political economy, and nation building, but their enthusiasm was always much more specifically, and less abstractly, focused. William McKeen, for example, recognized the improvers' historic mission, and perhaps few of the local correspondents so succinctly caught the full flavour of their duties and rewards. After detailing some of the improvements already visible – better use of manures, turnips "beyond all conception," and other new productions "which had always been deemed impracticable" – McKeen maintained that "yet these are only foretastes of what we may expect from a well regulated society ... By unabated exertions and perseverance we may expect to make our country flourish and ourselves respectable." McKeen was emphasizing the combination of individual and national progress that lay at the heart of improvement. Few, however, captured the gravity of the cause like D.B. McNab, provincial surveyor and secretary of the Little Baddeck Agricultural Society, who argued that "to rescue the country from a state of impending ruin is the duty of every person who feels an interest in its welfare." These men understood their class's civic duty.[24]

Science was more frequently addressed, although not in a much more sophisticated fashion. Its general importance was assumed across the province and throughout the decades of improvement. "Industry, Experiments, inquiry and a creative impulse to improve every Agricultural Advantage must be the lever to depend on to secure success," wrote Martin MacPherson from Inverness, "Otherwise your Legislative Aid will be a Pail of water to saturate the Myriad Sands on Africa's desert ... no Corn will be in Egypt, no renovation manifest there." Few correspondents were so loquacious. Most, however, felt that it was important to situate themselves within the framework of science, although it was not something that required much in the way of elaboration. In the 1820s, in particular, society members emphasized the importance of science, often waxing effusively on its social and economic role. The society in Mabou was founded for the "express purpose of exciting a more lively spirit of industry and agricultural research," while the Parrsboro society enthused about how "the light of science began to illuminate the horizon."[25] Recalling his days travelling the countryside of Nova Scotia in 1842, Sir Charles Lyell claimed that he had "never traveled in any country where my scientific pursuits seemed to be better understood, or were more zealously forwarded than in Nova Scotia." As proof, he related the story of his experience with one "Blue Nose," "an entire stranger to me," who refused payment for the geologist's use of two teams of horses, "saying that he heard I was exploring the country at my own expense, and he wished to contribute his share towards the scientific investigations undertaken for the public good." Many agricultural society members were equally zealous. Simon Holmes, the secretary of the Springville society, took his scientific agriculture quite seriously, travelling to the United States for "a few months" in order to acquire "some further knowledge of agricultural Chemistry." Few could afford such a leisured pursuit. Fewer still, however, took their science so seriously as some in the Wallace society, who "carr[ied] the principle of Animal Physiology so far [as] to govern their own persons in accordance with its laws."[26]

Lectures appear to have been the most important means of communicating the latest advances in agricultural science. Most society meetings usually included either a lecture or a debate on "this important branch of improvement." In Pictou County in the 1840s the West River Agricultural Society could draw on young geologist J.W. Dawson, friend of Charles Lyell, future member of the Royal Society, and future chairman of the Geological Society of America, or perhaps on Thomas McCulloch, the Edinburgh-trained minister who taught most everything – including chemistry, geology, and political economy – at Pictou Academy; university-educated clergymen such as Alexander MacDonnell in Mabou and Thomas Trotter in Antigonish could also be called upon. Few societies were so well endowed with educated scientific men; most, however, had someone who felt qualified to speak. William McKeen, for example, had no formal scientific training, but in 1842 he delivered a "Speech on Chemistry" to the Mabou society. Similarly, James D.B. Fraser, the New Glasgow druggist, occasionally gave "highly interesting and popular" lectures to the East River Agricultural Society on chemistry. Or when one was pressed, articles from the *Encyclopaedia Britannica* could be read aloud.[27] Appearances would suggest that the authority to speak on such an occasion most often meant drawing on whoever was willing to step forward as an expert, invariably a man of high standing in both the agricultural society and the community: a merchant, a minister, a "gentleman," or someone else who signed himself "Esquire." This expertise was not uncontested. Judging at exhibitions, in particular, often drew charges of "partiality with all the ill-will and distrust following in its train." But the societies never acknowledged any bias. Judges, one writer explained, were "drawn from the most active and intelligent members," and this "very activity and intelligence enables them to draw the greater number of prizes." Such ill will may have further lessened the draw of both exhibitions and the societies, yet there was little indication that the societies themselves viewed this as a problem. Certainly, their repeated defences against such charges of partiality were expressions of their unshaken confidence in their own sagacity and disinterestedness.[28]

Some societies did generate scientific information of their own. Again, few of their actual results are available to us. Nonetheless, this drive for research was something that they clearly felt they needed to address, if only briefly. Most reports noted "experiments" or "trials" in which some members of the society were engaged, although the details were scanty. Many reports noted experiments with fertilizers (e.g., sea kelp, mussel mud, plaster of paris), and some societies even encouraged the invention or manufacture of farm equipment. One West River member built a "dynamometer," by which "the abilities of our plough-makers are brought to the test." Later reports were similarly lacking in detail. At Wallace, for example, members told of experiments with "scientific compost heaps" designed to "prevent the escape of amonical gases," but again the specifics were sketchy. Although the agricultural societies were constitutionally bound to engage in scientific experimentation, the closest thing to a report on any trials in Mabou in the 1840s was the report of McKeen's *financial* success in breeding sows.[29]

The societies provided popular science. The catholic, if clearly elite, participation was in part due to science's place in a still largely pre-professional society. As Martin Hewitt observes, pre-professional science still viewed itself as practical in the sense that its advancement was "sought through the widest possible diffusion of ... scientific knowledge."[30] Still, it is remarkable how little scientific information was put forth and how little diffusion actually occurred. McKeen's "Speech on Chemistry," for example, contained very little discussion of the chemical properties of anything; it was more a speech advocating the importance of knowing something of such matters. Indeed, while it might have inspired some to read more, it is hard to imagine anyone learning very much from the speech itself; rather, if our view of the societies is at all accurate, its reception could be best characterized as a reconfirmation of the social value of scientific knowledge. Thus society members' elevation as experts was an important symbolic act, and their activities positioned them as authorities. We might say that their authority gave them authority, reconfirming not only their

social positions but also their missionary function as purveyors of
proper conduct in both farming and daily life. For the agricultural societies, as for Young, scientific farming allowed one to stake out the
high ground.

The best judge of science was the market. Most annual reports freely
mixed discussions on the proper maintenance of "amonical gases" and
the virtues of agricultural chemistry with ones on profitability and the
state of the local market. The agricultural societies' correspondence
repeatedly emphasized the importance of market forces in determining the proper conduct for the "Scientific Agriculturalist." The societies experimented with new crops or seeds, made trials with fertilizers,
and extolled the efficiency of farm machinery, but the bottom line –
the measure of scientific proof – was always the same: whether the
product and method could be successful when used in farming "conducted as a business."[31] Both Young and later incarnations of the Central Board often pointed to flax as a potentially important crop, one
not only capable of clothing farm families but also suited to "industrial" uses. In Parrsboro, for example, members observed that while
flax had been "formerly cultivated very extensively," now, "in the absence of machinery and [given] the cheapness of cotton," both raising
the crop and making linen were not worth the "trouble and expence."
They understood that better markets lay elsewhere and that local economic factors precluded the use of flax: "until machinery [is] introduced to cheapen labor, it could not be extensively followed as a
business."[32] It is here that we best see the particular combinations of
science and political economy and of class and status as central to the
societies' functions.

There were a number of refrains in the reports of the local societies
over the course of forty years, but two stood out. The first, which was
economic, related to the problems posed by poor markets and weak
capital. The second, which was social, related to the firm division that
these men saw between improvers and everyone else. The first issue
was critical. Improvers all knew that without markets they could raise
no capital, and with no capital they could not improve their farms.
Robert Dawson of Pictou, for example, explained that a number of factors hindered the "progress of improvement" in the area but argued
that the "want of capital is the most formidable barrier ... to the improvement of Lands." For most, it was the apparently simple problem
of prices and markets that hindered improvement; as the secretary of
the River John Agricultural Society noted, the "want of a remunerating

price for cattle in the home market" meant that only the unstable New-foundland market was open, so few were willing to invest in new breeds. Similarly, John Stewart of New Glasgow regretted the lack of "progress" on the East River, a problem that he traced to the "low price of stock and grain – [and] the scarcity of money." There was, however, an additional and more pressing problem: poor markets were an obstacle, but "above all" the greatest problem was the "preju-dices existing in [nonmembers'] minds at innovations and a complete misunderstanding of the benefits at innovation and agricultural societ-ies."[33] For Stewart, and for many other improvers, better markets were both the means and the end, but ideas and attitudes mattered too.

The second major refrain that we see in the societies' correspondence was the improvers' clear sense of their own social positions, especially with respect to non-members. Such positions were marked by wealth, re-spectability, and the capacity to display one's superior taste and culture. The practice of emulation, then, meant that the enlightened few could point out the pitfalls of inferior methods to the unenlightened many. Al-though, as noted earlier, they were both less ambitious and less ostenta-tious than Young, local improvers nevertheless demonstrated a clear agreement with him on the role of leadership, and for the most part they too seemed to subscribe to a belief in a properly ordered society in which they formed the respectable element. Many, for example, shared something of Young's patrician vision of the countryside. Again, their images were not as grand as Young's, but they too believed that the farmer should seek not only subsistence but also "refinement." Agricul-tural improvement meant more than improved yields; it also meant an improved public appearance. Among the surer signs of improvement described by the Pictou society's report in 1843 was a "greater taste dis-played in the arrangement and performance of the farmer's duties." "Formerly," recalled the president of the Wallace society of the time be-fore his society's single year of existence, "everything connected with farming was done slovenly and without taste. Now horses must be in good order, harnesses neat, ridges straight and of equal width – whether potatoes or turnips – drawn with as much precision and taste; and alto-gether evincing a strong desire to become more and more acquainted with the Science of Agriculture." Like Young, these respectable inhabit-ants collapsed the science of improvement into a cultural position marked by the tasteful appearance of their farms and by the "good or-der" that they evinced.[34] For these farmers, improvement could be mea-sured in ways other than crop production.

Perhaps the best demonstrations of cultural superiority came in the various public displays of virtuous practice put on by societies in the 1840s and 1850s. The annual exhibitions were the most common and probably also the most important. Not only were the rewards of improvement reaped here in the form of premiums and prizes, but they were also public spectacles where these improvements and improvers could stand as such. In smaller centres, such as Mabou, the exhibitions were held on a member's farm, usually that of one of the executive. But in larger centres such as Pictou or Amherst, the fair was held in the town market. Exhibitions, of course, were locations where the products of improved agriculture could be displayed and where the theory of emulation might be put into practice in the most public, if not particularly effective, of manners. Although membership in the societies was consistently low and drawn from a narrow base, and although the prize winners comprised an even smaller cross-section of the population, the exhibitions opened the societies to a significantly greater audience. In the 1820s some ploughing matches and cattle shows drew fairly impressive crowds, although it is hard to tell exactly how large these crowds were.[35] By the 1840s the societies were charging a small admission; the West River society, for example, charged 3d (by 1857 this had increased to 7½d, with children being charged 4d). Judging by the concerns over rowdiness and the potential revenues from admission fees, in at least some cases the crowds must have been substantial.

Notable too were the annual inspections that the West River society made of members' farms between 1842 and 1861. Each autumn, members met at the home of one of the executive before proceeding to march up the river and then back down the other side inspecting the quality, the productivity, and of course the tastefulness of their own farms. And each year, members were always impressed with their own success: "Wherever your committee went they beheld a desire for improvement to prevail to an extent which they scarcely anticipated. They saw greater attention paid to the collection and performance of the farmer's duties. They saw greater attention paid to the collection and preservation of manures. Compost heaps were seen ... and they found that some of the improved agricultural implements which your society has been in a great measure the means of introducing were rapidly coming into general use." After the inspection the members retired, usually to a tavern, for the annual dinner (at a cost of 5s – two days wages for a farm labourer or an unskilled miner). There was much conviviality and no small amount of self-congratulation as the members toasted themselves and their cause. On one occasion, there were fifteen such toasts before the members dispersed at midnight; the secretary no doubt understated what had transpired when he noted that "much friendly feeling was evinced on the occasion." As Graeme Wynn comments on these inspections, visiting their own farms provided a "ready and usually satisfying yardstick of the advance of progress."[36] It seems important to add, however, that while these inspections served the purposes of self-affirmation and self-congratulation, they also served as ritual extensions of the public displays at the exhibitions. There must have been no small amount of theatricality in the view of society members parading out of town and across the countryside. Indeed, it is hard to come away from the West River society's papers without noting a greater concern with fraternity and the public display of the members' superior methods and good taste than with scientific agriculture. Not only was their own progress the best yardstick with which to measure improvement, but it was evidently the only one that stuck in their minds.

These displays of cultural superiority hinged primarily on class, being the means by which the improvers showed off their class's achievements, specifically what could be realized by the properly regulated activities of the enlightened. Such displays amounted to some men demonstrating their superiority over other men. Thus it is on one of these ritual traipses up the river that we encounter, very briefly, one of the few acknowledgments of the existence of women in the countryside. The tour of 1861 was "most agreeably and profitably spent" visiting the farms and homes of the members. In a list of these agreeable moments, the secretary included "conversing with the farmers' fair wives and daughters and ... enjoy[ing] their hospitality." That it took forty years for us to encounter the wives and daughters of these public-spirited men and that when we do they are providing hospitality in their kitchens might not surprise us. It seems clear that these women's positioning in the domestic sphere was yet another mark of the respectability, and class position, of their husbands and fathers; a concomitant of the men's public respectability was the representation of their wives' private propriety. These acts were public demonstrations of their wealth, influence, and respectability, and the West River society's minutes were the publicly recorded representation of these demonstrations.[37]

On only four other occasions do we meet women. In the first three cases, we find two women included in the prize lists for the Pictou Agricultural Society Exhibitions in each of the years 1842, 1843, and 1852.

In each instance, the women claimed first and second prizes in the butter and cheese competitions, but these were clearly extraordinary exceptions that saw a few women in the official, public record of the societies make brief forays beyond their consignment to the private realm. Although these women won in areas typically assumed to be female-dominated production, the fact remains that men won the same prizes – and claimed victory in other "female" employments such as cloth production – in every other year. The fourth encounter is also in Pictou, this time on the East River. In 1825 James MacGregor proudly announced the completion of a new flax mill upriver. The mill was constructed by Alexander Grant, who, despite the "powerful prejudices of his neighbours ... [and] no little scoffing ... finished it in workmanlike manner."[38] Much of this prejudice, MacGregor noted with a dry wit and a hint of misogyny, came from "many of the good women [who] were sure it would never answer." But "young" Grant was not discouraged. His "improving" "public spirit" triumphed, and "now [the women] strive for who will be foremost to it." Like the men who were not converted to agricultural improvement, these women for a time had stood as obstacles to, and the objects of, improvement.

TEMPERANCE AND OTHER IMPROVEMENTS

When the provincial pot ran dry, as it did in 1826 and then again in 1861, so too did institutional enthusiasm for the diffusion of agricultural knowledge. As their various demises illustrate all too clearly, the agricultural societies derived much of their existence less from an ideal of civic virtue than from their access to state largesse. Nonetheless, much of the improvers' energy and enthusiasm relied on an ideological program that charged them with a historic mission. The program for improvement did not die with the end of provincial funding.[39] Improvement was a much larger social program than simply agricultural societies, and a range of other improvement associations offset their demise.

Pictou County was the fraternal centre of the province. In the 1820s and 1830s residents could join the Caledonia Lodge (Masonic), the Dorcas Society (a "society of young ladies" making clothing for the poor), the Pictou Friendly Society, the Pictou Female Benevolent Society, the Pictou Squaremen's Society, the Pictou Sabbath School Society, the Pictou Auxiliary Bible Society, the West River Ladies' Society, the Pictou Temperance Society (with branches on both the East and West

Rivers), the Pictou Indian Civilization Society, or the Pictou Subscription Library Society. Some of these associations would continue into the 1840s and 1850s, when they would be joined by the reconstituted agricultural societies, mechanics' institutes, and the Pictou Literary and Scientific Society.[40] Like the agricultural societies, the Literary and Scientific Society was eclectic in its offerings; but within this eclecticism we still see the general emphasis on the progress of science and society, if with a thoroughly popular twist. A lecture "on gases ... accompanied by experiments of much interest and beauty" by "Dr Johnston" in February 1842 was more an entertainment than a demonstration of practical science: "After the lecture, the Exhilarating Gass [sic] was administered to several members, and afforded a good deal of amusement." The next week's lecture, however, returned to more serious matters with the Reverend McKinley's lecture on the "spirit of civilization." That members could move so effortlessly between the amusement provided by the "Exhilarating Gass" and the apparent gravity of the "spirit of civilization" suggests something of the leisured domain of improvement. Yet, while leisured, such events were not trivial. In Cape Breton, J.P. Ward presented a lecture to the Sydney Literary and Scientific Society on "Modern Improvements," wherein, one brief report noted, he offered a "comprehensive view of ... important modern inventions [and] showing the vast superiority of the conditions of the moderns." Ward's description of the "extraordinary progress" of the past century was intended to do more than pass the time.[41] Like so many men of his generation, Ward marvelled at these feats, but he also wished to align himself with their success. It would be difficult to think of a better prop for one's collective identity than a century's progress or the spirit of civilization.

Little else remains of these lectures or of the proceedings of these groups, but their spirit was almost certainly captured in the writings of numerous editorials and letters that appeared in the local press. The editors of the *Colonial Patriot* caught the instructive spirit with their description of the "purpose" of their newspaper: "it will invigorate the agricultural and other societies. It will diffuse solid information and correct morals, and prove to every individual a stimulation to exertion." This confident, paternal tone was as clear with poor farmers, women, "Indians," and other peoples mired in tradition and the "deepest shades of night."[42] Typically, newspapers detailed methods for improving economy and efficiency. The *Mechanic and Farmer*, for example, regularly featured news and columns of interest to its stated audience. The short-lived *Bee*,

edited by James Dawson, took its name and presumably its purpose from
a popular Scottish encyclopaedia, James Anderson's eighteen-volume *Bee*
("calculated to disseminate useful knowledge among all ranks of people
at a small expense"). The *Colonial Standard*, the *Colonial Patriot*, the *Pictou
Observer*, and the *Bee* regularly published (or, very often, republished) columns on practical farming matters, while Halifax papers, especially the
Acadian Recorder, the Sydney-based *Spirit of the Times*, and the *Cape Breton
News*, also featured agricultural news and advice. Indeed, anyone with access to a newspaper would have had plenty of agricultural information to
sort through.[43]

While published in towns, such newspapers published material that
emphasized their identification with the countryside, and each was
very much aware of its role in addressing local issues in an appropriately instructive manner. Pictou County newspapers, especially, illustrated a keen awareness of improvement, particularly as it applied to
the variety of forms of useful employment to be found in the area.
Each week the *Mechanic and Farmer* included two columns: "The Farmers' Department" and "The Mechanics' Department."[44] "Mechanics" –
that is, skilled workmen – played an important role in these papers'
representation of the improved society, occupying what the *Colonial
Patriot* described as the "middle rank" of society, which was "Equally removed from poverty and riches, from the expectations of wealth, and
the fear of destitution." Yet, as had been the case with Young's imagined settlers, there was a danger of complacency among the mechanics
as well, who might be tempted by the prospect of an easy subsistence in
freshly turned soil: "A mechanic with very little intelligence may creep
through life with comfort ... but every man should strive to reach the
top of his profession ... we wish therefore to urge upon every trades-
man the necessity of aspiring after something more than an ignoble
existence." Always didactic, newspapers, like the agricultural societies,
consistently sought the higher ground of instruction. Whether they
were addressing the drinking habits of miners and mechanics, or the
"*poor* fishermen" who "loiter about the shore, drinking bad rum, and
grumbling that our neighbours from the States are taking all the fish,"
or the farmers who were "embarrassed with debts," newspaper writers
met the challenges of the day by explaining the proper course of behaviour to their social inferiors.[45]

Improvement was not limited to the agricultural poor or to the labouring classes. Indeed, almost anything could be an "improvement":
a new road or a bridge, a new school or more money for schools, and

even geological change could mark an improvement.[46] But the idea was most fully embodied in the various societies dedicated to improving people. Mechanics' institutes, for example, also amounted to improvement programs, as did the literary and scientific societies and the societies for the propagation of the gospel. Here, education – that is, the diffusion of knowledge – underpinned improvement, although there was some variation in exactly what this meant. "B," writing from River John, saw the "diffusion of useful knowledge" as a class issue. Improvement could be a leveller, for without it, someone "should happen to get the start of numbers of his fellow men by having a little money in his pocket ... [while] others [could] be kept back." "A Friend of Improvement" saw it as important for "every patriotic lover of this country," especially as it was related to the maintenance of "proper government" and central to "the rise and fall of nations": "Remembering that upon the dissemination of useful knowledge, the formation of correct political opinion, the inculcation of honourable independence, and virtuous principles, rest the firm basis of a throne." This writer believed in the importance of "liberal and enlightened principles" that would help to "establish sound, firm, enlarged, liberal and correct ideas of political and religious things." His emphasis on things both useful and correct and his comment that "correct knowledge" would help to "root out the abominable spirit of radicalism and discontent without cause" suggested limits to his liberality.[47] Situated so broadly and resting on such disparate foundations, improvement came to possess a crucial importance within almost every level of colonial society. Moreover, to this breadth could be added a great moral depth.

Agricultural improvement might have appeared commonsensical, but it was given much greater weight through its location within a broader discourse of moral improvement. As a duty, improvement carried a strong moral component, one that could operate within numerous spheres of social life. "A Friend of Good Order" wrote specifically to congratulate the *Colonial Patriot* on its championing of "good" causes, at least as compared with the "evils ... of all the public prints in Halifax."[48] These evil "doctrines ... would destroy the good order of society, and terminate in an unhingement of our whole moral code." Here, there was an obviously Tory emphasis on order and morality, but this writer also noted that he and his fellows were also "friends of improvement" and that, as such, they were not adverse to change. The addition of a moral language meant that many in these organizations came to represent themselves as being driven by a proselytizing spirit.

Like the foreign missionary societies, whose tasks included evangeliz-
ing the "Heathen, Mohammedan, and Anti-christian countries," and
also like ancillary groups such as the Pictou Indian Civilization Society,
which sought to "encourage industry in agricultural pursuits ... to dis-
courage vice ... [and to provide] the most proper means of advancing
['Indian'] moral improvement," agricultural improvers too saw it as
their task to bring the word to the unimproved "heathens" around
them.[49] It mattered little whether it was the word of God or the word
of science: those who felt morally and intellectually secure in their
worldviews disseminated improvement.

Temperance provides the best illustration. While temperance was
much more clearly centred on moral improvement, the overlap in
both membership and language between temperance and agricultural
societies suggests a high degree of cross-fertilization. Many officials in
the agricultural societies were also leaders in the temperance societies.
In Antigonish, in addition to his many other functions, the Reverend
Thomas Trotter was president of the Sydney County Temperance Society; in Inverness, William McKeen, the president of the Mabou Agricultural Society, also presided over the local Temperance Society. In
Pictou we see the range of usual names all serving on the executives of
one or both of the Pictou Temperance Union or the Pictou County
Temperance League – James MacGregor, Ebenezer McLeod, Robert
Dawson, James Dawson, George Smith, Robert McKay, Abraham
Patterson, Robert Grant, and James D.B. Fraser – while J.W. Dawson
was a founder of the later (1850s) Pictou Total Abstinence Society and
wrote pamphlets for the cause. Much the same was true in Cumberland County.[50] And not surprisingly, when the literary societies and
mechanics' institutes took off in the 1840s and 1850s, we again find
many of the same names.[51]

Whether the object of improvement was religiosity, temperance, agricultural practice, or other moral behaviours – and whether the "heathens" were foreign or domestic – improvement societies employed
much the same language to describe their context, their actions, and
their purpose. Like agricultural improvement, temperance was a duty.
Above and beyond not drinking, the duty of temperance advocates was
to join temperance societies so that they might further the cause. Here
too the example provided by the enlightened was crucial. The St Mary's
Temperance Society (in eastern Pictou County) utilized the prevailing
combination of enlightenment and mission; "believing that [they were]
in the path of duty," the society's members described temperance as a

"glorious cause" and an "enlightened" activity.[52] In their logging and farming community, where "few places afforded darker prospects for success," they had to "combat the long established custom" of drinking rum while working. Many were of the "opinion that some stimulant is necessary to enable a person to undergo hard labour." Their methodology too was similar; like members of the agricultural societies, they relied on a selfless leader to step forward and initiate the dissemination process. "No active measures," this writer continued, had been taken against this "vice ... until the truly laudable exertions of W. Taylor." A "gentleman actuated by a noble zeal," Taylor started the first temperance organization in their community, and now "men [were] become[ing] more enlightened and more alive to their true interests ... the light [of 'enlightened temperance'] is gradually diffusing itself."[53]

An important difference in the temperance societies was that more scope was allowed for women to participate, although this was contentious. The *Colonial Patriot* could criticize women "who make high pretensions of being patrons of every good work," but when it came to the "Temperance cause," they were criticized for "remain[ing] behind their gauzes and ribbons, as if drunken husbands and children and brothers was no concern of theirs."[54] "A Friend of Propriety," on the other hand, wished to "exclude women altogether" because it was "folly" for women to be "publicly binding themselves to refrain from tippling." If women wanted to have such an influence, they were urged to utilize their "charms" by "reserv[ing] their smiles for the sober and temperate."[55] While disagreeing over whether women should participate, both understood the basis of any woman's actions to be the home; the issue was simply whether, in a case that so connected the private and public spheres, women could take an ever-so-slight step into the public. Women's presence was often simply erased. In dismissing the St Mary's Temperance Society's claims of success, Alexander Lewis could observe that in claiming "upwards" of forty members, the society had misled the public by including "twenty female subscribers." Thus its account "[left] but a small balance." "A Friend of Propriety" understood why women might wish to join – as he understood why men might seek female influence in this "grovelling and unfeminine" matter – but he believed that their influence would be best exerted from within the home and marriage. To bring them out of this "bond" was to "tempt the more virtuous and amiable half of our race to throw away that high sense of propriety which is their greatest charm, and on which their influence to purify and polish us chiefly depends." In the public record, temperance allowed some space for women but offered them only a highly restricted role.

Women, however, did more than attend temperance meetings. They were often aggressive public campaigners for temperance. As Gail Campbell demonstrates was the case in New Brunswick, women signed temperance petitions and generally attempted to maintain pressure on politicians.[56] But as more men stepped forward to claim a share of public space, they increasingly pushed women into the background, even on an issue in which they grudgingly admitted that women had some interest. These contests would have important repercussions within the mid-nineteenth-century process of state formation, insofar as it entailed what some writers have referred to as the "imposition and consolidation of masculine rule."[57] Middle-class men in this period increasingly pushed their claim to political power on the basis of their civic (that is, public) virtues; these virtues, both of the above writers surely would have agreed, were masculine domains. Although women were not formally disfranchised until the middle of this period, details of the particular forms that liberal democracy would assume were being debated here. As middle-class men strove for a more secure place in the politics of this emerging country, aspects of the very ways that it was coming to define itself were coming to define a liberal government as a masculine preserve. These men were crafting a broader, more participatory politics, but lines of exclusion were still being drawn. As we have already seen, this was certainly the case in terms of property and an ongoing concern over democratic tendencies; it was also clear that the patriarchal-state model was firmly imbedded, as the new politics clung tenaciously to the masculine ideals of the patriarchal form. Let the societies admit women, argued "A Friend of Propriety," but "only as nature has so far conformed to our sex by adding to them the masculine appendage of the beard."[58]

Agricultural improvement and temperance not only came to occupy the time and energy of the same peoples but also assumed a similar place within communities. In both cases, leaders represented themselves as possessing similarly noble goals, creating the same kind of enthusiasm for an undeniably good cause and exhibiting a mastery of their future-defining missions. Church-run missionary societies too premised the need for their activities on people's lacking the "means of instruction" (and here they meant missionaries as much as Bibles). For those who sought leadership roles, improvement provided precisely the kind of virtuous display that greatly enhanced both the legitimacy of one's claim to

virtue and the path to progress. In the societies' ability to define this
ground, they drew energy and resources from each other. As an Inverness County correspondent observed, "no Public Measure ... ever introduced in this district" had "met such a cordial and unanimous spirit
of Support" as the recently organized agricultural society, "except perhaps the Temperance Cause."[59] It mattered little that their actual numbers were small; the societies were not inconsequential. Even before the
temperance societies actually referred to their activities as "crusades,"
they pursued their goals with both militancy and a clear sense of mission: intemperance was an evil that had to be conquered.[60] Readers of
the *Missionary Register*, a monthly magazine of the Presbyterian Church
in Pictou, could read about the "Home Mission" on one page and then
turn to the "Foreign Mission" to read about the "low state" of religion in
Mabou and the "cruelties of heathenism" in Java. Indeed, one Cape Breton temperance speaker linked alcohol directly with the "Oriental"
threat to Western christendom.[61] In an age of moral certainty, an evil
could be readily identified; in an age of empire and colonization, a strategy of conquest could be quickly devised.

The parallels between these different improvement schemes – both
in terms of personnel and ideas – are striking. If men could simply assume the properly situated moral basis of their actions, wholly different – or at least clearly separable – locations for intervention could
effortlessly acquire the same moral force. Interestingly, however, improvement was not simply a one-way movement. It was not simply a
case of a clearly defined moral cause (such as temperance) adding to
the legitimacy of a much less clearly delineated issue (such as agriculture). Increasingly, secular improvement issues also came to assume a
moral standing.

In 1833 another "Friend to Improvement," this one from Antigonish, was pleased to observe the formation in his area of "a society ...
for the free discussion of practical points of political economy." Not
only, he maintained, would this society "invite the attention of our
young men to matters of great practical importance," but it would
also "likewise indirectly accomplish the objects of temperance without
any of that moral quackery and empiricism which is so much in
vogue." Invoking "principles of economy," another editorial praised
both temperance organizations and the efforts of good citizens battling "young villains." "S.N." argued that the "cupidity of gain" was a
cause of intemperance, and another decried intemperance as "a waste
of property," while numerous temperance writers measured the cost

of intemperance in pounds sterling. The Reverend John MacLean asked: "Can a Nation prosper with such a drain on her resources, and such a drawback on her industry, as the use of liquors occasions?"[62] Sounding very much like a reformed John Young, he said that it took "no argument to shew that the community would be very much more likely to rise to independence and comfort" if less money was spent on alcohol. Indeed, he went much further: "[D]oubtless much, very much, of the poverty to be found ... in this section of the Country ... may be traced to the intemperate habits of the people. It is doubtless owing to the awful waste of time and property, and the careless habits which the consumption of Ardent Spirits is everywhere producing, that our Fisheries and many of our farms are so unproductive, and ... do not improve the means of wealth which are within their reach, and have therefore little to give in exchange for the commodities of other countries."[63] Both temperance and improvement stood at the forefront of progress; indeed, this was the motto of the Pictou branch of the Temperance Watchmen in North America, formed on the West River in 1857: "Temperance, Humanity, Progress." Thus Richard Smith, the manager of the General Mining Association and no enemy of gain, could argue that the "road to illimitable degrees of wealth and prosperity is now open to our march, and nothing but intemperance and laziness can retard our progress."[64]

Jotham Blanchard, editor of the *Colonial Patriot*, provides us with a clear illustration of how material improvement could quietly assume a moral grounding. In early 1828 he authored a series of six editorials on the benefits of improvement and the value of mutual-improvement societies. The first of these outlined his general argument.[65] Both the moral and political benefits were posed against the threat of an ignorant population: "At this moment," Blanchard informed his readers,

in our country, thousands, and many thousands too ... are going rapidly to destruction for the want of some object of sufficient interest to divert their attention from places and practices calculated to fix upon them habits which will lead to their ruin with as much certainty as falling bodies are drawn toward the centre of the earth.

This sound moral basis – and its scientifically demonstrable counterscenario – was as important to the individual as to the "prosperity, and probably the existence, of a Government," for it was "from the ignorant that the aspiring demagogue acts to effect his designs and usurp the rights of a nation." It was paramount not only that the improvers offer these people "useful knowledge" but also that these "many thousands" be made useful. Blanchard, widely held up as a radical democrat, here sounds much like the arch-Tory Governor Wentworth. The reforming newspaperman further argued that the "most important consideration" was the improvement associations' promotion of good moral tendencies. But he did not, even in the paragraph devoted to moral tendencies, describe moral practices; he described "useful" practices:

> It is not frowns, it is not arguments, that will correct or prevent these practices. It is presenting a substitute which is not less interesting but more useful, that alone will prove an effectual bulwark against the vicious habits in the young, and set them in a way that leads to usefulness, respectability and happiness.

In effect, Blanchard was arguing that useful practices were moral practices. The final point was that moral and political improvement was economical – a point that may seem to be (and indeed may have been) intended only to argue that these associations need not cost money, although given the other advantages, this proviso should hardly have seemed necessary. But it *was* necessary because, as the editorial makes progressively clear, the task at hand was as much about economics and government as it was about morality:

> In many cases it would be an actual saving of expense; for as it would turn the attention of the members to subjects of general utility, it would consequently divert it from others which are more expensive, and less useful ... the expence of time or money would in no case be perceptible, and in many cases there would be an actual saving of both.

Blanchard's economic calculus of morality and governance positioned "use" at the centre of a properly regulated society; economic utility lit the path to harmony, righteousness, and good government. Knowledge and morality promoted industry, which encouraged order, and "the friends of temperance and good order," as the Pictou Temperance Society referred to its members, embodied all of these noble traits in their progressive vision of the future.[66]

Temperance also worked on the body and on the individual, those social bodies that in aggregate made up society. Citing prominent American and English physicians and scientists, Pictou's Rev. John MacLean minutely detailed the effects of alcohol on the liver, the blood, and the mind. He described autopsies in which a physician claimed to have drawn pure whiskey from a dead man's brain, and he asked whether it was surprising, then, that alcohol's permanent and temporary "derangements" caused "crime, poverty, and misery" as well as "that most terrible of diseases, insanity." Another writer linked the mind and the body, emphasizing the "[h]ealth of body, cheerfulness of mind, simple manners, unperverted feelings, and free influenced thoughts." However, this was a description not of the benefits of temperance but of the "rewards and recommendations of a life widely devoted to rural pursuits" and of agriculture as a "profession" worthy of "Young Men of Family." Not only were the effects similar, but so too were the larger outcomes. Indeed, this writer could link these effects as causes in weightier social matters:

> Our national prosperity would be established upon the most solid of all foundations: for agriculture itself would be immensely improved by it; and as the farms of these more enlightened occupiers would exhibit not only valuable course of experiment, but the most improved modes of husbandry, the neighbouring tenantry could not fail to observe and adopt whatever they saw practiced with success. It is hardly necessary to remark that from such a body of spirited, intelligent men, a provincial magistracy might be appointed with the greatest advantage to the country; as none are more likely to execute the laws with impartiality than those whose habits of life render them perfectly independent of the executive life. For the same reason, in the Representation, many of them would naturally be considered by the people as persons eminently qualified to become their public guardians and trustees ... On the encouragement which this mode of life holds out to early marriage among this worthy class, consequently to regular conduct and an increase of population, we could expatiate with pleasure.[67]

Here, farming was both public and private; it was being defined as the surest location where the two could be united. "Rural pursuits," at least as practised by the "more enlightened occupiers," encouraged the "regular conduct" of individuals and the family, envisioned as a sound corps from which to draw both the local magistracy and provincial representatives and as the foundation for the national prosperity. In short, all the levels of government – from the individual and the family to the local, the provincial, and finally the national – could be traced back to a sound rural economy. The farmer could be identified as the ideal liberal citizen: he was healthy in mind and body, he married young and had many children, he was a public servant, he contributed to the economy, he governed his own behaviour, and he was a he. The Reverend MacLean (and many others in the local agricultural societies) simply would have added that he was also temperate. This collapsing of the social and the biological was common in Victorian society, and we should not be surprised to find such reiterations in the colonial countryside. It brought together a modern discourse of science with the moral imperative of an improving world; it effectively rationalized moral regulation, simultaneously authorizing elite guidance and shifting responsibility onto the shoulders of the unimproved.

By the 1840s agricultural societies could be seen to embody all that was good in colonial society. The promotion of agriculture had not transformed government policy on matters such as tariffs or even on the more proximate question of funding for the societies. But the societies had succeeded in elevating agriculture, husbandry, and life on the land to the status of self-evident, civic virtues in public discourse. Whereas twenty years earlier public discussion had hinged on elevating the peasantry, now the agricultural "profession" was commonly put forward as the basis for individual self-government, the family, a proper politics, and the state.

CONCLUSION

Agricultural improvement, observed the secretary of the River John Agricultural Society late in the winter of 1845, had brought with it "wealth, comfort, and respectability ... [W]ith industry and perseverance the farming community can command all the necessaries of life within themselves."[68] It was undoubtedly true that many could provide all the "necessaries of life," but many were closer to this margin than others. Later that year, when potato blight struck much of north-eastern Nova Scotia, the staple of the poor rotted in the ground. By the winter of 1847 reports of people starving in backland settlements offered cruel reminders of the precarious bases of this "comfort." Petitions came from various parts of Pictou County describing "destitute families" and "desperate cases," including starving backlanders and Mi'kmaq, and warning of the "fearful consequences" that might occur if there was no intervention.[69] There were also crippling financial losses that pushed many farms over the edge. In general, of course, it was the poor who suffered most severely.

Local elites responded to the crisis – and some were hurt by it – but few suffered. Indeed, as we saw earlier, many merchants benefited from the record amounts of funds provided for relief.[70] The agricultural societies also turned their attention toward distributing new seed and occasionally provided some food relief. But even at the worst point in the famine, they were just as concerned with importing "superior" breeding stock, new machinery, and guano. While some people starved, others boasted about cattle exports and fretted over the high cost of labour.[71]

Improvement owed its reception and implementation to its adherents' place in the colonial world. In appealing to the enlightened men of the community, "Agricola" had asked the societies to take on a mission that accorded with his sense of natural social leadership. It seems clear that the local improvers too assumed a society organized by rank and had similar understandings of government. If, beyond their local sphere, these improvers might have recognized their subordinate positions, they also well understood their elite status within their communities. The societies' reports frequently asserted the much-anticipated "general improvement," but it was also clear that this was unattainable for some. Here, "general" appears to have meant improvement only within a certain segment of society. This was true in the 1820s, as the following analysis of the situation in Cumberland County attests:

> Your committee … cannot but congratulate the society on the obvious benefits derived from this institution in the improvements that have been made; and by the spirit of industry and enterprize that has been diffused. Gladly would your committee announce that these were universal, but this is evidently not the case; the indolent nothing can reclaim, no stimulus can excite, nor example arouse. In these we expect no reformation.[72]

And it remained true through the 1840s and 1850s. This was equally evident in campaigns to "civilize" the Mi'kmaq. Provincial government officials were quite confident that they had done as much to civilize "Indians" as possible: "if they do not avail themselves of the advantages thus offered, it is owing to their own nature and habits." The same sentiment is evident in this anonymous 1847 poem from a member of the Pictou Literary and Scientific Society:

> Not that I blame the present race of man
> For the sad lot of this devoted clan

Much has been done for the falling tree to raise,
And cheer the evening of their fleeting days ...
He looks around ... where once the altar stood,
Torn by the plough, and swept with harrows rude;
Sees the towers and spires in rich succession rise,
Where once their warriors bled – where now their chieftain lies.[73]

Despite the improvers' shared proselytizing spirit, their declared belief in emulation, and the possibilities for instruction, society members remained much more interested in fraternity than in equality, and most of their correspondence fully dripped with disdain for the unimproved. In all these cases – the poor law, Indian policy, and the unimproved – the improvers were saying: we can only demonstrate, not make them emulate; if they fail, it is their own fault.

Most writers have assumed that agricultural societies were simply not necessary in colonies where land was cheap and labour dear.[74] This was less true in Nova Scotia, with its limited agricultural land and no immediate frontier. But as we have seen, the problem that hindered the success of the provincial societies was not that the adaptation of European *farming* technologies was necessarily inappropriate to the Nova Scotia environment but the assumption that European *social* technologies were appropriate for a colonial society. If, as has been argued here, the assumption of a free but ordered society of men underpinned both the larger program and its local implementation, then it seems that the societies ultimately served only to reinforce and in some cases to strengthen the social positions of their principals. Agricola may or may not have been correct in believing that the problem with Nova Scotia farmers was the indolence allowed them by still young soils and relatively easy circumstances, but he was certainly onto something. The relative ease of circumstances for many Nova Scotia farmers also meant that they did not need to join agricultural societies, read agricultural treatises, parade their virtuosity, or even listen to the advice of their self-appointed guides to wellbeing. Of course, Nova Scotia's climate offered no easy subsistence, and the potato famine made clear how perilous this equation was. But the simple fact remained that improvement's audience was limited not only by the choices of the province's peoples but also by the fact that many farmers simply had no pressing need to accept another's idea of what constituted improvement. This material context is crucial and an important reminder that there is little evidence of a distinct culture that we can describe in opposition to that of the improvers. Undoubtedly, many were not impressed by the public displays and the often clearly selfish motivations of some of the elite, but the evidence suggests a more inchoate opposition.

The societies' emphasis on status and economic returns highlights one of the key features of improvement *not* emphasized by its Nova Scotia adherents: the improvement of the soil through manure and a proper system of convertible husbandry. Both Young and to a lesser extent the local improvers noted the importance of these factors, but in none of their writings does the permanent improvement of the soil displace returns in cash or status as the ultimate end. Local reports faithfully repeated their claims that farmers were paying greater attention to manures, and some evidence includes discussions of replenishing fertility. But few backed up this talk with cash. A few societies offered prizes for fallow and manure in the 1820s, but by the 1840s this issue had been displaced by the weightier matters of importing livestock and machinery. In Nova Scotia it would not be possible to claim, as Steven Stoll does for the eastern United States, that improvers' saw permanent productivity as their central goal.[75] Young discussed fertility, manures, and convertible husbandry, and he wanted to build Nova Scotia's prosperity "on the solid and permanent basis of Agricultural improvement."[76] But maintaining this prosperity was never as important as achieving it. Unlike in the US, where declining productivity was the problem, in Nova Scotia the issue was raising it. Not only was Nova Scotia not as good a location for agriculture as Pennsylvania, but it was also a much younger colony. A century of poor habits had robbed many American farms of their fertility; Nova Scotia improvers appeared more intent on catching up. If the improvers possessed a guiding ethic, it was rooted more in productivity than in permanence. As we saw earlier, by mid-century many Nova Scotia farms had achieved some level of prosperity. Undoubtedly, part of this had come about through the use of some of the ideas and technologies advocated by the improvers. But given that few farmers actively took up Young's patriotic call, their success suggests that they were much less bound by bad habits and ancient prejudices than the improvers believed.

Still, the societies were important. The critical issue here is the role that improvement societies played in shaping a middle-class discourse of governance. Specifically, we have focused on middle-class men's persistent efforts to stake their claim on "the public" through public service. We have also seen, however, that agricultural societies were, in effect, state agencies. Not only were they funded by and responsible to the state, but they also comprised in large part the very people who represented the state within the numerous communities of the area. That these societies maintained some autonomy did not alter their part in the fabric of rule. That they represented only a tiny segment of the population did not make them inconsequential. These were the same men who disbursed road monies every spring and the same men who might (or might not) serve the court order that represented the end of a family's credit. Some were the same men for whom thousands of others voted in provincial and local elections. As such, these men may not have required either the possible material rewards of agricultural-society membership or the status that such activities engendered, but they certainly felt that they did. It would be far too crass to argue simply that the alignment between state officials and improvement-society members proves our case here, just as it would be too cynical to argue that these men's various public services were driven only by selfish motivations and a desire for power. Whether we are examining evidently genuine efforts toward a general improvement or the evidently selfish motivations of someone like William McKeen in Mabou, most believed that improvement would be a greater good. That they could see this while talking only among themselves was, however, an indication of their acceptance of a society governed by those who stepped forward. They saw what their social locations allowed them to see.

To emphasize the quest for status and social position while acknowledging only that such status was class-based is surely to miss the ways that, and the means by which, status was also configured in particular forms of "manly" behaviour. Terms such as "enlightened" and "improved" carried associations of status that combined elements of gender and class – often in not clearly separable ways. Such public-spirited enterprises were, as John Young observed, not only "useful in setting a noble example" and encouraging the "national prosperity" but also "more manly." Not to improve, he maintained, "betrayed a want of manly firmness."[77] In relation to other men – that is, the nonimproving "plodholes" – the improvers demonstrated their superiority as a class. In relation not only to women but also to less manly men, this very public-spiritedness was a reaffirmation of improvers' hold on masculine superiority. Together, unimproved confirmed these men's hold on the proper relations of authority in private and public domains. Certainly, among the elite, but probably also among others, all of this was situated within a view that understood such order to be basic and essential to a society that was ordered, naturally, into hierarchical ranks. For some, joining a society was an act of extending one's already existing position within the public domain, but for many others, it was a means to extend one's private patriarchal privileges into public view.

This ordered, patriarchal view was changing, although slowly. This was evident in the changed programs and shifting emphases. Increasingly, the connection was being made between the individual desire for self-improvement and the broader goals of agricultural improvement. But part of this had been present forty years earlier. It was also present in the improvers' language. The constancy with which we see the easy conflation of – or effortless movement between – terms such as "science," "agriculture," "agricultural science," "political economy," "progress," and "improvement" suggests that their understanding of these issues operated as much through belief as through knowledge. The core of this belief included a notion of progress and a clear sense of betterment – the idea that the "progressive advancement of society in general" was underway.[78] At the same time, the improvers did not see such change as inevitable. They believed that progress, like improvement, was a directed process. It came to those individuals who worked hard and persevered, and it came through knowing one's world. This knowledge was as attainable via the laws of political economy as it was via the scientific practice of agriculture. Here, the lack of what we might call scientific rigour is indicative not only of the improvers' broader ideological purpose but also of the continuities in their system of belief. Collapsing political economy, morality, markets, and science was an important underpinning of the work of the societies. That their scientific practices were based on demonstrable and unassailable facts was taken as clear proof of the importance of following their prescribed methods. Plough in straight lines, cover your manure heap, pay your debts, and keep your wife at home: the order that these men evinced in these public displays was clear proof that they understood the proper ordering of society. They could submit others to order, and they themselves were willing to submit to authority – their own, that of the state, and that prescribed by middle-class convention. In short, these men offered proof that those who understood the benefits of industry and improvement also understood government.

10

Antimonopoly

The improvers' focus on self-government highlighted a world where free individuals understood that they were governed by a natural order and that the improvers, in turn, governed those who did not understand. The General Mining Association (GMA) was an aberration; its monopoly was as glaring an example of improper regulation as "huddled" Acadians or the Highland hoe. The monopoly, the improvers maintained, was an unnatural creation, foisted upon the colony by another ancient tradition: the royal prerogative. In the mind of reforming improvers, it was a clear example of an ancient custom that denied colonial self-government. Twenty years of GMA operations had placed the province's coalmining industry on a much stronger footing, but the firm's monopoly also raised the ire of nascent industrial entrepreneurs and liberal nationalists within the province's government and elite. Years of petitions and constitutional wrangling later, the "mines question" was one of several taken up by the movement for political reform. Although this question was not settled for almost a decade after the province achieved "responsible government," the lease was finally altered in negotiations between 1856 and 1858. Within five years a new competitive-patronage system saw the emergence of over twenty new coal companies, and a wholly new era of coalmining capitalism was underway.

Across the cultural and economic fringes of the North Atlantic world, political and economic thought was increasingly concerned with the developmental possibilities of large-scale capitalist modernization.[1] Many in Nova Scotia looked on admiringly, some enviously, as Great Britain and the north-eastern United States underwent the commercial and industrial "revolutions" of the mid-nineteenth century. Inspired by these

visions, provincial elites saw in the GMA a model of what could be. Together, the wondrous achievements of monopoly capital and the political struggle to break its hold provided important lessons in the ways that
the elite might imagine the province's economic development and its
future politics. The new politics of the industrial countryside marked a
significant break in the role that coal had held in the more integrated vision of industrial colonization, and more significantly for the countryside it marked a departure from the small-propertied political imaginary
of the rural improvers. This chapter follows provincial politicians as they
struggled to refashion their political-economic futures.

DEVELOPING AN ARGUMENT

Opposition to the GMA came primarily from rival political and economic elites. From the moment the company's pending arrival was announced in the winter of 1826 until its monopoly was finally abrogated
over thirty years later, anyone wanting to develop any mineral resource
was blocked by the GMA and its inordinately restrictive lease. Opposition arose along two principal lines of critique. The first centred on the
injustice of this use of the royal prerogative. The imperial government
had "only to think that it is for Colonial benefit that grants of Mines are
made to chartered companies in order to grant them," observed the *Colonial Patriot*, but it "follows, therefore, that the right to judge of what is
for Colonial benefit must be conceded to the Colonial Legislature."[2]
Contrasting "privilege" with "the people," critics narrated a tale of arbitrary use of the royal prerogative and the "granting away all but the very
crust of the soil on which the people lived."[3] The second avenue of critique was a more strictly defined attack on the economic inefficiency of
the GMA's activities. Critics maintained that major negative impacts
were being felt across the province. Small coastal trading vessels, for example, could not make so many or such large shipments and were thus
unable to receive the discounts offered larger shippers. This meant that
fewer Nova Scotia and more New England vessels could take advantage
of the trade. Others argued that the massive works the firm had constructed might be appropriate for England but not Nova Scotia. In the
short term, they were certainly right. The two mining operations at Pictou and Sydney, together with their infrastructures, had cost about
£200,000. Most everyone understood, and accepted, that this investment had to earn a profit. But the critics maintained that this extrava-
gantly scaled project resulted in an excessive and unnecessary cost for

coal. Unlike every other mine dug previous to the coming of the GMA, these mines were meant to produce for the long term. The fixed cost was enormous by colonial standards – indeed, even by British standards these were costly mines[4] – but they were not extravagant. In 1842 John Buddle, England's leading mining engineer, had high praise for their planning and execution and found fault only with minor details of the mines' operation.[5]

All of these economic issues, however, could be (and were) brought back to the injustice of the lease, and the two lines of critique were typically employed in combination. Very often, the two issues converged; the argument against the "injustice" of the monopoly always operated together with a public-spirited self-interest. Thus, for example, some argued that additional developments would be good not only for individual entrepreneurs but also for the wider public. There was also the issue of the GMA "forcing" its coal on the American market – that is, giving large discounts to US customers in order to maintain its position in the US market, a practice that the company never denied.[6] Some noted the inefficiency of this as a business practice, but many more complained that this meant Nova Scotia consumers paid more for a Nova Scotia product than did their American counterparts. Due in part to the broader emancipatory rhetoric of the reformist 1840s and in part to the imagined riches of extensive industrial developments such as railways and ironworks, much of the province's liberal elite developed a new sense of purpose and eagerly promoted the public struggle for rights and economic freedoms. At the same time, across the province, small producers would lose similar battles because they lacked the ability to participate in the legal-juridical contests that shaped this part of the campaign. The liberal elite put "the coal question" on the same track as the successful struggle for responsible government and other constitutional matters. Imposing abstract notions of right and justice on "the Country," they came to maintain that "competition" was the means to progress. Individual entrepreneurs, they argued, should have the responsibility to promote both these political and economic ends. Whether attempting to attain the high road of the public good or maintaining the more easily traversed lines of self-interest, such critiques suggest that a new theme in the discourse of provincial political economy was emerging.

The struggle with the GMA did not introduce liberal economics into the province. But battling "monopoly" for thirty years taught many people the political value of the language of laissez-faire and more

particularly of competition. It is notable, for example, that in the
1820s and 1830s few spoke of competition. Opponents spoke of justice (or rather injustice), while supporters spoke of improvements,
the wonders of steam engines, the "enlarged plan upon which the
mines are now worked," and other changes that "could only have
been acquired by the diffusion of Capital." Forty years later Richard
Brown was not inventing memories when he recalled the enthusiasm
that had greeted the GMA's arrival. Recall that the ultra-liberal *Colonial
Patriot* was delighted with the event; after all, the GMA represented an
investment of the "surplus" capital of Britain in the colonies. Nova
Scotia sorely needed this investment, even if the adventure had been
secured in the most illiberal of manners.[7] Even those, such as Joseph
Howe, who would later be opponents of the GMA were very much impressed with the steam engines, the deep pits, and the stately homes of
the managers.[8]

Indeed, the provincial state made a dramatic turn-around in its approach to business. Earlier governments had proposed an extensive series of regulations to police private (and public) coal producers; such
regulation had specified which mines might be opened, the prices for
coal, the rates of royalty, and the appointment of inspectors.[9] This profoundly regulationist perception had also remained evident in the
free-port issue. Customs officials in Halifax argued that the best – or
rather, as the surveyor of customs argued, "the least objectionable" –
way to promote the trade was not to free it but to compel transhipment
through Halifax.[10] A good trade was a well-regulated trade. But there
would be little state-led regulation of coalmining in the GMA's first
thirty years of operation, as the Colonial Office's accommodating
stance toward the company gave the province much less room to manoeuvre. While, formally at least, the province led the 1825–26 negotiations with the newly formed GMA, in reality the only matter over
which there was any negotiation was the rent, and even in this Halifax
had very little bargaining power. After months of attempting to raise
the rent, the province finally relented, and in January 1829 a Committee of the Legislative Council recommended acceptance of the lease
and the GMA's terms. Through the entire process, the company's monopoly scarcely raised an eyebrow.

The committee, however, did make one regulatory gesture, and it
was directly related to the GMA's monopoly. In an effort to "temper"
the effects of the monopoly, and noting the company's rhetoric about
"improved management," "technique," and "steam machinery," the

committee members "urge[d]" a maximum pithead price for coal at the "traditional" level.[11] Regulations against hoarding or price fixing were still common in Nova Scotia.[12] But the fact that the committee "urged" such a measure is significant, and no attempt to enforce the recommendation was ever made. Five years later it was apparent that the regulatory spirit was still evident but that it had been transformed into something quite different. Following an alleged arson at Albion Mines in 1832, the province passed laws making it a felony to set fire to a coalmine (it was not made clear why the regular felony of arson was not adequate); eight years later it was made a felony to place "obstacles" across railways (there were only two in the province, both owned by the GMA).[13] Such laws themselves were nothing new, but their orientation and history were. Now, the regulatory spirit appears to have been expressed through the GMA, not at it. No one was ever convicted of these crimes, but their occurrence suggests something of the nature of local hostility toward the GMA.

Fifteen years later, in 1845, the province passed new anti-smuggling laws in direct response to the complaints of the GMA.[14] Artfully borrowing from the language of the company's opponents, Samuel Cunard, the GMA's general manager in Nova Scotia, insisted that it was "only justice … that [the GMA] be protected" given the "heavy royalty" the company paid. Before the end of the month the colonial government had appointed Richard Brown, Robert Bridge, Henry Poole, and David Dickson – four GMA agents – as customs agents for Sydney and Pictou. It is difficult to imagine a clearer illustration of the state acting at the behest of business.

Or was this in fact the case? Certainly, there were limits. The company's original request was for the province to provide additional men and ships to deal with smugglers. Smuggling had long been the bane of the government's connection with the coal trade, and it continued to be a major problem for the GMA.[15] Now, as then, the province was unwilling to spend much money to police smuggling. Although we do not know the precise reason for allowing the company a capacity normally reserved for the state, past expressions and ongoing concerns suggest that it may have had to do as much with shirking expenses as with bowing to capital. In addition, the new regulations also retained the customary limitation on petty offences. The officers were empowered only "to seize and take all such coals *not less than* two chaldrons."[16] Here, perhaps, was a palliative for the poor, those who mined coal on their land for their own, and possibly their neighbours', use. It is not at all clear that anyone was bowing here. If the company obtained what it wanted, it certainly had not done so in the way that it desired. And if the government was battling an "oppressive" agency, it was doing so very gingerly. What seems clearer, however, is that as far as the state was concerned, in none of these cases was the issue one of economics. Although the company saw it differently, it was not the smugglers' competition that the state identified as a problem; rather, it appears to have been a matter of government and police – of being seen to be ruling while also offering some accommodation to local sensibilities. Indeed, given the continuing battle between the province and the GMA, it is not surprising that Halifax resisted the demands of the company. But it could not be seen to allow smuggling. The outcome spoke to the nature of the contest. A paternalistic government, effectively stripped of part of its authority, asserted at least some measure of control; a regulatory company, legally limited in its ability to assert authority, attempted to legitimize and extend its existing means of control. It was an accommodation, although an uneasy one.

However we might qualify it, the fact remains that the government was in effect handing over state powers to the GMA. Event by event, part of this depended on whether a Tory- or reform-oriented government dominated the Assembly. The transfer of regulatory powers nonetheless continued under both. Whether this was (as a reformer might argue) making the GMA pay a price for its other privileges or (as a Tory might maintain) allowing the company the right to regulate its legitimate domain, the province was withdrawing from the normal activities of government. The thin efforts to regulate the regulators were never implemented (and we can probably safely surmise, given whom the inspectors were, that loads of coal under two chaldrons were summarily seized), but the impression of governing remained. In some cases, it appeared that the company did everything short of conducting its own trials in the prosecution of bootleg mines. In two cases from Cape Breton in 1850, the GMA had men arrested for digging coal on their own land and then managed to have the trials moved to Halifax, where J.W. Johnston – the company's lawyer, the province's solicitor general, and leader of the Tory caucus – conducted the cases. Defending the change in venue in the House, Tory MLA John Marshall observed that "it was thought that a fair trial could not be obtained where the cause of action originated" – certainly an interesting spin on the notion of a fair trial.[17]

The GMA won its case, but this egregious faculty to police bootleg mines also resulted in one of the government's first serious blows against the firm. Mines legislation made it a punishable offence to mine any amount of coal on one's own land, even for one's own use. Under the terms of the lease, and despite the Crown's formal ownership of all sub-surface minerals, this was a violation not of the Crown's rights but of the GMA's. In the 1851 session of the House of Assembly, William Young (John's son) introduced a measure that would strike the offending clause from the Act.[18] As the debate unfolded that Saturday morning, a range of positions emerged. Young, together with both his brother, George, and William Henry, argued that the law should simply be struck from the statutes and that no restriction should be placed on anyone's right to mine coal on his own land. Such a restriction, Young main-tained, was "a hardship upon the people," particularly property owners (those who happened to have coal under their land). Others, however, argued that a modification (leaving the offence but removing the pen-alty) was all that was necessary. Johnston – still effortlessly combining his positions as attorney general and GMA lawyer – defended the company against this offensive by arguing that the "power existed more in theory than in practice," apparently forgetting the proceedings that he had just conducted a few weeks earlier. John Marshall agreed, adding that the company had "expended large sums of money ... and done much bene-fit." Thus he did not see why "other persons" should have "greater privi-leges than were granted to [the GMA]," an interesting spin on the notion of privilege. Ultimately, the issue was allowed to die. Even William Young, undoubtedly with an eye to the future, conceded that the elimination of all rules might open the field too much. But for the reformers, the exchange had had good political effect. They had clearly illustrated the magnitude of the difference between the GMA and those who worked the bootleg mines while placing themselves on the right side – on the side of "the people."[19]

Even an oppositional government, such as the reform government of 1848, was limited in its ability to articulate a clear alternative to an imperially supported measure derived from the royal prerogative. While some state officials viewed the GMA's activities as operating within a certain code of politics and behaviour (determined, perhaps, by the self-policing inherent in laissez-faire or by the rights of granted privilege), others viewed both the resource and anyone who exploited it as subject to regulation. Should the state regulate this valuable re-source, or could the company do so on its own through the market? Although the Assembly had a regular Committee on Mines and Miner-als (chaired by George Young) from 1845 and appointed an inspector

when the Mines Act was revised in 1853, these measures were limited
to descriptive, not prescriptive, actions, being more ad hoc or politically opportune interventions than regulatory innovations. So free had
been the company's hand that later, after 1854, when serious negotiations with the GMA and the Colonial Office resumed, the province really knew nothing of the holdings, capacity, or any of the geological or
financial aspects of the company's operations.[20] The GMA had been
left to govern itself for almost thirty years, which, despite occasional
grumblings about weak support from the province, was really how the
company preferred things.

Because regulation had failed to allow the province any control over
its new industry, the provincial elite required new strategies. As noted
above, a fairly loose group of issues, emphasizing various combinations
of ineffectiveness or the monopoly, framed the early opposition to the
GMA. Its precise ideological or even political referents are, therefore, difficult to determine. Opponents of the company most commonly put
forth "competition" as a balm for the irritation caused by the "monopoly," but it is remarkable how complex this term could be. "Competition" was framed as much in terms of fairness and justice, or perhaps
moral economy, as it was in terms of political economy. James McGregor,
for example, spoke out against the firm's monopoly on the basis of its
unchallenged ability to sell exorbitantly expensive coal to local residents. In 1838 he recalled that over the past twenty-five years, until the
GMA arrived, "never over four pence half penny per bushel had been
paid at the pit mouth"; the GMA charged 6d.[21] Alexander Fraser of
Pictou argued that the company sold its coal to "foreigners ... at a
cheaper rate than they sold to natives born on the very surface of the
coal." Now, in 1838, the price of coal was "beyond the reach of the
poor" because the monopoly allowed the GMA to sell at whatever price
it wished. Similarly, Roderick McGregor observed that it was the "country people," those who had to have their coal carted some distance,
"who receive the injustice."[22] Here, the critique focused on the social
dangers of monopoly: it encouraged an abuse of the poor and, moreover, of Nova Scotia's poor. We might view such arguments with suspicion. That critics of the GMA deployed an argument rooted more in
public than in private interest and one that was proto-nationalist suggests that it had some currency not only in the popular imagination
but also among a paternalist and increasingly native-born elite.[23]
Whether they thought that this critique was the only argument to put
forward or simply the best one, men like Fraser and McGregor knew

that they had tapped into a vital issue. What value were the hundreds of thousands of pounds the GMA had invested if "the people" could not heat their homes?

"Anti-Monopolist," writing to the *Pictou Observer,* also raised the issue of national and individual fairness, but he did so by stressing the "common sense" economics of the issue. Quoting an unidentified GMA supporter, he asked for evidence of the supposed "advancement of the 'enlarged plan upon which the mines are now worked.'"[24] The result of such a plan, he argued, must be measured in terms of the "advantage to the public," of which he saw none. Ten years ago, he reminded his readers, Adam Carr – one of the first colliers on the East River – had sold coal from the pithead at 13s6d per chaldron, "the very price charged at this moment by the General Mining Association!!! Where then is the important feature ... so prominent in the increasing advancement of Nova Scotia?" Such an advancement could be shown only if a company's "gain or loss depended not upon the protection afforded by restrictive regulations, but upon the industry, economy and skill which they meet their rivals in the market and where the relative value of the article they furnish is subject to the ever changing and universal operating conditions of competition."[25] Clearly, this did not describe the GMA. Others, he noted, might argue that the immense capital brought to bear on the coalfield was enough. But this was an artificial arrangement, propped up by the "restrictive regulations" that supported a company otherwise unable to "meet their rivals" in fair competition under the "universal operating conditions" of the market.

These were fairly abstract issues; there were other issues, *effects* that were rooted more in the day-to-day concerns of many colonists. For local residents, "Anti-Monopolist" continued, there were no beneficial results to speak of or at least none that could not have been accomplished under earlier regimes. Again pointing to Adam Carr, he recalled a very different era:

The mines of Pictou were leased and successfully worked from 1820 to 1827 by an individual who could not boast of "an immense capital" to commence his operations; but can justly exalt in the more worthy pride of having demonstrated to Nova Scotians that without capital (comparatively speaking) but by mere industry, economy, perseverance, and practical knowledge of his business, he has acquired a respectable independence, and gained a name for honesty and integrity which is sure to outlive the lease of Rundell, Bridge,

& Rundell. These are not the trophies of niggardly transactions and the reward of "immense capital," nor the results of political influence, but the honest profits arising from free competition.[26]

Here, Carr was still being recalled as a yeoman-like figure, one marked by his honest independence. He had achieved a "respectable independence" and "honest profits" by "industry ... and practical knowledge," and he maintained this position as the embodiment of a mythological type within a political discourse. In a speech in 1845 William Young still described Carr as having "acquired a competency" by "dint of honest labour."[27] And, indeed, he was very much like the improving farmers. If we recall the early nineteenth-century era of "state-merchant enterprise," for Young to speak of Carr's characteristics as having been acquired in free and open competition was perhaps misleading, although the contrast undoubtedly seemed clear enough. Yet not everyone was impressed by these arguments.

Writing from Pictou, "Aristides" shifted the ground entirely to utility and progress. Was the price not the same, and were not the benefits visibly superior? Could Mr Carr's 40-foot mine and a horse be compared with the 250-foot shaft and the "expensive and costly steam engine" engaged by the GMA? The company was "deserving of the sincere thanks of all those interested in the speedy advancement of Nova Scotia, and for the progress they ha[d] made in the manufacturing of articles necessary for the comforts of civilized society"; such results, he reminded his readers, were always to be expected where "capital joined with superior science, industry, and prudent economy." "Aristides" was a modern, bourgeois writer who was impressed by results. "Knowledge and money," he enjoined, "is power, and may be considered the certain magicians for calling forth the dormant resources of this or any other Province."[28] Little else mattered.

Like John Young and Thomas McCulloch, "Aristides" and "Anti-Monopolist" represented two sides of a liberal coin. By raising "industry," "free competition," and the "universal operating systems of the market," "Anti-Monopolist" emphasized means: the liberal virtues of individual freedom and competition. By raising "progress," "civilization," and the combination of capital, science, and industry, "Aristides" emphasized results: the grandeur of the liberal vision of progress. These differently imagined futures resonated with different people, even within the same camp. For some, "Anti-Monopolist's" comparative point, which hinged on fairness, remained potent: placed beside the GMA, Carr was as David before Goliath, a yeoman before the "immense capital" of a foreign joint-stock company. For others, the crucial point may have been the issue of markets and the benefits of competition. However understood, the dominant argument in the 1830s was rooted in justice and fairness. These ideals of fair and reasonable competition between relative equals employed a yeoman-like language and were employed more often and in a more pronounced fashion than the economic argument about efficiency. The language of independence, fairness, and "honourable competition" resonated deeply across a broad cross-section of colonial society.[29] Most would have agreed with "Aristides" that the works were impressive; they might have found his argument less so. The way that the GMA's arrangement had been achieved was unseemly – perhaps un-yeomanly. Wealth and political influence had overridden "industry, economy, perseverance, and practical knowledge."[30] Part of the argument that "Anti-Monopolist" put forward might be recognizable to a twenty-first-century neoconservative, but part of it too was a small producer's resentment against the incursions of the wealthy and the powerful. Here was an abuse of power, one that the average settler could readily understand and with which he could identify. Few, however, appear to have risen to the fight. However the issue might be expressed, its visibility was limited to those people and places where some evidence of its effects might be seen. The GMA monopoly was an example of arbitrary rule, an abuse of the royal prerogative, but it was not the kind of issue that was going to fuel widespread popular unrest – except among liberal improvers.

More pragmatic concerns eventually came to the fore. Abraham Gesner, for example, argued in 1836 that "while competition is prevented ... the inhabitants of Nova Scotia are only permitted to gaze upon the treasures of their country."[31] Similarly, although adding flourish to Gesner's almost melancholy tone, Robert Holmes Smith refused to divulge the exact location of an iron mine that he had "discovered" in Hants County because no one could derive any advantage from any such disclosure "until the mines of the Province [were] *liberated* from the hands of a Monopoly and open to public *competition*."[32] Even within the existing trade, others gathered evidence of how the monopoly caused inefficiencies. James D.B. Fraser claimed that boats sat in Pictou harbour for an average of seventeen days while awaiting their turn at the Loading Ground's single wharf. He calculated an annual loss to merchants and the shipping captains of almost £12,000.

Such information, he argued, "ought to convince every person of the necessity for competition."[33] Such costs, although undoubtedly exaggerated for political effect, were effective indications of how the GMA hindered the broader development both of the coal trade and of the province's other mineral resources. Over the course of the 1840s, however, the argument developed an interesting turn toward the inefficiencies not just of the system engendered by the monopoly but also of the company itself as a monopoly-based firm. And it was here that the provincial government found a space within which it could assume a more strident and activist role in attempting to alter the terms.

Little beyond such public debates occurred over the course of the 1830s. At the political level, there was nothing like a sustained assault on the GMA, and the best that could be said was that such debates were laying the groundwork for a future politics. Even the infamous mob scenes throughout western Cape Breton during manager Richard Smith's failed bid for election in 1832 do not seem to have stirred the antimonopoly fire, except for among a few anti-GMA stalwarts, notably John Ross ("Anti-Monopolist") and more obviously Smith's opponent, William Young. Ross seems to have given up his public letter-writing campaign after 1833. But Young's fire burned more fiercely after the Legislature determined that he, not Richard Smith, had been the principal cause of the election disturbances during the previous autumn in Cape Breton.[34] With no seat in the Assembly, Young spent much of 1833 researching the common law and mineral rights as well as the royal prerogative while communicating with anyone who had either a knowledge of or an interest in the GMA's place in the province.[35] Nothing substantial was accomplished, but Young laid a strong framework of allies for the future, most notably with Lawrence Doyle, the member for Arichat Township, who would support all Young's reform measures into the 1850s. During this period, when Young was out of the House, Doyle appears to have been asking questions written by Young.[36] Unlike his brother, George, who jumped in and out of alliances with just about anybody, including company figures such as the Stewarts and Samuel Cunard, William Young maintained an almost single-minded determination to break the lease and must be regarded as the principal figure in maintaining the agitation against the GMA over so long a period.

Agitation was roused again in the late 1830s following the publication of Gesner's *Remarks on the Geology and Mineralogy of Nova Scotia* in 1836. Gesner's work highlighted a number of the key issues that would remain at the centre of the debate for the next twenty years. Pursuing some of the suggestive findings of the American naturalists C.T. Jackson and Francis Alger, Gesner's work was a walking tour of the mineral resources of the province, a boosterish assessment of their economic value, and an extended critique of the lease.[37] In simply detailing rich veins of unexploited iron, copper, manganese, coal, and building stones, Gesner did not have to rail against the lease, although he missed few opportunities.[38] Like "Aristides," the defender of the GMA, Gesner's argument employed science and the possibilities of capital investment, but instead he maintained that the monopoly hindered the nation's ability to make efficient use of its own resources. By repeatedly reminding his readers, over the course of almost two hundred pages, of the "vast amount of capital ... [which] lie[s] dormant in the hands of its possessors, when so many channels might be opened, and the surplus earnings of the country be retained among its inhabitants," he forcefully illustrated the potential loss represented by the lease. It was not just the capital applied to the resource but also the potential capital within the resource that might be of benefit. He critiqued what *was* with what *might be*, noting the loss both "to enterprise" and "to the Country." Minerals, he reminded his readers, were "objects of the greatest national importance ... [and] a knowledge of minerals is among the principal of those improvements which have elevated nations from a state of barbarism."[39] When the provincial Legislature publicly acknowledged Dr Gesner's work during the 1837 session, many undoubtedly were thanking him as much for his political contribution as for his geological endeavours. Unfortunately for the nearly always financially strapped geologist, more legislators also knew that there was no reason to grant him the £200 that a committee of the House recommended for a "Geological Survey of the Province."[40] Whatever his direct effects may or may not have been, by moving the discussion into the realms of nation, science, and improvement, Gesner offered the GMA's opponents a richer language from which to draw upon in their critiques. Here, outwardly at least, was a higher road, one that joined science to politics and public interest.

Gesner's contribution was but another salvo in a longer battle. But, at minimum, it certainly opened many eyes to unfulfilled possibilities and obligations. Between 1837 and 1841 pressure to reopen the issue mounted, and several attempts were made to open mines outside the lease. For the most part, these efforts involved people applying to the provincial government and eventually to the Colonial Office for permission to open unworked mines. Included here was Gesner himself. In 1838, having been outbid for a building-stone site at Apple River (near Minudie in Cumberland County), Gesner applied for permission to work an iron mine at another, undisclosed, location in the area.[41] Under the unworked-mines clause of the GMA's lease, anyone could apply for permission to open a mine, and so long as the company did not initiate mining activities on the site within the year, the licence was to have been granted. The Crown granted no such licences during the thirty-one years of the GMA monopoly. This was a problem for those interested in well-known, if unworked, mines such as the coal seam at the Joggins; but it was a much greater problem, as any geologist, prospector, or farmer with a shovel knew very well, for those concerned with mines as yet undiscovered or of uncertain value.[42] The Colonial Office twice rejected Gesner's petition as "too general and too comprehensive" (which it was, but this was the conundrum posed by the lease).[43] How, both the GMA and Colonial Office reasoned, could the lessees determine whether they intended to work a mine when the prospective lessee could not clearly indicate its location? Why, Gesner and others replied, should we do the GMA's prospecting? Gesner, like most others, did not attempt to clarify his claim.

Some made claims on perfectly well-known coal seams. In 1838 Gesner made a second application, this time for permission to work the seam at the Joggins. This application having been rejected, he continued his searching and claimed to have "discovered" a seam at Springhill, in the interior of the same county.[44] Gesner would continue his efforts to unite the iron and coal possibilities of Cumberland County for the next fifteen years, with no success.[45] In 1842 Amos Seaman, fresh from his victory over intruding squatters and rebellious tenants, resolved to take on the GMA as well by applying to work a seam at River Hebert, near his property at Minudie. In 1838 Alexander Fraser, whom we met above complaining on the part of the poor, petitioned to open an unworked seam on his farm across the East River from Albion Mines. Fraser's petition was made after the GMA tried to prosecute him for operating an illegal mine. This "collision," as it came to be known,[46] gave greater publicity to the limited benefits obtained by Pictou County residents through the company's operations. Fraser's petition too was rejected, but it is instructive to follow something of the debate here. Samuel Cunard, speaking for the GMA and basing his comments on those of the company's engineer, claimed that Fraser's was the same seam as that worked by the GMA, although this was clearly refuted by the statement of

Adam Carr, who had worked both seams for close to twenty years.[47] Moreover, Cunard continued, these were not mines anyhow but "merely holes dug at the outcrop." They were dangerous in that they flooded, which created the risk of cave-ins. All of this may have been true, but it had very little to do with the GMA's real concern that it not be undercut in local sales – almost 40 per cent of its revenue: if one such mine was allowed, many more would follow. On the issue of "foreigners" getting their coal cheaper than Nova Scotians, Cunard lied shamelessly, although artfully. He argued that because the company raised more than it could sell in the province, it was "compelled" to sell this "excess" overseas at a reduced rate.[48] It was a pathetic argument from the general manager of a firm that had always been clear that developing a position in the US market was vital to its future success.[49]

Additional difficulties were mounting for the GMA. As we saw in chapter 6, 1842 was not a good year. In London those on the Board of Directors were critical of several inefficiencies, and in both Sydney and Pictou we find the managers scrambling to reduce their costs.[50] Remarkably, after a successful strike the previous winter, these plans included a new wage cut. While wages formed only 40 per cent of the company's selling price, they were one of the few day-to-day cost factors over which management had any potential control. More drastic measures were forecast as well, including "giv[ing] notice to all the workmen employed at their principal colliery at Pictou, that they must hold themselves in readiness to quit the Mines in expectation of their being closed." Given the company's investment, these were probably threats designed to gain more leverage in wage negotiations and in the GMA's ongoing negotiations with the province and the Colonial Office for a reduction in the royalty.[51] Nonetheless, the "field" that the company had entered eighteen years earlier was certainly changing its shape. The completion of the Reading Railroad, the consequent reductions in the price of Pennsylvania coal, and new US import duties put the GMA at a severe price disadvantage; the GMA shipped about one-third as much coal in 1842 as it had in 1841.[52] That autumn Samuel Cunard was again petitioning for exemption of an additional 20,000 chaldrons from the royalty.[53] The following year the numbers recovered, but the decline highlighted the vulnerability of the Casual Revenue. Thus, although the company's sales increased over the course of the 1830s and 1840s, the province's revenue increased at a slower rate. Now, even the state could see that the company's purported lack of efficiency had material effects.

The pressure on the GMA increased through the early 1840s. During the miners' strike of 1842, Joseph Howe sent George Wightman, an engineer and personal friend of the new provincial secretary, to Pictou to investigate the company's claims of financial difficulties.[54] Wightman's mission in the winter of 1842 was to draw blood on one of the reformers' best examples of arbitrary and undemocratic British rule. The engineer was given considerable scope for his investigation, but the particular object was clear enough. While the first line of his instructions merely directed him to "investigate ... the causes of the losses sustained" by the GMA, the preamble emphasized the "injudicious proceedings" that characterized all of the company's operations. Thus Wightman's final instruction was to make recommendations on the "prospects which may exist for the further prosecution of the operations either by the Association or by other parties tending ultimately to profitable results." The engineer did not disappoint. A broader-ranging investigation into the North Atlantic coal market might have emphasized shifts in the production and transportation of coal in the United States, but Wightman was an attack dog, with his eyes fixed firmly on his target: the GMA. His investigation probed why the company had been inefficient, the problematic nature of the lease itself, and moreover, the deeper structural implications of monopolies.[55]

Wightman laid out six "classes" of problems: unnecessary speculations in matters unrelated or insufficiently related to mining, excessive "fluctuations" in the management, extravagant construction expenses, an excessive inventory, imperfections in the plan of the works, and "disadvantageous modes of carrying on the work." He detailed what he believed to be excessive speculations, expenditures, and inventories – totalling, he calculated, well over £61,000. Wightman then went on to describe and critique a number of smaller, although no less pernicious, faults in the management of the GMA's operation in Pictou County. His analysis suggested that these were symptoms of poor economy but not in themselves the cause of the company's ongoing malaise. The main cause identified by Wightman was not the lease or the monstrous capital of the firm but the "spirit of monopoly that reign[ed] among the workmen."[56]

Fully half of Wightman's report (and all of the fifth and sixth sections) attacked not the company but the colliers. He seems to have thought that the miners provided him with the clearest illustration of persistent cost problems – problems directly linking the lease, the GMA, and its imported practices: "The mistake by which this state of things was brought about, probably arose from applying the maxims and practices of England to a country under different circumstances. There, from the multitude of labourers every man is forced into a particular calling, and from which he cannot, if he wished it, easily escape. The facility with which men can turn to different employments at the same class is scarcely known, and hence it was thought necessary to import a class of regularly instructed miners." More curious, however, was his rather confused attribution of agency, in which the "system" and the colliers apparently combined to make the GMA act improperly. The company emerged from this analysis as made up of dupes and fools – dupes of the colliers and fools who misunderstood the ways of the colonies. The result, Wightman argued, was a perverse system whereby men who, in his estimation, were really no more than common labourers exercised a regulation of their own work completely without parallel in this colony. Not only were they "considered as tradesmen," but they also "fix[ed] their prices and w[ould] not admit any other person into their work."[57]

Wightman undoubtedly was drawn to what he saw as the revealing irony of one monopoly creating another. In terms of costs, which were the focus of the remainder of the report, the colliers did not figure in any of his calculations, but the colliers were certainly the topic that he felt most comfortable discussing. Wightman was unwilling to enter into any discussion of the GMA's system of marketing, pleading ignorance and a lack of information, but neither of these shortcomings prevented him from discussing the management of labour. As an engineer from Hants County, Wightman worked with what he knew and applied it wherever he could. Clearly, he knew much more about gypsum quarrying than coalmining, fully believing that digging a hole in the bank of a river was comparable to the work of a collier. In the terms that he emphasized – strength and "effort" – the two were comparable, but in terms of skill there was no comparison. In the Hants County operations, "A person hires or purchases a quarry and employs a few labourers who within a month become good quarry-men ... [Quarriers] hire by the month at four pounds, ten shillings and five pence, while the miners think themselves badly paid with less than thirteen pounds. The employer sells plaster at two shillings to two shillings and three pence per ton clear of rent and cartage and makes a living; the collier [*sic*] sells coals at more than double this sum, and sinks money. These facts of themselves are sufficient to create suspicion that there is mismanagement somewhere."[58] This final point was all that really mattered. Presumably, the long and detailed description was there merely to overwhelm the reader with as many evils as possible. Although in the winter of 1842 Cunard and Poole would have been hard-pressed to concede the point, they understood that Wightman knew little about his subject. While they might never have admitted it, their eventual relenting on that winter's strike bespoke a clear recognition of the value of their men's skills.

Wightman's report is most valuable to us for the way that it highlighted the peculiar place of colliers in the provincial labour market. Although many of his assessments were overdrawn or simply misinformed, he was certainly correct to note the colliers' high wages, their rather remarkable control over workplace issues, the apprenticeship system, the seasonality of their employment, and their very British ways. Most notable, however, is the way that Wightman, and implicitly his superiors, posed the entire problem. Although ostensibly there to investigate the GMA, Wightman was sent to Pictou during a long, and occasionally violent, strike that had provoked a fair amount of concern and comment. He did not address the strike, its related issues, or any of the winter's events in even one sentence of his extensive report. This was because – despite the way that he posed his argument – there was not a problem with labour at Albion Mines but a problem with the GMA; it was not the workers who had compelled his investigation but the way that the company organized its affairs. Not one of the newspaper accounts or the reports on the strikes at Albion Mines in 1840, 1841–42, or 1846 blamed the miners. If there was a labour problem at Albion Mines, it was the GMA's problem, not the government's or the people's. There was an assumption of responsibility here. If the colliers overextended their bounds, it was because their employers allowed it. This was Wightman's point. That he had to reproach the miners along the way was not simply his rhetorical strategy but also an expression of what he saw as fundamentally flawed management – in this case, the mismanagement of men: there were no independent yeomen here, just overpaid miners in a privileged system.

The political importance of Wightman's report lay not in his detailed descriptions but in his conclusions. Although he did not attempt to break down all these excess charges in terms of their effect on the prices charged for coal, there was no doubt that he viewed these economic practices, particularly the labour practices, as serious drains on the company's efficiency. His comments on whether the GMA was "forcing the market" were ambivalent, and as for "imperfections in the plan of the works," he could find none; indeed, the engineer gushed that the "workings [were] in as perfect a state as I suppose to be possible." But on the company's cost overruns and its extravagant labour policies, he was sure there was a problem that could be fixed: "I have no doubt," he concluded, "that were [the Albion Mines] in the hands of an individual who paid no more for the pits than fair valuation for the labour bestowed upon them, who took no more of the real estate than is really necessary for the working of them, and who paid for the railroad only so much as would bring the carriage by that channel equivalent in expense to what it would be by the old road and river, he would realise a very ample profit upon his investment." This was important, especially in the context of making the case that competition would cheapen the cost of production and therefore of fuel. But the "best method of obtaining the profit," he insisted, returning to the issue of the colliers, was the destruction of the miners' collectivity through the "establishment of a system of free contract." "[B]y this end," he added, "the spirit of monopoly that reigns among the workmen should be entirely got rid of so as to permit Contractors to get men from various parts of the country,"[59] thus permitting management to control some of its costs. Whatever the source of the problem might have been, labour emerged as Wightman's key illustration in his attack on the monopoly. In the short term, this argument had little impact, as both Cunard and Poole knew that he was wrong. Indeed, the colonial government was unconcerned with labour in any event. The company had proven its point that the labour problem in the mines was an effect, not a cause.

NEGOTIATING LIBERALISM

The pressure on the GMA began to have some effects. The combination of the increased number of petitions under the escape clause, the ongoing strikes and apparent inefficiencies, and increased pressure from a more reform-oriented House of Assembly after 1845 meant that the Colonial Office was also willing to put some pressure on the company, at least to open some new mines. The acceptance by the Assembly of a petition proposed by George Young in the 1845 session signalled the future course of the provincial government. The resolution was appropriately critical, emphasizing both the government's outrage at the injustice done to the province and the GMA's deleterious economic effects in fettering enterprise, limiting foreign trade, and impeding the introduction of manufacturing.[60] But the petition itself was weak, asking only under what conditions the GMA might alter or give up its lease. Although the reformers made good politics of the petition, its conclusion made clear that it was in fact only a weak testing of the waters. More notable was the amended resolution proposed by John Ross ("Anti-Monopolist"), which maintained that the GMA had "failed to fulfil any of the stipulations required" by the lease and that the province, not the company, should be setting the terms. He proposed allowing the GMA to maintain its current position but nullifying the lease, transferring all rights to the Assembly, and purchasing all of the company's "Building and other improvements." Although ultimately rejected, Ross's amended version found the support of about one-third of the Assembly. The matter was referred to a committee, chaired by George Young, and it became the first report of the Mines Committee. It was a remarkably tepid description of a number of "options" open to the province. Some of these carried a hint of threat – such as the first, which noted that any discussion of the value of the GMA would refer not to its financial statements but to the current value of its traded stocks – but no concrete steps were outlined. It was noteworthy, however, how few would now rise in public to defend the GMA. By 1852 even the usually cautious appointees in the Legislative Council were criticizing the lessee's manipulations of the escape clause by noting its frequent delays and regular "commencement of pretended operations."[61] Less remarkable was how the politicians, most notably the Youngs, were already tempering their language, acknowledging that, on the one hand, diplomacy could do more than anger and that, on the other, some comments might haunt them down the road when they had regained control of the mines.

Ultimately, the granting of responsible government in 1848 was the major turning point in the campaign against the GMA. For the first time, the provincial Legislature and, moreover, the executive had it within its power to alter the conditions under which the company acted. Among the reform government's first actions was to claim control of the Casual Revenue by promising the Colonial Office a new Civil List Act, an issue that had plagued all of these negotiations almost since the beginning.[62] By assuming responsibility for the civil list, the province was free to use the Casual Revenue (almost all of which came from the GMA) as a chip in any future negotiations with the company, especially if they proved difficult. With these issues out of the way, the province was in a better position to negotiate, so instead of rancour there were now clear signs of a willingness to negotiate.

Despite the changed conditions, the GMA retained support in both Halifax and London, and no major changes occurred until 1853. Having been rebuffed in its gestures toward negotiation and finding a "reasonable compromise,"[63] the provincial government took the dramatic step of unilaterally declaring its control of the province's mineral resources. The Mines and Minerals Act was amended to make the Assembly, not the British Treasury, the final arbiter on the escape clause. Henceforth, the Assembly would accept proposals for mines, notify the GMA, and determine whether the company was in fact mining at the specified location.[64] It was a bold step, and, perhaps to some surprise, neither the Colonial Office nor the Treasury objected. The province was being trusted to treat property in the manner that it demanded. Suddenly, the province had much more leverage, although in reality not the wide-ranging leverage suggested by the law. Any real step to deny the GMA its legal right in property and contract would surely have met with a firm response from London. Nevertheless, William Young was able to turn up the heat. In a letter to Robert Moser, the company's chair, Young made it clear that conditions had changed, as had the province's position: "I do not hesitate to say, that with the principle of self-government thoroughly naturalized in Nova Scotia, and the larger powers necessarily and wisely entrusted to its legislature and local government, it will be impossible for the general mining association [sic] to carry on its operation with advantage or comfort to themselves till a better feeling shall be restored."[65] The province was mostly posturing now, yet even in this rhetorical sphere it moved cautiously. Although the province notified the GMA of seven new applications for licences to mine coal, not one was approved. Having the legal ability to challenge the property rights of the company and doing so were two completely different matters.

Nonetheless, in effect, the battle had been won. The GMA was now under pressure from all sides to make an arrangement with the province. The position of those on the Board of Directors was now to make the best possible deal for themselves. Late in the autumn of 1854 the company offered the creditors of the Duke of York a straight buy-out of their arrangements: £120,000 for all their claims, a staggering sum of money simply to maintain its hold on its existing operations. The creditors accepted, although they claimed a "sacrifice" for the sake of expediency, and the Crown removed its objections as well. But things moved slowly in constitutionally complex colonial affairs. It was the following June before the British attorney general's office allowed that the actions of the province had been constitutional and returned the issue to Halifax for consideration.[66] Thus in 1856 Young secured from the Assembly the general guidelines by which it would accept surrender of the existing terms. Negotiations would occur the following summer in London.

Fate, however, was good to the GMA after all. An election in early 1857 returned J.W. Johnston's Tories. William Young, although he had led the political struggle and crafted the terms of surrender, was denied a seat at the negotiations in London. Johnston would lead Nova Scotia's delegation. No doubt, the GMA was pleased to see that its chief opponent in the upcoming negotiations would be its former solicitor and a director of its Nova Scotia bank. The terms negotiated fit the general tenor of compromise established in 1856, but rather too well. These terms suggested that the company would maintain its existing operations and receive a reduction in the royalty but would give up its exclusive right. The final agreement ensured just this, but mysteriously the GMA's existing operations had suddenly grown in number from four mines to six. A hole that Joseph Smith had dug at Springhill in the summer of 1852 (and just as quickly covered in) had grown to be a mine, while the shaft at Bridgeport in Cape Breton, which had been abandoned fifteen years earlier, was said to be back in operation. As the experience of the Joggins made clear, the company was not about to open mines at either of these places. But it was not going to allow anyone else to do so either.[67]

In their reports from the negotiations in London, Johnston and his negotiating partner, the moderate liberal Adams George Archibald, made a good show of demonstrating their tough bargaining skills. To their credit, they did reject the GMA's initial description of their existing workings as including almost the entire north-eastern quarter of Cape Breton Island, so the government managed to reserve everything east of the Mira River – that is, what would later become the coal towns of Victoria Mines, Reserve, New Waterford, Glace Bay, and Port Morien. But the negotiators otherwise exerted little pressure. Their reports from London narrated nice little moments of drama in which some difficulty or another "threatened to defeat the negociation." But anyone reading the final report could see both the untenably large starting point of the GMA and its very prompt acceptance of the provincial negotiators' next offer. That the company accepted quickly and "without qualification" was a sure sign that the Nova Scotians had caved. For the GMA's great "sacrifice," compensation was deemed to be warranted, so its rent was cut in half and the royalty reduced. While in 1857 the company would have had to pay over £6,000 into the Casual Revenue, the total instead would be about £3,000, less than had been paid in 1828. Richard Brown, one of the GMA's negotiators, buoyantly reported that the new arrangements were very good, as they allowed the company to "reduce their selling price and extend their operations." Moreover, he reminded the shareholders, the GMA could do so "perfectly confident in the security of their investments."[68] On the side of the province, J.W. Johnston certainly claimed to have done his best, but one wonders how firmly he negotiated. During the 1857 sitting of the House of Assembly, Joseph Howe dryly observed that "for years [Johnston] has been the counsel, and the advocate of the Mining Association ... We are in the position then at present [where] the Mining Association has not only got our Mines but our Attorney General too."[69] We can imagine a not-so-slight smile of self-congratulation on the faces of the GMA's directors as they departed the final meeting. The company had lost its monopoly, but it had extended the leases on all its existing mines, blocked new entrants from the best locations in the existing coalfields, reduced its charges, and guaranteed its legal rights. Such a "defeat" was truly bearable. In the winter session of 1858, William Young and Joseph Howe both ridiculed the agreement,[70] but there was no denying the Tory majority, and the agreement passed without amendment.

Ironically, what had been a large part of the province's leverage going into the negotiations – the GMA's overextended reach – had not been used to defeat the company. In some respects, this overextension argument strengthened the GMA's position. Whether the issue was smuggling, bootleg mines, or applications to open new legal mines, the company was ultimately pushed beyond even its quite impressive ability to police the entirety of the coalfields of Nova Scotia. Equally indicative of its limited capacity were its frequent requests for government support to suppress smuggling and its rather evident willingness to rely on the state for any support that it could get. In his 1853 petition Abraham Gesner attempted to make the reasonable point that to believe that "any one Company can improve and properly open all these resources is quite impracticable." He was right – and he might have added that it was quite impracticable for any company to even manage the resource throughout the entire province. In the end, this was as much the cause of the GMA's downfall as anything else. The company was big and powerful but not that big and powerful. Like

Gulliver, the GMA was brought down not with a mighty blow but by many small ones – some of which were apparently self-inflicted. This was the real irony of the Tory ministers' negotiations. Having put the company in a position where it simply could no longer reasonably justify its delays, excuses, and "pretended commencements" – that is, the years of petitions, reports, and complaints that kept the GMA on its feet trying to cover all angles – the ministers handed almost everything back. The company was overextended but profitable, and this was how it would remain.

Equally noteworthy, however, is the complete shift in the terms of the discussion. In all the materials generated during the last few years of the political campaign, the economic inefficiencies of the monopoly dropped from the centre of the argument. Downplaying the possible economic benefits that might accrue, the rights of "the people" replaced efficiency as the prize. But there was a change within this position too. The primary shift was back to justice, but now this ideal was expressed in terms of the national rights of the people; now the objects to be defended were the constitution and national self-determination. In 1856 Young railed against a company "who have no shadow of a claim on the resources and industry of the country." "The people" still figured in his comments, but the yeomanly figures of Adam Carr and John McKay had been replaced by national abstractions. Now Young wanted to "place the people in a better position with relation to their mines and minerals."[71] No one suggested that the price of coal was going to go down, and no one discussed economic benefits, except as these would benefit an abstract public, or "the people." Perhaps this was because of a growing awareness that few would derive any returns. To be fair to Young and Howe, neither of them (unlike many other members of the Assembly) held any interest in coalmines for the remainder of their lives, but they were certainly acting on behalf of many who did. Together with railways, coalmining became the hobbyhorse of the economic and, to a remarkably great extent, political elite of the province.[72]

The expected new developments in coalmining were slow in coming. In 1859, after only a single season of possibilities, the mines inspector was hard-pressed to work up a bit of enthusiasm for the "spirited and praiseworthy" efforts that he saw around him. He readily admitted that eight mines, from which barely 2,300 tons had been raised, represented a "feeble" effort.[73] Obtaining a licence to either search for or work a mine was relatively easy. It cost only $20,[74] covered one square mile, and could be had by applying to the inspector. Thus in these first years of state-regulated laissez-faire mining, what we see are many small mines, few of which lasted more than a year or two. For instance, the brothers Robert and George McKay (sons of John and William, "the colliers" whom we met in chapter 3) worked a small seam east of New Glasgow. In 1858 they raised 300 tons of coal "for home consumption" and sold it in the town for 8s4d per ton. Robert Smith, "with the laudable support of some gentlemen in the area," had dug a "shaft" 25 feet deep at Salmon River, in Colchester County, where he had a horse gin and a few men to excavate a level from which they raised almost 100 tons. As the subsequent history of coalmining in Colchester County can attest, this mine did not last long. But then few would in any county.[75] The newly negotiated position of the GMA left it clear control of the best sites and a truly superior position in its ability to control the market. Shafts of 25 feet producing a few hundred tons might be annoyances in the market, but they could not compete with the skills and capacities of hundreds of thousands of pounds of infrastructure and a thousand skilled miners. Smuggling and bootleg mines would continue, but the days of the yeoman were gone.

CONCLUSION

In an immediate sense, the GMA had two direct effects on the colony and on its government. First, the company brought to Nova Scotia far more capital than could ever have been brought together in the province at the time. Although local capital did exist, there was neither the will to bring it together in the form necessary for such a large undertaking nor the skill to manage this kind of investment or to build and operate an industrial-scale coalmine. Clearly, as we saw earlier, and as the history of any other coalmining district in this period would suggest, neither of these were necessary to initiate a coal industry. But the advent of such a highly capitalized operation meant that other potential paths were understood in terms only of what might have been. The enlarged scale meant that the company's ability to survive depended on maintaining its position in the Atlantic market at all costs. It was a large company with a large requirement for revenue, based on a tiny share of the North Atlantic market; it could allow no competition if it was to survive. The size of the GMA's operations – its equipment, the depth of the mines, the scale of development work, the skilled workforce, or more simply its capital – also meant that an unusually high threshold had been established for entry onto any reasonably level playing field. It would not be until late in the century before new operations could truly compete, much less play any kind of developmental role in the economy and society of the province.

The second direct effect of the GMA was the role that it played in shaping a liberal discourse of politics in Nova Scotia. Highlighting competition, independence, and senses of both individual and national right, the debate over the position of the GMA employed a liberal vocabulary and instructed many Nova Scotia residents in liberalism's political possibilities. The connections here to a fairly unsophisticated – indeed, crass – battle over access to the fruits of the emerging industrial-capitalist order are patently evident. Yet the battle over the "right" of "the people" to "improve" themselves and to better not only their own individual conditions but also that of the province as a whole through "competition" opened opportunities for political debate, discussion, and ultimately, in true parliamentary fashion, closure. The patterned series of decisions that accompanied these contests set the context for how these issues might be decided upon in the future and thus the context for the nature of government itself. Here too the size of the GMA's plantation mattered. Ironically, the liberalism that emerged victorious from this debate was closer to that of "Aristides" than to that of "Anti-Monopolist." Results, in the end, came to matter more than means, and national self-determination (and national economic development) emerged as more important elements than either competition or the primacy of the individual. These debates were not restricted to the mines question. In debates over railway financing in the 1850s, reform politicians argued for "the People's Line" – that is, a government financed railway – over a "monster Monopoly" controlled by an "English Company of bankers and speculators." When Charles Fairbanks argued against "permitting any private company to monopolize our great thoroughfare," his tone and his terms resonated clearly for any liberal nationalist.[76] Railways, like the mines, would be tools of nationalism and state formation. National ends, and a strong state, would be underpinnings of Nova Scotia's Victorian liberalism.

The critique of the GMA was a part of what we might call (borrowing from and modifying French historian William H. Sewell Jr's expression) a rhetoric of *colonial* bourgeois revolution.[77] Provincial liberal's use of the terms of this debate not only asserted the place of right and justice but also linked them to a particular political economy and made them central to a liberal politics. The debate acknowledged and accepted the power of capital; the issue was to nationalize it, or more accurately to get it into the hands of an indigenous middle class. If, as Phillip A. Buckner argues, the transition to responsible government was as much a transfer of power to the executive as a transfer to the colony itself, the struggle against the GMA can help us to better see the special place envisioned for capital within the new political order.[78] Without wishing to overstate the position of the coal question in the province's struggle for responsible government, it is clear that at certain times it played a materially and symbolically powerful role in the debate, an immediate reminder of arbitrary rule, imperial illiberality, and Nova Scotians' ultimately limited capacities as freeborn, and propertied, British citizens. Much as John Young successfully centralized rural political power in the capital, so too did his son William and the other reformers manage to make coalmines, and later railways, tools of a centralized political elite. Both achieved their ends through a language of liberalism that was enamoured more with economic freedoms for some than with broad-based principals of liberty and democratic reform. These were important effects, as important to the history of the province as any of the monopoly's allegedly debilitating effects on the development of the Nova Scotia economy.

Conclusion

The making of liberal government in rural Nova Scotia was less a particular program than a broad-based contestation of the nature and legitimacy of authority. Politically, this included debates over imperial strategy, colonial autonomy, democratization, and how these reflected understandings of colonial and individual self-government. But there was also a profoundly important material context, one shaped by class struggles over the legitimacy of power, contests over the appropriate nature of manliness and ethnic capacities, and competition for scarce resources – most notably coal and the province's notoriously limited availability of good farmland. To reduce this to its barest form, if political debates over improvement and reform formed the discursive context for this study, then rural Nova Scotia's limited agricultural resources, its rich beds of coal, and the combined effects of these on capital and class formation meant that the colony remained less democratic, more paternalistic, and still further removed from the centres of centralized power. As elites came to dominate the narrow channels of civil society, they embarked on projects whose effects paralleled, reinforced, and legitimated the enclosures of material resources. The pattern was clear. Whether it was Edward Mortimer's ability to draw (or to "concuss") trade, the GMA's industrial colonization program, Amos Seaman's capacity to consolidate an entire basin's land, production, and trade, William McKeen's ability to exercise political and economic domination, or any number of other smaller stories of consolidation and control, we can see that enclosure reduced poor settlers' abilities to achieve a basic competency. In a society where property, competency, and self-government defined political subjects, the poor found themselves increasingly removed from emerging democratic debates.

The state was the single most identifiable agent of both stability and change here. Reluctant to pass any but the smallest matters over to local control, it was that much more unwilling to pass major resources over to private hands. In the eighteenth and early nineteenth centuries, the grindstone, the gypsum, and to some extent the coal trades offered clear examples of local peoples controlling resources through use and local regulation. For a time, the state allowed – and to some extent even encouraged – small producers to maintain these places, always cognizant that the consolidation of such resources entailed a threat to political power, especially when these economic centres were beyond the surveillance of Halifax. In the case of coal, state-merchant enterprise offered the province's capital a managerial technique that nicely satisfied the political concerns of the state and the private ambitions of some merchants. Enclosure was not part of this agenda, until capitalists, with the support of the imperial state, forced the issue. Yet even here, Halifax found ways to bridge the older mercantilist vision with its elites' increasing aspirations. It is impossible to underestimate the role played by the example of the GMA's wealth and power in the vision of Nova Scotia politicians. At the same time, we should not underestimate the importance of the broader contestation of ideas and resources across the colony's industrial countryside. The GMA provided moments of clarity and focus but only moments. The political campaign over liberal government was wider, deeper, and more pronounced than we have imagined.

Improvement's legacy was mixed. To be sure, in its emphasis on innovation and progress, combined with its idealization of the role of individual betterment, it offered a powerful mix of economic progress and liberal-democratic possibilities. But as we have seen, these democratic possibilities were more often expressed as abstract principles than as practical political programs. Just as the supporters of the GMA emphasized the monopoly's economic benefits over the principles of antimonopoly, improvers maintained that ends mattered. Economic growth mattered; wealth mattered. "Wherein ... is the advantage of this famous Responsible Government?" asked Pictou's *Colonial Standard* in 1862. The answer, part of a larger comment on "the evils of unlimited democracy," emphasized the improvers' ends: "It cannot be discovered in the improved condition of the country, in increased wealth, developed resources, or a more happy and contented population."[79] Here was the improvers' favoured index. The *Colonial Standard*, we should observe, was a Tory paper, trumpeting the virtues of

Premier J.W. Johnston, denigrating the old reformer Howe, and routinely reminding its readers that the "truest ... sense of the word government necessarily implied gradations of rank in the social scale."[80] But as we've seen, reformers too perceived ranks and contentedly proscribed rights and prescribed improvements for those below. The distinction between Grits and Tories could be fine. The reason for this, it now seems clear, lies in the nature of colonial Nova Scotia's liberalism, a liberalism that sought a balance of freedom and authority closer to an older British model than to the American model to the south and one that offered fewer resources (both political and material) for middle-class mobilization. More mercantilist than republican, more statist than democratic, it continued to seek government more through elite-led regulation than through popular self-government. It is in this particular balance that industry and improvement most powerfully left their marks on Nova Scotia.

In Britain combinations of capital formation, class conflict, agrarian improvement, and liberal and utilitarian political ideas fundamentally changed the country and demanded that the models and practices of governance re-form in ways completely unforeseen a half-century earlier. By the nineteenth century the drive for overseas dominion was propelled by a sense of "the expansion of England," by a class, race, and gender-specific compulsion, a nationalist/colonialist dream, to recreate Britishness abroad. We can see in the directors of the GMA, in men like the Stewarts and Samuel Cunard, and in the men who ran the Colonial Office a vision of an imagined empire that logically flowed from the drive to plant England overseas. Much the same was understood by players on the western side of the Atlantic. Colonial officials and those of a nascent, colonial-bourgeois class were aware of the same basic issues and desirous of many of the same results. The Nova Scotia elite were well aware of their place in the empire, but they imagined a still grander New World order: a state with the capacity to organize and govern property and production, a state that could allow the elite to set their own course, a state where Victorian men could advance themselves, their families, communities, colonies, and nations. In this context, the local elite would set their own course; they would do so in ways learned from the "parent country," facilitated by colonial capital, and often resisted by the poor.

Industry and improvement left their marks on the Nova Scotia landscape. As surely as strata were forming across the social geography of the province, new physical landscapes were emerging too, imprinting the land with marks of improvement's many different forms and differential effects. The imagined landscapes of John Young and Richard Smith – the "verdant meadow" and the industrial valley, Sussex and Staffordshire – were ideals, and by mid-century reasonable facsimiles certainly could be located in numerous locations across the province. But the countryside's landscape articulated a fantastic range of circumstances from the magnificent Champs-élysées and the extensive croplands of the West River to the hundreds of middling farms scattered across our study area, and from the stony upland and backland farms behind Mabou, Margaree, and Middle River to the rocky shores, stone-littered quarries, and blackened landscapes of the mining and quarrying centres across the country of coal from Cow Bay to Mabou Coal Mines and from the East River to the Joggins. Durham, on the West River of Pictou County, the transplanted centre of the Pictou Agricultural Society, was certainly at the heart of the area's best farming districts, not only outproducing most centres in northern Nova Scotia but also proudly exhibiting its superior social and political acumen in a number of public locations. To this day, one can drive along the valley of the West River and still see the clear evidence of improvement in the rich green fields, the classic patchwork pattern of fenced fields, the farm equipment, and a number of sprawling country homes. Few of these homes were built in the period discussed here – most date from the turn of the century – but undoubtedly they are products of capital generated by these same lands, of surplus accumulated from the labour of any number of "plodholes," and of plans and practices that emerged from the rich discourse of improvement.

But conquering the landscape was the least of these elite colonists' concerns. The major obstacles to liberalizing colonial Nova Scotia were its decidedly illiberal peoples, particularly their annoyingly stubborn habits of acting in ways other than those prescribed by the public-spirited enterprise of the improvers. Whether it was an individual farmer's unwillingness to give up his "old hoe," the quarriers' refusal to surrender their worksites, or the persistent obstinacy of so many in rejecting the orderly expectations of others, there were any number of contexts from which the commonsense of liberal practice simply made no sense. Resisted by "the Fraternity," rioting miners, "congregating" peasants, and the innumerable "collusions" and "combinations" of peoples who sought only a modest independence (sometimes propertied, sometimes not) and who were accustomed to exercising dominion over their own lives and families, liberals did not follow an easy course. These were the people of the country of coal. Together with the colony's metropolitan colonizers, modernizing state officials, local improvers, and petty enclosers, they comprised an acutely uneven and variegated social landscape, one characterized by a capricious climate and a varied resource base but above all by a people of varied ideals, expectations, and needs. Aspects of these ordinary people's ideas and practices would survive but not fully intact. A history of nineteenth-century Nova Scotia must reinstate these people at the centre of the province's story. If they lost, they nevertheless altered the story; if their legacy is no longer evident, their story can remind us of the costs exacted in securing liberal capitalism as the cornerstone of the New World order.

Improvers were participants in the process of creating a governable society, a point that they themselves clearly understood. Although only indirectly part of the process of state formation, they were very much a part of making the state governable, of making liberal government. Tories and reformers alike recognized that the government of any society was the place of enlightened men who accepted their duty as citizens, so both took up the banner of improvement with great enthusiasm. Whether a particular contest was over responsible government, tariff policy, when one should marry (and whom), the location of a road, an evaluation of the best breed of cattle, or the appropriate membership of a temperance society, part of this duty was not only to step forward but also to participate in the broader contest for the occupation, definition, and ultimate control of the public spaces wherein these issues would be decided. In this sense, we can see Young's "letters," the societies' parades and competitions, mechanics' institutes, and workingmen's libraries, the contests over females in temperance, or any of the local agricultural societies' reports as both discrete and linked moments in the ongoing process of defining and claiming these spaces. Upholding the banner of improvement was a key component, but it was only part of a larger process. Occupying these locations allowed these men not only to reinforce their sense of social position but also to put themselves and their fellows forward as men (as defined against a vague, shapeless other) who were doing their duty. The societies' correspondence, we must remember, represents only slices of these men's lives. But when, for example, we situate their reports of their own immediate successes (as compared with most others' alleged failures) and their self-descriptions as enlightened men (versus the "peasants" around them), we see men attempting to legitimate their claim on these public spaces. Many, undoubtedly, would have argued that obtaining an appointment as justice of the peace did not allow one an unambiguous claim on respectability. Standing up for God, country, science, and progress – in short, for the public duty of improvement – might not do so either, but it usually added solid proof of one's service. Even where it was understood that an ordered society was natural, such activities served to individualize actions and social positions – implicating some and elevating others, individually. With civil society so completely linked to, and dependent on, the colonial state, local politics in rural Nova Scotia remained an elite preserve, further weakening avenues for the emergence of a broader popular democratic politics.

The improvers' greatest achievement was their ability to represent, politically and symbolically, the central place of civic virtues such as the independence of property across a range of diverse social locations and to attach these virtues so clearly to measurable indices such as wealth and property. So much, of such great importance, could be demonstrated to depend on the linchpin of a propertied independence. Our examination of the structure of wealth suggests a significant range of material (in)security or economic capacity among the province's rural population. A propertied independence offered more than material security; it marked the base point for an independent citizenry. This citizenry posited virtuous public and private behaviour, industriousness, manliness, temperance, and respectability as the features that began to define the liberal subject.

Outside this public sphere of political negotiations and elite discourse, the improvers' ideas also reinforced private capitalists' individual rights and freedoms against the inconvenient impositions of the poor, the dispossessed, and more generally those who continued to adhere to illiberal habits. For the poor, government meant a diverse bundle of practices directed toward attaining independence, interdependence, and self-regulation. For the liberal improvers, government meant the regulation of social being, the orderly relations of property and authority, and under the strictest senses of proper conduct, the government of the self. As the improvers made clear, many settlers were showing themselves to be out of step with the programmatic advancement of the new liberal order. State-based improvers from John Young to J.W. Dawson worked tirelessly to reinvigorate the colony by stressing the value of education, proper conduct, the correct use of manures, and the judicious application of capital. Samuel Cunard and his fellows on the board of the GMA also wished to discuss improvement and capital. They were concerned much less with propriety and a propertied independence than with the independence of property. Their long battle with the province provided many lessons in the strength and importance of property and "immense capital," a shining example for the developmental period that would begin after Confederation.

Notes

INTRODUCTION

1 Dipesh Chakrabarty, "Postcoloniality and the Artifice of History," 21.
2 Lucy Maud Montgomery, *Anne of Green Gables*, 12.
3 Raymond Williams, *The Country and the City*, 165–81. See also Janice Kulyk Keefer, *Under Eastern Eyes*.
4 Ian McKay, "The 1910s," 228; Daniel Samson, "Dependency and Rural Industry," 104–59; E.R. Forbes, *Maritime Rights*.
5 Daniel Vickers, *Farmers and Fishermen*; Allan Kulikoff, *From British Peasants to Colonial American Farmers*; N.E.S. Griffiths, *From Migrant to Acadian*; James W. St G. Walker, *The Black Loyalists*; Carolyn Merchant, *Ecological Revolutions*.
6 William Cronon, *Changes in the Land*, 54–81; William C. Wicken, *Mi'kmaq Treaties on Trial*, 169–211.
7 This is a point also made, although in quite different ways, by Richard Judd, *Common Lands, Common People*; by R.W. Sandwell, *Contesting Rural Space*; by John Weaver, *The Great Land Rush and the Making of the Modern World, 1650–1900*; and by Rusty Bittermann, *Rural Protest on Prince Edward Island*.
8 For very different perspectives that nevertheless share an emphasis on "transition," see Christopher Clark, *The Roots of Rural Capitalism*; and Winifred Barr Rothenberg, *From Market-Places to a Market Economy*. Steven Maynard, "Between Farm and Factory," emphasizes the centrality of non-market activities in rural Pictou County households well into the industrial era. See also Béatrice Craig, Judith Rygiel, and Elizabeth Turcotte, "The Homespun Paradox."
9 Steven Hahn and Jonathan Prude, *The Countryside in the Age of Capitalist Transformation*.

10 Daniel Vickers, "Competency and Competition"; Daniel Vickers, "'Those Damned Shad.'" Compare Richard L. Bushman, "Markets and Composite Farms in Early America"; and Kulikoff, *From British Peasants.*

11 Sandwell, *Contesting Rural Space*; Daniel Samson, "Visions du libéralisme et de 'l'amélioration' dans la Nouvelle-Écosse rurale, 1820–1848."

12 Horace Miner, *St. Denis, a French-Canadian Parish*; Robert Redfield, *Peasant Society and its Culture.*

13 Charles W. Dunn, *Highland Settler*, 122–35.

14 Ibid., 119–21, also emphasizes women's roles and how women succumbed to a love of "finery," "dancing," prepared foods, and domestic labour-saving devices.

15 Ian McKay, *The Quest of the Folk*, 30–42.

16 Colin McKay, "The New Brunswick Farmer," esp. 259–61.

17 See, for example, D. Campbell and R.A. MacLean, *Beyond the Atlantic Roar*; Richard Apostle and Gene Barrett, *Emptying Their Nets*; Maynard, "Between Farm and Factory"; and Michael J. Troughton, "From Nodes to Nodes."

18 T.W. Acheson, "The National Policy and the Industrialization of the Maritimes, 1880–1910"; D.A. Muise, "'The Great Transformation'"; Ian McKay, "The Crisis of Dependent Development."

19 Rusty Bittermann, "The Hierarchy of the Soil"; Béatrice Craig, "Le développement agricole"; Debra McNabb, "The Role of the Land in Settling Horton Township, Nova Scotia."

20 T.W. Acheson, "The Great Merchant and Economic Development in Saint John, 1820–50"; Eric Sager, with Gerald E. Panting, *Maritime Capital*, 23–46; Stephen J. Hornsby, *Nineteenth-Century Cape Breton*, 85–110.

21 David Frank, "The Country of Coal."

22 Marilynn Gerriets, "Agricultural Resources, Agricultural Production, and Settlement at Confederation."

23 Julian Gwyn, *Excessive Expectations*, 72–3, 109–16.

24 Royden Harrison, ed., *The Independent Collier.*

25 Ian McKay, "'By Wisdom, Wile or War'"; D.A. Muise, "The Making of an Industrial Community"; and David Frank, "The Industrial Folk Song in Cape Breton."

26 C.B. Fergusson, *The Labour Movement in Nova Scotia before Confederation*; Hornsby, *Nineteenth-Century Cape Breton*, 95–109.

27 The general point about the effect of the monopoly is made by most writers. The most effective treatment – and from where I borrow the use of the term "enclave" – is McKay, "The Crisis."

28 The following draws upon Elizabeth Mancke, "Imperial Transitions"; Elizabeth Mancke, "Early Modern Imperial Governance and the Origins

of Canadian Political Culture"; and G.A. Rawlyk, *The Canada Fire.* See also
J.M. Beck, *The Government of Nova Scotia.*

29 Ian McKay, "The Liberal Order Framework."

30 Raymond Williams, *Keywords,* 320.

31 J.M. Neeson, *Commoners,* 30–1, 34–52; E.P. Thompson, *Customs in Common,*
99–126; Eric Richards, *A History of the Highland Clearances,* vol. 2, 25–31; T.C.
Smout, "Problems of Nationalism, Identity and Improvement in Later Eighteenth-Century Scotland." In Steven Stoll, *Larding the Earth,* 20–5, note the different use of improvement as having a sustainability, or conservationist,
dimension that Stoll argues is distinctly American. Certainly, part of this difference can be explained by the unique circumstances of Nova Scotia agriculture, but I would maintain that in rescuing a "permanent" vision, Stoll
downplays the improvers' elite politics.

32 C.A. Bayly, *Imperial Meridian,* 121–5.

33 Daniel Samson, "'The Yoke of Improvement.'" James Livesay, "Agrarian
Ideology and Commercial Republicanism in the French Revolution," discusses how the revolutionary government of France sought a similar
balance.

34 Michel Foucault, "On Governmentality." This is the first discussion of the
term "governmentality," but the notion is evident as well in Foucault's
Discipline and Punish, 213–28, and in his *The History of Sexuality,* vol. 1,
135–45.

35 Foucault, "On Governmentality," 87–8. Two strains emerge within the governmentality literature, one more attentive to the government of the liberal
self and one more attentive to the administration of liberal societies. On the
liberal self, see Patrick Joyce, *The Rule of Freedom,* and on administration, see
Mary Poovey, *Making a Social Body,* and Bruce Curtis, *True Government by Choice
Men?* and "Foucault on Governmentality and Population."

36 In this specifically Foucauldian context, see Patrick Joyce, *Democratic Subjects.*
B. Anne Wood picks up on some of this as a specifically middle-class
tension in her *Evangelical Balance Sheet.* More generally, see Joyce E.
Chaplin, *An Anxious Pursuit;* Christopher L. Tomlins, *Law, Labor, and Ideology
in the Early American Republic;* James Vernon, *Politics and the People;* E. Jane
Errington, *The Lion, the Eagle, and Upper Canada;* and Joyce Appleby, *Liberalism
and Republicanism in the Historical Imagination.*

37 This, of course, is a massive simplification of a complex and historiographi-
cally contentious process. See, however, Anthony Arblaster, *The Rise and Decline of Western Liberalism,* 162–202; Jean-Marie Fecteau, *Un nouvel ordre des
chose;* and Jeffery McNairn's important study on the development of public
opinion, *The Capacity to Judge.*

38 Rawlyk, *The Canada Fire*; Nancy J. Christie, "'In These Times of Democratic Rage and Delusion.'"

39 See, for example, the editorials and letters on the Navigation Acts and the Reform Bill in the *Colonial Patriot*, 18 January 1828, 25 January 1828, 19 November 1831, 26 November 1831, and 15 May 1832.

40 "What is Liberalism?" *Cape Breton Spectator*, 14 August 1847. For an attempt by William Young and Herbert Huntington to define "what we mean by a 'Liberal' in Nova Scotia," see Nova Scotia, *Journals of the House of Assembly* (1840), appendix 21. McNairn's work on Upper Canada, *Capacity to Judge*, emphasizes a more sophisticated discussion of politics.

41 Gordon Darroch, "Scanty Fortunes and Rural Middle Class Formation in Nineteenth Century Central Ontario"; Marvin MacInnis, "The Size and Structure of Farming in Canada West, 1861"; Rusty Bittermann, Robert A. MacKinnon, and Graeme Wynn, "Of Inequality and Interdependence in the Nova Scotian Countryside, 1850–70." Evidence in Sandwell, *Contesting Rural Space*, 213–24, suggests still greater inequality on Saltspring Island, British Columbia, although such subregional variation should be expected.

42 See D.A. Muise, "The Federal Election of 1867 in Nova Scotia"; and Brian Tennyson, "Economic Nationalism and Confederation."

43 Kenneth G. Pryke, *Nova Scotia and Confederation, 1864–1875*, 14; Rosemarie Langout, "Developing Nova Scotia." For an account that significantly deepens this focus, see David A. Sutherland, "Voluntary Societies and the Process of Middle-Class Formation in Early Victorian, Halifax, Nova Scotia."

44 Curtis, *True Government?*; Fecteau, *Un nouvel ordre*.

45 Allan Greer and Ian Radforth, "Introduction," in Allan Greer and Ian Radforth, eds, *Colonial Leviathan*, 10–11.

46 Graeme Wynn, "Ideology, Society, and State in the Maritime Colonies of British North America, 1840–1860," 313–18; Bruce Curtis, "The Canada 'Blue Books' and the Administrative Capacity of the Canadian State, 1822–67."

47 For the Canadian context, see Tina Loo, *Making Law, Order, and Authority in British Columbia, 1821–1871*; Sandwell, *Contesting Rural Space*; and Adele Perry, *On the Edge of Empire*. Among the broader colonial literature, I have also been influenced by the visions, if not always the methodologies, of Ranajit Guha, *Elementary Aspects of Peasant Insurgency in Colonial India*; Gilbert M. Joseph and Daniel Nugent, eds, *Everyday Forms of State Formation*; and James C. Scott, *Weapons of the Weak*.

48 Curtis, *True Government?* 8–11, 101–24. See also J.I. Little, *State and Society in Transition*; and McNairn, *Capacity to Judge*, esp. 63–115.

49 Bittermann, *Rural Protest*; Allan Greer, *The Patriots and the People*.

CHAPTER ONE

1 Joseph Howe, *Western and Eastern Rambles,* 142–3, this section originally published in Howe's newspaper, the *Novascotian,* 4 February 1830.

2 Ibid., 153, 189, 193–4.

3 Ibid., 191.

4 W.S. Moorsom, *Letters from Nova Scotia,* 330–1.

5 Ibid., 141–3.

6 Ibid., 336–8.

7 Graeme Wynn, "A Region of Scattered Settlements," 342–5; Bernard Bailyn, *Voyagers to the West.*

8 See, for example, Graeme Wynn, "Late Eighteenth-Century Agriculture on the Bay of Fundy Marshlands"; Alan R. MacNeil, "The Acadian Legacy and Agricultural Development in Nova Scotia, 1760–1861"; D.A. Muise, ed., "A Descriptive and Statistical Account of Nova Scotia and Its Dependencies," 92; and Debra McNabb, "The Role of the Land in Settling Horton Township, Nova Scotia."

9 Elizabeth Mancke, "At the Counter of the General Store."

10 See D.B. Cann and R.E. Wicklund, "Soil Survey of Pictou County, Nova Scotia"; D.B. Cann, J.I. MacDougall, and J.D. Hilchey, "Soil Survey of Cape Breton Island"; and J.I. Nowland and J.I. MacDougall, *Soils of Cumberland County, Nova Scotia.*

11 Rusty Bittermann, "The Hierarchy of the Soil," 54.

12 "Pictou County Deeds," books 4 and 5 (1810–11), RG 47, Nova Scotia Archives and Records Management (NSARM).

13 See R.G. Riddell, "A Study of the Land Policy of the Colonial Office, 1763–1855"; Stephen J. Hornsby, *Nineteenth-Century Cape Breton,* 51–2; and Rusty Bittermann, "Economic Stratification and Agrarian Settlement."

14 Hornsby, *Nineteenth-Century Cape Breton,* 51–7; "Petition of a number of people of the East River of Pictou," 20 July 1810, no. 87, vol. 225, RG 1, NSARM.

15 This was a particularly grave problem for women, especially widows; see Petition of Ulalie Paon, Arichat, 6 May 1820, and Petition of Eleanor Poirier, 6 May 1820 [the dates appear to have been added; the petitions seem to date from 1816], Colonial Office records for Nova Scotia (hereafter CO) 217/133; Swayne to Bathurst, 26 July 1814, CO 217/132; Crawley to George, 5 April 1837, "C," vol. 54, RG 20, NSARM.

16 L.F.S. Upton, *Micmacs and Colonists,* 84–8.

17 This is nicely illustrated in Hornsby's map of settlement (1800) and Crown-land grants (1786–1820), in *Nineteenth-Century Cape Breton,* 4, 49.

18 *Colonial Patriot*, 28 December 1827. See also John Young, *The Letters of Agricola on the Principles of Vegetation and Tillage*, 120–1.

19 Howe, *Western and Eastern Rambles*, 170. See also Bailyn, *Voyagers to the West*, 390–7; and George Patterson, *A History of the County of Pictou, Nova Scotia*, 121–2.

20 Patrick C.T. White, ed., *Lord Selkirk's Diary, 1803–1804*, 46.

21 Ibid., 47.

22 Ibid., 37–9. For a discussion of Selkirk's view on Highlanders, see Eric Richards, *A History of the Highland Clearances*, vol. 2, 36–43.

23 White, ed., *Lord Selkirk's Diary*, 50–1.

24 See James McGregor to John Young, 17 January 1825, no. 151, vol. 6, RG 8, NSARM; Alexander Stewart to James Johnston, 13 November 1828, no. 58, vol. 1539, MG 1, NSARM. See also Rusty Bittermann, "Farm Households and Wage Labour in the Northeastern Maritimes before 1850," 38–9; and Peter A. Russell, "Forest into Farmland," 326–39.

25 James McKenzie, cited in Great Britain, *Parliamentary Papers* (1839), vol. 17, 144–5. Some farms in Cumberland County sold for between £1,500 and £3,250 in the late 1810s; see Cumberland County, book G, RG 47, NSARM. Graeme Wynn, *Timber Colony*, 78–81, estimates that between £30 and £40 were necessary in New Brunswick but that between £100 and £300 would buy a farm on a good site with some land already cleared. As in Nova Scotia, prime land sold for about £15 per acre, and a very good farm could sell for between £2,000 and £3,000. Robert Leslie Jones, *History of Agriculture in Ontario, 1613–1880*, 67, estimates £100 as a minimum in Ontario in about 1840; Robert E. Ankli and Kenneth J. Duncan, "Farm Making Costs in Early Ontario," 48, regard Jones's estimate as "most reliable," adding that they find it "hard to believe that anyone could have started with less and have had any prospect of success."

26 Hornsby, *Nineteenth-Century Cape Breton*, 48–51.

27 On the ideal of the yeoman, see Bittermann, "Farm Households"; and Joyce Appleby, *Liberalism and Republicanism in the Historical Imagination*, 255–60.

28 George Ross to John Young, 22 February 1822, no. 137, vol. 6, RG 8, NSARM.

29 Thomas McCulloch, *The Mephibosheth Stepsure Letters*. See also *Colonial Patriot*, 12 November 1828, 22 October 1831, and 12 March 1833; and Patterson, *History of the County of Pictou*, 86, 246. The important corrective here is Wynn, *Timber Colony*.

30 Gerald Sider, *Culture and Class in Anthropology and History*, 12–38, 58–73, 146–8.

31 Daniel Vickers, *Farmers and Fishermen*, 100; Wynn, *Timber Colony*, 114–16;
    Douglas McCalla, "Rural Credit and Rural Development in Upper Canada,
    1790–1850."

32 See Wynn, *Timber Colony*; and Alan R. MacNeil, "Society and Economy in
    Rural Nova Scotia, 1761–1861," 221–58.

33 James Luttrell DesBarres to Isabella DesBarres, 20 July 1815, vol. 25, MG
    23, National Archives Canada (NAC), DesBarres Papers, vol. 2 (hereafter
    DesBarres Papers), 4793–5. Tenants on the DesBarres estate at Tatama-
    gouche often paid their rent in timber. See, for example, "Bond" of James
    Mattatal, 24 June 1800 [13 tons at 15s per ton], DesBarres Papers, 4185;
    and "Bond" of David Mattatal, 5 August 1806 [10 tons squared and butted
    for £15], DesBarres Papers, 4190.

34 A.A. Johnston, *A History of the Catholic Church in Eastern Nova Scotia*, vol. 1,
    458–9; David Stewart journal, 14 July 1831, 3209/28, Public Archives of
    Prince Edward Island (PAPEI); *Colonial Patriot*, 3 September 1831 and
    11 June 1833. See also Bittermann, "Farm Households," 50–4.

35 White, ed., *Lord Selkirk's Diary*, 45–7.

36 Patterson, *History of the County of Pictou*, 250–5, quotation at 251. In one
    seven-week period, his bookkeeper told George Patterson some years later,
    he shipped £35,000 worth of timber.

37 Ibid., quotation at 251; *Colonial Patriot*, 11 January 1828; petition of the
    inhabitants "on the shore of the Gulf of St Lawrence," "P," vol. 16, RG 5,
    NSARM.

38 Susan Buggey, "Edward Mortimer," 611.

39 Patterson, *History of the County of Pictou*, 252.

40 Pictou County Quarter Sessions, 5, "P," vol. 318, RG 34, NSARM. See, for ex-
    ample, the cases of Alexander Graham (39 lashes), 17 May 1815; and
    George Clegson (24 lashes), 24 July 1816.

41 Lewis M. Wilkins to Peleg Wiswall, [c. 1815], Peleg Wiswall Papers, no. 3,
    folio 7, vol. 979, MG 1, NSARM. See also Wynn, *Timber Colony*, 111–12.

42 William Matheson Papers, 289, Micro: Biography: William Matheson,
    1824–29, NSARM.

43 "Account of Timber Purchased," 1829–31, 10 November 1831, William
    and George Harper Papers (1829–31), d58, MG 24, NAC; Helen Harper
    Steeves, *The Story of Moncton's First Store and Storekeeper.*

44 William Harper to James King, 27 October 1831, d58, MG 24, NAC.

45 See Robert Plunkett to James Luttrell DesBarres, 25 October 1815,
    DesBarres Papers, 5010–11. See also *Colonial Patriot*, 21 December 1827.

46 The following is from "Fort Lawrence Business Papers," Thomas Roach,
    Account Book, 1801–13, no. 1, vol. 119, MG 3, NSARM.

47 A current list from 1807 indicates 277 accounts totalling £2,746.7.9 in out-
standing charges. Most of the accountholders, we must presume, came
from Amherst Township, but the list includes at least 22 accounts for individuals from across the basin in either Minudie or Maccan. See "Account,
1807," no. 7, vol. 119, MG 3, NSARM.

48 See accounts for Benjamin Wilson and Jesse Converse, "Fort Lawrence
Business Papers," Thomas Roach, Account Book, 1801–13, no. 1, vol. 119,
MG 3, NSARM. One firkin equals nine UK gallons, approximately seventy-
five pounds.

49 The quotation is from "Fort Lawrence Business Papers," Thomas Roach,
Account Book, 1801–13, no. 1, vol. 119, MG 3, NSARM.

50 Labour exchange: Jesse Bent (page 7), William Brown (17), Thomas
Merrill (21), and numerous others. Grindstones: Maximin Burk (a
Minudie tenant), who received £6.1.6 for ninety-six grindstones and £3 for
"2 months work" (181), James Beaumont (15), Samuel Hicks (30), John
Boss, another Minudie tenant (59), William Read (88), John Leblong
(Leblanc) (99), Benjamin Read (102), Ezra Barnes (109), William
Easterbrook (110), Peter Melanson (150), Joseph Sears (157), Maximin
Burk (181), Myer Ayre (230), and Hugh Boyd (265), in Thomas Roach,
Account Book, 1801–13, no. 1, vol. 119, MG 3, NSARM.

51 See the accounts for Mark Thompson (page 69), grain and road money;
William Donkin (71), grain bounty; Robert Donkin Jr (76), road money;
Mrs George Niles (107), land; and George Newton (27), in Thomas Roach,
Account Book, 1801–13, no. 1, vol. 119, MG 3, NSARM. In all likelihood, the
labourer never saw his money; it was simply credited against his account, usu-
ally against goods charged at the credit price. See also "An Old Inhabitant,"
Pictou Observer, 7 March 1832; "A Friend to Man," *Pictou Observer,* 15 February
1832; and "Thistle" from Cape Breton, *Colonial Patriot,* 30 July 1828.

52 For timber contracts, see accounts of Peter McElman (page 29), George
Graves (96), Charles Chapple (163), William Donkin Jr (268), and William
Chapman (296) in Thomas Roach, Account Book, 1801–13, no. 1,
vol. 119, MG 3, NSARM. See also Muise, ed., "Descriptive and Statistical
Account"; and MacNeil, "Society and Economy."

53 See Bailyn, *Voyagers to the West,* 391–6; Elizabeth Mancke, "Corporate Structure
and Private Interest," 161; Winthrop Bell, *The "Foreign Protestants" and the Settlement of Nova Scotia;* J.M. Bumsted, *The People's Clearances;* Hornsby, *Nineteenth-
Century Cape Breton,* 41–7; and Patterson, *History of the County of Pictou,* 46–78.

54 On the failed schemes of the eighteenth century, Bailyn's *Voyagers to the West*
is most useful. However, attempts continued into the nineteenth
century; see Viscount Falkland to Lord John Russell, Halifax, 21 December

1841; and H.W. Crawley to John Whidden, Provincial Secretary, 27 October 1841, both reprinted in "Correspondence Related to Emigration," in Public Record Office, London, England, *British Parliamentary Papers*, vol. 16, 462–97; Wentworth to Hobart [secretary of state], 1 February 1804, 479–81, vol. 53, RG 1, NSARM.

55 Bailyn, *Voyagers to the West*, 406.

56 John Robinson and Thomas Rispin, *A Journey through Nova-Scotia*, 33–4.

57 The following is pieced together from a number of letters and legal papers in the Harrison Papers, vol. 427, MG 1, NSARM.

58 Luke Harrison to William Harrison, 189–91, vol. 427, MG 1, NSARM; book G, 10 March 1818, Cumberland County, RG 47, NSARM. The mortgage stipulated payments of £87 per year, which included 6 per cent interest per year calculated on the original £525. See also Elijah Purdy to John Young [list of officers and committee], 12 January 1820, no. 158, vol. 6, RG 8, NSARM.

59 "Agreement," pg. 202, book F, Amherst Township, RG 20, NSARM.

60 Cape Breton Land Papers, 1820, nos 2405, 2425, 2618, NSARM. Bittermann, "Farm Households," 37, also notes former PEI tenants settling to the rear of St Peter's in southeastern Cape Breton in 1818.

61 White, ed., *Lord Selkirk's Diary*, 37–9; Bittermann, "Economic Stratification," 73–5.

62 Patterson, *History of the County of Pictou*, 130.

63 List of land grants from 1809–10, January 1811, CO 217/88.

64 Rosemary E. Ommer, "Primitive Accumulation and the Scottish *Clann* in the Old World and the New."

65 Bailyn, *Voyagers to the West*, 373–90; Robert J. Morgan, "Joseph Wallet Frederick Desbarres"; G.N.D. Evans, *Uncommon Obdurate*, 27–42.

66 See the map "Distribution of population in the Maritimes, 1750," in N.E.S. Griffiths, *The Contexts of Acadian History, 1686–1784*, 65. Griffiths also notes that the term "aboiteaux" is specifically Acadian (58–9).

67 See Israel Longworth, *History of Colchester County, Nova Scotia*, 88.

68 Petition from the Residents of Tatamagouche, 2 September 1795, DesBarres Papers, 4179–80.

69 Captain John Macdonald, "Conditions of Settlement at Tatamagouche, Nova Scotia, 1795," xxviii; F.L. Pigot, "John Macdonald of Glenaladale."

70 Macdonald, "Conditions of Settlement," xli; Rusty Bittermann, *Rural Protest on Prince Edward Island*, 21–3.

71 Macdonald, "Conditions of Settlement," xxxviii–xxxix.

72 DesBarres to Haliburton, 3 September 1815, DesBarres Papers, 4908–10.

73 Ainslie to Bathurst, 3 July 1817, CO 217/135; Draft of Address of the Assembly, 1 April 1815, no. 3, vol. 305, RG 1, NSARM.

74 Macormick to Sydney [secretary of state], 5 September 1788, CO 217/105.

75 Wentworth to Hobart, 10 September 1802, CO 217/76/475–9.

76 Wentworth to Portland, 27 July 1801, CO 217/75/91.

77 William Haliburton to Nathaniel Atcheson, 20 August 1812, CO 217/97/79–83, original emphasis.

78 See also the similar ethnic hierarchy outlined by Samuel Cunard in "Report from the Select Committee of the House of Lords appointed to consider the Means by which Colonization may be made subsidiary to other measures for the Improvement of the social condition of Ireland," in Great Britain, *Parliamentary Papers*, vol. 6 (1847), minutes of evidence, 74; the comments of "Father Manseau" on the "negroes of Tracadie," in Johnston, *History of the Catholic Church*, vol. 1, 337–8; and Moorsom's disparaging comments on the lack of "industry" displayed by African Americans, Acadians, and the Highland Scots, in *Letters from Nova Scotia*, 127–8, 334, 344. There is also, of course, the vicious racism of T.C. Haliburton's Sam Slick novels.

79 Draft of Assembly to the Lt Governor [expressing concerns over the immigration of "refugee negroes"], no. 3, vol. 305; and Wentworth to Castlereagh [secretary of state], 3 February 1806, 78–83, vol. 54, both in RG 1, NSARM.

80 *Colonial Patriot*, 21 December 1827. See also Moorsom, *Letters from Nova Scotia*, 127–8; and Report of the Committee on the "Probability of Employment for Emigrant Laborers to Nova Scotia," 26 November 1831, 368–75, vol. 195, RG 1, NSARM.

81 MacNeil, "Society and Economy," 78–9; Moorsom, *Letters from Nova Scotia*, 130.

82 See James W. St G. Walker, *The Black Loyalists*, 18–32.

83 Ward Chipman, quoted in Robin W. Winks, "Negroes in the Maritimes," 461; Walker, *Black Loyalists*, 42–9; Draft of Address of the Assembly, 1 April 1815, no. 3, vol. 305, RG 1, NSARM; Harvey Amani Whitfield, "Black Refugee Communities in Early Nineteenth Century Nova Scotia."

84 G.A. Rawlyk, "The Guysborough Negroes."

85 For Acadians, the figure was 28.2 acres; see "Township of Tracadie," Census Returns, 1827, vol. 447, RG 1, NSARM.

86 Moorsom, *Letters from Nova Scotia*, 127–31; I.E. Bill, *Fifty Years with the Baptist Ministers and Churches of the Maritime Provinces*, 87, 238, 289–90; C.B. Fergusson, *A Documentary Study of the Establishment of the Negroes in Nova Scotia*, 2–3.

87 Sir Colin Campbell to Lord Glenelg, 25 August 1837, 55–7, vol. 115, RG 1, NSARM.

88 See Walker, *Black Loyalists*, xi; George Elliott Clarke, ed., *Fire on the Water*, 12–6; and G.A. Rawlyk, *The Canada Fire*, 33–43.

89 Griffiths, *Contexts of Acadian History*, 56–61, quotation at 27.

90 McCulloch, *Mephibosheth Stepsure Letters*.

91 Appleby, *Liberalism and Republicanism*, 56.

92 "Minudie," DesBarres Papers, 22–3.

93 DesBarres Papers, 39–40.

94 Report of James Chalmers, 1805, DesBarres Papers, 4124–5; Stephen Oxley to John Young, River Philip, 16 December 1818, reprinted in Young, *Letters of Agricola*, 224–7. See also Thomas Chandler Haliburton, *Historical and Statistical Account of Nova Scotia*, vol. 1, 64–5; and "Sketch of the character, mode of living &c., of the Acadians," Hugh Graham to Dr Brown, 9 September 1791, CO 217/110.

95 Haliburton, *Historical and Statistical Account*, vol. 2, 229.

96 J.B. Uniacke, quoted in "Report from the Select Committee of the House of Lords appointed to consider the Means by which Colonization may be made subsidiary to other measures for the Improvement of the social condition of Ireland," in Great Britain, *Parliamentary Papers*, vol. 6 (1847), minutes of evidence, 48.

97 Ommer, "Primitive Accumulation," 131–4; Maureen Molloy, "'No Inclination to Mix with Strangers.'"

98 Rev. Thomas Trotter, cited in J.S. Martell, "The Achievements of Agricola and the Agricultural Societies, 1818–1825," 17; Young, *Letters of Agricola*, 224–7.

99 Orders to quit, in DesBarres Papers: John Henry (p. 4128), John Seamans [*sic*] (4132), Nicholas Seamans (4134), and W. Terris (4834). On *all* the tenants of Minudie, see J.F.W. DesBarres to W.D. Haliburton, 27 November 1813, DesBarres Papers, 4865–67. See also in DesBarres Papers: James Glennie to DesBarres, 10 April 1813 (p. 4828); W.H.O. Haliburton to Peter Brine and others, January 1815 (4835–6); and Haliburton to DesBarres, 29 July 1813 (4847–8).

100 DesBarres to Haliburton, 4 June 1815, DesBarres Papers, 4903–4, original emphasis.

101 See the new leases and evictions, dated 1815, in DesBarres Papers, 5235–38.

102 "Minudie," 1827, no. 103, vol. 446, RG 1, NSARM.

103 "Diary of Capt. John Huston, 1793–1801," vol. 493, MG 1, NSARM. This is an incorrect identification; Huston was dead by 1790.

104 In DesBarres Papers: J.W. McDonald to James Luttrell DesBarres, Minudie, 23 November 1810 (p. 3925–7); "Bond" of John Seamans and James Glenie with J.F.W. DesBarres, 15 December 1808 (4144–49); "Bond" between Peter Brine Sr et al. and DesBarres, 17 October 1815 (5235–8); "Rents at Minudie," May 1811 (4174).

105 Hornsby, *Nineteenth-Century Cape Breton*, 70, 75–8. See also Charles W. Dunn, *Highland Settler*, 24–33, 150–2; and D. Campbell and R.A. MacLean, *Beyond the Atlantic Roar*.

106 Hornsby, *Nineteenth-Century Cape Breton*, 71; Dunn, *Highland Settler*, 28, 31, 63; Mary Byers and Margaret McBurney, *Atlantic Hearth*.

107 Douglas McCalla, *Planting the Province*, 6–7.

CHAPTER TWO

1 John Young, *The Letters of Agricola on the Principles of Vegetation and Tillage*, 44.

2 D.C. Harvey, "The Intellectual Awakening of Nova Scotia."

3 Stanley MacMullin, "In Search of the Liberal Mind," 85.

4 Thomas McCulloch, *The Mephibosheth Stepsure Letters*.

5 Graeme Wynn, "Exciting a Spirit of Emulation among the 'Plodholes,'" 5–9.

6 D.C. Harvey, "Pre-Agricola John Young"; R.A. MacLean, "John Young."

7 Anonymous to Young, 3 November 1819, I 204, MG 24, National Archives Canada (NAC); William Young to "Mother," 4 July 1815, no. 6, vol. 731, MG 2, Nova Scotia Archives and Records Management (NSARM). On Young and Sinclair, see J.S. Martell, "The Achievements of Agricola and the Agricultural Societies, 1818–1825," 9; and John Young, *Report of the Provincial Agricultural Society*, 11.

8 John Young, *An Inquiry into the Impolicy of Fixing Wages by Law*. I have found references to this book, but no British libraries hold a copy.

9 Young, *Letters of Agricola*, 19–22.

10 Vernon C. Fowke, *Canadian Agricultural Policy*, 32–9; Martell, "Achievements of Agricola," 1–2.

11 Young, *Letters of Agricola*, 40–1.

12 Ibid., 19, 143.

13 Ibid., 20–1. For a general view of the regional economy and responses to the decline, see David A. Sutherland, "The 1810s: War and Peace," 247–50, 258–60; and Wynn, "Exciting a Spirit of Emulation," 43–53.

14 Young, *Letters of Agricola*, 456.

15 Ibid., 44, 460.

16 Ibid., 460.

17 Ibid., 20–1.

18 Ibid., 18, original emphasis.

19 Ibid., 20–1, 30.

20 See T.C. Smout, "Problems of Nationalism, Identity and Improvement in Later Eighteenth-Century Scotland"; J.M. Neeson, *Commoners*, 15–52; and Leonore Davidoff and Catherine Hall, *Family Fortunes*, 416–49.

21 Donald Winch, "Adam Smith"; Young, *Letters of Agricola*, 207–8.

22 See R.L. Meek, "Smith, Turgot, and the 'Four-Stages' Theory"; and Neeson, *Commoners*, 30–1. In Adam Smith, *An Inquiry into the Nature and*

Causes of the Wealth of Nations, the stages are best observed generally in book 3, chapter 4, and in book 5, chapter 1, part 1.

23 Young, *Letters of Agricola*, 23, 25, 219.

24 Ibid., 18, original emphasis.

25 Ibid.

26 Ibid., 63; see also 60, 391.

27 Ibid., 60, 447.

28 Ibid., 444–7.

29 Ibid., 44, 257, 388.

30 Ibid., 44, 219, 28.

31 Ibid., 219.

32 Ibid., 22–3.

33 Ibid., 454–60; Smith, *Wealth of Nations*, bk 3, ch. 1, "Of the Natural Causes of Opulence."

34 Young, *Letters of Agricola*, 58.

35 Smout, "Problems of Nationalism," 15.

36 Young, *Letters of Agricola*, 37.

37 Ibid., 41, 454–5.

38 Ibid., 452.

39 Ibid., 449, 460.

40 T.C. Smout, *A History of the Scottish People, 1560–1830*, 298.

41 Young, *Letters of Agricola*, 261–6.

42 See Smout, "Problems of Nationalism," 19. A similar story is told by "A Scotsman," in *Pictou Observer*, 2 March 1832.

43 Young, *Letters of Agricola*, 38; Martell, "Achievements of Agricola," 9.

44 Sir John Sinclair, *The Statistical Account of Scotland*, 20 vols. On Sinclair, see Eric Richards, *A History of the Highland Clearances*, vol. 2, 25–31; and Rosalind Mitchinson, *Agricultural Sir John*.

45 The word "statistical" has two meanings. The first derives from the use of "statist," an early modern term still current in the mid-nineteenth century, to denote "one skilled in state affairs, one having political knowledge, power, or influence." The suffixes *–ic* and *–al* give the meaning "of or pertaining to statecraft." See *Oxford English Dictionary* (1991), which also notes Sinclair's usage as one of the earliest (1798). The shift to something more akin to twentieth-century usage occurred in the late eighteenth and early nineteenth centuries with the ascendance of the term "statistic" to denote statecraft's inclusion of facts of the state and also, but not exclusively, to denote simply "a quantitative fact or statement." Thus knowledge of statecraft and knowledge of state could point to wholly different matters, or they could be two components of the same matter. The second use of

"statistical" derives its meaning from this more ambiguous form. Note, however, the contemporary uses of "Statistic science" to mean "Political Geography" (1789) and Bentham's discussion of "statistic use" in *Rational Judicial Evidence* (1824) to denote the "sort of collateral use thus being derived from any article of official evidence," both of which centre on knowledge of and within states. See also an anonymous book reviewer's definition, in the *Critical Review* (1787), of a work as "properly statistical" because it "consist[ed] of different tables, containing a general comparative view of the forces, the government, the extent and population of the different kingdoms of Europe." In this context, Young's admiration for Du Quesnay's *Tableau Economique* seems very much a product of his mentor's apparently similar opinion.

46 Sinclair's usage of the term "statistical" borrowed from the German, but he regarded its German meaning as slightly different from his own. In Germany "statistical" denoted "an inquiry for the purpose of ascertaining the political strength of a country, or questions respecting *matters of state*; whereas, the idea I annex to the term, is an inquiry into the state of a country, *for the purpose of ascertaining the* quantum *of happiness enjoyed by its inhabitants, and the means of its future improvement.*" See Sinclair, *Statistical Account of Scotland*, vol. 20, xiii, original emphasis. On the European context, see Keith Tribe, *Governing Economy*; and Daniel Samson, "'The Yoke of Improvement.'"

47 Young, *Letters of Agricola*, 38.

48 Ibid., 389–90.

49 Ibid., 60.

50 Ibid., 28, 447, 290.

51 Ibid., 455.

52 Ibid., 454–5. See also Thomas Chandler Haliburton, *Historical and Statistical Account of Nova Scotia*, vol. 2, 358–9, for comments on the "ill-judged attempt to make the formation of towns precede the cultivation of the land."

53 Young, *Letters of Agricola*, 60–1.

54 Thus Young elevated husbandry to the role of "prime mover" in a society, not only abandoning Smith here but also critiquing Smith's dismissal of the physiocrats; see Young, *Letters of Agricola*, 449–52. Young's use of physiocratic ideas was not unusual, and many British writers on political economy continued to borrow heavily from the physiocrats well into the nineteenth century; see R.L. Meek, *The Economics of Physiocracy*, 345–63.

55 Young, *Letters of Agricola*, 63.

56 C.A. Bayly, *Imperial Meridian*, 121–6; Smout, *History of the Scottish People*, 291–301.

57 Young, *Letters of Agricola*, 218–9.

58 Ibid., 59.

59 Ibid., 388, emphasis added.

60 Ibid., 444.

61 Ibid., 210, 444.

62 Ibid., 34 (quotation), 122, 398.

63 The phrase "shovelling out paupers" actually belongs to Wakefield's associate, Charles Buller; see H.J.M. Johnston, *British Emigration Policy, 1815–1830*, 168.

64 Young, *Letters of Agricola*, 38. See also Timothy Mixter, "The Hiring Market as Workers' Turf."

65 Donald Winch, *Classical Political Economy and Colonies*, 52–72, 90–104; Johnston, *British Emigration Policy*, 163–74.

66 Young, *Letters of Agricola*, 456–7.

67 See the discussion of Adam Smith in Albert O. Hirschman, *The Passion and the Interests*, 100–13.

68 Young, *Letters of Agricola*, 18, original emphasis.

69 Ibid., 219.

70 Ibid., 388, 446.

71 McCulloch, *Mephibosheth Stepsure Letters*, 68–9, 71.

72 Ibid., 153, original emphasis.

73 Ibid., 97–101, 145–6.

74 Ibid., 117–18.

75 Ibid., 143–4.

76 Ibid., 40, original emphasis.

77 Ibid., 120.

78 Ibid., 121–2.

79 Ibid., 142. See also George Patterson, *A History of the County of Pictou, Nova Scotia*, 224–5; and *Colonial Patriot*, 3 June 1829.

80 McCulloch, *Mephibosheth Stepsure Letters*, 142.

81 Ibid., 185.

82 Ibid., 153–4.

CHAPTER THREE

1 George Patterson, *A History of the County of Pictou, Nova Scotia*, 198.

2 See ibid., 193–9. See also J.M. Beck, *Politics of Nova Scotia*, vol. 1, 58–67; and Brian Cuthbertson, *Johnny Bluenose at the Polls*, 39–42.

3 Judith Tulloch, "William Cottnam Tonge," 779–83; Judith Tulloch, "James Fulton," 268; and Judith Fingard, "Sir John Wentworth," 848–52.

4 J.S. Martell, "Early Coal Mining in Nova Scotia," 156.

5 For a brief overview, see ibid., 157.

6 David A. Sutherland, "Halifax Merchants and the Pursuit of Development, 1783–1850."

7 Eli Heckscher, *Mercantilism*, vol. 2, 13–23, quotation at 15.

8 Richard Brown, *A History of Cape Breton*. Grants prior to 1783 did not reserve coal or iron, a loophole that the Annapolis and later the Londonderry iron mines attempted to exploit.

9 Brown, *History of Cape Breton*, 374; Macormick to Sydney, 11 December 1788, Colonial Office records for Nova Scotia (hereafter CO) 217/105.

10 Joshua M. Smith, *Borderland Smuggling*.

11 Miller to Portland, 26 September 1796, CO 217/133/547–51.

12 James Miller to Duke of Portland, 27 August 1794, CO 217/110/537; Miller to Portland, 21 November 1795, CO 217/11/261; Wentworth to Hobart, Halifax, 10 September 1802, CO 217/76/475–9.

13 George Leonard to Portland, Saint John, New Brunswick, 2 November 1800, CO 217/74/525–30. On Leonard, see Ann Gorman Condon, "George Leonard," 394–6.

14 See Nova Scotia Archives and Records Management (NSARM) Micro: Places: Cape Breton – Courts: Supreme Court, September and December 1814; and Miller to Portland, 27 August 1794, CO 217/110/537ff; Attorney-General's report, n.d., CO 217/134; *Saint John Gazette and Weekly Advertiser,* 23 November 1798, cited in H.A. Innis and A.R.M. Lower, eds, *Select Documents in Canadian Economic History, 1783–1885*, 398; and *Royal Gazette and Weekly Advertiser,* 19 May 1814 and 3 September 1816.

15 Macormick to Sydney, 11 December 1788, CO 217/105/531. See also Wentworth's description of the Cumberland County coalfields in his letter to Hobart, 17 June 1803, CO 217/78/63–71; Gerald S. Graham, "The Gypsum Trade of the Maritime Provinces"; and W.S. W.S. MacNutt, *New Brunswick*, 173–6.

16 Crawley estimated that eleven vessels that he knew of had smuggled "not less than 1000 chaldron" in the past year; see Crawley to George, 5 January 1821, nos 63 and 64, vol. 458, RG 1, NSARM. Governor Ainslie estimated about 3,000 chaldrons; see Ainslie to Bathurst, 14 March 1817, CO 217/135. See also Richard Brown, *The Coal Fields and Coal Trade of the Island of Cape Breton*, 66.

17 Crawley to George, 5 January 1821, nos 63 and 64; and Crawley to George, 19 June 1821, no. 71, both in vol. 458, RG 1, NSARM; Miller to Portland, [October 1795], CO 217/112/263; Thomas Roach, Account Book, 1801–13, no. 1, vol. 119, MG 3, NSARM; Joshua Lee to Thomas N. Jeffery, 8 November 1822, no. 43, vol. 458, RG 1, NSARM.

18 The customs house at Halifax first recorded sales of Pictou coal in 1815; see the abstracts in Nova Scotia, *Journals of the House of Assembly* (1823), 137.

19 Wentworth to Hobart, 17 June 1803, CO 217/78/63–71; Petition of Adam Carr, 20 January 1817, no. 5; and Carr to Rupert George, 10 January 1827, no. 123, both in vol. 458, RG 1, NSARM.

20 Petition of Edward Mortimer and others, 20 February 1817, no. 4, vol. 458, RG 1; and George Smith to John Young, 12 April 1820, no. 130, vol. 6, RG 8, both in NSARM. See also Robert Dawson to John Young, West River, Pictou County, 12 November 1820, no. 121; and James MacGregor to Young, East River, Pictou County, 6 January 1820, no. 129, both in vol. 6, RG 8, NSARM.

21 Petition of Adam Carr, 20 January 1817, no. 5, vol. 458, RG 1, NSARM; Patterson, *History of the County of Pictou*, 198; W.S. Moorsom, *Letters from Nova Scotia*, 345; George Smith to Rupert D. George, 13 July 1820, no. 28, vol. 458, RG 1, NSARM.

22 See Innis and Lower, eds, *Select Documents*, 237–8; Pierce S. Hamilton, *History of the County of Cumberland*; Peter Latta, "The Lower Cove Grindstone Quarries"; and G.N.D. Evans, *Uncommon Obdurate*, 27–42.

23 Vol. 25, MG 23, National Archives Canada (NAC), DesBarres Papers, vol. 2 (hereafter DesBarres Papers), 3110, 3578.

24 "Manudie [*sic*] Rent Amounts" (1799), DesBarres Papers, 4111–18; see also the rent lists for 1810 and 1811, DesBarres Papers, 4174–5, 4176. See the affidavits of Thomas Chapman (no. 153), William Chapman (no. 154), and especially "Petition from Minudie, Against Mr Seaman's claim to the shore ...," with 127 signatures (no. 160), all in vol. 243, RG 1, NSARM. A number of affidavits were presented in support of Seaman's petition, although these were by no means unequivocal on the issue of possession and the foreshore; see the affidavits of Nehemiah Ayer, Joseph Brine, John Burk, and Oliver Barnes (all in no. 166) and those of William Hayes and John Holmes (both in no. 167), vol. 243, RG 1, NSARM. See also "Bond" between John Seamans [*sic*] and J.F.W. DesBarres and another between James Glennie and J.F.W. DesBarres, 15 December 1808, DesBarres Papers, 4136–9, 4144–9.

25 DesBarres Papers, 4136–9, 4174; McDonald's memo, 20 June 1810, DesBarres Papers, 4157; Affidavit of Simon Newcomb, 7 September 1836, no. 155, vol. 243, RG 1, NSARM; Helen Harper Steeves, *The Story of Moncton's First Store and Storekeeper*. In 1838 "A Farmer" claimed that over 200 men worked under Seaman, but the context of the letter makes it clear that even this number is far short of the total; see "A Farmer" to Lord Glenelg, February 1838, CO 217/168/11–14.

26 See Bonnie M. McCay, *Oyster Wars and the Public Trust*; Stuart A. Moore, *A History of the Foreshore*, esp. 434–538, 667–94; and "Abstract of DesBarres grant at Minudie," copy, dated 5 May 1765, no. 148, vol. 243, RG 1, NSARM.

27 "A Farmer" to Glenelg, 11 February 1838, CO 217/168/11–14; Moses H. Perley, *Reports on the Sea and River Fisheries of New Brunswick*, 144–6.

28 Statement of Thomas S. Black, 12 October 1836, no. 151, vol. 243, RG 1, NSARM. See also Affidavit of Thomas Chapman, 25 August 1836, no. 153, vol. 243, RG 1, NSARM. Listed in Thomas Roach's ledger, there is also a Thomas Chapman, "Blacksmith," who sold Roach grindstones between 1803 and 1806; it is probably the same man.

29 See James Christie's discussion of the process in his affidavit dated 2 January 1837, no. 166, vol. 243, RG 1, NSARM.

30 Affidavits of Simon L. Newcomb, 7 September 1836, no. 155; William Chapman, [1836], no. 154; and Thomas Chapman, 25 August 1836, no. 153, all in vol. 243, RG 1, NSARM.

31 On "strangers," see affidavits of John Burk, 25 January 1837, no. 166; James Christie, 2 January 1837, no. 166; and William Hayes, 24 January 1837, no. 167, all in vol. 243, RG 1, NSARM; and J.M. Neeson, *Commoners*, 110–33.

32 "Fort Lawrence Business Papers," Thomas Roach, Account Book, 1803–13, vol. 119, MG 3, NSARM. The Roach account book also notes Nathan Seamans (timber, butter, grindstones), Captain Richard Grose (freight on his vessel, butter, oats, and one-third share of "plaster"), Nathaniel Embree (cash, butter, "plaster"), William White (grindstones, butter, oats, timber), Josiah Hicks, John Lablong [LeBlanc], Titus Thornton, and Peter Melonsong [Melanson].

33 "Fort Lawrence Business Papers," Thomas Roach, Account Book, 1803–13, vol. 119, MG 3, NSARM: John Morse, John Boss, William Read, John Henry, Benjamin Read, Joseph Ward, Ezra Barnes, William Easterbrook, William Henry, Peter Melonsong [Melanson] Jr, Thomas Whitten, John Harper, Maximin Burk, Charles Melonsong [brother of Peter, above], William McGear, Kersimer Melonsong (one-quarter share), Myer Ayre, and Hugh Boyd. See also Steeves, *Story of Moncton's First Store*, esp. 26–8, 43–7, 62–70.

34 George Leonard's report of November 1800, CO 217/74; Wentworth to Hobart, 10 May 1803, CO 217/78; Ainslie to Bathurst, 5 July 1817, CO 217/135; Wentworth to Hobart, 19 June 1802, CO 217/76; Wentworth to Hobart, 14 April 1804, CO 217/79.

35 Wentworth to Hobart, 10 May 1803, CO 217/78.

36 Tulloch, "William Cottnam Tonge."

37 MacNutt, *New Brunswick*, 137–9.

38 David Allison, *History of Nova Scotia*, vol. 2, 576; Wentworth to William Windhaus, ["One of His Majesty's Principal Secretaries of State"], 4 April 1807, CO

217/81; Margaret Ells, "Governor Wentworth's Patronage," 67; Wentworth to Windhaus, 4 April 1807, CO 217/81, emphasis added.

39 Wentworth, cited in Graeme Wynn, "1800–1810," 229; Wentworth to Thomas Millidge and John Ruggles (Annapolis County sheriffs), 1 May 1807, 162–3, vol. 54, RG 1, NSARM.

40 Ells, "Governor Wentworth's Patronage"; Brian Cuthbertson, *The Loyalist Governor*, 2–28; Fingard, "Sir John Wentworth."

41 Wentworth to Hobart, 10 May 1803, CO 217/78; Wentworth to William Windhaus, 4 April 1807, CO 217/81. George Leonard argued much the same in New Brunswick; see MacNutt, *New Brunswick*, 139. Between 1812 and 1816 the legislatures of both Nova Scotia and New Brunswick debated a series of measures to regulate the illicit trade; see the comments of Hon. Ward Chipman (New Brunswick), 16 July 1813, no. 89, vol. 226, RG 1, NSARM; Peleg Wiswall, no. 77, vol. 21, "A," RG 5, NSARM; and Copy of the "Plaister of Paris Act," 21 March 1816, CO 217/98. New Brunswick attempted to impose a tax on gypsum going *into* Charlotte County (which borders the Passamaquoddy); see MacNutt, *New Brunswick*, 173–6; and Graham, "Gypsum Trade."

42 See Robert Hale, "A Voyage to Nova Scotia"; and A.G. Doughty, ed., *The Journal of Captain John Knox.*

43 "Petition of Tremain & Stout," 20 September 1796, CO 217/112/238; Robert J. Morgan, "Orphan Outpost"; Stephen J. Hornsby, *Nineteenth-Century Cape Breton*, 15–18.

44 Brown, *Coalfields and Coal Trade*, 66–72.

45 Macormick to Sydney, 23 October 1787, CO 217/105/101.

46 Henry Dundas, Secretary of State, to James Miller, 27 June 1793, CO 217/109/231–4; Portland to Miller, 4 November 1794, CO 217/110/565.

47 Statement of Revenue, His Majesty's Coal Mines, Sydney, 1820, no. 87, vol. 458, RG 1, NSARM; J.B. Brebner, *The Neutral Yankees of Nova Scotia*, 204–42.

48 Macormick to Dundas, 6 October 1792, CO 217/109.

49 James Miller to the Duke of Portland, 20 March 1796, CO 217/112/295. See also "Account of Coals Shipped," 6 July 1794, CO 217/110/387–8; and "Account of Coals Shipped," 26 January 1975, CO 217/111/77–9.

50 Mathews to Portland, 10 December 1796, CO 217/113/57.

51 See Miller to Portland, 12 November 1798, CO 217/117/707; Miller to Portland, 27 August 1794, CO 217/110/521, enclosure; Mathews to Portland, 23 September 1796, CO 217/112/240–1, enclosure; Petition of Tremain and Stout, 5 July 1798, CO 217/116/5; Portland to Miller, 4 November 1794, CO 217/110/565; and Portland to Macormick, 1 June 1795, CO 217/111/95–101.

52 We could also note the importance of Lawrence Kavanagh and the other Jersey merchants, but their interests in Cape Breton were limited almost entirely to the fish trade and to matters directly relating to their supply of fish producers. See Kavanagh to Murray, enclosed in Murray to Portland, 25 October 1799, CO 217/117/527; Robert J. Morgan, "Laurence Kavanagh," 370–1; and David A. Sutherland, "Richard Tremain," 891.

53 See Miller to Portland, 26 September 1796, CO 217/113/551; Miller to Portland, 29 September 1796, CO 217/113/556; Miller to Jonathan King, Undersecretary of State, 10 June 1797, CO 217/113/842; and Memorial of Ingram Ball et al., 27 June 1797, CO 217/113/897.

54 Macormick to Sydney, [1787], CO 217/105/1 and CO 217/105/117; Murray to Portland, 6 July 1799, CO 217/117/240; Miller to Jonathan King, 13 August 1799, CO 217/117/313; Macormick to Dundas, 28 March 1792, CO 217/109/71; Miller to Portland, 10 July 1795, CO 217/111/503.

55 Miller to Portland, 20 September 1796, CO 217/112/443; "Minutes of Council," January 1797, CO 217/113/103; Miller to Portland, 31 October 1794, copy, CO 217/112/447; "Account with Tremain & Co.," 1811, no. 211, vol. 2, RG 11, NSARM; Miller and Ingram Ball to Portland, 27 June 1795, CO 217/113/905; Miller to Portland, 20 September 1796, CO 217/112/443.

56 Miller to Portland, 20 March 1796, CO 217/112/289; Miller to Portland, 25 June 1796, CO 217/112/417; Mathews to Portland, 14 February 1797, CO 217/113/111; Miller to Portland, 21 November 1795, CO 217/112/261; Miller to Portland, 7 January 1797, CO 217/113/599.

57 Miller to Portland, 14 July 1795, CO 217/111/499; Miller to Portland, 21 November 1795, CO 217/112/261.

58 "Account Current of His Majesty's Colliery at Spanish River," [August 1800], CO 217/118/277–8.

59 "Monthly Pay List of Persons Employed in Working the Colliery of His Majesty's Coal Mines near Sydney in the Island of Cape Breton commencing the 11th Day of Feb'y and ending the 15th Day of March 1800," CO 217/118. See also nos 147 and 149, vol. 1, "A," RG 21, NSARM.

60 However, it should be noted that many mines in Britain at this time operated on similarly low levels of technology and unrefined divisions of labour; see Robert Colls, *The Pitmen of the Northern Coalfield*, 25–6, 51–74; and B.R. Mitchell, *Economic Development of the British Coal Industry, 1800–1914*, 70–81, 99–104.

61 Coal cut to the deep followed the seam downward, away from the shaft, and thus tended to be of better quality and had to be hauled farther.

62 Miller to Portland, 20 September 1797, CO 217/116/169; Miller to Richard Stout, 15 September 1796, CO 217/112/449; Stout to Miller, [c. August 1796], copy in Miller to Portland, 20 September 1796, CO 217/112/443;

Mathews to Portland, 17 October 1797, CO 217/113/495; Miller to Portland, 20 September 1797, CO 217/116/169.

63 Petition of Adam Carr, Pictou, 20 January 1817, no. 5, vol. 458, RG 1, NSARM.

64 "Report of the Committee on the Probability of Employment for Emigrant Laborers to Nova Scotia," nos 368–75, vol. 195, RG 1, NSARM.

65 Mathews to Portland, 23 September 1796, CO 217/112/233. John McKay noted that expanded markets and higher wartime prices were the reasons why he expanded his works on the East River between 1813 and 1815; see Memorial of John McKay, 28 September 1819, no. 13, vol. 458, RG 1, NSARM.

66 Wentworth to Hobart, 10 August 1802, CO 217/76/433; Wentworth to Hobart, 17 June 1803, CO 217/78/63–71.

67 See David A. Sutherland, "Lawrence Hartshorne," 312–14; David A. Sutherland, "James Forsyth," 327–9; and Hobart to Wentworth, 2 November 1802, CO 217/76/481–4.

68 Wentworth to Hobart, 17 June 1803, CO 217/78/63–71.

69 Wentworth to Castlereagh (secretary of state), 14 February 1806, no. 86, vol. 54; and Windham to Wentworth, 10 May 1806, no. 90, vol. 60, both in RG 1, NSARM.

70 "Extracts of the Halifax Committee of Trade," no. 79, vol. 304, RG 1, NSARM; Statement of William Sabatier and Others, [December 1810], CO 217/88/9–17.

71 Prevost to Liverpool, 19 January 1811, CO 217/88/5–7; Sutherland, "Halifax Merchants"; "Opinion of Richard Uniacke on Mines," 24 December 1816, no. 2, vol. 460, RG 1, NSARM.

72 Draft of Address of the Assembly, 1 April 1815, no. 3, vol. 305, RG 1, NSARM. See also Sherbrooke to Bathurst, 6 April 1815, CO 217/96.

73 Extract of a letter from the Secretary of State (Bathurst) to Sherbrooke, 16 June 1815, no. 103, vol. 288, RG 1, NSARM.

74 *Royal Gazette*, 14 December 1816; Petition of Hartshorne, Boggs & Co., 31 December 1816, no. 3, vol. 458, RG 1, NSARM. A memo attached to this petition, initialled "GRD" (George Ramsay, Lord Dalhousie), endorses McKay's bid "to work the Coal Mine ... on which he has been employed for the last year" for one additional year.

75 Memorial of John McKay, 28 September 1819, no. 13, vol. 458, RG 1, NSARM. See also the statements of Alexander Prentice, 31 January 1818, no. 12; and James Dixon, 4 August 1820, no. 16, both in vol. 458, RG 1, NSARM.

76 Memorial of John McKay, 28 September 1819, no. 13, vol. 458, RG 1, NSARM. See also Patterson, *History of the County of Pictou*, 400–1.

77 Memorial of Edward Mortimer, S.G.W. Archibald, S.B. Robie, and William Lawson, 20 February 1817, no. 4, vol. 458, RG 1, NSARM.

78 Patterson, *History of the County of Pictou*, 251; "Coals dug and raised by John McKay," 1 January to 31 December 1817, no. 6, vol. 458, RG 1, NSARM.

79 Memo signed by Dalhousie, 10 February 1819, no. 12, vol. 460, RG 1, NSARM. For McCully's lease, see Minutes of the Legislative Council, 15 February 1819, no. 9, vol. 214½, (A), RG 1, NSARM. McCully's lease was "on the same terms and conditions by which Mr Mortimer is bound to work those [mines] in the District of Pictou."

80 See McKay's bid in no. 5, vol. 460, RG 1, NSARM; Memo of Lord Dalhousie, [c. January 1817], no. 6, vol. 460, RG 1, NSARM; and Sutherland, "Lawrence Hartshorne."

81 See Patterson *History of the County of Pictou*, 193–9. See also Beck, *Politics of Nova Scotia*, vol. 1, 58–67; Tulloch, "William Cottnam Tonge"; and Fingard, "Sir John Wentworth."

82 Statement of John Taylor and Others, 7 April 1820, no. 18, vol. 458, RG 1, NSARM.

83 Undated statements of Adam Carr, no. 5; Alexander Prentice, no. 12; James Dixon, no. 16; and Peter McCallum, no. 21, all in vol. 458, RG 1, NSARM. Three of the four men identified themselves as a "miner," while the other, Alexander Prentice, referred to himself as a "yeoman."

84 Statement of Peter McCallum, "clark," 20 January 1820, no. 21; Statement of James Dickson [Dixon], collier, 20 January 1820, no. 22, both in vol. 458, RG 1, NSARM.

85 Richard Stewart to James Kempt, 29 May 1821, no. 78; Samuel McCurdy to [James Kempt], 15 June 1821, no. 79, both in vol. 458, RG 1, NSARM.

86 Amherst Township, Census of 1827, NSARM; Nicholas H. Meagher, "Life of Hon. Jonathan McCully, 1809–1877."

87 Petition statements of Adam Carr, 20 January 1817, no. 5, vol. 458, RG 1, NSARM. See also undated petition statements of Alexander Prentice, no. 12; James Dixon, no. 16; and Peter McCallum, no. 21, all in vol. 458, RG 1, NSARM.

88 Joyce Appleby, "Commercial Farming and the 'Agrarian Myth' in the Early Republic"; Daniel Vickers, "Competency and Competition."

89 "An Ordinance to Prevent the Exportation of Gypsum or Plaister of Paris from the Island of Cape Breton ...," [1811], no. 87, vol. 4, RG 11, NSARM.

CHAPTER FOUR

1 Richard Stewart to Sir James Kempt, Digby, 29 May 1821, no. 78, vol. 458, RG 1, Nova Scotia Archives and Records Management (NSARM). See also Stephen Oxley to John Young, River Philip, 16 December 1818, reprinted

in John Young, *The Letters of Agricola on the Principles of Vegetation and Tillage*, 224–7.

2 Dipesh Chakrabarty, *Rethinking Working-Class History*; Ranajit Guha, "The Prose of Counter-Insurgency"; and William C. Wicken, *Mi'kmaq Treaties on Trial.*

3 See C.A. Bayly, *Imperial Meridian*, 81–9, 109–20; and Gwyneth Tyson Roberts, "'Under the Hatches.'"

4 Assembly petition of Uniacke and Croke, 3 April 1815, no. 108, vol. 288, RG 1, NSARM.

5 R.J. Uniacke [attorney general] to Bernard, 29 November 1803, no. 53, vol. 303, RG 1, NSARM.

6 W.S. MacNutt, *New Brunswick*, 173, asserts that merchants and politicians believed that "controls" were "always to be viewed with distrust." This is true, but it was a political rather than ideological point. They did not fear the regulations but the people who might benefit by them. Regulation of the gypsum trade was never in question, only the methods.

7 Ibid., 173–6.

8 Samuel Cunard to Sir James Kempt, 9 January 1826, Colonial Office records for Nova Scotia (hereafter CO) 217/146. Some merchants and state officials also viewed coal as a potential means of improving Halifax's status as the dominant entrepot for trade between British North America and the West Indies. Canada also lacked its own coal reserves, and surplus production in Nova Scotia would bring more wheat and flour shipped through Halifax. See H.A. Innis, *The Cod Fisheries*, 227–71.

9 J.M. Neeson, *Commoners*, 110–57; Bonnie M. McCay, "Old and New World Fisheries."

10 E.P. Thompson, *Customs in Common*; James C. Scott, *The Moral Economy of the Peasant*. For critiques, see Winifred Barr Rothenberg, *From Market-Places to a Market Economy*, 25–55; and Samuel L. Popkin, *The Rational Peasant*, 17–31.

11 Johnston was also a member of the House of Assembly for Cumberland County and would soon become leader of the conservatives (a position that he would hold almost to Confederation) and premier. Stewart is less well known, but some biographical detail can be obtained in the *Dictionary of Canadian Biography* entry for his brother and partner, Alexander Stewart, the other member for Cumberland County. Bliss was a New Brunswick lawyer. See David A. Sutherland, "James W. Johnston," 383–8; J.M. Beck, "Alexander Stewart," 746–8; and W.A. Spray, "Henry Bliss," 71–2.

12 A.A. MacKenzie, "Amos Peck Seaman," 709–10.

13 This is an unattributed passage found in the card catalogue at the Public Archives of Nova Scotia. I believe it was written by Will R. Bird, but I have been unable to substantiate this.

14 Even during the downturn following the Franco-American wars, some
   farms in the area sold for £750 to £1,500; see deeds for Robert Blinkhorn,
   191, and for Samuel McCully and Thomas Roach, 204, book G, Cumberland County, RG 47, NSARM.

15 DesBarres's legal estate was a disaster; he left several wills – and several families – and the estate was still in dispute in the 1860s. See the collection entitled "Estate of J.F.W. DesBarres," vol. 1539, MG 1, NSARM.

16 Seaman to J.W. Johnston, Henry Bliss and James Stewart, Minudie,
   30 October 1825, no. 13, vol. 1539, MG 1, NSARM; vol. 25, MG 23, National
   Archives Canada (NAC), DesBarres Papers, vol. 2 (hereafter DesBarres
   Papers), 5909–16.

17 See "Rents at Minudie," [c. 1810 or 1811], DesBarres Papers, 4174; "Bond
   of Tenants," 18 November 1808, DesBarres Papers, 4126 (see also 4140–
   3); "Agreements," 21 January 1813, DesBarres Papers, 5203–10; and
   "Bond between Peter Brine [Sr], Peter Brine Jr, Peter Como, [and oth-
   ers]," 17 October 1815, DesBarres Papers, 5235–8.

18 "A list of rents for the Jogins [sic] 1827," no. 48, vol. 106, MG 1, NSARM.

19 Amos Seaman to Sir Colin Campbell, 15 March 1837, enclosed with
   Campbell to Lord Glenelg, 31 March 1837, CO 217/163. On stimulants to
   open new markets for trade, see Amos Seaman to Moses Moses H. Perley,
   11 September 1850, reprinted in Moses H. Perley, *Reports on the Sea and River
   Fisheries of New Brunswick*, 152–3.

20 On evictions, see James Stewart to J.W. Johnston, Amherst, 27 August 1825,
   no. 10; Stewart to Johnston, 16 April 1827, no. 41; Stewart to Johnston,
   6 December 1827, no. 49; Stewart to Johnston, Amherst, 13 November 1828,
   no. 58; Stewart to Johnston, 4 May 1829, no. 62; and Stewart to Johnston and
   Bliss, 7 December 1831, no. 105, all in vol. 1539, MG 1, NSARM; and Stewart
   to Johnston, 3 October 1832, no. 119 vol. 1539, MG 1, NSARM.

21 James Stewart to J.W. Johnston and Bliss, Amherst, 10 August 1829, no. 63,
   vol. 1539, MG 1, NSARM. In this same letter Stewart mentions the case of
   "Mattatal," which appears to have been unresolved in 1832; see Stewart to
   Louisa DesBarres, 8 May 1832, DesBarres Papers, 5866–9. See also the case of
   David Blenkhorn's widow, in Stewart to Johnston, 6 December 1827, no. 49,
   vol. 1539, MG 1, NSARM. Stewart claimed to have sold thirty-five lots the year
   before; see Stewart to Johnston, 13 November 1828, no. 58, vol. 1539, MG 1,
   NSARM. For illustrations of other tenants resisting removal, see Stewart to
   Johnston, 13 October 1828, no. 57, vol. 1539, MG 1, NSARM; and Johnston
   to Stewart and Bliss, 10 August 1829, no. 63, vol. 1539, MG 1, NSARM.

22 Schedule of Lands (Tatamagouche), 12 October 1842, no. 165, vol. 1539,
   MG 1, NSARM.

23 Welch did not seem to know that Stewart was Johnston's partner, as he appears to have been writing to Johnston in his capacity as an MLA; see James Welch Sr to J.W. Johnston, 7 March 1838, no. 152, vol. 1539, MG 1, NSARM.

24 See J.W. Johnston to James Stewart, 7 November 1832, no. 121, vol. 1539, MG 1, NSARM; and Johnston and Stewart to Robert B. Dickey, 8 December 1838, no. 157, vol. 1539, MG 1, NSARM.

25 See no. 21, vol. 31; and no. 57, vol. 112, both in MG 100, PANS; and James Glennie to Augustus W. DesBarres, 4 December 1826, no. 34, vol. 1539, MG 1, NSARM.

26 See J.W. Johnston to Thomas Roach, 5 February 1827, no. 35, vol. 1539, MG 1, NSARM; and Roach to Johnston and Bliss, 2 March 1837, no. 36, vol. 1539, MG 1, NSARM. Roach himself petitioned for a grant of a quarry at Franklin Manor in 1813; see Roach to Charles Morris, 12 October 1813, no. 107, vol. 86, "C," RG 20, NSARM; and no. 14, vol. 146, MG 100, NSARM. This would fit the general pattern described for Prince Edward Island in Rusty Bittermann, "Women and the Escheat Movement."

27 For expressions of fear that excessive actions might drive away the tenants en masse, see James Stewart to J.W. Johnston, 27 August 1825, no. 10, vol. 1539, MG 1, PANS; Stewart to Johnston and Bliss, 30 August 1830, no. 87, vol. 1539, MG 1, NSARM.

28 James Stewart to J.W. Johnston, 4 May 1829, vol. 1539, MG 1, NSARM

29 Johnston, Stewart, and Bliss to Augustus W. DesBarres, 22 August 1833, DesBarres Papers, 5896–7; James Stewart to Louisa DesBarres, 8 May 1832, DesBarres Papers, 5866–9.

30 James Stewart to Louisa DesBarres, 8 May 1832, DesBarres Papers, 5866–9.

31 J.W. Johnston to Augustus Wallet DesBarres, Halifax, 22 August 1833, DesBarres Papers, 5896–7, original emphasis.

32 James Stewart to J.W. Johnston, 7 December 1831, no. 105, vol. 1539, MG 1, NSARM; Johnston to Stewart, 20 December 1831, no. 109, vol. 1539, MG 1, NSARM.

33 J.W. Johnston to James Stewart, 14 December 1831, no. 106, vol. 1539, MG 1, NSARM; Johnston to Stewart, 20 December 1831, no. 109, vol. 1539, MG 1, NSARM.

34 As described in Petition of Amos Seaman, 15 September 1834, no. 146, vol. 243, RG 1, NSARM. See also "Proclamation of the Supreme Court at Amherst, June 1836," where the lawyers attempted to overturn an 1832 lower court finding for some tenants at Minudie, in Estate of J.F.W. DesBarres, no. 148, vol. 1539, MG 1, NSARM.

35 James Stewart to J.W. Johnston, 23 December 1831, no. 110; and Stewart to Johnston, 8 December 1831, no. 106, both in vol. 1539, MG 1, NSARM; Johnston to Stewart, 20 December 1831, no. 109, vol. 1539, MG 1, NSARM.

36 James Stewart to J.W. Johnston, 23 December 1831, no. 110, vol. 1539, MG 1, NSARM.

37 See James Stewart to Charles Twining [lawyer for one of DesBarres's heirs], 28 August 1833, no. 127, vol. 1539, MG 1, NSARM; and MacKenzie, "Amos Peck Seaman." For a copy of the deed, dated 2 February 1834, see no. 144, vol. 243, RG 1, NSARM.

38 Francis O'Regan to Abraham Gesner, 2 November 1837, reprinted in Nova Scotia, *Journals of the House of Assembly* (hereafter *JHA*) (1840), appendix 24, document 17.

39 *JHA* (1840), appendix 24, document 1.

40 Petitions of William Chapman, 29 September 1836, no. 154, vol. 243, RG 1, PANS; and Simon L. Newcomb, 7 September 1836, no. 155, vol. 243, RG 1, NSARM.

41 Statement of Thomas Chapman, 25 August 1836, no. 153, vol. 243, RG 1, NSARM.

42 Neeson, *Commoners*, 110–33.

43 Statement of Thomas S. Black, 12 October 1836, no. 151, vol. 243, RG 1, NSARM.

44 See also the statements by Thomas Chapman, 25 August 1836, no. 153, vol. 243, RG 1, NSARM; and William Chapman, 29 Septmber 1836, no. 154, vol. 243, RG 1, NSARM.

45 James Stewart to J.W. Johnston, 23 December 1831, no. 110; Memorandum of Robert M. Dickey, [n.d.] October 1833, no. 133; and Proclamation of the Supreme Court at Amherst, June 1836, no. 148, all in vol. 1539, MG 1, NSARM; Stewart to Provincial Secretary, 4 May 1839, no. 22, vol. 253, RG 1, NSARM; James F. Gray to Provincial Secretary, 3 May 1839, no. 21, vol. 253, RG 1, NSARM.

46 James Stewart to J.W. Johnston, 23 December 1831, no. 110, vol. 1539, MG 1, NSARM, original emphasis.

47 Report of John Spry Morris, 17 February 1835, reprinted in *JHA* (1840), appendix 24, document 5.

48 Sir Colin Campbell to Lord Glenelg, 13 July 1835, CO 217/161.

49 Quotation from Petition of James Soy, Isaac Tipping, George Newton, and Joseph Read, 16 December 1833, reprinted in *JHA* (1840), appendix 24, document 3. Adam Smith, *An Inquiry into the Nature and Causes of the Wealth of Nations*, 145, uses just such an example to explain the price of land: "[The landlord] sometimes demands rent for what is altogether incapable of

human improvement. Kelp is a species of sea-weed, which, when burnt, yields an alkaline salt, useful for making glass, soap, and for several other products. It grows in several parts of Great Britain, particularly in Scotland, upon such rocks only as lie within the high water mark, which are twice every day covered by the sea, and of which the produce, therefore, was never augmented by human industry. The landlord, however, whose estate is bounded by a kelp shore of this kind, demands a rent for it as much as his corn fields."

50 "Opinion of the Crown Officers [Charles R. Fairbanks and R. MacDonnell], upon the Matter of the Quarries at Minudie," 18 September 1832, no. 143, vol. 243, RG 1, NSARM. See also Stuart A. Moore, *A History of the Foreshore*, 434–538, 667–94.

51 See petitions of Thomas S. Black, no. 151; Thomas Chapman, no. 153; William Chapman, no. 154; and Simon L. Newcomb, no. 155; as well as "Petition from Minudie," no. 160, all in vol. 243, RG 1, NSARM. See also petitions of James Soy and others, no. 7; James Soy and Isaac Tipping, no. 2; Francis O'Regan, no. 19; and James Soy, no. 20, all in vol. 253, RG 1, NSARM.

52 Petition of Amos Seaman, 12 August 1836, no. 175, vol. 243, RG 1, NSARM; James Stewart to Charles Twining, 4 October 1833, no. 129, vol. 1539, MG 1, NSARM.

53 See affidavits of Nehemiah Ayer, Joseph Brine, James Christie, John Burk, and Oliver Barnes, all in no. 166, vol. 243, RG 1, NSARM; Gilbert Seaman, Edward Baker, James Barnes, William Hayes, and John Holmes, all in no. 167, vol. 243, RG 1, NSARM; W.W. Pride and Joshua Chandler, no. 167, vol. 243, RG 1, NSARM; and D. Shaw and Samuel Gay, no. 169, vol. 243, RG 1, NSARM.

54 Affidavit of Nehemiah Ayer, 21 January 1837, no. 166, vol. 243, RG 1, NSARM.

55 See the petition of Joshua Chandler, 6 February 1836, reprinted in *JHA* (1840), appendix 24, document 12.

56 Petition of James Soy and others, 16 December 1833, no. 3; and Petition of James Soy and others, 16 April 1835, no. 4, both in vol. 253, RG 1, NSARM; James Soy to Sir Colin Campbell, 30 March 1836; and Francis O'Regan to Abraham Gesner, 2 November 1837, both reprinted in *JHA* (1840), appendix 24, documents 11 and 17.

57 Report of Henry Huntington, Joseph Howe, and Hugh McDonald, reprinted in *JHA* (1840), appendix 74. The Read Company Papers are a large collection housed at the Provincial Archives of New Brunswick.

58 "Petition from Minudie, Cumberland, against Mr Seaman's claim to the Shore," n.d. [added 30 April 1837], no. 160, vol. 243, RG 1, NSARM.

59 See also Petition of James Soy and others, 16 December 1833, no. 3, vol. 253, RG 1, PANS; and Petition of James Soy and others, 16 April 1835, no. 4, vol. 253, RG 1, NSARM. Most of the petitions from vol. 253, NSARM, are reprinted in *JHA* (1840), appendix 24. An 1836 memo, unsigned, also made an antimonopoly argument, urging that the "shore ought to be thrown open to the commerical industry of the whole province," but again this was clearly in the context of competitive bidding for Crown lands; see the unsigned, undated memorandum enclosed with Sir Colin Campbell to Lord Glenelg, 13 August 1836, CO 217/161.

60 See "Petition from Minudie, Cumberland, against Mr Seaman's claim to the Shore," n.d. [added 30 April 1837], no. 160, vol. 243, RG 1, NSARM; and the petitions of James Soy and eleven others, 3 December 1833; and James Soy and sixteen others, 15 April 1835, both reprinted in *JHA* (1840), appendix 24, documents 1 and 6.

61 Petition of Amos Seaman, 7 January 1839, no. 2, vol. 253, RG 1, NSARM.

62 Petition of Amos Seaman, 12 August 1836, no. 175, vol. 243, RG 1, NSARM.

63 Amos Seaman to James Stewart, 23 February 1839, no. 14, vol. 253, RG 1, PANS; Petition of Amos Seaman, [n.d.] July 1836, no. 150, vol. 243, RG 1, NSARM.

64 The position was given to Joshua Chandler, the high sheriff of Cumberland County; see his reports in nos 70–5, vol. 459, RG 1, NSARM. See also Amos Seaman to James Stewart, 23 February 1839, no. 14; Seaman to Stewart, 27 February 1839, no. 15; and Stewart to Sir Rupert D. George, Provincial Secretary, 7 March 1839, no. 16, all in vol. 253, RG 1, PANS; and Stewart to George, 14 March 1839, no. 16, vol. 253, RG 1, NSARM. Three years later, after Lord Glenelg authorized Seaman's claim, the Legislature passed "An Act Respecting the Measuring of Grindstones in the County of Cumberland" (6 Vict., Cap. 22), which attempted to recoup revenue by inspecting stones at the rate of ½d per stone.

65 See Amos Seaman to Lord Glenelg, [n.d.] July 1836, no. 150, vol. 243, RG 1, NSARM; "Report of the Surveyor General" [John Spry Morris], 7 December 1833; and "Surveyor-General's Report on Petition No. 2," 17 February 1835, both reprinted in *JHA* (1840), appendix 24.

66 Colin Campbell to Lord Glenelg, 10 January 1837, CO 217/163.

67 Phillip A. Buckner, *The Transition to Responsible Government*, 273–4. On the utilitarian governors, see Catherine Hall, "Imperial Man," esp. 133–44; and Ian Radforth, "Sydenham and Utilitarian Reform."

68 Sir Colin Campbell to Lord Glenelg, Halifax, 13 August 1836, CO 217/161.

69 See Sir Colin Campbell to Lord Glenelg, 13 July 1836, CO 217/161; Campbell to Glenelg, 3 August 1836, CO 217/161.

70 Sir Colin Campbell to Lord Glenelg, 20 January 1839, CO 217/170;
Sir Colin Campbell to Sir Rupert George, 14 December 1838, enclosed
with Sir Colin Campbell to Lord Glenelg, 20 January 1839, CO 217/170.

71 Petition of James Soy and sixteen others, "Manudie," 16 April 1835, reprinted in *JHA* (1840), appendix 24, document 6.

72 Sir Colin Campbell to Lord Glenelg, 13 August 1836, CO 217/161.

73 The Expulsion remained firmly placed in the Acadian tenants' collective
memories. The Reverend Ferdinand Gauvreau was the parish priest across
the Cumberland Basin at Memramcook, New Brunswick, and also tended
to Minudie. In describing his parishioners' fishing habits, he notes that
they told him these were the same techniques and locations that they had
used "even before the invasion of the province by the English"; quoted in
Perley, *Reports on the Sea*, 145–6.

74 Petition of Amos Seaman, [n.d.] July 1836, no. 150, vol. 243, RG 1, NSARM.

75 Seaman's deed to the DesBarres estate specifically mentioned the shad fishery as part of the property, but of course at this point he had no more claim
on the weirs than he had on the grindstones; see "Copy of deed of sale,"
2 February 1834, no. 144, vol. 243, RG 1, NSARM; *Cape Breton Spectator*,
18 June 1846; Perley, *Reports on the Sea*, 152–3; "Petition of Amos Seaman,
Merchant," 26 Febraury 1842, no. 100, vol. 459, RG 1, NSARM; and
MacKenzie, "Amos Peck Seaman."

76 Annual Report of the Cumberland Agricultural Society, 1852, no. 158,
vol. 14, RG 8, NSARM.

77 All quotations in this paragraph are from Amos Seaman to Moses H. Perley,
11 September 1850, reprinted in Perley, *Reports on the Sea*, 152–3.

78 See Seaman's petitions for drawbacks on flour – a refund of the duty of 3s
per barrel, for which supplies to the fishery were eligible – in *JHA* (1842),
appendix 52 (Committee on Trade and Manfactures).

79 Assembly petition of Uniacke and Croke, 3 April 1815, no. 108, vol. 288,
RG 1, NSARM.

80 Moore, *History of the Foreshore*, 460–1, notes that the law was increasingly
weakened under a series of decisions between 1795 and 1829 but that a
new Crown Lands Management Act in 1830 (10 Geo. 4, Cap. 50) briefly
reasserted the right of the Crown. The spirit of this act, in combination
with the law's assumption of Crown ownership, probably explains the
reluctance of the Colonial Department to take action. See also the
broader discussion in Philip Girard, "Land Law, Liberalism, and the
Agrarian Ideal."

81 Thomas James [deputy provincial secretary] to "Gentlemen," 14 October
1836, no. 159, vol. 243, RG 1, NSARM.

CHAPTER FIVE

1 See J.S. Martell, "Early Coal Mining in Nova Scotia"; D.A. Muise, "The General Mining Association"; Marilynn Gerriets, "The Impact of the General Mining Association on the Nova Scotia Coal Industry, 1826–1850"; Marilynn Gerriets, "The Rise and Fall of a Free-Standing Company in Nova Scotia"; Ian McKay, "The Crisis of Dependent Development"; and Stephen J. Hornsby, *Nineteenth-Century Cape Breton*, 95–107.

2 Memo by W. Vernon Smith, Colonial Office, enclosed with GMA to Lord John Russell, Secretary of State for Colonies, 27 November 1840, Colonial Office records for Nova Scotia (hereafter CO) 217/176.

3 Richard Brown, *The Coal Fields and Coal Trade of the Island of Cape Breton*, 54.

4 McKay, "Crisis of Dependent Development," 14–17.

5 *Colonial Patriot*, 14 December 1827; R.P. Fereday, "The Career of Richard Smith."

6 Eric Hobsbawm, *Industry and Empire*, 109–14.

7 Carlos Marichal, *A Century of Debt Crises in Latin America*, 43–67; Frank Griffith Dawson, *The First Latin American Debt Crisis*; Boyd Hilton, *Corn, Cash, Commerce*, 202–31; Leland Hamilton Jenks, *The Migration of British Capital*, 25–64.

8 *Annual Register, or A View of the History, Politics, and Literature of the Year 1825* (London: Baldwin and Craddock, 1826), 2–4; Henry English, *A Complete View of Joint Stock Companies*, 31–2.

9 T.C. Haliburton to Peleg Wiswall, 10 May 1825, in Richard A. Davies, ed., *The Letters of Thomas Chandler Haliburton*, 31.

10 *Annual Register, or A view of the History, Politics, and Literature of the Year 1827* (London: Baldwin and Craddock, 1828), 2–14, 230–1.

11 Treasury Minutes, 29 March 1825, enclosed with Sir James Kempt to William Huskisson, 13 May 1828, CO 217/148; *Annual Register … 1827*, 8–14; *Gentleman's Magazine* (London) 96, no. 1 (January 1826): 58; Jenks, *Migration of British Capital*, 42–4.

12 The senior Rundell, Philip, had retired in 1822 and was probated at more than £1,200,000 (not including real estate) when he died in February 1827 (just more than a month after the duke died). The Latin American stocks were languishing. They were issued at £5 and had traded as high as £16 but were selling for £1¼ in January 1827. While capitalized at £2,000,000, only £100,000 was actually paid up. See English, *Complete View of Joint Stock Companies*, 3.

13 See, however, the vaguely accusative comments in Henry English, *A General Guide to Companies Formed for Working Foreign Mines*, 86–8. On Rundell, see *Annual Register … 1827*, 230–1. See also the General Mining Association Limited, "Deed of Settlement," 5–6.

14 General Mining Association, "Deed of Settlement," 6; Copy of lease, dated
11 July 1826, in document 9, vol. 460, RG 1, Public Archives of Nova Scotia
(PANS); and Dawson, *First Latin American Debt Crisis*, 100.

15 J.R. McCulloch, *A Dictionary, Practical, Theoretical, and Historical, of Commerce
and Commercial Navigation*, 801.

16 The original lease from 1788 does not appear to have been extant at the
time. Instead, officials appear to have used a copy dated 1792. See "Case
respecting the lease of Mines in Nova Scotia to His late Royal Highness the
Duke of York and Albany," Treasury Minutes, copy, 29 March 1825, enclosed in James Kempt to William Huskisson, 13 May 1828, CO 217/148.

17 Cape Breton's place in the lease was not clear. In 1788 the Island was a separate colony and therefore apparently not part of the lease. But after reports
of potentially lucrative seams of coal near Sydney, the duke's solicitors immediately attempted to make the case that Cape Breton was part of the lease.
The Treasury insisted that Cape Breton was not part of Nova Scotia at the
time of the grant and therefore "certainly not intended to be included." Nevertheless, a new arrangement was negotiated to suit the purpose. A map in
the package, with no clear provenance, shows an area including eastern New
Brunswick, which raises the possibility that someone conceived of Nova Scotia
as embracing the ancient boundaries of post-1713 British Acadia or of the
1621 Scottish grant. See John Parkinson [solicitor to the Duke of York] to the
Duke of York, copy, 3 April 1826; Parkinson to T. Frankland Lewis (Treasury),
6 November 1827; and E.G. Stanley (Treasury, for Huskisson) to
William Hill (Colonial Office), 14 December 1827, all enclosed with
Sir James Kempt to William Huskisson, 13 May 1828, CO 217/148.

18 The annual rent of £3,300 on the first 20,000 chaldrons per year (and 2s per
chaldron beyond 20,000) was for the already existing mines that they had assumed, while the remaining "reserved" mines were subject to an immediate
royalty of 2s per chaldron on every chaldron produced; see R.W. Hay (Colonial Office) to the General Mining Association, 24 January 1835, no. 10; and
"Memo on Coal Returns," [c. 1835], no. 11, both in vol. 460, RG 1, PANS.

19 I was not able to locate any of these records, but letters reprinted in the *Journals of the House of Assembly* in the 1850s between the attorney solicitor general
and solicitors for both the estate of the duke and the GMA suggest that this
was the basis for the action; see H. Merivale to Gaspard LeMarchant, Lieutenant Governor, 7 February 1855, reprinted in Nova Scotia, *Journals of the House
of Assembly* (hereafter *JHA*) (1856), appendix 12; and Farrer, Ouvry, and
Farrer, solicitors for the Estate of the Duke of York, to Merivale, 4 December
1856, reprinted in *JHA* (1857), appendix 54. To see how truly incestuous this
entire affair was, note that Thomas Farrer, here acting on behalf of the creditors of the estate of the duke in a suit against the GMA, was (and may here still

be) a director of the GMA. Note too that Rundell was also one of the creditors, as was the Crown (the duke died owing the Crown almost £122,713). The chancery trial, then, pitted the creditors against the GMA and the Crown, but the Crown and some board members of the GMA were also creditors. In effect, people were suing themselves. Thomas Ferrar held the most problematic position; he was acting as solicitor for a group of which he was in fact a part in a suit against another group of which he was also a part. The final settlement had the GMA pay the creditors £120,000, £30,000 of which went to the Crown. See the letters between Farrer, Ouvry, and Farrer and Merivale from 4 December 1856 and 12 January 1857, also reprinted in *JHA* (1857), appendix 54.

20 See George Smith to Sir James Kempt, [n.d.], enclosed in Kempt to Huskisson, 14 December 1827, CO 217/147.

21 Samuel Cunard to Sir James Kempt, 9 January 1826, enclosed in Kempt to R. Wilmot Horton, Undersecretary of State for the Colonies, 13 February 1826, CO 217/146.

22 Sir James Kempt to William Huskisson, 13 May 1828, CO 217/148. The GMA also managed to sneak the much larger Newcastle chaldron into the lease rather than the much more commonly employed Winchester chaldron. This allowed the company to reduce significantly its payments to the Crown. See Gerriets, "Impact of the General Mining Association," 62–5.

23 Smith and Liddell requested an end to their lease and £1,000 compensation for the loss of the mines; see Petition of George Smith and William Liddell, 9 May 1828, CO 217/148. They obtained the first but not the latter; see J. Stewart, Treasury, to R.W. Hay, 22 July 1828, CO 217/148.

24 *JHA* (1839), appendix 50, lists 915 employees at Pictou alone (including those working on the South Pictou Rail Road). The works at Pictou are described at some length in Joseph Howe, *Western and Eastern Rambles*, 159–69. On brick exports, see the weekly shipping returns for Pictou, printed in the *Colonial Patriot*, which regularly note ships carrying bricks to PEI, Cape Breton, and New Brunswick (Miramichi).

25 P.J. Cain and A.G. Hopkins, *British Imperialism*.

26 See the shareholders listed in English, *General Guide to Companies*, 35–6. Both Rundell and Bridge, however, made it into the "missing persons" volume published by Oxford in 1994; see C.S. Nichols, ed., *Dictionary of National Biography, Missing Persons*, 87–8, 574–5.

27 John Wright to George Renny Young, London, 25 June 1850, f1/757, vol. 723, MG 2, PANS; James A. Jaffe, *The Struggle for Market Power*, 85.

28 Littleton was a Tory, although a "moderate reformer," until moving to Huskisson's support and sitting with the Whigs in the "Reform Ministry";

see G.F.R.B., "Edward John Littleton," 369–71; A. Aspinall, ed., *Three Early Nineteenth Century Diaries*, ix-xi; and Fereday, "Career of Richard Smith," chs 1 and 2.

29 Belcher would return to Halifax in 1829 to "assume personal direction of his
surviving business interests" and the position as Halifax agent for the GMA in
Halifax; see David A. Sutherland, "Andrew Belcher," 62–4.

30 Aspinall's account suggests that Littleton had very little influence prior to
aligning himself with Huskisson in 1827 and never acquired much in the following years. He was always on the fringes of the Cabinet but was never actually
offered a position. He was finally offered a new peerage – Baron Hatherton –
in 1835. See Aspinall, *Three Early Nineteenth Century Diaries*; and Sir Bernard
Burke and Ashworth P. Burke, eds, *Genealogical and Heraldic History of the Peerage
and Baronetage, the Privy Council, Knightage and Companionage*, 963–5.

31 Littleton inherited his uncle's estate but also married well; see Aspinall, *Three
Early Nineteenth Century Diaries*, ix.

32 Petition of the [GMA], 22 December 1842, no. 104; and "Memorial of the
Chairman and Directors of the General Mining Association," 30 April 1831,
no. 36, both in vol. 459, RG 1, PANS. The directors for 1829 are listed in General Mining Association, "Deed of Settlement," 1.

33 Richard Brown Correspondence, vols 151–9, MG 1, PANS. The Act of 1858
specifically notes Farrer as the negotiator for Mary Ann Rundell and Edmond
Strong, executrix and executor respectively; see Nova Scotia, *The Statutes of
Nova Scotia* (1858), 78.

34 Robert Stewart to George Renny Young, 3 December 1836, Robert Stewart's
Letterbook, 2316/2, Public Archives of Prince Edward Island (PAPEI). My
thanks to Rusty Bittermann for alerting me to the Stewart papers.

35 See entries from 5 July 1831 onward for David Stewart's activities in Pictou
and Sydney with Richard Smith, in David Stewart's Journal, 3209/28, PAPEI.
See also David Stewart to Thomas Farrer [GMA], 17 September 1831; David
Stewart to G.V. Duval [GMA], 17 September 1831: David Stewart to John
Bainbridge [provincial agent for Nova Scotia], 21 January 1832; and David
Stewart to John Bainbridge, 12 March 1832, all in Stewart Letterbook,
2316/1, PAPEI.

36 See E.N. Kendall, Commissioner, *Reports Nos. 1 and 2 on the State and Condition
of the Province of New Brunswick with some observations on the Company's Tract*
(London: W. Day, 1835); and North American Colonial Association of Ireland, *Report of an Extraordinary Meeting of the Shareholders of the North American
Colonial Association of Ireland held at the Company's Office, Broad Street* (London:
M'Kewan, 1844). The company's Lower Canadian project grew out of the
earlier program for Canada and Nova Scotia, originally outlined by the Stewarts as early as 1832. See David Stewart to John Bainbridge [New Brunswick

and Nova Scotia Land Company], 18 April 1832; David Stewart to J. Lawson [New Brunswick and Nova Scotia Land Company], 20 April 1832, both in Stewart Letterbook, 2316/1, PAPEI; Robert Stewart to D. Henchy, 18 June 1835; Stewart to George Renny Young, 1 February 1836; and Stewart to Young, 3 December 1836, all in Stewart Letterbook, 2316/2, PAPEI.

37 Bainbridge was also the agent for the New Brunswick and Nova Scotia Land Company; see New Brunswick and Nova Scotia Land Company, *Report of the Directors of the New Brunswick and Nova Scotia Land Company*; David Stewart to John Bainbridge [New Brunswick and Nova Scotia Land Company], 18 April 1832, Stewart Letterbook, 2316/1, PAPEI; and Great Britain, House of Commons, *First Report of the Select Committee on the Means of Improving and Maintaining the Foreign Trade of the Country*, 44–50. See also Graeme Wynn, *Timber Colony*, 121; and Phyllis R. Blakeley, "Samuel Cunard," 176.

38 GMA directors the Hon. Edward Blount and Ambrose Humphreys were also directors, with John Bainbridge, of the New Brunswick and Nova Scotia Land Company; see Kendall, *Reports Nos. 1 and 2*. Another GMA director, Felix Ladbroke, joined the Stewarts, Edward Gibbon Wakefield, the Rt. Hon. Edward Littleton, and the Earl of Durham as directors of the North American Colonial Association of Ireland; see the list of investors in North American Colonial Association, *Colonization of the County of Beauharnois*. See also David Stewart's letters to Alexander Baring, 20 April 1832, and to Lord Viscount Goderich, 22 March 1832; Robert Stewart's letters to R.W. Hay, 24 September 1833, to Sir George Seymour, to John Angerstein, MP, to Lord James Townshend, MP, and to John Walter, MP, all dated 9 July 1835, lobbying to get the North American Colonial Association bill through; and Stewart to "Miss Fanning," 7 August 1835, all in Stewart Letterbook, 2316/2, PAPEI.

39 Blakeley, "Samuel Cunard"; "Communications on the subject of the Shubenacadie Canal, Nova Scotia," 6 May 1830, CO 217/149.

40 "List of Subscribers, Shubenacadie Canal, Nova Scotia," 27 March 1829, CO 217/149. See also the list of subscribers for the Quebec and Halifax Steamship Company (1831), which included Rundell, Bridge, Belcher, Cunard, and George and William Young, in Sandford Fleming, "Notes on Ocean Steam Navigation," 167–8.

41 Kendall, *Reports Nos. 1 and 2*; Stewart to Bainbridge, 20 January 1832 and 21 January 1832, Stewart Letterbook, 2316/1, PAPEI; Stewart to George Renny Young, 3 December 1836, Stewart Letterbook, 2316/2, PAPEI.

42 On David Stewart's visit, see particularly entries for 7 July 1831 (in the works with Smith), 8 July 1831 (meets local politicians), 10 July 1831 (surveys the farmlands around the mines), 11 July 1831 (arranges land sale), and 14 July (walks the proposed route of the canal at St Peter's), in David Stewart's

Journal, 3209/28, PAPEI. See also Charles Fairbanks and John Bainbridge to R.W. Hay, 27 March 1830, copy, in "Communications on the subject of the Shubenacadie Canal, Nova Scotia," 6 May 1830, CO 217/149.

43 Robert Stewart to "D Henchy Esqr," 12 March 1835; Stewart to John Hill, 19 March 1835; and Stewart to Andrew Colville, 15 August 1835, all in Stewart Letterbook, 2316/2, PAPEI. In the letter to Hill, in which Stewart was trying to buy land from him, Stewart used the good price that the land company had obtained from the New Brunswick government (2s3d per acre) as leverage, noting that such large purchases nearby were keeping downward pressure on land prices.

44 He at least met Richard Smith, Joseph Smith, William Davis, Peter Crerar, Hugh Denoon, George Smith and Thomas Dickson (the two MLAs), George Renny Young, and a number of the magistrates and other prominent people of the district; see David Stewart's Journal, 3209/28, PAPEI.

45 Robert Stewart to George Renny Young, 1 February 1836; and Stewart to Young, 3 December 1836, both in Stewart Letterbook, 2316/2, PAPEI; George R. Young, *Upon the History, Principles, and Prospects of the Bank of British North America*; Bank of British North America, *Alphabetical List of the Proprietors of the Bank of British North America*; Blakeley, "Samuel Cunard."

46 Blakeley, "Samuel Cunard." Richard Smith defeated William Young in Cape Breton in 1832. The election was marked by several riots and excessive spending; see Brian Cuthbertson, *Johnnny Bluenose at the Polls*, 276–9.

47 Joseph Schull and J. Douglas Gibson, *The Scotiabank Story*, 6–49. Uniacke eventually headed the first post-reform government in the province, but in the 1830s he, like Joseph Howe, was still a Tory.

48 Sutherland, "Andrew Belcher," 64. Fortunately for Cunard, Belcher was dead by the time Cunard's debts almost caught up with him. In 1842 the Banks of Nova Scotia and British North America cooperated in loaning Cunard £45,000 so that he might gain some security against his £130,000 in debts; see Schull and Gibson, *Scotiabank Story*, 43–4.

49 Robert Stewart to John Bainbridge, 6 August 1835, Robert Stewart's Letterbook, 2316/2, PAPEI. On William Young, see the extensive series of notes on the law of mines and minerals, the terms of the lease, and his speeches on the "evils" of the monopoly, in nos 155–70, vol. 732, MG 1, PANS. We will see more of these papers below.

50 Atlantic and St Lawrence Railroad Company, *Report of the Provisional Committee of the Atlantic & St. Lawrence Railroad*. Cunard was not the only connection here. Five years later, John Wright, an original investor in and board member of the GMA, was pitching for the Halifax and Quebec Railway and its related land company, the Canadian Land and Railway Association; see John Wright

to George Renny Young, 25 January 1850, George Young Papers, f1/757, vol. 723, MG 2, PANS. See also "[Proposed] Bill to Incorporate the Canadian Land & Railway Association," George Young Papers, f1/771, vol. 723, MG 2, PANS. The full scheme is laid out in Canada Land and Railway Association, *Report & outline of a plan by which an extensive railway may be constructed in the British North American colonies.*

51 H.J.M. Johnston, *British Emigration Policy, 1815–1830*; Donald Winch, *Classical Political Economy and Colonies.*

52 See, for example, Robert Stewart to Henchy, 18 June 1835, Stewart Letterbook, 2316/2, PAPEI.

53 M.P. Cowen and R.W. Shenton, *Doctrines of Development*, esp. 21–41.

54 Winch, *Classical Political Economy*, 51–72, 144–8.

55 Edward Gibbon Wakefield, "A Letter from Sydney," in M.F. Lloyd Prichard, ed., *The Collected Works of Edward Gibbon Wakefield*, 163–6.

56 "Address of the Shubenacadie Canal Co.," 20 May 1829, CO 217/149.

57 George Cawston and A.H. Keane, *The Early Chartered Companies, A.D. 1296–1858*, 152–3, 190–1.

58 Treasury Minutes, copy, in Sir James Kempt to William Huskisson, 13 May 1828, CO 217/148.

59 Treasury Minutes, copy, in Sir James Kempt to William Huskisson, 13 May 1828, CO 217/148, emphasis added.

60 Edmund Waller Rundell to R.W. Hay, "Personal," 29 November 1828, CO 217/148.

61 Cited in Cawston and Keane, *Early Chartered Companies*, "Preface." Note too this expression in Wakefield's description of Australian colonization as "an extension of the old society," in Wakefield, "Letter from Sydney," in Lloyd Prichard, ed., *Collected Works*, 165.

62 Petition of Rundell, Bridge, and Rundell, 22 January 1828, CO 217/148; Winch, *Classical Political Economy*, 65–92; Michel Foucault, "On Governmentality," 98–101.

63 Petition of the General Mining Association [signed by Edmund Waller Rundell], 30 April 1831, no. 36, vol. 459, RG 1, PANS.

64 Report of George Wightman on the GMA, 10 March 1842, no. 37, vol. 3, RG 21, PANS. For examples of other petitions employing the same strategy, see General Mining Association to Lord John Russell, Secretary of State for the Colonies, 27 November 1840, CO 217/176; and Memorial of [GMA], [1828], no. 32; and Petition of [GMA] [signed by Cunard], 22 December 1842, no. 104, both in vol. 459, RG 1, PANS.

65 Muise, "General Mining Association"; McKay, "Crisis of Dependent Development"; Gerriets, "Impact of the General Mining Association."

66 Samuel Cunard to Sir James Kempt, 9 January 1826, enclosed in Kempt to R. Wilmot Horton, Undersecretary of State for the Colonies, 13 February 1826, CO 217/146.

67 Petition of the [GMA] [signed by Edmund Waller Rundell], 30 April 1831, CO 217/153.

68 "GMA Letterbook, 1827–1833," MG 14, 19 D.8.a, Beaton Institute (BI).

69 Petition of Richard Smith for the General Mining Association, 4 June 1827, no. 11, vol. 459, RG 1, PANS. The General South American Mining Association sent out George Backwell in the spring of 1826; see Sir James Kempt, Lt Governor, to Wilmot Horton, 16 April 1826, CO 217/146; and George Backwell to William Huskisson, 7 March 1828, CO 217/148. See also Brown, *Coal Fields*, 56–7.

70 Jonathan Parkinson to the Duke of York, copy, 3 April 1826, enclosed in Sir James Kempt to William Huskisson, 13 May 1828, CO 217/148.

71 *Colonial Herald*, 4 May 1839, cited in Rusty Bittermann, "Farm Households and Wage Labour in the Northeastern Maritimes before 1850," 56.

72 See the discussion of ordering for stores in Richard Brown Sr to Richard Brown Jr, 19 January 1866, no. 1, vol. 151, MG 1, PANS. Richard Smith commented on rope being expensive in Halifax compared with Britain; see Richard Smith to M.B. Almon, 21 June 1827, Pictou Letterbook, RG 002/01/0001/0000/0001, Bank of Nova Scotia Archives. There were two ropeworks in Halifax in the 1820s and 1830s, including the Stanyon works, which were founded in the same year as the GMA; see David A. Sutherland, "The Stanyon Ropeworks of Halifax, Nova Scotia."

73 Account Book of John G. Grant, 1847–77, vol. 117, MG 3, PANS. For Sydney, see the timber contracts in a list dated December 1854 for "perfectly hewed, exactly of the dimensions specified, and delivered by the 15th of April on the roadside leading from the No. 3 pit ... at 10/ [10s] per 100 feet," in "GMA Timber Contracts, 1854–64," D.16, MG 14, 19, BI. Similar contracts for the same period exist for the Lingan mine as well.

74 See "Account of Expenditure at the Albion Coal Mines, in the County of Pictou, in the Year ending on the 31st December, 1838," copy of "Return Marked F," in *JHA* (1839), appendix 50; and Belcher to Richard Brown, 10 April 1833, no. 37, D.9.a, MG 14, 19, BI.

75 Joseph Smith, "Return Marked C," reprinted in *JHA* (1839), appendix 50; "Diary, Richard Brown," June 1830 to February 1832, no. 8, vol. 40, "A," RG 21, PANS; Richard H. Brown Sr, Diary, 29 December 1849, no. 9, vol. 38, "A," RG 21, PANS. The GMA occasionally advertised its need for oats; see *Cape Breton News*, 17 November 1852. There was, of course, an incentive for coal shippers to return if they had a cargo for the mines; see Richard Brown to George L. Deblois, 24 May 1833 (hay), no. 18a; [unsigned letter dated at Boston] to

Richard Smith, 22 June 1833 (oats), no. 20b; Andrew Belcher to Richard Brown, 20 April 1833 (English leather), no. 32; Belcher to Brown, 10 April 1833 (rope and shovels), no. 37; and Deblois to Smith, 14 July 1832 (hay), no. 60, all in D.9.a, MG 14, 19, BI; and Smith to Rupert Cochrane, 31 August 1832; and Smith to Deblois, 6 September 1832, both in D.8.a, MG 14, 19, BI.

76 James Primrose to M.B. Almon, 18 April 1839 and 17 August 1839; Primrose to James Forman, 14 April 1842, all in Pictou Letterbook, RG 002/010001/0000/0001, Bank of Nova Scotia Archives.

77 Henry Poole, in "Report," vol. 35, "R," RG 5, PANS; *Colonial Patriot,* 14 March 1828. Local shipping figures are based on a one-in-two sample (fifty-one weeks) of clearances from Pictou harbour between April 1831 and December 1833 as reported in the *Colonial Patriot.* See also Primrose to Almon, 11 March 1839, Halifax Letterbook, RG 002/01/0001/0000/0001, Bank of Nova Scotia Archives. Despite the changes to Pictou's and Sydney's status, for merchant-capitalists outside Halifax, the free-port issue remained significant; see William Young to the Earl of Durham, item no. 3, appendix A, in "Report on the Affairs of British North America from the Earl of Durham," in Great Britain, *Parliamentary Papers,* vol. 17 (1839).

78 Edmund Waller Rundell to R.W. Hay, "Personal," 29 November 1828, CO 217/148, emphasis added. It was this same argument that the Shubenacadie Canal Company used the following year. A commentary in the *Novascotian,* 18 October 1827, emphasized the domestic market for coal in a cold province and the wider possibilities for export of coal, iron, and even steel. It also made the link between the increased population of the area and the domestic and export markets for both coal and iron.

79 Edmund Waller Rundell to R.W. Hay, 29 November 1828, CO 217/148; this is *not* the same letter as in the previous note.

80 Sir James Kempt to Wilmot Horton, 8 April 1827, CO 217/147.

81 The Hay letter is not in the file; these observations are based on Rundell's reply. See Edmund Waller Rundell to R.W. Hay, 6 December 1828, CO 217/148.

82 Sir James Kempt to R. Wilmot Horton, 28 October 1826, CO 217/146; Kempt to Horton, 8 April 1827, CO 217/147.

83 Petition of General Mining Association [Samuel Cunard], 22 December 1842, no. 104, vol. 459, RG 1, PANS. See F.W. Taussig, *The Tariff History of the United States,* 131–5.

84 Petition of the [GMA], 22 December 1842, no. 104, vol. 459, RG 1, PANS; Robert Moser to Lord Stanley, 5 January 1844, London, reprinted in *JHA* (1845), appendix 1; William Young to Moser, 31 July 1854, reprinted in *JHA* (1855), appendix 3.

85 McKay, "Crisis of Dependent Development," 29.

CHAPTER SIX

1 Report of George Wightman, 10 March 1842, no. 37, vol. 3, RG 21, Nova Scotia Archives and Records Management (NSARM).

2 J.M. Beck, *Joseph Howe*, vol. 1, 236-9; Ian Ross Robertson, *The Tenant League of Prince Edward Island, 1864-1867*, 34-5, 301-2.

3 The first census that we might use (1827) is missing for both Sydney Mines and Albion Mines. The 1838 census nicely identifies miners for us but sadly does not tell us much more than that they were there and the size of their families.

4 These approximate proportions are based on the description supplied by H.S. Poole, "Cost of Raising Coal at Albion Mines," 7 February 1842, file: "Correspondence, 1842," vol. 7, "A," RG 21, Public Archives of Nova Scotia (PANS).

5 Bettina Bradbury, "Pigs, Cows, and Boarders"; Louise A. Tilly and Joan W. Scott, *Women, Work, and Family*, 53-4.

6 Alan Campbell, *The Lanarkshire Miners*, 108-9.

7 Michael Haines, *Fertility and Occupation*, 142-4; Béatrice Craig, Judith Rygiel, and Elizabeth Turcotte, "The Homespun Paradox." Commissioned outwork does not seem to have been common in the northern counties, although some women clearly worked full time at weaving and fulling. We will return to this in the next chapter. On occupational opportunities for women in a French mining town, see Tilly and Scott, *Women, Work, and Family*, 84-6. See also K.D.M. Snell, *Annals of the Labouring Poor*, 348-50; and R.E. Pahl, *Divisions of Labour*, 33-9, 67-73.

8 This is based on an assumption of 6d per yard, although prices varied. Archibald and Company, for example, offered as much as 1s6d in the 1820s, but this was high; see Archibald & Co. Ledger, "A," MG 14, 45, Beaton Institute (BI); and the accounts for Betsy McDonald (Big Judique) and Mary McDonald, "Account Book, 1865-1870," William McKeen Papers, no. 1459, vol. 109, MG 12, BI.

9 Robert Grant, *East River Worthies*, 23; *Pictou Observer*, 14 October 1834.

10 See Michael Hanley (p. 353), Henry Lawler (376), Daniel Lawler (379), and Thomas Phelan (437), all in book R, RG 47, PANS; and Angus MacInnis (p. 150), and John McLean (465), both in book U [1952], RG 47, PANS.

11 See, for example, the court-ordered property assessments in May 1850 in George Laurence Papers, vol. 541, MG 1, PANS; and John Murphy to Samuel Fairbanks, 26 January 1857, reprinted in Nova Scotia, *Journals of the House of Assembly* (hereafter *JHA*) (1857), appendix 71.

12 W. Ouseley, quoted in C.B. Fergusson, ed., *Uniacke's Sketches of Cape Breton*, 173.

13 L.D. McCann, "The Mercantile-Industrial Transition in the Metals Towns of Pictou County, 1857-1931"; L.D. McCann and Jill Burnett, "Social Mobility and the Ironmasters of Late Nineteenth Century New Glasgow," 66–70.

14 Rosemary E. Ommer, "Anticipating the Trend"; James M. Cameron, *Industrial History of the New Glasgow District.*

15 We might note here that our sample missed William Davies, the man who was recruited to run the foundry for the GMA in the 1830s and who now owned it. His "probable value" was listed at £1,500.

16 *Colonial Patriot*, 18 January 1828.

17 Campbell, *Lanarkshire Miners*, 20–1; Robert Colls, *The Pitmen of the Northern Coalfield*, 123–33. On letters from abroad, see Snell, *Annals of the Labouring Poor*, 9–14.

18 See Peter Barrett, "Twelve Years in North America, Containing a Brief Sketch of the Life, Trials and Persecutions of Peter Barrett, an English Immigrant, in Nova Scotia, Canada, Written by Himself," unpublished manuscript, 1879, PANS; and Allan C. Dunlop, "Peter Barrett's Pictou County."

19 James Madison to "Brother and Sister" [envelope addressed to John Stevenson], 28 December 1835, no. 7, vol. 185, MG 100, NSARM.

20 Some also returned from the US; see Walter R. Johnson, *The Coal Trade of British America*, 21.

21 *Pictou Observer*, 14 March 1832; *Cape Breton Spectator*, 6 May 1848.

22 Royden Harrison, *The Independent Collier.*

23 Arthur Redford [c. 1860], quoted in Haines, *Fertility and Occupation*, 9.

24 Report of George Wightman, 10 March 1842, no. 37, vol. 3, RG 21, NSARM.

25 See H.B. Jefferson, "Mount Rundell, Stellarton, and the Albion Railway of 1839." Mt Rundell was destroyed late in the century.

26 Richard Brown, *The Coal Fields and Coal Trade of the Island of Cape Breton*, 50–2, 62–8.

27 Some ships carpenters near Pictou were reportedly earning as much as 7s6d per day. On local wage rates, see "Return showing the Average Wages of Mechanics and Others in Pictou, Nova Scotia, for the Three Months ended 10 October 1842," enclosure no. 7 in Viscount Falkland to Lord Stanley, 3 February 1843, reprinted in "Correspondence Related to Emigration," in Great Britain, *Parliamentary Papers*, vol. 16, 483. Data on colliers' wages and the employment of sons are from Henry Poole, "Cost of Raising Coal at Albion Mines," 7 February 1842, vol. 7, "A," RG 21, NSARM. Data on housing and coal are from George Smith, "Report on Riots at Albion Mines," 19 November 1841, Report, vol. 35, "R," RG 5, NSARM. Coal was usually free for employees.

28 "Report on Riots at Albion Mines," 19 November 1841, Report, vol. 35, "R," RG 5, NSARM; Barret, "Twelve Years in North America," 6; Frederic S. Cozzens, *Acadia, or A Month with the Blue Noses,* 186.

29 George Smith, for example, noted that although the men were well paid by the day, this might not amount to much by the month. Two miners told him that although they earned 10s per day, they might earn as little as £2 per month. See George Smith, "Report on Riots at Albion Mines," 19 November 1841, vol. 35, "R," RG 5, NSARM.

30 "Diary, Richard Brown," 5 and 6 July 1830 (mustering); 8 September 1830 (fired miner for refusing an order); 13 September 1830 (fired cooper for misconduct); 28 September 1830 (fired someone for "not working more industriously"); 15 November 1830 (fired three men for "bad treatment of some strangers"); and 8 and 9 July 1831 (mustering), no. 8, vol. 38, "A", RG 21, NSARM. On the incident in 1834, see Brown to Sir Rupert George, 3 September 1834, no. 111, vol. 458, RG 1, NSARM.

31 "Diary, Richard Brown," 29 April 1845, no. 8, vol. 38, "A," RG 21, NSARM.

32 R.H. Brown Sr, Diary, 29 April 1845, 16 and 17 March, 26 and 28 June, 13–15 and 29 August, and 15 November 1849, no. 8, vol. 38, "A," RG 21, NSARM. In 1830 Brown also noted a number of men taking "Holy Days"; see 29 June 1830 and 25 March 1831, no. 8, vol. 40, "A," RG 21, NSARM. See also Walter Johnson's brief description of one such negotiation in his *Coal Trade of British America,* 20.

33 Richard Smith, quoted in "Report of the Select Committee of the House of Commons on Accidents in Mines," in Great Britain, *Parliamentary Papers,* vol. 5 (1835), 223–37, 249–53, 276–84, quotation at 276. Compare this with Cozzens's description of Sydney Mines – "this nest of Beelzebub" – in his *Acadia,* 186–99.

34 Smith, quoted in "Report of the Select Committee," 276–7.

35 *Colonial Patriot,* 31 December 1833.

36 Bryan D. Palmer, *Working-Class Experience,* 41–8, 76–8.

37 *Colonial Patriot,* 31 December 1833.

38 It is worth noting that Sunday, 30 December 1833, was the anniversary, but the commemoration occurred on Monday.

39 *Colonial Patriot,* 31 December 1833.

40 Many parades in New York were explicitly supportive of the politics of economic expansion; see Sean Wilentz, *Chants Democratic,* 87–91.

41 *Colonial Patriot,* 31 December 1833.

42 "Report on the Fire at Pictou," 1833, vol. 1625, "S," RG 5, NSARM.

43 *Colonial Patriot,* 11 January 1828; *Mechanic and Farmer,* 25 September 1839; *Cape Breton Advocate,* 13 January 1841; *Spirit of the Times,* 21 June 1844 and

11 January 1845; "Diary, Richard Brown," 28 June 1849, no. 9, vol. 38, "A," RG 21, NSARM.

44 The following description of the celebration and the parade is taken entirely from *Mechanic and Farmer,* 25 September 1839.

45 "Mr. Buddle's Report on The Sydney Mines Railway," no. 32, vol. 39, "A," RG 21, NSARM, original emphasis. See also Jefferson, "Mount Rundell."

46 "Diary, Richard Brown," 5 July 1830 and 8 July 1831, no. 8, vol. 40, "A," RG 21, NSARM. However, see also Brown's apology to the president of the council for the refusal of the men to·muster, in Brown to Sir Rupert George, 3 September 1834, no. 111, vol. 458, RG 1, NSARM.

47 These strikes are discussed later in the chapter.

48 *Eastern Chronicle,* 12 May 1864.

49 Many of these men would have been disenfranchised under changes passed by the (Liberal-dominated) House of Assembly but rejected by the (Tory) Legislative Council in 1854; see Beck, *Joseph Howe,* vol. 2, 169–70.

50 Wilentz, *Chants Democratic,* 87–91.

51 Reports from *The Home and Foreign Missionary Record for the Church of Scotland,* July 1839 to December 1841, quoted in Laurie Stanley, *The Well-Watered Garden,* 137–8; and in Alexander Farquharson, *Sketch of the Missionary Proceedings at Cape Breton from August 1833 to October 1834,* 8–10.

52 *Spirit of the Times,* 24 May 1844; Mrs Roderick G. Bain, compiler, "History of Sydney Mines," unpublished manuscript [1951], 29–30, BI. Farquharson, *Sketch of the Missionary Proceedings,* 8, estimated that the mining population was 60 per cent Presbyterian and 40 per cent Catholic.

53 See *Colonial Patriot,* 3 September 1833 and 24 September 1833.

54 See the case of the Queen versus David Sutherland [hostler at Albion Mines], tried for the murder of Alexander McKenzie [bankman at Albion Mines], 1841, Pictou County, "C," RG 39, NSARM.

55 Brown, *Coal Fields and Coal Trade,* 54.

56 *Spirit of the Times,* 1 March 1845; *Cape Breton News,* 16 March 1853; "Petition of Miners and Others Resident at Albion Mines [27 February 1841]," in *JHA* (1841), 66.

57 D.B. McNab to J.B. Uniacke, 3 January 1857, reprinted in *JHA* (1857), appendix 71.

58 "Diary, Richard Brown," 4 April, 14 April, 21 April, 3 May, and 1 September 1831, no. 8, vol. 40, "A," RG 21, NSARM.

59 I have found no contemporary description of the 1840 walkout. This description is based on commentary comparing the 1841–42 strike with that of two summers earlier; see *Mechanic and Farmer,* 2 February 1842. The tactic, however, was the same used six years later in another strike at Pictou, during

which "several masters of the vessels protested against the Company," presumably out of their own interest, not that of the miners; see *Novascotian*, 12 October 1846. See also Johnson, *Coal Trade of British America*, 20.

60 On the GMA's economizing, see "Cost of Raising Coal at Albion Mines," 7 February 1842, file: "Correspondence, 1842," vol. 7, "A," RG 21, PANS; and Petition of the GMA [authored by Cunard], 22 December 1842, no. 104, vol. 459, RG 1, NSARM. The length of the strike is not clear. The *Mechanic and Farmer* described it as ten weeks old on 2 February 1842, two weeks before it ended, while George Wightman, who was sent to investigate for the province, described it as two months.

61 *Mechanic and Farmer,* 26 January 1842.

62 Henry Poole, cited in George Smith, "Report on Riots at Albion Mines," 19 November 1841, vol. 35, "R," RG 5, NSARM.

63 We might know a fair bit more if the *Pictou Observer* had published a letter that it received from "A Miner" sometime in January. The editor agreed that the "Association's agents are pursuing an erroneous course towards the unfortunate men" but felt that they should delay publication of the letter "until we learn the result of Mr. Cunard's next visit to the mines." Unfortunately (for us), the strike was settled the day of the next issue, so the letter was not published. See *Pictou Observer,* 25 January and 3 February 1842.

64 Henry Poole, cited in George Smith, "Report on Riots at Albion Mines," 19 November 1841, vol. 35, "R," RG 5, NSARM.

65 *Mechanic and Farmer,* 2 February 1842; and *Pictou Observer* 25 January 1842.

66 Henry Poole, cited in George Smith, "Report on Riots at Albion Mines," 19 November 1841, vol. 35, "R," RG 5, NSARM.

67 Poole became a manager and promoter in the postmonopoly period; see Henry S. Poole, *Notes on the Coal Field of Pictou*; and Henry S. Poole and J. Campbell, *Additional Papers on the Nova Scotia Gold Fields.*

68 See the comments of George Smith and Henry Poole in George Smith, "Report on Riots at Albion Mines," 19 November 1841, vol. 35, "R," RG 5, NSARM.

69 George Smith, "Report on Riots at Albion Mines," 19 November 1841, vol. 35, "R," RG 5, NSARM; *Mechanic and Farmer,* 9 February 1842. The *Pictou Observer,* 3 February 1842, claims that the 2d cut that the men accepted was their initial position and, therefore, that they had won the strike. On the other hand, the acceptance of a cut of 2d per cubic yard instead of a 4d cut certainly sounds like "splitting the difference." The paper also credited not Cunard but Poole with the negotiations; Poole was described as the "local agent." It is actually not clear what Poole's exact position was at this time; he would have been only twenty-eight in 1842. Joseph Smith was the manager in

Pictou, and Cunard was the general agent in Halifax; presumably, then, Poole
was Smith's or Cunard's assistant.

70 *Mechanic and Farmer,* 2 February 1842. A petition from Egerton Township
officials requesting additional poor-relief funds also noted that a number of
striking men had "fled for the United States" and left their families behind;
see "Petition from Egerton Township," 3 February 1842, no. 114, vol. 81, "P,"
RG 5, NSARM. The quotation is from "Petition from Egerton Township,"
no. 17, vol. 8(a), "P," RG 5, NSARM.

71 "Petition from Egerton Township," no. 17, vol. 8(a), "P," RG 5, NSARM. See
also *JHA* (1844), 4 February 1843, 381.

CHAPTER SEVEN

1 Stephen J. Hornsby, *Nineteenth-Century Cape Breton,* 41–7, 57–74; D.C. Harvey,
"Scottish Immigration to Cape Breton."

2 *Cape Breton Spectator,* 13 November 1847.

3 Graeme Wynn, "A Region of Scattered Settlements."

4 The provincial population (123,630) listed in the returns for 1827 does not
include Cape Breton. The Cape Breton figures (19,000) were included in
Sir James Kempt to William Huskisson, 12 May 1828, Colonial Office records
for Nova Scotia (hereafter CO) 217/148.

5 This calculation does not include Antigonish County, which in 1827 was half
of Sydney County.

6 On emigration from Pictou, see George Patterson, *A History of the County of
Pictou, Nova Scotia,* 441–2. Thomas Crawley, the Crown surveyor for Cape
Breton, also noted Pictou residents arriving in Cape Breton in the 1830s;
see T.C. Crawley, "Short Account of the Settlements of Cape Breton," no. 24,
vol. 334, RG 1, Nova Scotia Archives and Records Management (NSARM).

7 H.J.M. Johnston, *British Emigration Policy, 1815–1830: "Shovelling out
Paupers."* See also W.S. Shepperson, *British Emigration to North America,*
192–234.

8 Report of Committee on the "Probability of Employment for Emigrant Laborers to N. Scotia," council minutes, 26 November 1831, 368–75, vol. 195,
RG 1, NSARM.

9 Viscount Falkland to Lord John Russell, Halifax, 21 December 1841; H.W.
Crawley to John Whidden, Provincial Secretary, 27 October 1841, reprinted
in "Correspondence Related to Emigration," in Great Britain, *Parliamentary
Papers,* vol. 16, 462–97, quotation at 465. See also the comments on absentee
landholders by Titus Smith, Richard Brown, and even Samuel Cunard in
their presentations before the Durham Commission, appendix B, in "Report

on the Affairs of British North America from the Earl of Durham," 21, emphasis added, in Great Britain, *Parliamentary Papers*, vol. 17 (1839).

10 William Young to the Earl of Durham, Quebec, 20 September 1838, appendix to "Report on the Affairs of British North America," copy, no. 203, vol. 732, MG 2, NSARM; Falkland to Russell, 19 July 1841, in Great Britain, *Parliamentary Papers*, vol. 16, 466.

11 John Spry Morris to Sir Rupert George, 17 February 1837, enclosed with Sir Colin Campbell, Lt Governor, to Lord Glenelg, Undersecretary for the Colonies, 14 February 1837, CO 217/163; Charles Buller to Earl of Durham, appendix B, in "Report on the Affairs of British North America from the Earl of Durham," 21, in Great Britain, *Parliamentary Papers*, vol. 17 (1839).

12 Viscount Falkland to Lord John Russell, Halifax, 21 December 1841; H.W. Crawley to John Whidden, Provincial Secretary, 27 October 1841, both in Great Britain, *Parliamentary Papers*, vol. 16, 469.

13 "Quarterly Returns: Immigrants," J.C. Boggs, Sub-Collector of Customs, Pictou, reprinted as enclosure 5, despatch 7, Viscount Falkland to Lord Stanley, 3 February 1843, in Great Britain, *Parliamentary Papers*, vol. 16, 479–83.

14 See T. Fred. Elliot and Edward E. Villiers to Lord Stanley, [n.d.] February 1842, enclosure 6 of Stanley to Viscount Falkland, 15 March 1842, in Great Britain, *Parliamentary Papers*, vol. 16, 475–9.

15 Charles Buller to Earl of Durham, appendix B, in "Report on the Affairs of British North America from the Earl of Durham," 21, emphasis added, in Great Britain, *Parliamentary Papers*, vol. 17 (1839).

16 Viscount Falkland to Lord John Russell, Halifax, 21 December 1841; H.W. Crawley to John Whidden, Provincial Secretary, 27 October 1841, both in Public Record Office, *British Parliamentary Papers*, vol. 16, 469.

17 John Spry Morris to Sir Rupert George, 17 February 1837, enclosed with Sir Colin Campbell, Lt Governor, to Lord Glenelg, Undersecretary for the Colonies, 14 February 1837, CO 217/163.

18 Falkland to Russell, 19 July 1841, in Great Britain, *Parliamentary Papers*, vol. 16, 464–9.

19 See T. Fred. Elliot and Edward E. Villiers to Lord Stanley, [n.d.] February 1842, enclosure no. 6 of Stanley to Viscount Falkland, 15 March 1842, in Great Britain, *Parliamentary Papers*, vol. 16, 475–9.

20 Hornsby, *Nineteenth-Century Cape Breton*, 56; W.S. MacNutt, *The Atlantic Provinces*, 228–9; D.C. Harvey, "The Civil List and Responsible Government in Nova Scotia."

21 Report of Committee on the "Probability of Employment for Emigrant Laborers to N. Scotia," council minutes, 26 November 1831, 368–75, vol. 195, RG 1, NSARM. See also Hornsby, *Nineteenth-Century Cape Breton*, 53–5.

22 Nova Scotia, *Journals of the House of Assembly* (hereafter *JHA*) (1859), appendix 7.

23 H.W. Crawley, as reported in Falkland to Russell, 21 December 1841, in Great Britain, *Parliamentary Papers*, vol. 16, 465–6.

24 John Murphy to Samuel Fairbanks, 26 January 1857, reprinted in *JHA* (1857), appendix 71; Falkland to Russell, 19 July 1841, in Great Britain, *Parliamentary Papers*, vol. 16, 466. Such changes were never simply benevolent but rather more utilitarian. As pointed out in Harvey, "Civil List," it was also hoped that the changes would generate badly needed revenue.

25 John Wright to George Renny Young, 25 January 1850, f1/757, vol. 723, MG 2, NSARM; "[Proposed] Bill to Incorporate the Canadian Land & Railway Association," George Young Papers, f1/771, vol. 723, MG 2, NSARM.

26 J.I. Little, *Nationalism, Capitalism, and Colonization in Nineteenth-Century Quebec*, 147–57.

27 Thomas Keefer, *The Philosophy of Railroads*.

28 "Report from the Select Committee of the House of Lords appointed to consider the Means by which Colonization may be made subsidiary to other measures for the Improvement of the social condition of Ireland," in Great Britain, *Parliamentary Papers*, vol. 6 (1847), minutes of evidence, 49. See also Canada Land and Railway Association, *Report & outline of a plan by which an extensive railway may be constructed in the British North American colonies*, esp. 37–47.

29 See "Report from the Select Committee of the House of Lords appointed to consider the Means by which Colonization may be made subsidiary to other measures for the Improvement of the social condition of Ireland," in Great Britain, *Parliamentary Papers*, vol. 6 (1847), minutes of evidence, 51–60, quotation at 59. Dan Bunbury, "Safe Haven for the Poor?" esp. 29–30, notes the agrarian vision behind the provincially sponsored saving banks.

30 J.M. Beck, *Joseph Howe*, vol. 2, 39–40; *JHA* (1857), appendix 71; Abraham Gesner, *The Industrial Resources of Nova Scotia*, 313–29.

31 *JHA* (1850), appendix 80; and (1857), appendix 71; Hornsby, *Nineteenth-Century Cape Breton*, 118–20.

32 In the 1850s the province encouraged squatters to take out grants; see Hornsby, *Nineteenth-Century Cape Breton*, 123–8.

33 Rusty Bittermann, Robert A. MacKinnon, and Graeme Wynn, "Of Inequality and Interdependence in the Nova Scotian Countryside, 1850–70," 15–16, 24.

34 Douglas McCalla, *Planting the Province*, 67–91. Rusty Bittermann, "The Hierarchy of the Soil," suggests that profitable Nova Scotia farms may have been more dependent on the cow than Upper Canadian farms were on wheat.

35 The following discussion is based on a one-in-three sample of the household-level returns for seven of the twenty-two census districts of Pictou County in 1851. These include the three districts on the lower West River, districts 6

(Mount Dalhousie and Roger's Hill), 7 (Hardwood Hill), and 8 (Greenhill and West River), and the four districts along the lower half of the East River, districts 12 (Albion Mines), 13 (New Glasgow), 16 (East Branch East River), and 17 (Hopewell).

36 See chapter 2 for a discussion of Thomas McCulloch, *The Mephibosheth Stepsure Letters.*

37 See D.B. Cann and R.E. Wicklund, "Soil Survey of Pictou County."

38 Bittermann, MacKinnon, and Wynn, "Of Inequality and Interdependence," 20–1; F. Lewis and M. McInnis, "Agricultural Output and Efficiency in Lower Canada." Prices are median figures obtained from the *Mechanic and Farmer,* 31 August 1842, 30 November 1842, and 26 July 1842; and Account Book of John G. Grant, "East River," [1847], vol. 117, MG 3, NSARM.

39 This was based on 4d per pound. The prices quoted in the *Mechanic and Farmer* ranged from 1d to 7d per pound in Pictou. The lower figure was noted as "unusually low" (30 November 1842), and most reports listed the prices as ranging from 4d to 6d per pound.

40 Many farm products were excluded from the census, but timber was clearly the most important. Pictou County was not a major hay producer; based on a standard estimating number of 1.2 tons per cow, our average farm's 7.6 tons came up well short of the 12.7 required. Such a farm may have purchased or exchanged to make up for this shortfall (shipping returns indicate some imports of hay from Prince Edward Island), although rough forage in the woods probably accounted for part of it as well.

41 Looms were counted and valued in the 1851 census.

42 Between 1847 and 1855 John Grant paid his female servants 2s6d per week. Typically, day rates for labour ranged from 1s3d for daughters, 1s6d for sons or "your wife," 2s6d or 3s for an adult male, and up to 6s6d for working with horses or oxen; see passim, vol. 117, MG 3, NSARM. In the 1840s the Reverend Alexander MacLeod of Mabou paid his female day servants 4s every two weeks; his "man servant" was paid 20s on being hired and 10s per month thereafter (on top of room and board); two others were hired for a year at £15 and £10. See entries for Widow McDonald and Catherine McKinnon (both of whom entered his service 28 June 1843) and for John Beaton and Dugald McMaster (June 1845), in Journal of Reverend Alexander MacLeod, 1835–48, vol. 564, MG 1, NSARM.

43 This is the same general conclusion reached by Bittermann, MacKinnon, and Wynn, "Of Inequality and Interdependence." That this should be the case is not surprising, however, given that part of our data (district 7, Hardwood Hill on the West River) comprises half of theirs (Hardwood Hill and Middle River, Victoria County).

44 Interestingly, only about one in ten households owned their own hand-looms in 1851. This is a much lower frequency than Kris Inwood and Phyllis Wagg uncovered in their work on the same area in the 1870s, suggesting that increased market penetration after 1851 facilitated home production by allowing households to purchase a loom and factory-spun cotton thread; see their "The Survival of Handloom Weaving in Rural Canada, ca. 1870," 350–2.

45 John Murray calculated his sales at about £70 and his expenditures at £45; see Graeme Wynn, "Ideology, Society, and State in the Maritime Colonies of British North America, 1840–1860," 295.

46 Rosemary E. Ommer, "Merchant Credit and the Informal Economy."

47 Julian Gwynn and Fazley Siddiq, "Wealth Distribution in Nova Scotia during the Confederation Era, 1851 and 1871."

48 See D.B. McNab and others in reply to R.G. Haliburton's 1861 questionnaire, in C.B. Fergusson, ed., *Uniacke's Sketches of Cape Breton*, 160, 168, 173.

49 See, for example, the accounts of Angus Link, Angus McDonald, Effy McPherson, Archy McDonald, and Murdoch Ferguson, in John Beamish Moore Account Book, 1848-67, Micro Biography, NSARM.

50 John G. Grant Papers, vol. 117, MG 3, NSARM. See especially the accounts of Donald McKenzie, Farquer Fraser, Hugh McKenzie, William Fraser, Alexander Fraser, Finly Fraser, James Cameron, Hugh Cameron, William Sutherland, John McKenzie, Margaret McIntosh (weaving), Catherine Sellars (weaving; Duncan Sellars also had an account that he paid off in cloth), Widow McLennan (butchering), and two "servant girls," in James Barry Papers, vol. 1216, MG 1, NSARM.

51 Unsigned report, in Fergusson, ed., *Uniacke's Sketches*, 161.

52 Rusty Bittermann, "Farm Households and Wage Labour in the Northeastern Maritimes before 1850."

53 Abraham Gesner, quoted in Fergusson, ed., *Uniacke's Sketches*, 173. See also Betsy Beattie, *Obligation and Opportunity*, 25–41.

54 D.B. McNab, quoted in Fergusson, ed., *Uniacke's Sketches*, 172.

55 Supreme Court Records contain numerous such cases. See, for example, James Wylie, William Blair, and John Blair vs James Fitzpatrick, June [then moved to October] 1841; Governors of King's College vs George McDonald, Donald McDonald, and Donald McLeod, June 1842; and Isabella Ann Fraser vs Roderick McNeil, 1843, all in "Pictou, 1839–1843," RG 39, NSARM. See also the report of Peter Crerar, the Deputy Surveyor of Crown Lands for Pictou County, in *JHA* (1854), appendix 19.

56 Examination of Neil McFadgeon, Garden of Eden, Pictou Co., 26 September 1848, no. 180, vol. 257, RG 1, NSARM.

57 See W. Peter Ward, *Courtship, Love, and Marriage in Nineteenth-Century English Canada*; and Ellen M.T. Gee, "Marriage in Nineteenth-Century Canada," 318–20.

58 Peter Gossage, "Family Formation and Age of Marriage in Saint-Hyacinthe, Quebec, 1854–1891." For a helpful discussion of the "selection mechanisms" by which some families remained, while others migrated, see Bruno Ramirez, *On the Move*, 22–32, 111–37.

59 Marvin MacInnis, "Women, Work and Childbearing."

60 Gee, "Marriage in Nineteenth-Century Canada," 320. Using slightly earlier figures, David Gagan, *Hopeful Travellers*, 76–7, notes a rise in Peel County.

61 Bettina Bradbury, "Pigs, Cows, and Boarders"; Richard L. Bushman, "Family Security in the Transition from Farm to City, 1750–1850."

62 The foregoing refers to British North American currency.

63 Nova Scotia Estate Papers, nos 467 (Bogg), 1263 (Donnely), and 1864 (Balfour), reel 969, RG 48, NSARM.

64 Nova Scotia Estate papers, nos 47 (McLean) and 199 (Scott), vol. 6, RG 48, NSARM.

65 The following figures for Pictou and Cape Breton Counties, 1865 and 1870, are based on a one-in-five sample of all marriages in which the male identified himself as a farmer and on a 100 per cent sample of all marriages in which the male described himself as a miner. Compare this with figures for Ontario in Gee, "Marriage in Nineteenth-Century Canada," 320, which show males marrying at 28.4 on average and females at 25.0.

66 Michael Haines, *Fertility and Occupation*, 23–7, 138–48; E.A. Wrigley, *Industrial Growth and Population Change.*

67 Nancy Grey Osterud, *Bonds of Community*, 62–7, 92–4; Leonore Davidoff and Catherine Hall, *Family Fortunes*, 321–43. In neighbouring Prince Edward Island, however, many women remained spinsters all their lives; see Michelle Stairs, "Matthews and Marillas."

68 See Haines, *Fertility and Occupation*, 143–6, 152–4; and Adele Perry, "Bachelors in the Backwoods," 180–94.

69 Inverness and Cape Breton Counties had the most stable figures (closest to 1.0 male per female), although both had more males than females in most age categories. These county figures are drawn from the tables printed with the returns for 1871, in *Census of 1871*, vol. 4.

70 Andrew Blaikie, "Coastal Communities in Victorian Scotland," finds similar sex ratios for fishers in north-eastern Scotland in the mid-nineteenth century, although ages of marriage there were lower than we see here.

71 Patterson, *History of the County of Pictou*, 224–5.

72 Osterud, *Bonds of Community*, 93.

73 Ibid., 124.

74 *Spirit of the Times*, 3 February 1844.

75 *Spirit of the Times*, 30 August 1844.

76 *Mechanic and Farmer*, 7 August 1839; *The Bee*, 3 February 1836.

77 McCulloch, *Mephibosheth Stepsure Letters*, 113–18.

78 "Family Economy," *Colonial Patriot*, 3 June 1829.

79 *Mechanic and Farmer*, 7 August 1839. See also the reprinted article "Force of Example," *Mechanic and Farmer*, 5 June 1839; and "Domestic Duties," *Colonial Patriot*, 4 February 1834.

80 *Colonial Patriot*, 14 December 1827.

81 *Spirit of the Times*, 30 August 1844. See also A.J. Babington's letter on "the government of families," in *Cape Breton News*, 17 November 1852.

82 McCulloch, *Mephibosheth Stepsure Letters*, 40, 61, 138; *Spirit of the Times*, 20 September 1844; *The Bee*, 2 December 1835; Laurie Stanley, *The Well-W atered Garden*, 61–2.

83 McCulloch, *Mephibosheth Stepsure Letters*, 61; "A.Z.," *The Bee*, 2 December 1835.

84 J.I. Little, *Crofters and Habitants*, 198–200; and compare Gérard Bouchard, "La sexualité comme practique et rapport social chez les couples paysans du Saguenay, 1860–1930."

85 See Rosalind Mitchison and Leah Leneman, *Sexuality and Social Control*, 99–133; and T.C. Smout, "Scottish Marriage, Regular and Irregular, 1500–1940." On illegitimacy in agricultural areas, see Leah Leneman and Rosalind Mitchison, "Girls in Trouble."

86 See, for example, notices in *Colonial Patriot*, 3 March 1832, 9 April 1833; *Mechanic and Farmer*, 7 August 1839; and *Spirit of the Times*, 30 January 1845.

87 Peter Barrett, "Twelve Years in North America, Containing a Brief Sketch of the Life, Trials and Persecutions of Peter Barrett, an English Immigrant, in Nova Scotia, Canada, Written by Himself," 13, unpublished manuscript, 1879, NSARM.

88 Nova Scotia Vital Statistics, RG 32, NSARM.

89 Osterud, *Bonds of Community*, 56–72, 92–6, 275–89; and Steven Maynard, "Between Farm and Factory."

90 *Eastern Chronicle*, 13 May 1873. Seven years later forty-six more men died in the adjoining seam; see James M. Cameron, "Disasters in the Pictou Collieries."

91 *Eastern Chronicle*, 13 May 1873; Pictou County Marriage Records, RG 32, NSARM. See also *Mechanic and Farmer*, 12 June 1839 and 21 August 1839, for reports of the deaths of two mineworkers. Katie Pickles, "Locating Widows in Mid-Nineteenth Century Pictou County, Nova Scotia," does not pursue industrial employments.

92 Bittermann, MacKinnon, and Wynn, "Of Inequality and Interdependence".

93 Joyce Appleby, "Commercial Farming and the 'Agrarian Myth' in the Early Republic."

94 See, in varying degrees on all these issues, D. Campbell and R.A. MacLean, *Beyond the Atlantic Roar*, 101–10; Charles W. Dunn, *Highland Settler*, 124–5; and Hornsby, *Nineteenth-Century Cape Breton*, 186–200.

95 Campbell and MacLean, *Beyond the Atlantic Roar*, 101–2.

96 Dunn, *Highland Settler*, 132.

CHAPTER EIGHT

1 Nova Scotia, *Journals of the House of Assembly* (hereafter *JHA*) (1855), appendix 1. In order and rounded off, the export values were: fishery products, £419,000; forest products, £220,000; shipbuilding, £144,000; agriculture, £134,000, and mines, £63,000. These figures, however, bear no resemblance to revenue sources, as the coal industry still provided two-thirds of all the Casual Revenue.

2 Pictou duty returns, *JHA* (1823), 138.

3 Mary Byers and Margaret McBurney, *Atlantic Hearth*, 302–3.

4 Robert Hill to William McKeen, 12 June 1839, no. 90, vol. 109, MG 12, Beaton Institute (BI).

5 Angus McLellan to William McKeen, Port Hood Ga[o]l, 6 April 1834, no. 36; Robert Hill to McKeen, Broad Cove, 17 April 1839, no. 84; and Hill to McKeen, Broad Cove, 14 May 1839, no. 80, all in vol. 109, MG 12, BI.

6 Hill to McKeen, 14 May 1839, no. 80, vol. 109, MG 12, BI.

7 Robert Hill to William McKeen, 16 September 1839, no. 102, vol. 109, MG 12, BI.

8 Richard Brown, *A History of Cape Breton*, 425.

9 Hill to McKeen, 7 September 1840, no. 122, vol. 109, MG 12, BI.

10 Hill to McKeen, 19 October 1840, no. 128, vol. 109, MG 12, BI.

11 Robert Hill to William McKeen, 7 September 1840, no. 122, vol. 109, MG 12, BI. There are notations for several dozen of McKeen's suits – including orders to send people to gaol – in George Laurence Papers, vol. 541, MG 1, Nova Scotia Archives and Records Management (NSARM).

12 Robert Hill to McKeen, 14 November 1840, no. 130; Hill to McKeen, 16 September 1839, no. 102; and Hill to McKeen, 11 September 1839, no. 889, all in vol. 109, MG 12, BI. Hill sent McKeen one load of eight casks in the summer of 1839, which he described as the "best to ever leave B[road] C[ove]" but which fetched only 8d per pound; see Hill to McKeen, 22 June 1839, no. 870, vol. 109, MG 12, BI.

13 See, for example, Wm H. Thomas to McKeen, St John's Newfoundland,
17 July 1830, no. 242; James Fergus & Co., St John's, Newfoundland, to
McKeen, 24 June 1834, no. 285; and Fergus to McKeen, 17 July 1834,
no. 294, all in vol. 109, MG 12, BI. See also Hill to McKeen, 14 November
1840, no. 130, vol. 109, MG 12, BI, in which Hill attempts to make the farmers fatten their swine more; despite his efforts, "few dos attend to it."

14 Fergus to McKeen, 25 August 1834, no. 299, vol. 109, MG 12, BI.

15 See, for example, John Barss to McKeen, Halifax, 1 October 1842, no. 138,
vol. 109, MG 12, BI, which provides a detailed inventory from one auction in
Halifax of 86 quintals of codfish, 30 quintals of haddock, 7 barrels of salmon,
4 barrels of mackerel, 2 barrels of seal oil, 19 firkins of butter, and an unspec-
ified quantity of pork.

16 The estimate is based only on Hill's correspondence; see Robert Hill to
William McKeen, 24 July 1839, no. 97, vol. 109, MG 12, BI. A few weeks earlier, Hill had purchased as many cattle as he could and was writing McKeen to
send him more money if he wanted more cattle; see Hill to McKeen 16 September 1839, no. 102, vol. 109, MG 12, BI.

17 W.C. Delany (Clerk of Supreme Court) to McKeen, Arichat, 25 April 1834,
no. 197, vol. 109, MG 12, BI. It is also notable that this case took place outside
of Inverness County.

18 See, for example, the nearly twenty-year struggle of Mary Ann MacKay
et al. vs James Murdoch, June 1861, no. 10, vol. 2, Pictou County, "C,"
RG 39, NSARM.

19 John Den vs John DeCoste, May 1842 (these files are not numbered
but are in rough chronological order); Richard [illegible] vs Andrew
MacDonald, May 1842; and John Doe vs James Pringle, 22 July 1850,
all in George Laurence Papers, vol. 541, MG 1, NSARM.

20 The papers of county sheriff George Laurence contain numerous such incidents, sometimes for very small sums. See, for example, the file for cases
brought forward in August 1850, which indicates that Angus Murphy was
gaoled for £1.6.1 owed to Roderick McDonald, Port Hood; Hugh McEachen
was gaoled for £8.14.6; and Angus McIsaac was gaoled for £4.5.9 owed to
Angus McDonald. John McLean successfully sued Donald Stewart for 12s9d
plus £15.10.6 in court costs, putting Stewart in gaol. These cases are all in the
file marked "1850s," George Laurence Papers, vol. 541, MG 1, NSARM.

21 Robert Hill to William McKeen, 24 July 1839, no. 97; Hill to McKeen, 22
June 1839, no. 870; and Hill to McKeen, 11 August 1840, no. 117, all in
vol. 109, MG 12, BI.

22 Robert Hill to William McKeen, 5 June 1840, no. 113, vol. 109, MG 12, BI.
See also D.B. McNab to McKeen, 27 June 1836, no. 184, vol. 109, MG 12, BI.

23 Robert Hill to William McKeen, 16 September 1839, no. 102; and Hill to McKeen, 18 August 1840, no. 119, both in vol. 109, MG 12, BI.

24 Robert Hill to William McKeen, 17 April 1839, no. 87; Hill to McKeen, 16 September 1839, no. 102; and Hill to McKeen, 1 June 1842, no. 154, all in vol. 109, MG 12, BI.

25 Hill to McKeen, 29 October 1839, no. 904; and Hill to McKeen, 22 September 1840, no. 123, both in vol. 109, MG 12, BI.

26 See McKeen's suits against Donald Sutherland (Broad Cove, November 1840, for £40); Donald Morrison (Mabou, October 1841, for £200); and John Decoste (n.p., June 1840, for £46), in George Laurence Papers, vol. 541, MG 1, NSARM.

27 D.B. McNab to William McKeen, 18 August 1834, no. 206, vol. 109, MG 12, BI. See also Charles Dunn, *Highland Settler*, 33, which comments on the "violence with which Highlanders disputed property rights."

28 The following is from the statement of Hugh Johnston in the case of Laurence vs Donald MacDonald and Angus MacDonald, file marked "1830s," George Laurence Papers, vol. 541, MG 1, NSARM.

29 For another store break-in in which the entire family participated, see the charges for theft against Neil Jameson, Mary Jameson ("his wife"), and others, brought by Martin McPherson, merchant, Broad Cove, March 1834, in George Laurence Papers, vol. 541, MG 1, NSARM.

30 The quotation is from a story about a constable rebuffed at gunpoint in *Spirit of the Times*, 28 December 1844.

31 Stephen J. Hornsby, *Nineteenth-Century Cape Breton*, 54–5; Rusty Bittermann, "Women and the Escheat Movement."

32 On the Mt Rundell incident, see chapter 6, pages 184–5.

33 Letter from C.H. Harrington, *Cape Breton News*, 15 September 1852; letter from "An Inhabitant," *Cape Breton News*, 22 September 1852.

34 Robert Hill to William McKeen, 28 January 1842, no. 143; and Hill to McKeen, 1 June 1842, no. 154, both in vol. 109, MG 12, BI.

35 Charge of break and enter and assault against John Henley and others, in George Laurence Papers, file marked "1850s," vol. 541, MG 1, NSARM.

36 Byers and McBurney, *Atlantic Hearth*, 307.

37 Robert Grant, *East River Worthies*, 20.

38 *Colonial Herald*, 4 May 1839, cited in Rusty Bittermann, "Farm Households and Wage Labour in the Northeastern Maritimes before 1850," 56.

39 See the discussion of ordering for stores in Richard Brown Sr to Richard Brown Jr, 19 January 1866, no. 1, vol. 151, MG 1, NSARM. There were at least two ropeworks in Halifax in the 1820s and 1830s, including the

Stanyon works, which were founded in the same year as the GMA; see David A. Sutherland, "The Stanyon Ropeworks of Halifax, Nova Scotia."

40 Account Book of John G. Grant, 1847–77, vol. 117, MG 3, NSARM.

41 These timbers were not for pit props but appear to have been for the construction of a large building, perhaps a pithead. See the order dated December 1854 for timber "perfectly hewed, exactly of the dimensions specified, and delivered by the 15th of April on the roadside leading from the No. 3 pit ... at 10/ [10s] per 100 feet," in "GMA Timber Contracts, 1854–64," D.16, MG 14, 19, BI. This contract is on the first page; the next five seem to record payment and delivery. Similar contracts for the same period exist for the Lingan mine as well.

42 See, for example, Joseph Smith, "Return Marked C," in *JHA* (1839), appendix 50.

43 See "Diary, Richard Brown," June 1830 to February 1832, no. 8, vol. 40, "A," RG 21, NSARM; and "Diary, Richard Brown," 29 December 1849, no. 9, vol. 38, "A," RG 21, NSARM. The GMA occasionally advertised its need for oats; see *Cape Breton News*, 17 November 1852.

44 See, for example, Richard Brown to George L. Deblois, 24 May 1833 (hay), no. 18a; [unsigned letter dated at Boston] to Richard Smith, 22 June 1833 (oats), no. 20b; Andrew Belcher to Richard Brown, 20 April 1833 (English leather), no. 32; Belcher to Brown, 10 April 1833 (rope and shovels), no. 37; and Deblois to Smith, 14 July 1832 (hay), no. 60, all in D.9.a, MG 14, 19, BI; and Smith to Rupert Cochrane, 31 August 1832; and Smith to Deblois, 6 September 1832, both in D.8.a, MG 14, 19, BI.

45 On Pictou, see the statement by Henry Poole, in "Report," vol. 35, "R," RG 5, NSARM; on Sydney, see the discussion of Archibald and Co., below.

46 See "Account of Expenditure at the Albion Coal Mines, in the County of Pictou, in the Year ending on the 31st December, 1838," copy of return marked "F," in *JHA* (1839), appendix 50. This account, however, may be deceptive. In 1833, for example, Andrew Belcher was buying rope and shovels in Halifax, but they were manufactured in the United States; see Belcher to Richard Brown, 10 April 1833, no. 37, D.9.a, MG 14, 19, BI.

47 Eric Sager, with Gerald E. Panting, *Maritime Capital*, 174–92; Bittermann, "Farm Households," 50–1; Graeme Wynn, *Timber Colony*, 72–84, 155–67.

48 *Colonial Patriot*, 14 March 1828.

49 See Gerald S. Graham, *Sea Power and British North America, 1783–1820*, 195–215. Ten years later, in the province's submission to the Durham Commission, William Young noted the free-port issue as one of Nova Scotia's major persisting concerns; see William Young to the Earl of Durham, item no. 3, appendix A, in "Report on the Affairs of British

North America from the Earl of Durham," in Great Britain, *Parliamentary Papers*, vol. 17 (1839).

50 For a copy of the 1827 petition, the petitioners' argument, and references to the earlier efforts, see *Colonial Patriot*, 11 and 18 January 1828. Sydney had previously enjoyed free-port status but had lost it with Cape Breton's reunification with Nova Scotia.

51 *Royal Gazette*, 22 October 1827. Kempt had been instructed to insert some such message; see Sir James Kempt to Wilmot Horton 12 June 1827, Colonial Office records for Nova Scotia 217/147.

52 *Colonial Patriot*, 21 May 1828. The insertion of "*sic*" here may be inappropriate. In a letter dating from 1832, Smith claimed that while the works and the coal were owned by the GMA, the "wharf and premises are my own"; see Richard Smith to Thomas Tremain (Charlottetown, PEI), 28 August 1832, D.8.a, MG 14, 19, BI.

53 A collection of GMA letters contains a detailed correspondence with the Halifax agent, Andrew Belcher, and the Boston agent, J.L. Deblois, and makes mention of some of the other agents; see "Richard Smith, letters, 1831–1833," D.8.a, MG 14, 19, BI.

54 The following is based on a one-in-two sample (fifty-one weeks) of clearances from Pictou harbour between April 1831 and December 1833, as reported in the *Colonial Patriot*.

55 The survey shows 61 vessels chartered by Ross and Primrose; 47 of these carried coal, 6 carried bricks or coke (manufactured by the GMA), 2 carried timber, 1 carried stone, and 6 carried other cargoes. The firm also ran a weekly advertisement in the *Colonial Patriot* from 16 April 1831 to the end of the shipping season: "Wanted for Charter: Vessels of any burthen, to load coal at Pictou for New York and other places in the United States."

56 The sample identifies 368 vessels, of which 152 carried coal. Cargoes were identified for 317 of 368 vessels, so coal represented slightly less than half of all cargoes. Of the 152 coal shipments, Ross and Primrose was the agent for 48, the GMA was the agent for 40, George Smith sent 4, various ships' masters sent 7, the agents for 39 were unidentified, and the remaining 13 were divided among other merchants.

57 This percentage is based on an assumption of 100 tons of coal per shipment for brigs, brigantines, and barques (surely a low estimate, as most of the recorded vessels of this type carried between 110 and 150 tons), 50 tons for schooners, and 30 tons for sloops and shallops. Of those coal shipments for which we know both the vessel's type and agent, Ross and Primrose sent 50 schooners, 35 brigs, and 14 smaller vessels – by my estimate, 6,420 tons.

58 Archibald had occasional dealings with Thomas and William Bown, and his account with them for 1824 has one transaction involving coal, in which the Bowns gave Archibald 32 chaldrons for £36.16.0. While we might expect that the Bowns were important, even vital, customers for Archibald, he does not seem to have suffered for the thin relationship. Their other major items of exchange with Archibald in 1824 were £11 worth of iron and £75 in cash that they had "received from Captain Dodd." That Archibald could get £75 out of the cash-starved, market-hungry merchants suggests that the relationship was tilted toward their supplier rather than toward capitalists such as themselves. See Archibald & Company Papers, MG 14, 45, "A," BI (entries for 1825 only).

59 This analysis is clearly very cautious, but my concerns over records are very real; we need to be careful to separate what the firm became from what it was at this point. The Archibald ledger for the mid-1820s begins in April 1824; these figures are drawn from 1825. The totals and all sums presented here are based on a one-in-five sample of the 320–page book. This sample yielded total sales of £399.10.11 (hence approximately £2,000). This surely underestimates total sales, as there are other accounts in both the earlier and later developing ledgers, as well as other entries for larger accounts carried from and to these older and newer ledgers. See Archibald & Company Papers, MG 14, 45, "A," BI.

60 Archibald & Co. Ledger, "1840–42," ["B"], MG 14, 45, BI. See, for example, the account of William Fife, who purchased needles, cloth, soap, leather, and some foodstuffs in exchange for repairing two pairs of boots (2s), resoling some shoes (3s6d), and performing one day of labour (2s); Peter Morrison bought rum, tea, butter, cloth, and clothing in exchange for a small amount of butter, 40 bushels of potatoes, a half ton of timber, and five and a half days of rafting (still leaving him short at the end of the year); while Michael Kelly purchased a small amount of household supplies, such as flour, sugar, rum, and tea, and paid off half of this debt with some fish oil (£1.14.4) and one whole and two half days of butchering animals.

61 Archibald & Co. Ledger, "1840–42," ["B"], MG 14, 45, BI.

62 John P. Parker, *Cape Breton Ships and Men*, 48–54. An article in the *Spirit of the Times*, 19 January 1844, described eight sealing vessels leaving Sydney harbour bound for Newfoundland and noted that six of the vessels belonged to "those enterprising individuals" Archibald and Co.

63 "Diary, Richard Brown," 15 January 1845, no. 8, vol. 38, "A," RG 21, NSARM.

64 See the examples of James Moore (rough carpentry work, p. 106) and Murdoch Beaton (occasional employment in and around the sawmill, 93), in Archibald & Co. Ledger, "1840–42," ["B"], MG 14, 45, BI.

65 Sydney Mines, "Company Store Book," 11 November to 29 April 1854, C.2.a.1, MG 14, 19, BI; Sydney Mines, "Company Store Book," September to December 1831, C.2.a, MG 14, 19, BI. Although the GMA had its own supply store at the mines, men were apparently able to buy supplies elsewhere. In 1867 Richard Brown remembered having attempted "many years ago" to open a cooperative store at Sydney Mines, but it failed because of poor management; see Richard Brown Sr to Richard Brown Jr, 6 July 1867, no. 26, vol. 151, MG 1, NSARM.

66 See, for example, the accounts of Robert McKay (p. 69), Jerry Desmond (88), James Lamey (89), and John Smith (92), in Archibald & Co. Ledger, "1840–42," ["B"], MG 14, 45, BI.

67 Charles Archibald was reported to have floated a scheme to operate a second "iron and steel" manufactory at Londonderry, "contiguous to" Gesner's operation; see *Cape Breton Spectator*, 2 June 1849.

68 See Donald Macgillivray, "Henry Melville Whitney Comes to Cape Breton"; and Ian McKay, "Industry, Work and Community in the Cumberland Coal Fields, 1848–1927," 180–289.

69 George Patterson, *History of Victoria County*, 111–12, 114–15, 119, 187; Rusty Bittermann, "The Hierarchy of the Soil," 44–5; Parker, *Cape Breton Ships and Men*, 61–2, 65–6.

70 Here and below, the reference is to British North American currency. *JHA* (1858), appendix 18, 18–19; (1864), appendix 18, 18–19; and (1865), appendix 6, 10.

71 Allan C. Dunlop, "Pharmacist and Entrepreneur." He also ran at least one sealing vessel out of Sydney and imported Peruvian guano (perhaps for the East River Agricultural Society); see *Spirit of the Times*, 20 September 1844. See also James D.B. Fraser to "Kedelove," Glasgow, 30 June 1843; Fraser to Gilbert Seaman, Boston, 11 May 1844; Fraser to Joseph Austen, New York, 10 October 1844; and Fraser to Hemshaw, Ward, & Co., Boston, 28 May 1845, all in Fraser Papers, vol. 319(b), MG 1, NSARM.

72 James D.B. Fraser, Account Book, October 1838 to September 1840, Dalhousie University Archives, MS-4-28; advertisement in *Colonial Patriot*, 18 June 1828; James D.B. Fraser to William Foran, Esq., Saint John, 30 July 1838 and 9 August 1838, vol. 319(b), MG 1, NSARM.

73 See Fraser to "Kedelove," Glasgow, 30 June 1843; Fraser to Gilbert Seaman, Boston, 11 May 1844; Fraser to Joseph Austen, New York, 10 October 1844; Fraser to Hemshaw, Ward, & Co., Boston, 28 May 1845; Fraser to Messrs McKinney and Liston, Boston, 18 August 1840; and Fraser to "Morton," [Saint John], 4 March 1841, all in vol. 319(b), MG 1, NSARM.

74 Abraham Gesner, *Remarks on the Geology and Mineralogy of Nova Scotia*, 141, noted that the Pictou County stones were "much inferior" to the Cumberland County stones.

75 See Douglas McCalla, *Planting the Province*, 141–7.

76 Ross's papers contain about thirty letters between Fraser and Ross on this enterprise, spanning the period April 1859 to November 1864; see Alexander Ross Papers, nos 24 through 66, vol. 2466, MG 1, NSARM. Specific references follow.

77 James D.B. Fraser to Samuel Fairbanks, 3 February 1864, extracts reprinted in *JHA* (1864), appendix 18; Fraser to Ross, 6 April 1859, no. 37; Fraser to Ross, 20 April 1859, no. 40; and Fraser to Ross, 23 November 1859, no. 43, all in vol. 2466, MG 1, NSARM.

78 Fraser to Ross, 23 January 1860, no. 43(a), vol. 2466, MG 1, NSARM.

79 James McKeagney, Inspector of Mines, to Provincial Secretary (Howe), 31 August 1860, document 125, vol. 7, "A," RG 21, NSARM; Fraser to Ross, 15 November 1859; no. 42; and Fraser to Ross, 27 January 1860, no. 45, both in vol. 2466, MG 1, NSARM.

80 Fraser to Ross, 23 January 1860, no. 43(a); and Fraser to Ross, 27 January 1860, no. 45, both in vol. 2466, MG 1, NSARM. See also Kenneth G. Pryke, "James Carmichael," 126–8.

81 Fraser to Ross, Providence, RI, 17 September 1863, no. 50; Fraser to Ross, 18 April 1863, no. 51; and Memorandum of Sale of Fraser Mine, 22 October 1864, no. 62, all in vol. 2466, MG 1, NSARM.

82 *JHA* (1865), appendix 6. McKeen's political connections also facilitated getting the province to pay for dredging the harbour, a necessary appendage to his "submarine" mine; see *JHA* (1865), appendix 30.

83 Submarine Mining Co., Accounts, "1863–64," no. 1458, vol. 109, MG 12, BI.

84 Of course, there was the issue of the increasing cost of raising the coal as the mines got deeper, but this charge would not become significant until later in the century. At mid-century, the most important expenses were developmental, not operational.

85 Annual report of the River John Agricultural Society, 1845, no. 122, vol. 18, RG 8, NSARM.

86 In general, see *JHA* (1846), appendix 77. On conditions in some of the "back settlements" of Pictou County, George Young's papers (from which specific references are cited below) are very good. On the famine, see Hornsby, *Nineteenth-Century Cape Breton*, 111–20; Robert J. Morgan, "'Poverty, wretchedness, and misery'"; L.F.S. Upton, *Micmacs and Colonists*, 92–3; Howard S. Russell, *A Long Deep Furrow*, 215–17; and T.M. Devine, *The Great Highland Famine*.

87 D.M. McGregor (Bailey's Brook) to George Renny Young, 2 March 1848, f2/ 367; and John Johnston (Blue Mountain) to Young, 8 March 1848, f2376, both in vol. 721, MG 2, NSARM.

88 James Henderson and others (Merigomish) to Young, 27 September 1848, f2/456, vol. 721, MG 2, NSARM.

89 George Smith to George Young, 12 May 1848, f3/418, vol. 721, MG 2, NSARM. For a nice illustration of how the spectre of starving voters and the imperatives of bridge construction could be combined, see also Walter Murray to George Young, Merigomish, 14 November 1848, f3/476, vol. 721, MG 2, NSARM.

90 *Cape Breton Spectator*, 13 May 1848. On Pictou, see James McDonald et al. to George Renny Young, "Back Settlements, Gulf," 7 March 1848, f2/374; John Johnston to Young, 8 March 1848, f2/376; and D.M. McGregor to Young, 2 March 1848, Bayley's Brook, f2/367, all in vol. 721, MG 2, NSARM; Petition of Residents of Bailey's Brook, 3 February 1849, f1/535; Petition of the Undersigned Inhabitants of the Township of Maxweltown [*sic*], 9 March 1849, f1/602; Thomas Carmichael to Young, f1/581; Captain Alexander Grant to Young, Barney's River, 6 March 1847, f1/593; and Alex Fraser to Young, 16 March 1849, f2/623, all in vol. 722, MG 2, NSARM. On the distribution of food during famines, see Amartya Sen, *Poverty and Famines*, 39–45.

91 James Crichton to Geore Renny Young, 8 March 1849, f1/599; and James D.B. Fraser to Young, f1/598, both in vol. 722, MG 2, NSARM.

92 See also the private-sector plan of Alexander Brown, of nearby Durham, who sought to overcome the problem by encouraging people in the "back settlements" to bring their wood out in the spring so that "it could be taken in exchange for Bread Stuffs." He was quite sure that if Young could either forward a few hundred barrels of meal or a loan of £100, "a company (I think) would soon start on the West River to enter into the speculation." In either case, "much immediate relief could be given to hundreds of persons who are now bordering almost on a State of Starvation," and the cost to the government would be nil. See Alexander Brown to George Young, 23 February 1849, f1/575, vol. 722, MG 2, NSARM.

93 Rev. Norman MacLeod, quoted in Dunn, *Highland Settler*, 30. See also Morgan, "'Poverty, wretchedness, and misery'"; Hornsby, *Nineteenth-Century Cape Breton*, 111–20; and the brief transatlantic account in James Hunter, *A Dance Called America*, 122–41.

94 See *JHA* (1847), appendix 83; and (1848), appendix 39.

95 *Cape Breton Spectator*, 13 May 1848. The issue of the previous week contained a grisly description of bare-footed starving women begging food door-to-door at St Ann's Bay.

96 Morgan, "'Poverty, wretchedness, and misery,'" 91–2.

97 W. Ouseley to Titus Smith, Sydney Agricultural Society, 19 November 1846, no. 141; Ouseley to Smith, 11 January 1848, no. 143; Roderick MacKenzie to Smith (Baddeck), 29 December 1847, no. 185; and MacKenzie to Smith, 29 December 1848, no. 192, all in vol. 16, RG 8, NSARM.

98 There is no clear account of exactly how many died. Morgan, "'Poverty, wretchedness, and misery,'" 92, notes a number of reported deaths. Hornsby, *Nineteenth-Century Cape Breton*, 119–20, remarks only that "very few died." It would seem that perhaps ten adults died of starvation during the famine. But the effect on the old, the sick, the weak, the young, and the unborn cannot be estimated and would surely push the figure much higher, probably into the hundreds.

99 Morgan, "'Poverty, wretchedness, and misery,'" 98–9.

100 The following are from Inverness County, Deed Books G-K, RG 47, NSARM. As we are without an account book for this period, it is impossible to link positively each of these to either the famine or debts incurred to McKeen because of the famine. Even without such an account book, however, it is very difficult not to see an obvious connection. Bittermann, "Hierarchy of the Soil," 44–5, notes Victoria County merchants mortgaging farms for food.

101 Unsigned response (first of three) from Inverness County to R.G. Haliburton's survey of December 1861; see C.B. Fergusson, ed., *Uniacke's Sketches of Cape Breton*, 185.

102 H.D. Sellon, quoted in *Cape Breton Spectator*, 6 May 1848. Morgan, "'Poverty, wretchedness, and misery,'" 93, also notes that "force had to be used to prevent supplies being seized" but offers no evidence.

103 Morgan, "'Poverty, wretchedness, and misery,'" 98. Similarly, see the description of desperate men milling about the wharves at North Sydney in *Cape Breton Spectator*, 13 May 1848. On the power of the physical and moral influence of the crowd, see E.P. Thompson, *Customs in Common*, 207–16.

104 *Cape Breton Spectator*, 13 May 1848

105 *Presbyterian Witness*, 16 July 1853, cited in Laurie Stanley, *The Well-Watered Garden*, 205–6n26; Morgan, "'Poverty, wretchedness, and misery,'" 98.

106 Fraser ran twice for the House, first in 1844, a controversial contest against Martin Wilkins, and again in 1863, against Charles Tupper (later Sir), being defeated both times. Fraser's petition to have the 1844 election overturned is reprinted in *JHA* (1845), 309–10. See also Dunlop, "Pharmacist and Entrepreneur," 10–1; and Brian Cuthbertson, *Johnny Bluenose at the Polls*, 256–7.

107 Fraser to George R. Young, 1 March 1849, f1/584; and Fraser to Young, 8 March 1849, f1/598, both in vol. 722, MG 2, NSARM.

108 James D.B. Fraser to Young, 14 March 1849, f1/613, vol. 722, MG 2, NSARM. At the same time, on the East River, James Grant had already

invested several hundred pounds and was trying to obtain a £300 legislative grant for the completion of his mill; see Grant to Young, f1/548, vol. 722, MG 2, NSARM.

109 Fraser to Young, 11 February 1848, f2/335, vol. 721, MG2, NSARM. See also the correspondence regarding the division of the county into townships, a matter that hinged most directly on the costly issue of poor relief, in Fraser to Young, 1 March 1849, f1/584, vol. 722, MG 2, NSARM.

110 Reverend Alex MacDonnell to William McKeen, Judique, 10 May 1832, no. 5; and William Young to McKeen, 25 March 1834, no. 1, both in vol. 109, MG 12, BI; *Spirit of the Times,* 26 December 1843.

111 William Young to William McKeen, 10 April 1848, no. 188; and Young to McKeen, Halifax, 16 Nov 1836, no. 72, both in vol. 109, MG 12, BI; J.M. Beck, *Joseph Howe,* vol. 2, 17.

112 On temperance, see W.B. Mullin to William McKeen, Ship Harbor, 16 January 1833, no. 8; John Peabody to McKeen, Antigonish, 4 March 1833, no. 12; and extracts from McKeen's speech on temperance, 7 March 1840, no. 105, all in vol. 109, MG 12, BI. McKeen could also unite temperance and politics, as when he lobbied Young for "uniting the Temperance Mission and that of Common School Education"; see McKeen to William Young, [c. 1840], no. 180, vol. 109, MG 12, BI.

113 *Spirit of the Times,* 26 December 1843. Five of the seven on the executive were named McKeen, his sons David and John as well as three nephews, sons of Lewis and James.

114 "Public Meeting at Port Hood," *Cape Breton Advocate,* 11 November 1840.

115 Sir John Harvey to Earl Grey, 1 April 1847, reprinted in *JHA* (1848), appendix 39.

116 Abraham Gesner, *The Industrial Resources of Nova Scotia,* 12; Morgan, "'Poverty, wretchedness, and misery,'" 100.

117 See chapter 7.

CHAPTER NINE

1 Annual Report, River John Agricultural Society, 21 December 1842, no. 111, vol. 18, RG 8, Nova Scotia Archives and Records Management (NSARM).

2 See Leonore Davidoff and Catherine Hall, *Family Fortunes,* 419–49; R.J. Morris, *Class, Sect, and Party,* 161–203, 249–61, 318–31; Mary Ann Clawson, *Constructing Brotherhood;* David A. Sutherland, "Voluntary Societies and the Process of Middle-Class Formation in Early Victorian Halifax, Nova Scotia"; and Jean-Marie Fecteau, "État et associationnisme au XIXe siècle québécois." Compare Jeffery McNairn, *The Capacity to Judge,* esp. 63–115.

3 Uniacke to Young, 29 February 1820, no. 62, vol. 2, RG 8, NSARM.

4 *Acadian Recorder,* 19 December 1818, reprinted in John Young, *The Letters of Agricola on the Principles of Vegetation and Tillage,* 206–13. The directors included much of the mercantile-political elite of the capital.

5 Young, *Letters of Agricola,* 353; Daniel Samson, "'The Yoke of Improvement.'"

6 *Acadian Recorder,* 19 December 1819, reprinted in Young, *Letters of Agricola,* 206–13.

7 William McKeen to John Young, Mabou, 10 March 1821, no. 121, vol. 7, RG 8, NSARM; William McKeen to Titus Smith, 18 June 1841, no. 287, vol. 16, RG 8, NSARM. See also a similar tale in Cumberland County, "Report for 1841," [January 1842], vol. 14, RG 8, NSARM.

8 J.S. Morse to Young, Amherst, 7 January 1819, reprinted in Young, *Letters of Agricola,* 257–8. See also Alexander Stewart to Young, Amherst, 2 January 1821, no. 175, vol. 6, RG 8, NSARM; Reverend Thomas Trotter to Young, 20 January 1819, Antigonish, reprinted in Young, *Letters of Agricola,* 283–4; and Graeme Wynn, "Exciting a Spirit of Emulation among the 'Plod-holes,'" 36–8, 49.

9 James MacGregor to Young, 20 October 1820, no. 141, vol. 6; John McLennan to Central Board, Middle River, 12 December 1854, no. 221, vol. 16; James Jenks to Caleb Lewis, Cumberland Agricultural Society, 2 January 1821, no. 174, vol. 6; Report of the River John Agricultural Society, 1842, no. 111, vol. 18; and Report of the Pictou Agricultural Society (PAS), 1843, no. 1, vol. 22, all in RG 8, NSARM; Stephen Oxley to John Young, 16 December 1818, reprinted in Young, *Letters of Agricola,* 224–7.

10 PAS, 1843, no. 1, vol. 22, RG 8, NSARM. See also Maxwelton Society, Report for 1849, no. 153, vol. 18; Report of the River John Agricultural Society, 1844, no. 122, vol. 18; and McKeen to Young, 1 August 1821, no. 126, vol. 7, all in RG 8, NSARM.

11 See John M. Weir to John Young [Cumberland], 12 January 1824, no. 104; Ebenezer McLeod to Young, 4 June 1822, [West River, Pictou], no. 109; Ebenezer McLeod to Young, 18 January 1821, no. 120; and James MacGregor to Young, 26 January 1821, [East River, Pictou], no. 131, all in vol. 6, RG 8, NSARM; and J.S. Martell, "From Central Board to Secretary of Agriculture."

12 A.F. Haliburton to Titus Smith, Sydney, 16 January 1843, no. 122, vol. 16; James Doyle (Mabou) to Young, 27 December 1823, no. 135, vol. 7; Report of the Wallace Agricultural Society, 1842, no. 289, vol. 14; and Report of the Wallace Agricultural Society, 1850, no. 271, vol. 14, all in RG 8, NSARM. Wynn, "Exciting a Spirit of Emulation," notes a heavier

emphasis on cattle on the West River compared with the East, and Rusty Bittermann, "Hierarchy of the Soil," 35–8, argues that Middle River's agricultural economy was "overwhelmingly centred on the cow." In Antigonish in 1841, £28,877 of £29,527 worth of agricultural exports came from cattle, pork, sheep, or butter; see Charles [Creed?] to Titus Smith, 11 January 1842, no. 7, vol. 15; and Report, 1842, no. 111, vol. 18, both in RG 8, NSARM.

13 Edward Sutherland to Titus Smith, [Sydney], 17 May 1841, no. 108, vol. 16, RG 8, NSARM. See also Report of the Pictou Agricultural Society, 1842, no. 1, vol. 22; J.L. Tremain to Titus Smith, [Mabou], 3 February 1842, no. 293, vol. 16; John Jones to James Irons, [Baddeck], 27 December 1852, no. 254, vol. 16; and Report of the Combined Branch, Inverness Agricultural Society, 1842, no. 311, vol. 16, all in RG 8, NSARM.

14 Report of the River John Agricultural Society, 1846, no. 127, vol. 18; Simon Holmes to James Irons, [Springville], 11 November 1852, no. 208, vol. 18; J.L. Tremain to Titus Smith, 3 February 1842, no. 293, vol. 16; Hiram Blanchard to Smith, 15 January 1845, no. 299, vol. 16; and "Account of Implements, Stock, Seeds &c imported and Sold by the Inverness Agricultural Society," 1842, no. 291, vol. 16, all in RG 8, NSARM.

15 Patterson to Titus Smith, 20 January 1844, no. 20, vol. 18, RG 8, NSARM. See also Patterson to Smith, 18 January 1845, no. 27, vol. 18, RG 8, NSARM; and John Stiles to Smith, 28 November 1843, no. 18, vol. 18; report on annual dinner, [January 1843], no. 1, vol. 22; Report of the River John Agricultural Society, 1846, no. 127, vol. 18; and D.B. McNab to Smith, 16 April 1844, no. 238, vol. 16, all in RG 8, NSARM. The Sydney society purchased some threshing machines made in Baddeck "for the encouragement of our Island Manufactures," but they "proved to be inferior to the Machines made in Pictou"; see W. Ousley to Smith, 11 January 1848, no. 143, vol. 16, RG 8, NSARM. The "old Hoe" quotation is from E. Sutherland to Titus Smith, no. 112, vol. 16, RG 8, NSARM, original emphasis.

16 Report of the North Sydney Agricultural Society, 1855, no. 279, vol. 16; Report of the Maxwelton Agricultural Society, 1858, no. 174, vol. 18; and "Constitution of the Agricultural Society Established at Antigonishe [sic], 1841" [printed at Halifax, 1852], no. 1 vol. 15, all in RG 8, NSARM.

17 William McKeen to Titus Smith, 18 June 1841, no. 287, vol. 16; and Hiram Blanchard to Titus Smith, Report for 1843, [c. January 1844], no. 298, vol. 16, both in RG 8, NSARM. See also J.M. Beck, *Politics of Nova Scotia*, vol. 1, 159–60.

18 "Constitution" of the Coal Mines, Broadcove, and Margaree Combined Branch Inverness Agricultural Society, 14 August 1841, no. 309, vol. 16, RG 8, NSARM. See also the locational disputes within the Maxwelton (or as

some had it, the Merigomish) society, in James McKay and George Murray to Central Board of Agriculture, 20 February 1854, no. 168, vol. 18, RG 8, NSARM. These disputes are also discussed in Wynn, "Exciting a Spirit of Emulation," 47; and in Martin MacPherson to Titus Smith, 28 August 1845, no. 308, vol. 16, RG 8, NSARM. The break-off society that was formed in North Sydney was directly attributed to disputes over the available largesse; see William Ousley to Smith, 3 January 1849, no. 148, vol. 16, RG 8, NSARM.

19 *Free Press*, 17 December 1819; Young, *Letters of Agricola*, 20–1; R.A. MacLean, "John Young," 932.

20 William Fraser to "Agricola," 28 February 1820, no. 61, vol. 2, RG 8, NSARM. Similarly, see Petition of the West River [Pictou] Agricultural Society, 14 January 1821, no. 134; John Weir to Young, Londonderry, 12 January 1824, no. 104; James MacGregor to John Young, 26 January 1821, no. 131; and Alexander Stewart to John Young, 2 January 1821, no. 175, all in vol. 6, RG 8, NSARM.

21 See, for example, the membership reports from Sydney, no. 107 (1841) and no. 110 (1843); and from Middle River, no. 174 (1846), both in vol. 16, RG 8, NSARM. The New Glasgow society peaked at sixty members in 1847, but fell to thirty-five two years later; see Annual Report for 1847, no. 101; and Annual Report for 1849, no. 103, both in vol. 18, RG 8, NSARM.

22 Wynn, "Exciting a Spirit of Emulation," 36–8. Compare John Taylor to Titus Smith, 23 June 1847, no. 39; and John Harris to William Scott, 14 January 1848, no. 40, both in vol. 18, RG 8, NSARM. In Maxwelton the figure was les than 12 per cent; see John Mitchell to Titus Smith, 19 March 1842, no. 136; Robert Murray to Smith, 22 August 1845, no. 141; and Report of the Maxwelton Agricultural Society, 1854, no. 171, all in vol. 18, RG 8, NSARM; and Jenks to Young, 3 January 1825, no. 211, vol. 6, RG 8, NSARM.

23 "An Experienced Farmer" to John Young, Cumberland, 16 November 1820, no. 233, vol. 2, RG 8, NSARM, spelling as in original.

24 McKeen to Young, 22 March 1823, no. 132, vol. 7; and McNab to Titus Smith, 16 April 1844, no. 238, vol. 16, both in RG 8, NSARM. See also *Colonial Patriot*, 3 March 1832 and 23 April 1833.

25 Martin MacPherson to Titus Smith, [n.d.] 1841, no. 310, vol. 16; "Rules and Regulations," Mabou Agricultural Society, 10 March 1821, no. 123, vol. 7; and Annual Report, 1825, Parrsborough Agricultural Society, no. 219, vol. 6, all in RG 8, NSARM.

26 Charles Lyell, *Travels in North America in the Years 1841–42*, 193–4; Simon Holmes to James Irons, 11 November 1852, no. 208, vol. 18; John Holmes to William Scott, no. 210, vol. 18; and Wallace Agricultural Society, Annual

Report, 1851, no. 307, vol. 14, all in RG 8, NSARM. See also *Colonial Phrenological Journal* (Pictou), May 1860; *Pictou Observer,* 9 December 1834; George Patterson, *A History of the County of Pictou, Nova Scotia,* 395–6; and *Cape Breton Advocate,* 7 April 1841.

27 See J.W. Dawson, *Contributions toward the Improvement of Agriculture in Nova-Scotia;* "Speech on Chemistry," McKeen Papers, vol. 109, MG 12, Beaton Institute (BI); Patterson, *History of the County of Pictou,* 396ff; PAS, October 1842 and December 1850, no. 1, vol. 22, RG 8, NSARM.

28 Report of the Springville Agricultural Society, 1854, no. 219, vol. 18, RG 8, NSARM. See also Robert Stewart, John Bonnyman, and John Oliver to Young, 6 December 1820, no. 124, vol. 6, RG 8, NSARM.

29 William McKeen to Young, Mabou, 1 August 1821, no. 126, vol. 7; and Ebenezer McLeod to Young, West River, 18 January 1821, no. 120, vol. 8, both in RG 8, NSARM; and PAS, 14 November 1838, trials with various lime-stones, 43, no. 1, vol. 22, RG 8, NSARM. On guano, see Sydney, no. 141, vol. 16; Pictou, Report for 1850, no. 1, vol. 22; and Hiram Blanchard to Titus Smith, 15 January 1845, no. 299, vol. 16, all in RG 8, NSARM.

30 Martin Hewitt, "Science, Popular Culture, and the Producer Alliance in Saint John, N.B.," 244.

31 Report of the Parrsboro Agricultural Society, 1850, no. 224, vol. 14; George Smith to John Young, 12 April 1820, no. 130, vol. 6; and James MacGregor to Young, 19 April 1822, no. 144, vol. 6, all in RG 8, NSARM.

32 Parrsboro, no. 220 (1851); and no. 224 (1850), vol. 14; William Smith to James Irons, Merigomish, 9 June 1847, no. 155, vol. 18; and "Annual Report for 1852," no. 161, vol. 18, all in RG 8, NSARM.

33 Robert Dawson to Young, 12 November 1820, no. 121, vol. 6; "Scheme for Encouragement," Amherst, 1824, no. 214, vol. 6; "Report of the River John Agricultural Society," 28 December 1843, no. 112, vol. 18; and John Stewart to Titus Smith, New Glasgow, 22 December 1841, no. 90, vol. 18, all in RG 8, NSARM.

34 PAS, 1843, no. 1, vol. 22, RG 8, NSARM; D. Macfarlane (Wallace) to Titus Smith, 7 July 1841, no. 283, vol. 14, RG 8, NSARM; "Report for 1858," vol. 22, RG 8, NSARM; C.H. Belcher, *The Farmer's Almanack* (Halifax: Belcher, 1824).

35 As the Cumberland Agricultural Society noted in its 1842 report, its annual meeting was "not numerously [but] respectably attended"; see no. 148, vol. 14, RG 8, NSARM. See also A.F. Haliburton (Cape Breton County Agricultural Society) to Titus Smith, 16 January 1843, no. 124, vol. 16, RG 8, NSARM. See Graeme Wynn's discussion of prizes in "Exciting a Spirit of Emulation," 32–7.

36 PAS, 1843, no. 1, vol. 22, RG 8, NSARM. For more detail on the inspection, see PAS, 1842, 82, no. 1, vol. 22, RG 8, NSARM. See also page 52 of the

1842 report, which recounts that following their spring 1841 meeting, they "dined together in the Masonic Hall"; and Wynn, "Exciting a Spirit of Emulation," 38.

37 Report of the Visiting Committee, 3 March 1861, no. 1, vol. 22, RG 8, NSARM. See also Rusty Bittermann, "Women and the Escheat Movement"; and Davidoff and Hall, *Family Fortunes*, 416–49.

38 See the entries for 18 October 1842 and 6 October 1843, no. 1, vol. 22; and MacGregor to Young, 28 October 1825, no. 141, vol. 6, both in RG 8, NSARM.

39 Some societies continued to exist beyond the denial of funds in the spring of 1826; see reports in *Colonial Patriot*, 8 October 1828; and *Pictou Observer*, 20 July 1831.

40 See *Pictou Observer*, 30 January 1833, 9 December 1834, and 22 February 1842; *Colonial Patriot*, December 1827, 18 January 1828, 25 January 1828, 14 March 1828, 8 October 1828, 22 October 1831, 23 January 1832, and 3 March 1832; Pictou Female Benevolent Society Papers, no. 22, vol. 206, MG 100, NSARM; and *The Spirit of the Times*, 19 December 1843, 19 January 1844, 24 May 1844, 21 June 1844, 20 September 1844, and 29 November 1844.

41 *Pictou Observer*, 22 February 1842; Patterson, *History of the County of Pictou*, 395–7; *The Bee*, 10 Janaury 1838; *Spirit of the Times*, 8 February 1845.

42 See also their praise for the "variety of plans ... for the improvement of the labouring classes," in *Colonial Patriot*, 18 January 1828; and Member of the Pictou Literary and Scientific Society, *The Pictou Indians: An Original Poem* (1847), 6.

43 It should also be noted that illiteracy may not have been that great an obstacle. "Simon," writing to the *Colonial Patriot*, 28 March 1828, described weekly community gatherings in his (unnamed) back-country settlement, which centred on one person reading to the assembled audience. Such evenings were by no means passive affairs, for as Simon observed those in attendance routinely offered "various and singular opinions" on those expressed in the paper. See also *Cape Breton Advocate*, 2 December 1845.

44 See, for example, "Is Farming Profitable in Nova Scotia?" *Mechanic and Farmer*, 5 June 1839. Occasionally, however, the paper would reprint columns from the Society for the Diffusion of Useful Knowledge or from the *Prince Edward Island Gazette*; see *Mechanic and Farmer*, 3 July 1839 and 7 August 1839.

45 *Colonial Patriot*, 11 January 1828, 28 May 1831, and 22 October 1831; *Pictou Observer*, 14 April 1835.

46 On general "improvements," see *Colonial Patriot*, 7 May 1831; *Spirit of the Times*, 8 February 1845; and Thomas Trotter, *A treatise on geology*, iv-v. Improvement could be the object of satire and social critique. For

example, in reference to juvenile delinquency, family degeneration, and intemperance, the *Colonial Patriot*, 18 February 1829, stated: "That this is an age of universal improvement is attested by innumerable facts."

47 *Colonial Patriot*, 28 December 1827 and 28 May 1828; "Brittanicus," *Colonial Patriot*, 18 February 1832. See also Beck, *Politics of Nova Scotia*, vol. 1, chs 4 and 5; and B. Anne Wood, "The Significance of Evangelical Presbyterian Politics in the Construction of State Schooling."

48 *Colonial Patriot*, 28 May 1828.

49 Report of the East River Evangelical Society, reprinted in *Colonial Patriot*, 7 May 1833; "Pictou Indian Civilization Society," *Colonial Patriot*, 14 March 1828; L.F.S. Upton, *Micmacs and Colonists*, 166–7; reports of the Pictou Auxilliary Bible Society, reprinted in *Colonial Patriot*, 22 February 1828 and 26 March 1833.

50 W.B. Mullin to McKeen, Ship Harbor, Strait of Canso, 16 January 1833, McKeen Papers, no. 8, vol. 109, MG 12, BI; *Colonial Patriot*, 17 March 1832; C.H. Belcher, *The Farmer's Almanack* (Halifax: Belcher, 1848), 88; J.W. Dawson, *The testimony of the Holy Scriptures respecting wine and strong drink*. See also the membership lists in *Colonial Patriot*, 22 February 1828 and 7 May 1833; and C.H. Belcher, *Nova-Scotia Temperance Almanack* (1836).

51 *Cape Breton News*, 3 November 1852; *Spirit of the Times*, 31 May 1844 and 18 January 1845; Belcher, *Farmer's Almanack* (1848), 88. Generally, see C.B. Fergusson, *Mechanics' Institutes in Nova Scotia*.

52 Report of the St Mary's Temperance Society, signed John McDonald, reprinted in *Colonial Patriot*, 14 May 1831. See also the editorial on "the prevailing vice of the day," in *Colonial Patriot*, 17 September 1828; and Patterson's description of logging and drinking, in *History of Pictou County*, 245–50.

53 The reference may be to Wentworth Taylor, a justice of the peace and the commissioner for "taking special bails"; see "The King's Ministers," in C.H. Belcher, *The Farmer's Almanack* (Halifax: Belcher, 1828), 48–50, 53.

54 *Colonial Patriot*, 24 September 1833. The literary and scientific societies seem to have allowed women to attend but not to join; see *Spirit of the Times*, 24 May 1844 and 25 January 1845. See also the very brief report on A.O. Dodd's lecture before the Sydney Mechanics' Institute on "The Rights of Woman," in *Cape Breton News*, 24 November 1852.

55 All quotations in this paragraph are from *Colonial Patriot*, 14 May, 28 May, and 23 July 1831.

56 See Gail Campbell, "Disfranchised but Not Quiescent"; and Nova Scotia, *Journals of the House of Assembly* (hereafter *JHA*) (1841), 21 January 1840, 669.

57 Lykke de la Cour, Cecillia Morgan, and Mariana Valverde, "Gender Regulation and State Formation in Nineteenth-Century Canada," 165.

58 *Colonial Patriot*, 28 May 1831.

59 See Alexander Farquharson, *Sketch of the Missionary Proceedings at Cape Breton from August 1833 to October 1834*, 3; Joshua Marsden, *The Narrative of a Mission to Nova Scotia, New Brunswick, and the Somers Islands*, 30–1; and Martin MacPherson to Titus Smith, 28 August 1841, no. 305, vol. 16, RG 8, NSARM.

60 *Colonial Patriot*, 24 September 1833, 14 May 1831, 23 July 1831, and 21 January 1832. Andrew Belcher, *Nova-Scotia Temperance Almanack* (1838), lists 362 members. If correct, then the numbers show a dramatic increase from any figures reported in the early 1830s. See also "The Temperance Armies," poem, *Mechanic and Farmer*, 12 January 1842.

61 *The Missionary Register of the Presbyterian Church of Nova Scotia* (Pictou), vol. 1, no. 9 (September 1850), 130–1; and vol. 1, no. 11 (November 1850), 164–6. "Judge Marshall," speaking at the St Ann's Temperance Society, claimed that it was a known fact that alcoholic beverages were "invented by the Arabian chemists intentionally to eradicate the Christian religion"; see *Spirit of the Times*, 28 June 1844.

62 "A Friend to Improvement," *Colonial Patriot*, 23 April 1833; *Colonial Patriot*, 28 May 1828, 19 March 1833, and 24 September 1833. See also *Colonial Patriot*, 26 March 1831, 23 April 1831, and 14 May 1831; and John MacLean, *An Address Delivered at a Quarterly Meeting of the Pictou and West River Temperance Societies in October 1833*, 10–14.

63 MacLean, *Address Delivered*, 10–14; William McKeen, "Speech on Temperance," n.d. [enclosed with a letter dated 7 March 1840], William McKeen Papers, no. 105, vol. 109, MG 12, BI. See also William Garvie, cited in Janet Guildford, "Creating the Ideal Man," 21–2.

64 Temperance Watchmen in North America, *Ritual of the Brotherhood of Temperance Watchmen in North America*; *Colonial Patriot*, 14 March 1828.

65 *Colonial Patriot*, 4 January 1828.

66 *Colonial Patriot*, 4 August 1832 and 17 September 1833.

67 MacLean, *Address Delivered*, 3–6; *Mechanic and Farmer*, 22 May 1839; "Elias Homespun," *Commercial Herald* (Sydney), 12 January 1850.

68 Annual report of the River John Agricultural Society, 1845, no. 122, vol. 18, RG 8, NSARM.

69 *JHA* (1846), appendix 77; Upton, *Micmacs and Colonists*, 92–3. The problem of Mi'kmaq crop failures continued; see *JHA* (1853), appendix 30.

70 See *JHA* (1847), appendix 83; and (1848), appendix 39.

71 W. Ouseley to Titus Smith, Sydney Agricultural Society, 19 November 1846, no. 141; Ouseley to Smith, 11 January 1848, no. 143; Roderick MacKenzie to Smith (Baddeck), 29 December 1847, no. 185; and MacKenzie to Smith, 29 December 1848, no. 192, all in vol. 16, RG 8, NSARM.

72 James Jenks to John Young, Cumberland Agricultural Society, 3 January
   1825, no. 216, vol. 6, RG 8, NSARM.

73 Member of the Pictou Literary and Scientific Society, *The Pictou Indians:
   An Original Poem* (1847), 17–18, original emphasis.

74 Wynn, "Exciting a Spirit of Emulation"; Steven Stoll, *Larding the Earth.*

75 Stoll, *Larding the Earth.*

76 Young, *Letters of Agricola,* 44.

77 Ibid., 63.

78 Unattributed quotation used by Forrester in his report on the societies
   in 1859, "Agriculture," *JHA* (1860), 613.

CHAPTER TEN

1 Paul Gootenberg, *Imagining Development,* 18–20, 58–64; Joseph E. Love and
  Nels Jacobsen, eds, *Guiding the Invisible Hand.*

2 *Colonial Patriot,* 5 March 1833.

3 Lawrence Doyle, 24 March 1845, quoted in *Spirit of the Times,* 12 April
  1845. See also *Novascotian,* 24 February 1851; G.R. Young, "The Coal Question," broadsheet, [c. 1845], no. 38, vol. 9, "P," RG 5, Nova Scotia Archives
  and Records Management (NSARM); and Memo, Sir Rupert George,
  24 August 1840, no. 61, vol. 459, RG 1, NSARM.

4 By way of comparison, the GMA's fixed cost clearly would have placed the
  company in the upper end of collieries in Britain in the 1820s. While there
  were a few mines valued at between £350,000 and £700,000, the vast majority were estimated to be worth less than £50,000; see M.W. Flinn, *The
  History of the British Coal Industry,* vol. 2, 190–211.

5 "Mr Buddle's Report on the Sydney Colliery in the Island of Cape Breton,"
  no. 33, vol. 39, "A," RG 21, NSARM. Richard Brown was, understandably,
  very proud of these mines, and he crowed just a little about these qualities
  in his *The Coal fields and Coal Trade of the Island of Cape Breton,* 50–68.

6 See Samuel Cunard's defence of the company's practices in *Cape Breton
  News,* 23 November 1850, reprinted from *Halifax Sun,* 11 November 1850.

7 The editor, Jotham Blanchard, ran a series on colonial political economy;
  see in particular *Colonial Patriot,* 25 January 1828.

8 Report of the Halifax Board of Trade, in *Pictou Observer,* 22 February 1832;
  Brown, *Coal Fields and Coal Trade,* 77–8. For Joseph Howe's views, see his
  Western and Eastern Rambles, especially his reply to those "who carp and cavil
  at this valuable and highly respectable company" (159–70) and his defence
  of the GMA (163–4). See also the enthusiastic editorials in the *Colonial
  Patriot,* 14 December 1827, and the *Novascotian,* 19 October 1827. An

exception here was the cautious comment in the *Acadian Recorder,* 16 June
1827, which argued that "mines should be kept in operation in as many
quarters and to as great an extent as possible, as competition will be ever
serviceable to industry."

9 See "Report of His Majesty's Council, to whom was referred a Letter from
the Right Honourable Earl Bathurst to His Excellency the Lieutenant Governor on the Subject of the Coal Mines in this Province," 23 May 1815,
no. 1, vol. 460, RG 1, NSARM.

10 See the comments attributed to "Mr Woodhouse," surveyor of customs, in
Sir James Kempt to Wilmot Horton, 8 April 1827, Colonial Office records
for Nova Scotia (hereafter CO) 217/147. See also Kempt to Horton,
28 October 1826, CO 217/146.

11 Report of Committee of House of Assembly, 17 January 1829, no. 155,
vol. 458, RG 1, NSARM. It may have been a very small gesture: most were
expecting that the improved production would actually lower the price.
See *Colonial Patriot,* 14 December 1827; and *Novascotian,* 18 October 1827.

12 Grain tolls were still regulated, and the counties still regularly set an assize
for bread; see, for example, *Pictou Observer,* 9 June 1835 and 7 July 1835;
and Daniel Dickson, *A Guide to Town Officers,* 176–84, 189–96.

13 Nova Scotia, *Statutes,* 1840, Cap. 18, "An Act to Prevent Injury to Rail Roads."

14 Samuel Cunard to Sir Rupert George, 13 December 1845, no. 113,
vol. 459, RG 1, NSARM.

15 William Cook to M.B. Almon, 19 November 1828, D.8.a, MG 14, 19,
Beaton Institute (BI); Richard Smith to Sir James Kempt, 27 July 1832,
no. 159, vol. 458; and memo signed by Sir Rupert George, 24 August 1840,
no. 61, vol. 459, both in RG 1, NSARM.

16 Unsigned, undated memos, nos 114–15, vol. 459, RG 1, NSARM, emphasis
added. This had been part of the original 1815 act as well. It was widely regarded that such minor infractions would never meet with conviction by a
jury. See *Novascotian,* 24 February 1851; and James Miller (superintendent
of mines at Sydney) to Portland, 27 August 1794, CO 217/110.

17 "Notes on GMA prosecutions," William Young Papers, no. 292(a), vol. 732,
MG 2, NSARM; *Novascotian,* 24 February 1851. In response to charges that
this was a law passed for the GMA, the attorney general rightfully noted that
this law, like the smuggling laws, predated the company's existence, although he might have added that the techniques of enforcement did not.

18 The following is based on the "Debates and Proceedings" as reported in
the *Novascotian,* 24 February 1851.

19 William Hall, a conservative member from King's County, said that the reformers should watch their actions, as they might regret such a sweeping

change when the day came when there was not a monopoly; see *Novascotian*, 24 February 1851.

20 These lacunae became more evident later, but one can read Young's frustrations with the technical issues put forth in negotiations in London in 1854; see his account in a letter to Rev. Alexander MacDonald, Mabou, 1 November 1854, no. 592, vol. 732, MG 2, NSARM.

21 Statement of James McGregor, 13 July 1838, no. 56, vol. 459, RG 1, NSARM. Similarly, James D.B. Fraser noted that the GMA sold unscreened coal at the mine for a higher price than it charged for screened coal that had been conveyed by rail to the dock; see Fraser to George Young, vol. 5, "A," RG 21, NSARM.

22 Roderick McGregor to George Young, 4 March 1848, vol. 5, "A," RG 21, NSARM.

23 A critic, "Aristides," described such arguments as "high sounding patriotism"; see *Pictou Observer*, 14 March 1832.

24 "Anti-Monopolist," *Pictou Observer*, 22 February 1832. He was quoting a report in a Halifax newspaper from the Halifax Board of Trade. "Anti-Monopolist" was John Ross, a Colchester County merchant who several times ran for the Assembly. Ross was also the author of letters signed "Freeholder" in the *Pictou Observer*, 14 March 1832, and "Monopoly" in the *Free Press*, 10 November 1829. See also John Ross to William Young, 14 February 1833, William Young Papers, vol. 732, MG 2, NSARM; and Brian Cuthbertson, *Johnny Bluenose at the Polls*, 242–5.

25 "Anti-Monopolist," *Pictou Observer*, 14 March 1832.

26 Ibid.

27 William Young, "Speech on Coal," no. 168, vol. 732, MG 2, NSARM.

28 "Aristides," *Pictou Observer*, 14 March 1832.

29 The phrase "honourable competition" is from John Young, *The Letters of Agricola on the Principles of Vegetation and Tillage*, 27.

30 *Pictou Observer*, 22 February 1832.

31 Abraham Gesner, *Remarks on the Geology and Mineralogy of Nova Scotia*, 154. Gesner and Ross would later be partners in a Londonderry iron-mining company; see Abraham Gesner and John Ross, *Report on the Londonderry Iron and Coal Deposits*.

32 Petition of Robert Holmes Smith, 15 January 1846, no. 112, vol. 459, RG 1, NSARM, emphasis added.

33 James D.B. Fraser to George Young, 4 March 1848, vol. 5, "A," RG 21, NSARM. Fraser, using figures obtained from the US consul in Pictou, determined that 108 American vessels docked at the Loading Ground between 17 August and the close of shipping (late December to early January). He

claimed that their "*average* detention" was seventeen days, whereas five days was proper (original emphasis). Therefore, 108 boats at 12 days per boat, at £4 per day demurrage, equalled a loss of £5,784, or close to £12,000 for the year. His math is wrong (£5184, not £5784) and doubling it is misleading, as more ships came in the second half of the year than in the first.

34 "Report on Controverted Elections," Assembly Papers, 1833, vol. 22, "R," RG 5, NSARM; James D.B. Fraser to George Young, 4 March 1848, vol. 5, "A," RG 21, NSARM.

35 See William Bown to William Young, 4 February 1833, no. 155; and John Ross to Young, 14 February 1833, no. 157, both in vol. 732, MG 2, NSARM. See also various memos, notes, and speeches "On the Coal Question," all from 1833, in nos 156-63 and 167-8, vol. 732, MG 2, NSARM.

36 See the memo dated 6 February 1833, no. 156, vol. 732, MG 2, NSARM.

37 Gesner, *Remarks on the Geology*; F. Alger and C.T. Jackson, "Remarks on the Geology and Mineralogy of Nova Scotia."

38 See Gesner, *Remarks on the Geology*, x, 62-3, 65, 93, 101-5, 153-4.

39 Ibid., x, iv.

40 *JHA* (1837), 11 April 1837, 189.

41 Petition of Abraham Gesner, 24 September 1838, no. 62; Gesner to Provincial Secretary, 19 April 1839, no. 64, both in vol. 459, RG 1, NSARM.

42 Almost twenty years later J.W. Dawson, *Acadian Geology*, 3, would still be making the same point.

43 G.D. Pennington [Treasury] to James Stephen, 13 June 1839, copy, no. 109, vol. 459, RG 1, NSARM.

44 Memorial of Gesner on behalf of himself and others [directed to Lt Governor LeMarchant], [c. January 1853], enclosure in Gesner to Joseph Howe, Provincial Secretary, dated at New York, "Office of the Asphaltum Mining and Kerosene Gas Company, 497 Broadway," 26 December 1853, no. 60, vol. 461, RG 1, NSARM; Gesner, *Remarks on the Geology*, 146-7.

45 Petition of Abraham Gesner, [iron mines in Cumberland], 24 September 1838, no. 62, vol. 459, RG 1, NSARM. Gesner's position is confused, somewhat, by his apparent retraction in his *The Industrial Resources of Nova Scotia*, where he claimed that he had been "misled" earlier and now praised the "extensive and skilful operations of the company" as well as the "indomitable skill and perseverance" of Cunard (see esp. 273, 277, 283-4, and 286). But less than four years later he was back in the struggle and engaged in a nasty and personal battle with Samuel Cunard; see E.F. Sanderson et al. to Gesner, New York, 19 February 1853, no. 51; Joseph Howe to Samuel Cunard, "Agent of the [GMA]," Halifax, 17 March 1853, no. 52; and Gesner to Howe, 26 December 1853, no. 60, all in vol. 461, RG 1, NSARM; and Gesner and Ross, *Report on the Londonderry*.

46 *Pictou Observer*, 12 June 1838; Adam Carr to Alexander Fraser, 28 June 1838, no. 54, vol. 459, RG 1, NSARM.

47 Samuel Cunard to Sir Rupert George, 3 March 1838, no. 67, vol. 459; and Statement of Adam Carr, 28 June 1838, no. 54, vol. 469, both in RG 1, NSARM; *JHA* (1839), appendix 50.

48 Samuel Cunard to Sir Rupert George, 16 January 1839, no. 68; and Cunard to George, 3 March 1838, no. 67, both in vol. 459, RG 1, NSARM; Roderick McGregor to George R. Young, 4 March 1848, file: "Correspondence, 1848," vol. 5, "A," RG 21, NSARM. Cunard's argument did not fool anyone in Pictou; some quickly pointed out that local residents bought the unscreened run-of-mine coal (i.e., a mixture of large pieces and small gravel-like coal that burns too hot and very quickly), while the "excess" to which Cunard referred was the superior screened product.

49 On the company's market intentions, see the petition of Rundell, Bridge, and Rundell, [August 1831], CO 217/153, where they note that they were "not solely" interested in the markets of Nova Scotia and that from the "outset ... [the GMA] was chiefly encouraged by the hope of establishing Nova Scotia coal in the markets of the United States." See also Cunard's own testimony before the "Select Committee of the House of Commons appointed to inquire into the condition of the Islands and Highlands of Scotland, and into the practicability of affording the people relief by means of Emigration," 24 May 1841, reprinted in *Colonial Herald*, 30 April 1842; and Petition of GMA [Cunard to Lord Falkland], 22 December 1842, no. 104, vol. 459, RG 1, NSARM, where Cunard bemoaned the devastating effect that new tariffs in the US had had on the company's present year and future prospects.

50 See Joseph Smith, "Cost of raising coal at Albion Mines" [which contains doubled columns of wages – one with existing wages and one with reduced scale], 7 February 1842, file: "1842, Reports and Correspondence," vol. 7, "A," RG 21, NSARM; "Estimate of Wages, Bridgeport," [Richard Brown], 1842, vol. 7, "A," RG 21, NSARM; and Cunard's brief note that the company was "now preparing a reduced scale of wages," in Petition of the [GMA], 22 December 1842, no. 104, vol. 459, RG 1, NSARM. Walter R. Johnson, *The Coal Trade of British America*, 16–19, estimated that the cost of labour for coal delivered on board the ship was approximately 40 per cent of the selling price in New England.

51 In general, see the correspondence between Robert Moser ["Chairman" GMA] and Lord Stanley and between Samuel Cunard and Lord Stanley reprinted in *JHA* (1846), appendix 1; quotation from Moser to Stanley, 5 January 1844.

52 Petition of General Mining Association [Samuel Cunard], 22 December 1842, no. 104, vol. 459, RG 1, NSARM. See also F.W. Taussig, *Tariff History of the United States*, 131–5; and Grace Palladino, *Another Civil War*, 16–42.

53 Petition of the [GMA], 22 December 1842, no. 104, vol. 459, RG 1,
   NSARM; Robert Moser to Lord Stanley, 5 January 1844, London, reprinted in *JHA* (1845), appendix 1. The results of this petition are
   unclear. The next item in file no. 104, vol. 459, RG 1, NSARM, is an expression of gratitude from Cunard, but correspondence reprinted in
   1844 and 1845 suggests that no augmentation was given until 1845, and
   it was for 6,000 chaldrons, not 20,000; see *JHA* (1844), appendix 1. See
   also William Young to Moser, 31 July 1854, reprinted in *JHA* (1855),
   appendix 3.

54 See J.M. Beck, *Joseph Howe*, vol. 1, 236–9.

55 See the preamble to Report of George Wightman on the GMA, 10 March
   1842, no. 37, vol. 3, RG 21, NSARM. Wightman must have developed a rep-
   utation as a good investigator. Later, in the mid-1850s, he was chief engineer on the Shubenacadie Canal project, and in 1861 he was hired by the
   commission investigating the land issue in Prince Edward Island, where he
   became known as "the spy"; see Ian Ross Robertson, *The Tenant League of
   Prince Edward Island, 1864–1867*, 34–5, 301–2.

56 His calculation included £7,000 for real estate, £12,000 for "buildings" (including everything from workmen's houses to pithead structures), £30,000
   for overruns on the railway, £2,740 for the now unused foundry, and "excess" inventory of £9,755; see Report of George Wightman on the GMA,
   10 March 1842, no. 37, vol. 3, RG 21, NSARM.

57 Ibid.

58 Ibid.

59 Ibid.

60 See *Spirit of the Times*, 12 April 1845, which contains the debate.

61 Report from the council's Committee on Mines and Minerals, *JHA* (1852),
   appendix 96.

62 *JHA* (1849), appendix 10. See Beck, *Joseph Howe*, vol. 2, 10–18; and D.C.
   Harvey, "The Civil List and Responsible Government in Nova Scotia."

63 See George Young in *JHA* (1849), appendix 37.

64 "An Act to Amend An Act to Regulate the Mines and Minerals of Nova Scotia," (16 Vict., Cap. 15).

65 William Young to Robert Moser, President, GMA, 31 July 1854, reprinted in
   JHA (1855), appendix 3.

66 See Merivale to A.E. Cockburn and Richard Bethell, 7 February 1855; and
   Cockburn and Bethel to Merivale, 18 June 1855, both in *JHA* (1856), appendix 12.

67 Jonathan McCully to George Smith, 21 March 1848, vol. 7, RG 21,
   "A," NSARM. For a description of the GMA "squatting" on the mines in

Cumberland County, see Ian McKay, "Industry, Work, and Community in the Cumberland Coal Fields, 1848–1927," 25–34.

68 Brown, *Coal Fields and Coal Trade*, 77–8, 83–4.

69 Nova Scotia, *Debates and Proceedings of the House of Assembly* (1857), 205. The following day Johnston announced that he had retired as counsel for the GMA.

70 Beck, *Joseph Howe*, vol. 2, 124–5.

71 Nova Scotia, *Debates and Proceedings of the House of Assembly* (1856), 61.

72 See Rosemarie Langout, "Developing Nova Scotia"; McKay, "Industry, Work, and Community," 66–99; Kenneth G. Pryke, *Nova Scotia and Confederation, 1864–1875*; and D.A. Muise, "The Federal Election of 1867 in Nova Scotia."

73 *JHA* (1859), "Mines Report."

74 In British North American currency.

75 Ibid. The measures, for both coal and cash, do get confusing here. This price (using currency, but on weight not volume) looks good. But assuming McKay's ton to be 2,200 pounds (as it was in all the negotiations), it cost only 6d less than the 13s6d that the GMA had been charging for a 30 hundred-weight chaldron. For a discussion of coalmines in Antigonish County (and their politician owner), see J. Campbell, *Report on the Antigonish Oil-Coal Mines*.

76 *Cape Breton News*, 16 February 1853.

77 William H. Sewell Jr, *A Rhetoric of Bourgeois Revolution*.

78 Phillip A. Buckner, *The Transition to Responsible Government*, 67–71, 237–8, 334–5.

CONCLUSION

1 *Colonial Standard*, 8 April 1862.

2 *Colonial Standard*, 7 January 1862.

Bibliography

PRIMARY SOURCES

Beaton Institute (BI), Cape Breton University, Sydney, Nova Scotia
- William McKeen, MG 12, 109.
- General Mining Association, MG 14, 19.
- Archibald Family Papers, MG 14, 45.

Dalhousie University Archives
- James D.B. Fraser, MS-4–28.
- Acadia Coal Co., MS-4–149.

National Archives Canada
- William and George Harper Papers (1829–31), vol. 58, MG 24.
- J.F.W. DesBarres Papers, vol. 25, MG 23.

Public Archives of New Brunswick
- New Brunswick Land Petitions, reels f9043, f1047, f10838, f10839.

Nova Scotia Archives and Records Management (NSARM)
- Government record group (RG) 1, vols 243, 253, 458, 459, 460, 461, 462; RG 5, Legislative Papers, ser. P (petitions) and ser. R (reports); RG 8, Agriculture; RG 11, Cape Breton as a Separate Colony; RG 21, Mines; RG 32, Vital Statistics; RG 47, Land Records.
- Private papers, manuscript group (MG) 1, Private: Richard Brown, vol. 151; A.C. Dodd, vol. 242B; James D.B. Fraser, vol. 411; John Huston, vol. 493; Estate of J.F.W. DesBarres, vol. 1539; Alexander Ross, vol. 2466.
- Private papers, MG 2, Political: M.B. Almon, vol. 18; William Young, vols 732–3; George Young, vols 719–25.
- Private papers, MG 3, Business: John Grant, vol. 117; Thomas Roach, vol. 119; Martin Wilkins, vol. 272; Peter Smyth, vol. 284.
- Private papers, microfilm (not grouped): Davison Family Papers; William Matheson.

Public Archives of Prince Edward Island (PAPEI)
– Robert Stewart Letterbooks, 2316/1.
– David Stewart's Journal, 3209/2.
Public Record Office, London, England
– *British Parliamentary Papers: Reports, Correspondence and Other Papers Relating to the Affairs of Canada, 1842–46.* Vol. 16. Shannon, UK: Irish University Press, 1968.
– Colonial Office records for Nova Scotia (CO) 217, 1790–1860. Microfilm in National Archives Canada.

Government Documents

Great Britain, House of Commons. *First Report of the Select Committee on the Means of Improving and Maintaining the Foreign Trade of the Country.* London: n.p., 1821.
Nova Scotia. *Debates and Proceedings of the House of Assembly.* Halifax, 1855–65.
– *Journals of the House of Assembly (JHA).* Halifax, 1800–1865.
– *The Statutes of Nova Scotia.* Halifax: J.S. Thompson, 1852–67.
"Report on the Affairs of British North America from the Earl of Durham." In Great Britain, *Parliamentary Papers,* vol. 17 (1839), minutes of evidence, Nova Scotia.
"Report of the Select Committee of the House of Commons on Accidents in Mines." In Great Britain, *Parliamentary Papers,* vol. 5 (1835), minutes of evidence, testimony of John Buddle and Richard Smith.
"Report from the Select Committee of the House of Lords appointed to consider the Means by which Colonization may be made subsidiary to other measures for the Improvement of the social condition of Ireland." In Great Britain, *Parliamentary Papers,* vol. 6 (1847), minutes of. evidence, Samuel Cunard and George Young.

Newspapers and Periodicals

Acadian Recorder (Halifax), 1815–25
Annual Register (London), 1825–30
The Bee (Pictou), 1835–36
Cape Breton Advocate, 1840–41
Cape Breton News, 1850–53
Cape Breton Spectator, 1846–49
Colonial Patriot (Pictou), 1827–35
Colonial Standard (Pictou), 1858–65

Eastern Chronicle (New Glasgow), 1843–50

Farmers' Almanack, (Halifax), later *Belcher's Farmers' Almanack*

Journal of Agriculture (also *Nova Scotian Journal of Agriculture*) (Halifax), 1866–70

Journal of Education and Agriculture (Halifax), 1858–62

Mechanic and Farmer (Pictou), 1838–44

Missionary Register of the Presbyterian Church of Nova Scotia (Pictou), 1850–55

Novascotian (Halifax), 1815–25

Pictou Observer, 1831–35, 1838–40

Spirit of the Times (Sydney), 1842–46

Published Eighteenth- and Nineteenth-Century Manuscripts

Algar, F. *A Handbook for the Colony of Nova Scotia.* London: Canadian News, 1864.

– and C.T. Jackson. "Remarks on the Geology and Mineralogy of Nova Scotia." *American Academy of Arts and Science* n.s. 1 (1833): 279–330.

Allison, David. *History of Nova Scotia.* Vol. 2. Halifax: A.W. Bowen, 1916.

Anderson, James. *The Bee, or Literary Weekly Intelligencer, consisting of original pieces and selections from performances of merit, foreign or domestic: A work calculated to disseminate useful knowledge among all ranks of people at a small expense.* Edinburgh: Mundell and Son, 1791–93.

Aspinall, A., ed. *Three Early Nineteenth Century Diaries.* London: Williams and Norgate, 1952.

Atlantic and St Lawrence Railroad Company, Provisional Committee. *Report of the Provisional Committee of the Atlantic & St. Lawrence Railroad.* Halifax: Gossip and Coade, 1845.

Bank of British North America. *Alphabetical List of the Proprietors of the Bank of British North America.* London: Teape and Son, 1842.

Belcher, C.H. *Nova-Scotia Temperance Almanack.* Halifax: Belcher, 1836.

Bill, I.E. *Fifty Years with the Baptist Ministers and Churches of the Maritime Provinces.* Saint John: Barnes, 1880.

Bligh, Harris H., QC. *The Nova Scotia Law Index, Embracing All the Private and Local Legislation of the Province of Nova Scotia down to and Including the Year 1900 (1758–1900).* Halifax: McAlpine, 1901.

Bourinot, J.G. "Notes on a Ramble through Cape Breton." *New Dominion Monthly* 2, no. 2 (May 1868): 87–92.

Boyd, Frank Stanley, ed. *McKerrow: A Brief History of the Coloured Baptists of Nova Scotia, 1783–1895.* 1896. Reprint, Halifax: Afro-Nova Scotian Enterprises, 1977.

Brown, Richard. *The Coal Fields and Coal Trade of the Island of Cape Breton.* London: Sampson, Low, Marston, Low and Searle, 1871.

– *A History of Cape Breton, with some account of the discovery and settlement of Canada, Nova Scotia and Newfoundland.* London: Sampson, Low, Son and Marston, 1869.
– "On the Geology of Cape Breton." *Proceedings of the Geological Society* 4 (London, December 1843): 23–6.

Campbell, J. *Report on the Antigonish Oil-Coal Mines, the property of Hon. John McKinnon, M.E.C., and Wm. Chisholm, Esq., Nova Scotia.* Halifax: n.p., 1865.

Canada Land and Railway Association. *Report & outline of a plan by which an extensive railway may be constructed in the British North American colonies, combining its execution with an enlarged scheme of colonization and reclamation of waste lands, and executing the works so that the company and emigrants shall be mutually benefited.* London: J. Bradley, 1850.

Carmichael-Smyth, Robert. *The employment of the people and capital of Great Britain in her own colonies, at the same time assisting emigration, and penal arrangements.* London: W.P. Metchim, 1849.

Cawston, George, and A.H. Keane. *The Early Chartered Companies, A.D. 1296–1858.* London: E. Arnold, 1896.

Chambers, William. "Things as They Are in America, Nova Scotia." 1853. Reprinted as "A Friendly Scot Looks at Nova Scotia in 1853," ed. D.C. Harvey, *Collections of the Nova Scotia Historical Society* 27 (1947): 81–100.

Cozzens, Frederic S. *Acadia, or A Month with the Blue Noses.* New York: Derby and Jackson, 1859.

Davies, Richard A., ed. *The Letters of Thomas Chandler Haliburton.* Toronto: University of Toronto Press, 1988.

Dawson, J.W. *Acadian Geology: An Account of the Geological Structure and Mineral Resources of Nova Scotia and Portions of the Neighbouring Provinces of British America.* Edinburgh: Oliver and Boyd, 1855.
– *Contributions toward the Improvement of Agriculture in Nova-Scotia, with Practical Hints on the Management and Improvement of Live Stock compiled from Youatt, Johnston, Young, Peters, Stephens, &c.* 2nd ed. Halifax: R. Nugent, 1856.
– "On the Lower Carboniferous Rocks or Gypsiferous Formation of Nova Scotia." *Proceedings of the Geological Society* 4 (London, December 1843): 26–35.
– *Practical hints to the farmers of Nova-Scotia on the management and improvement of livestock, and on general husbandry.* Halifax: R. Nugent, 1854.
– *Report on the Geological Structure and Mineral Resources of Prince Edward Island.* Montreal: J. Lovell, 1871.
– *The testimony of the Holy Scriptures respecting wine and strong drink, being the substance of a course of lectures delivered before the Pictou Total Abstinence Society.* Pictou: Pictou County Temperance League, 1858.

Dickson, Daniel. *A Guide to the Town Officers, shewing their appointment, duties, liabilities, and privileges, according to the laws of the province.* Pictou: The Bee, 1837.

Doughty, A.G., ed. *The Journal of Captain John Knox.* 1757. Reprint, Toronto: Champlain Society, 1914.

Drummond, Robert. *Minerals and Mining in Nova Scotia.* Stellarton, NS: Mining Record Office, 1918.

English, Henry. *A Complete View of Joint Stock Companies formed during the years 1824 and 1825, being six hundred and twenty-four in number, shewing the amount of capital, number of shares, amount advanced, present value, amount to be called, fluctuation in price, names of bankers solicitors &c., with a general summary and remarks, and an appendix giving a list of companies formed antecedent to that period, with amount of capital, number of shares, dividends, &c.* London: Boosey, 1827.

‒ *A General Guide to Companies Formed for Working Foreign Mines, with their prospectuses, amount of capital, number of shares, names of directors, &c., and an appendix shewing their progress since their formation, obtained from authoritative sources, with a table of the extent of their fluctuations in price, up to the present period.* London: Boosey, 1825.

Fairbanks, Charles R. *Reports and papers relating to a canal intended to connect the harbour of Halifax with the Basin of Mines, remarks on its nature and importance, and a plan and section; also, the report of a survey for canals between St. Peter's Bay and Bras d'Or Lake in Cape Breton, and the Bay of Fundy and Bay of Verte.* Halifax: J.S. Cunnabell, 1826.

Farquharson, Alexander. *Sketch of the Missionary Proceedings at Cape Breton from August 1833 to October 1834.* Edinburgh: n.p., 1835.

Fergusson, C.B., ed. *"The Old King is Back": Amos "King" Seaman and His Diary.* Halifax: Public Archives of Nova Scotia, 1972.

‒ ed. *Uniacke's Sketches of Cape Breton and Other Papers Relating to Cape Breton Island.* Halifax: Public Archives of Nova Scotia, 1958.

Fleming, Sandford. *The Intercolonial: A Historical Sketch of the Inception, Location, Construction and Completion of the Line of Railway Uniting the Inland and Atlantic Provinces of the Dominion.* Montreal: Dawson Brothers, 1876.

General Mining Association Limited. "Deed of Settlement, dated 10th April, 1829, as altered by Resolutions of Extraordinary Meetings of the Proprietors, held 2nd and 19th August 1870." Westminster: Bircham, Dalrymple, Drake, Bircham and Burt, 1870.

Gesner, Abraham. *The Industrial Resources of Nova Scotia, comprehending the physical geography, topography, geology, agriculture, fisheries, mines, forests, wild lands, lumbering, manufacturing, navigation, commerce, emigration, improvements, industry, contemplated railways, natural history, and resources of the province.* Halifax: A. & W. MacKinlay, 1849.

‒ *Remarks on the Geology and Mineralogy of Nova Scotia.* Halifax: Gossip and Coade, 1836.

– and John Ross, *Report on the Londonderry Iron and Coal Deposits and a Prospectus with a View to Form a Company to Work the Same, by the proprietor, John Ross.* Halifax: Gossip and Coade, 1846.

G.F.R.B. "Edward John Littleton." In *Dictionary of National Biography,* vol. 33, 369–71. London: Oxford University Press, 1888.

"G.H." *The American Mines, Shewing their Importance in a National Point of View, with the Progress and Present Position of the Real Del Monte Company, and Cursory Remarks on Other Similar Undertakings in South America.* London: Effingham Wilson, 1834.

Grant, Robert. *East River Sketches, historical and biographical, with reminiscences of Scottish life.* New Glasgow: S.M. MacKenzie, 1895.

– *East River Worthies.* New Glasgow: Scotia Printers, 1895.

Hale, Robert. "A Voyage to Nova Scotia." *Historical Collections of the Essex Institute* 42 (1906): 217–43.

Haliburton, R.G. *The Coal Trade of the New Dominion.* Halifax: T. Chamberlain, 1868.

– *Explorations in the Pictou Coal Field.* Halifax: T. Chamberlain, 1868.

Haliburton, Thomas Chandler. *A General Description of Nova Scotia, illustrated by a new and correct map.* Halifax: Royal Acadian School, 1823.

– *Historical and Statistical Account of Nova Scotia.* 2 vols. Halifax: Howe, 1829.

– *The Old Judge, or Life in a Colony: A Selection of Sketches.* 1849. Reprint, Ottawa: Tecumseh Press, 1978.

Hamilton, Pierce S. *History of the County of Cumberland.* [Halifax]: n.p., 1880.

– *Nova-Scotia Considered as a Field for Emigration.* London: J. Weale, 1858.

Harvey, D.C., ed. *Holland's Description of Cape Breton Island and Other Documents.* Halifax: Public Archives of Nova Scotia, 1935.

Heatherington, Alexander. *A Practical Guide for Tourists, Miners, and Investors, and All Persons Interested in the Development of the Gold Fields of Nova Scotia.* Montreal: J. Lovell, 1868.

Hind, Henry Youle. *Eighty Years of Progress of British North America, showing the wonderful development of its natural resources by the unbounded energy and enterprise of its inhabitants, giving in a historical form, the vast improvements made in agriculture, commerce, and trade, modes of travel and transportation, mining and educational interests, etc., etc.* Toronto: L. Stebbins, 1863.

– *Report on the Sydney Collieries, Cape Breton.* Halifax: Nova Scotia Printing Company, 1871.

Homer, John. *A brief sketch of the present state of the province of Nova Scotia, with a project offered for its relief.* Halifax: n.p., 1834.

Howard, John Henry. *The Laws of the British Colonies in the West Indies and Other Parts of America Concerning Real and Personal Property and Manumission of Slaves, with a view of the constitution of each colony.* London: Butterworth, 1827.

Howe, Joseph. *Speech of Joseph Howe on Inter-Colonial Railroads and Colonization.* Halifax: R. Nugent, 1851.

– *Western and Eastern Rambles: Travel Sketches of Nova Scotia.* Ed. M.G. Parks. Toronto: University of Toronto Press, 1973.

Johnson, Walter R. *The Coal Trade of British America, with Researches on the Characters and Practical Values of American and Foreign Coals.* Washington, DC: Taylor and Maury, 1850.

Keefer, Thomas. *The Philosophy of Railroads, published at the request of the directors of the Montreal and Lachine Railroad.* Toronto: A.H. Armour, 1850.

Kendall, E.N., Commissioner. *Reports Nos. 1 and 2 on the State and Condition of the Province of New Brunswick, with some observations on the Company's Tract.* London: W. Day, 1835.

Knight, Thomas F. *Nova Scotia and Her Resources.* Halifax: A. & W. MacKinlay, 1862.

Longworth, Israel. *History of Colchester County, Nova Scotia.* 1886. Reprint, Truro, NS: Book Nook, 1989.

Lyell, Charles. *Travels in North America in the Years 1841–42, with Geological Observations on the United States, Canada, and Nova Scotia.* New York: Wiley and Putnam, 1845.

– and J.W. Dawson, "On the Remains of a Reptile (Denrepton Acadianum, Wyman and Owen) and of a Land Shell Discovered in the Interior of an Erect Fossil Tree in the Coal Measures of Nova Scotia." In Proceedings of the Geological Society, *Quarterly Journal* 9 (1853): 58–63.

Macdonald, Captain John. "Conditions of Settlement at Tatamagouche, Nova Scotia, 1795." In Government of Canada, Department of Archives, *Report*, xxvii-xliii. Ottawa: King's Printer, 1945.

MacLean, John. *An Address Delivered at a Quarterly Meeting of the Pictou and West River Temperance Societies in October 1833.* Halifax, W. Cunnabell, 1834.

Marsden, Joshua. *The Narrative of a Mission to Nova Scotia, New Brunswick, and the Somers Islands.* Plymouth-Dock, UK: J. Johns, 1816.

McCulloch, J.R. *A Dictionary, Practical, Theoretical, and Historical, of Commerce and Commercial Navigation.* London: Longman, Rees, 1834.

McCulloch, Thomas. *The Mephibosheth Stepsure Letters.* Ed. Gwendolyn Davies. Ottawa: Carleton University Press, 1990.

– *The nature and uses of a liberal education illustrated, being a lecture delivered at the opening of the building, erected for the accommodation of the classes of Pictou Academical Institution.* Halifax: A.H. Holland, 1819.

"Mechanic." *A Word in Season to the Fishermen and Famous of Nova Scotia.* Pictou: Colonial Patriot Office, 1833.

Moore, Stuart A. *A History of the Foreshore and the Law Relating Thereto, with a Hitherto Unpublished Treatise by Lord Hale, Lord Hale's "De Jure Maris," and*

Hall's Essay on the Rights of the Crown in the Sea-shore. London: Stevens and Hayes, 1888.

Moorsom, W.S. *Letters from Nova Scotia, comprising sketches of a young country.* London: H. Colburn and R. Bentley, 1830.

Mulhall, M.G. *The English in South America.* 1877. Reprint, New York: Arno, 1977.

Munro, A.H. *Characteristics of the Present Age, and the Duties of the Educated Classes.* Halifax: Christian Messenger, 1865.

New Brunswick and Nova Scotia Land Company. *Report of the Directors of the New Brunswick and Nova Scotia Land Company, Submitted to the Stockholders at a General Meeting Held at the London Tavern, on Monday, 2d July, 1832.* London: A. Taylor, 1832.

North American Colonial Association. *Colonization of the County of Beauharnois, on the south bank of the St. Lawrence, near the city of Montreal, and the junction of Lower and Upper Canada with the state of New York, together with the terms and conditions of sale of an extensive territory and diverse valuable properties in the said county of Beauharnois and the township of Clifton, including lands reserved for villages and towns, numerous houses, farm buildings, mills, farming stock, etc, etc.* London: Smith, Elder, 1840.

North American Colonial Association of Ireland. *Report of an Extraordinary Meeting of the Shareholders of the North American Colonial Association of Ireland Held at the Company's Office, Broad Street.* London: M'Kewan, 1844.

Patterson, George. *A History of the County of Pictou, Nova Scotia.* 1877. Reprint, Belleville, ON: Mika, 1972.

– *History of Victoria County.* 1885. Reprint, ed. W. James MacDonald. Sydney, NS: University College of Cape Breton Press, 1978.

Perley, Moses H. *Reports on the Sea and River Fisheries of New Brunswick.* 2nd ed. Fredericton: J. Simpson, 1852.

Poole, Henry S. *Notes on the Coal Field of Pictou.* N.p., 1860.

– and J. Campbell. *Additional Papers on the Nova Scotia Gold Fields.* Halifax: n.p., 1862.

Robinson, John, and Thomas Rispin, *A Journey through Nova Scotia, Containing a Particular Account of the Country and Its Inhabitants, with Observations on the Management in Husbandry, the Breed of Horses and Other Cattle, and every thing Material Relating to Farming to which is added an Account of several Estates for Sale in different Townships of Nova Scotia, with their Number of Acres, and the Price at which each is set.* York, UK: C. Etherington, 1774.

Rutherford, John. *A Letter to P.S. Hamilton, Esq., Chief Commissioner of Mines.* Halifax: A. Grant, 1867.

Sinclair, Sir John. *The Statistical Account of Scotland.* 20 vols. Edinburgh: Wm. Creech, 1798.

Smith, Adam. *An Inquiry into the Nature and Causes of the Wealth of Nations.* New York: Modern Library, 1937.

Smith, Titus. *Lecture on Mineralogy, delivered by Mr. Titus Smith, on March 5 1834, before the Halifax Mechanics' Institute.* Halifax: Cunnabell, 1834.

Society for Promoting Agriculture in the Province of Nova-Scotia. *Letters and papers on agriculture, extracted from the correspondence of a society instituted at Halifax, for promoting agriculture in the province of Nova-Scotia, to which is added a selection of papers on various branches of husbandry, from some of the best publications on the subject in Europe and America.* Halifax: Howe, 1791.

Taussig, F.W. *The Tariff History of the United States: A Series of Essays.* New York: G.P. Putnam, 1895.

Temperance Watchmen in North America. *Ritual of the Brotherhood of Temperance Watchmen in North America, initiated at Durham, Maine, 1849, revised in a new draft by the central committee, December 14, 1853, again revised by general convention at Durham, Nova Scotia, July 22, 1857.* Pictou: J.D. McDonald, 1860.

Trotter, Thomas. *The Principles of Meteorology.* Pictou: The Bee, 1837.

– *A treatise on geology, in which the discoveries of that science are reconciled with the scriptures and the ancient revolutions of the earth are shown to be sources of benefit to man.* Pictou: Geldert and Patterson, 1845.

White, Patrick C.T., ed. *Lord Selkirk's Diary, 1803–1804: A Journal of His Travels in British North America and the Northeastern United States.* Toronto: Champlain Society, 1958.

Young, George R. *Upon the History, Principles, and Prospects of the Bank of British North America and of the Colonial Bank, with an inquiry into colonial exchanges, and the expediency of introducing "British sterling and British coin" in preference to the "dollar" as the money account and currency of the North American colonies.* London: Wm. S. Orr, P. Richardson, and J. Ridgeway, 1838.

Young, John. *An Inquiry into the Impolicy of Fixing Wages by Law.* Glasgow: R. Chapman, 1813.

– *The Letters of Agricola on the Principles of Vegetation and Tillage, written for Nova Scotia and published first in the Acadian Recorder.* Halifax: Holland, 1822.

– *Letters of the Local Agricultural Societies, in reply to a circular of the Central Board.* Halifax: n.p., 1826.

– *Report of the Provincial Agricultural Society.* Halifax: n.p., 1823.

SECONDARY SOURCES

Reference

Burke, Sir Bernard, and Ashworth P. Burke, eds. *Genealogical and Heraldic History of the Peerage and Baronetage, the Privy Council, Knightage and Companionage.* 72nd ed. London: Harrison and Sons, 1913.

Dictionary of Canadian Biography. Vols 4–12. Toronto: University of Toronto Press, 1972–90.

Dictionary of National Biography. London: Smith, Elder, 1885–1904.

Dominion of Canada. *Report of the Department of Archives.* Ottawa: Dominion of Canada, 1894–96, 1945–48.

Elliot, Shirley B. *The Legislative Assembly of Nova Scotia, 1758–1983: A Biographical Directory.* Halifax: Province of Nova Scotia, 1984.

Ells, Margaret, comp. *A Calendar of Official Correspondence and Legislative Papers, Nova Scotia, 1802–1815.* Halifax: Public Archives of Nova Scotia, 1936.

An Etymological Dictionary of the Scottish Language. Paisley: Alexander Gardner, 1880.

Fergusson, C.B., ed. *Place-Names and Places of Nova Scotia.* 1967. Reprint, Belleville, ON: Mika, 1974.

Innis, H.A., and A.R.M. Lower, eds. *Select Documents in Canadian Economic History, 1783–1885.* Toronto: University of Toronto Press, 1933.

Nichols, C.S., ed. *The Dictionary of National Biography, Missing Persons.* Oxford: Oxford University Press, 1994.

Oxford English Dictionary. Oxford: Clarendon Press, 1961.

Robinson, Mairi, ed. *The Concise Scots Dictionary.* Aberdeen: Aberdeen University Press, 1987.

Books and Articles

Acheson, T.W. "The Great Merchant and Economic Development in Saint John, 1820–50." *Acadiensis* 8, no. 2 (Spring 1979): 3–27.

– "The National Policy and the Industrialization of the Maritimes, 1880–1910." *Acadiensis* 1, no. 2 (Spring 1972): 3–28.

– *Saint John: The Making of a Colonial Urban Community.* Toronto: University of Toronto Press, 1985.

Allison, David. *History of Nova Scotia.* Vol. 2. Halifax: A.W. Bowen, 1916.

Ankli, Robert E., and Kenneth J. Duncan, "Farm Making Costs in Early Ontario." *Canadian Papers in Rural History* 4 (1984): 33–49.

Apostle, Richard, and Gene Barrett. *Emptying Their Nets: Small Capital and Rural Industrialization in the Nova Scotia Fishing Industry.* Toronto: University of Toronto Press, 1992.

Appleby, Joyce. "Commercial Farming and the 'Agrarian Myth' in the Early Republic." *Journal of American History* 68 (1982): 833–49.

– *Liberalism and Republicanism in the Historical Imagination.* Cambridge, MA: Harvard University Press, 1992.

Arblaster, Anthony. *The Rise and Decline of Western Liberalism.* Oxford: Basil Blackwell, 1984.

Bailey, A.G. "The Historical Setting of Haliburton's Reply." In Thomas Chandler Haliburton, *A Reply to the Report of the Earl of Durham*, ed. A.G. Bailey, 1–7. Ottawa: Golden Dog Press, 1976.

Bailyn, Bernard. *Voyagers to the West: A Passage in the Peopling of America on the Eve of the Revolution*. New York: Vintage, 1986.

Baron, Ava. "Gender and Labor History: Learning from the Past, Looking to the Future." In Ava Baron, ed., *Work Engendered: Toward a New History of American Labor*, 1–46. Ithaca: Cornell University Press, 1991.

Bayly, C.A. *Imperial Meridian: The British Empire and the World, 1780–1830*. London: Longman, 1989.

Beattie, Betsy. *Obligation and Opportunity: Single Maritime Women in Boston, 1870–1930*. Montreal and Kingston: McGill-Queen's University Press, 2000.

Beck, J.M. "Alexander Stewart." In *Dictionary of Canadian Biography*, vol. 9, 746–8. Toronto: University of Toronto Press, 1976.

– *The Government of Nova Scotia*. Toronto: University of Toronto Press, 1957.

– *Joseph Howe*. Vol. 1, *Conservative Reformer, 1804–48*. Montreal and Kingston: McGill-Queen's University Press, 1984.

– *Joseph Howe*. Vol. 2, *The Briton Becomes Canadian*. Montreal and Kingston: McGill-Queen's University Press, 1985.

– "Jotham Blanchard." In *Dictionary of Canadian Biography*, vol. 12, 81–5. Toronto: University of Toronto Press, 1984.

– *Politics of Nova Scotia*. Vol. 1, *1710–1896*. Tantallon, NS: Four East, 1985.

Bell, Winthrop. *The "Foreign Protestants" and the Settlement of Nova Scotia: The History of a Piece of Arrested British Colonial Policy in the Eighteenth Century*. Toronto: University of Toronto Press, 1961.

Belshaw, John Douglas. *Colonization and Community: The Vancouver Island Coalfield and the Making of the British Columbia Working Class*. Montreal and Kingston: McGill-Queen's University Press, 2002.

Berman, Marshall. *All That Is Solid Melts into Air: The Experience of Modernity*. New York: Simon and Schuster, 1982.

Bittermann, Rusty. "Economic Stratification and Agrarian Settlement: Middle River in the Early Nineteenth Century." In Kenneth Donovan, ed., *The Island: New Perspectives on Cape Breton History*, 71–87. Fredericton: Acadiensis Press, 1990.

– "Farm Households and Wage Labour in the Northeastern Maritimes before 1850." In Daniel Samson, ed., *Contested Countryside: Rural Workers and Modern Society in Atlantic Canada, 1800–1950*, 34–69. Fredericton: Acadiensis Press, 1994.

– "The Hierarchy of the Soil: Land and Labour in a 19th Century Cape Breton Community." *Acadiensis* 18, no. 1 (Autumn 1988): 33–55.

- *Rural Protest on Prince Edward Island: From British Colonization to Escheat Movement.* Toronto: University of Toronto Press, 2006.
- "Women and the Escheat Movement: The Politics of Everyday Life on Prince Edward Island." In Janet Guildford and Suzanne Morton, eds, *Separate Spheres: Women's Worlds in the 19th-Century Maritimes*, 23–38. Fredericton: Acadiensis Press, 1994.
- Robert A. MacKinnon, and Graeme Wynn. "Of Inequality and Interdependence in the Nova Scotian Countryside, 1850–70." *Canadian Historical Review* 74, no. 1 (1993): 1–43.
Blaikie, Andrew. "Coastal Communities in Victorian Scotland: What Makes North-East Fisher Families Distinctive." *Local Population Studies* 69 (2002): 15–31.
Blakeley, Phyllis R. "Samuel Cunard." In *Dictionary of Canadian Biography*, vol. 9, 172–86. Toronto: University of Toronto Press, 1976.
Bouchard, Gérard. "Co-integration et reproduction de la societié rurale: Pour un modele sagueayen de la marginalité." *Recherches sociographiques* 29 (1988): 283–309.
- "Economic Inequalities in Saguenay Society, 1879–1949: A Descriptive Analysis." *Canadian Historical Review* 79, no. 4 (1998): 660–90.
- "Family Reproduction in Rural Areas: Outline of a North American Model." *Canadian Historical Review* 75, no. 4 (1994): 475–510.
- "La sexualité comme practique et rapport social chez les couples paysans du Saguenay, 1860–1930." *Revue d'histoire lAmérique Francaise* 54, no. 2 (2000): 183–217.
Boydston, Jeanne. *Home and Work: Housework, Wages, and the Ideology of Labor in the Early Republic.* Oxford: Oxford University Press, 1990.
Bradbury, Bettina. "Pigs, Cows, and Boarders: Non-Wage Forms of Survival among Montreal Families, 1861–1891." *Labour/Le Travail* 15 (Spring 1985): 7–22.
- "Widowhood and Canadian Family History." In Margaret Conrad, ed., *Intimate Relations: Family and Community in Planter Nova Scotia, 1759–1800*, 19–41. Fredericton: Acadiensis Press, 1995.
Brebner, J.B. *The Neutral Yankees of Nova Scotia: A Marginal Colony during the Revolutionary Years.* New York: Columbia University Press, 1937.
Brenner, Robert. "Agrarian Class Structure and Economic Development in Pre-Industrial Europe." In T.H. Aston and C.H.E. Philpin, eds, *The Brenner Debate: Agrarian Class Structure and Economic Development in Pre-Industrial Europe*, 10–63. Cambridge, UK: Cambridge University Press, 1985.
Brun, Régis, comp. "Un registre de l'état civil des habitants de Franklin Manor, des Champs-élysées, de Maccan et de Nappan." *Cahiers de la Societe Historique Acadienne* 2, no. 3 (October 1966).

Buckner, Phillip A. *The Transition to Responsible Government: British Policy in British North America, 1815–1850*. Westport CT: Greenwood Press, 1985.

Buggey, Susan. "Edward Mortimer." In *Dictionary of Canadian Biography*, vol. 5, 434–5. Toronto: University of Toronto Press, 1983.

Bumsted, J.M. *The People's Clearances: Highland Emigration to British North America, 1770–1815*. Winnipeg: University of Manitoba Press, 1982.

Bunbury, Dan. "Safe Haven for the Poor? Depositors and the Government Savings Banks in Halifax, 1832–67." *Acadiensis* 24, no. 2 (Spring 1995): 24–48.

Bushman, Richard L. "Family Security in the Transition from Farm to City, 1750–1850." *Journal of Family History* 6 (Fall 1981): 238–55.

– "Markets and Composite Farms in Early America." *William and Mary Quarterly* 55, no. 3 (1998): 351–74.

Byers, Mary, and Margaret McBurney. *Atlantic Hearth: Early Homes and Families of Nova Scotia*. Toronto: University of Toronto Press, 1994.

Cain, P.J., and A.G Hopkins. *British Imperialism: Innovation and Expansion, 1688–1914*. London: Longman, 1993.

Cameron, James M. "Disasters in the Pictou Collieries." In Nova Scotia Historical Society, *Collections* 38 (1973): 127–56.

– *Industrial History of the New Glasgow District*. New Glasgow: n.p., 1970.

Campbell, Alan. *The Lanarkshire Miners: A Social History of the Their Trade Unions, 1775–1974*. Edinburgh: John Donald, 1979.

Campbell, D., and R.A. MacLean. *Beyond the Atlantic Roar: A Study of the Nova Scotia Scots*. Toronto: McClelland and Stewart, 1974.

Campbell, Gail. "Disfranchised but Not Quiescent: Women Petitioners in New Brunswick in the Mid-19th Century." *Acadiensis* 18, no. 2 (Spring 1989): 22–54.

Campbell, R.H. "The Enlightenment and the Economy." In R.H. Campbell and Andrew S. Skinner, eds, *The Origins and Nature of the Scottish Enlightenment*, 8–25. Edinburgh: John Donald, 1982.

Cann, D.B., J.I. MacDougall, and J.D. Hilchey. "Soil Survey of Cape Breton Island, Nova Scotia." In *Nova Scotia Soil Survey*. Report no. 12. Truro, NS: Federal Department of Agriculture, 1963.

– and R.E. Wicklund. "Soil Survey of Pictou County, Nova Scotia." In *Nova Scotia Soil Survey*. Report no. 4. Truro, NS: Federal Department of Agriculture, 1950.

Chakrabarty, Dipesh. "Postcoloniality and the Artifice of History: Who Speaks for Colonial 'Indian' Pasts?" *Representations* 37 (Winter 1992): 1–26.

– *Rethinking Working-Class History: Bengal, 1890–1940*. Princeton: Princeton University Press, 1989.

Chaplin, Joyce E. *An Anxious Pursuit: Agricultural Innovation and Modernity in the Lower South, 1730–1815*. Chapel Hill: University of North Carolina Press, 1993.

Christie, Nancy J. "'In These Times of Democratic Rage and Delusion': Popular Religion and the Challenge to the Established Order, 1760–1815." In George Rawlyk, ed., *The Canadian Protestant Experience, 1760–1990*, 9–47. Burlington, ON: Welch, 1990.

Clark, A.H. *Three Centuries and the Island: A Historical Geography of Settlement and Agriculture in Prince Edward Island*. Toronto: University of Toronto Press, 1959.

– "Titus Smith, Junior, and the Geography of Nova Scotia in 1801 and 1802." In Association of American Geographers, *Annals* 44, no. 4 (December 1954): 291–314.

Clark, Christopher. *The Roots of Rural Capitalism: Western Massachusetts, 1780–1860*. Ithaca: Cornell University Press, 1990.

Clarke, George Elliott, ed. *Fire on the Water: An Anthology of Black Nova Scotian Writing*. Lawrencetown Beach, NS: Pottersfield, 1991.

Clawson, Mary Ann. *Constructing Brotherhood: Class, Gender and Fraternalism*. Princeton: Princeton University Press, 1989.

Cohen, Marjorie Griffin. *Women's Work, Markets, and Economic Development in Nineteenth-Century Ontario*. Toronto: University of Toronto Press, 1988.

Colls, Robert. *The Pitmen of the Northern Coalfield: Work, Culture, and Protest, 1790–1850*. Manchester: Manchester University Press, 1987.

Cottrell, P.L. *British Overseas Investment in the Nineteenth Century*. London: Macmillan, 1975.

Courville, Serge. "Croissance villageoise et industries rurales dans les seigneuries du Québec (1815–1851)." In François LeBrun and Normand Séguin, eds, *Sociétés villageoises et rapports villes-campagnes au Québec et dans la France de l'Ouest, XVIIᵉ-XXᵉ siècles*, 205–19. Trois-Rivières: Centre de recherches en Études québécoises, 1987.

– "Un monde rural en mutation: Le Bas-Canada dans la première moité du XIXᵉ siècle." *Histoire sociale/Social History* 40 (1987): 237–58.

– Jean-Claude Robert, and Normand Séguin. "The Spread of Rural Industry in Lower Canada, 1831–1851." *Journal of the Canadian Historical Association* (1991): 41–70.

Cowen, M.P., and R.W. Shenton. *Doctrines of Development*. London: Routledge, 1996.

Craig, Béatrice. "Le développement agricole dans la haute vallée de la riviere Saint-Jean en 1860." *Journal of the Canadian Historical Association* 3 (1992): 13–26.

– "Solder les comptes: Les sources de credits dans les magasins generaux ruraux de l'est canadien au milieu du XIXᵉ." *Journal of the Canadian Historical Association* 13 (2002): 23–47.

– Judith Rygiel, and Elizabeth Turcotte. "The Homespun Paradox: Market-
Oriented Production of Cloth in Eastern Canada in the Nineteenth Century." *Agricultural History* 76, no. 1 (2002): 28–57.

Cronon, William. *Changes in the Land: Indians, Colonists, and the Ecology of New
England.* New York: Hill and Wang, 1983.

Cross, Michael. "'The Laws Are Like Cobwebs': Popular Resistance to Authority in Mid-Nineteenth Century British North America." In Peter Waite, San-
dra Oxner, and Thomas Barnes, eds, *Law in a Colonial Society: The Nova Scotia
Experience,* 103–23. Toronto: Carswell, 1984.

– ed. *The Frontier Thesis and the Canadas: The Debate on the Impact of the Canadian
Environment.* Toronto: Copp Clark Pitman, 1970.

Curtis, Bruce. "The Canada 'Blue Books' and the Administrative Capacity of
the Canadian State, 1822–67." *Canadian Historical Review* 74, no. 4 (1993):
535–65.

– "Foucault on Governmentality and Population: The Impossible Discovery."
Canadian Journal of Sociology 27, no. 4 (Fall 2002): 505–33.

– *The Politics of Population: State Formation, Statistics, and the Census of Canada,
1840–1875.* Toronto: University of Toronto Press, 2001.

– *True Government by Choice Men? Inspection, Education, and State Formation in
Canada West.* Toronto: University of Toronto Press, 1992.

Cuthbertson, Brian. *The First Bishop: A Biography of Charles Inglis.* Halifax: Waeg-
woltic Press, 1987.

– *Johnny Bluenose at the Polls: Epic Nova Scotian Election Battles, 1758–1848.* Halifax:
Formac, 1994.

– *The Loyalist Governor: A Biography of Sir John Wentworth.* Halifax: Petheric
Press, 1983.

Darroch, Gordon. "Scanty Fortunes and Rural Middle Class Formation in
Nineteenth Century Central Ontario." *Canadian Historical Review* 79, no. 4
(1998): 621–59.

– and Lee Soltow. *Property and Inequality in Victorian Ontario: Structural Patterns
and Cultural Communities in the 1871 Census.* Toronto: University of Toronto
Press, 1994.

Davidoff, Leonore, and Catherine Hall. *Family Fortunes: Men and Women of the
English Middle Class, 1780–1850.* Chicago: University of Chicago Press, 1987.

Dawson, Frank Griffith. *The First Latin American Debt Crisis: The City of London
and the 1822–25 Loan Bubble.* New Haven: Yale University Press, 1990.

Day, Gordon, ed. *Geographical Perspectives on the Maritime Provinces.* Halifax: St Mary's
University Press, 1988.

de la Cour, Lykke, Cecillia Morgan, and Mariana Valverde. "Gender Regulation and State Formation in Nineteenth-Century Canada." In Allan Greer

and Ian Radforth, eds, *Colonial Leviathan: State Formation in Mid-Nineteenth Century Canada*, 163–91. Toronto: University of Toronto Press, 1992.

DesBarats, Catherine. "Agriculture within the Seigneurial Regime of Eighteenth-Century Canada: Some Thoughts on the Recent Literature." *Canadian Historical Review* 73, no. 1 (1992): 1–29.

Devine, T.M. *The Great Highland Famine.* Edinburgh: John Donald, 1988.

– *Improvement and Enlightenment: Proceedings of the Scottish Historical Studies Seminar.* Edinburgh: John Donald, 1989.

– "Social Responses to Agrarian 'Improvement': The Highland and Lowland Clearances in Scotland." In R.A. Houston and I.D. Whyte, eds, *Scottish Society, 1500–1800*, 149–68. Cambridge, UK: Cambridge University Press, 1989.

Dunlop, Allan C. "Peter Barrett's Pictou County: From the Fenian Scare to the Drummond Colliery Explosion." *Nova Scotia Historical Review* 14, no. 1 (1994): 135–52.

– "Pharmacist and Entrepreneur: Pictou's J.D.B. Fraser." *Nova Scotia Historical Quarterly* 4, no. 1 (1974): 1–22.

Dunn, Charles W. *Highland Settler: A Portrait of the Scottish Gael in Cape Breton and Eastern Nova Scotia.* Toronto: University of Toronto Press, 1953.

Ells, Margaret. "Governor Wentworth's Patronage." *Collections of the Nova Scotia Historical Society* 25 (1942): 49–74.

Errington, E. Jane. *The Lion, the Eagle, and Upper Canada: A Developing Colonial Ideology.* Montreal and Kingston: McGill-Queen's University Press, 1987.

Evans, G.N.D. *Uncommon Obdurate: The Several Public Careers of J.F.W. Desbarres.* Salem, MA: Peabody Museum, 1969.

Fecteau, Jean-Marie. "État et associationnisme au XIXe siècle québécois: Éléments pour une problématique des rapports État/société dans le transition au capitalisme." In Allan Greer and Ian Radforth, eds, *Colonial Leviathan: State Formation in Mid-Nineteenth-Century Canada*, 134–62. Toronto: University of Toronto Press, 1992.

– *Un nouvel ordre des chose: La pauvreté, le crime, l'État au Québec, de la fin du XVIIIe siècle à 1840.* Outremont, QC: VLP Éditeur, 1989.

Fereday, R.P. "The Career of Richard Smith." Published in *Acorn*, the house magazine of Round Oaks Steel Works, Limited, Brierly Hill, West Midlands, United Kingdom. Available at the NSARM Library, call no. V/F V.282 #22.

Fergusson, C.B. *A Documentary Study of the Establishment of the Negroes in Nova Scotia.* Halifax: Public Archives of Nova Scotia, 1948.

– *The Labour Movement in Nova Scotia before Confederation.* Halifax: Public Archives of Nova Scotia, 1964.

– *Mechanics' Institutes in Nova Scotia.* Halifax: Public Archives of Nova Scotia, 1960.

Ferleger, Lou, ed. *Agriculture and National Development: Views on the Nineteenth Century.* Ames: Iowa State University Press, 1990.

Fingard, Judith. "Sir John Wentworth." In *Dictionary of Canadian Biography,* vol. 5, 848–52. Toronto: University of Toronto Press, 1983.

Fleming, Sandford. "Notes on Ocean Steam Navigation." *Transactions of the Canadian Institute* 3 (1891–92): 167–8.

Flinn, M.W. *The History of the British Coal Industry.* Vol. 2, *1700–1830: The Industrial Revolution.* Oxford, Clarendon Press, 1984.

Forbes, E.R. *Maritime Rights: The Maritime Rights Movement: A Study in Canadian Regionalism, 1919–1927.* Montreal and Kingston: McGill-Queen's University Press, 1979.

– and D.A. Muise, eds. *The Atlantic Provinces in Confederation.* Toronto: University of Toronto Press, 1993.

Foucault, Michel. *Discipline and Punish: The Birth of the Prison.* 1975. Reprint, New York, Pantheon, 1979.

– *The History of Sexuality.* Vol. 1, *Introduction.* New York: Pantheon, 1990.

– "On Governmentality." In Graham Burchell, Colin Gordon, and Peter Miller, eds, *The Foucault Effect: Studies in Governmentality,* 87–104. Chicago: University of Chicago Press, 1991.

Fowke, Vernon C. *Canadian Agricultural Policy: The Historical Pattern.* Toronto: University of Toronto Press, 1946.

Fox-Genovese, Elizabeth, and Eugene Genovese. *Fruits of Merchant Capital: Slavery and Bourgeois Property in the Rise and Expansion of Capitalism.* New York: Monthly Review, 1984.

Frank, David. "The Country of Coal." *Labour/Le Travail* 21 (Spring 1988): 233–42.

– "The Industrial Folk Song in Cape Breton." *Canadian Folklore canadien* 8, nos 1–2 (1986): 21–42.

– "Richard Smith." In *Dictionary of Canadian Biography,* vol. 8, 730–2. Toronto: University of Toronto Press, 1985.

Gaffield, Chad. *Language, Schooling and Cultural Conflict: The Origins of the French-Language Controversy in Canada.* Montreal and Kingston: McGill-Queen's University Press, 1987.

Gagan, David. *Hopeful Travellers: Families, Land, and Social Change in Mid-Victorian Peel County, Canada West.* Toronto: University of Toronto Press, 1981.

Garner, John. *The Franchise and Politics in British North America, 1755–1867.* Toronto: University of Toronto Press, 1969.

Gee, Ellen M.T. "Marriage in Nineteenth-Century Canada." *Canadian Review of Sociology and Anthropology* 3 (1982): 311–25.

Gerriets, Marilynn. "Agricultural Resources, Agricultural Production, and Settlement at Confederation." *Acadiensis* 31, no. 2 (2002): 129–56.

- "The Impact of the General Mining Association on the Nova Scotia Coal Industry, 1826–1850." *Acadiensis* 21, no. 1 (Autumn 1991): 54–84.
- "The Rise and Fall of a Free-Standing Company in Nova Scotia: The General Mining Association." *Business History* 34, no. 3 (July 1992): 16–48.

Girard, Philip. "Land Law, Liberalism, and the Agrarian Ideal: British North America, 1750–1920." In John McLaren, A.R. Buck, and Nancy E. Wright, eds, *Despotic Dominions: Property Rights in Settler Societies*, 120–43. Vancouver: University of British Columbia Press, 2005.

Gootenberg, Paul. *Imagining Development: Economic Ideas in Peru's "Fictitious Prosperity" of Guano, 1840–1880*. Berkeley: University of California Press, 1993.

Gossage, Peter. "Family Formation and Age of Marriage in Saint-Hyacinthe, Quebec, 1854–1891." *Histoire sociale/Social History* 47 (1991): 61–84.

Graham, Gerald S. "The Gypsum Trade of the Maritime Provinces: Its Relation to American Diplomacy and Agriculture in the Early Nineteenth Century." *Agricultural History* 12, no. 3 (1938): 209–23.
- *Sea Power and British North America, 1783–1820: A Study in British Colonial Policy*. Cambridge, MA: Harvard University Press, 1941.

Greer, Allan. "Introduction." In Allan Greer and Ian Radforth, eds, *Colonial Leviathan: State Formation in Mid-Nineteenth Century Canada*, 3–16. Toronto: University of Toronto Press, 1992.
- *The Patriots and the People: The Rebellion of 1837 in Rural Lower Canada*. Toronto: University of Toronto Press, 1993.
- and Ian Radforth, eds. *Colonial Leviathan: State Formation in Mid-Nineteenth Century Canada*. Toronto: University of Toronto Press, 1992.

Griffiths, N.E.S. *The Contexts of Acadian History, 1686–1784*. Montreal and Kingston: McGill-Queen's University Press, 1992.
- *From Migrant to Acadian: A North American Border People, 1604–1755*. Montreal and Kingston: McGill-Queen's University Press, 2005.

Guha, Ranajit. *Elementary Aspects of Peasant Insurgency in Colonial India*. Delhi: Oxford University Press, 1983.
- "The Prose of Counter-Insurgency." In Ranajit Guha and Gayatri Spivak, eds, *Selected Subaltern Studies*, 45–86. New York: Oxford University Press, 1988.

Gunn, Simon. "From Hegemony to Governmentality: Changing Conceptions of Power in Social History." *Journal of Social History* 39, no. 3 (Spring 2006): 705–20.

Gwyn, Julian. *Excessive Expectations: Maritime Commerce and the Economic Development of Nova Scotia, 1740–1870*. Montreal and Kingston: McGill-Queen's University Press, 1998.
- "'A Little Province Like This': The Economy of Nova Scotia Under Stress, 1812–1853." *Canadian Papers in Rural History* 6 (1988): 192–225.

– "The Mi'kmaq, Poor Settlers, and the Nova Scotia Fur Trade, 1783–1853." *Journal of the Canadian Historical Association* 14 (2003): 65–91.

Gwynn, Julian, and Fazley Siddiq. "Wealth Distribution in Nova Scotia during the Confederation Era, 1851 and 1871." *Canadian Historical Review* 73, no. 4 (1992): 435–52.

Haines, Michael R. *Fertility and Occupation: Coal Mining Populations in the Nineteenth Century and Early Twentieth Centuries in Europe and America.* Ithaca: Western Societies Program, Occasional Papers, Cornell University, 1975.

– *Fertility and Occupation: Population Patterns in Industrialization.* New York: Academic Press, 1979.

Hall, Catherine. *Civilising Subjects: Colony and Metropole in the English Imagination, 1830–1867.* Chicago: University of Chicago Press, 2002.

– "Imperial Man: Edward Eyre in Australasia and the West Indies, 1833–66." In Bill Schwarz, ed., *The Expansion of England: Race, Ethnicity, and Cultural History,* 133–44. London: Routledge, 1996.

Hall, Stuart. "Cultural Identity and Diaspora." In Jonathan Rutherford, ed., *Identity: Community, Culture, Difference,* 222–37. London: Lawrence and Wishart, 1990.

Hahn, Steven, and Jonathan Prude, eds. *The Countryside in the Age of Capitalist Transformation: Essays in the Social History of Rural America.* Chapel Hill: University of North Carolina Press, 1985.

Hardy, René. *La Sidérurgie dans le Monde Rural: Les Hauts Fourneaux du Québec au XIXe Siècle.* Quebec: Press de l'Université de Laval, 1995.

– and Normand Séguin. *Forêt et société en Mauricie: La formation de la région de Trois-Rivières, 1830–1930.* Montreal: Boréal, 1944.

Harrison, Royden, ed. *The Independent Collier: The Coal Miner as "Archetypal Proletarian" Reconsidered.* New York: St Martin's, 1979.

Harvey, D.C. "The Civil List and Responsible Government in Nova Scotia." *Canadian Historical Review* 28, no. 4 (December 1947): 365–82.

– "The Intellectual Awakening of Nova Scotia." *Dalhousie Review* 13 (1933): 1–22.

– "Pre-Agricola John Young, or A Compact Family in Search of Fortune." *Collections of the Nova Scotia Historical Society* 32 (1959): 125–59.

– "Scottish Immigration to Cape Breton." *Dalhousie Review* 22 (1941): 313–24.

Heckscher, Eli. *Mercantilism.* Vol. 2. 1931. Reprint, London: George Allen and Unwin, 1955.

Hewitt, Martin. "Science, Popular Culture, and the Producer Alliance in Saint John, N.B." In Paul A. Bogaard, ed., *Profiles of Science and Society in the Maritimes prior to 1914,* 243–75. Fredericton: Acadiensis Press, 1990.

– "Science as Spectacle: Popular Scientific Culture in Saint John, New Brunswick, 1830–1850." *Acadiensis* 18, no. 1 (Autumn 1988): 91–119.

Hilton, Boyd. *Corn, Cash, Commerce: The Economic Policies of the Tory Governments, 1815–1830.* Oxford: Oxford University Press, 1977.

Hirschman, Albert O. *The Passion and the Interests: Political Arguments for Capitalism before Its Triumph.* Princeton: Princeton University Press, 1977.

Hobsbawm, Eric. *Industry and Empire: From 1750 to the Present Day.* Harmondsworth: Penguin, 1969.

Hornsby, Stephen J. *Nineteenth-Century Cape Breton: A Historical Geography.* Montreal and Kingston: McGill-Queen's University Press, 1992.

Howkins, Alun. *Reshaping Rural England: A Social History, 1850–1925.* London, Harper Collins, 1991.

Hunter, James. *A Dance Called America: The Scottish Highlands, the United States, and Canada.* Edinburgh: Mainstream, 1994.

Innis, H.A. *The Cod Fisheries: The History of an International Economy.* 1940. Reprint, Toronto: University of Toronto Press, 1954.

– and A.R.M. Lower, eds. *Select Documents in Canadian Economic History, 1783–1885.* Toronto: University of Toronto Press, 1933.

Inwood, Kris, ed. *Farm, Factory and Fortune: New Studies in the Economic History of the Maritime Provinces.* Fredericton: Acadiensis Press, 1993.

– and Phyllis Wagg. "The Survival of Handloom Weaving in Rural Canada, ca. 1870." *Journal of Economic History* 53, no. 2 (1993): 356–8.

– and Phyllis Wagg. "Wealth and Prosperity in Nova Scotia Agriculture, 1851–71." *Canadian Historical Review* 75, no. 2 (1994): 239–64.

Jaffe, James A. *The Struggle for Market Power: Industrial Relations in the British Coal Industry, 1800–1840.* Cambridge, UK: Cambridge University Press, 1991.

Jefferson, H.B. "Mount Rundell, Stellarton, and the Albion Railway of 1839." *Collections of the Nova Scotia Historical Quarterly* 34 (1966): 81–120.

Jenks, Leland Hamilton. *The Migration of British Capital to 1875.* New York: Knopf, 1927.

Jones, Robert Leslie. *History of Agriculture in Ontario, 1613–1880.* Toronto: University of Toronto Press, 1946.

Johnston, A.A. *A History of the Catholic Church in Eastern Nova Scotia.* Vol. 1, *1611–1827.* Antigonish, NS: St Francis Xavier University Press, 1960.

Johnston, H.J.M. *British Emigration Policy, 1815–1830: "Shovelling out Paupers."* Oxford: Clarendon Press, 1972.

Joseph, Gilbert M., and Daniel Nugent, eds. *Everyday Forms of State Formation: Revolution and the Negotiation of Rule in Modern Mexico.* Durham: Duke University Press, 1994.

Joyce, Patrick. *Democratic Subjects: The Self and the Social in 19th-Century England.* Cambridge, UK: Cambridge University Press, 1994.

– *The Rule of Freedom: Liberalism and the Modern City.* London: Verso, 2003.

Judd, Richard. *Common Lands, Common People: The Origins of Conservation in Northern New England.* Cambridge, MA: Harvard University Press, 1997.

Kealey, G.S., ed. *Class, Gender, and Region: Essays in Canadian Historical Sociology.* St John's: Committee on Canadian Labour History, 1988.

Keefer, Janice Kulyk. *Under Eastern Eyes: A Critical Reading of Maritime Fiction.* Toronto: University of Toronto Press, 1987.

Kernaghan, Lois D. "A Man and His Mistress: J.F.W. DesBarres and Mary Cannon." *Acadiensis* 11, no. 1 (Autumn 1981): 23–42.

Kincaid, Barbara. "Scottish Immigration to Cape Breton, 1758–1838." MA thesis, Dalhousie University, 1964.

Kulikoff, Allan. *From British Peasants to Colonial American Farmers.* Chapel Hill: University of North Carolina Press, 2000.

Langout, Rosemarie. "Developing Nova Scotia: Railways and Public Accounts, 1848–1867." *Acadiensis* 14, no. 2 (Spring 1985): 3–28.

Latta, Peter. "The Lower Cove Grindstone Quarries." *Journal of the Society for Industrial Archaeology* 11 (1985): 67–72.

Leneman, Leah, and Rosalind Mitchison. "Girls in Trouble: The Social and Geographical Settling of Illegitimacy in Early Modern Scotland." *Journal of Social History* 22, no. 3 (1988): 483–97.

Lewis, F., and M. McInnis. "Agricultural Output and Efficiency in Lower Canada." *Research in Economic History* 9 (1984): 45–87.

Little, J.I. *Crofters and Habitants: Settler Society, Economy, and Culture in a Quebec Township, 1848–1881.* Montreal and Kingston: McGill-Queen's University Press, 1991.

– *Nationalism, Capitalism, and Colonization in Nineteenth-Century Quebec: The Upper St Francis District.* Montreal and Kingston: McGill-Queen's University Press, 1989.

– *State and Society in Transition: The Politics of Institutional Reform in the Eastern Townships, 1838–1852.* Montreal and Kingston: McGill-Queen's University Press, 1997.

Livesay, James. "Agrarian Ideology and Commercial Republicanism in the French Revolution." *Past and Present* 157 (November 1997): 94–121.

Lloyd Prichard, M.F., ed. *The Collected Works of Edward Gibbon Wakefield.* Glasgow: Collins, 1968.

Loo, Tina. *Making Law, Order, and Authority in British Columbia, 1821–1871.* Toronto: University of Toronto Press, 1994.

Love, Joseph E., and Nels Jacobsen, eds. *Guiding the Invisible Hand: Economic Liberalism and the State in Latin America.* New York: Praeger, 1988.

Macgillivray, Donald. "Henry Melville Whitney Comes to Cape Breton: The Saga of a Gilded Age Entrepreneur." *Acadiensis* 9, no. 1 (Autumn 1979): 44–70.

MacInnis, Marvin. "The Size and Structure of Farming in Canada West, 1861." *Research in Economic History*, supplement 5, part B (1989): 313–29.

– "Women, Work and Childbearing: Ontario in the Second Half of the Nineteenth Century." *Histoire sociale/Social History* 48 (1991): 237–62.

Macintyre, Stuart. *A Colonial Liberalism: The Lost World of Three Victorian Visionaries*. Melbourne: Oxford University Press, 1991.

MacKenzie, A.A. "Amos Peck Seaman." In *Dictionary of Canadian Biography*, vol. 9, 709–10. Toronto: University of Toronto Press, 1976.

MacKinnon, Robert A. "Roads, Cart Tracks, and Bridle Paths: Land Transportation and the Domestic Economy of Mid-Nineteenth-Century Eastern British North America." *Canadian Historical Review* 84, no. 2 (2003): 177–216.

MacLean, R.A. "John Young." In *Dictionary of Canadian Biography*, vol. 5, 930–5. Toronto: University of Toronto Press, 1983.

MacMullin, Stanley. "In Search of the Liberal Mind: Thomas McCulloch and the Impulse to Action." *Journal of Canadian Studies* 23, nos 1–2 (Spring/Summer 1988): 68–85.

MacNeil, Alan R. "The Acadian Legacy and Agricultural Development in Nova Scotia, 1760–1861." In Kris Inwood, ed., *Farm, Factory and Fortune: New Studies in the Economic History of the Maritime Provinces*. Fredericton: Acadiensis Press, 1993.

– "Society and Economy in Rural Nova Scotia, 1761–1861." PhD thesis, Queen's University, 1990.

MacNutt, W.S. *The Atlantic Provinces: The Emergence of Colonial Society, 1712–1857*. Toronto: McClelland and Stewart, 1965.

– *New Brunswick: A History, 1784–1867*. Toronto: MacMillan, 1963.

Mancke, Elizabeth. "At the Counter of the General Store: Women and the Economy in Eighteenth-Century Horton, Nova Scotia." In Margaret Conrad, ed., *Intimate Relations: Family and Community in Planter Nova Scotia, 1759–1800*, 167–81. Fredericton: Acadiensis Press, 1995.

– "Corporate Structure and Private Interest: The Mid-Eighteenth Century of New England." In Margaret Conrad, ed., *They Planted Well: New England Planters in Maritime Canada*, 161–77. Fredericton: Acadiensis Press, 1988.

– "Early Modern Imperial Governance and the Origins of Canadian Political Culture." *Canadian Journal of Political Science* 32, no. 1 (1999): 3–20.

– "Imperial Transitions." In John G. Reid et al., eds, *The "Conquest" of Acadia, 1710: Imperial, Colonial, and Aboriginal Constructions*, 178–202. Toronto: University of Toronto Press, 2004.

Marichal, Carlos. *A Century of Debt Crises in Latin America: From Independence to the Great Depression, 1820–1930*. Princeton, Princeton University Press, 1989.

Martell, J.S. "The Achievements of Agricola and the Agricultural Societies, 1818–1825." *Bulletin of the Public Archives of Nova Scotia* 1, no. 3 (1940).

- "Early Coal Mining in Nova Scotia." *Dalhousie Review* 25, no. 2 (1945): 156–72.
- "From Central Board to Secretary of Agriculture." *Bulletin of the Public Archives of Nova Scotia* 2, no. 2 (1940).
Maynard, Steven. "Between Farm and Factory: The Productive Household and the Capitalist Transformation of the Maritime Countryside, Hopewell, Nova Scotia, 1869." In Daniel Samson, ed., *Contested Countryside: Rural Workers and Modern Society in Atlantic Canada, 1800–1950*, 104–59. Fredericton: Acadiensis Press, 1994.
McCalla, Douglas. *Planting the Province: The Economic History of Upper Canada, 1784–1870*. Toronto: University of Toronto Press, 1993.
- "Rural Credit and Rural Development in Upper Canada, 1790–1850." In Rosemary Ommer, ed., *Merchant Credit and Labour Strategies in Historical Perspective*, 255–72. Fredericton: Acadiensis Press, 1990.
McCann, L.D. "The Mercantile-Industrial Transition in the Metals Towns of Pictou County, 1857–1931." *Acadiensis* 10, no. 2 (Spring 1981): 29–64.
- ed. *People and Place: Studies of Small Town Life in the Maritimes*. Fredericton: Acadiensis, 1987.
- and Jill Burnett. "Social Mobility and the Ironmasters of Late Nineteenth Century New Glasgow." In L.D. McCann, ed., *People and Place: Studies of Small Town Life in the Maritimes*, 59–77. Fredericton: Acadiensis, 1987.
McCay, Bonnie M. "Old and New World Fisheries." In Bonnie M. McCay and James M. Acheson, eds, *The Question of the Commons: The Culture and Ecology of Common Resources*, 195–216. Tuscon: University of Arizona Press, 1987.
- *Oyster Wars and the Public Trust: Property, Law, and Ecology in New Jersey History*. Tucson: University of Arizona Press, 1998.
- and James M. Acheson, eds. *The Question of the Commons: The Culture and Ecology of Common Resources*. Tuscon: University of Arizona Press, 1987.
McIntosh, Robert. "The Family Economy and Boy Labour in Sydney Mines, 1871–1901." *Nova Scotia Historical Review* 13, no. 2 (1993): 68–71.
McKay, Colin. "The New Brunswick Farmer: How the Capitalist System Levies Tribute upon the Product of His Labour." In Ian McKay, ed., *For a Working-Class Culture in Canada: A Selection of Colin McKay's Writings on Sociology and Political Economy, 1897–1939*, 259–61. St John's: Committee on Canadian Labour History, 1996.
McKay, Ian. "'By Wisdom, Wile or War': The Provincial Workmen's Association and the Struggle for Working-Class Independence in Nova Scotia, 1879–1897." *Labour/Le Travail* 18 (Fall 1986): 13–62.
- "The Crisis of Dependent Development: Class Conflict in the Nova Scotia Coalfields, 1872–1876." In Greg Kealey, ed., *Class, Gender, and Region: Essays in Canadian Historical Sociology*, 9–48. St John's: Committee on Canadian Labour History, 1988.

– "Industry, Work, and Community in the Cumberland Coal Fields, 1848–1927." PhD thesis, Dalhousie University, 1983.

– "The Liberal Order Framework: A Prospectus for a Reconnaissance of Canadian History." *Canadian Historical Review* 81, no. 4 (2000): 617–45.

– "The 1910s: The Stillborn Triumph of Progressive Reform." In E.R. Forbes and D.A. Muise, eds, *The Atlantic Provinces in Confederation*, 192–229. Toronto: University of Toronto Press, 1993.

– *The Quest of the Folk: Antimodernism and Cultural Selection in Twentieth-Century Nova Scotia*. Montreal and Kingston: McGill-Queen's University Press, 1994.

– "The Realm of Uncertainty: The Experience of Work in the Cumberland Coal Mines, 1973–1927." *Acadiensis* 16, no. 1 (Autumn 1986): 3–57.

– ed. *For a Working-Class Culture in Canada: A Selection of Colin McKay's Writings on Sociology and Political Economy, 1897–1939*. St John's: Committee on Canadian Labour History, 1996.

McNabb, Debra. "The Role of the Land in Settling Horton Township, Nova Scotia." In Margaret Conrad, ed., *They Planted Well: New England Planters in Maritime Canada*, 151–60. Fredericton: Acadiensis Press, 1988.

McNairn, Jeffery. *The Capacity to Judge: Public Opinion and Deliberative Democracy in Upper Canada, 1791–1854*. Toronto: University of Toronto Press, 2000.

Meagher, Nicholas H. "Life of Hon. Jonathan McCully, 1809–1877." *Collections of the Nova Scotia Historical Society* 21 (1927): 73–114.

Meek, R.L. *The Economics of Physiocracy*. Cambridge, MA: Harvard University Press, 1962.

– "Smith, Turgot, and the 'Four-Stages' Theory." *History of Political Economy* (1971): 9–27.

Merchant, Carolyn. *Ecological Revolutions: Nature, Gender, and Science in New England*. Chapel Hill: University of North Carolina Press, 1989.

Merriman, John. *The Margins of City Life: Explorations on the French Urban Frontier, 1815–1851*. Oxford, Oxford University Press, 1991.

Miller, Virginia. "The Micmac: A Maritime Woodland Group." In R. Bruce Morrison and C. Roderick Wilson, eds, *Native Peoples: The Canadian Experience*, 324–52. Toronto: McClelland and Stewart, 1986.

Millward, Hugh. "Mine Operators and Mining Leases on Nova Scotia's Sydney Coalfield, 1720 to the Present." *Nova Scotia Historical Review* 13, no. 2 (1993): 67–86.

Miner, Horace. *St. Denis, a French-Canadian Parish*. Chicago: University of Chicago Press, 1939.

Mitchell, B.R. *Economic Development of the British Coal Industry, 1800–1914*. Cambridge, UK: Cambridge University Press, 1984.

Mitchinson, Rosalind. *Agricultural Sir John: The Life of Sir John Sinclair of Ulbster, 1754–1835*. London, Geoffrey Bles, 1962.

– and Leah Leneman. *Sexuality and Social Control: Scotland, 1660–1780.* New York: Blackwell, 1989.

Mixter, Timothy. "The Hiring Market as Workers' Turf: Migrant Agricultural Laborers and the Mobilization of Collective Action in the Steppe Grainbelt of European Russia." In Esther Kingston-Mann and Timothy Mixter, eds, *Peasant Economy, Culture, and Politics of European Russia, 1800–1921,* 294–340. Princeton: Princeton University Press, 1991.

Molloy, Maureen. "'No Inclination to Mix with Strangers': Marriage Patterns among Highland Scots Migrants to Cape Breton and New Zealand, 1800–1916." *Journal of Family History* 11, no. 3 (1986): 211–43.

Montgomery, Lucy Maud. *Anne of Green Gables.* 1908. Reprint, Toronto: McClelland and Stewart, 1992.

Morgan, Robert J. "Joseph Wallet Frederick DesBarres." In *Dictionary of Canadian Biography,* vol. 6, 192–7. Toronto: University of Toronto Press, 1987.

– "Lawrence Kavanagh." In *Dictionary of Canadian Biography,* vol. 6, 370–1. Toronto: University of Toronto Press, 1987.

– "Orphan Outpost: Cape Breton Colony, 1784–1820." PhD thesis, University of Ottawa, 1972.

– "'Poverty, wretchedness, and misery': The Great Famine on Cape Breton, 1845–56." *Nova Scotia Historical Review* 6, no. 1 (1986): 88–104.

Morris, R.J. *Class, Sect, and Party: The Making of the British Middle Class, Leeds, 1820–1850.* Manchester: Manchester University Press, 1990.

Muise, D.A. "The Federal Election of 1867 in Nova Scotia: An Economic Interpretation." *Collections of the Nova Scotia Historical Society* 36 (1968): 327–51.

– "The General Mining Association and Nova Scotia's Coal." *Bulletin of Canadian Studies* 6, no. 1 (1983): 70–87.

– "'The Great Transformation': Changing the Urban Face of Nova Scotia, 1871–1921." *Nova Scotia Historical Review* 11, no. 2 (1991): 1–42.

– "The Making of an Industrial Community: Cape Breton Coal Towns, 1867–1900." In Don Macgillivray and Brian Tennyson, eds, *Cape Breton Historical Essays,* 76–94. Sydney, NS: University College of Cape Breton Press, 1980.

– ed. "A Descriptive and Statistical Account of Nova Scotia and Its Dependencies." *Acadiensis* 2, no. 1 (Autumn 1972): 82–93.

Neeson, J.M. *Commoners: Common Right, Enclosure and Social Change in England, 1700–1820.* Cambridge, UK: Cambridge University Press, 1993.

Neill, Robin. *A History of Canadian Economic Thought.* London: Routledge, 1991.

Nowland, J.I., and J.I. MacDougall. *Soils of Cumberland County, Nova Scotia.* Ottawa: Department of Agriculture, 1973.

Ommer, Rosemary E. "Anticipating the Trend: The Pictou Ship Registry, 1840–1889." *Acadiensis* 10, no. 1 (Autumn 1980): 67–89.

- "Merchant Credit and the Informal Economy: Newfoundland, 1919–1929." In Canadian Historical Association, *Historical Papers* (1989): 167–89.
- "Primitive Accumulation and the Scottish *Clann* in the Old World and the New." *Journal of Historical Geography* 12, no. 2 (1986): 121–41.
- ed. *Merchant Credit and Labour Strategies in Historical Perspective.* Fredericton: Acadiensis Press, 1990.

Osterud, Nancy Grey. *Bonds of Community: The Lives of Farm Women in Nineteenth-Century New York.* Ithaca: Cornell University Press, 1991.

Palladino, Grace. *Another Civil War: Labor, Capital, and the State in the Anthracite Regions of Pennsylvania, 1840–68.* Urbana: University of Illinois Press, 1990.

Palmer, Bryan D. *Working-Class Experience: Rethinking the History of Canadian Labour, 1800–1990.* Toronto: McClelland and Stewart, 1991.

Parker, John P. *Cape Breton Ships and Men.* Toronto: s.n., 1967.

Pahl, R.E. *Divisions of Labour.* Oxford: Blackwell, 1984.

Payne, Abraham Martin. "Life of Sir Samuel Cunard." *Collections of the Nova Scotia Historical Society* 19 (1918): 75–92.

Perry, Adele. "Bachelors in the Backwoods: White Men and Homosocial Culture in Up-Country British Columbia, 1858–1871." In R.W. Sandwell, ed., *Beyond the City Limits: Rural History in British Columbia,* 180–194. Vancouver: University of British Columbia Press, 1999.

- *On the Edge of Empire: Race and Gender in the Making of Colonial British Columbia, 1851–1871.* Toronto: University of Toronto Press, 2002.

Phillipson, N.T., and R. Mitchison, eds. *Scotland in the Age of Improvement: Essays in Scottish History in the Eighteenth Century.* Edinburgh: University of Edinburgh Press, 1970.

Pickles, Katie. "Locating Widows in Mid-Nineteenth Century Pictou County, Nova Scotia." *Journal of Historical Geography* 30 (2004): 70–86.

Pigot, F.L. "John Macdonald of Glenaladale." In *Dictionary of Canadian Biography,* vol. 5, 514–17. Toronto: University of Toronto Press, 1983.

Poovey, Mary. *Making a Social Body: British Cultural Formation, 1830–64.* Chicago: University of Chicago Press, 1995.

Popkin, Samuel L. *The Rational Peasant: The Political Economy of Rural Society in Vietnam.* Berkeley: University of California Press, 1979.

Pryke, Kenneth G. "James Carmichael." In *Dictionary of Canadian Biography,* vol. 8, 126–8. Toronto: University of Toronto Press, 1976.

- *Nova Scotia and Confederation, 1864–1875.* Toronto: University of Toronto Press, 1979.

Radforth, Ian. "Sydenham and Utilitarian Reform." In Allan Greer and Ian Radforth, eds, *Colonial Leviathan: State Formation in Mid-Nineteenth-Century Canada.* Toronto: University of Toronto Press, 1992.

Ramirez, Bruno. *On the Move: French Canadian and Italian Migrants in the North Atlantic Economy, 1860–1914.* Toronto: McClelland and Stewart, 1991.

Rawlyk, G.A. *The Canada Fire: Radical Evangelicalism in British North America, 1775–1812.* Montreal and Kingston: McGill-Queen's University Press, 1994.

– "The Guysborough Negroes: A Study in Isolation." *Dalhousie Review* 48 (1968–69): 24–36.

Redfield, Robert. *Peasant Society and Its Culture.* Chicago: University of Chicago Press, 1963.

Richards, Eric. *A History of the Highland Clearances.* Vol. 2, *Emigration, Protest, Reasons.* London: Croom Helm, 1985.

Riddell, R.G. "A Study of the Land Policy of the Colonial Office, 1763–1855." *Canadian Historical Review* 18 (1937): 385–405.

Roberts, Gwyneth Tyson. "'Under the Hatches': English Parliamentary Commissioners' Views of the People and Language of Mid-Nineteenth-Century Wales." In Bill Schwarz, ed., *The Expansion of England: Race, Ethnicity, and Cultural History,* 171–97. London: Routledge, 1996.

Robertson, Ian Ross. *The Tenant League of Prince Edward Island, 1864–1867: Leasehold Tenure in the New World.* Toronto: University of Toronto Press, 1996.

Rothenberg, Winifred Barr. *From Market-Places to a Market Economy: The Transformation of Rural Massachusetts, 1750–1850.* Chicago, University of Chicago Press, 1992.

Russell, Peter A. "Forest into Farmland: Upper Canadian Clearing Rates, 1822-1839." *Agricultural History* 57, no. 3 (July 1983): 326-39.

Russell, Howard S. *A Long Deep Furrow: Three Centuries of Farming in New England.* Hanover, NH: University Press of New England, 1982.

Sager, Eric, with Gerald E. Panting. *Maritime Capital: The Shipping Industry in Atlantic Canada, 1820–1914.* Montreal and Kingston: McGill-Queen's University Press, 1990.

Samson, Daniel. "Dependency and Rural Industry: Inverness, Nova Scotia, 1899–1910." In Daniel Samson, ed., *Contested Countryside: Rural Workers and Modern Society in Atlantic Canada, 1800–1950,* 104–59. Fredericton: Acadiensis Press, 1994.

– "Visions du libéralisme et de 'l'amélioration' dans la Nouvelle-Écosse rurale, 1820–1848." *Bulletin d'histoire politique* 14, no. 2 (Winter 2006): 35–50.

– "'The Yoke of Improvement': John Young, Sir John Sinclair, and the Improvement of the Scotlands, New and Old." In Thomas Summerhill and James C. Scott, eds, *Transatlantic Rebels: Agrarian Radicalism in Comparative Perspective,* 87–116. East Lansing: Michigan State University Press, 2004.

– ed. *Contested Countryside: Rural Workers and Modern Society in Atlantic Canada, 1800–1950.* Fredericton: Acadiensis Press, 1994.

Sandberg, L. Anders. "Dependent Development, Labour and the Trenton Steel Works, Nova Scotia, c. 1900–1943." *Labour/Le Travail* 28 (Fall 1991): 127–62.

Sandwell, R.W. *Contesting Rural Space: Land Policy and the Practices of Settlement, Saltspring Island, British Columbia, 1859–1891.* Montreal and Kingston: McGill-Queen's University Press, 2005.

– "Rural Reconstruction: Towards a New Synthesis in Canadian History." *Histoire sociale/Social History* 27 (1994): 1–32.

Saunders, Ivan J. "The New Brunswick and Nova Scotia Land Company and the Settlement of Stanley, New Brunswick." MA thesis, University of New Brunswick, 1969.

Scott, James C. *The Moral Economy of the Peasant: Rebellion and Subsistence in Southeast Asia.* New Haven: Yale University Press, 1976.

– *Weapons of the Weak: Everyday Forms of Peasant Resistance.* New Haven: Yale University Press, 1985.

Schull, Joseph, and J. Douglas Gibson. *The Scotiabank Story.* Toronto: Macmillan, 1982.

Sen, Amartya. *Poverty and Famines: An Essay on Entitlement and Deprivation.* Oxford: Oxford University Press, 1981.

Sewell, William H., Jr. *A Rhetoric of Bourgeois Revolution: The Abbé Sieyes and What Is the Third Estate?* Durham: Duke University Press, 1994.

Sheets-Pyenson, Susan. "Sir William Dawson: The Nova Scotia Roots of a Geologist's Worldview." In Paul A. Bogaard, ed., *Profiles of Science and Society in the Maritimes prior to 1914,* 83–99. Fredericton: Acadiensis Press, 1990.

Shepperson, W.S. *British Emigration to North America: Projects and Opinions in the Early Victorian Period.* Minneapolis: University of Minnesota Press, 1957.

Siddiq, Fazley, and Julian Gwynn. "The Importance of Probate Inventories in Estimating the Distribution of Wealth." *Nova Scotia Historical Review* 11, no. 1 (1991): 103–18.

Sider, Gerald. *Culture and Class in Anthropology and History: A Newfoundland Illustration.* Cambridge, UK: Cambridge University Press, 1986.

Smith, Joshua M. *Borderland Smuggling: Patriots, Loyalists, and Illicit Trade in the Northeast, 1783–1820.* Gainesville: University Press of Florida, 2006.

– "Problems of Nationalism, Identity and Improvement in Later Eighteenth-Century Scotland." In T.M. Devine, ed., *Improvement and Enlightenment,* 1–21. Edinburgh: Edinburgh University Press, 1988.

– "Scottish Marriage, Regular and Irregular, 1500-1940." In R.B. Outhwaite, ed., *Marriage and Society: Studies in the Social History of Marriage,* 204-36. New York: St Martin's, 1981.

Snell, K.D.M. *Annals of the Labouring Poor: Social Change in Agrarian England, 1660-1900.* Cambridge, MA: Cambridge University Press, 1985.

Spray, W.A. "Henry Bliss." In *Dictionary of Canadian Biography,* vol. 10, 71-2. Toronto: University of Toronto Press, 1972.

Stairs, Michelle. "Matthews and Marillas: Bachelors and Spinsters in Prince Edward Island in 1881." In Nancy Christie and Michael Gauvreau, eds, *Mapping the Margins: The Family and Social Discipline in Canada, 1700-1975,* 247-72. Montreal and Kingston: McGill-Queen's University Press, 2004.

Stanley, Laurie. *The Well-Watered Garden: The Presbyterian Church in Cape Breton, 1798-1860.* Sydney, NS: University College of Cape Breton Press, 1983.

Steeves, Helen Harper. *The Story of Moncton's First Store and Storekeeper: Life around "The Bend" a Century Ago.* Saint John: J. & A. MacMillan, 1924.

Stoll, Steven. *Larding the Earth: Soil and Society in Nineteenth-Century America.* New York: Hill and Wang, 2002.

Sutherland, David A. "Andrew Belcher." In *Dictionary of Canadian Biography,* vol. 7, 233-4. Toronto: University of Toronto Press, 1976.

– "The 1810s: War and Peace." In Phillip A. Buckner and John G. Reid, eds, *The Atlantic Region to Confederation: A History,* 234-60. Toronto: University of Toronto Press, 1994.

– "Halifax Merchants and the Pursuit of Development, 1783-1850." *Canadian Historical Review* 59 (1978): 1-17.

– "James Forsyth." In *Dictionary of Canadian Biography,* vol. 5, 327-9. Toronto: University of Toronto Press, 1983.

– "James W. Johnston." In *Dictionary of Canadian Biography,* vol. 10, 383-8. Toronto: University of Toronto Press, 1972.

– "Lawrence Hartshorne." In *Dictionary of Canadian Biography,* vol. 6, 312-14. Toronto: University of Toronto Press, 1987.

– "Richard Tremain." In *Dictionary of Canadian Biography,* vol. 9, 891-2. Toronto: University of Toronto Press, 1976.

– "The Stanyon Ropeworks of Halifax, Nova Scotia: Glimpses of a Pre-Industrial Manufactory." *Labour/le Travail* 6 (1980): 149-58.

– "Voluntary Societies and the Process of Middle-Class Formation in Early Victorian Halifax, Nova Scotia." *Journal of the Canadian Historical Association* n.s. 5 (1994): 237-57.

Tennyson, Brian. "Economic Nationalism and Confederation: A Case Study in Cape Breton." *Acadiensis* 2, no. 1 (Autumn 1972): 38–53.

Thompson, E.P. *Customs in Common.* London: Merlin, 1991.

– *The Making of the English Working Class.* Harmondsworth: Penguin, 1963.

Thornton, Tamara Plakins. *Cultivating Gentlemen: The Meaning of Country Life among the Boston Elite, 1785–860*. New Haven: Yale University Press, 1989.

Tilly, Louise A., and Joan W. Scott. *Women, Work, and Family*. New York: Holt, Rinehart, and Winston, 1978.

Tomlins, Christopher L. *Law, Labor, and Ideology in the Early American Republic*. Cambridge, UK: Cambridge University Press, 1993.

Tribe, Keith. *Governing Economy: The Reformation of German Economic Discourse, 1750–1840*. Cambridge, UK: Cambridge University Press, 1988.

– *Land, Labour, and Economic Discourse*. London: Routledge and Kegan Paul, 1978.

Troughton, Michael J. "From Nodes to Nodes: The Rise and Fall of Agricultural Activity in the Maritime Provinces." In Gordon Day, ed., *Geographical Perspectives on the Maritime Provinces*, 25–46. Halifax: St Mary's University Press, 1988.

Tulloch, Judith. "James Fulton." In *Dictionary of Canadian Biography*, vol. 6, 268. Toronto: University of Toronto Press, 1987.

– "William Cottnam Tonge." In *Dictionary of Canadian Biography*, vol. 6, 779–83. Toronto: University of Toronto Press, 1987.

Upton, L.F.S. *Micmacs and Colonists: Indian-White Relations in the Maritimes, 1713–1867*. Vancouver: University of British Columbia Press, 1979.

Vernon, James. *Politics and the People: A Study in English Political Culture, 1815–1867*. Cambridge, UK: Cambridge University Press, 1993.

Vickers, Daniel. "Competency and Competition: Economic Culture in Early America." *William and Mary Quarterly* 47, no. 1 (1990): 3–29.

– *Farmers and Fishermen: Two Centuries of Work in Essex County, Massachusetts, 1630–1850*. Chapel Hill: University of North Carolina Press, 1994.

– "'Those Damned Shad': Would the River Fisheries of New England Have Survived in the Absence of Industrialization?" *William and Mary Quarterly* 61, no. 4 (2004): 685–712.

Wagg, Phyllis. "The Bias of Probate: Using Deeds to Transfer Estates in Nineteenth-Century Nova Scotia." *Nova Scotia Historical Review* 10, no. 1 (1990): 74–87.

Wahrman, Dror. *Imagining the Middle Class: The Political Representation of Class in Britain, ca. 1780–1840*. Cambridge, UK: Cambridge University Press, 1995.

– *The Making of the Modern Self: Identity and Culture in Eighteenth-Century England*. New Haven: Yale University Press, 2004.

Walker, James W. St G. *The Black Loyalists: The Search for the Promised Land in Nova Scotia and Siera Leone, 1783–1860*. Toronto: University of Toronto Press, 1992.

Ward, W. Peter. *Courtship, Love, and Marriage in Nineteenth-Century English Canada*. Montreal and Kingston: McGill-Queen's University Press, 1990.

Weaver, John C. *The Great Land Rush and the Making of the Modern World, 1650–1900*. Montreal and Kingston: McGill-Queen's University Press, 2003.

Whitfield, Harvey Amani. "Black Refugee Communities in Early Nineteenth Century Nova Scotia." *Journal of the Royal Nova Scotia Historical Society* n.s. 6 (2003): 92–109.

Wicken, William C. *Mi'kmaq Treaties on Trial: History, Law, and Donald Marshall Junior.* Toronto: University of Toronto Press, 2002.

Wilentz, Sean. *Chants Democratic: New York City and the Rise of the American Working Class, 1788–1850.* New York: Oxford University Press, 1984.

Williams, Raymond. *The Country and the City.* London: Chatto and Windus, 1973.

– *Keywords: A Vocabulary of Culture and Society.* 2nd rev. ed. London: Flamingo, 1983.

Winch, Donald. "Adam Smith: Scottish Moral Philosopher as Political Economist." In Hiroshi Mizuta and Chuhei Sugiyama, eds, *Adam Smith: International Perspectives,* 85–111. New York: St Martin's, 1993.

– *Classical Political Economy and Colonies.* Cambridge, MA: Harvard University Press, 1965.

Winks, Robin W. "Negroes in the Maritimes: An Introductory Study." *Dalhousie Review* 48 (1969): 453–71.

Wood, B. Anne. *Evangelical Balance Sheet: Character, Family, and Business in Mid-Victorian Nova Scotia.* Waterloo, ON: Wilfred Laurier University Press, 2006.

– "The Significance of Evangelical Presbyterian Politics in the Construction of State Schooling: A Case Study of the Pictou District, 1817–1866." *Acadiensis* 20, no. 2 (Spring 1991): 62–85.

Wrigley, E.A. *Industrial Growth and Population Change: A Regional Study of the Coalfield Areas of North-West Europe in the Later Nineteenth Century.* Cambridge, UK: Cambridge University Press, 1961.

Wynn, Graeme. "1800–1810: Turning the Century." In Phillip A. Buckner and John G. Reid, eds, *The Atlantic Region to Confederation: A History,* 210–33. Toronto: University of Toronto Press, 1994.

– "Exciting a Spirit of Emulation among the 'Plodholes': Agricultural Reform in Pre-Confederation Nova Scotia." *Acadiensis* 20, no. 1 (Autumn 1990): 5–51.

– "Ideology, Society, and State in the Maritime Colonies of British North America, 1840–1860." In Allan Greer and Ian Radforth, eds, *Colonial Leviathan: State Formation in Mid-Nineteenth Century Canada,* 284–328. Toronto: University of Toronto Press, 1992.

– "Late Eighteenth-Century Agriculture on the Bay of Fundy Marshlands." *Acadiensis* 8, no. 2 (Spring 1979): 80–9.

– "A Region of Scattered Settlements and Bounded Possibilities: Northeastern North America, 1775–1800." *Canadian Geographer* 31, no. 2 (Summer 1987): 98–113.

– *Timber Colony: A Historical Geography of Nineteenth Century New Brunswick.* Toronto: University of Toronto Press, 1979.

Index